Memoirs from Eldred, New York, 1800-1950

Book 2

Echo Hill and Mountain Grove

Stories of Families and Boarding Houses in the Town of Highland, New York

1880-1920

Louise Elizabeth Smith

HALFWAY BROOK

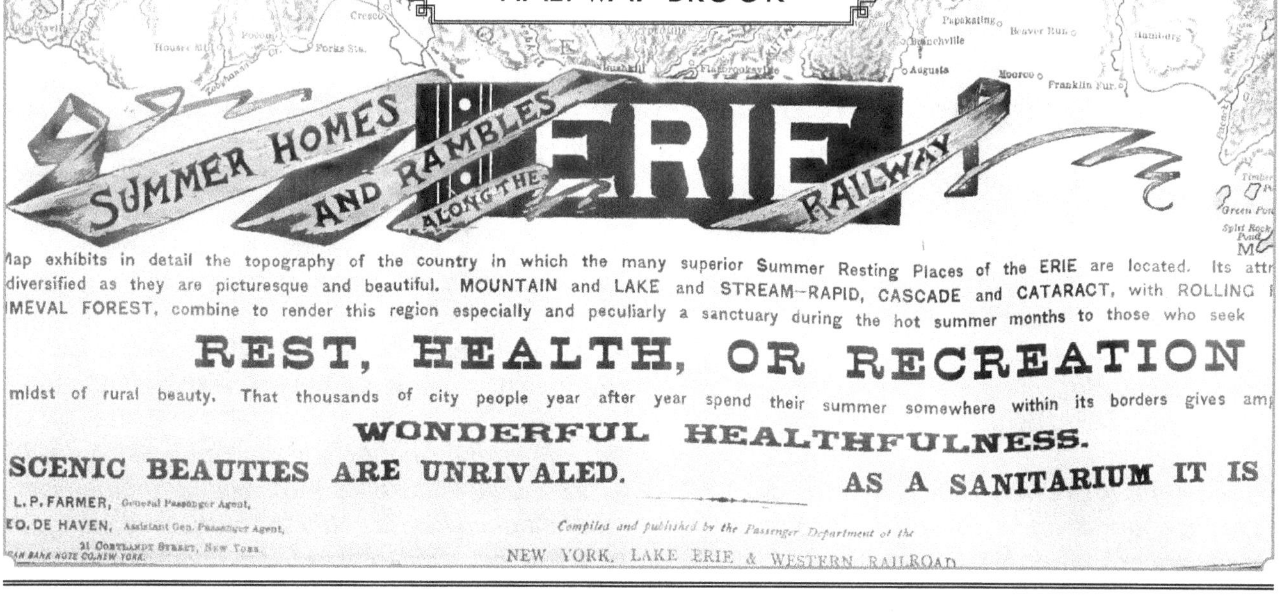

Photo: Cynthia Leavenworth Bellinger.

Published by Halfway Brook *Publishing*
Cave Creek, Arizona

Family information online:
halfwaybrook.com: Halfway Brook community blog, on-going projects, resources

weezy.info: Stories and information about the Crabtree-Higginson, Austin-Leavenworth, Smith-Corbridge, and Fallin-Williams families

Photo and text contributions:
Mary Briggs Austin, Melva Austin Barney, Cynthia Leavenworth Bellinger, Katherine Calkin Traxler, Ken Bosch, Kevin Marrinan, Chuck Myers, Christena Stevens Myers, and Gary D. Smith

Cover, interior design, and maps:
Gary D. Smith (PerformanceDesign.net)

Editing:
Gary D. Smith, Cynthia Leavenworth Bellinger

Copyright © 2011 by Louise E. Smith
Printed in the United States of America
ISBN: 978-0-9826374-2-5

Other books by Louise Elizabeth Smith:
The Mill on Halfway Brook
Grandma and Me
Aida Austin's 1881 Diary

Cover photos are repeated and credited in the book. Title page background: Farmer, L.P., Picturesque Erie Summer Homes, *N.Y., L.E. & W.R.R., 1890.*

I would like to thank:

Richard O. Eldred for permission to quote from his book, *The Eldred Family: Elisha Eldred of Minisink, New York, and His Descendants*, Baltimore: Gateway Press, Inc., 1988.

Minisink Valley Historical Society for permission to use photos.

John Hull for permission to use the memoirs of Daniel Rowlee Schoonover.

Hawley Library for use of the Louis Hensel print.

The Proctor Family for permission to use photos, information, and Charles Proctor's *Travelogue* contributions.

Tom Gibson for permission to use information from his site, shohola.org.

Herb Wolff for permission to use Lou Kloss's *Memoirs.*

John Conway for permission to quote: *Retrospect, Sullivan County Democrat*, October 8, 2010.

All rights Reserved. Please contact the author for permission to reproduce any part of this book.

Disclaimer: Information and sources were recorded as accurately as possible. Incorrect information is unintentional. Please notify the author regarding errors so they can be corrected in the next edition.

Table of Contents

Preface and Acknowledgments iv

Map of Northeast United States viii

Town of Highland's Boarding House Locations x

Dedication, Ecclesiastes 3 xii

Echo Hill and Mountain Grove Introduction xiii

Map of the Town of Highland xiv

Chapter 1: Lumber and Bluestone, 1880 1

Chapter 2: Dear Diary, 1881–1882 25

Chapter 3: Picturesque Highlands, 1880s 65

Chapter 4: Paths Diverge, 1883–1889 89

Chapter 5: Sublime Scenery, 1890–1900 131

Chapter 6: An Old Bachelor, 1890–1900 165

Chapter 7: Turn of the Century, 1900–1905 201

Chapter 8: Homestead Cottage, 1906–1910 241

Chapter 9: Echo Hill Farm House, 1910–1916 283

Chapter 10: Dear Soldier Boy, April 1917–May 1918 319

Chapter 11: Another Soldier Boy, May 1918 361

Chapter 12: Mountain Grove House, 1919–1920 401

Bibliography 436

Appendix 437

Index 475

About the Author 496

Preface

Every family has a story. But I did not know my Austin family story as I never knew my grandparents, Mort and Jennie Leavenworth Austin, who grew up in the village of Eldred. Even though I knew very little about them, I surmised they were gentle, kind people as they were the parents of my father Art Austin, whom I very much admired.

In 2007 I set out to put together a short booklet about Mort and Jennie's family. I had wisely enlisted the help of my cousin Cynthia Leavenworth Bellinger. (Cynthia's grandfather Garfield Leavenworth was a brother to my grandmother Jennie Austin.)

Cynthia and I wondered how we could write about our grandparents with so few photos and very little information. Two events took away that concern.

First, unknown to me, my mother Mary Briggs Austin and my cousin Melva Austin Barney each had a vast assortment of Austin papers and photos. The family archives they sent me included letters as old as 1845, and information on the location of the James Eldred home near Halfway Brook (which became the title of Book 1).

Second, I realized that as early as 1811, some of the ancestors of my Austin grandparents had lived in the part of the Town of Lumberland which became the Town of Highland, Sullivan County, New York.

The *Memoirs from Eldred, New York* series starts in 1800. It tells the story of my grandparents, their relatives, friends, and neighbors, and the towns they lived in. My account ends in 1950, around the time my parents moved to Michigan.

The Austin treasure boxes from my mother and Melva, along with the information and photos Cynthia provided, grew to 600 pages. At that point, the narrative became three books.

The Mill on Halfway Brook, the first book, was published in April 2010.

The story of the astounding amount of information sent to me and the people who sent it can be read in the Acknowledgments.

Acknowledgments

It is not possible to adequately express my appreciation to the generous people (many of them descendants of relatives and townsfolk) whose help made this book possible. I am very grateful to these relatives and new friends for taking their valuable time to assist in a variety of ways. They shared (collectively) an immense wealth of material, answered multiple questions, proofread excerpts, offered encouragement, and made excellent suggestions.

Austin Family
Included in the wonderful, large, varied collection of my mother Mary Briggs Austin, was Aida Austin's small, leather-covered 1881 Diary; Mort Austin's Autograph Book; the delightful 1918 Lone Scout WWI letters; the WWI letters of McKinley; and Jennie Austin's Scrapbook. My mother also answered a multitude of questions, as did my cousin Melva Austin Barney.

Melva's eclectic family treasure contained Mary Ann Austin's scrapbook; letters to Lon Austin from his friends out west, Proctor family members, and Daisy; Lon's poignant story in Chapter 6; and Aida Austin's Autograph Book, her handwritten story about the Eldred schoolhouse, and her WWI research. Tania Leigh Gaete, Melva's granddaughter, kindly emailed me Melva's old Austin photos.

Melva and her sisters, Joan Austin Geier, Margie Austin Maglione, and Dawn Lee Austin Segarra, shared their dad Raymond Austin's WWI letters. Joan, Margie, and Dawn Lee also took time from their busy schedules to send me their Austin family photos.

Margie and her husband Andy emailed me an excerpt from her dad's 1961 Diary, which told the story of his grandpa Henry Austin's death. Joan's daughter Liz Geier sent me two CDs of the Austin photos she had scanned for her mother. Dawn Lee's son

Joseph Segarra relayed my email messages to her.

My siblings—Charles Arthur Austin, Mary M. Austin, and Carol J. Austin—have been very supportive and encouraging of this project. Carol sent a copy of her interview with our dad Art Austin, on what it was like to grow up in Eldred.

Newly found Austin relative Katherine (Kathy) Calkin Traxler took a considerable amount of her time to scan and email a significant number of exciting old photos. She also mailed two boxes of materials from her Austin family archive which was fortunately saved by her grandmother Lillie Austin Calkin.

My Austin branch had lost contact with Cousin Lillie's family, so it was very exciting to meet Kathy in person, and to talk on the phone to her aunt Dorothy (Dot) Calkin Hale.

Dot, a delightful lady and daughter of Cousin Lillie, gave Kathy the fantastic Austin treasury Lillie had collected. It included Jennie Crandall's newsy letters about Eldred; much needed photos of Maria, Lon, Aida, and Mort Austin; and photos of Augustus and Maria Austin, and their descendants.

I was very glad to hear from Darren Foster, the only descendant of Augustus and Maria Eldred Austin that I have been able to locate. Darren, who is related to little Archie Paton (Buddy in Aida's 1881 Diary), sent me his updated family line.

Schoonover and Kloss Memoirs

The memoirs of Daniel Rowlee Schoonover and Lou Kloss make the years from 1880–1900 come alive, especially when combined with the photos shared by the Minisink Valley Historical Society.

Rowlee's father, O.P. (Perry) Schoonover (mentioned in *The Mill on Halfway Brook*), was an uncle to Aida Austin (and her siblings), as his first wife was Ann Mary Austin. After Ann Mary died, Perry married Mary Murray Parker, a widow with three children: George, Laura, and Kate Parker. Perry and Mary had children of their own: Emily and Rowlee. Aida Austin called Rowlee, Emily, and the Parker children *cousin*, though technically they were not related.

It was very exciting to meet (by email) John Hull (descendant of Rowlee Schoonover) and Richard James (descendant of Laura Parker Britt). John Hull took time from his full calendar to copy and send family photos and the adventurous memoirs Rowlee Schoonover wrote for his daughter Justina. John's sister Marjorie Hull Huwa provided paperwork for Deyo Hull. Richard James also took time from his busy life to update his family line and email some wonderful Parker and Britt scans which included photos that belong to his sister Barbara Kate James Stowell.

I was very glad to get the descriptive memoirs of Lou Kloss, from his nephew Herb Wolf. The photo of Herb and Margaret's cut glass bowl made at the Barryville Glass Factory, and Herb's great Glass Factory Pond story are in Chapter 8.

James Eldred Descendants

It has been enjoyable to converse with Richard O. Eldred who has been so enthusiastic about this book. Richard was able to locate the death dates of our relatives, Augustus and Maria Eldred Austin. Richard graciously gave permission to quote from his book, *The Eldred Family*, which updates the location of the descendants of James and Polly Mulford Eldred.

Marnette Hart Click sent me an envelope with photos and articles about her ancestor, Lewis Carmichael, son of Zophar and Sarah Eldred Carmichael.

Leavenworth Relatives

Linda Leavenworth Bohs contributed the Civil War letters of our great-grandfather Sherman S. Leavenworth, which are in Book 1. Linda and her husband Norman Bohs continued to answer questions and contribute Leavenworth stories, photos, and encouragement, even with Linda's jam packed schedule.

Cynthia's husband Richard Bellinger, her mother Gisele Rouillon Leavenworth, her siblings Nancy Leavenworth Leo and David Leavenworth were very helpful behind the scenes. Kelly Leavenworth Kuhn, David's daughter, tracked down the foundation of the sawmill across from the Jane Ann Myers home.

Charlee Hirsch Schroedel answered questions about her parents, Anthony and Christina Leavenworth Hirsch, and her grandfather Sherman S. Leavenworth. The Leavenworth Bible pages were provided by Ric Schroedel. Matt Schroedel also answered questions.

It has been some time since there had been contact with the descendants of Harriet Leavenworth Palmer. So it was quite exciting to "meet" Edythe King Westerfield and her daughter, Pamela Westerfield, who shared some photos and updated information on the Palmer and Ewart families.

Marion Connors Woods Hansen shared stories about her mother Hazel Sergeant Connors.

Marialyce Koenig Kornkven and her brother Gerald Koenig, descendants of John Leavenworth and Amelia Bradley, took time from their busy lives to send some very welcome photos and correct family information.

Cynthia shared the family research of Madelyn Meyers Busse. Madelyn was the sister of Bill Meyers Jr. who marries Anna Leavenworth in Book 3. Madelyn's mother Lottie Scott Meyers was a granddaughter of Isaac M. and Joanna Bradley.

Myers Relatives
Great Aunt Aida mentioned Howard, Emily, and Tina Stevens in her 1940s Diary. So it was very exciting to talk with Christena Stevens Myers and communicate by email. Teenie, as she is affectionately known, shared many photos and gladly answered a gazillion questions. I was delighted to get two photos from Teenie of her as a little girl with my grandmother, Jennie Austin. Teenie's husband Martin D. Myers Jr. is the grandson of George W.T. Myers, Jennie Austin's uncle. Teenie also shared Helen Myers Hulse's thorough family research.

The information of Eleanor Myers Rizzuto, daughter of Charles Cripps Myers, was shared by Stuart and Geraldine Mills Russell. Stuart sent me a CD with photos of the boarding houses of Jane Ann Myers, the Mills, and the Asendorfs.

Chuck Myers, from a different Myers family (related to my Austin cousins, Melva, Joan, Margie and Dawn Lee), and his wife Ruth Worzel (good friends of my parents) supplied numerous photos. Chuck answered only about a million questions.

Others who helped
A huge thank you (in no specific order) to many others who took time from their busy lives to help.

The Proctor Family included some delightful scans of photos (many from glass negatives) from the early 1900s, along with their family photos, information, and permission to use Charles Proctor's *Travelogue*.

Kevin Marrinan was also very helpful. He loaned photos and postcards (some from Pam Fischetti Defeo), suggested people to contact, copied Pam's 1910 Highland tax records, spent a good deal of time finding answers to questions (including locations of boarding houses), and tracked down the elusive Ed Grotecloss for photos and details about Ed's Greig ancestors.

Ken Bosch was enthusiastic about the project and took time from his busy life to share the Maier and Bosch information and photos he had diligently compiled. Ken's extensive, well researched collection included: photographs from the Ed Bosch Collection of Alice Bosch Reisen; photographs and anecdotes from Margo Bosch Meyer and Bobby Bosch; anecdotes and stories verified by Fred Bosch; photographs from the collection of Charles W. Bosch, Ken's grandfather; an audio interview of Lena Bosch from his brother Bill; interviews of family members; some wonderful stories of Ted Wicks; documents from Dorothy Brodmerkel Weber; Ken's research from ancestry.com and his three trips to Germany; and Vicki Kohler's trove of photos, negatives, and documents, that her grandparents, Herman and Mary Horton Bosch had saved.

It was neat to "meet" Vicki Kohler, as my great aunt Aida Austin mentions Herman and Mary Bosch in her 1940s Diary. Vicki Kohler's engaging emails included the story of Herman and Mary rescuing some of the Maier records that are in this book. Vicki also emailed me photos, documents, and sent some WWI and other items via U.S. mail.

Bob and Beatrice Behrens Nelson made a special trip to Monticello to track down Pelton land information. A descendant of William Kerr, Bob was very helpful with getting me precise information.

Emily Knecht Hallock (May 1934–July 30, 2011) and her friendly, prompt, helpful emails will be greatly missed. Emily had quite a cache of obituaries which she very willingly shared. She had the original newspaper obit on Daniel Hallock. Emily emailed many photos of the Clarks and Hallocks. Carolyn Hallock Clark and her husband Vernon Clark tracked down answers to a horde of questions about the Clark and Hallock families.

Emily's sister Dorothy Knecht Foster answered all the questions I asked about her husband's grandmother, Jennie Hallock Foster. It was neat that Jennie Hallock's wedding invitation to the Austins was in Melva's Collection.

Emily's cousin, Edey LaBarr Werman shared the cemetery files she researched years ago, and quickly answered questions about the Middaugh, Lilley, and LaBarr families.

Berniece Wells Haas graciously answered inquiries about her family and where she lives—near the original James Eldred home. Berniece's daughter-in-law, Darlene Sutherland Haas lives nearby. Darlene generously helped with answers and shared information about her Sutherland and Drake ancestors (the Drakes being in Mongaup pre-1800).

Charles Paulus (a Sutherland cousin of Darlene) loaned me his prized color slide of Glass Factory Pond for scanning.

I enjoyed getting emails from William (Bill) Erwin Horton (also related to the Sutherland family). Bill sent me Avery, Bradley, and Horton family photos and stories, and answered questions. Sue Horton Cloud (Bill's daughter), was also very helpful with answers. Earl and Sharon Stewart Lilley (friends of Bill and Lucille Horton) contributed both Ort and Lilley family trees.

Kathy Datys shared hours of research as well as images of the Spring House in Barryville.

Bill Ihlo furnished Toaspern and Straub photos including the super photograph of Straub's Hotel in Chapter 8. Bill was also instrumental in getting Straub and Toaspern family information and/or photos from his sisters, Betty Ihlo Morganstern and Barbara Ihlo Sardone; and their distant cousin, Marion Lass Guenther, and Marion's daughter, Linda Anderson.

I appreciated Ivan J. and Jana Tether taking the time to email helpful Tether information and photos.

Arlene Wolff Bennett explained about some of the boarding houses near Washington Lake. Helen Hensel Oset shared postcards and information about the boarding houses in the Yulan area, much of which will be in Book 3. Richard (Dickie) Haas also answered a slew of inquiries.

Ron Flieger confirmed that his relatives owned Mountain Top Cottage. Joe Arlt contributed Clark information and a photo of George James Clark. James C. Clark confirmed that his relatives, the Costellos, sold land to the Maiers, and provided information on George James Clark in WWI.

Even with a busy schedule, George J. Fluhr, historian of Pike County, Pennsylvania, took time to scan several historical photos and send me nine booklets he had written. George also suggested some excellent additions and changes to the narrative.

David Weidner emailed more details about the Millers and Edith Kalbfus who ran Highland Cottage. Judy Gumaer Testa sent Cuddeback family information for Eliza Ann Gardner Cuddeback.

Virginia West Palmer emailed a description of West Farm and a photo of her relatives, Theodore and Charles West.

I am grateful to Alice Willis who showed me around my great-grandparents Echo Hill Farm House, in 2007, and still keeps in touch by email. Eddie Mellan shared the story of his mother Mary Mellan's birth in the U.S. in 1911.

I received scans of the old Ira Austin home from Christina Watts. Christina also rescued the 1884 Clouse marriage certificate (with Aida Austin's signature as witness) from Reber's, and mailed it to me.

My thanks also to Larry Stern for the use of the postcards on his ecki site; and to the Town of Highland for the use of their postcards and Austin Smith's History Scrapbook.

Frank V Schwarz, Lumberland historian, was one of the first people I talked to for information on the area. Frank answered questions, supplied information on the MacKenzie family, his own family, and emailed a scanned photo of his grandfather's Glen Spey boarding house.

I was excited to "meet" two Kyte descendants. Barbara Waite Wilkinson sent me a scanned photo of some of her Kyte ancestors. Bronwyn Kyte provided information on the descendants of Felix and Eliza Greiger Kyte.

An Arizona friend, Louisa Gray LeSatz, shared her Colorado photos which showed the area near where the John Leavenworth family lived.

Thank you, too, to others not mentioned who helped in other ways; and to my many friends who encouraged me and never complained about my short or non-existent emails, or that all I talk about is "the book I am working on."

Cynthia Leavenworth Bellinger
What would I have done without the generous and immense help of Cynthia Leavenworth Bellinger? As in *The Mill on Halfway Brook*, Cynthia enthusiastically helped. She researched censuses, drove to Eldred to get (and scan) photos from Teenie, Chuck, Helen, and Kevin; offered encouragement; suggested great sources; gave helpful comments on countless rough drafts; tracked down correct information; typed over 1,500 names for the index; and once again helped with indexing (which took seven days). My hat's off to you Cynthia. Thank you so much.

Gary Smith
This book would not exist without my husband Gary's technical help, design expertise, editing skills, and his encouragement that this immense project could be completed. Gary created another superb cover and interior design, retouched close to 1,000 photos, spent days creating maps, and added his professional touch to make this book a real treasure for my family and the many new friends I have met. Thank you so very much, Gary.

VIII • ECHO HILL AND MOUNTAIN GROVE

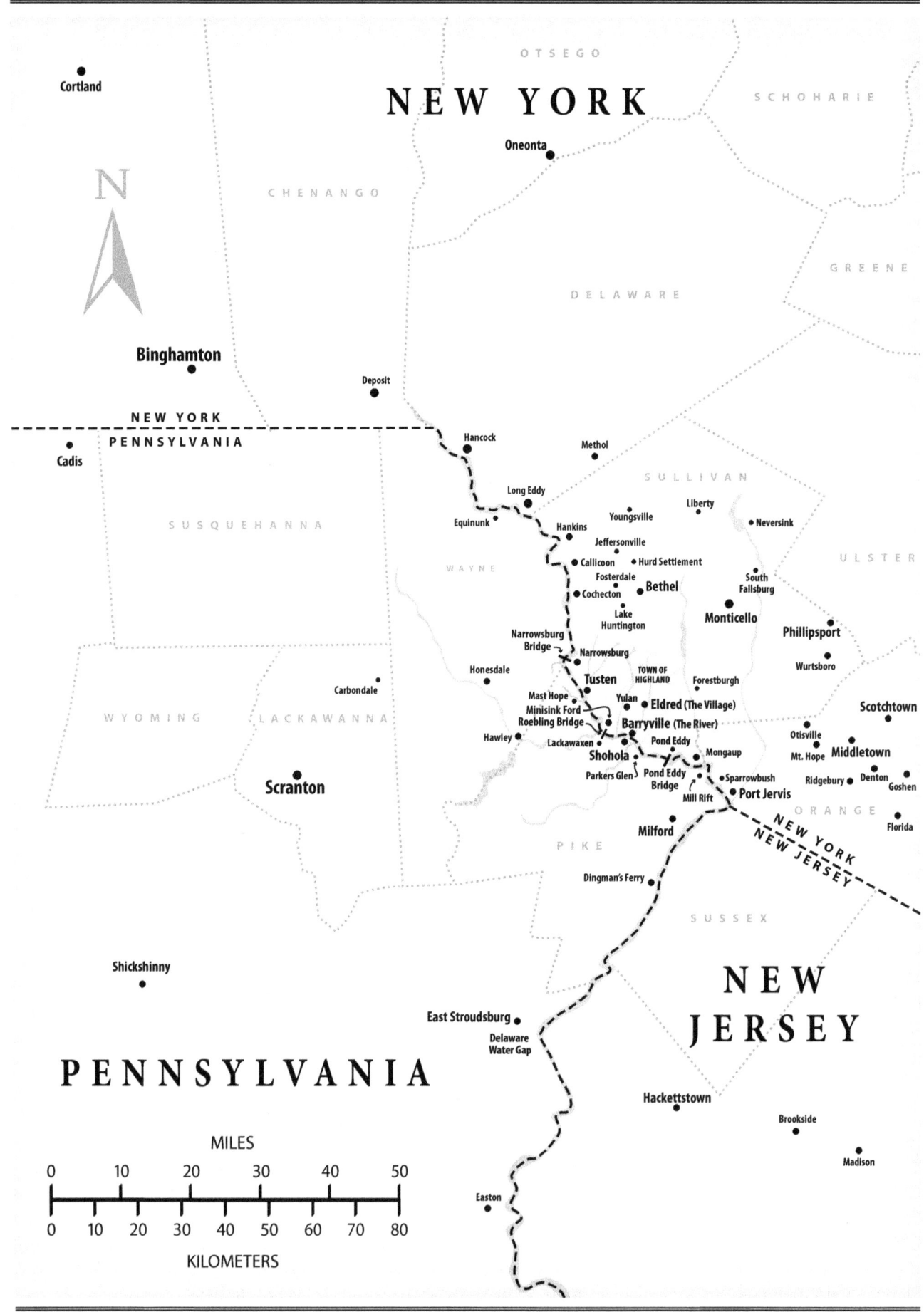

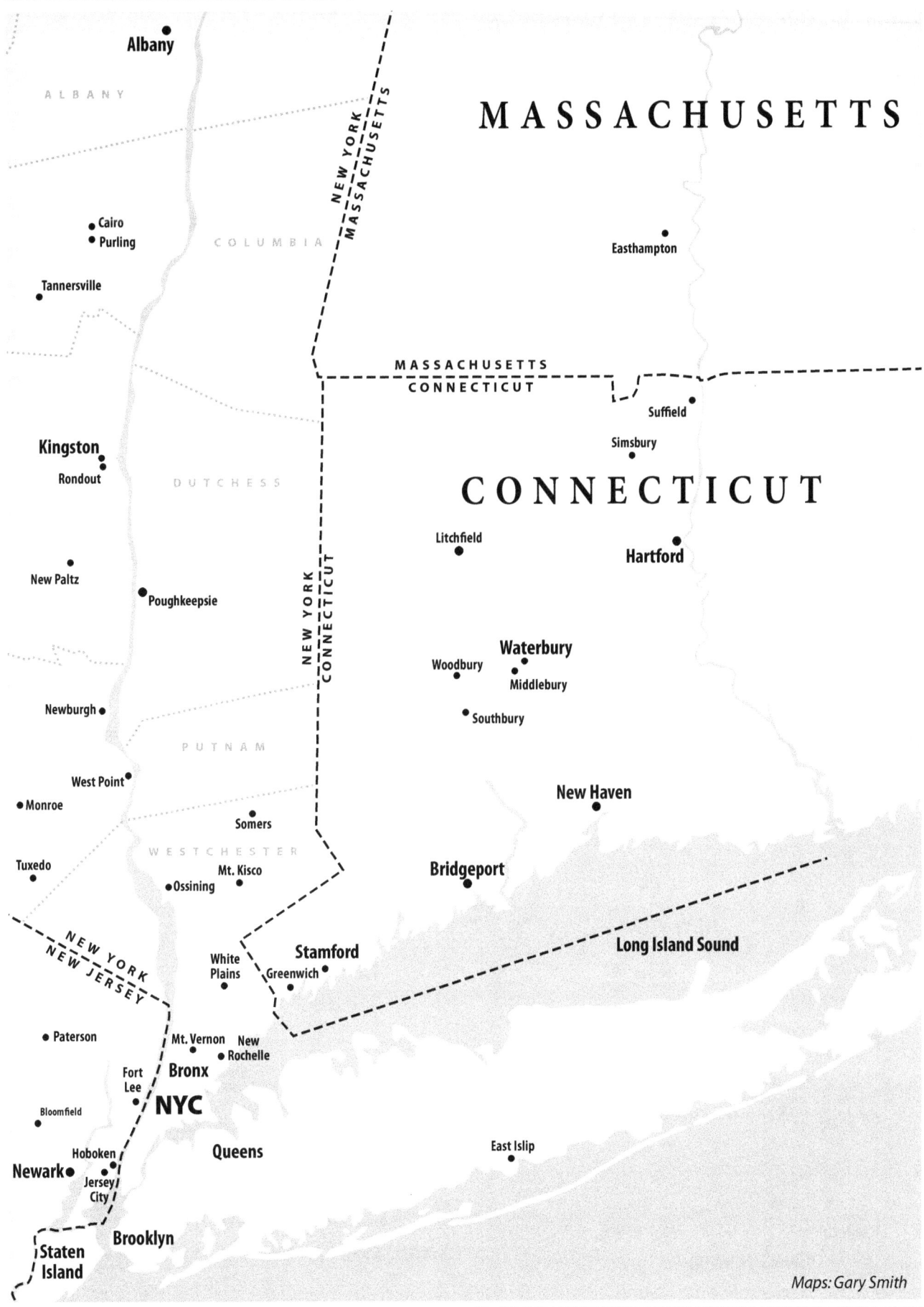

x • ECHO HILL AND MOUNTAIN GROVE

Yulan, Washington Lake, and West Eldred

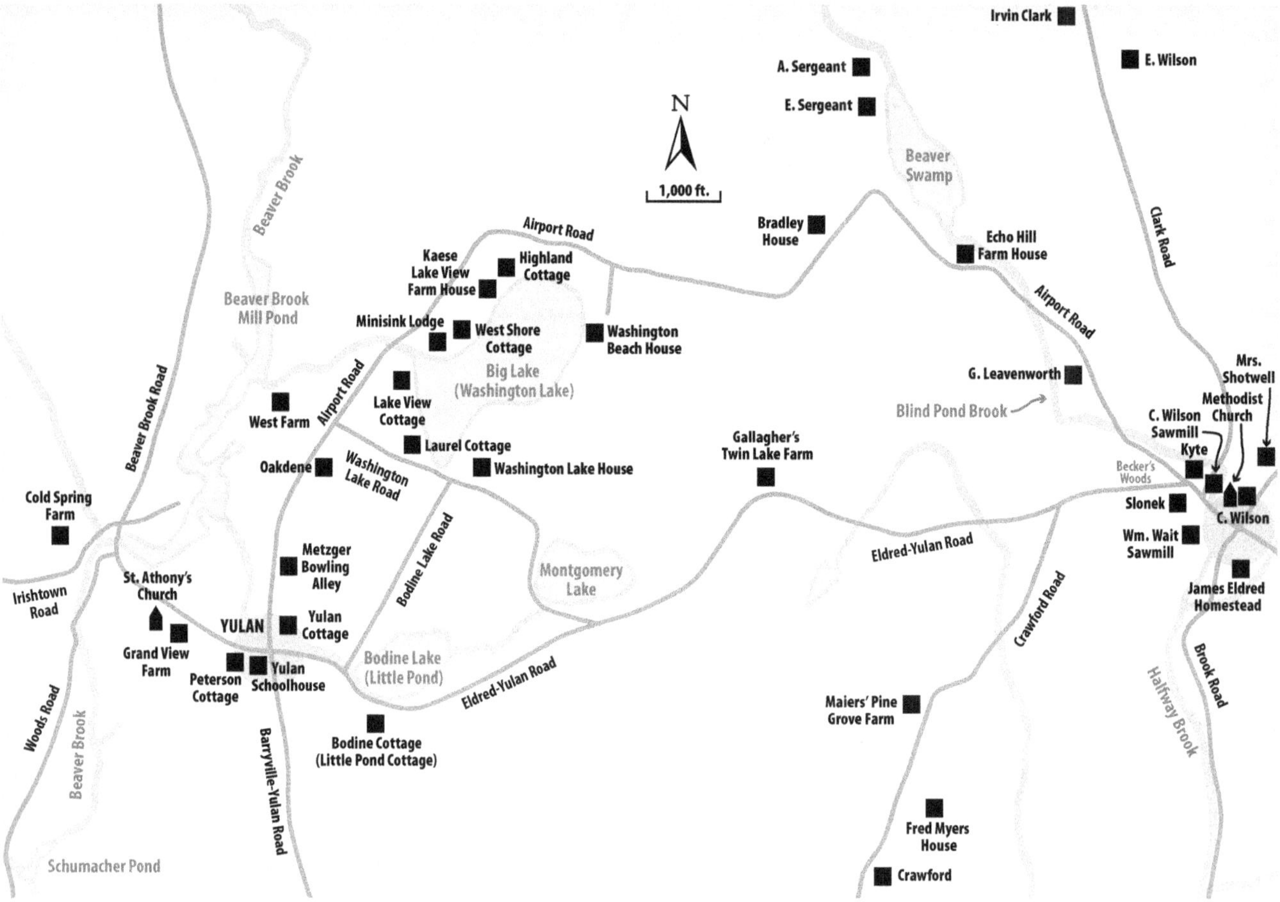

Minisink Ford and Lackawaxen

Barryville (the River) and Shohola

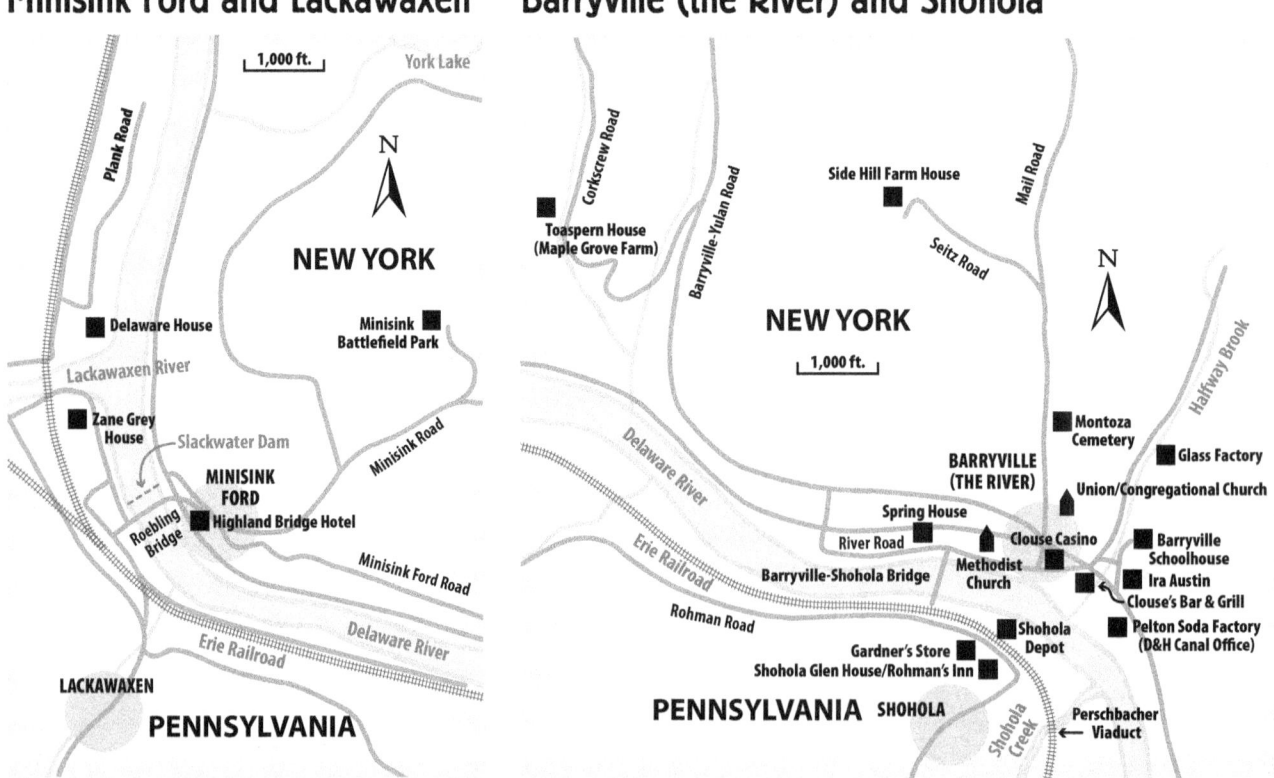

Town of Highland's Boarding House Locations • XI

Eldred (East and North) and Venoge (Highland Lake)

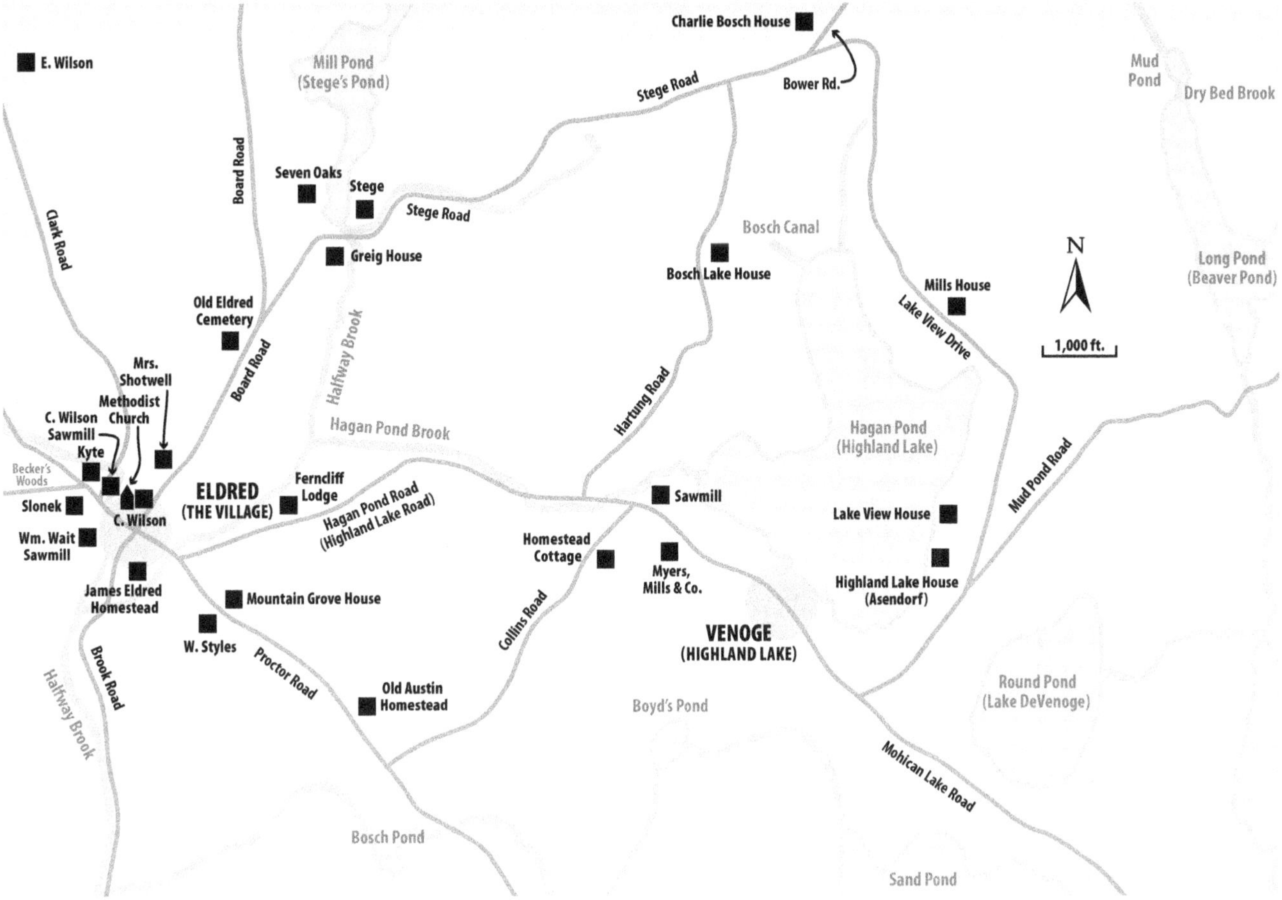

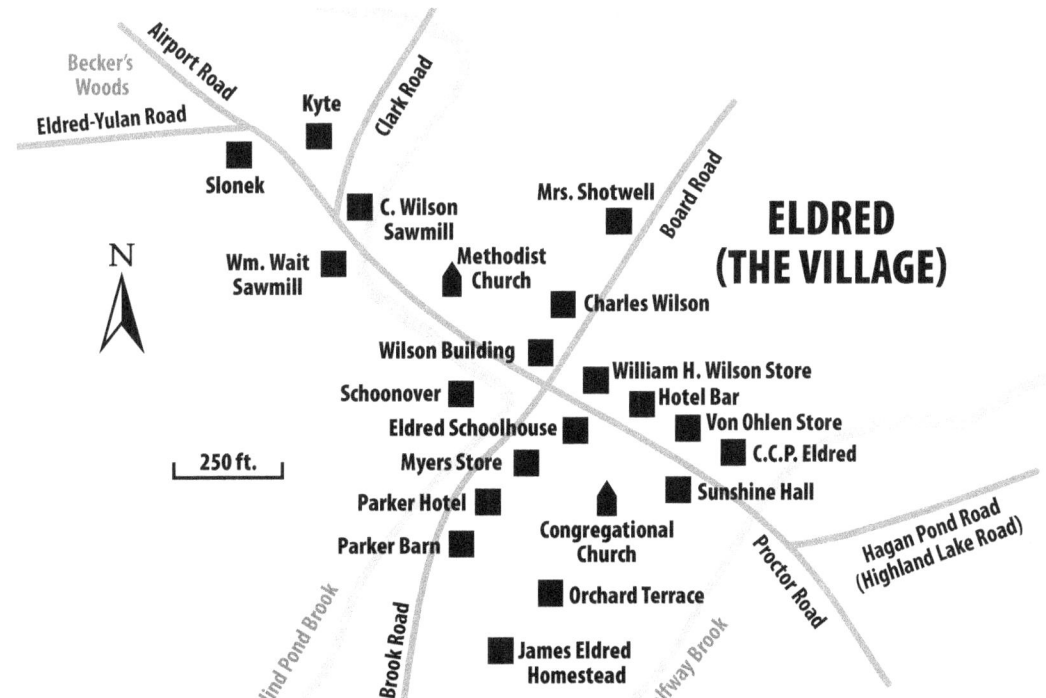

Maps: Gary Smith

Eldred (the Village)

Dedicated To:

Mary Briggs Austin

Melva Austin Barney

Cynthia Leavenworth Bellinger

Other Austin and Leavenworth relatives who preserved family histories

*The many people of the Town of Highland
who have graciously shared their information and photos of the area,
thereby making it possible for this book to be written
to honor the memory of my Austin grandparents,
Charles Mortimer Austin and Jennie Louisa Leavenworth*

To Everything There is a Season

To every thing there is a season, and a time to every purpose under the heaven:

A time to be born, and a time to die; a time to plant, and a time to pluck up that which is planted;

A time to kill, and a time to heal; a time to break down, and a time to build up;

A time to weep, and a time to laugh; a time to mourn, and a time to dance;

A time to cast away stones, and a time to gather stones together; a time to embrace, and a time to refrain from embracing;

A time to get, and a time to lose; a time to keep, and a time to cast away;

A time to rend, and a time to sew; a time to keep silence, and a time to speak;

A time to love, and a time to hate; a time of war, and a time of peace.

What profit hath he that worketh in that wherein he laboureth?

I have seen the travail, which God hath given to the sons of men to be exercised in it.

He hath made every thing beautiful in his time: also he hath set the world in their heart, so that no man can find out the work that God maketh from the beginning to the end.

I know that there is no good in them, but for a man to rejoice, and to do good in his life.

And also that every man should eat and drink, and enjoy the good of all his labour, it is the gift of God.

I know that, whatsoever God doeth, it shall be for ever: nothing can be put to it, nor any thing taken from it: and God doeth it, that men should fear before him.—*Ecclesiastes 3:1–14*

Echo Hill and Mountain Grove
Introduction for Book 2

Little brook! Little brook!
You have such a happy look
Such a very merry manner, as you swerve and curve and crook.
And your ripples, one and one,
Reach each other's hands and run
Like laughing little children in the sun!
—From The Brook Song, by James Whitcomb Riley.

Postcard entitled "Laughing Waters, Eldred, New York," courtesy of Katherine Calkin Traxler.

Charles Mortimer Austin and Jennie Louisa Leavenworth (my grandparents) grew up near brooks on opposite sides of the lovely, charming hamlet of Eldred, in the Town of Highland, Sullivan County, New York.

The Leavenworth home near Blind Pond Brook on the west, would become Echo Hill Farm House. The Austin family would build Mountain Grove House near Halfway Brook, on the east side.

The Town of Highland with its 50-plus square miles of hilly, rugged terrain overlooked the Delaware River. With an abundance of brooks, rivers, lakes, ponds, and springs, and only 107 miles from New York City, the town (as well as the whole region) was perfect for sportsmen and vacationers.

The Mill on Halfway Brook told the story of the ancestors of Mort and Jennie, and the settling of Eldred, first called Halfway Brook Village, in the Town of Lumberland, New York.

Echo Hill and Mountain Grove continues that narrative from 1880 to 1920, years of change.

Many of Highland's farmers turned their farmhouses into boarding houses, and continued to farm. The main financial base related to lumber, the D&H Canal, or bluestone quarries, was replaced with that of boarding houses in the picturesque hamlets of Barryville (*the River*), Minisink Ford, Yulan, Eldred *(the Village)*, and Venoge (Highland Lake).

Summer boarders arrived at the Shohola Railway Station in Pennsylvania, conveniently located across the Delaware River from Barryville.

Memoirs, newspapers, diaries, documents, letters, grocery books, scrapbooks, biographies, photos, and postcards shared by my Austin and Leavenworth relatives, and many friends of Eldred, help to tell the history of the townsfolk and Boarding Houses in the Town of Highland.

I hope you will enjoy this excursion back to 1880 as we get reacquainted with relatives, friends, and neighbors from *The Mill on Halfway Brook,* as well as meet some newcomers in a town that really did and does exist.

xiv • Echo Hill and Mountain Grove

The Town of Highland's hamlets: Eldred (the Village), Venoge (Highland Lake), Yulan, Barryville (the River), and Minisink Ford; and nearby Towns of Bethel, Tusten, and Lumberland. Jennie Leavenworth was born and grew up on the west side of Eldred, near Blind Pond Brook. Mort Austin grew up on the east side on the Austin land in the triangle bordered by Collins, Hagan Pond, and Proctor Roads. Map: Gary Smith.

Chapter 1
Lumber and Bluestone
The Town of Highland, New York, 1880

Pa never missed a spring that he did not steer rafts down the Delaware River from the time he was 22 years old until he was 72.

Now when I was 9 years old, Pa said, "Bub, when you are grown up, there will be no more rafting down on the Delaware and I want you to say, 'My pop took me down the River on a raft.'"
—Daniel Rowlee Schoonover.

This photograph, made from a glass plate, was taken along the Delaware River and shows the front end of a raft. Flattened horseshoes and long saplings (seen in the foreground) were used to bind sections of logs into one huge raft. The canal wall is in the background. Photo courtesy of Minisink Valley Historical Society.

Just as Daniel's Pa predicted, lumber rafting on the Delaware River would come to an end.

The nearby Delaware and Hudson (D&H) Canal, which shipped lumber and bluestone from Honesdale, Pennsylvania, to Rondout, New York, would be closed by 1900.

The area's economy had depended on lumbering and the D&H Canal, but that was changing. Soon it would be based on boarding houses that provided lodging for vacationers and sportsmen from New York City.

But in the 1880s, lumbering, rafting, and stone quarrying were still a part of everyday life.

Perry and Rowlee's Trip
Pa (Perry Schoonover), a big man at over 6 foot 2 inches and 200 pounds, was 61 when he took his son Rowlee for a raft trip down the Delaware River.

Perry's first wife, Ann Mary Austin had died young and Perry had married Mary Murray Parker (Rowlee's mother), a widow with 3 children—George, Kate, and Laura Parker. Daniel Rowlee Schoonover continued his story:

So Mother started along about the first of the year, 1881, to make me salve for sore lips you are sure to get from drinking river water, and new clothes—all homemade.

Pa bought me a new pair of calf skin boots with red tops and brass toes that I had to save for the trip and had to wear the old cow hides to go to school and to work in.

And every morning, Ma had to grease them with the mutton tallow that she kept in a saucer with a rag in, that was always hot. But when we went out in the cold and snow, they would turn as white as the snow.

We pulled out of Barryville on a double raft on the Saturday before Easter, 1881, at daybreak. How the wind did blow, and it was a steady pull all the time.

We landed at Dingman's Ferry [in Pennsylvania, about 17 miles south of Port Jervis] at dark, and stayed there over Easter Sunday for the wind was

This photograph, possibly taken during a spring freshet (notice the ice on rocks in the background), shows the enormous size of the rafts that traveled along the Delaware River. The rowboat in the center of the raft and loose logs in the river may have been the result of a raft that broke up further upstream. Photo courtesy of Minsink Valley Historical Society.

so high that it was not safe to start out. By Monday the water had gone down, so we had to wait for higher water.

I remember Pa got my board at the Hotel for half price for I was only 9 years old, and it being Easter they had hard boiled eggs for breakfast and I ate mine for that meal.

The wind stayed high and the water low, so Pa said, "Come Bub. We won't raft as I promised you, but we can go all the way on the train."

So we took the D.E. & W.R.R. and got in New York about 11. We went to the old Smith Hotel and went to bed.

I remember coming down in the morning to the dining room and I had on the new calfskin boots and what a noise they made on the marble floor.

We sat down to the table and a feller came and asked us what we would have and Pa said, "Give us some prunes and ham and eggs."

And they was the best prunes I ever ate. They had cooked them with molasses or something that made them taste different than anything Ma ever cooked and I told Pa that I sure was going to tell Ma about how them prunes tasted.

Pa said, "Bub, you know we don't have the sugar and molasses to cook the same as these folks do."

By late that p.m., we landed in Brooklyn and there was my sister Kate [Parker] to meet us. But Pa had to go right back, so he left me with Kate until he returned to take me home.

Well, the first thing Kate did was to take me out and buy new shoes and a new suit of clothes and the next day we had to go to the Barnum Circus that was at Madison Square Garden and that was something to take back to Eldred.

I stayed with Kate for a week or so until Pa came for me and we went home on the Emigrant train that got to Shohola at 1 a.m. and then we had to walk up the Brook Road to Eldred which was 5 miles and I did not mind for I was so full of everything that I had to tell Ma and Em [his sister] that I did not think of getting tired.
—Daniel Rowlee Schoonover.

Rowlee also described how the lumber rafts were built:

And now hold your hat, for to understand rafting, you have to go in some details to make it clear enough to understand.

The building of a sawed lumber raft is somewhat of an intricate piece of work. You must remember these rafts had to go down a river that was full of hazards that would make a rodeo look like a camp meeting.

First the logs are cut and drawn down to the mill or on the side of the road to the approach to the mill.

At that time there was no circular saws. They were using the old up and down saws which ran by water power.

The lumber was drawn to the river and piled in large piles on the bank of the river and left until spring. And when high water came, then all Hell was let loose, for everybody that could navigate at all turned out and got $1.00 or so a day for shoving lumber down from piles to the water edge where the men were making the rafts.

Every little sapling that was over 2 inches [called grubs] was also taken down to the river and was ready to commence to raft.

After the lumber gets to the river, you need the grubs.

Now they had the boring machine which a man sat down, and straddled. It had a 2-inch auger and he used a template that was made of an 18-foot board with a hole in both ends and he would fit that on top of 6 other boards and bore the holes so they would all be the same.

Now they would take them and put a grub up through these holes and tie them together, and they would fit them in the water and float them in place and they were called cribs or colts.

Now the cribs was floated out and put end to end. So that made a raft 64 feet long by 32 feet wide and also gave it flexibility for going through the rifts and over dams. If the raft was rigid you could not handle it.

Now I know you will want to know how these rafts were handled. First there was a big beam 12 by 12 that was mounted on the raft opposite from the way the river ran, and there was a big pin 2 inches in diameter. The oars was hung on their pins and almost balanced.

The oar shanks were about 25 feet long with an oar blade of 12 feet set in the heavy end so they balanced on the pin and a man could take hold of the small end and walk across the raft and dip the blade in the water and push the oar back.

They have four oars to a double raft and when they want to go around a bend or to keep the raft in the channel, the steersman cries out, "Two or more strokes for Pennsyvany." And if they want to go the other way, hollars the same, only he says Jersey, of course.

When oarsmen pull Pennsylvania on the front, the back pull Jersey and that brings the raft around.—Daniel Rowlee Schoonover.

Lumber Rafts on the Delaware, 1880

The Delaware River is lined with rafts on their way to Philadelphia. Although the winter was unfavorable for the lumber trade, and the high winds prevalent further up, the stream drove the rafts against rocks and sand-bars, causing many wrecks. Old citizens say they never saw the trade better.

It is estimated that there are now over 2,000 rafts between Lackawanna and Easton [in Pennsylvania]. Each raft contains about 60,000 feet of lumber, so that a total of 120,000,000 feet is on the way to Philadelphia.

By the end of the week, if high water continues, there will be scarcely a raft left in the upper waters of the Delaware.

Lumber has advanced very materially since last year, causing the working men along the river to feel highly elated.

One firm in this town has gone into the pine and hemlock region intending to purchase an extensive tract of first-class log timber, float it down here, and manufacture it in their steam saw-mill.—The New York Times, *April 30, 1880.*

"The oars was hung on their pins and almost balanced. The oar shanks were about 25 feet long with an oar blade of 12 feet set in the heavy end so they balanced on the pin."—Daniel Rowlee Schoonover. This photograph shows a raft on the Delaware River near Port Jervis, New York, at the end of the 19th century. Photo courtesy of Minisink Valley Historical Society.

Looking east towards Eldred. First building on the left is the Methodist Church. The Congregational Church is in the distance on the right. The old school is in the middle of the photo. There are tree stumps all around. C.C.P. Eldred's house is on the left in the distance. Village/Proctor Road was later changed to a different route. Photo courtesy of Chuck Myers.

The Effects of Heavy Lumbering
The Town of Highland had been part of the Town of Lumberland's 300,000 acres of rolling hills carpeted by a continuous forest of huge, old, and valuable trees. The area had been heavily lumbered since before 1800 and the effects were starting to show, as can be seen in some older photos of the area. The highly-prized white pine were mostly gone, but there were other trees—chestnut, oak, butternut, buttonwood, fir, hemlock, and silver birch.

The fine chestnut trees were scattered in every nook and corner, and along fences. In the fall, we always had our pockets full of chestnuts and hickory nuts, and boy did they taste fine. There were also lots of butternuts.
—Lou Kloss Memoirs.

Abundant Wildlife
The Town of Highland's many animals, colorful birds, and fish still made the area a favorite spot for hunters and fisherman in the 1880s. Wildlife included squirrels, chipmunks, foxes, pheasants, ducks, turkeys, partridges, rabbits, coyotes, bald eagles, and rattlesnakes. Deer were still abundant and so were fish. Bears and wildcats were not as plentiful, but they could still be found.

We saw many gray squirrels, red squirrels, and chipmunks; also pheasants. And when they would fly away we would often get a good scare as they made a noise like a shot or thunder. We also saw an occasional deer or fox, even a skunk at times. These we, of course, gave plenty of time to get away.
The chipmunks used to hide the nuts in piles of stone and fences for future use. And many times when we drew these stones to the fence to be built up, we would find one of these chipmunk hoards and fill our pockets.
The blue jays were also great for taking the nuts out of the pods or burrs on the trees and hiding them in hollow trees.
There was a big swamp here which was filled with jack rabbits in the winter. I caught about a dozen rabbits every winter.
In the fall we would see ducks on the river; also plenty of muskrats.—Lou Kloss Memoirs.

There used to be an old woman that lived near our place. Her name was Mrs. Shotwell. She lived all alone and I do not think she was afraid of anything. I know one night, she heard her chickens making a big noise. She was in her nightgown when she went out to see what the trouble was.
She opened the chicken house door and there was a big wild cat in the coop. She backed out and went to the wood pile and got a club and went back and went in the coop and closed the door behind her and killed Mr. Cat.
She got pretty well scratched up. But she said, "I killed the varmint anyway."—Daniel Rowlee Schoonover.

Chapter 1: Lumber and Bluestone, 1880

Occupations and Family Life

In 1880 the main occupations were related to lumber (sawyer, lumberman, carpenter); the canal (boatman, lock tender, worker, foreman, contractor, baggage master); the railroad; the bluestone quarry (quarry man, stone mason, stone cutter); and farming (including women farmers: Amanda Kelso, Elizabeth Winslow, Sarah Masher, Sara Shotwell, and Martha Adams).

Other jobs listed on the 1880 census were laborer, huckster (sales person), watchman, blacksmith, teamster, store keeper, store clerk, physician and surgeon, shoemaker, telegraph operator, keeping house, servant, teacher, dressmaker, and baker. Children of course were at school.

The people of the town included: descendants of settlers from the early 1800s; families from Orange County, New York, or nearby Pennsylvania; and immigrants from European countries including Sweden, Prussia/Germany, Alsace, France, Russia, Holland, Scotland, Ireland, and England.

Lou Kloss and his parents arrived in New York City from Germany around 1880. The family moved to Tusten in 1884.

Perry (O.P.) Schoonover had lived in Barryville or Eldred for almost 40 years. Aida Austin called him Uncle Perry and his second wife, Aunt Mary; and their children, cousins. Uncle Perry raised Aunt Mary's three children—George, Kate, and Laura Parker—as his own.

Uncle Perry and Aunt Mary Parker Schoonover had two children. In 1880 Emily was 11 and Daniel Rowlee was 8.

It was in 1880, and I was 8 years old that things was pretty tough: no work anywhere and Pa who was good at most any kind of a job, hired out to a man named Madison who lived over on the back road to Barryville from Yulan.

Butcher wagons went through the country for those days you had to buy everything from the peddler wagons. There was John Bower, the butcher, and Joe Sturns, the peddler, with everything from crown combs to Jew's harps and they took all the rags, bottles, and boxes that we had saved up in part payment.

So we moved over to the Madison Place and Pa did the butchering and what a big time Em and I had.

I remember we had the attic strung full of bladders blown up and dried. And Ma used to bind the tops with red tape and put strings in them and give them away for tobacco pouches for Christmas presents.

The family stayed that winter and came back home to Eldred early the next spring, for Pa would never let a spring go by without going down the river on a raft.—Daniel Rowlee Schoonover.

Though a number of the young men (John Leavenworth, Ell and Lon Austin, and others) had gone west for work (ranching, farming, and mining), there was still work available with the Delaware and Hudson (D&H) Canal, the Erie Railroad, and bluestone quarries.

The D&H Canal continued to transport not only coal from Honesdale, Pennsylvania, to Rondout, New York, but wood, bluestone, brick, and other items.

Many Irish and German workers had been employed to dig and build the canal or railroad, and a number of those families had stayed in the area.

By 1880 the canal channel was 6 feet deep and 32 feet wide. Boats 15 feet wide and 90 feet long carrying 130 tons of coal could fit through the passageway.

It was 78 miles from Lock 68 (in 1880) in Barryville on the Delaware River to Roundout

"On the back road to Barryville from Yulan." Postcard shows Yulan Road near Barryville, possibly near where the Schoonovers lived at one time. Courtesy of Kevin Marrinan.

A canal boat on the Delaware River. Running a canal boat was often a family business out of necessity to make a living. The wife and children would work very long days alongside the husband/father who was a boatman. Photo courtesy of Minisink Valley Historical Society.

on the Hudson River. The coal was unloaded at Rondout (near Kingston), New York, and sent by steamship to market.

The coal was mined around Honesdale, and all the way to Carbondale, Pennsylvania, and further. It was brought from there by narrow switchback R.R., a narrow gauge line.

Where there were steep hills, they had what they called planes. These were tracks up a steep grade with a powerhouse above.

There were heavy wire cables stretched all the way up several inches thick. Wheels were placed every little way up to hold the cables. There were double sets of tracks so that one set of cars could be pulled up while the other was let down at the same time.
—Lou Kloss Memoirs.

Canal Boats and the D&H Canal
The canal boats were pulled by mules and traveled 1 to 3 miles an hour. It took 7 to 10 days to take the round trip from Honesdale.

In *Reminiscences*, Johnston commented that boatmen were often forced to run the boat as a family business due to the D&H Canal Company policies. Out of necessity to make a living, the boatman's wife and children would work over 12 hours a day alongside him on his canal boat.

The canal boats were drawn by a team of horses or mules going tandem, attached to about 100 feet of inch rope. There was a wheel attached about 15 feet from the team so that they could go together or single file, as when they came to a narrow bridge. One side of the bridge was generally so narrow that only one could pass at a time.

The boats had to go through about a 100 locks on the way to the Hudson River at Rondout, in which they were raised up or let down from 15 to 20 feet, which was done by hand. The men worked at 12 hour turns.

It was here that the Delaware River was dammed up by the Canal Company. The company had to have what they called feeders to supply the canal with water at different places along the way.

The dam here was all the way across the river, and raised the water level at least 10 feet in summer, as in winter the boards that held back the water were taken out and stored to dry for the next spring.

These boards were placed behind heavy iron upright bars, fastened to the heavy planks and held upright by wooden braces. The bars were about 6 feet apart, and the boards a little longer, and were stacked up on one another. The water held them in place by

West Shore Bridge, Kingston, New York. Kingston is near Rondout, New York, on the eastern end of the D&H Canal. Postcard courtesy of the Austin Family.

pressing against them.

It kept a carpenter busy most of the winter making new ones for the ones that were worn out or washed away by the floods. Also the heavy floods washed away the reinforcements of heavy rocks that were placed below the dam (spillway) to keep it in place.

Nearly every year they had to have a gang of 100 to 150 Italians to blast out the rocks from the mountainside half a mile up the river and load it onto scows and take it to the dam where they dumped it behind the dam.

Some years they had to work at this all summer to repair the damage done by extra heavy floods. This dam made a fine stretch of water for over 2 miles and was a fine place for boating and fishing.—Lou Kloss Memoirs.

There was a very tough element that followed the canal. The most of them was Irish and would rather fight than do anything else to pass away the time and they had plenty of time on their hands for the speed was about 4 miles per hour.

There was 2 locks at Barryville and the Canal was a wonderful place for the boys of the town to swim. The canal bridge was a great place to dive from. It was about 40 feet from the top to the water and we used to jump from the top down, feet first and strike the bottom of the canal.

The Delaware River was another great place to swim and dive. I remember my mother used to say that my hair was not dry from June until October.

It used to be great sport to get onto a loaded boat when it came out of the lock and ride down to Pond Eddy and come back on a light boat back home.

I suppose you wonder how the two boats passed each other going in opposite directions and the mules that pulled the boats both on the same side of the canal.

The loaded boat had the right of way and when the loaded boat met the light or empty boat, the team that was pulling the light boat would stop and let the slack of their tow rope sink to the bottom of the canal and the loaded boat would pass over the rope as there was no crew. The boys used to know all the old captains that ran the canal boats and they got to know the boys.
—Daniel Rowlee Schoonover.

Roebling Aqueduct
Minisink Ford and the Roebling Aqueduct were west of Barryville.

The Aqueduct, designed and constructed in 1847 by John A. Roebling (who also designed the Brooklyn Bridge), eased the congestion of lumber rafters and canal boats on the Delaware River.

The Roebling Aqueduct connected the D&H Canal at Lackawaxen on the Pennsylvania side, to Minisink Ford, New York. Log rafters went under the aqueduct without canal boats getting in the way. Canal travel became faster by up to a day.

Cliffs along the Delaware River below Barryville. Postcard in the Defeo Collection, courtesy of Kevin Marrinan.

Canal posts were used as a guide to put a rope around to keep boats from hitting the wall. Photographed in 2010 by Cynthia Leavenworth Bellinger.

Slackwater Dam

A six-foot high slackwater dam existed below the confluence or juncture of the Lackawaxen and Delaware Rivers before the Roebling Aqueduct was built in 1847. The dam, which caused a calm section over a mile long, was raised to 16 feet after the Aqueduct was completed. The extra height was helpful for the canal, but treacherous for the lumber rafters.

When a raft went over the dam, the bow oarsmen disappeared from the stern oarsmen under a swirl of white water. Many rafts of lumber were lost on this section of the river, and the Delaware and Hudson paid the damages.

In an attempt to aid raftsmen, the D&H provided guides to lead rafts through this dangerous section, but this was not done without a payment to the canal company.—Osterberg, Matthew, The Delaware and Hudson Canal and the Gravity Railroad, p. 53.

Once over the Aqueduct, canal boats made a sharp right at Minisink Ford, New York, and went through Locks 72, 71, and 70 (some of the lock numbers have been changed). There were 16 locks before they reached Port Jervis.

Railroads and Railway Stations

Railways played a huge role in the economy of the area. But they also played a part in the demise of the D&H Canal because it was easier to ship logs and bluestone by rail.

The New York, Lake Erie and Western Railroad converted from 6-foot broad gauge, to standard gauge in June 1880, so that it could connect with other railroads. This made it possible for the Erie Railroad to ship vast quantities of the blue flagstone quarried along the Delaware River.

There was a Railway station at Lackawaxen, Pennsylvania, and one in Shohola, Pennsylvania, opposite Barryville.

The Shohola Railway Station, built in the early 1860s, was where New York City vacationers and sportsmen arrived to be taken to the boarding house of their choice in the Town of Highland.

Railroad stations were constructed in Pond Eddy, Middaugh's, Parkers Glen, Handsome Eddy, and a beautiful Victorian depot constructed

The Roebling Aqueduct is just downstream from where the Delaware and Lackawaxen Rivers join. The slack water dam (to the right of the Aqueduct in this photo) caused a 1-1/4 mile calm section in the river. The photo was taken around 1880 from the New York side of the Delaware River. Photo courtesy of the Minisink Valley Historical Society.

This photo (also taken around 1880) provides a closer view of the slack water dam from the Pennsylvania side just upstream of the Roebling Aqueduct. The dam was raised from 6 feet to 16 feet after the Aqueduct was finished. It was a very treacherous place for the raftsmen. The Delaware House is in the background. Photo courtesy of the Minisink Valley Historical Society.

in Shohola (see p. 80).

The creation of the railroad bed in Shohola township was a fantastic feat of engineering, costing more than $1,000,000 to blast and cut along the rocky shores of the Delaware River.

An original wooden trestle for a single broad gauge line was replaced by a large single arch viaduct constructed of hand cut stone by Jacob Perschbacher of German Hill in 1870 [see p. 48 and 49].

The new viaduct allowed two standard gauge (4-feet 8.5-inches) lines to cross the Shohola Creek, eliminating the last of the dangerous single track gauntlets, and creating a double track on the entire main line.
—shohola.org.

A Tavern, a Bridge, and a Store
Around 1826 Garret Wilson had managed a sawmill on some 4,000 acres of land in Shohola. Later, Chauncey Thomas became owner of that acreage. Chauncey had built Thomas Tavern in 1849 and the Barryville-Shohola Suspension Bridge in 1856. Next to the Tavern Thomas had built a store.

When Chauncey Thomas died in October 1882, Stephen St. John Gardner (grandson of James Eldred), Chauncey's administrator, purchased the right of the heirs and "became the owner of a larger part of the bridge."—*Johnston, John W., Reminiscences, p. 351.*

John F. Kilgour, the Bluestone King, became owner of Thomas's, Shohola acreage. We'll talk more about the Tavern (Shohola House in 1880), the bridge, the store, Shohola, and Shohola Glen, Pennsylvania, in Chapters 2 and 3.

Large bluestone quarries were located along the Delaware River, in Pond Eddy, Parkers Glen, and Shohola.

Erie train. It was easier to ship logs and bluestone by train than on the D&H Canal. Postcard in the Defeo Collection, courtesy of Kevin Marrinan.

Parkers Glen Bluestone

On a tract of 1600 acres, Kilgour and Parker began their new venture by employing 15 woodcutters to clear the land. During the winter of 1883, 12 teams of horses each hauled 1,000 feet of oak and pine daily to a sawmill. The newly constructed sawmill was 60 feet by 29 feet, and stood three stories high…

Adjoining the sawmill was a stone mill for cutting, planing, and polishing the bluestone, operations formerly done in New York City. The stone mill, 100 by 48 feet, contained two stone planes, two sets of stone saws, and rubbing and polishing machines. A new loading dock, 400 feet long was built, and a large office building was erected. Barns for the huge Percheron [*powerful draft horse, originally from France*] that could pull four to six tons, a blacksmith shop, and a carpenter shop were added to the complex. The total initial investment was over $25,000.

For the employees who worked at sixteen quarries in Parkers Glen, Kilgour erected cottages and later a schoolhouse and a church…

By 1885 over 800 men were employed at Parkers Glen where several mills cut and polished stone day and night—electric lights having been introduced. That year the Kilgour Bluestone Company owned over 6,000 acres of land, leased an additional 6,000 acres and operated 23 quarries along the Delaware from Hancock to Mill Rift, and up the Lackawaxen River as far as Hawley. An average of 95 loaded freight cars were shipped each week, with the Erie collecting $10,000 per month for freight. Annual business of the Company amounted to approximately a million dollars, with monthly payrolls over $20,000.
—*Fluhr, George, J., Quarries, Kilgour, and Pike County, Pennsylvania, 1984, p. 10, 11.*

Carr's Rock, Parkers Glen
Parkers Glen was originally named Carr's Rock. Carr, a raftsman, had been stranded there one night after his raft had been wrecked, according to George J. Fluhr, Historian for Pike County, Pennsylvania.

In April 1868, there had been a terrible train accident at Carr's Rock. Forty people died and 75 were injured. To try and erase that memory, the name was changed to Parkers Glen to honor

Barryville-Shohola Suspension Bridge which connected Shohola, Pennsylvania, with Barryville, New York, until 1941. Postcard in the Defeo Collection, courtesy of Kevin Marrinan.

Parkers Glen Railway Station. Photo courtesy of Minisink Valley Historical Society.

"Parkers Glen fountain was accidentally created by the Erie Railroad when they wanted to establish a railroad stop at Parkers Glen Village."—Osterberg. Postcard courtesy of Kevin Marrinan.

Elijah Strong Parker, a partner of John Fletcher Kilgour.

Parkers Glen [has] a stone plant for the purchase, manufacture, and sale of building and other stones.

There is a number of tenement houses, a store house, a depot of the Erie Rail Road Company, a well equipped stone mill for planing, rubbing, and shaping stone after almost any required pattern.

Connected with it is a large tract of land from where a vast quantity of stones have been quarried and hauled to the mill and the dock.

The business was first put in operation by John F. Kilgour, who soon after persuaded a Mr. Parker, formerly of New York City, to become his partner.

Parker was an honest, confiding man, who...by reason of his naturally innocent... disposition, was the least of all men fitted to enter such a partnership with safety...After 2 or 3 years trial, he left it a poor man...From him the place was named...—Johnston, pp. 224, 225.

Parkers Glen Fountain
Parkers Glen Fountain was accidentally created by the Erie Railroad when they wanted to establish a railroad stop at Parkers Glen Village. They put a strainer in a long pipe at the base of the Walker Lake Falls and ran the pipe under the railroad track to ensure the tracks would be safe from running water.

The gravitational force of the water created the fountain, which was a wondrous sight to behold on the Delaware River...—Osterberg, Matthew M., Matamoras to Shohola, p. 19.

Parkers Glen bluestone dock in the early 1900s. Photo courtesy of Minisink Valley Historical Society.

New York Curbstones

Just before you get in Barryville, going west, there is a house on your right with gingerbread trim which was the custom of that period in building. It belonged to a party by the name of William Hickok and it was at the time that the Bluestone Business was at its height.

Vanderbilt was building their mansion on 5th Avenue [in New York City]. It stood on the NW corner of 57th St. and 5th Avenue and ran to 58th St., and they was searching the country for the largest flagstones they could find for the sidewalks and they wanted them so thick that they would form their own curbstones.

They located them at Barryville in Hickok's quarry. They was 14 inches thick and was from 12 to 15 feet square. After they had located the stone, it was a case of how they was to get them to New York.

Of course there was the old Delaware and Hudson Canal running, but if they put a 15-foot stone on a canal boat, it would be so wide that it could not pass another boat, for the canal was only wide enough for 2 boats to pass, and the boats was 10 feet wide and they could not get them across to Shohola to the Erie R.R., for the bridge across the river was too narrow. And besides, it could not take the weight.

They made a new canal boat so they could put the stones in edge ways and they shipped them from Barryville in a special built boat to Roundout on the Hudson. Then they was taken in tow to New York.

Well, Bill Hickok made enough off them stones to retire; and the old quarry is still there to see.

While I am telling about that

Cart loaded with a large bluestone from the Goble Quarry in Rio, New York. The stone was sold to Alexander's Hotel in Sparrowbush. This photo, taken between 1905 and 1907, is courtesy of Minisink Valley Historical Society.

The 1871 Pond Eddy Suspension Bridge across the Delaware River was near Lock 63. Photo courtesy of Minisink Valley Historical Society.

Hawk's Nest Road view of the Delaware River and Cherry Island. It was still a dirt road until the 1930s. Photo courtesy of Kevin Marrinan.

Pond Eddy's suspension bridge, built in 1871, was near Lock 63. On the Pennsylvania side was an Erie Railway station.

There were some stores in Barryville and Eldred, but townsfolk continued to travel to Port Jervis for the household items they needed. The way to Port Jervis, still a one lane dirt road, included a very scenic section, known as the Hawk's Nest.

Port Jervis was a major center for both the D&H Canal and the railroad. John B. Jervis, for whom Port Jervis was named (it had been called Carpenter's Point), was the chief engineer of the D&H Canal.

Jervis was one of the great 19th century engineers. He designed and oversaw the construction of the Croton Aqueduct and water system built to serve New York City. He was involved in several major railroad projects and the iron industry. —minisink.org.

From Port Jervis to Shohola
Mr. Kloss narrated a trip traveling northwest from Port Jervis, New York, to Shohola, Pennsylvania:

At Port Jervis is the Tri-States Rock in the middle of the river where the three states come together—New Jersey, New York, and Pennsylvania. The Erie used to build some of their cars here at Port Jervis.

One mile above Port Jervis we come to the little town of Sparrowbush. Here is the end of the big yards of the Erie where in the heyday of the coal business stood many coal trains at a time to be taken to coast towns. Also trains of flagstones and timber.

We cross the Delaware at Sparrowbush into Pennsylvania.

part of my life, I must tell you about a house down in Parkers Glen where they used to have boarders that worked in the stone mills. The houses was no more than shanties and the boarders was all seated at the breakfast table one morning.

Down the side of the mountain came rolling the tire from a locomotive that was going by on the Erie. The tire struck the house and went through it from one side, upset the breakfast table and out on the other side and down in the river and did not hurt anyone. But they was a scared bunch. The house was halfway down the side of the mountain between the R.R. and the river.—Daniel Rowlee Schoonover.

Port Jervis, New York
East of Parkers Glen, the next hamlets on the way to Port Jervis were Pond Eddy (later Flagstaff), Pennsylvania, and Pond Eddy, New York.

First we come to Mill Rift at the other end of the bridge which was quite a flagstone center. Across from here, a little farther up the river on the New York side, is what is called the Hawk's Nest.

At the Hawk's Nest we pass several hundred feet high above the river and you get dizzy looking down at the river and the silvery tracks of the Erie.

Next we come to Pond Eddy, which was also a large bluestone center. Next was Parkers Glen; all did a large business. The fountain piped down from the hill to near the river that sprouts a 100-feet high, is at Parkers Glen.

Then next comes Shohola which was a great vacation center.—Lou Kloss Memoirs.

The Klosses Move to a Farm
Moving to the area and getting settled could be an adventure. Mr. Kloss told the story of his family moving by train from New York City to Tusten, around 1884.

We left West New York on a very raw and windy day after the middle of October. The weather was very raw. Our relations took us to the train and soon we were on the way for the great adventure.

When we arrived, there were several neighbors down with their ox teams and wagons at the bridge. One took us and the other took our furniture (as it had arrived in the meantime) up, up among the hills to, I think, the rockiest farm in the county that father could pick out.

The wagons were the regular farm wagons and only a board for a seat—no springs—and you can imagine the shaking up we got by the time we rode the 3-1/2 miles over rocks and stones.

As we left the river we went

The original Erie Train Depot in Port Jervis, New York. This structure was replaced in 1889 and rebuilt in 1892 (see p. 174). Photo from Defeo Collection, courtesy of Kevin Marrinan.

Erie Railroad yards, Port Jervis, New York, looking east. Photo from the Defeo Collection, courtesy of Kevin Marrinan.

Tri-States Rock showing the intersection of New York, New Jersey, and Pennsylvania state boundary lines. Postcard in the Defeo Collection, courtesy of Kevin Marrinan.

Photo shows the D&H Canal by Pond Eddy. In the distance is the Pond Eddy Suspension Bridge which was built in 1871. Photo courtesy of Minisink Valley Historical Society.

down a little hill and across a small bridge made of about a dozen planks about 14 feet long, which were placed over beams across the small brook that flowed all the way from past our future home and started about a mile above where we lived.

As soon as we crossed the bridge we started climbing up and up hill. First we saw the home and barn that belonged to the mill property. From there we went through the woods past a watering trough with ice cold water. Everybody had a drink. We went over another bridge and past a farm house. At the road was a 1-room log house with a 6-foot wide and 10-foot-high chimney on the outside.

On this farm stood as fine a stand of timbers as I have ever seen—such a fine standing of white pine trees. Many of them were 3 feet or more through and 100 feet long; fine yellow pine and oak and other trees.

The next year the son sold all the timber on this over a hundred acres for $500.00 to a lumberman from up the river who must have made a fine profit on the deal.

Families in Pond Eddy and Places Nearby

Sears and Mary Keen Gardner moved to Pond Eddy around 1800. In 1880 two of their children were living, Lettie Sergeant and Eliza Ann Young.

Eliza's son Coe Finch Young, a lumberman and dairy farmer, his wife Adaline Sweezy, and their daughter Jennie Dusenbery Young, lived in Pennsylvania.

The Hallocks and Van Tuyl families settled along the Delaware River, less than 5 miles west of Pond Eddy, in an area called Handsome Eddy, which was opposite Parkers Glen, Pennsylvania.

In 1880 Samuel Jesse Hallock, 9, lived with his parents Oliver Blizzard and Emma Schwab Hallock, and sister Adelia. Samuel's future wife Anna May Buchanan lived in New Jersey.

In the western corner of Lumberland, north of Handsome Eddy, was a very hilly, rugged area called Hillside. There the Kerrs had bought 100 acres from Mary Rider Hallock around 1870. They had been headed west when their wagon wheel broke, and decided to settle there.

Potato Hill, a section of Hillside, had root cellars built directly into the mountain where potatoes and other vegetables were stored.

Young Napoleon B. Quick and his family lived in Lumberland. Napoleon would marry Frances White. And my mother Mary Briggs Austin would meet them in the 1940s when she went to Pond Eddy to visit her good friend Ruth Worzel, the Quicks' granddaughter.

The Sutherland and Drake families, some of whom are a part of this story, lived in Lumberland.

They cut the white pine trees into logs 20 to 30 feet long and peeled them. The yellow pine they cut full length, piled them up on big piles and as soon as snow came, hauled all the logs to the river bank where there were mighty piles of logs.

All the fields were piled high with logs along the river. They were taken down the hills on bobsled piled 5 or 6 high and 1 or 2 behind fastened to the ends of logs with irons. And this way a tremendous pile of logs were taken off that property.

The yellow pine logs were used as piling and to drive into the mud banks along the rivers in the cities for ferry slips, etc.

The logs were rafted to Philadelphia or Trenton where there were big sawmills, and there they were cut up into lumber. I understand he got about 12 or 14 big rafts out of this timber.

They also cut about 2,000 cross ties and about 12 sets of railroad switch ties, all of oak timber—6 by 7 inches, and 8-1/2 feet long for cross ties; and 8 feet to 15 feet 8 inches, for the switch ties; all bark had to be peeled off.

This lumbering gave a lot of men work that winter in the woods. We, personally, and some neighbors got quite a number of top logs and a lot of firewood that lasted us for several years.

The logs we had sawed into boards could always be used on the farm as the lumbermen only took the logs to where the big limbs started, and the rest they left in the woods as the sawmills down the river didn't want knots. My father then prophesied that within 40 years there would be very little wood to be had in this neighborhood, the way it was being cut and wasted; also by the forest fires.

Canal along the Delaware River at Pond Eddy. Notice the telegraph poles. Photo courtesy of Minisink Valley Historical Society.

It took much less time than that. They soon had to go to the south for their pine and soon after, they started to bring lumber from California and the Pacific coast 3,000 miles away.

With the board from those logs, we built the kitchen addition to the old house while our neighbor built a two-story addition to his house.

From the cutting of the railroad ties we got many, many chips—some as big as two feet long and over a foot wide. It took us all winter and longer to get the wood out as I had only Saturdays to work in. And father took the

Stone Quarry on the Bank of the Delaware below Barryville, New York. Large quarries were located in Pond Eddy, Parkers Glen, and Shohola, with smaller quarries located all along the railroad and river. Postcard in the Defeo Collection, courtesy of Kevin Marrinan.

Four corners, Yulan, New York, not too far from where the Kloss family lived in Tusten. The back of Yulan Schoolhouse can be seen on the right. Postcard courtesy of Helen Hensel Oset.

logs to the sawmill 4 miles away. Then there was the job of cutting up the wood for the stoves.

There were many farms, houses, barns, wagon sheds, and corn cribs in this section at that time. All that is left today [1950s] are stone walls 5 or 6 feet high and from 3 to 6 or more feet thick.

You come across these walls often, as each farmer fenced in from 10 to 20 fields. It took each farmer months and years to build these fences; they thought sons would have it easier with their fields.

It was backbreaking work to build them I can assure you. The stones were drawn to where the stone walls would be built by ox teams, mostly. Oxen could walk better in rough ground than horses and were cheaper. They just needed to be turned out to pasture and given a little feed. But horses had to be cleaned, curried, and harnessed.

Later they dug out the stumps. The stones they drew to places where they soon built miles of stone walls all around that crisscrossed through their property. They worked 16 or more hours every day and even Sundays and holidays.—Lou Kloss Memoirs.

Old Dan Tucker and Other Stories
Rowlee Schoonover told a number of stories from the time when he lived in Eldred and Barryville.

I was 4 years old when my parents moved to Eldred, 4 miles up the brook, into a house that was all dolled up for my mother, Mary Murray Schoonover, that belonged to my grandfather, Peter Schoonover.

We moved on a hay rack. I being a big shot, the first thing I remember doing was to take a piece of board and nail it fast to the floor. Which to my mother of course was terrible. But Pa thought it was very smart for a boy four years to do.

I remember the first high water we had when the cellar was flooded and my mother put me in a wooden washtub and I had to pull myself up to get the food from the shelf that held all the goods Mother had canned, for they were not bought at the store.

There was an old man they used to call old Dan Tucker who lived all alone in a shanty up near Hagan Pond (which is now Highland Lake) and the town had to take care of him.

One day, someone found him dead in the road, and of course, the town had to bury him. They came to Pa to make the coffin. Pa had some dry butternut boards in the shed and he planed them up and made the coffin and my mother trimmed it with an old black silk

One of several bridges over Halfway Brook near Eldred, New York. Postcard in Defeo Collection, courtesy of Kevin Marrinan.

1880s: James and Polly V. Mulford Eldred Descendants

James and Polly Mulford Eldred settled near Halfway Brook at a location that became the southeast corner of Eldred, New York. (You can read more about them in *The Mill on Halfway Brook*.)

Some of the descendants of James and Polly Eldred's children are known thanks to, *The Eldred Family*, written by Richard O. Eldred.

Charles C.P. (C.C.P.) Eldred and Mary Ann Eldred Austin (daughter of James Eldred and his second wife, Hannah Hickok) lived in Eldred. Eliza Eldred Gardner, a widow, lived in Barryville. Phebe Maria Eldred Austin lived in New York City.

Abraham Mulford Eldred had died young. His widow, Elizabeth Wheeler Eldred Travis and some of his descendants lived or would live in Pennsylvania. Sarah Eldred Carmichael lived in Middletown, New York.

Sarah Eldred Carmichael

Zophar and Sarah Eldred Carmichael lived at the farm Zophar inherited from his parents. Many of Zophar and Sarah's 10 children lived in New York or Iowa.

Lewis Carmichael, a widower, was a railroad contractor, and lived in Iowa. His daughter Lina would marry Frank Watson.

Decator and Phebe Linkletter Carmichael lived in New York. They would have a son, Floyd Decator Carmichael, who would marry Cora Hardcastle Eldred, a descendant of Charles C.P. Eldred.

Sarah Eldred Carmichael, daughter of James and Polly Mulford Eldred, died at her home near Middletown, in August 1882. She had had several years of poor health.

Zophar then lived with his daughter Eliza and her husband, Egbert Puff. Zophar died in October 1885.

Abraham Mulford Eldred's Descendants

Mulford and Elizabeth's daughter Amelia Eldred was married to John Hancy. The Hancy family lived in Cleveland, Ohio, and had six children.

Mulford and Elizabeth's son, Benjamin Franklin (Frank) Eldred was married to Almira Barnes. The family lived in West Damascus, Pennsylvania, where Frank had close to 40 acres of land.

Descendants of two of Frank and Almira's 13 children—John Franklin and Lewis Laforde Eldred—are part of this story.

Charles C.P. Eldred

Charles Cotesworth Pickney Eldred was a farmer, lumber dealer, and Postmaster. He had been Postmaster on February 12, 1873, when the name of the Post Office was changed from Halfway Brook Village to Eldred, to honor his father. At least that is one of the stories.

C.C.P. or Cortzi was married to Effa Caroline Van Tuyl. Their son George W. Eldred had died at a young age and left 3 sons. Two of those grandsons, James Eldred and Herbert L. Eldred, lived with C.C.P. and Effa.

Marietta West, the widow of George W. Eldred, lived at the home of her parents, Samuel and Mary West, with her youngest son George.

Rebecca, daughter of C.C.P. and Effa, taught school and worked in her father's Post Office. Rebecca later lived in Philadelphia, Pennsylvania, and Galveston, Texas.

James Daniel Eldred, son of C.C.P. and Effa, was married to Frances Payne. Abram W. Rundle, a farmer, lived with them.

C.C.P. and Effa's daughter Polly Vanorsdol Eldred and her husband George Egbert Mapes moved to Philadelphia when George became an associate editor of the *Philadelphia Times*.

C.C.P. and Effa's daughter Maria Adeline Eldred married Charles Kendall, an oil operator. Their children were Nellie and Charles Kendall.

C.C.P. and Effa's daughter Sarah Jane Eldred Wait had died in May, 1879.

Eliza Eldred Gardner

Four of James K. and Eliza Eldred Gardner's 11 children lived into adulthood: Stephen St. John Gardner, James E. Gardner, Ann Eliza Cuddeback, and Maria Calkin.

Eliza Eldred Gardner, a widow, lived in Barryville with her son Stephen St. John Gardner, his second wife Margaret Terns, and his children from his first marriage: James K., Katie, Mary L., and Myers Gardner. His son Herbert died of scarlet fever in 1880. *(See p. 445 for news articles about Stephen and his family.)*

Stephen St. John Gardner seems to have been quite a businessman. Stephen was in the lumber business in Mongaup for 12 years. He sold that business and ran the general store in Shohola, Pennsylvania, that Chauncey Thomas had built. Later, Stephen had a partnership at that store with his son James K. Gardner.

James E. Gardner and his wife Rebecca Rider had three children: Charles F. Gardner, Susan Gardner, and Anna Gardner. James E. Gardner was a grocery man.

Ann Eliza Gardner and her husband Lewis Cuddeback had 3 children, but only Mary Cuddeback lived to adulthood.

Maria Gardner and her husband Oliver Calkin had children: James, Lilly, Charles, and Alonzo Calkin.

—*Stephen Gardner information from: J.H. Beers & Co., Commemorative Biographical Record of Northeastern Pennsylvania, 1900.*

The Delaware River below Barryville, New York. Postcard in Defeo Collection, courtesy of Kevin Marrinan.

dress. She had put brass headed tacks all around and I remember Pa saying that is the nicest bed Dan Tucker has ever laid in.

Old Ben Williams was a good fiddler and I used to like to hear him fiddle. His shop was down across the brook from our house and Pa had forbid me going down there. I used to sneak away and go down to get Ben to play for me. He thought a lot of me.

One time I went down to his shop and he was fiddling away and he looked up and said, "Here comes your dad. You get under the bench." I crawled under the bench and he stood up in front of me and kept on fiddling. My father came in. He said, "Ben, did you see anything of Rowlee?"

Ben said, "Hmm, No, Perry." Pa went out of there and up to Abe Myers's store. And I legged it across the brook and home. I was always getting myself in bad.

View above the dam on Halfway Brook, Barryville, New York. Postcard courtesy of Kevin Marrinan.

At the time of my boyhood here, there was one General Store that was run by Abe Myers that you could buy most anything you would want and no one thought of paying for what they got until spring when the lumber business got under way and the rafting started and the Delaware and Hudson canal opened up for the summer.

One time Abe Myers had a watermelon patch up back of the church and we went up to see if they were ripe. We plugged one or two and they were green.

I said, "Boys, come on. Aunt Effy [wife of C.C.P. Eldred] has got a patch down across the brook."

So we went down and waded the brook and there was a stone wall we had to climb over before we got in the garden. I said, "Keep still, for old Effie may be down here weeding the garden."

I climbed up on the wall and she raised up and said, "Yes, old Effie is here."

We all nearly broke our necks getting out of there, but it was too late. She had seen me and she was good friends with my folks and sure enough, she went and told mother about me stealing her melons and then Abe Myers told how someone had been in his melons and of course I got the blame for it all.

Ma made me go and tell Pa and I was going to kill myself, but when I told Pa, he laughed and said, "Bub, Mother will have to take care of you." So I began to cry and holler before she ever touched me. But I got a good strapping that day.

One time Pa had to work out his road taxes. Them days every man had to put in 2 or 3 days on the road if he owned any property. My father had 3 days' work to serve. So he took me along to help him, not that I could do any good, but more for company.

We had been cutting brush along the road all the forenoon and we stopped to eat our lunch in an old house that nobody lived in and Pa said, "Bub, go and get the dinner pail full of fresh water."

I took the pail and started out. I happened to walk up the road and I saw the worst old woman coming up the road. I stood and looked at her for a little while and the more I watched her, the more I got scared. I could see her sunbonnet. She had a cane in her hand and she was wobbling from one side to the other. I was scared. I went back to Pa and he laughed and said, "Come on Bub, We'll see who she is."

He took me by the hand. We walked up the road and I kept saying, "Don't you see her?"

He kept saying, "No."

We went on and when we got to what I thought was the old woman, there was a big round bush that we had cut that morning and the wind was blowing it from one side to the other. Don't tell me there is nothing in imagination.

We later moved to Barryville and lived in the old Lilley house, just below where I was born.

I had a friend named Chester Hulse (called Chet) who was the same age as myself who lived on the other side of the brook and he and I rigged up a telephone across the brook for it was about that time that we was hearing about the telephone. We had a wire made of haywire across the brook and tied one end in the woodshed and he had the other to a chickdale [outhouse].

Now on the ends of the haywire was two condensed milk cans with a nail on a loop across the bottom of the can

Barryville in 1880

James D. Eldred took the 1880 Highland Census. James was the son of C.C.P. and Effa Eldred, and grandson of James and Polly V. Mulford Eldred.

Ira McBride Austin (the other Austin family), a wagon maker, had a blacksmith shop. Ira and his wife Minerva Drake had 6 children: Nellie, Minnie, Frank, Mabel, Lou, and Bertha; and a servant, in 1880. Baby Bertha died in 1880 at 3 months old.

Mabel Austin would marry Ed Smith. Their son Austin Smith would be the Town of Highland Historian and record some helpful history that was used in this book. Ira Austin's home is still standing.

Ira's father Benjamin C. Austin lived with them, but died in November 1880, at the age of 72. Benjamin C. Austin was buried in the old Eldred Cemetery.

Augustus (Gus) Osier was a hoop maker. He wrote a letter to Lon Austin in 1879. In 1880 Gus lived with two sisters, a niece, and a brother. In January 1881, Gus married Phebe J. Lee of Barryville. Several Austin letters mention Gus Osier.

Mary Rixton, a widow, had a bakery in Barryville. Her children: William, a baker; John, a laborer; Herman, a school teacher; and Martin, 16, a laborer. Henry, Mary, Caroline, Charles, Joseph, and Anna went to school.

Susanna Clouse was a widow with children: August, Jacob, William, Lizzie, Lewis, and Solomon. Jacob, 19, worked on the canal.

John W. Johnston was a counsellor at law. In his book, *Reminiscences*, Mr. Johnston mentioned many of the people who lived in Barryville (but rarely in a very positive way).

Henry Christian (Chris) and Ida Heyen Toaspern from Germany and some of their children play a part in our story. Their children born by 1880: Edith, Anna, and Meta. Chris was listed as farming.

William H. Whitney was a farmer and painter.

Frederick Schwab was a boatman on the canal. Fred and his wife Margery would run a boarding house. They were listed with their daughter and a servant, John Webb.

The Schumachers, their children, and 3 servants lived in Barryville. There seem to be two Schumacher boarding houses—one in Barryville and another one northwest of Barryville by Schumacher Pond.

There also was a Schoonmaker family in the area at some point.

Samuel Hulse was a laborer. He and his wife Elizabeth had 4 children: Frederick, Mary, Henry, and Chester. Chester was Rowlee's friend.

Gotlieb Metzger, a farmer, would have a boarding house by 1900. Follett Metzger, a farmer, was listed with his wife Regina, mother Barbara, and sons, Robert and Christian.

Anna Mistenas, the school teacher, boarded with Perry and Mary Murray Parker Schoonover, and their children: Emily and Daniel Rowlee Schoonover. George, Kate, and Laura Parker were not mentioned in the census. Laura and Kate seem to be in Eldred in the summer of 1881, as Aida Austin mentioned the girls in her 1881 Diary.

Perry Schoonover's friend Daniel H. Rowley (spelled Rowlee in the 1870 census), 60, was a farmer. His wife Mary, 60, had been injured by a fall.

John Hickok, 30, was a telegraph operator. Benjamin Parker, 62, was a millwright and surveyor.

Herman and Belle Barber farmed, but would have a boarding house by 1900.

Enos Smith, 54, was a farmer and shoemaker. He and his wife Caroline had 10 children at home. Two sons were quarrymen, and one son was a farmer.

The first Parker Hotel built by James Y. Parker. It was near the northeast corner of the center of Eldred. Photo courtesy of James Y. Parker's granddaughter, Christena Stevens Myers.

and we could hear each other very plain.—Daniel Rowlee Schoonover.

Lumber to Boarding Houses
As mentioned earlier, the Town of Highland was changing from a lumber-based economy to one dependent on summer boarders.

The seasonal visitors, often from New York City, arrived by train to enjoy the natural beauty of the area. They looked forward to a relaxed life style in the fresh mountain air and home-cooked meals made with fresh ingredients from nearby farms.

Chapters 3 and 5 discuss the boarding houses and occasional hotel in the Town of Highland in more detail; introduce us to old and new neighbors and relatives; and reacquaint us with the Leavenworth family who lived on the west side of Eldred.

The Austin family (who we read more about in Chapters 2, 4, and 6) lived on the east side of Highland, less than a mile east from the center of Eldred or Eldred Corners.

James Y. Parker built his first Parker Hotel near Eldred's northeast corner.

James Y. Parker and his wife Emily Payne Parker had a daughter Adelaide and a son William Parker. Their son James Y. Parker had died young.

William Parker would have a son Andrew who would some years in the future be the owner of Andy Parker's Store.

James and Emily Parker would have a granddaughter, Christena Stevens, who would marry a great-grandson of Jane Ann Myers, and provide photos and information for this book.

The Beck and Greig families, both from England, lived less than a mile north of Eldred Corners near Mill Pond (later called Stege's). Their houses were not far from Board Road which went north to Bethel, New York, some 13 miles from Eldred Corners.

The Greigs had owned knitting mills in Manchester, England, and lost all their ships running the blockade during the Civil War. In 1869, they paid all their debts and sailed for New York.

Both the Greigs and Becks lived in Eldred by 1870. We will visit them again in Chapter 5 when they each own a huge boarding house.

Proctor Road started at Eldred Corners and went southeast on its way to Glen Spey, in the Town of Lumberland. The road passed the Parker Hotel, C.C.P. and Effa Eldred's home; crossed Halfway Brook bridge; and came to a Y in the road.

The Y formed one corner of the triangular piece of Austin property. Glen Spey could be reached by going either way.

To the left Hagan Pond Road went northeast to the thumb of

Tusten and Bethel, 1880s

The LaBarr family had settled to the west of Highland, in Beaver Brook, Town of Tusten. In May 1880, Calvin LaBarr married Elizabeth Rice. Calvin's father Gordon R. LaBarr died that year. Gordon had been a Postmaster in his later years. Calvin and Elizabeth's son Jacob Daniel LaBarr would be born in 1886.

North of Highland, was the Town of Bethel where the Crandall and Ort families lived.

Jacob Ort and his wife Catherine had children: Frank, Mary, and Katie.

Ezekiel and Betsy Crandall had children: Milton, Mary, John, Henry, and Robert (and possibly David).

Later, some of the Ort and Crandall children play a part in the Town of Highland.

Frank Ort marries Mary Crandall; Milton Crandall has a boarding house near Yulan; and Robert Crandall marries Nellie Simpson, who would be a good friend of my grandmother, Jennie Leavenworth Austin.

1880 New York State Census: Farms

FARMER	ACRES	VALUE	HAY	WORK ANIMALS	HONEY	MILCH COWS/BUTTER
C.C.P. Eldred	262 acres	$2,775	10 tons	2 horses	—	4/200 pounds
Wm. H. Austin	100 acres	$2,675	18 tons	4 horses	—	2/10 other/100 pounds
James Collins	100 acres	$2,685	4 tons	6 horses, 1 mule	—	2/150 pounds
Alexander Mills	126 acres	$2,710	2 tons	1 horse	—	2/137 pounds
James Boyd	65 acres	$2,275	7 tons	2 oxen	—	2/160 pounds
Abel S. Myers	87 acres	$1360	—	2 horses	—	4/100 pounds
G.W.T. Myers*	177 acres*	$3,470	7 acres	2 horses, 1 mule	—	6/400 pounds
Leon DeVenoge	1,302 acres	$5,300	29 tons	3 horses	—	8/720 pounds
George Bunce	101 acres	$960	3 tons	1 horse, 1 mule	—	—
Mahlon I. Clark	50 acres	$2,775	9 tons	2 horses	—	4/100 pounds
George Clark	50 acres	$2,470	11 tons	2 oxen	—	2/7 other/300 pounds
David Hickok	170 acres	$4,900	50 tons	2 mules	—	6/6 other/350 pounds
Ethel B. Sergeant	150 acres	$1,750	15 tons	2 oxen	—	2/2 other/160 pounds
Alvah Sergeant	43 acres	$585	5 tons	—	—	1/2 other/80 pounds
S.B. Leavenworth	150 acres	$2,500	12 tons	4 oxen	—	3/3 other/560 pounds
Isaac M. Bradley	66 acres	$4,495	15 tons	2 horses, 1 mule	50 pounds	3/300 pounds
Joseph Tether	229 acres	$6,020	28 tons	2 oxen, 1 horse	—	4/8 other/300 pounds
Justin Bodine	90 acres	$1,850	15 tons	1 horse	—	1/100 pounds
David Ayers	240 acres	$3,500	20 tons	—	100 pounds	7/1200 pounds
Daniel Wells	394 acres	$2,620	15 tons	1 horse, 2 mules	150 pounds	3/470 pounds
John W. Johnston	190 acres	$10,200	40 tons	1 horse	400 pounds	2/60 pounds

*rent/share

FARMER	SHEEP/SWINE	POULTRY/EGGS/DOZ.	OATS ACRES/BU.	BUCKWHEAT ACRES/BU.	RYE ACRES/BU.	IRISH POTATOES ACRES/BU.	INDIAN CORN ACRES/BU.	APPLE TREES ACRES/BU.
C.C.P. Eldred	7/4	29/80	2/40	3/43	6/36	1/100	6/150	30/2/157
Wm. H. Austin	4/1	29/50	6/190	10/136	4/80	1/70	4/150	20/2/60
James Collins	12/60 lb.**	16/48	3/60	2/37	2/10	1/80	3/75	10/2/20
Alexander Mills	—/1	15/60	—	3/32	4/13	1/2 A/65	3/55	20/3/100
James Boyd	—/2	30/90	—	2/36	—	1/2 A/64	3/55	60/2/100
Abel S. Myers	—/2	11/35	—	—	7/70	2/100	—	—
G.W.T. Myers	—6	12/48	2/40	1/25	1/5	—	5/100	30/2/10
Leon DeVenoge	—/2	65/100	—	6/110	1/10	1/120	6/180	—
George Bunce	—/—	30/40	1/20	3/60	2/20	1/50	1/20	70/1/130
Mahlon I. Clark	2/—	20/75	2/40	4/80	2/40	1/80	4/50	20/1/100
George Clark	—/15	16/80	—	8/65	—	1/100	1/41	30/1/75
David Hickok	7/3	8/20	8/80	5/154	6/85	—	4/200	—
Ethel B. Sergeant	—/—	10/40	—	2/24	2/10	1/4 A/15	—	25/1/25
Alvah Sergeant	—/1	20/100	—	2/15	—	1/3 A/20	—	—
S.B. Leavenworth	—/4	20/150	—	5/105	4/50	1/80	2/60	12/1/30
Isaac M. Bradley	—/—	20/100	—	2/40	—	1/100	5/257	60/2/35
Joseph Tether	—/1	25/350	4/150	1/32	—	1/85	4/200	—
Justin Bodine	—/—	20/100	—	—	—	1/31	—	50/2/100

**fleece

Maney's Mill (in 1917) and Proctor Road approach the entrance to Sand Pond. Photo courtesy of the Proctor Family.

Hagan Pond. At the thumb, the road headed southeast, continued past Hagan Pond and Round Pond on the left, and Sand Pond on the right (to the south), and eventually ended up at Glen Spey where the MacKenzie family lived (at least part time).

MacKenzie, Proctor, and Singer
In 1880 George R. MacKenzie (the Vice President of Singer Manufacturing Company), his wife Rebecca, and children: Edward, James, Alexander, Hugh, and Rebecca, were listed in Lumberland. They had 3 servants, and 2 laborers.

The MacKenzie mansion, *The Homestead*, was built in the late 1860s. Mr. MacKenzie had also built the church and school in Glen Spey.

Back at the Y in the road, Proctor Road to the right continued past the Austin Property and Collins Road on the left; Loch Ada on the right; Maney's Mill (built in 1787); and then the hamlet of Glen Spey in the Town of Lumberland.

During the summer months, the William F. Proctor family lived in Lumberland on their Lochada Estate. Mr. Proctor's wife, Vouletti Theresa Singer, was the daughter of Isaac Merritt Singer, the originator of the Singer Company.

William F. Proctor worked for Singer for decades helping to create a world wide enterprise. Eventually Singer left the United States to live in England and turned over the full operations of the company to George Ross MacKenzie as President and William as Vice President.

The two men became good friends...[They] apparently recognized Sullivan County as an ideal location to build their summer estates, each only a few miles from the river in the town of Lumberland. Access was by horse and carriage and roads were gravel or rutted dirt.

What made the land so attractive was the proximity to New York City via the Erie Railroad to Port Jervis, N.Y. or to Shohola, Pennsylvania. Still, it was an all day trip when William and George built their country homes.

William F. and Vouletti Singer Proctor had three children: William Ross, Charles Edward, and Ada Olive. The Ross middle name was to honor his good friend, George Ross MacKenzie.
—sandpond.org.

Loch Ada and Sand Pond
In 1880 the Proctor family had 3 servants, 7 carpenters, 3 painters, and 2 paper hangers.

Around 1870 William Fash Proctor had purchased several thousand acres of land that included Haggai's Pond and Sand Pond. He changed the name of Haggai's Pond to Loch Ada to honor his daughter, Ada. The English Tudor home he built was called Lochada. (Half of Sand Pond, half of Round Pond, and all of Haggai/Loch Ada were located in the Town of Lumberland.)

In the 1880s Charles E. Proctor, son of William F. Proctor, kept a travel diary when he visited a number of local places, including, Haggai, Round, and Sand Ponds.

We will also have time to visit Sand Pond, the most beautiful sheet of water in Sullivan, the property of Mr. W.F. Proctor whose superb summer home is but a mile distant.

The waters of Sand Pond are as cold as ice and as clear as crystal—sand being clearly seen at a depth of 30 feet. A sounding has been taken to the depth of 70 feet, but no bottom was found.

This lake is connected by an underground passage with Round Pond, but a quarter of a mile to the northeast. This small lake is without doubt the deepest in the county being touched at a depth of 90 feet.

In both these lakes there is good fishing especially in Sand

"Sand Pond, the most beautiful sheet of water in Sullivan," near the Proctor Lochada Estate. Photo is courtesy of the Proctor Family.

Pond where the gamiest and strongest bass in the state are caught. Salmon trout of good size have been taken, but in late years they seem to have diminished, until now they are rarely caught.

These lakes being private, it is necessary to get permission before fishing can be indulged in. One mile to the south is Haggai's Pond or "Loch Ada" also on the property of Mr. Proctor. Here is situated his summer home by far the most beautiful and expensive house.—Charles E. Proctor.

Over the years the Proctor family provided many jobs for people in the area. We will visit the Proctor family in the 1890s when my great uncle Lon Austin worked for William F. Proctor at Lochada.

Congregational and Methodist Churches

The congregations of the Methodist and Congregational Churches had been in Eldred for many years.

The Methodist Church just northwest of Eldred Corners, had been built in 1859. M. Lambert was the Methodist minister in 1880.

The Congregational Church southeast of Eldred Corners had been started in 1799 by Isaac Sergeant. A number of Rev. Sergeant's descendants play a part in this story.

Rev. Felix Kyte, originally from Lydd, England, had been the pastor of the Congregational Church for 46 years. After Felix died in 1878, the Church seemed to have difficulty finding another pastor.

E.W. Fisher was the pastor in 1880, the year a Congregational parsonage was purchased. When the Fisher family moved several years later, E.W.'s wife Lucy continued to correspond with Aida Austin.

One source said that neither church had a steeple until 1900. According to an 1879 letter of Mary Ann Austin, the Congregational Church in Eldred planned to put on a steeple in July 1879. There are two photos (taken from opposite sides of Eldred), that show both churches without steeples.

1880s Church News

1880–1890 Congregational Church Pastors
E.W. Fisher, 1880–1883
J.E. Perine, 1883–1884
H.P. Hamilton, 1885–1888
J.R. Taylor, 1888–1888
W.C. Wilcox, 1888–1889
E.A. Smith, 1889–1892

Congregational Church New Members
Ida Quick, January 1880
Sarah Webb, 1881
Ida Barnes, 1881
S. St. John Gardner, September 1881
Aida A. Austin, 1882
Mrs. Hugh Quick, 1883
Mrs. Priscilla Owens (Kilpatrick), 1883
William H. Whitney, February 1884
Libbie Sergeant, 1888
Henry Ladore Austin, 1889

Methodist Episcopal Church Pastors
M.S. Lambert, 1880–1882
H. Litts, 1883–1889
W.H. Carson, 1886

M.E. Church Baptisms by M.S. Lambert, 1880, Eldred
Olin Hickok
Charles M. Austin
Katie B. Parker
Minnie C. Kelso
Laura C. Parker
Theresa Osier
Ella J. Kelso
Joanna Bradley

M.E. Church Baptisms by M.S. Lambert, 1880, Barryville
Ella Calkin
Alice J. VanTuyl
Amelia E. Hallock

The Pond Eddy United Methodist Church built around 1882 by George W. Maney, included beautiful stained glass windows.

View of Eldred looking west. The Congregational Church minus a steeple is on the left. The old school building which the Austin sisters disliked, is the small building just below the Congregational Church. The Methodist Church is the next white building in the distance, also minus a steeple. C.C.P. Eldred's home is on the far right, across from the barns. Photo courtesy of Chuck Myers.

Area Residents in the 1880s

Abel S. Myers and his family lived behind the Congregational Church and the schoolhouse. Abel had a store and also farmed. His first wife had died and Abel had married Maria Hankins. In 1880 the Myers household included their children: Jackson, 3, Sarah (Lulu), 1, and Edwin V. Myers (from Abel's first marriage); and their servant, Mary Raub. Edwin Myers, a store clerk, probably in his father's store, was a very good friend of my grandfather, Mort Austin.

Mort (Charles Mortimer), 15, and his brother Ladore (Dory), 13, and their sister, Henrietta, 30, lived with their parents William Henry and Mary Ann Austin on the old Austin Homestead.

In 1870 the 260 acre triangle piece of land formed by Hagan Pond, Proctor, and Collins Roads seems to have belonged to Henry Austin. Henry owned at least 100 acres of land in 1880. His property with buildings was valued at $2,675.

Henry Austin had not been able to continue his trucking or carting business in New York City with his brother Augustus. By 1880 Henry Austin had been farming full time for 4 years.

The 1880s letters indicate there were financial problems for Henry still, and that he was discouraged with his farm and wanted to sell it. Eventually, that creates other problems for the family.

The older Austin brothers, Lon (Albert A. Austin) and Ell (James Eldred Austin), were in Kansas.

Ell, in Saline County, worked as a brakeman on the railroad and lived at the Railroad Hotel with 40 others. He would soon be working for Henry Parmenter who owned quite a bit of land in Kansas.

Lon was in Solomon City where their sister Emma had died in November 1879. Lon was a laborer and lived on Poplar Street with Charles Evenoe also from New York. But in 1881, letters indicate Lon traveled to Oregon and California.

For a number of years, Henry and Mary Ann Austin's family in Eldred had traveled by train to New York City to be with their Eldred-Austin cousins in the winter. In late June the cousins took the cars (as the train was called) to Eldred where they spent the summer.

In January 1881, the Austin sisters Aida, 19, and Maria, 27, were in New York City with their Eldred-Austin cousins, according to the 1881 Diary that Aida Austin kept.

Chapter 2
Dear Diary
Aida Austin's 1881 Diary

Saturday, January 1
"A bad beginning makes a good ending?" I hope that is true for I have made a very bad beginning.

Tom took the boys around to Net's this afternoon. Harry and I went to Central Park after supper. There was no skating, so we called at Mrs. Braisted's. It was 11 o'clock when we got home.

Lil came around this afternoon. She found out there was no skating and told Ida, and she has been laughing at me ever since.

Aida Austin a few years before she wrote her 1881 Diary. Photo courtesy of Katherine Calkin Traxler.

So wrote Aida Antoinette Austin at the start of the year in her small, leather-covered 1881 Diary.

Aida, 19, lived in New York City with Uncle Augustus and Aunt Maria Eldred Austin. Almost every day Aida wrote about the weather or daily life. She often mentioned her sister Maria, who also lived with Eldred-Austin relatives.

Aida's father Henry Austin was the brother of Uncle Augustus Austin. Aida's mother Mary Ann Eldred was a half sister of Maria Eldred, wife of Uncle Augustus.

Summer in Eldred, New York
In the summer, Aida and some of her New York City relatives travelled some 107 miles by train to Shohola, then to Eldred, where they most likely stayed at the old Austin homestead with Aida's parents Henry and Mary Ann; and brothers Mort and Dory Austin.

When Aida was in Eldred, she wrote about raking hay on their farm, spending time with friends in Eldred (the Village), and visits from relatives who lived in the area: Uncle C.C.P and Aunt Effa who lived nearby; Uncle Irv and Aunt Laura Clark on the west side of Eldred; the Gardner and Calkin families in Barryville.

Winter in New York City
During the winter and fall months when Aida was in New York City, she described skating, sailing, shopping, going to the dentist and doctor, enjoying nearby Central Park, getting the mail, celebrating holidays, visiting people (often relatives), studying, and playing checkers (a very Austin activity).

Uncle Augustus and Aunt Maria
At the start of 1881, Aida lived with Uncle Augustus, Aunt Maria, Cousin Ida Belle, and possibly Cousin Ed, on Grouverneur Boulevard in New York City. Ed was a night watchman; Ida was a teacher. Uncle Augustus and Aunt Maria lived with or next to their daughter, Cousin Addie Austin Thompson and her family.

Addie's husband Thomas J. Thompson was an accountant. Their sons Gussie (Augustus), 7, and Tommy, 5, kept things lively. Harry, 15, was listed as a son working in Tom Sr.'s office.

When Tommy was a baby, he had been cared for by Aida's sister Emma. It had only been a year and a month since Emma had died of tuberculosis in Kansas, but Aida did not mention Emma's death in her diary. Tommy Thompson still visited and sometimes stayed with Aida's family in Eldred, New York.

Aida may have watched the boys for Addie, who she called Ad, in her diary. Or perhaps Aida was attending school.

The first week of 1881 started off with plumbing problems at the home of Uncle Augustus and Aunt Maria. It took several return trips over a few days before the plumbing was fixed.

N.Y.C., Monday, January 3, 1881
Mr. Buckbee was here this morning. He is going to send the plumber here tomorrow.

N.Y.C., Tuesday, January 4, 1881
The plumbers have been here all day and I have not got a bit of sewing done.

N.Y.C., Wed., January 5, 1881
The plumbers have been here again all day.

N.Y.C., Thurs., January 6, 1881
Maria came over this afternoon. I was just going out. I called down at Mrs. B.'s to see if she would go to Central Park Saturday evening with Harry and I.

The plumbers were here again this morning until eleven o'clock.

Some People in New York City
Aida often talked about the Braisted family. Mrs. B. was Laura Braisted. Laura, her husband William Braisted, and their sons George and William, lived in the 12th Ward of New York City. William Braisted was an assistant foreman at the fire department. Mr. and Mrs. Braisted Sr. and their son Otis, 15, also lived there.

Some of the other Eldred-Austin cousins (who are often mentioned in the diary): Mortimer Bruce (Mort) Austin, Net Austin Clinton, Rand Austin Paton, and their families lived within 3 miles of the senior Austins and the Thompson family.

Aida's sister Maria may have lived with and helped out her cousin Net Clinton. Other relatives will be introduced as we meet them in the diary.

The rest of this chapter will be excerpts from Aida's 1881 Diary, interspersed with letters from or to her family, and information on events and places in New York City or Eldred, New York.

N.Y.C., Saturday, January 8, 1881
Harry and I went to Central Park. Mrs. Braisted and George went with us.

N.Y.C., Sunday, January 9, 1881
I have written to Mother and Dora West this afternoon.

N.Y.C., Mon., January 10, 1881
I have studied and sewed and taught the children. Mrs. Trimble has been here making Ida's dress.

N.Y.C., Tues., January 18, 1881
Net and Cousin Mary had letters from Alaska today. Harry and I have been in the yard skating. Little Net came down this afternoon.

Alonzo Eugene Austin Family, Missionaries in Sitka, Alaska
The letters were from the Alonzo Eugene Austin family. Alonzo E. was the oldest child of Uncle Augustus and Aunt Maria.

Alonzo E. Austin, his wife Belle

Cover of Aida Austin's 1881 Diary. It's 2-3/4 inches wide and 4-inches high.

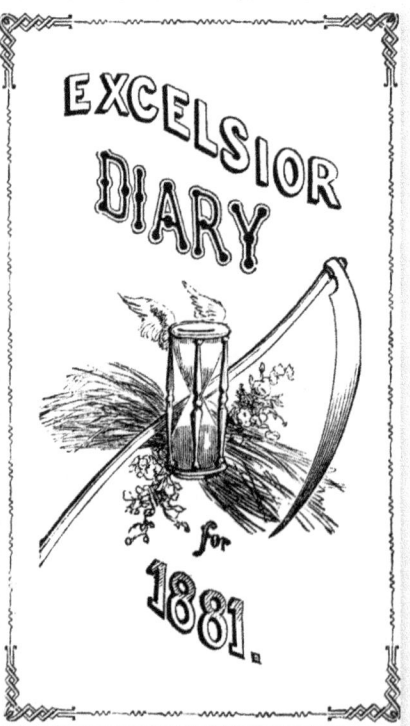
Title page of Aida Austin's 1881 Diary. Courtesy of Mary Briggs Austin.

Camp, and their children Olinda, Henrietta, and Alonzo E. Austin Jr. lived in Sitka, Alaska, in 1881.

Sitka was west of British Columbia on the Alaskan Panhandle. In 1867 the U.S. purchased the Alaskan Territory from the Russian Empire for $7.2 million dollars. Sitka was kept as the capital.

Alonzo E. Austin went to Sitka in 1879 as a missionary for the Presbyterian Church. He had traveled the 4,000 mile trip at the urging of his seminary friend, John Brady.

Alonzo's wife and children: Belle, Olinda (Linnie), Henrietta, and Alonzo Jr., joined Alonzo in Alaska by early 1880.

Belle and daughters Olinda and Henrietta taught in an elementary school that the Austins may have started in Sitka.

By 1883 a boarding school (now part of Sheldon Jackson College) was opened for the Native boys. Sheldon Jackson, a Presbyterian Missionary and later a political leader, became the First General Agent of Education in Alaska.

A Sheldon Jackson School document states that the first building (called Austin Hall) was a 5,000 square foot, two-story building built from "salvaged lumber from an abandoned fish cannery at Old Sitka, the site of the Russians' first fort in the region."—*Information from: Sikes, Art,* Austins in Alaska, Alonzo Eugene Austin, *Austin Families Newsletter,* September 2008; alaskahistoricalsociety.org; yukonpresbytery.com; askart.com; and wikipedia.org.

Henrietta Marries Walter Styles
Henrietta Austin seems to have married Walter Styles by 1881. Walter lived in the area of Sitka

Uncle Augustus and Aunt Maria Austin. Photo courtesy of Katherine Calkin Traxler.

and Hoonah from 1880 to around 1885, where he was a missionary-teacher. He was also Sitka's Postmaster for two years.

Walter was an accomplished artist. His paintings recorded the life among the Tinglit people of Alaska and were widely published in the late 1800s.

We will meet Walter and Henrietta Austin Styles later on in this book, but not under happy circumstances. Walter would become a town leader in the village of Eldred.

N.Y.C., Friday, January 21, 1881
Rained all day. Tommy was going to have his birthday party. He is five years old, but no one came. It has been such a bad day.

Possibly Alonzo Eugene Austin, son of Uncle Augustus. Cynthia Leavenworth Bellinger Collection.

Tommy Thompson's Birthday
N.Y.C. Sat., January 22, 1881
Tommy had his party today. Nettie and Buddie, Willie and George, and Bertie and Georgie Ackwell. Willie has a new pair of skates.

Archie and Rand Austin Paton
Nettie and Buddie (little Archie) Paton, were children of Archie and Rand Austin Paton *(see p. 32)*. Apparently little Ida was not at the party. The Paton family lived on East 8th Street in New York City. Archie Paton was a carpenter.

Unfortunately, there are no photos of the Paton children.

Willie and George were sons of the Braisteds.

On Saturday Aida had started a letter to her brother Lon in Kansas. She continued to write it on Sunday.

Aida Austin, N.Y.C. to Lon Austin
Sunday, January 23, 1881
Dear Brother Lon,

I have been so very busy that you will have to forgive me for not answering your letter before. Tommy is having his birthday party. Nettie and Buddie and Georgie and Willie Braisted are here and a little girl and the boy from across the way are coming. So you can imagine the lively time we are having.

The little girl and boy from across the way came and I had to stop writing and amuse the children.

They played games until supper and then they went up in the parlor and spoke pieces and sang and then played games until eight, when George and Willie went home.

Net and Buddie stayed all night and have just gone home.

Maria, Mrs. Braisted, Willie, and I are going to the Park someday next week. I wish you were here to go with us.

How I do wish I could see you. I have so much to talk about. Where is Ell [their brother] and how is he getting along?

We have had some very cold weather and a great deal of snow. I think they must have had some fearful weather in Sullivan. I have not heard from them in sometime.

I am going to have some pictures as soon as I can get out and if they are decent, I will send you one of them. I hope you will get some of yours and send one to me. Write soon. With much love, I remain your affectionate sister,
Aida

Wm. Sutherland, Lawrence, Kans., to Alonzo Austin, Solomon City, Kans.
Sunday, January 23, 1881
Friend Lon,

When Sunday comes, I find myself thinking more than on other days of my acquaintances in Solomon and it becomes natural that I should have a short 'talk' with some of them.

There are two families on each side of us who are having considerable trouble. One of the husbands gets drunk and his wife has threatened to leave him and she went so far one day as to send the furniture downtown to an auction store, but by the efforts of friends, she was persuaded to try him once more.

The other husband wants to leave his wife, but she won't divide the plunder, so he has threatened to kill her and then kill himself.

Snow is falling today, but not very fast. There is not enough for sleigh riding. Skating is the principle outdoor exercise down here. The skaters sometimes get up carnivals and wear costumes.

Tommy Thompson, the birthday boy. Photo courtesy of Katherine Calkin Traxler.

Albert Alonzo (Lon) Austin, Aida's brother who was out west. Photo courtesy of Katherine Calkin Traxler.

The first session of school will soon be over and I will have to buy some more books.

This is a great town for churches and schools. This morning I heard 3 bells ringing at one time. When they get through ringing, they toll the bell slowly as if for the dead. I suppose that it is a warning for the living to turn aside from their wicked ways.

The End of the World has been prophesied for 1881. But it may be that there is some mistake about that being so.

A comet has been seen, I believe fooling around in the sky "seeking whom he may devour."

That which is in the place where a mustache should flourish, is looming up, down, sideways, crossways and so forth. Lizzie says that I am in style for the color of it is old gold and that shade seems to be the rage.

Autographs is the rage with the girls at school at present. I have written in 10 or 12 autograph books, I guess.

There's music in the air. A young man downstairs plays the banjo. This city is well supplied with music; Three or four bands besides stringed instruments.

We live opposite the Congregational Church. They have a big pipe organ. I think that I'll go over to church tonight.

Fare Ye Well, Yours truly, Wm. G. Sutherland

The Sutherland Family
Stephen and Phoebe Warner Sutherland and their children, Anne Agnes, Irving, William, Alfred, Martha, Catherine, Norman W., and Washington, lived in Lumberland in 1880. It isn't clear if Wm. G. Sutherland was the son of Stephen and Phoebe.

Catharine Sutherland would marry William Horton. They would be the grandparents of William Erwin Horton, a great-grandson of Isaac M. and Joanna Bradley.

Norman W. Sutherland would be the grandfather of Darlene Sutherland Haas.

N.Y.C., Mon., January 24, 1881
Gussie stayed upstairs nearly all day and little Tom and I have had a very peaceful time. Mort (Aida's cousin) stopped in tonight.

N.Y.C., Tues., January 25, 1881
Ad went to Rand's this afternoon. I finished my letter to Lon.

N.Y.C., Wed., January 26, 1881
Mrs. Braisted, Georgie, and Willie and I went to Central Park this afternoon. We had a splendid skate. Mr. Braisted is home again sick.

N.Y.C., Tues., February 1, 1881
It has snowed all day so we did not go to the Park. I had a letter from mother today. She cannot come down. I have commenced studying again.

N.Y.C., Wed., February 2, 1881
It has been fearful cold today; went to the Park.

N.Y.C., Thurs., February 3, 1881
It has not been quite so cold today. Ida frosted her big toe yesterday. Maria was here this afternoon. She is going to stay with Mary. They are going to give her 12 dollars a month.

N.Y.C., Wed., February 9, 1881
Rand and the children and Net and Lil around today.

Lil may be Lillie Calkin, daughter of Oliver and Maria Gardner Calkin. Maria was the daughter of Eliza Eldred Gardner.

Eldred-Austin Cousins in 1881

Grouvernour Ave., N.Y.C.
Uncle Augustus and Aunt Maria Austin; Edward Austin; Ida Belle Austin; and Thomas J., Addie Austin, Gussie, Tommy, and Harry Thompson.

Brooklyn, New York
Mortimer (Mort) Bruce and Mary Millspaugh Austin, and their children: Mary Isabelle, Charles Augustus, and John Mortimer Austin.

East Broadway Street, N.Y.C.
Henry and Net Austin Clinton, and their baby.

East 8th Street, N.Y.C., N.Y.
Archibald and Miranda (Rand) Austin Paton, and children: Nettie, Mary, Ida, and Archibald R. (Archie/Buddie).

Sitka, Alaska
Alonzo Eugene and Belle Camp Austin; Olinda, Henrietta, and Alonzo Eugene Austin Jr.

New York City, N.Y.
Tina Austin Laing, a widow.

Eldred, New York
Uncle Irvin and Aunt Laura Austin Clark and their sons: Ellsworth, Elbert, and Robert Clark.
Uncle Perry and Aunt Mary Murray Parker Schoonover; George, Kate, and Laura Parker; and Daniel Rowlee and Emily Schoonover.
Uncle C.C.P. and Aunt Effa Eldred, Rebecca (Becca) Eldred, and James D. Eldred.

Barryville, New York
Aunt Eliza Eldred Gardner and her children: Maria Gardner Calkin, Stephen St. John Gardner, James E. Gardner, and their families. Eliza's daughter, Ann Eliza Gardner Cuddeback, her husband Lewis Cuddeback, and their children lived in Orange County, New York.

From Mary Ann Austin's Scrapbook

Great-Grandmother Mary Ann Austin had a scrapbook in which she kept many poems, newspaper articles, photos, and pictures.

The poems from 1879 (the time of her daughter Edith Emogene Austin's death) and before are in, *The Mill on Halfway Brook*.

This chapter has the newspaper articles on the deaths of President Garfield and the poet Henry Wadsworth Longfellow, as well as a few of the many other poems that were in her scrapbook. Other poems are in the Appendix, pp. 449, 450.

Special thanks to Melva Austin Barney for sharing the scrapbook.

To an Old Coat

Poor coat, well loved for many
   reasons,
Since both of us grow old, Be true;
This hand has brushed you for ten
   seasons.
E'en Socrates no more could do.

Whilst Time your thin and white-
   seamed stuff
Keeps on attacking without end.
Wisely, like me, his blows rebuff;
And never let us part, old friend.

That birthday flown, when first I
   wore you,
I mind well—memory yet
   is strong
My friends around to honour
   bore you,
And poured their welcome forth
   in song.

Your shabby plight—of which I'm
   vain—
Hinders them not an arm to lend.
They'd freely feast us now again;
So never let us part, old friend.

You're patched behind, an ancient
   rending;
That, too, recalls a past delight:
One night to run from Jane
   pretending,
I felt her soft hand clutch me tight.

Torn were you, and that frightful tear
It took my Jane two days to mend,
Whilst I was held her captive there;
So never let us part, old friend.

Have you been steeped in musk
   and amber,
Which fops sniff, looking in
   the glass?
Or pushed along an ante-chamber.
For swells to sneer at as we pass?

Throughout all France by faction rent.
   Ribbons and stars fell strife
   can send—
A field-flower is your ornament;
So never let us part, old friend.

Fear no more days of idle ranging.
When our two fates became as one.
Of pleasure with pain interchanging.
Of intermingled rain and sun.

For the last time I soon shall doff
My clothes, just wait! and we
   will wend
Together, gently going off;
So never let us part, old friend.

—Pierre Jean de Beranger, translated by F. Doyle.

N.Y.C., Thurs., Feb. 10, 1881
I have a very bad cold and feel terrible.

N.Y.C., Friday, February 11, 1881
They went around to Net's this morning and stayed until most dark. My teeth commenced aching so I got Ida to stay with the children and I went to the dentist and had two out. I took the gas and I had to go to bed I felt so bad.

Henry and Net Clinton
Henry and Net Austin Clinton lived on East Broadway Street in New York City. Henry was a brass finisher. Henry and Net had married in 1878. They had a little one that Aida sometimes called Little Dot. Henry and Net's daughter Ida Clinton was the only one of their three children that lived into adulthood.

N.Y.C., Sat., February 12, 1881
My cold is worse. Rand stayed up to her mother's today.

N.Y.C., Mon., February 14, 1881
My cold is so bad I can hardly see.

N.Y.C., Tues., February 15, 1881
My cold is better. I went out this afternoon. I bought 8 valentines, 4 comic ones and 4 nice ones.

I stopped into Net's. The baby is awful cunning. I took a comic valentine down to Mrs. Braisted. She is going to send it to Harry for me so he will get it tomorrow.

N.Y.C., Wed., February 16, 1881
Harry's valentine came today. He was fearful mad until I made him think it was not me and then he did not care much.

N.Y.C., Thurs., Feb. 17, 1881
Maria was over this afternoon. She bought mother a new black dress.

N.Y.C., Friday, February 18, 1881
I must study and drive away these shadows. How dark and cold they fall around my path tonight.

Every one seems false and heartless. I sit and think such bitter things until ambitious hatred touching my heart and brain bids them be.

N.Y.C., Sat., February 19, 1881
Tommy was vaccinated today.

Harry and I went down to Mrs. Braisted's. We stopped at Lizzy Brown's to see where Ida was.

N.Y.C., Sun. February 20, 1881
Peace and love hover around my path tonight. I went to Brooklyn this afternoon and Maria and I went out for a ride. Harry and I went to Rand's after tea. Arch and the girls were going to church so we went with them.

Wm. Sutherland, Lawrence, Kans., to Lon Austin, Kans.
February 20, 1881
Friend Lon,
   My mustache is looming up grand and gloomy. How is yours flourishing?
   Wm. G. Sutherland

N.Y.C., Mon., February 21, 1881
Snowed all the forenoon but cleared off very nice this afternoon. I commenced making my blue wrapper. I am not going to study tonight. I am too tired.

N.Y.C., Thurs., Feb. 24, 1881
It has been very cold today. Ad, Aunt Maria, and Lil went up to Rand's this forenoon and Ida went after school. She is teaching again. Maria was over this afternoon.

N.Y.C., Friday, Feb. 25, 1881
I wrote to Mother today. I have come down in the parlor to study, but I can't seem to get my mind settled to it, so I will write a little and go to bed. It snowed all the forenoon but cleared off very nice this afternoon.

George Lovee, Brookside, N.J., to Alonzo Austin
February 25, 1881
Friend Alonzo,
   I received your letter this day and was very glad to hear from you and that you are still alive and enjoying good health.
   You said that you want to go out to Oregon the first of April. Well I do not know whether I will go there or not. My uncle does not want me to go so far away, but if I can not get a place that suits me I am with you for Oregon. There is not any staying here now.
   I have not had a sleigh ride yet. It has been so warm and rainy here. It is all mud and has been for nearly two weeks. My folks has just told me not to tell you that I will come. They think I will do better here than out there.
   I think that I will be along one of these days. Write and say when you want to start for certain.
   This from your friend,
   George A. Lovee

N.Y.C., Sat., February 26, 1881
Little Net and Buddie brought little Ida down this afternoon. Their mother let them take her out for a walk. She didn't think of them walking her clear down here

Ida Belle Clinton may be the baby mentioned in Aida's diary. Photo courtesy of Melva Austin Barney.

Net Austin's husband, Henry Clinton. Photo courtesy of Melva Austin Barney.

Net (Cousin Nettie) Austin Clinton. From the Melva Austin Barney Collection.

[maybe 2 miles]. Aunt Maria kept her down and sent Bud and Net right back to tell their mother.

N.Y.C., Sun., February 27, 1881
Ida and I took little Ida home this afternoon. We stayed to tea.

Archibald Paton, husband of Rand Austin Paton. Photo courtesy of Melva Austin Barney.

A young Charles Mortimer Austin. Photo courtesy of Katherine Calkin Traxler.

Mort Austin, Eldred, to Lon Austin
Winter, early 1881
Dear Brother Lon,

I begin to think you have forgotten me or are enamored with some nice young lady. I got tired waiting for you to answer my letter, so I will write a few lines.

Father is gone down to Canfield's to spend the evening. It is very pleasant without him. It is like a hush before the thunderstorm.

Scarlet fever is around here. There has 5 been killed with it (see p. 445). The teacher has stopped his school. I am sorry for I want to learn all I could this winter. I like the teacher first rate.

This winter has been the hardest in 25 years. The snow is 3 feet deep and it was outrageous cold yesterday. Today is the first warm day we have had in 12 weeks.

We are all quite well. Father is cross as coal but he is quite good to me now, but it won't last long. I am getting so tired of it.

I wish it was spring so I can get away from here. I go to meeting 3 nights out of a week, so takes away some of the lonely hours. It is getting late. I am getting tired. I must go. Much love to you all. Write soon.
Ever your brother,
Charles M. Austin

N.Y.C., Saturday, March 5, 1881
The door bell has rung about fifty times I guess today.

N.Y.C., Sunday, March 6, 1881
Tired, tired, tired. Arch stopped in this morning just about noon with Nettie, Buddie, and Ida. I took Gussie and Tom around to Net's this afternoon.

Miranda (Rand) Austin Paton. Photo courtesy of Katherine Calkin Traxler.

N.Y.C., Monday, March 7, 1881
Not a very bad beginning for Monday. I took the children to Wood's this morning to get their pictures, but I did not get them. Doctor Lang came this afternoon and vaccinated Harry again.

N.Y.C., Tuesday, March 8, 1881
Net, Lil, and the baby came around to dinner today. I went out this afternoon and took Little Archie out for a walk.

N.Y.C., Wed., March 9, 1881
Rained all day. Ad went around to Net's to dinner and stayed all the afternoon. Gussie went up to his Grandma's, so I brought Tommy up in the parlor and practiced. I am getting so nervous I am almost afraid to go to bed. It seems I should wake up if I went to sleep. I will see Dr. DeVenoge next week.

N.Y.C., Thurs., March 10, 1881
Rand brought little Ida down to Aunt Maria's this afternoon and

has left her down all night. Maria was over this afternoon. Her cold seems to be better. She had a letter from Mother and Dora.

N.Y.C., Friday, March 11, 1881
Ad has been a bed nearly all day. She has such a terrible cold. Ida is going to a ball with Arch and Rand tonight.

N.Y.C., Saturday, March 12, 1881
Little Ida has been down here all the afternoon. Buddie is around to Net's and she has been around two or three times. I have been copying all my papers in a book. They are such a nuisance. I have not studied.

As indicated in Mort's letter to his brother Lon, the Austin home had some stress going on, seemingly because of Henry Austin. Perhaps the pressure of not enough income was getting to him.

It is hard to match up Great-Grandpa Henry as being hard to live with and grouchy, with any of the loving, endearing letters he wrote to his children.

There is a letter dated March 1881 from Ell Austin to his father. It says that Ell had left home without saying good bye.

Ell Austin, Solomon City, Kans., to W.H. Austin, Eldred
March 14, 1881
Dear Father,
I take pen in hand to tell you that I am sorry that I was angry and I did not speak to you when I left home. Also that card I sent you when Mother was here. (Mother tried to keep me from sending it, but I was proud and willful, so she couldn't do anything with me.)

I know it was wrong then for I write to ask you to forgive me.

New York Street-Car Etiquette

A few hints, boiled down, the observance of which will tend to promote the comfort and welfare of that large class of fellow-sufferers who are obliged to spend from thirty minutes to two hours of each day in those necessary evils called street cars.

Gentle hint No. 1 and of importance first:
Always chew tobacco when riding. If you have not acquired that most elegant habit, do so at once, or you will thereby lose one of the best opportunities of showing your independence and utter disregard of the decencies of life, and of your neighbors' clothes.

No. 2
Never give up your seat to anyone, especially to ladies, thereby showing that you were brought up with a proper regard of your own importance and comfort. Should you have a weakness in that respect, however, and should you wish to give up your seat to a lady, be particular that she is young, good-looking and well dressed, and always select the time when some poor washer-woman or tired shop-girl has been hanging on the strap in front of you for half an hour or more. You will thus show that you have a proper regard for what is due to the different classes in society.

No. 3
When standing, always take the first seat vacated. Never mind the ladies; they can do the same. You know your rights; take them. Sit down like a man, and if you have a paper become immediately absorbed. Take no notice of any little mean remarks that may be made by those around you—you might get kicked out of the car if you did.

No. 4
Should a good-looking girl be seated anywhere near you, that is alone, (Be particular about that), stare at her—they like it—and it may lead to—personals in the *Herald*, which object and end should be your highest ambition.—*From Mary Ann Austin's scrapbook.*

Fifth Avenue, New York City. Postcard in the collection of Mary Briggs Austin.

Mary Ann Eldred Austin with one of her children as a baby. Photo courtesy of Katherine Calkin Traxler.

I don't expect we will ever meet again on this earth, but I want to meet you in heaven.
I hope you will write and tell me that you forgive me.
Hoping that this will find you well and will close.
Your aff. son,
J. Eldred Austin

Mary Ann Austin, Eldred, to Lon Austin
(Date unknown)
Dear Son Lon,
You don't write to me, but I will write you a few lines. A Mother may be forgot, but children never. I do want to know just how you get along.
Your father says if you and Ell, or you alone could raise $500 and pay his debts, he would give you the deed of the place. I wish you could. If we had not owed most, tried to borrow half of, and made your father wait for the other half. I think he is so sick of the place. He would rather you boys have it at any rate.
Your loving
Mother

It is unclear as to what happened regarding the Austin property. Records indicate that Ell bought the place or some of it for a $500 mortgage, which causes some family troubles later on.

N.Y.C., Tuesday, March 15, 1881
After tea, Harry and I went out. I stopped to see Dr. Lang. He says it is my heart, that I am nervous. He gave me a bottle of medicine.

N.Y.C., Wed., March 16, 1881
I think that medicine is helping me. I feel better.

George Lovee, Brookside, N.J., to Lon Austin
March 20, 1881
Dear Friend,
I will not go out to Oregon this spring as my uncle does not want me to go. He is getting old and he would rather I would not go.
So far it is raining here and every day, nearly mud without end. I am going in the woods to cut wood.
I don't want to work on a farm. If I was offered 18 dollars amount the year around, I would not take it.
I am going to have a good old time this summer in New Jersey. Next spring I will leave for Oregon and I want you to write to me when you get out there. I was very near leaving this morning with two boys from here for Arkansas, but I backed out.
Well, I have not got much time to write as I have agreed to go and see a pair of black eyes.
All well from your friend,
George A. Lovee

N.Y.C., Monday, March 21, 1881
Sewed a little, drew pictures, and that is about all. Cousin Mort stopped in for his clothes tonight and had a game or two of checkers with Cousin Ida.

N.Y.C., Wed., March 23, 1881
I went to see Dr. Lang. He changed my medicine.

N.Y.C., Thurs., March 24, 1881
I have felt a great deal better today. Maria was over this afternoon. Ad has been out again. Aunt Maria and Ida went up to Rand's.

N.Y.C., Saturday, March 26, 1881
I have not felt very good today. I am afraid his medicine is not helping much after all.

N.Y.C., Sunday, March 27, 1881
Cousin Mort stopped in this morning to bid us good bye. He is going away tomorrow.

Cousin Mort Austin's Family
Mortimer (Mort) Bruce Austin, his wife Mary, and their children Mary Isabelle, Charles Augustus, and John Mortimer Austin lived on South 8th Street in Brooklyn. Cousin Linda Gardner, 16, helped with the housekeeping. Mortimer was a wholesaler of notions and had something wrong with his leg.
Linda Gardner may have been Mary L. *(see p. 445)* daughter of Stephen St. John Gardner, who was the son of Aunt Eliza Gardner.

Mary Ann Austin, Eldred, to Lon Austin, Solomon City, Kans.
March 27, 1881
My dear Son,
Your long looked for letter has arrived. It is very welcome, for indeed I thought you had forgot your Mother and I was afraid you was sick, as Eldred [Ell] did not

say anything about you.

How I do wish you was working to Proctors and boarding home. Gus Osier has moved on his father-in-law's place so that he will be nearer Proctor. But George Parker lives near his father, so he has a good way to walk.

They say that this man that has bought near Proctors is worth the most so that it will make plenty work.

George Hickok came home last week dressed like a gentleman and set some crazy to leave this place. Bill R. and H. Sprague expect to leave for Catheray in a few weeks. Olin Hickok went last Monday.

Wells's wife came out with George. George says he gets $100 a month driving a gypsy wagon, is doing well; and Wells makes money. But he has bad luck losing horses I think.

Tom [Collins] and Gus [Osier] find it cost them more married than single. Kelso and his team don't look as though they could stand up to the school boys who hollar at him, "Take that team to the boneyard." Kelso threatened to arrest them and take them to Monticello where they would learn manners.

Rob [Kelso] is home yet to help build a new house on the hill again.

Mr. Middaugh is our neighbour in the Parker house. They buried their little boy a few weeks ago. Miss Emma Middaugh (I suppose you are acquainted with her) who was home to the funeral, went back to her work.

Our Congregational minister lives in the Newcomb house. Dr. DeVenoge has moved back.

I have told all the news I can think of except Henry Lily's wife is dead. Her daughter, Mrs. Parker, moved out there about four weeks before she died, but they do not like it there and have moved to Kansas City.

I received a letter from Mrs. Wells. She likes it very much in Tennessee. Says they are making gardens. It is anything but that here. It is very cold and the wind is blowing. A very hard March. Came in like a Lion and stays like a roaring Lion.

I do hope you will have success. Mortie is sick.

Please write to your loving Mother

N.Y.C., Thurs. March 31, 1881
Maria was over this afternoon. She had a letter from Mother. Mort [Charles M., her brother] has the bilious fever. Rob Kelso is going to stay home all summer. They are going to build a new house on the hill again.

The Kelso Family
Rob Kelso wrote Aida a couple of endearing letters in 1879 when he went out west. The Kelso family lived in Eldred and were friends of the Austins at one time, though there seemed to be some disagreement later. The Kelso house had burned down in 1878.

N.Y.C., Tuesday, April 5, 1881
A fearful windy day.

N.Y.C., Wednesday, April 6, 1881
Ad went to a matinee this afternoon with Net. The children and Rand have been down nearly all the afternoon. Tom and I have been playing checkers. He beat me four and I beat him six.

N.Y.C., Thursday, April 7, 1881
Had a letter from Dora West this morning. Maria was over this afternoon. She did not stay to tea. Ad went out this morning with Rand. They left Archie here and

Aida's 1881 Diary mentions Mortimer Bruce Austin often playing checkers. Photo courtesy of Melva Austin Barney.

Ida up to Aunt Maria's. He is the sweetest little fellow ever was. Annie C. [Collins from Eldred] has been to see Maria.

N.Y.C., Friday, April 8, 1881
Harry and I went down to Mrs. Braisted's after supper. There was a fearful big rat in the hall. Her brothers killed it.

G. Lovee, Brookside, N.J., to A. Austin, Solomon City, Kans.
April 13, 1881
Friend Alonzo,
Yours was received yesterday and was varry much surprised. I had thought that you were in Oregon by this time. How is it that you did not go out there?

Uncle Augustus Austin. "Uncle Gustus and Mrs. Fanning danced a jig." Photo courtesy of Katherine Calkin Traxler.

Aunt Maria Eldred Austin. "Aunt Maria and Eliza went to Middletown." Photo courtesy of Katherine Calkin Traxler.

It is raining here today and it did yesterday. I am cutting wood and getting out railroad ties. I make $1.25/day. Sometimes I wish that I was out there. Jersey ain't big enough for me. This is my last summer in it.

Well, you must come home and stay this summer and next winter and then we'll go where ever you want to go.

Give my best regards to all of the boys. I am your friend, George A. Lovee

N.Y.C., Thursday, April 28, 1881
Maria is going to stay here. Net and Bud came down after school.

N.Y.C., Monday, May 2, 1881
Rained a little today. I beaded the lace for my hat.

N.Y.C., Wednesday, May 4, 1881
I went to Ridley's this forenoon. Took the children and got their shoes. This afternoon Ida, Annie, Gus, Tommy, little Ida, and I went to the Park. I tried to find the kind dentist with Gussie. Ad had a letter from Cousin Mort today, saying he will be here tonight about ten o'clock.

N.Y.C., Thursday, May 5, 1881
Mort came last night. He is going to board here. Tom and I played checkers with him tonight. He beat us terrible.

N.Y.C., Saturday, May 7, 1881
Tom [Addie's husband] took Gussie [their son] to have his tooth pulled this forenoon. After tea Maria and I went out to see a picture, "The Inn Keeper's Daughters."

N.Y.C., Tuesday, May 10, 1881
I took Tommy out this afternoon. We got some ice cream first.

N.Y.C., Friday, May 13, 1881
Cousin Susie [Gardner] came down just at dinner time. She brought her friend Mrs. Fanning with her. After, we all went in the parlor. We sang and Ida spoke two pieces. We had a splendid time. Uncle Gustus and Mrs. Fanning danced a jig.

N.Y.C., Saturday, May 14, 1881
Susie and Mrs. Fanning went home this forenoon. Net brought her baby around this afternoon, fun! Eliza and Charley Gardner came down this forenoon.

N.Y.C., Monday, May 16, 1881
It rained nearly all the forenoon and it has been cloudy all day so Net did not get around with her baby.

N.Y.C., Wednesday, May 18, 1881
Have sewed all the afternoon. Mort has gone traveling again.

Tom came home early tonight and said he had tickets for Daily's Theater and we had to hurry around. We got there just as the curtain rose.

N.Y.C., Thursday, May 26, 1881
Cousin Tina took dinner to Net's today and she came around to Aunt Maria's to tea. Net had the baby's picture taken. Ad went over to Mary's.

Tina Austin Laing
Ranny Laing, Tina (Justina) Austin Laing's husband, died before 1880. Tina must have been ill in 1880. The census listed her as a widow and seamstress in the women's hospital in New York.

N.Y.C., Sunday, May 29, 1881
Aunt Eliza [Gardner], Aunt Maria, Uncle Gustus, and Maria went to church this morning. Tommy and Gussie went to Sunday School this afternoon with Harry. They seemed to like it very much.

N.Y.C., Monday, May 30, 1881
Ad and Tom, Uncle Gustus and Aunt Maria, Gussie and Aunt Eliza went to Rockaway this afternoon, and Ida, Lil, and I went to Brighton Beach.

N.Y.C., Tuesday, May 31, 1881
Maria had a letter from home this morning. Mother is sick and wants Maria to come home. She is going Thursday. Mort came back just before tea.

N.Y.C., Wednesday, June 1, 1881
Maria and I were out this morning shopping.
Maria left for Eldred on Thursday.

N.Y.C., Friday, June 3, 1881
It has been dark and cold and rainy all day. I had grown almost discouraged. It seemed as if everything was going wrong. They are making little Tom so bad. While we were eating supper the children got to playing and making such a noise.

N.Y.C., Saturday, June 4, 1881
I had a letter from Maria this morning. She says she found Mother very sick, but she thinks she is a little better.

N.Y.C., Sunday, June 5, 1881
Tommy and Gussie went to Sunday School twice.

This next letter, from Maria to her brother Lon, is typical of the Austin dry sense of humor. A fun surprise from "quiet" Maria who was in Eldred to care for her mother who was ill.

The Austin neighbors Robert and Amanda Kelso had at least 6 children. Emma, the oldest, had recently married Tom Collins. Minnie may be Minnie Kelso. Rob Kelso (mentioned earlier) had been *sweet* on Aida. Edward Kelso was the doctor. Mr. Kelso in the following letter was Robert Sr.

Maria Austin, Eldred, to Lon Austin
June 6, 1881
Dear Brother Lonie,
We have just received a postal card from you. Mother has been wanting me to write to you ever since I came home, but haven't had anytime for writing or any thing else as she has been quite sick, but is better now, but not able to write.
Thursday, I left the folks all well in New York. Aida is wondering why you do not write. She is soon coming home.

Tina Austin Laing. "Cousin Tina took dinner to Net's today." Photo courtesy of Katherine Calkin Traxler.

I wish you were here. I am sorry you are so far from home. Ell—we haven't heard from him since you left Kansas. I hear Alfred Skinner is home.
The country looks very nice. I haven't heard any news to write you as I haven't been out since I came home, so you must excuse a short letter and all mistakes as I haven't much time for writing, for there is no one here nearly all the time.
Mr. T.K. Collins has just been here. I haven't seen him since he was married. I don't know if I could stand the pressure as Minnie said. She heard I was grieving myself to death over Tom and that Mother said if he had only married one of her girls, she wouldn't have cared which one, only so that he would have been in the family.
Dr. Kelso is home practicing on Mrs. Gregg. Rob has sideboards and is practicing on a lumber pile. Mr. Kelso is practicing law—

Ridley's

Aida Austin often talked about Ridleys.

Edward Ridley Sr., an English immigrant, founded Ridley's in 1849. The store started as a small building on Grand Street. By 1883 Mr. Ridley's store included the entire street-front on Grand from Orchard to Allen. According to some sources, it was the country's largest retail store.

Ridley was one of the Lower East Side's most important retailers. At one time, the store had five acres of floor space and up to 2,400 employees.

Visitors at the well-known establishment of Edward Ridley & Sons, corner of Grand and Allen Streets, yesterday, found themselves in the midst of a bewildering array of Fall and Winter goods.

It was the opening of the three days' exhibition of all the novelties which the firm have recently imported from Europe, and the new designs that the ingenuity of foreign artists had produced were displayed in tasteful profusion.—The New York Times, October 6, 1880.

his mark is Uncle Perry. He has sued him three times. Perry beat everytime.

Ever your affectionate sister,
Maria

Uncle Perry and Aunt Mary
Uncle Perry was the father of Daniel Rowlee Schoonover who we met in Chapter 1. Uncle Perry, his wife Aunt Mary Murray Parker, and their children, Emily and Daniel Rowlee Schoonover, lived in Eldred in 1881. Mary's daughters Kate and Laura Parker must have been in Eldred for the summer, as they picked huckleberries with Aida in July.

N.Y.C., Tuesday, June 7, 1881
Net, Lil, and the baby came around to dinner and Aunt Eliza came down. It commenced to rain almost as soon as they got here.

N.Y.C., Thursday, June 9, 1881
Lil went home today. Aunt Maria and Eliza went to Middletown. It has rained all the afternoon. I went to Ridley's.

N.Y.C., Tuesday, June 14, 1881
I was around to Net's. We had quite a long talk. I guess I will come back with her in the fall.

N.Y.C., Thursday, June 16, 1881
Ad went out this forenoon just before dinner and did not get back until nearly supper time. Cousin Mort has gone traveling again, and will not be back until Monday night.

N.Y.C., Sunday, June 19, 1881
Harry and I went on the Long Branch this morning to Newburgh for a sail. We bumped into another boat at Newburgh, but it did not do much damage, only broke the railing and some of the beams. No one was hurt.

Maria Austin, Aida's sister. Photo courtesy of Katherine Calkin Traxler.

N.Y.C., Monday, June 20, 1881
Ad and I went to Macy's and to Lord & Taylors this afternoon. She bought the children linen suits.

N.Y.C., Thurs., June 23, 1881
Had a card from Lon this morning.

N.Y.C., Friday, June 24, 1881
Took little Tom out this afternoon and got him a pair of boots.

Aida and Her Cousins in Eldred
In June, Cousins Ida Belle, Addie, and Addie's son, Tommy, went with Aida to her home in Eldred (the Village), some 100 miles away by train.

Eldred, Saturday, June 25, 1881
Came home today. It seems so nice to be home once more. Mother seems a great deal better. Every thing looks splendid.

Eldred, Sunday, June 26, 1881
I was going down to church this morning with father, but it rained, and this afternoon I was too lazy to go.

We have had 6 or 7 callers: Mr. Collins and Annie, Mr. Sergeant, Uncle Perry and Aunt Mary, George Myers and his wife. I wrote to Ad and Ida.

J.E. Austin, Solomon City, Kans., to His Brother
June 26, 1881
Dear Brother,
I was glad to hear from you and learn that you like it where you are and are doing well.
We had a hailstorm here 2 or

Dr. Kelso's house in Callicoon, New York. Postcard courtesy of Mary Briggs Austin.

3 weeks ago that done a good deal of damage. I thought it hurt my corn fearfully, but it has come out all right and looks first rate.

I have had to cultivate all alone and I am just about tired out. I am getting a little thin. I've got down to 126 pounds. I tell you, I will be glad when the corn is laid by so I can get a little rest.

The cyclone that they had in Solomon City scared the folks so badly that a good many have made them dugouts to go in, in case of another.

We have had a good deal of hard wind and rain since. Every time a storm comes up, most everybody goes in the cellar.

Our last trial at Salina has cost me about $35 or $40.

I begun this letter a week ago but have been so busy and tired that I could not finish it before.

I received a letter from Maria the other day which I will enclose in this.

If I can raise the money, I think I will go home for a week or two in September.

Please write soon and tell me all about the county.
Your aff. brother,
J. Eldred Austin

Eldred, Monday, June 27, 1881
It has been rainy most all day. Tommy and I went to the village this morning to post Ad's letter. Aunt Eliza and Myers Gardner came up to dinner. They stayed to tea. It was raining quite hard when they started for home and it is raining hard yet.

Gardner Relatives
Aunt Eliza Gardner, the sister of Maria Austin and Mary Ann Austin, lived in Barryville with her son Stephen St. John Gardner and his family. James K., Katie, Mary L., and Myers Gardner were

Mary Murray Parker Schoonover in her later years feeding turkeys. Photo courtesy of Richard James, great-great-grandson.

Stephen's children. Stephen had married his second wife Margaret (Maggie) Terns, in November 1880. A month later his son Herbert had died at age 12, from Scarlet Fever *(see p. 445)*.

James E. Gardner and Maria Gardner Calkin, both of Barryville, or nearby, were also children of Aunt Eliza. Other Gardners mentioned in the diary were probably related to Eliza.

Eldred, Friday, June 28, 1881
Dora West came down a little while this afternoon and Annie Collins stopped in a few minutes. We had a very hard shower. After tea Maria and I went out for a walk. Collins' colt was down here and we took it home.

Aida Austin, Eldred, to Lon Austin
Tuesday, June 28, 1881
Dear Brother Lon,
I received your postal last Thursday, but was busy getting ready to come home. It rained nearly all day yesterday and it was cloudy all day Sunday so I did not go to church, but it is very pleasant today and everything looks splendid.

I do wish you were here. It is so nice. I have not seen anyone hardly yet and have not heard much news.

Maggie Terns, second wife of Stephen St. John Gardner. Photo courtesy of Katherine Calkin Traxler.

Lord & Taylor

Opening Day at Lord & Taylor at Broadway and 20th Street. "Ladies ascending in the elevator." Wood engraving in Frank Leslie's Illustrated Newspaper, v. 35, Jan. 11, 1873, p. 289. Source: Library of Congress, Prints and Photographs Division: LC-USZ62-121663.

Aida Austin shopped at Lord & Taylor in New York City. It would be interesting to know if she knew that her neighbor in Eldred, Jane Ann Myers, was a niece to George Washington Taylor who along with Samuel Lord started the store.

Elizabeth Van Pelt (my great-great-great-grandmother), mother of Jane Ann Myers, was Mr. Taylor's half sister.

Jane Ann Myers named one of her sons George Washington Taylor Myers. George W.T. Myers would have a large, beautiful boarding house on Hagan Pond.

George W. Taylor, of Lord & Taylor, died at age 72, in March 1879, in Manchester, England.

Lord & Taylor Store, 20th St. and Broadway, around 1870. Photo: Library of Congress, W.W. Lytle, STEREO U.S. GEOG File: USZ62-92647.

Mr. Kelso and Uncle Perry have been to law two or three times. Uncle Perry beat every time.

He is going to turn Mr. Kelso out of church if he can. I never saw such people in my life as there are here. They are quarreling the whole time.

Mother wants to know what you have done with everything. She has been worrying about them for fear you have sold them.

She seems better, but she is not out of danger. Any little thing most would kill her. I feel so worried about her.

Let us know how you are getting along and if you hear anything from Ell.

We are all well excepting mother. With much love, I remain your loving sister,
Aida

Eldred, Wed., June 29, 1881
Maria and I called at Mrs. Collins and Dubois. Mrs. D. and Henry walked back with us. They were going down to Kelso's.

Mr. Fisher [the minister] called to see mother. We saw the comet tonight. Mrs. Camping was up a little while this afternoon.

1881 Comet
The 1881 Great Comet (Tebbutt III) appeared in late May to July. It could be seen in the southern sky without a telescope.

Eldred, Thursday, June 30, 1881
Becca called to see us this afternoon. Then she went on to Collins and Dubois. She took tea at Collins.

Henrietta went up to Mary Jane's this afternoon and Ella came back with her. Emma Kelso, or Collins I should say, called for their maid. I did not see her as I was upstairs.

Becca (Rebecca) Eldred was the daughter of Aida's Uncle C.C.P. and Aunt Effa Eldred.

Eldred, Friday, July 1, 1881
It has been very pleasant all day. I have finished fixing my room to study in. It looks real nice. I have taken out the carpet and painted the floor. I am going to commence studying next week. Ida is coming up tomorrow.

Eldred, Saturday, July 2, 1881
Mort and I went down for Cousin Ida this afternoon. I stopped at Lambert's and got my album. The train was two hours behind.
I saw Clara Clark, Mary Wilson, and Becca when we went through the Village. They were fixing the house for a festival they are going to have Monday. Ellsworth and Elbert [Clark] stopped here first after supper. They were coming home from Pond Eddy.
President Garfield was shot this morning at 20 minutes past 9 by one who pretends to be crazy.

Eldred, Sunday, July 3, 1881
It has been very warm all day and I have not been to church once. Maria went down in the afternoon after supper. Her and I went to Dr. DeVenoge's. We saw Mrs. DeVenoge and a young lady that is staying there.

Eldred, Monday, July 4, 1881
They had a festival in the Village today. Ida and I went down this morning. We came home about dinner time and had a cup of tea, something to eat, and a good rest. After the shower we went back again and did not come home until nearly eleven. We had a splendid time.

Eldred, Tuesday, July 5, 1881
It has been terrible warm. Mort and father had a quarrel at the dinner table. I was not there. Dory was telling us about it.
Mort went up to Aunt Laura's. Maria, Ida, and I went down for the mail and to Myers' store. Elbert [Clark] and Mort came up from the Village with us.

Aunt Laura's Family
Aunt Laura Austin Clark, her husband Uncle Irvin Clark, and their sons Ellsworth, Elbert, and Robert lived on the west side of Eldred, north of the Leavenworth family. Laura was a sister to Henry and Augustus Austin.

Eldred, Wednesday, July 6, 1881
Ida, little Tom, and I went up on the hill for berries this morning, but it was so warm we did not stay long. Annie Collins came down for the mail. It was after dark when she went home. I went up to their road with her. Maria and Ida was down to prayer meeting.

Annie Collins
Annie Collins was a sister to Tom Collins and Robert Collins. The Collins siblings had lived on Collins Road when they were young and were neighbors of the Austins. Their parents James and Isabelle Collins were listed in the 1880 census.

Eldred, Thursday, July 7, 1881
It has been rather cloudy today. Maria, Tommy, and I went up on the hill for berries. We got about 4 quarts all together. This afternoon Ida and I went out in the woods to read. She only stayed a few minutes, but it was nearly six when I got home. Met Minnie and Alice.

Eldred, Friday, July 8, 1881
Dory, Cousin Ida, and I went down to the River for the grist. It rained

President Garfield Assassinated

President Garfield had been President for barely 4 months when he was shot.

Garfield became concerned that the stress of living in the White House contributed to his wife Lucretia's ill health. So in mid-June the President took her to the train station to travel to a seaside resort.

On July 2, 1881, President Garfield was again at the Railroad Station. He was with two of his sons, and James Blaine and Robert Todd Lincoln. The President was to travel first to New Jersey to see his wife; then give a speech at Williams College, his Alma Mater. But President Garfield was shot before he could get on the train.

Charles J. Guiteau, for reasons of his own, felt he should be rewarded with an ambassadorship when Garfield was elected. When he was continually rejected, he decided God told him to kill the president. That is the story that is told.

Guiteau had bought a revolver with $15, and trailed Garfield to the Baltimore and Potomac Railway station. There he shot President Garfield twice from behind.

The July 3, 1881 article in the *New York Herald* said that when Guiteau surrendered to the authorities, he claimed: "I am a Stalwart of the Stalwarts. Arthur is president now!"

The Stalwarts were a New York faction of the Republican Party. Chester Arthur, the Vice President, was a Stalwart, but was not implicated in the assassination.

The second shot hit the first lumbar vertebra. Garfield faced a long, painful battle with infections from which he would not recover. One source indicated that the infections were possibly caused by the unwashed hands of the physicians and their non-sterilized instruments.—*From several sources including wikipedia.org.*

Annie Collins, at one time a neighbor of the Austin family. Photo courtesy of Katherine Calkin Traxler.

Ellsworth Clark, son of Irvin and Laura Austin Clark, and cousin to the Austins. Photo courtesy of Katherine Calkin Traxler.

Eldred, Friday, July 8 1881
The papers begin to go against Grant. The Republican Papers—father don't know hardly what to say.

Eldred, Saturday, July 9, 1881
I went over and stayed with old Mrs. Collins. She was all alone. I went over to the pond for a sail.

Eldred, Sunday, July 10, 1881
Maria, Ida, and I went down to church this morning. Mr. Fisher gave us a terrible long sermon. Just as we were sitting down to supper, Aunt Laura, Ellsworth, and Robbie came.

Eldred, Monday, July 11, 1881
We had a fearful hard shower this morning but it cleared off this afternoon. Dory brought up the mail. He brought Cousin Ida a letter from someone.

Mary Ann Austin, Eldred, to Lon Austin
Sunday, July 1881
My Dear Son Lon,

I have been very sick eight weeks and am very thankful I am once more able to get outdoors. I began to think I never would, the time seemed so long I was kept indoors.

I was very much surprised to get your postal saying you were on your way to Oregon. I felt as if I should never see you again. I wished I could have gone with you.

The winters here are more than I can stand with all kind of trouble to boot. It is very pleasant here now. The girls are home, but I suppose Aida has told you all the news.

I shall be very glad to see you home again. Your Father has had terrible spells, but is quite calm just now, only he says he is determined *to sell, but I guess it will be like all other of his sells. He offered the place to Maria for $500. I've talked of trying to raise it, but I suppose it is useless to try.*

Mortie has written to Ell today to get him a place in Kansas. I can neither persuade Mortie to stay home or your father to go with him. I fear Mort has the consumption, although he has not coughed any to speak of since

---

Kate's Ideal

You say he must be handsome
With a grand, commanding air.
A voice of liquid sweetness
And a wealth of curling hair.
The blood of noble kindred
Must course within his veins
And added to his worldly goods
Must be a stock of brains.

We differ, friend, and widely,
I'll risk your great surprise,
And value not the flashes
That dart from glorious eyes.
I could gaze unmoved forever
On a figure of a face,
And the honeyed words do linger
Long as those in sand we trace.

O! disregard the bank account
And stretch of yielding lands,
Ignore the dazzling whiteness
Of the small and dainty hands;
The blood that flows down ages
In a blue unbroken stream
May be tainted heritage
Of which you little dream.

And look for richer treasures
In the depth of heart and mind,
A love that knows no change
And a voice that's ever kind;
A heart that knows no falseness
From first to final breath
Is the heart to which, fair dreamer,
Thou should'st yield thine till death.
—Mary K. Hanly. Poem in Mary Ann Austin's scrapbook.

---

nearly all the way down and back.

Ida and I went down to the Village this afternoon for the mail and to the store.

warmer weather; a change of climate may cure him.

He knows more about farming than any other work. I guess he thinks he won't miss being away from home if he is with one of you boys. He is to work for Uncle Courtsworth [C.C.P. Eldred] for a month. He seems too young to go off so far alone without any learning.

Your Father tried to drive him off last fall and had I been downstairs, I could have stopped the quarrel before he ordered Mortie to leave.

If he could only get work with Uncle C.C.P.E., I would not mind it. I coaxed him to come home Saturday night. He hates to leave his colt. It is a beauty. I am most a mind to sell it for him. I suppose your Father could get it back if Mortie sold it.

I wish the children would club together and keep the place. If none of you would ever marry, but all live together, it would be nice. This place is lovely and if managed right, money to be made with it.

Mother

Uncle C.C.P. and Aunt Effie Eldred

In the following letter, Cortzie was Charles Courtsworth Pinckney Eldred. C.C.P., as he was often called, was an uncle to the children of his sisters: Maria Austin, Mary Ann Austin, and Eliza Gardner.

Uncle C.C.P., Aunt Effa, and Cousin Becca, lived in Eldred, to the west of Henry and Mary Ann Austin. C.C.P. Eldred's grandsons, James Eldred and Herbert Eldred, helped on his farm.

In Chapter 1, Aunt Effie was the lady who told Perry Schoonover that his son Rowlee was stealing watermelons from her garden.

Kate and Laura Parker when they were younger. "We are going huckleberrying tomorrow with Kate and Laura Parker." Photo courtesy of Barbara Kate James Stowell, named in honor of her aunt Kate Parker.

Eldred, Tuesday, July 12, 1881
Mort went to work for Uncle Cortzie.

We are going huckleberrying tomorrow with Kate and Laura Parker. I had a letter from Addie.

Kate and Laura Parker

There is a cute photo of Kate and Laura Parker when they were young. In 1881 Kate was around 21, and Laura was 18.

Rowlee Schoonover mentioned in Chapter 1 that after his raft trip in the spring of 1881, he had stayed with his sister Kate in New York City.

Eldred, Wed., July 13, 1881
We slept until after nine o'clock this morning. Kate and Laura were here before we were up. Went huckleberrying with them. I had a pretty good time only it was fearful hot.

Eldred, Friday, July 15, 1881
Ida and I got up early enough for the mail this morning. We met Aunt Effie, Aunt Mary, and Kate Parker going huckleberrying. We went to Myers' store.

Eldred, Saturday, July 16, 1881
Lillie, Myers Gardner, little Mary, Lonnie, and Charley came up this morning. Ad went home with Lil. Mort came home tonight.

Eldred, Sunday, July 17, 1881
It has been real cool all day. I have not been to church once.

The Austin cousins at the Austin homestead in Eldred, New York. Photo from Mary Ann Austin's scrapbook, courtesy of Melva Austin Barney.

Eldred, Monday, July 18, 1881
Maria and I had a letter from Lon today. It has been so cold today. Mother and I went upon the hill to pick huckleberries.

Eldred, Tuesday, July 19, 1881
We moved the stove this morning and I answered Lon's letter.

This afternoon I went out with father and Dory and raked hay until six o'clock. Henrietta came over to stay all night.

Eldred, Wed., July 20, 1881
I took old Fan [their horse] and went down for Ida this morning. Dinner was ready when I got back.

After I got through eating, I went to sleep and slept until nearly supper time. Maria, Ida, Dory, and I went down to church this evening.

Eldred, Thursday, July 21, 1881
I went out in the hay field with Dory and father and raked hay until suppertime.

After supper, Ida and I went down for the mail. Mort was turning the cows away. We waited for him. Then we went over to Myers' to get me a big straw hat.

Eldred, Friday, July 22, 1881
Ida and I went out to rake hay this afternoon. When we got through I went to bed and took a nap. Cousin Ida got another letter from that fellow. Annie Collins came down for her mail.

Eldred, Saturday, July 23, 1881
Ida and I took old Fan this morning to the store to get some things. Ella was down and gave her a ride up to Greig's. We drew in one load of hay this afternoon. Ida, Tommy, and I had to ride on it.

Mort, Ida, and I went up the Hagan Pond Road for a walk. We met Mary DeVenoge [Dr. DeVenoge's daughter] and Miss DeVogue, Rob Kelso, and Maurla Brunette. Went up to Collins. Annie was down for her mail.

Eldred, Sunday, July 24, 1881
Ida, Maria, Mort, and I went down to church this morning. The school teacher from Barryville preached a very good sermon.

After dinner Ida and I went up to Aunt Laura's. When [we] came home, we met Rob and Miss Burnett over by Mr. Kyte's.

Eldred, Monday, July 25, 1881
I have commenced studying again.

Ida and I went for the mail this afternoon. Had a letter from her mother and I had one from Lon. We met Rob, Ed, Minnie, and May just the other side of the bridge.

Eldred, Tuesday, July 26, 1881
Becca, Ida, and I went over to Dubois this afternoon.

Eldred, Wed., July 27, 1881
Ida and I went down for the mail this afternoon. We went up in the fields to see Mort. Had two rides on the hay. Ed and Mort took us over for a sail on Hagan [Pond].

Eldred, Thursday, July 28, 1881
Lil, Ida, and I went up to see Henrietta this morning. This afternoon we went down to Aunt Effie's to tea. Had one ride on a load of hay.

Eldred, Friday, July 29, 1881
Ida, Lil, Laura Parker, and I went up to Aunt Laura's to paper. We had a lovely time. Elbert [Clark] brought us home in the evening.

It rained in the afternoon and the trees were very wet yet when we came home. We shook the branches when they came over the road.

Eldred, Saturday, July 30, 1881
Mort came home tonight. Kate N., Becca, Ad and her husband, and little Nell came up to tea.

Eldred, Sunday, July 31, 1881
Showery all day. Maria went down to church this afternoon.

Maria, Ida, Dory, Mort, Mrs. Cam, and I went down to church, but there was none. Stayed in Aunt Effie's a while and sang.

Mary Ann Austin, Eldred, to Lon Austin
July 1881
Dear Lon,

I am very glad you have your health so good. It must be a healthy place. I do so hope you can come home this fall. Your Father thinks it will cost you nearly 100 to come home.

He is very sweet to Aida. She goes out and rakes hay. Cousin Ida goes out sometimes with her. Your Father took them up to Laura's yesterday. Maria went to Glen Spey with Rebecca and little Jim drove.

Went to dinner with Eddie M. He came up to tea and Mortie went back and stayed with Eddie as he was alone.

The things in the world matter but little as we are journeying to a better or worse land and so let us live as to enjoy a better, for this world is so full of trouble. Yet we cling to it as long as we can, but the old must die. My stay here is short.

I hope my dear son that you live in the enjoyment of God's love. Don't neglect prayer, the only safe guard against tarnation.

With much love to you I close, Your loving Mother

Eldred, Monday, August 1, 1881
Maria went to New York this morning and I guess Mother went with her. Tommy rode to Barryville with them. It rained terrible when he and Dory were coming back. They were both wet to the skin.

Eldred, Tuesday, August 2, 1881
Father has been up to Uncle Irv's all day. Ed and Mort came up. We went for a walk.

Eldred, Wed., August 3, 1881
Father went to Dunlap's today to help him draw in his hay. Mort came up tonight and Ida went to church and Dory. I had a letter from Maria and Ad. They want mother to stay until a week from Saturday.

The Lewis Dunlap Family
Lewis Dunlap and his son Lewis Oliver Dunlap had been in town at least since 1840. In 1880 Lewis Dunlap, 74, a farmer, and his wife Emily, 66, were listed with son George, 20. Lewis Oliver Dunlap, 49, was listed with his wife Catharine, 39, and their 6 children.

Eldred, Thurs., August 4, 1881
Ida has gone to Aunt Effie's to a surprise party. I was too lazy. I have written to Lon. Terrible warm.

Eldred, Friday, August 5, 1881
Another warm day. Father to Uncle Irv's.

Ida went to the village after supper and rode up with father when he came home.

Eldred, Saturday, August 6, 1881
Busy the whole day. Father at home. Mort came up tonight. Henry Webb is up from the City; has been telling a mess of lies to Ed Myers. Mort would not tell me half he said as he promised Ed he would not. I could have wrung his neck.

Henry Webb
Henry Webb seems to be a son of Charles Cripps Webb and Sarah Shotwell. Charles C. Webb was the son of Jane Ann Webb Myers. Jane Ann lived across from Hagan Pond

Mary DeVenoge, daughter of Dr. Leon and his wife Catharine DeVenoge. "I went up the Hagan Pond Road for a walk. We met Mary DeVenoge." —Aida Austin. Photo courtesy of Mary Briggs Austin.

Henry Ladore (Dory) Austin, Aida Austin's youngest brother, as a child. Photo courtesy of Katherine Calkin Traxler.

near Collins Road, not far from the Austin family. (Ed Myers was the son of Abel S. Myers and not related to Jane Ann Myers.)

Eldred, Sunday, August 7, 1881
William Wilson here to dinner.

The Delaware River near Port Jervis, New York. Erie Railway's 1881 Summer Excursion Routes *Booklet.*

A scene on the Delaware River near Callicoon, New York. In Erie Railway's 1874 Summer Tourist *and 1881* Summer Excursion Routes *Booklets.*

Ad in the Erie Railway's 1881 Summer Excursion Routes *Booklet. Mort wanted to see Kansas.*

Ida and Mort went to church in the forenoon. Ida and I went in the afternoon. Mort and I have been out for a walk. Had a long talk.

Eldred, Monday, August 8, 1881
Ida went to Aunt Laura's this morning. I went for the mail and over to the store. Henry Webb came in while I was there. Tried to be very pleasant.

Eldred, Tuesday, August 9, 1881
Cloudy all day but pleasant. Father has a very sore eye.

Eldred, Wed., August 10, 1881
Henry Webb and his friend Mr. Black called and wanted me to go out to White Lake tomorrow to a picnic. Mort has not been asked and I am not going.

George Lovee, Brookside, N.J., to Alonzo (Lon) Austin
August 10, 1881
Friend Alonzo,
You seem to talk as if you did not think much of the people out there in that state. I am glad that I did not go out there with you.
Well we have just finished harvest here. We threshed in the field all of our oats. Peaches are ripe now and apples and pears.
It has been hot and dry here all summer and the corn is all dried up. Some fields won't have 10 bushels in.
Potatoes are all dried through.
I am thinking of renting 66 acres of land for 8 years and set it all in peach trees. There is money in it at $1.50 a basket. A neighbor here has 1,000 baskets.
This is what she wrote to me:
Fall from the ship mast to the deck
Fall downstairs and break your neck
Fall to the earth from heaven above
But never oh never fall in love.
Your friend,
George A. Lovee

Eldred, Thurs., August 11, 1881
Mort and I went to Lackawaxen after dinner. Elbert went with us. Had a real pleasant ride.

Eldred, Friday, August 12, 1881
Ed was up in the afternoon and played croquet after tea. Mort and I went over to Mrs. West's and went to the Village.

Eldred, Sat., August 13, 1881
Busy all day. Mother came home this afternoon. [Mary Ann Austin had been in New York City.]

Eldred, Sunday, August 14, 1881
Ed, Mort, Ida, and I went up to Aunt Laura's this afternoon. Came back to tea and went to church.

Eldred, Monday, August 15, 1881
Busy all the forenoon. Went down to school this afternoon. Annie walked up nearly to Campfield's to Net and Maria.

Eldred, Tues., August 16, 1881
Mort and Ida went to the Village this morning. Ida, Mort, and I went to the Village this afternoon.

Eldred, Wed., August 17, 1881
Mort started for Kansas. Ed took him to Lackawaxen. Ida and I went with him. We started from here about 6 and had to wait up there until 10.
We got Mort's ticket $3 less than we thought we could. Ed broke the whipple tree when we were going up.
Uncle Irv and Elbert have been working here today.

Eldred, Thurs., Aug.18, 1881
Mother has been sick all day but seems a little better tonight.

Eldred, Friday, August 19, 1881
It has been rainy all day. Father

went to the mill this morning and has just got back.

Eldred, Sunday, Aug. 21, 1881
Callers Elbert, Ellsworth, Robbie, and Aunt Laura, Cousin Bee and Jimmie Gardner and their two little girls.

Mary Ann Austin, Eldred, to Lon Austin
Sunday, August 1881
My dear Son,
   Your very welcome letter came while I was in the city. I only stayed two weeks, and they sent for me to come home before Mort went to Kansas.
   He left Wednesday. I could not persuade him to wait until you came home as he had made up his mind to go. I think he would have done better here. He could get work plenty, but he wanted to see Kansas. The change of climate may do him good.
   I was real sick that night he went, and for a day or two, but am much better now, only my heart seems bleeding at every pore and the trials and sorrows of my married life come o'er me like the rushing of mighty waters and it seems as though the brittle thread of life must surrender with one more drop in the bitter cup.
   Yet God hath sustained me so far, and will until he sees fit to call me home.
   I had to stop writing for company. Jim Gardner and wife called. I have been so busy I have not time to think of all my troubles.
   We have heard from Mort. He reached Solomon safe and is with Ell. I hope you can come home.
   With much love to my dear Lon. Mother

Eldred, Monday, Aug. 22, 1881
A lovely day. Old Mr. West here to

The Old Pastor's Dismissal

"We need a younger man to stir the
   people and lead them to the fold."
The deacons said: "We ask your
   resignation,
Because—you're growing old."
The pastor bowed his deacons out in
   silence,
And tenderly the gloom
Of twilight hid him and his bitter
   anguish
Within the lonely room.

Above the violet hills the sunlight's
   glory
Hung like a crown of gold,
And from the noble church the
   organ's anthem
Above the stillness rolled.
Assembled were the people for
   God's worship;
But in his study chair
The pastor sat unheeding, while the
   south wind
Caressed his snow-white hair.

A smile lay on his lips. His was
   the secret
Of sorrow's glad release,
Upon his forehead shone the
   benediction
Of everlasting peace.
"The ways of Providence are most
   mysterious,"
The deacons gravely said,
As wondering eyed, and scared, the
   people crowded
About their pastor—dead.

"We loved him!" wrote the people on
   the coffin,
In words of shining gold:
And 'bove the broken heart they set
   a statue
Of marble, white and cold.
The end? Ah no, the undiscovered
   country
Somewhere in brightness lies;
Though only space and stars may be
   discerned
By man's short-sighted eyes.

—Elizabeth Cumings. Found in Mary Ann Austin's scrapbook.

---

dinner. I got a letter from Maria.

Eldred, Tues., August 23, 1881
I took some letters to the post office this morning and stayed to dinner at Aunt Effie's.
   I went down this afternoon for the mail. Ida and I went to see Henrietta but she had gone to the Village.

Eldred, Wed., August 24, 1881
Mammie has been here all day to help mother. Father and Dory have been working on the road.
   Ida had a letter from Mort. He has reached Solomon all safe.

Shohola Glen, Pennsylvania
Friday, August 26, 1881
Lil, Ida, Addie, Lon, and I have gone out for a morning walk.

Lil and I are resting here on the bridge while Addie, J.K., and Ida are exploring the glen.
   We all got back from the glen about eleven or half a past.

The lower Shohola Glen and its walking paths was 5 or so miles from the Austin home.
   The Shohola Creek, which wound its way through the glen, started in the mountain tops of Pike County, Pennsylvania, and took a *tortuous and extremely precipitous* course to the Delaware River. The creek fell almost 1,000 feet over its last 8 miles, according to the Erie train brochures of the 1880s.
   The Erie Railway traveled across the creek on the large arch viaduct Jacob Perschbacher had

Aerial photo of railway bridge over Shohola Creek near Shohola, Pennsylvania, 1971. "In its descent from the mountaintops of Pike County to the Delaware, the course of the Shohola Creek is tortuous and extremely precipitous, so that during the last 8 miles of its length, its fall is nearly 1,000 feet."—Summer Homes and Rambles on the Picturesque Erie, 1886. Photo: Jack E. Boucher; Library of Congress, Historic American Engineering Record: HAER PA,52-SHOH, 1-8.

made of hand cut stone in 1870. Most likely, this was one of the sights Aida and her cousins saw at the Glen.

In 1881 George Layman owned the hotel Shohola House which was advertised as a "new and commodious hotel near the depot," in Charles Hallock's 1877 *The Sportsman's Gazetteer and General Guide*.

George Layman (according to John W. Johnston) originated the idea of the Glen as a place for a resort when George built paths alongside the mountains and steps so his guests could get from one ledge to another. George may have gotten the idea from Chauncey Thomas, the original owner.

Chapter 3 will talk more about the Shohola Glen Resort, the original modern theme park, and the inn Mr. Layman owned in Barryville, in 1885.

Henrietta, in the next diary entry, may have been Aida's oldest sister, Mary Henrietta Austin.

Eldred, Sat., August 27, 1881
Henrietta came home today.

Wm. Sutherland, Solomon City, Kans., to Lon Austin
August 27, 1881
Friend Lon,
I write hoping that this letter may reach you. Your brother told me that you are living in

Stockton, California.

Times are rather dull at present here. This is Saturday and hardly any trade in town. We have been having very hot weather this summer and not much rain, so crops both of corn and wheat are short but the elevators are paying good prices for grain.

Corn is worth from 5 cents up per bushel and wheat from 1 upwards. Hogs and cattle are held at high figures.

I suppose you have heard your other brother arrived here some time ago and I think is staying with Jack.

There have been a great many arrivals and departures since you left the sunny vale of the Solomon.

Whooping cough has carried off several babies in town. Arthur lost his and Mr. Marvin lost one.

The mill is not yet running, but the water is now running over the dam. There are now three brickyards near town. My father is building a brick residence north of the Presbyterian Church.

Now Lon, tell me how you are fixed and what kind of a country you are in.

Yours truly,
Wm. G. Sutherland

Eldred, Sat., August 27, 1881
President sinking very rapidly.

Eldred, Sunday, August 28, 1881
News came this morning the president was dead, but Mr. Fisher told tonight he was still alive.

Henrietta started for the Dr.'s this morning. Stopped for Mom. I had been to church. Mr. Fisher preached a splendid sermon text: "Mary hath chosen the better part."

Eldred, Monday, August 29, 1881
Terrible warm.

Looking from the East, the Great Shohola Viaduct on Shohola Creek. "The dance floor was located under the Great Shohola Viaduct built by Jacob Perschbacher in 1870. The floor was 25 feet above the water of the Shohola Creek and 15 feet below a balcony where the bands played."—shohola.org. Photo: Jack E. Boucher; Library of Congress, Historic American Engineering Record: HAER PA, 52-SHOH, 1-6.

Eldred, Tues., August 30, 1881
Warmer than yesterday if possible. Down to Aunt Effie's until school was out. Then over to see Annie. Met Vic Desilva.

Eldred, Wed., August 31, 1881
Ida started for Middletown this afternoon. Ed took her to the Depot. Tommy has been down to Middaugh's all day.

Eldred, Friday, Sept. 2, 1881
Had a good time playing croquet.

Eldred, Sat., September 3, 1881
Took Net's letter to the Post Office. Stopped to see Minnie and then went on down to old Billy Myers' and Dan Clark's. Had a game of croquet at Mrs. Beck's.

Detail showing the east side of Shohola Viaduct brickwork of Jacob Perschbacher. Photo: Jack E. Boucher; Library of Congress: HAER PA, 52-SHOH, 1-4.

The Great East River Suspension Bridge

A Currier & Ives chromolithograph from 1885. "Grand bird's eye view of the Great East River connecting New York and Brooklyn." Photo: Library of Congress: LC-DIG-pga-03205.

The Great East River (Brooklyn) Suspension Bridge, the first land connection between Manhattan and Brooklyn, was also the first steel-wire suspension bridge. It was the longest (5,989 feet) suspension bridge in the world from 1883 (when it opened), until 1903.

John A. Roebling, who designed and constructed the Roebling Aqueduct in Lackawaxen, Pennsylvania, was the initial designer of the Brooklyn Bridge.

Very unfortunately, Mr. Roebling's foot was crushed when he surveyed a possible bridge site. His toes had to be amputated. Soon after, he died of a tetanus infection.

John's son Washington Roebling was then put in charge of the bridge. Washington and his wife Emily had gone to Europe as newlyweds. There they learned how to use caissons (watertight structures) to work on the foundation of the bridge.

On January 3, 1870, construction started on the bridge using caissons. Washington Roebling and several others ended up with decompression sickness or caisson disease. Some workers died. Washington became bedridden.

For the next 12 or 13 years, Emily Roebling played a major role in the completion of the Brooklyn Bridge. With Washington's help, she learned about the math, calculations, materials, bridge specifications, and cable construction information necessary to build the bridge.

Emily relayed directions and information from her husband Washington, to his assistants working on the bridge; and reported the progress to her husband.

In 1882 when her husband's position as chief engineer was questioned, Emily wrote down her husband's statement as to why he should not be removed, and spoke to the American Society of Civil Engineers. Washington Roebling was permitted to remain as Chief Engineer.

When the bridge was opened May 24, 1883, Emily Roebling rode with President Chester Arthur. Later President Arthur went to the

Close-up view of construction of Brooklyn Bridge over East River, New York City. Photo: Library of Congress: LC-US62-108446.

Roebling home and shook hands with Washington who had been unable to attend the ceremony.

1,800 vehicles and 150,300 people had crossed the East River on the Brooklyn Bridge.

One story was that a week after the opening, there was a rumor that the bridge would collapse. The resulting stampede crushed and killed 12 people.

A year later, P.T. Barnum led a parade of 21 elephants over the bridge, helping to end doubts about the bridge's stability and publicizing his famous circus at the same time.
—*wikipedia.org and asce.org.*

Chapter 2: Dear Diary, 1881–1882 • 51

Eldred, Tuesday, Sept. 6, 1881
Very warm all day. I have been sick. A letter from Lon. He has gone to Cuffey's Cove, California.

Eldred, Wed., Sept. 7, 1881
Fearful warm. Sick. Better this afternoon. Rode to the Village with father for the mail. Nothing, only a paper.

Eldred, Thurs., Sept. 8, 1881
Felt better today. Not so warm.

Eldred, Friday, Sept. 9, 1881
Cloudy all day. Father sold Mort's colt to Mr. Gallagher. Mother and I had a letter from Maria. I had a paper from "Harper's Bazaar."

Eldred, Saturday, Sept. 10, 1881
Pleasanter today. I went to the Village this afternoon.

Eldred, Sunday, Sept. 11, 1881
*Rainy all day. No church.
Ellsworth stopped this afternoon to bid me a good by.*

The next we hear from Aida's cousin Ellsworth Clark, will be a letter to his brother in 1906.

Eldred, Monday, Sept. 12, 1881
Very pleasant all day. I have got all my clothes ready to go back tomorrow.

**Aida Leaves for New York City
N.Y.C., Tuesday, Sept. 13, 1881**
Came down today. Train an hour behind time. Ten o'clock when I got to the depot. No one there to meet me. Went to Net's. Could not get in there so I came around here. Aunt Maria got up and let me in. Ida, Mary, Ada, Tom, and Mort to Coney Island.

**290 East Broadway, N.Y.C.,
Wed., September 14, 1881**
Did not get around until after ten

Caisson Disease

Illustrations of the inside of an East River Bridge caisson. Frank Leslie's Illustrated Newspaper, v. 31, no. 785, October 15, 1870, p. 76; Library of Congress, Prints and Photographs Division: LC-USZ62-124944.

Caisson, French for box, is a sealed underwater structure.

Caisson disease (decompression illness) occurred in construction workers when they ascended back to the surface (and normal air pressure) from the compressed atmosphere of the caisson too rapidly.

The Brooklyn Bridge was built with the use of caissons. A number of workers were killed or permanently injured by caisson disease during its construction. Washington Roebling suffered greatly from Caisson Disease.
—wikipedia.org.

1880s chromolithograph by L.W. Schmidt showing a bird's-eye view of New York City with the Hudson River and the New Jersey waterfront on the left; New York Harbor and Governor's Island in the right foreground; Battery Park, Manhattan, the East River, Brooklyn Bridge, and the borough of Brooklyn at center. Photo: Library of Congress, Prints and Photographs Division: L.W. Schmidt; LC-DIG-pga-04130.

The City of New York around 1884. Currier & Ives chromolithograph, with watercolor; Library of Congress: LC-DIG-ppmsca-07831.

Aida Austin's signature and address on the inside cover of her diary. Aida lived with Henry and Net Austin Clinton, at 290 East Broadway St., when she went back to New York City.

o'clock. Then went out to Ridley's with Maria. Net went up to Rand's so I stayed around to Ad's until she came back about five.

After supper Maria and I went to the doctors. I stopped at Ad's and got my letters. Harry came around with me and so the first day is ended. God help me.

Aida lived with Henry and Net Austin Clinton, at 290 East Broadway St., when she went back to New York City. Aida wrote the address on the inside of her Diary cover.

Seventy-two years later, Aida's great niece, Joan Austin Geier, worked in the area of 290 East Broadway.

In 1953, I worked at the American Thread Company at 260 Broadway. The building is still there. It stands right in the middle of East Broadway or between two streets, one of which would be East Broadway.

When I worked there the area

seemed to be light industrial (although American Thread was a national headquarters building) with a smattering of small restaurants. As I remember, all the buildings were old, attached brick but stories high; and it seems to me that most of them had probably been private homes originally.

When I worked there the area was clean and safe, but neither quaint nor residential.
—Joan Austin Geier.

N.Y.C., Thurs., Sept. 15, 1881
Terrible windy. All day around to Ad's and on Grand Street this afternoon. Around to Ad's again tonight. Have just got home. Harry came with me.

Sutherland, Solomon City, Kans., to A. Austin, Cuffey's Cove, Calif.
September 15, 1881
[Stockton CA, crossed out]
Friend Lon,
A great many of our Solomon folks have been down to Bismarck attending the fair. A 20-mile race was run at Bismarck between a Kansas girl and a Missouri girl on (ponies) horses.

The Kansas girl had 7 horses and the other girl had 2 or 3 more than that number. The time of the race including stops and changing from one horse to the other was 46 minutes—fastest on record.

The judge decided the race in favor of the Missouri girl as she came under the string half a length ahead of the Kansas girl. But many of those present claim that 'our' girl won by rights and all admit that she rode much nicer than 'their' girl. The purse was advertised as $10,000.

A fire yesterday destroyed the main exhibition hall on the Kansas City fair grounds and several people are reported killed. We have not yet learned the particulars.

Arthur's little girl died of spasms brought on by whooping cough sometime ago. Also, Mr. Marvin lost his little boy.

September 29. Tonight we are going to have a dance if it don't rain. The mill is again in operation and is doing lots of good to the town.

I think that I will stay in Solomon most of this winter excepting maybe 2 or 3 weeks trapping trip on the Solomon River.

What are you doing? What is the wages of clerks as near as you can tell?

How is your neighborhood for fire and how many girls to one boy are there?

Yours respectfully,
Wm. G. Sutherland
Office of Sutherland and Co.,
Dealers in General Merchandise

E. Rainer, West Oakland, Calif., to Lon Austin
1881
Friend Austin,
I left Stockton shortly after you did and came down to Oakland and stayed about two months and then I got a job in a flour mill at Benicia and I have worked there ever since until last Friday.

They shut down to put in some new machinery, so I will be idle for about two months. I am getting $2.50 per day for 11 hours work and always in the house. I think I like it better than ranching.

That place that I worked at in Stockton wasn't much better for grub. I don't think I will work on ranches much more for wages. There is nothing in it, but men was awful scarce this summer at Stockton. I heard they got $3.00 a day to drive wagon and couldn't get them for that.

There is lots of grain that ain't thrashed yet and won't be for two months upon the islands.

I remain as ever Your Friend,
E.M. Rainer

N.Y.C., Friday, Sept. 16, 1881
Rainy all day. Quite pleasant.

N.Y.C., Sat., September 17, 1881
Quite pleasant today. Tina here to dinner. She and Net went to Ridley's. The baby's pretty good with me. Growing so. Pretty and cunning.

N.Y.C., Sunday, Sept. 18, 1881
Lovely day. Round to Ad's after dinner.

N.Y.C., Monday, Sept. 19, 1881
Maria and I were on Grand this afternoon. Very warm all day. President worse.

N.Y.C., Tuesday, Sept. 20, 1881
President died last night 10:35.
Have not been out today. Net

Coney Island

There were so many rabbits on the island (now a peninsula) in southernmost Brooklyn, that the Dutch called it, Conyne Eylandt or Rabbit Island. That is one story.

After the Civil War, when excursion trains, steamboats, and city streetcars could reach the area, Coney Island became a resort with hotels, beaches, horse racing, and amusement parks.

In 1876 Mr. Looff, a Danish Woodcarver, built the first carousel at Coney Island. It cost 5 cents to ride.

Between about 1880 and World War II, Coney Island was the largest amusement area in the United States, attracting several million visitors per year.—wikipedia.org.

President Garfield 1831–1881

President Garfield. From Mary Ann Austin's scrapbook courtesy of Melva Austin Barney.

The following newspaper articles about President Garfield were in Mary Ann Austin's scrapbook.

The Dead President
Tomorrow will be laid in his eternal bed one of the noblest of American citizens. James A. Garfield, after struggling patiently, calmly and heroically with death for 80 days, was beaten in the contest, and he now takes his place with our well-loved Lincoln in the affection and reverence of the American people.

It is strange that these two men—Lincoln and Garfield—should have been chosen by assassins as victims. They both sprung from the very poorest of our people, by the hardest endeavor achieved education and position in life, and were chosen by their fellow-countrymen to rule over them.

There was nothing in the character of these two men of the people to arouse enmity or create hatred. The honors which they had fairly won they wore with gentle humility and they were kindly, generous and charitable in all their ways. Toward their bitterest opponents they exhibited no animosity, and when they had occasion to rebuke they did so as to leave no sting behind.

They will remain forever among the most revered and loved of American citizens.

The Last Resting Place
In accordance with a wish often expressed of late years, President Garfield will be buried in Lake View Cemetery, at Cleveland, Ohio. This cemetery lies upon a high wooded ridge in the outskirts of that city, overlooking the waters of Lake Erie.

It possessed peculiar attractions for President Garfield, says a writer in the *New York Tribune*: "Within the sight of the highest ground in the cemetery is the place where the farmer boy whom destiny had marked for great achievements and great suffering first saw the lake while chopping wood to earn money to educate himself, and was fitted by the sight of its restless shining waves to know the great world and mingle in its large affairs.

Mrs. Garfield. From Mary Ann Austin's scrapbook courtesy of Melva Austin Barney.

"About 10 miles to the south is the site of the log cabin where he was born and there is still standing the plain little frame house which he and his brother built with their own hands for their widowed mother when their sturdy toil had lifted the family out of the pinching straits in which it was left by the death of their father."

Lake View Cemetery, Cleveland, Ohio. Photographed by Thomas S. Sweeny. From Mary Ann Austin's scrapbook, courtesy of Melva Austin Barney.

ate her supper early and took the baby out. Quite a long talk on heaven and hell.

President Garfield's Death
President Garfield was fighting blood poisoning and bronchial pneumonia. Then he had a massive heart attack. He died on September 19 at 10:35 p.m.

Chester A. Arthur then took the oath of office of the president.

The following handwritten poem was in Mary Ann's scrapbook.

On the Death of Garfield
*A gloom is o'er our nation
A shadow is o'er her cast
The gaze with breathless motion
For we see the flags half mast.*

*The bells they toll the story
That the long, long struggle's o'er
For our noble chief is dead
And we'll hear his voice no more.*

*Yes he's crossed oblivion's ocean
Where many thousand sailed
  before.
And he's anchored in the harbor
On that bright celestial shore.*

N.Y.C., Wed., Sept. 21, 1881
Cooler today. Maria stopped in tonight. She has a very bad cold.

N.Y.C., Thursday, Sept. 22, 1881
A little cooler today and cloudy. I went around for Maria and we went up to 15th Street to see the building draped in mourning. Looked very pretty.

Net has come upstairs to sleep and I have gone down.

N.Y.C., Sat., September 24, 1881
Very warm. Net and Clinton out tonight buying groceries. Home all day. A letter from Maria. Maria Calkin [in Barryville] received money all right.

N.Y.C., Sunday, Sept. 25, 1881
Quite warm. Went to church with Harry and Maria. Willett Street Church. Mr. Stansbury had a very good sermon. Spoke so nice of Mr. Garfield.

N.Y.C., Monday, Sept. 26, 1881
Terrible warm. Went to Willett St. Church this afternoon with Ida, Nettie and Net, Maria, Ad, Harry. Buddie, Gussie, and Aunt Maria were there. Around to Ad's tonight.

N.Y.C., Tuesday, Sept. 27, 1881
Warm this forenoon. Showers this afternoon. Went to Benedict's to get my watch fixed. Stopped at Ridley's coming back. Jumped on a Grand Street Car going faster than I thought. Came near getting thrown under it. A gentleman caught me.

N.Y.C., Thursday, Sept. 29, 1881
Net and I went around to Ad's for dinner. Stayed until five o'clock.

Mary Ann Austin, Eldred, to Lon Austin
October 1, 1881
My Dear Son Lon,

I'm so glad that you are coming home. If your Father doesn't let you take the place, he has got to do different from what he does now. The way he has treated Mortie makes me almost hate him. He is the selfishest man I ever see. He hires Elbert Clark for 10 dollars a month only. I think that is more than Mortie got in 2 years. Mortie was so mad when his Father threatened of kicking him outdoors. Your Father finds fault with him all the time. I think he will let you take the place. I have Dora West to help me.

I don't want you to send me money to go to the city, but if you have a mind to send some home, I will keep it for you without your Father knowing.

There are so many sailboat robberies. There was another one last week. They not only robbed the safe, but all the passengers. The robberies are mostly on the Rock Island South, but I suppose you see it in the papers.

When you come, take Wabash South, that is the quickest and best. Be very careful of your money or you will get robbed.

There was a grand singing here in the Congregational Church Wednesday night, but I will save the news until I see you. I want to see you so much.

Write soon to your loving Mother

N.Y.C., Sunday, October 2, 1881
Warm. I went around for Maria. She, Buddy, and myself went to Willett St. Church. Text was 1st Corinthians, Chapter 2, verse 1.

N.Y.C., Tuesday, October 4, 1881
Cloudy and clear by turns. Quite windy tonight. Net, Baby, and I arrived to Aunt Maria's all day.

N.Y.C., Wed., October 5, 1881
Terrible cold today.

Aida Austin, N.Y.C., to Lon Austin
October 6, 1881
Dear Brother Lon,

Lon, I am afraid you don't get half of my letters. I am sure you did not get my last letter I sent you at San Jouquin.

You are such a rover. I do hope you will come home soon and you must come right on here for a visit. Just think how long it will be before I can see you if you don't. You know how much I want to see you.

I am feeling better than I have for a long time; we have had some very warm weather, but it is

Boat House, Central Park, New York. Postcard in the collection of Mary Briggs Austin.

Willett Street Church information in Mary Ann Austin's scrapbook. "Went to Willett St. Church this afternoon."—Aida Austin. Courtesy of Melva Austin Barney.

considerable cooler now.

Do write soon. With lots of love, I remain,

Your ever loving sister, Aida

N.Y.C., Friday, October 7, 1881
Warmer today. Maria in a little while this afternoon.

Net out with the baby. I have been around to Ad's a little while. Just written to Lon.

N.Y.C., Sat., October 8, 1881
Quite warm today. Maria was here. Net and Clinton had gone out.

N.Y.C., Mon., October 10, 1881
Very windy. Aunt Maria went to Paterson and has been around to see Maria and Ida. A very large fire up town somewhere. Harry and Ed gone to it.

N.Y.C., Tues., October 11, 1881
Cloudy and damp. Got my watch this afternoon.

N.Y.C., Wed., October 12, 1881
Ad and Maria down to dinner. Rainy all the afternoon.

They did not bring Gus so we had a very peaceable time.

N.Y.C., Thurs., October 13, 1881
I have had quite a cold.

N.Y.C., Friday, October 14, 1881
My cold worse. I have slept nearly all the day. Net out with the baby.

N.Y.C., Sat., October 15, 1881
Cold a great deal worse. I can scarcely see.

N.Y.C., Sunday, October 16, 1881
Maria here tonight.

N.Y.C., Tues., October 18, 1881
A letter from Lon this morning. Coming home in November.

N.Y.C., Wed., October 19, 1881
Not very pleasant. Net, baby, and I around to Ad's. Maria and I went out this afternoon.

N.Y.C., Friday, October 21, 1881
Real pleasant after dinner. Net, Baby, and I around to Ad's. Rand, Net, Ad, Buddy, Gussie, and the baby went to Ridley's.

N.Y.C., Sunday, October 23, 1881
Damp. Took a good long sleep this afternoon.

Around to Ad's after supper. Nettie was there with Ida all the afternoon.

N.Y.C., Mon., October 24, 1881
Rainy all day. Net stopped to Mr. Rowe again about getting in Cooper's Institute to take lessons in drawing. Tired, oh so tired.

N.Y.C., Tues., October 25, 1881
Cloudy the greater part of the day. Down to see Mrs. B. Net, George, and Will coming home from school.

Stopped to see Maria. Ad out. Clinton is working overtime. Nettie was not home to tea.

N.Y.C., Wed., October 26, 1881
Cold. Net and I went up to Rand's to dinner. Ad and the Greek lady came in the afternoon.
Little Arch is growing so pretty. Looks, acts so much like dear little Tom.

N.Y.C., Thurs., October 27, 1881
Warmer. Maria and I sent the package with Tommy's clothes and some groceries for mother.
Mr. Rowe says he can surely get one in Cooper's Institute. I am so tired and sleepy.

N.Y.C., Mon., October 31, 1881
Rainy. Around to Ad's again tonight. Played checkers with Cousin Ed and Tom. Got beat.

N.Y.C., Wed., November 2, 1881
Misty. I went around to Ad's to do a little stitching for Net and to see Ad's blue velvet. I am going to buy it. I think it is very pretty.

N.Y.C., Sun., November 6, 1881
Not very pleasant. Rather cold. Around to Ad's all the afternoon. Down to Willett St. Church with Maria this evening. A very good sermon. Text: "Thou son of David have mercy upon me."

Mary Ann Austin, Eldred, to Lon Austin
November 6, 1881
My Dear son Lon,
I wish you and Aida would stay home this winter and go to school. It commences next week. If you don't have to get your ticket through to New York, you better get it to Lackawaxen on account of your trunk.
Your Father says he thinks you ought to have half of the sheep if you take the place. I hope you will come home as soon as you get through working there.
I miss Mortie very much. Dory is so much like his Father, hateful to everything it seems to me.
I will be very happy when you get home. I wrote to Eldred that your father talked of letting you take the place. Did he say anything to you about it?
I received yours Friday. It found us all well as I hope this dispatch will find you my dear son.
Don't neglect to pray God to help you to love as you will wish you had when you come to die. Try my dear child to live for a better and brighter world than this.
Write soon to your loving Mother

It seems that Henry and Mary Ann may have sold or mortgaged 100 acres to Ell at some point. A land document of March 1884, indicates Ell sold that 100 acres back to his mother for $500.

N.Y.C., Tues., November 8, 1881
Election day. Mr. Clinton home. Nettie to work half of the day, the other half home. Harry has just gone home. He brought me a letter from Lon.

N.Y.C., Wed., November 9, 1881
Rainy all day. I went around to Ad's to do some stitching. She had a lady there using the machine so I went down to Mrs. Braistead's.

N.Y.C., Fri., November 11, 1881
Pleasant today. Net and I took the baby on Grand Street and had her pictures. We met Ad and Gussie.
I played checkers with Tom and cousin Mort. Got beaten terrible. I did some studying this afternoon.

N.Y.C., Sunday, Nov. 13, 1881
Net and I went to church this morning. Very pleasant. Net and the baby went around to Aunt Maria's and stayed to dinner. Went around to Ad's after dinner.

N.Y.C., Wed., Nov. 16, 1881
Very pleasant today. I went to the butcher and stopped into Ad's quite a little while. Ida was there.

N.Y.C., Thurs., Nov. 17, 1881
Very pleasant. Net went across town this morning. Got back a

Groceries 1881

There are a number of grocery book ledgers in the Austin Collection. The following seems to have been bought from Abel S. Myers who had a store in town.

January
443 lbs. B. flour $8.86
18 bushel oats.................. 9.00
3 doz. eggs........................ .54

February
333 lbs. B. Flour 6.66

March
5 lbs. 2 oz. butter 1.28

April
4 lbs. butter....................... .68
4 dozen eggs..................... .60
4 doz. eggs........................ .60

May
4 doz. eggs........................ .50
1 egg beater .... .30
1 illustrated Lord's Prayer.... .40
6 bushels potatoes........... 3.00

August
Work on road, district No. 13:
Team: 6.5 hours 2.44

September
1 cow................................ 25.00
1 check.............................. 25.00
Goat to Wm. Gallagher..... 67.50

little after one. The baby slept until twelve. I went around to Ad's a few minutes. Read one of Mort's letters to Ida. Went to school.

N.Y.C., Sunday, Nov. 20, 1881
Very pleasant. Net and I started for the Baptist Church this morning, but hated to go in, so went to All Saints. After dinner I went around to Ad's. After tea Maria and I went to Willett St. Church.

N.Y.C., Monday, Nov. 21, 1881
Rather cloudy all day. Been sewing on my dress.
Went to the butchers about four o'clock. Stopped into Ad's. She was out with Poll and Annie. Tom bound to have little Tom home. I am so tired.

N.Y.C., Tuesday, Nov. 22, 1881
Very cold. Maria and I out all the afternoon. A letter from Mother. Father wants me to come home.

N.Y.C., Wed., Nov. 23, 1881
Very cold a little snow this morning but it soon turned to rain and is rainy yet tonight.

N.Y.C., Thursday, Nov. 24, 1881
Thanksgiving Day. All home to dinner. Mort, Mary, Uncle Gussy, Aunt Maria here this evening. And Harry, Mr. Clinton and I have been playing checkers. Very cold.

Sutherland, Abilene, Kans., to A. Austin, Cuffey's Cove, Calif.
November 24, 1881
Friend Lon,
Today is Thanksgiving. The stores have closed from 10 a.m. to 5 p.m.
I am now working for Sterl and Zahner of this city. Have been here a week or ten days.
There is going to be a Grand Ball here in Abilene tonight. I am staying at present at Mr. Merchant's Hotel here.
I would like to go to the Pacific Coast next spring and hope to hear from you occasionally between now and then.
How's your girl?
I am not making as much money here as in Solomon, but I had a racket with Arthur and would rather work for less here, but if I stay, I will try and get a raise. I have to put in long hours here, about 7:30 a.m. to 9:30 p.m.
The weather has been very nice for this time of year. Have hardly any snow or ice yet.
The boys in Solomon are getting along in the same old way.
Henry Whitley has built a nice bridge over the "race" for to cross his carriage or wagon.
If I would come out to California or Oregon, do you think I would have much trouble in finding work at good or fair pay? I would like to strike a good position in a bank.
Write soon.
From your friend,
Wm. G. Sutherland

N.Y.C., Friday, Nov. 25, 1881
Cold. Net up to Rand's with Cousin Mary. Went this morning. Not back until five. Baby pretty good. Tina in a few minutes to see Net.
Maria and Gussie have been in.

Wm. H. Austin, Eldred, to Aida Austin, N.Y.C.
November 25, 1881
Dear Daughter,
We are all well but your mother. She is not vary well, but is around most of the time.
Tommy says he won't go to New York. If his Father does come after him he will run and hide. He is well and grows fast. He is gitting too big for his clothes. I got him a pair of boots and you would laugh to see how much he thinks of them.
School has commenced here and I think you had better come home and go to school this winter and next summer here and then I think I could send you to Monticello a year.
I think if you ever intend to teach school, it is time you was studying for it, but you must do as you think best.
If you will come and go to school, I will help you all I can. Please let me know soon if you will come.
With much love from your Father, Wm. H. Austin

N.Y.C., Sunday, Nov. 27, 1881
Pleasant. Net Sick. Maria was sick with a cold but Ad, Tom, Cousin Mort and Mary went to Willett Street Church.

N.Y.C., Tuesday, Nov. 29, 1881
Around to Ad's this afternoon to get a pattern. Rand there.

N.Y.C., Wed., Nov. 30, 1881
Ad stopped in this afternoon to try on Net's gray silk.

N.Y.C., Sat., December 4, 1881
Rainy all day. Wrote to Mort.

N.Y.C., Thurs., Dec. 8, 1881
Net and I around to Ad's all day. Aunt Julia and her little nephew came there to dinner.

Aunt Julia was the widow of Uncle James Austin, brother of Augustus and Henry Austin.

N.Y.C., Sat., Dec. 10, 1881
Cold. Harry around tonight. Mr. Clinton and I have been playing checkers. Both beat about the same.

Henry Wadsworth Longfellow

Henry Wadsworth Longfellow died March 24, 1882, at his home in Cambridge, Massachusetts.

My dad Art Austin often quoted three of Mr. Longfellow's poems: *The Children's Hour*, *Paul Revere's Ride*, and *The Song of Hiawatha*.

The following newspaper article commemorating the famous poet Henry Wadsworth Longfellow (1807–1882), was in Great-Grandma Mary Ann Austin's scrapbook.

The unexpected death of Mr. Longfellow, following so soon upon the remarkable honors paid to him on his seventy-fifth birthday, has called forth tributes of love and sorrow from all the countries to which his fame and works have extended, and has caused a profound sensation throughout the United States and England, where his name for so many years has been a household word.

"Mad River in the White Mountains" was Longfellow's Last Poem.

This poem, on a well-known White Mountain stream, was corrected, in proof by the poet only a day or two before his death, and is now printed in the May Atlantic.*—The Atlantic Monthly.*

Mad River in the White Mountains

Traveller
Why dost thou wildly rush and roar,
Mad River, O Mad River?
Wilt thou not pause and cease to pour
Thy hurrying, headlong waters o'er
This rocky shelf forever?

What secret trouble stirs thy breast?
Why all this fret and flurry?
Dost thou not know that what is best
In this too restless world is rest
From over-work and worry?

Henry Wadsworth Longfellow. Woodcut in Mary Ann Austin's scrapbook, courtesy of Melva Austin Barney.

The River
What wouldst thou in these
    mountains seek,
O stranger from the city?
Is it perhaps some foolish freak
Of thine, to put the words I speak
Into a plaintive ditty?

Traveller
Yes; I would learn of thee thy song,
With all its flowing numbers,
And in a voice as fresh and strong
As thine is, sing it all day long,
And hear it in my slumbers.

The River
A brooklet nameless and unknown
Was I at first, resembling
A little child, that all alone
Comes venturing down the stairs of
    stone,
Irresolute and trembling.

Later, by wayward fancies led,
For the wide world I panted;
Out of the forest dark and dread
Across the open fields I fled,
Like one pursued and haunted.

I tossed my arms, I sang aloud,
My voice exultant blending
With thunder from the passing cloud,
The wind, the forest bent and bowed,
The rush of rain descending.

I heard the distant ocean call,
Imploring and entreating;
Drawn onward, o'er this rocky wall
I plunged, and the loud waterfall
Made answer to the greeting.

And now, beset with many ills,
A toilsome life I follow;
Compelled to carry from the hills
These logs to the impatient mills
Below there in the hollow.

Yet something ever cheers and
    charms
The rudeness of my labors;
Daily I water with these arms
The cattle of a hundred farms,
And have the birds for neighbors.

Men call me Mad, and well they may,
When, full of rage and trouble,
I burst my banks of sand and clay,
And sweep their wooden bridge
    away,
Like withered reeds or stubble.

Now go and write thy little rhyme,
As of thine own creating.
Thou seest the day is past its prime;
I can no longer waste my time;
The mills are tired of waiting.
—*Henry Wadsworth Longfellow.*

1886 lithograph of a busy scene on Broadway in New York City entitled, "A glimpse of New York's dry goods district; The largest in the world, covering a space of 135 acres; containing 4,500 firms; employing $800,000,000 capital."—Source: Library of Congress, Prints and Photographs Division: LC-USZ62-2662; 3a06318.

N.Y.C., Sunday, Dec. 11, 1881
Real cold.

Maria, Clinton, and I went around to Willett St. Church tonight. Had a very good sermon.

Mary Ann Austin, Eldred, to Lon Austin
December 11, 1881
My dear Son,

Your letter made me very happy. I was so afraid you had given up coming home. My health has been miserable for a good while, but I am better now.

Mortie wrote me you were going to be married. At first I felt awful. I thought I should never see you again.

Mortie said Ell was going to take the Parmenter place, so guess he has given up coming home this winter.

I want to go to the city shortly after New Year's. If you get a ticket through, will it let you stay a night home, or if I went down with you, would I have to meet you at Port Jervis? You can have your baggage left at Lackawaxen.

News when I see you which I hope will be soon.

Your loving Mother

Wm. Sutherland, McPherson, Kans., to Lon Austin
December 11, 1881
Friend Lon,

You will wonder no doubt who is writing to you from McPherson. It is I, Wm. G. Sutherland, who having had a "racket" with Arthur Sutherland of Sutherland & Co., is now in a land of strangers.

I came here last Thursday. Before that time I was working in a store at Abilene for three weeks. I am now with E.G. Clarke of McPherson, learning the Banking Business. It was with the consent and approval of my parents.

I room above the bank and board at a restaurant. Hoping to hear from you soon.

I remain yours truly,
Wm. G. Sutherland

N.Y.C., Monday, Dec. 12, 1881
Net out this afternoon. I met Ad and the two Greek girls in Ridley's. Harry around tonight. It is raining.

N.Y.C., Thursday, Dec. 15, 1881
A letter from Mort. Quite pleasant. Harry around tonight.

I had to go out to the grocery for some ham, so stopped in to see Maria. Uncle Gustus opened the door for me. It was quite late when I came in. Harry brought me some cards.

N.Y.C., Sunday Dec. 18, 1881
Very pleasant. Net had little "Dott" around home a little while this morning. Mrs. B., Willie, Maria, and I went around to the Baptist Church tonight.

N.Y.C., Monday, Dec. 19, 1881
Net out nearly all day. Baby very good. Tina stopped in a few minutes this afternoon.

N.Y.C., Tuesday, Dec. 20, 1881
Answered Mort's letter. I went to Ridley's this morning. Took a sleep this afternoon.

N.Y.C., Thursday, Dec. 22, 1881
Ad and Net were going out but it has been too rainy.

I went to sleep this afternoon when Baby did and did not get up until nearly six.

I am so tired. God help me. Is all over now. I must be strong.

N.Y.C., Saturday, Dec. 24, 1881
Net out this forenoon. Maria and I over to Macy's this afternoon. Harry and I have just got in from Ridley's.

N.Y.C., Sunday, Dec. 25, 1881
Quite pleasant. We went to Willett St. after all, speaking and singing.

N.Y.C., Monday, Dec. 26, 1881
Net, Baby, and I around to Ad's this afternoon to the Christmas tree. It was very nice. We all got some nice presents.

Ida, Uncle Gustus, Aunt Maria, and I went around to the Baptist Church to Lizzy Brown's wedding. Back to Ad's. I had to dress up as Santa Claus.

James Brown
There is an Eliza Brown, 23, listed in the home of James Brown, 51, a widower in the 1880 census. The family lived in the 7th Ward.

There was a son James Brown, a bookkeeper who was 18 in 1880. Cousin Ida Belle Austin married a James Brown, though it is unknown when.

N.Y.C., Tuesday, Dec. 27, 1881
Rainy and damp all day. I was around to Ad's this morning for some of my things.

Arch was down. Rand fell last night and cut her head fearful. I stopped in to Ad's tonight. They had not heard anything more from Rand.

N.Y.C., Thursday, Dec. 29, 1881
Rained all day. Buddie and I went around to the church (Baptist) tonight. They had some good speaking and singing and old Santa Claus. Tom, Ad, Maria, the youngest Greek girl, Harry, and Gussie went.

N.Y.C., Friday, Dec. 30, 1881
Quite pleasant. I went to Ridley's this afternoon. Got me a box of drawing tools.

N.Y.C., Saturday, Dec. 31, 1881
"A bad beginning" and has it? I only know I am safe. Feet are on the solid rock. God keep me ever.

N.Y.C., Sunday, Jan. 1, 1882
Rather cold. I went around for Maria tonight to go to church. A very good sermon.

N.Y.C., Monday, January 2, 1882
Cold. Busy all the morning. Willie came up to see me this afternoon. I took him around to the Christmas tree and to Gussie.

N.Y.C., Tuesday, January 3, 1882
Fearful cold. Tina in a few minutes this morning. Maria in tonight. She and Ad had a letter from mother. Wants me to come home.

Aida Austin, N.Y.C., to her brother
January 4, 1882
Dear Brother,

I expect to start for home next week. Father wrote for me sometime ago to come home and go to school and mother says he is fearful mad, so I think it is better for me to go and I wish you would stop home first, if you come at all.

I am beginning to think you don't intend to. You promised me so faithfully. What made you? But I will hope a little longer for I want to see you so much.

When you write, direct your letter either to 25 Gouverneur St. or Eldred, Sullivan County, New York. Mother is not well and I think I better go as soon as possible.

Your loving sister, Aida

N.Y.C., Thurs., January 5, 1882
Around to Ad's tonight. Took Buddie with me. We went to the stationery store on Grand St.

N.Y.C., Friday, January 6, 1882
Rainy all day. Rand came down and took Buddie home. I have been around to Ad's a little while.

N.Y.C., Thurs., January 12, 1882
I have been sick. Went out today for the first time. The doctor was here Saturday, Sunday, and Monday. Maria stayed with me until Tuesday.

This morning I went around to Ad's. Net came around and we stayed all day.

I am going home Saturday.

James Brown, husband of Ida Austin. Photo courtesy of Melva Austin Barney.

Ida Belle Austin married James Brown. Courtesy of Melva Austin Barney.

1878 wood engraving of the first train on the Gilbert Elevated Railroad passing through Sixth Avenue. Source: Library of Congress, Prints and Photographs Division: USZ62-127248; 3c27248.

George says for me not to go and little Will says to hurry back. He wants to go with me.

N.Y.C., Friday, January 13, 1882
Rainy all day. Around to Ad's this morning. Out with Maria this afternoon. Left her on Grand St. and went down to Mrs. Braisted's. It was dark when I got back.

Am going to stay here to Ad's all night. I go tomorrow. Am so tired. God help me.

Edward Wilson's Family
The Edward Wilson family mentioned in the next letter lived west of Mill Pond on Clark Road. Edward Wilson was a farmer and weaver. His sons Charles and William Wilson play a part in this story. In *The Mill on Halfway Brook*, Aida tried to encourage her brother Lon to go out with Annie Wilson (Edward's daughter).

Aida Austin, Eldred, to Maria Austin
January 19, 1882
Dear Sister Maria,
I suppose you have heard of the burning of Mr. Wilson's house. The fire broke out in the upper part of it, about noon, just a week ago.

They saved a few things, but nothing of much account. Almost every particle of the girls' clothing was destroyed, but Will and Mr. Wilson, I believe, saved the most of theirs. I understand one of the girls is going to the City; and that the other will keep house for Will and Mr. Wilson in the old house.

The Ladies' Aid Society of the Eldred Congregational Church is going to have a tea party at Aunt Effie's next Thursday evening for Annie and Mary. And I think we will raise quite a little money. I hope so anyway.

We held a Sociable at Will Kyte's last night. Mother and Father, Mort, Lon, and I were down. I had a good time and I guess everyone else did. There were about 50 out. The next one to be held at Mrs. Myers', two weeks from yesterday.

I have not been over to see Mrs. Collins very much lately; but I guess she is well. How is Annie? We have not heard a word from her since she went back.

How is little Tom getting along? Tell him Ida sends lots of love and kisses to her dear little friend, Tommy Edward Thompson; and that his pups are well and growing like weeds.

I have not heard from Mrs. Braisted in some time. If you see her before I write to her, I wish you would tell her to write.

Mother intended writing to you, but she says she is too tired tonight and so will wait until some other time.

With love to all, I remain your loving sister, Aida

It seems that Tommy Thompson was in Eldred soon after Aida wrote the above letter.

Addie Thompson, N.Y.C., to Tom Thompson, Eldred
January 23, 1882
Dear Little Tom,
Gussie [his brother] wants me to write you a little letter to tell you that he wishes you would come home as he wants to see you very much. He says for you to never mind about bringing the pup home, he thinks it will grow big faster if you leave it up there and he says you can have his Velocipede all day while he is at school and he thinks you will like the little horse that Santa Claus brought you very much.

You will have to hurry if you want to see that Christmas Tree as it is getting so dry we shall have to take it down pretty soon. You must coax Aunt Mary to come down with you as we all want to see her very much.

Gussie wants you to write a letter and tell him what day you are coming home. I will not write anymore as I am most sick tonight.

Papa, Gussie, and Mama all

send you lots of love and kisses and hope we will see you home now very soon.

Be a good boy and do not be saucy to Aunt Mary.

Good night and many kisses from, Mama [Addie]

The next letter was in the Austin Collection, but it is not known who Katie and Mary were.

Katie, Beaver Brook, N.Y., to Mary
February 7, 1882
Dear Mary,

There was a terrible accident happened today. The train was wrecked and only two cars saved. So I suppose the mail train was destroyed and just to think neither one nor Mary can hear from our beaux…

Write soon, Katie

Mary Ann Austin, Eldred, to Lon Austin
February 14, 1882
My Dear Son,

I began to be afraid you had gone on to Alaska, or that you was sick or dead until Aida received your letter. She said we might look for you anytime.

Why don't you come home? What can keep you? Can't you get your pay, get enough to get home on some way. There is plenty of work here this winter. Come and see.

Your Father said to tell you that if you wanted to see me alive, you better come home. I guess by that he wants to see you and oh, I want to see you more than words can express.

Aida is going to school yet, but I won't tell my news hoping that you may hear all by word of mouth.

Don't forget your loving Mother, M.A.

W. Sutherland, Central Bank, McPherson, Kans., to Lon Austin
March 11, 1882
Friend Alonzo,

I like banking very well and if I do well, expect to stick to it.

We have had a heavy snow storm and it has now nearly melted off but there are only 2 or 3 small sleighs here and so we didn't have much fun, but the snow has been of immense value to the wheat crop.

There has been some entertainment here this winter such as surprise parties, several dances, and theatricals.

Last night I took my violin and went up to E.G. Clarke's residence. We had music and singing and then snowballed each other on the way home.

Solomon has improved very much in the last year and promises well for the future.

Well Lon, you have not yet told me what you are doing. I should infer that you are chopping down trees, or some such thing in a lumber camp. Is that it?

I hope some day to travel through California and other western states and territories and have a good time.

What are a young man's chances in the west? And what wages do they pay in the different trades and professions? What do you know of banking out there?

Yours Respectfully,
Wm. G. Sutherland

J.E. Austin, Solomon City, Kans., to Lon Austin
April 30, 1882
Dear Brother Lon,

I was glad to hear from you again. I was quite surprised to learn that you had gotten home again. I had begun to think that the Indians had scalped you or

Addie Austin Thompson. "Gussie wants me to write you a little letter to tell you that he wishes you would come home." Photo courtesy of Katherine Calkin Traxler.

else you had got a hair puller and she would not let you write.

I think you must have got rich pretty quick to be able to go home and stay all summer. I only made a little more last year than expenses and enough to pay what I went behind the year before.

Have you another wagon? I can't pay very well until fall. I have got the money now, but I will have to use a good deal this season.

Since Mortie came here, I have paid him $99.25 and I owe him for one month's work now.

I am going to plant 25 acres more of corn this year than I did last and no one to help me but Mort.

I waited for Elbert [Clark] to come until it was too late to get any help here, so I am out. Elbert got Mort to send him the money to come and then backed out and kept the $10 of the money. I don't believe he was intending to come.

Mort says he wrote and will not write to you again unless you answer his letter.

Gussie (Augustus) Thompson, son of Tom and Addie Austin Thompson. "I have a nice time going to school." Photo courtesy of Katherine Calkin Traxler.

Your sister-in-law wants to know if you have got your bride with you. It is late so I must close.
Write soon to your affec. Brother, Jas. E. Austin

Gussie Thompson, N.Y.C., to Aida Austin, Eldred
December 10, 1882
Dear Ida [Aida Austin],
Maria says that she will answer your letter when her eyes get better. Tom says how is Jack and the pups? How is Aunt Mary? Mort also. How is Lonso and Tom.
I have had a slay [sleigh] ride Thanksgiving. I have a nice time going to school. All send love, good by, write soon,
Gussie Thompson
(The letter included a horse and rider drawing. See p. 451.)

Gussie Thompson, N.Y.C., to Aida Austin, Eldred
Dear [Aida Austin],
Tommy is playing with his horse. I am going to school also. I am lernt how to right good. I like to go to school much.
Tommy wants to know how his pup is.
Tommy and I are coming up to Aunt Mary if we are good.
I hope you will right some. From your little friend,
Gussie
(The letter included a Gunner Boat drawing. See p. 451.)

Austin and Leavenworth Relatives
The Austin family of my grandfather Mort Austin lived on the east side of Eldred. We will visit them again in Chapter 4.

Mort Austin was the future husband of Jennie Louisa Leavenworth, born in 1880. The Leavenworths lived on the west side of Eldred, but Jennie's grandmother, Jane Ann Van Pelt Webb Myers, had a boarding house near Hagan Pond, northeast of the Austin property.

Erie Railway Booklets Promote Boarding Houses
The Myers boarding house, 7 miles from the Shohola Station (across the river from Barryville), was first listed in the New York, Lake Erie and Western Railroad Booklet of 1882. The 1881 *Summer Excursion Routes* brochure mentioned visiting Highland Lake, Shohola, and Lackawaxen.

Previously, boarders in Highland were school teachers, widowed family members, or hired workers who lived in an extra room the family had.

With the promotion of the area, first by Railway Books and then by New York City newspapers, large farm houses were turned into places for boarders.

Some rented out a room that had been added on. Others built a boarding house for the new means of income.

Chapter 3
Picturesque Highlands
Boarding Houses of Highland, 1880s

Shohola, Pennsylvania, on the banks of the Delaware, 1,000 feet above the sea, is the station from which a picturesque portion of Sullivan County, in the vicinity of Eldred—among the Sullivan highlands and lakes—is reached by an enjoyable drive of five miles.

Nine mountain lakes reached easily, the farthest being six miles distant. Hagan, Hagai, Big, Montgomery, Sand, and York, in Sullivan County are all stocked with bass and pickerel.—Summer Homes and Rambles on the Picturesque Erie, *N.Y., L.E. & W.R.R., May, 1886.*

The railroad bridge across Shohola Creek. Photo: Jack E. Boucher; Library of Congress: HAER PA.52-SHOH.1-1.

Summer visitors to Sullivan County's picturesque Town of Highland arrived at the Shohola Railway Station, across the Delaware River and opposite Barryville.

The New York, Erie and Western Railroad Company (which became Erie Railroad in 1895) published booklets in the 1880s encouraging vacationers, sportsmen, and New York City businessmen with their families, to travel their railroad to locations along the Delaware River, in New York and Pennsylvania.

The Delaware Highlands
Homes and hotels along the Delaware River were featured in the *Delaware Highlands* Section of the Erie Railroad's brochures which described the places as: *a romantic village; the finest mountain scenery of the Delaware Valley; picturesque mountain scenery; ponds and streams, ravines and glens in profusion; picturesque in the extreme;* or *provides delightful rambles.*

Highland's summer homes were mainly in one of four places: close to a group of ponds on its east side; near a cluster of lakes and ponds on the west side; near the center of Eldred; or near Barryville on the Delaware River.

To the east of Eldred were Hagan, Sand, Round, and Haggai (Loch Ada) Ponds; some of them bordered on or were in Lumberland. We'll visit that area later in this chapter.

Washington, Montgomery and Little (Bodine) Lakes, and Beaver Brook Mill and Schumacher Ponds were close to Yulan on the west side of Highland near the Town of Tusten.

Washington Lake (perhaps the Big Lake referred to in the Erie brochure), was the larger lake shaped like a fish. Beers 1870 map shows the Gallaghers east of the lake, the Tether and Owen families near the southern tip of the tail, and the West family to the west, near Beaver Brook Mill Pond.

Montgomery Lake, south of Washington Lake, was a natural pond fed by ice cold springs. It was 50 feet deep, full of bass, and ran into Little Pond.

Schumacher's Pond near Yulan, New York, was a section of Beaver Brook that Mr. Schumacher dammed up. Postcard courtesy of Kevin Marrinan.

Little Pond, or Bodine Lake, was a natural lake which Justin Bodine stocked with pickerel, bass, perch, and other fish.

A story is told that during the winters in the late 1800s, the men would place a small pine tree in Bodine Lake and make bets as to what day the tree would fall through the ice.

Beaver Brook flowed from the Town of Tusten on the west of Highland into the long, thin Beaver Brook Mill Pond. Beaver Brook Bridge was nearby.

Beaver Brook flowed out of the Mill Pond, headed south running through Schumacher Pond, and ended southeast of York Pond between Minisink Ford and Barryville where it spilled into the Delaware River.

Schumacher Pond was a section of Beaver Brook that Mr. Schumacher dammed up. One story said that at one time there was coal on Schumacher Pond Road. It was hand dug from pits 20 to 30 feet deep.

Blind Pond was less than 2 miles northwest of Washington Lake. Blind Pond Brook flowed out of the pond through or near the Clark and Sergeant properties, then slowed down as it went through Beaver Swamp, not far from the Leavenworth homestead.

Beaver Swamp
Many of the names of the area's landmarks had "beaver" in them because they were so prevalent.

As far as I know, Beaver Swamp has been here long before

Beaver Brook Bridge in Yulan, New York. Photo courtesy of Kevin Marrinan.

Families who Lived near Blind Pond Brook, 1880s

Several of the families we met in *The Mill on Halfway Brook*, lived in the northwest area of the Town of Highland, close to Blind Pond Brook.

In 1880 George and William Bunce, bachelor farmers and the last of the Bunce family in the area, still lived northeast of Blind Pond. George died in 1885, and that is all that is known of the Bunce family in Eldred.

The Ed Wilson family lived south of the Bunce brothers. Charles Wilson had or would have a sawmill. He married Christina Mills in 1886. William H. Wilson would also marry a local girl and have Wilson's Store.

You may remember Wilmot and Mary Van Auken Clark who lived just southeast of Blind Pond, and west of the Wilson family. Descendants of their sons Irvin and George Clark are part of this story.

Irvin and Laura Austin Clark had 3 sons: Ellsworth, Elbert, and Robert.

George and Harriet Clark had 9 children. Four of them are a part of this story: Martin Dominick Clark, George Malcome Clark, Clarissa Clark, and Ella Clark.

Martin Dominick and Mary Costello Clark's son George James Clark was born in New York City in 1885. He would fight in WWI.

George Malcome and Elizabeth Hoatson Clark's daughter Georgia would be a teacher in Eldred.

Clarissa Clark would marry Frank Roberts Sergeant. Their daughter would marry a son of Sherman S. Leavenworth. Ella Clark and her second husband Myron Howe would move to Massachusetts, where she would later care for her niece.

Some descendants of Rev. Isaac Sergeant (who had started what became the Congregational Church in Eldred) lived on the southwest side of Blind Pond Brook.

In 1880 Alvah and Phebe Owen Sergeant's sons Morgan and Alvah T. were still at home with them. Their son Frank R. Sergeant boarded with his sister Jane Livingston's family.

Alvah Sergeant had been a deacon in the Congregational Church for 13 years. Alvah's parents Ethel and Lettie Gardner Sergeant lived next door to them. Ethel and Lettie's children: Isaac Sergeant, 46, a carpenter and Caroline Sergeant, 27, a dressmaker; and grandson James W. Sergeant, lived with them in 1880.

The homestead of Rev. Felix Kyte (pastor of the Eldred Congregational Church from 1832–1878) was near Blind Pond Brook, but closer to Clark Road. Felix's widow Eliza Greiger Kyte lived with her son William, his second wife Mary Alice Whitney, and their young children, Herbert, Mary Alice, and Felix J. Kyte. Aida Austin talks about Mary A. Kyte (Wormuth) in her 1940 Diary, in Book 3 of this series.

Felix and Eliza Kyte's son, Charles Eldred Kyte (most likely named after Charles C.P. Eldred), and his wife Sarah Crouch lived in Illinois.

The Charles Eldred Kyte Family in Rock Island County, Illinois, in 1892. Left to right: Charles Eldred, Lena Leota, Charles Colony, John Felix, and Sarah Viola Crouch Kyte. Photo courtesy of Barbara Wilkinson.

They had a son Charles Colony Kyte. Charles Eldred Kyte had been slightly wounded in the Civil War. He and his friend Corporal John Colony had made a pact to name one of their children after each other. John D. Colony had named one of his sons, Charles Kyte Colony.

Waterwheel on Kyte property near Blind Pond Brook. Photo courtesy of Chuck Myers.

Erie Train Stations Near the Delaware River

Excursion tickets were valid for continuous passage either going or returning on the date of issue or anytime within the next 30 days.

Package tickets of 10, 20, or 25 were good for either direction until used.

Commutation tickets were valid for continuous passage between the stations named on the tickets, if the train stopped at said station. The limit was 60 rides between the stations during the month named on the ticket.

Trains brought vacationers from New York City to scenic locations near the Delaware River. Photo from the Defeo Collection, courtesy of Kevin Marrinan.

Miles from New York City

Callicoon, New York 136	Lordville, New York 153-1/2
Cochecton, New York 130-3/4	Middletown, New York 67
Deposit, New York 177	Narrowsburg, New York 122-1/4
Goshen, New York 59-3/4	Parkers Glen, Pennsylvania 102-1/4
Hancock, New York 163-3/4	Paterson, New Jersey 16-3/4
Hankins, New York 143	Pond Eddy, Pennsylvania 99
Hawley, Pennsylvania 127	Port Jervis, New York 88-1/4
Honesdale, Pennsylvania 136	Shohola, Pennsylvania 107
Lackwaxen, Pennsylvania 111	Sparrowbush, New York 90-3/4
Long Eddy, New York 146-3/4	Tuxedo, New York 38-1/2

Erie Depot and Hotel Oakland in Narrowsburg, New York. Postcard courtesy of Mary Briggs Austin.

white men ever settled here. I know this because where Goldie Leavenworth's house is now, there was an old house there before. They dug down 7 feet for the foundation and found fresh beaver wood preserved in the muck.

It would have made an ideal location for the lumber company to set up a mill—which they did behind the Leavenworth homestead. Besides, it also made it convenient to float logs as was often done back in those times.

Much of this existing Beaver Dam is made of stone, which probably means that at one point man had a hand in it—meaning repairing it. The beavers were trapped out many times. They had to find their own way downstream and to the dam.
—Norman Bohs.

The Leavenworth Homestead

It is not known when the Leavenworth homestead became a boarding house called Echo Hill Farm House. Perhaps because it was a smaller home, it was advertised more by word of mouth.

Echo Hill Farm House, once a bunkhouse for lumberjacks near the sawmill on Blind Pond Brook, was where Sherman Buckley and his wife Charlotte Ingram lived.

By 1880 there was a two-story house which seems to have been attached to the original one-story cabin. In 1880 Libby Owen *(photo p. 447)* was listed as a servant.

Buckley had farmed some 250 acres of land for about 30 years, and still used the sawmill powered by Blind Pond Brook.

Two of the four trees which had been planted during the Civil War for the Leavenworth sons—Hezekiah, Atwell, Sherman S. and John—had been growing close to 20 years. Atwell and Hezekiah had died near the end of the war, and two of the trees had been cut down.

Sherman S., John E., and Harriet Palmer were the only three of Buckley and Charlotte Leavenworth's nine children still living.

Henry and Harriet Palmer
Henry and Harriet Palmer and their 3 children lived in Port Jervis in 1880. Henry ran a wood yard; Harry clerked in the grocery store; Edith taught school (as had Harriet at one time); and James, the youngest, attended school.

Sherman and Maria Leavenworth
Sherman S. Leavenworth and his wife Maria Myers had lived with Buckley and Charlotte probably since their marriage in December 1874. At the beginning of 1882, Sherman and Maria had 3 children: Anna Mae, 6, Truman Ellis, 3, and my grandmother, Jennie Louisa, almost 2.

John Ellis Leavenworth
In 1867 at age 16, John Ellis Leavenworth had left Eldred (called Halfway Brook Village at the time).

I believe that I read that John Leavenworth wanted to enlist as a flag bearer in the war, but was rejected as too young. My impression is that he did not serve and that he was exhorted in the letters to stay home and get the spring crops in.—Gerald Koenig.

John served in the Army of the West with Custer after the Civil War, according to his great-nephew, Robert C. Austin. John then mined in Colorado.

Charlotte Leavenworth Dies
The first week of June 1882, Charlotte Ingram Leavenworth died. Perhaps her son John returned from mining in Colorado for her funeral.

James Garfield Leavenworth Born
Sherman and Maria Myers Leavenworth's son James Garfield Leavenworth was born June 22, 1882. Garfield, as he came to be called, would grow to be at least 6 foot 6 inches tall. Most likely the new little one was named for the president who had died in 1881.

John Leavenworth Marries Anna Amelia Bradley
In August 1882 John E. Leavenworth married the girl next door, Anna Amelia Bradley, at Barryville. Rev. M.S. Lambert was the preacher.

Hazel Leavenworth, my mother, said he came back to Eldred to marry with a lot of gold from his mining activities.—Gerald Koenig.

John Ellis Leavenworth, son of Sherman B. and Charlotte Leavenworth. Photo courtesy of his grandson, Gerald Koenig.

John and Amelia seem to have returned to Colorado. In May 1883 their daughter Florence was born.

The Bradley Family of Eldred
The Bradley family of Eldred lived between Washington Lake and the Leavenworths. They had access to the lake from the northeast.

Letters indicate that Isaac M. Bradley had built a house for his family during the Civil War.

Isaac M. and Joanna Brown Bradley, and their 7 children: Amelia, Viola, Mary Francis, Isaac N., Lottie, Atwell, and little Norah, play a part in this story.

Isaac M. Bradley, a farmer, had 70 acres of land in 1880. (He was listed with 368 acres in 1875).

Isaac M. Bradley's father Isaac Bradley from Connecticut, had died in 1873. Isaac Bradley Sr. had lived in what was then Lumberland, from 1840.

Mary Bradley and John Bradley
Mary Larkin Bradley, wife of Isaac Bradley Sr., and mother of Isaac

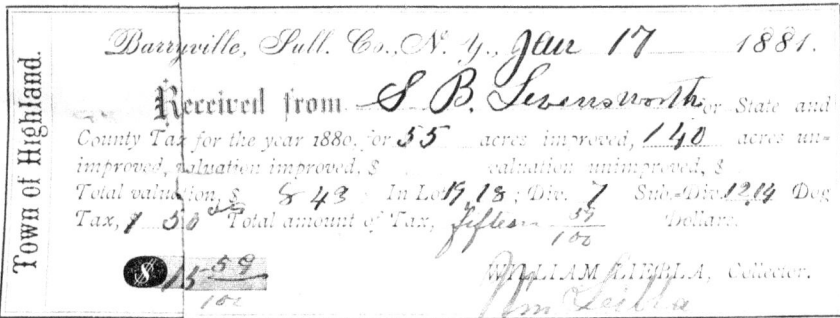

Sherman B. Leavenworth's receipt for $15.59 for taxes paid to the Town of Highland on 195 acres of land in 1880. Courtesy of Cynthia Leavenworth Bellinger.

Washington Lake, Yulan, New York. Beers 1870 map shows the Gallaghers located east of the lake and the Tether and Owen families near the southern tip of the tail. Postcard courtesy of Kevin Marrinan.

M. Bradley, had died in 1846. Four years later Isaac Sr. had married Charlotte Perry.

Isaac Sr. and Charlotte had a son, John Perry Bradley, half brother to Isaac M. Bradley.

In 1883 Charlotte Perry Bradley, a widow of 10 years, and her son John Bradley lived in West Brookfield, Massachusetts. Both John and Charlotte Bradley wrote to Isaac M. and his wife Joanna, from Massachusetts, in 1883.

J. Bradley and C. Bradley, West Brookfield, Mass., to Isaac and Joanna Bradley, Eldred
May 13, 1883

1881 New York, Erie and Western Railroad: Mountain Resorts

The New York and Erie Railroad originated in 1832, became the New York, Lake Erie and Western Railroad in 1878, and the Erie Railroad in 1895.

The Shawangunk Mountains cross the state of New York in a north eastward direction through the counties of Orange, Sullivan and Ulster. They are a continuation of the Blue Mountains of New Jersey and Pennsylvania. The main line of the New York, Lake Erie and Western Railroad begins the ascent of the Shawangunks 65 miles from New York, and crosses them at Otisville, at an elevation of 1,500 feet above tide…

Shohola, with its wonderful streams and glen; Lackawaxen, girded about by hills and mirrored in the broad Delaware; Narrowsburg, with its picturesque old bridge and unfathomable eddy in the river; Cochecton, Callicoon, Hancock, and Deposit; all crowded by the high mountains of the Upper Delaware Valley, offers rare attractions to the lover of the wild and rugged in nature and of true life among the mountains.

The Glen on the Shohola Creek, at Shohola, is a remarkable collection of natural curiosities discovered in 1876…

From Shohola by stage, several resorts in the western Sullivan County mountains are reached, Highland Lake being the most popular. It is seven miles from the Erie Railroad station.—Summer Excursion Routes, N.Y., L.E. & W.R.R., 1881, p. 90.

1883 Cover of New York, Lake Erie and Western Railroad's Summer Homes and Rambles.

1881 Cover of New York, Lake Erie and Western Railroad's Summer Excursion Routes.

Dear Brother and Sister,
I have had considerable work through the winter and I am working now for one of the neighbors for 13 dollars a month. I am to work about 7 months.

Isaac, what do you find to busy yourself about these times? Have you begun to plan yet or is it cold weather there yet and a backward Spring?

How are your folks? Are the girls to home yet? Have you heard anything from Mary and her husband? We sent a letter to Amelia; have not heard from her yet. If you write to her, tell her that we would like to hear from her.

John P. Bradley

Sunday morning, May 20, 1883
Dear Son and Daughter,
John commenced this letter last Sunday and I will try and finish it today if I can. My health is very poor and I never expect to be any better. I have a cancer and it grows quite fast.

We calculated to go to see you last fall. John had got all ready to go and I was almost ready and in less than a week before we were ready to start, I was taken sick. I did not write you about it for I thought perhaps we might go yet. I have given up all hopes of going unless something should turn up in my favor.

Isaac, I want you and Joanna to come if you possibly can and if Joanna can't come, I want you to come if you can. Your children are old enough to leave. You can't think how I want to see you.

My brother John lives in the Village. Write and tell me what day you will come and what train you will come on and John will meet you there.

I think the fare from New York is 4 dollars and 3 cents. It seems as if I can't give up but what I must see you. I hope you can both come. Write soon. I shall expect you.
From your Mother,
Charlotte Bradley

Charlotte Perry Bradley died in September 1883.

Town of Highland Boarding Houses
Boarding Houses in the Town of Highland first appeared in Erie Railway's 1882 Brochure.

Bradley Farm
Isaac M. Bradley, Proprietor
In 1880 the Colwell (possibly Colville) family of 4 boarded with the Bradleys in 1880. (Lottie Bradley would later marry Charles Colville.)

The Bradley House, on what is now Airport Road, was first advertised in the Erie Railway's 1882 *Mountain Lake and Cataract* booklet. The Bradley Farm continued to be advertised by the Railway Brochures throughout the 1880s.

Isaac and Joanna's son Isaac N. Bradley would marry Jessie Tether, the daughter of Joseph and Anne Barber Tether, who lived south of the Bradleys.

Washington Lake House
Joseph Tether, Proprietor
Joseph Tether had 220 acres on

Delaware Highlands Boarding Houses from 1882

These listings appeared in the 1882 and 1883 Erie Railway publications.

Shohola, 108 miles from New York, is beautifully located among the mountains, overlooking the Delaware. It is in the heart of the famous hunting and fishing regions of Pike and Sullivan Counties.

Isaac M. Bradley
6 miles from Shohola. Carriage, single passenger, $2; family $3. Accommodates 18; 11 rooms; 1 in room $8; 2 $7 each; $1.25 per day. Center of trout, perch, and pickerel fishing. Boats free. Deer, bear, partridge, rabbit, woodcock, wild pigeon shooting. Deer hounds and setters furnished. $2 per day. Croquet ground. Meet parties at Shohola when notified. Headquarters for sportsmen. Fresh vegetables, milk, eggs, and butter. Guides obtained.

Myers, Mills & Co.
7 miles from Shohola. Conveyance, 75 cents for one; 50 cents. 2 or more; trunks, 25 cents. Accommodates 30; 5 single rooms; 12 double; $6 to $8; $12 to $16; $1.25 per day. Discount for season. Lake in front of house; 5 others within one mile. 2 boats free; others 25 cents a day.

Little Pond Cottage, J. Bodine
4 miles from Shohola. Accommodates 15; 10 rooms, double piazzas all around; $8 per week; $1.50 per day. Pond in front of house; 2 other ponds near. Boats and fishing free. Conveyance $1 per person from Depot. French cooking. Fresh vegetables, milk, eggs, etc.

Source: Abbott, John N., Mountain Lake and Cataract; Summer Homes and Rambles Along the Erie Railway; *New York, Lake Erie and Western Railroad Company, Hopcraft & Co., N.Y., 1882, pp. 53 to 55; and 1883, pp. 26, 27.*

Justin and Adele Bodine owned Little Pond Cottage on Bodean (Bodine) Pond/Lake, northeast of Yulan. Postcard courtesy of Helen Hensel Oset.

the east side of Washington Lake. Starting in 1885, Joseph and Anne advertised their new farmhouse and its large airy rooms near the tail of Washington Lake, in the newspaper and Erie Railroad's *Summer Homes and Rambles*.

Joseph Tether advertised good hunting and fishing for sportsmen in the *Brooklyn Daily Eagle* in the fall of 1888.

Joseph Tether and Anne Barber had both been born in England. Joseph had arrived from England with his parents Edward and Elizabeth Peet Tether, in 1850. The Tethers settled in Highland around 1860, and are shown on the 1870 map just south of Washington Lake. In 1880 Mary Kerr, the school teacher, boarded with Joseph and Anne Tether.

Descendants of Edward and Elizabeth Tether's children: Marianne Whitney, Elizabeth Owen, and Joseph W. Tether play a part in this story.

William and Marianne Tether Whitney's daughter Mary Alice Whitney married William Kyte, son of Rev. Felix and Eliza Greiger Kyte. William and Mary Alice's daughter Mary Kyte (Wormuth) would be a friend to Aida Austin.

Robert and Elizabeth Tether Owen lived south of the Tether family. Their children Mabel Louise, William, and Frank are part of this story.

Mabel L. Owen would marry Edwin Van Schoick Myers. They would be parents of my aunt Gladys Myers Austin. William Owen would marry Phoebe Middaugh. They would have a lovely 4-story boarding house called Oakdene. Their daughter Pearl would marry Fred Defeo Sr. Frank Owen would also have a boarding house.

Little Pond Cottage
J. Bodine, Proprietor
East of the Owen family was Little Pond (Bodean/Bodine Pond), where Justin and Adele Bodine lived. Their Little Pond Cottage started in 1880 as a small farm boarding house for 12 guests.

Twin Lake Farm, J.P. Gallagher, Proprietor, and Highland Farm, S. Gallagher, Proprietor
Montgomery Lake was a bit northeast of Little Pond. Twin Lake Farm seems to have been on Eldred-Yulan Road, northeast of Montgomery Lake. Both Gallagher homes were advertised in the 1886 Erie Booklet.

Spring House, Barryville
George Layman, Proprietor
George Layman's Spring House in Barryville was advertised in the 1885 Erie Railway booklet.

George Layman had been listed in the Erie Brochures of 1882 and 1883 as proprietor of the Shohola House in Shohola, Pennsylvania.

In 1885 Mr. Layman ran the Spring House across the Delaware River in Barryville, New York. The Spring House was originally built around 1850 and was first a farmhouse. Gardner Forgerson (in 1845) sold the property to Hiram Quick, who built a home, barn, and well on the land. Hiram added 4 more lots for a total of about 3 acres.

Threatening his Rescuers

There was an interesting news item in the June 1886 edition of the *The New York Times*.

George Layman, proprietor of a large summer boarding house at Barryville, Sullivan County, tied a rope around his neck, to which was attached a large stone, on Wednesday, and then waded out into the Delaware River to drown himself. His movements were observed, and he was dragged ashore.

This greatly incensed Layman, and seizing a large stone, he threatened to kill anyone who interfered with him. His menaces were so alarming that the crowd fell back, and he then plunged into the river again.

Finally, the man was rescued and taken home. Layman has been acting irrationally of late, and is believed to be insane. He has no business or domestic troubles so far as ascertained.—The New York Times, *June 4, 1886.*

Later it would be learned that Mr. Layman suffered many years from Bright's disease. Perhaps Mr. Layman was experiencing severe pain in the event reported in the June 1886 news article.

The premises was beautifully located, the land smooth and well shaped; but Hiram possessed neither the requisite taste nor money for its improvement. He became involved, conveyed the property to N.B. Johnston and removed to Virginia where he died.—Johnston, p. 352.

Quite sadly, Napoleon (N.B.) Johnston committed suicide in August 1884. His son John W. Johnston (nephew of the author of *Reminiscences*) had become the owner of the property in 1880. Young J.W. Johnston built a new house, but failed in business.

George Layman then became the owner of the property which became the Spring House in Barryville—only a 5 minute walk from Shohola, across the Barryville-Shohola Bridge.

The Spring House was made larger and offered guests:

...an excellent waterfront, well-shaded lawns, and everything conducive to health and comfort.—Johnston, p. 352.

Lake View Farm House
Edward Prange, Barryville
Edward Prange's Lake View Farm House mentioned in the 1886 *Summer Homes and Rambles*, would later belong to Alfred Kaese.

Laurel Valley House
Charles Hickok, Proprietor
Charles Hickok had a home two miles north of Barryville. Quite possibly Charles was a descendant of Justus and Mary Wells Hickok. Justus was an uncle of Mary Ann Eldred Austin.

Other Barryville
Boarding Houses
Between 1886 and 1889, several

Spring House was owned by George Layman. "An excellent waterfront, well-shaded lawns, and everything conducive to health and comfort." Photo courtesy of Kathy Datys.

Barryville houses were added to the Erie Railway's list of places to stay in the Delaware Highlands: D.H. Heyen, D.W. Bogert, W.W. Cortright's River View House, Mrs. Charles Frace, and Charles Racine's West Shore Cottage.

Near Hagan Pond/Highland Lake
The boarding houses of Jane Ann Myers and Dr. DeVenoge mentioned in the 1880s railroad brochures, were the only two located on the east side of the Town of Highland.

Myers, Mills & Co.
Jane Ann Myers
The 1882 *Mountain Lake and Cataract* included the Myers, Mills & Co. near Hagan Pond. The Myers family were country neighbors of the Austin family and relatives of the Leavenworths on the west side of Eldred. Jane Ann Van Pelt Webb Myers was the mother of Maria Myers Leavenworth and grandmother of Jennie Louisa Leavenworth.

Jane Ann Myers ran the Myers

Hancock, New York, view of the Delaware from the 1881 Erie Railway Brochure.

boarding house near Collins and Hagan Pond Roads. Her son Gus Myers, and other son George W.T. Myers and his wife Martha Mills helped.

Jane Ann Myers's home had been built in the early 1850s. By 1880 there seems to be two houses

Myers, Mills & Co.

Jane Ann Myers Boarding House. Photo courtesy of Stuart and Geraldine Mills Russell.

Jane Ann Myers, Gus Myers, and George W.T. and Martha Mills Myers lived northwest of the Proctor Property in Lumberland.

Sometime in 1881 Charles E. Proctor wrote about the walk he took from Black Lake (about 9 miles north of Eldred) to several locations in the Town of Highland. Charles Proctor mentioned that he stayed and ate at the home of Mrs. Myers (my great-great-grandmother Jane Ann Van Pelt Webb Myers).

[We'll be] in the neighborhood for a day or two. We will get the best accommodations to be had at Highland Lake.

To reach which we turn to the left and after passing through the village and across the brook which once was famous for its trout, we ascend for the next two miles in the road to the left.

When having reached the summit, we suddenly come upon Hagan or Highland Lake, securely hemmed in by beautifully wooded hills. This splendid body of water is almost 1-1/2 miles long and 1/2 wide and almost 1,400 feet altitude.

Here fine fishing is to be had and good boats can be obtained from Mrs. Myers whose comfortably situated house is on the right and facing the lake. Here it is our intention to put up during our stay...

To the left of the house we are well prepared to partake of the excellent repast set before us.
—Charles Edward Proctor.

Jane Ann Van Pelt Myers on the right. Photo courtesy of Cynthia Leavenworth Bellinger.

with a laundry area and summer kitchen between the two.

Jane Ann Myers and her son Augustus (Gus) lived in one house. George Washington Taylor Myers and his wife Martha Mills lived in the other.

George W.T. and Martha Mills Myers had two sons, Charles and Martin D. Myers. Soon George and Martha would build a huge, beautiful boarding house on Highland Lake.

Jane Ann Myers's other daughter Lottie Myers Darling and her husband Charles Darling had three daughters: Agnes, Ida, and Edith Darling. They lived north of Binghamton, New York.

L. DeVenoge, M.D., Eldred

Southeast of Hagan Pond was Round Pond where Dr. Leon, his wife Catherine, and daughter Mary lived on over 1,000 acres. They had three servants and a boarder, in 1880. Their boarding house was featured in the 1889 *Picturesque Erie Summer Homes*.

Alexander Mills Family Boarding House

Alexander Mills's boarding house was north of Hagan Pond's little finger. The Mills Boarding House, built in 1850 (with additions), was not listed in the Erie Brochures. But at some point the Mills home became a boarding house.

Alexander Mills, a carpenter, and his wife Margaret Gillies' five children, Martha, Margaret, Mary, George, and Christina Mills, play a part in this story.

James Boyd Family Boarding House

James and Margaret Mills Boyd had six children. James and Margaret would have a boarding house before 1900. Three of the Boyd descendants, Bertha, Isabelle,

Delaware Highlands Boarding Houses from 1885

These listings first appeared in Erie Railway publications from 1885–1889.

Washington Lake House
Joseph Tether, Proprietor
Accommodates 30; 20 rooms, adults $6 to $8; children half price; servants $5; transient $1.25 per day. Discount for season. Transportation adults $1; children, half price. Lake of 200 acres only 2 minutes' walk. Perch, pickerel, bass. Surrounded by forest. Raises vegetables. Plenty milk, eggs butter and poultry.

Spring House, Barryville
George Layman Proprietor
5 minutes walk *from Shohola*. Accommodates 30; 20 rooms; adults $7 to $8; children under 12, half price; servants $6; transient $1.25 per day. Discount for season. Transportation, $1. Raises vegetables. Plenty fresh milk, butter, eggs and poultry.

Laurel Valley Farm House
Charles Hickok, Proprietor
Accommodates 20; 10 large rooms; adults $7; children $3.50; transient $1.50 per day. Transportation free to weekly boarders. 3 miles from Shohola Glen. Good livery. Will meet guests in response to telegrams. Raises vegetables. Plenty of butter, eggs, milk and poultry.

Lake View Farm House
Edward Prange, Proprietor
Accommodates 20; 13 rooms; adults $7; children $3; servants $5; transient $1.25 per day. Discount for season. Transportation, $1. Raises vegetables. Plenty fresh milk, butter, eggs and poultry.

River View House
W.W. Cortright, Proprietor
1/4 mile *from Shohola*. Conveyance 25 cents. Accommodates 20; 11 rooms; adults, $6 to $8; children under 12 years, half price; servants, $5; transient $1.50. Good livery near. Good fishing and gunning. Guides $1.50 per day. Raises vegetables. Plenty of fresh milk, eggs and poultry.

D.H. Heyen, Barryville
2 miles *from Shohola*. Accommodates 10; 5 rooms; adults $5 to $8; children, half price; servants $5. Conveyance 50 cents. Good fishing. Raises vegetables. Plenty of fresh milk, eggs and poultry.

D.W. Bogert, Barryville
1/4 mile *from Shohola*. Accommodates 6; 3 rooms; adults, $8 to $10; no children or servants. Good fishing near. Raises vegetables. Plenty of fresh milk, eggs and poultry. House on the bank of Delaware River.

Twin Lake Farm
J.P. Gallagher, Proprietor
5 miles *from Shohola*. Transportation, $1; children half price. 2 single, 11 double rooms; adults $6 to $8; children, $4–$6; servants, $6; transient, $1.50/day. Boats free. Piano, croquet, archery, and other amusements free to guests. Covered dancing pavilion; picnic grounds, and excursions organized to all parts of the county. Raises vegetables; plenty of fresh milk, eggs and poultry.

Highland Farm
S. Gallagher, Proprietor
5 miles *from Shohola*. Transportation free to season guests. Accommodates 8 to 10; 5 rooms; adults, $6 to $7; children half price; $1 per day. Discount for season. Good fishing. Raises vegetables. Plenty of fresh milk, eggs and poultry. House new.

Chas. C. Racine
10 miles *from Shohola*; conveyance, $1. 1 double, 6 single rooms; adults, $7; children, half price; servants, $7; $1 per day; discount for season. Boats, $1 per day; own livery.

Mrs. Chas. C. Frace, Barryville
1/2 mile *from Shohola*. 2 single, 6 double rooms; adults, $6; children under 10 years, half price; servants, $5; $15.0 per day. Excellent fishing and gunning. Splendid tennis and croquet lawn.

L. DeVenoge, M.D.
Eldred, Sullivan County, N.Y.
7 miles from Shohola; transportation $1.60 double rooms; adults $8 to $12; servants $8; discount for season. Good fishing; boats free.

Sources: Abbott, John N., Summer Homes and Rambles on the Picturesque Erie, *New York, Lake Erie & Western R.R., 1885, pp. 60, 61; and 1886, pp. 87, 88. Farmer, L.P.,* Picturesque Erie Summer Homes, *Passenger Department, N.Y., L.E. & W.R.R., 1888, pp. 94–96; and 1889, pp. 92–94.*

and Floyd, are a part of this story.

Bertha Boyd would marry William H. Wilson. Isabelle Boyd would marry Henry Asendorf. The Asendorfs would have a huge boarding home and play a part in the life of her uncle George and aunt Martha Myers' grandson.

Floyd Boyd would one day have a garage in town with his cousin Alexander Wait. Alexander's parents were George and Mary Mills Wait.

The John Horton Family
The John Horton family also lived on Hagan Pond. Several of their descendants play a part in this story. John and Anne Stanton Horton's grandson Charles Horton would marry Beatrice Avery, a granddaughter of Isaac M. and Joanna Brown Bradley.

John and Anne Horton's daughter Mary Elvira Horton

Young Julius Maier (second from the left) and Anna Maier (behind Julius) were children of Joseph and Juliana Maier. Photo courtesy of the Bosch Family.

(born in 1900) would marry Herman Bosch, a son of Wihelm and Mary Maier Bosch.

Wilhelm and Mary Maier Bosch

Wilhelm and Mary Maier Bosch, and daughters, Wilhelmina and Juliana, moved from New York City to Hagan Pond sometime in 1880. They would have a boarding house by 1900.

Heinrich Wilhelm Bosch emigrated to the United States about 1871. His German name had been Boesch.

Pop [Wilhelm] had a job as a sailor. He went from Germany to all different ports. It got time for him to go in the German Army, so Pop skipped off the ship when it landed in New York City, and got a job driving a coal cart.

One night in New York City, Pop was in a bar room drinking and Grandpa [Joseph Maier] was there too. Grandpa wanted to know if anyone could milk cows, as he had bought a farm in the country [Eldred]. Pop said he knew how to milk.

So Grandpa hired him and he went up here in Eldred, New York. Grandpa had two daughters [Mary and Anna Maier] and one boy [Julius Maier]. After Pop worked for a year or so, he married one of the girls [Mary]. So Pop and Ma started a family of their own.

Pop bought 50 acres of land [near Hagan Pond] for $150 and built a one-room house, quite a large one. We all lived in the one-room house for years. It had a curtain to make two rooms.

We also had 2 cows and a horse and chickens and a pig. Pop worked for Dr. DeVenoge for a long time and a dozen other men. They got 40 cents for 10 hours work. This is what was told to me.
—Ed Bosch, son of Wilhelm and Mary Maier Bosch.

Maier's Pine Grove Farm

Joseph Maier and his wife Juliana emigrated from Bavaria in 1859. Joseph, a successful furniture maker in New York City, bought an 111-1/2 acre farm southwest of Eldred, on Crawford Road in 1875.

The land deed shows that Juliana Maier made the actual purchase from Alfred and Elizabeth Costello for $5,450. This was the location of the Maier's Pine Grove Farm Boarding House.

Alfred and Elizabeth Costello had purchased the property from Samuel and Elizabeth Myers in the fall of 1872 for $3,500. Alfred and Elizabeth were the parents of Mary Costello who married Martin Dominick Clark, whose son George James Clark we will meet in Chapters 6, 10, 11, and 12.

Pine Grove Farm was 3 miles from the Shohola Depot. We will hear more about Joseph, Juliana, Annie, and Julius Maier in later chapters.

Parker Hotel and Bar

The Parker Hotel and Bar was a bit southeast of Eldred Corners. It was the home of James and Emily Payne Parker and their children

Alexander Mills' home. Photo courtesy of Stuart and Geraldine Mills Russell.

Delaware House

Delaware House, 1882
Mrs. M.A. Holbert Proprietor; F.J. Holbert, Manager. 1/3 of a mile on banks of Delaware at junction of Lackawaxen. Conveyance free. Accommodates 100; 15 single rooms; 50 double rooms; $10 to $12; $2 per day. Discount for season. Two cottages attached. Boating for a mile on river. Black bass fishing in front of house. Boats free. Livery furnished; $5 per day. Best of references. Fresh vegetables, butter, eggs, milk, etc. from farm. Guides obtained.
—*Erie Railway Brochure, 1882.*

Delaware House, 1884
A popular Summer resort on the Erie Road and banks of the Delaware and Lackawaxen Rivers; everything first class; boating, bathing and fishing; boats free; reduced rates for June and September; circular. F.J. Holbert, Agent.—Brooklyn Daily Eagle, June 11, 1884.

View from New York, looking towards Pennsylvania where the Lackawaxen River joins the Delaware River. The Erie Railroad track and bridge crossing the Lackawaxen River is behind the Delaware House on the right. Photo courtesy of Minisink Historical Society.

View of the Roebling Bridge from the Delaware House in Pennsylvania. Photo: Library of Congress, Prints and Photographs Division: HAER, PA, 52-LACK, 1-23.

This delightful unidentified photo is courtesy of the Bosch Family. Possibly Wilhelm Bosch bent over on the right and Joseph Maier sitting down.

William and Adelaide. A delightful surprise arrives at the James and Emily's home, but not until the early 1890s.

The Parker Hotel had a bar and the first liquor license in town. Emily Parker saved her tip money and had a cute cottage built behind the hotel for a winter home. (Boarding house families often had a smaller winter home they lived in during the cold months.)

Minisink Ford and Lackwaxen
Most boarding houses in Highland were located near Eldred, Yulan, Barryville, or Hagan Pond (called Venoge in 1897). At some point at least two hotels/houses were located in the other hamlet, Minisink Ford, about 4 miles west

Parker House built by James Y. Parker. Photo courtesy of Christena Stevens Myers.

The house Emily Parker had built with her tip money. Photo courtesy of Christena Stevens Myers.

Wilhelm Stops for a Drink

Straub's Bar in the following story was originally the Parker Hotel. Most likely Wilhelm Bosch had also been to the bar when James Y. Parker owned the Parker House.

Wilhelm could be very ornery when he was drinking. [Later in life, Wilhelm stopped drinking.] Wilhelm's grandchildren universally recalled Wilhelm's almost daily stops at Straub's Bar in Eldred.

When Wilhelm arrived, the other patrons were expected to exit and wait on the front porch until Wilhelm had his first drink. They would then be allowed to re-enter.

When Wilhelm's horse was parked by the terrace wall by the street in front of Straub's, students in the school across the street in the present Town Hall (including his children and later his grandchildren) would observe bar patrons milling about outside and know that Wilhelm stopped in for a drink. —Ken Bosch, great-grandson.

James Y. Parker (in the middle) at the bar in his first Parker House, which was later Straub's Hotel. Photo courtesy of Christena Stevens Myers.

of Barryville, near the Roebling Aqueduct.

The Lackawaxen and Delaware Rivers joined north of the Aqueduct on the Pennsylvania side. The large Delaware House *(shown on p. 77)* was built north of the Lackawaxen River by William Holbert in 1852. The Delaware House was advertised in the Erie Railway Booklets from 1882 on, and at least by 1884 in the newspaper.

Shohola Glen House and John F. Kilgour

The Shohola House, across from the Shohola Railway Station, was also featured in the Railway brochures.

Shohola House (first known as Thomas Tavern) and the store next to it, had been built by Chauncey Thomas in the mid-1800s. The Tavern burned down, but by 1875, George Layman had rebuilt it as Shohola House.

From its beginning in 1849, over the years, it has been a favorite stopping place for raftsmen, canalers, railroaders, quarrymen, and lumberjacks.

George Layman ran the

Villages and Houses Reached by the Erie Railway

View of the Delaware River from the Hawk's Nest mountain road. Postcard courtesy of Katherine Calkin Traxler.

The following descriptions are from Picturesque Erie: Summer Homes, *by L.P. Farmer, N.Y., L.E. &R.R., 1888. The distance is from New York City. Week days: 3–8 trains from and 5–8 trains back to N.Y.C. Sundays: 1–5 trains.*

Sparrowbush, N.Y., 90-3/4 miles
Fare: $2.80; round trip $3.80.

Sparrowbush is a romantic village two miles west of Port Jervis. It is in the midst of some of the finest mountain scenery of the Delaware Valley. The Hawk's Nest Mountain Road, which is one of the attractions of Sparrowbush, is an unequaled drive. There are many other natural and artificial attractions in the vicinity which commend Sparrowbush especially to the summer visitor.

Boarding houses: Geo. Terwilliger, John R. Patterson (Sparrowbush); and Mrs. Mary Rose.

Pond Eddy, Pa., 99 miles
Fare: $3.05; round trip $4.20

Situated in the Delaware Valley, in the midst of picturesque mountain scenery, with ponds and streams, ravines and glens in profusion.

Boating, bathing and fishing of the best. Population, 200. Comfortable and healthful place to spend the summer. Wm. Rixton Hotel.

Parkers Glen, Pa., 102-3/4 mi.
Fare: $3.15; round trip 4.40

A quiet and enjoyable resort among the mountains. Delaware River close at hand. The glen from which the town derives its name is picturesque in the extreme, and provides delightful rambles to those who locate in the vicinity. Population 75. Best of fishing and gunning, and good drives in every direction.

Shohola Glen House, Pa. J. F. Kilgour, Proprietor (1886)
Opposite depot. Accommodates 50; 35 rooms; adults, $8 to $10; children, reduced rates; servants, $4.50; transient, $2 per day. Cottages for camping parties. Raises vegetables; abundance of fresh milk, eggs, butter and poultry.

Lackawaxen, Pa., 111 miles
Weekdays: 8 trains from and to N.Y.C.; Sundays: 5 trains from, 4 trains to N.Y.C. Fare: $3.40 Round trip: $5.

The scenery is superb, and the view up and down the valley is of surpassing loveliness. It is on the Delaware and Lackawaxen Rivers. The attractions of this place are its pure air, its beautiful scenery, its fishing, its boating, and the general wildness that pervades the surrounding. No mosquitoes or malaria. Population 200.

Holbert's Delaware House, Buck's New York Hotel, National Hotel, and H.E. Twichell's Mt. Lake Farm House.

Mast Hope, Pa., 116-1/2 miles
Fare: $3.55; round trip: $5.30.

A picturesque and healthy locality (population of 200) situated amidst surroundings similar to Lackawaxen. It is very popular as a summer retreat, and has everything to recommend it to those who would spend the summer quietly in the midst of delightful surroundings.

Some boarding/farm houses: Mrs. Mary Hankins; Mrs. M. Dabron; W.H. Hankins; and F.C. Munger.

Narrowsburg, N.Y., 122-1/4 miles
Fare: $3.75; Round trip: $5.45.

At Big Eddy, the widest and deepest part of the Delaware River above tide. Population of 600.

There are lakes, and streams and mountains; splendid views and healthful air and water. Ten mountain lakes within eight miles, and numerous trout streams. Best of black bass fishing. Boating for two miles. Deer hunting on surrounding ridges. Partridge shooting good; splendid drives; livery near station. No mosquitoes or malaria; cool nights.

2 hotels; 13 boarding or farm houses.

Cochection, N.Y., 130-3/4 miles
Fare: $4; Round trip: $5.60

Cochecton village is neat and cozy, and there is an air of pastoral ease. Population 600. Several fine lakes in the mountains within four miles of the station. Both pickerel and trout fishing.

18 boarding or farm houses: DeWitt Knapp, Ezra Calkin, etc.

Callicoon, N.Y., 136 miles
Weekdays: 7 trains from and to N.Y.C.; Sundays: 4 trains from and 3 to N.Y.C. Fare: $4.15; Round trip: $5.75

Callicoon (population 1,200) is in the midst of surroundings of a wild and rugged character. Numerous lakes cluster in the hills on both sides of the river. No malaria.

Stage lines to North Branch: 50 cents; Callicoon: 75 cents, daily except Sundays.

40 hotels or boarding houses.

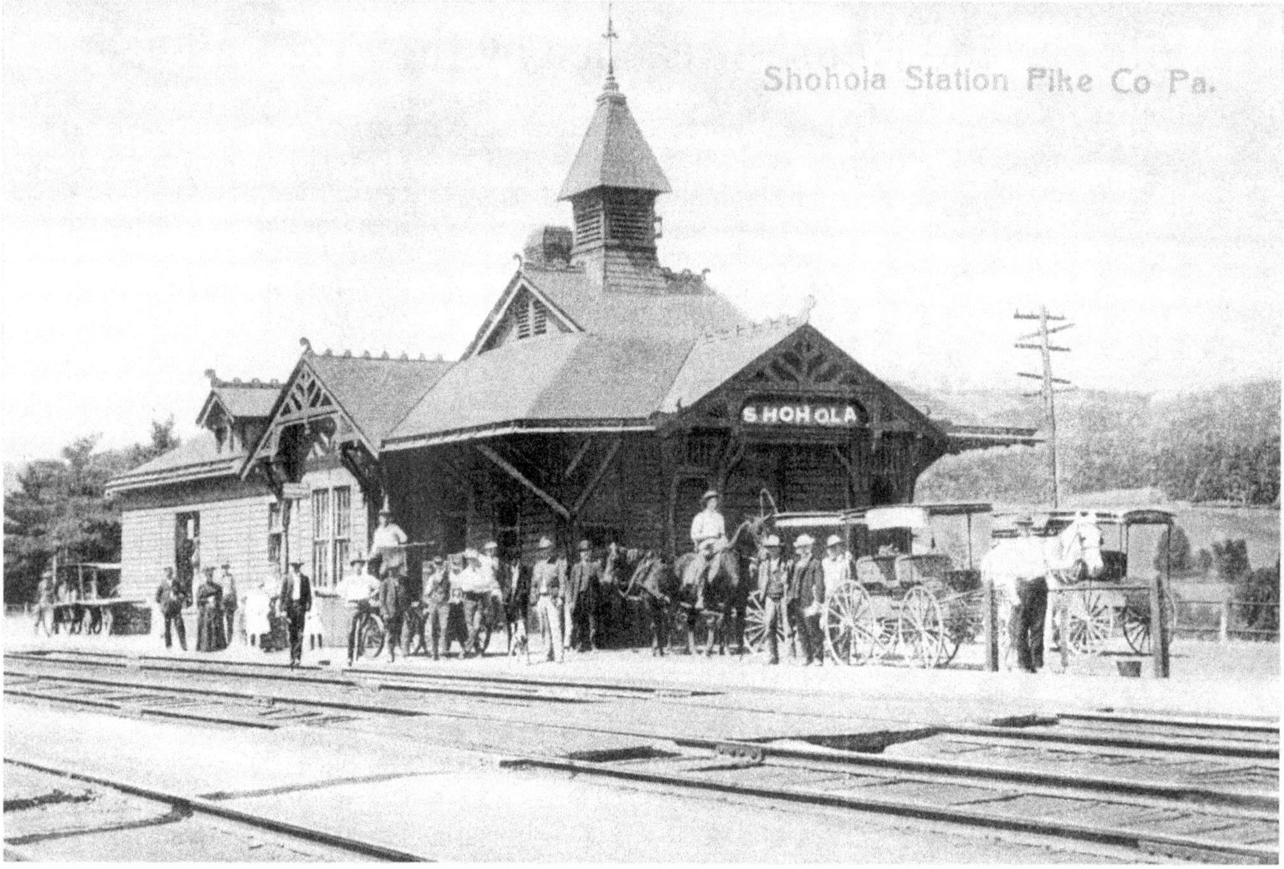

Shohola Depot in Shohola, Pennsylvania, across from the Shohola Glen House. Vacationers to the boarding houses in the Town of Highland were met at the Shohola Station. Photographer: Louis Hensel. Photo is in the Hensel Collection, courtesy of Hawley Library.

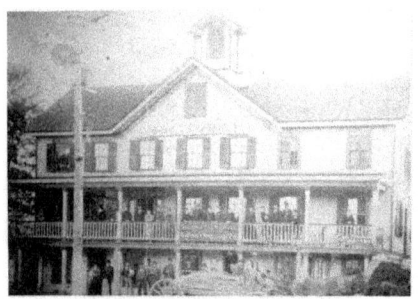

Shohola Glen House, owned by George Layman and then John F. Kilgour. Photo courtesy of George J. Fluhr, Historian for Pike County, Pennsylvania.

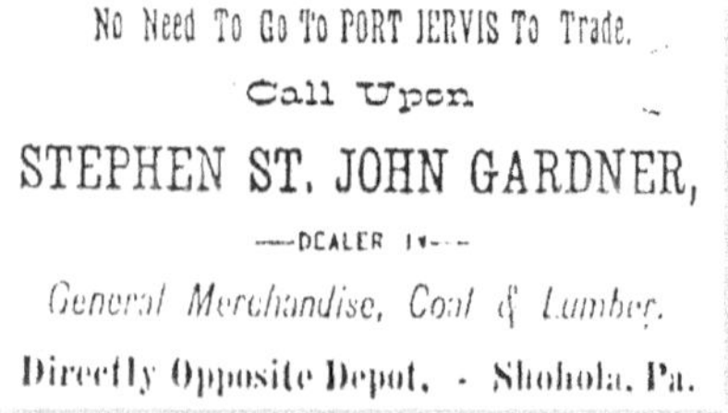

No Need To Go To PORT JERVIS To Trade.

Call Upon

STEPHEN ST. JOHN GARDNER,

—DEALER IN—

General Merchandise, Coal & Lumber.

Directly Opposite Depot, - Shohola, Pa.

Ad for Stephen St. John Gardner's store next to the Shohola Glen House. Courtesy of George J. Fluhr, Historian for Pike County, Pennsylvania.

rebuilt hotel-tavern for about 10 years and Chauncey probably had an interest in it. When Thomas died in 1882, Stephen St. John Gardner, another prominent businessman of the era, who was affiliated with a bank in Port Jervis, was executor of the estate.

Much of the estate was purchased by John F. Kilgour, who had been making a fortune by quarrying bluestone. In 1885, the hotel was transferred from Layman to Kilgour.—Fluhr, George J., Rohman's Inn, Shohola Glen Hotel, Shohola, Pa., 1849–1999, *p. 3.*

Starting in 1883 Stephen St. John Gardner, a cousin to the Eldred-Austin families, ran the general store next to the Shohola Glen House, but he and his family lived in Barryville.

Shohola Glen, a Local Attraction

Shohola Glen was a mile from the Shohola Depot. It was developed by the new owner, John Kilgour, of the Kilgour Bluestone Company in Parkers Glen. When George Layman owned the Shohola House, he had added paths for his guests.

Soon thereafter, John F. Kilgour became the owner of the once large lumber tract, mill, Glen and all. He was a large stone dealer and shipping considerable freight by the Erie Rail Road, secured an influence with that company.

Moved by the suggestion imparted by Layman's work, he proceeded at once to prepare the Glen as a place of general attraction and resort.

Using the water power at the old mill, he erected a machinery to haul two light cars up a considerable incline and lower them in return; and thus he constructed a gravity railroad, called the Switchback Road, from the Erie Depot to the top of the incline, for the easy and speedy conveyance of visitors to and from the Glen for 5 cents each way.

He cleared and ornamented the grounds, constructed enticing pathways through the groves, erected a dancing pavilion and other things for the pleasure of guests and visitors.

He also induced the Rail Road Company to build a first class depot at Shohola, to make it an extra stopping point for trains in summer, etc., and to run Sunday excursion trains from New York City to Shohola, for a charge of one dollar per round trip. As many as 2,500 excursionists have visited the grounds upon a single Sunday.—Johnston, p. 359.

Well, your granddad (Perry Schoonover) got the job to build the two stations for the switchback, the two hotels, the dancing pavilion, roller skating rink, the 250 stepstones way that went from Shiver DeFreeze to the Erie R.R. Under the culvert, over the Shohola Crick which the Erie crosses, he built a dance platform 100 feet by 40 feet, but that was a flop because the water dropped down from overhead and that was not so good. You can see it today, the iron work that held the bandstand against the side of the culvert.

I was 12 years old or there about when Shohola Glen was opened for pleasure spot and they ran excursion trains from N.Y. every Sunday for $1 round trip. There would be more than 1,000 people. They came on flat cars with seats on the side from the coal fields of Pennsylvania and what a time they would have. Everything was wide open. Beer stands down in what they called Shiver DeFreeze which was below the Glen.

How well I remember when the news came to Eldred that they was going to build Shohola Glen.

There was a man by the name of Abbot who was a promoter of pleasure places; the party that used to run the Star In Steamship Lines to Glen Island from New York City. He asked for bids for building the Switchback R.R. that ran from the Erie R.R. Station down to the Glen.

I will try and explain how the Switchback R.R. worked. It left Shohola and ran down along the side of the mountain by gravity to the Glen and from there was pulled up an incline to the top of the mountain by cable and cut loose from cable and ran back to Shohola by gravity.

I remember they had 4 old horse cars from New York that they used for rolling stock and the people would ride on top of the cars and hang on like flies. The run was about 1-1/2 miles.

They got the power to pull the cars up the incline from an old sawmill which they made over and used the water power from the Shohola Crick. They also put in a dynamo and they was the first electric lights that came in this part of the country.—Daniel Rowlee Schoonover.

The old mill (of Garret Wilson), and turbine that were used to generate the power that was required to pull the Shohola Glen Gravity Railroad. The cables used to pull the cars can be seen in the center of the photograph. Photo courtesy of Minisink Valley Historical Society.

Shohola was a great vacation center. The Erie ran as high as four trains of twelve cars each, every Sunday in summer, for one dollar the round trip. The 107 miles bringing 5,000 picnickers.

They had a switchback here that ran 1/2 mile to the Glen where were big shady pine trees and hemlocks and others, and the usual entertainment. They also had different salesmen as it was usually hot and the crowd was beer minded.—Lou Kloss Memoirs.

There were other boarding houses in the area before 1900. We will talk more about them and what else the guests did for entertainment in Chapter 5.

Sherman Stiles and Maria Myers Leavenworth

In 1886 Sherman S. and Maria Myers Leavenworth had 5 children

Aerial Ferry and Switchback Railroad, 1886

The novel Switchback Railroad which has been in course of construction for months between the Erie station here and Shohola Glen was opened today, and several thousand people from the country round were present and enjoyed a ride over the route.
—The New York Times, *Shohola, June 21, 1886.*

Among the attractions thus provided for the season of 1886 is a suspension cable tramway, or, more properly, perhaps, an Aerial Ferry.

Two large wire cables are suspended across the gorge at the head of the Glen running parallel with each other on a four-foot gauge. They are anchored in the solid rock on both sides.

Basket cars, suspended by wires or rods from four grooved wheels, into which the cables deeply fit, run across the chasm, carrying passengers to and fro. The cars have room for half a dozen persons. They run by gravity in one direction, and are drawn across in the other direction by an endless wire rope and a windlass, which is worked by a turbine water wheel taking its power from the stream. A horizontal iron bar, with enclosed pulleys at each end, fitting on and running along the cable, is attached to the running gear of the cars, to keep the gauge intact. This novel thoroughfare will give a sort of traveling-in-the-Andes air to explorations in the Glen.

Another new feature is the Switchback Railway, by which visitors will be given the exhilarating and exciting experiences.

The Switchback Railway starts from the Erie Railway, near the Shohola Glen House, and passes at first in a direction opposite to that by which the Glen is naturally reached.

It sweeps to the rear of the Kilgour summer residence and grounds, and circles gradually to the face of the cliff west of the village.

Shohola Glen Gravity Railroad car ascending the plane by use of steel cables which can be seen in the foreground. Photo courtesy of Minisink Valley Historical Society.

The switchback railroad around 1890. It cost a nickel to go from the main station to the glen entrance a mile away. Photo courtesy of the Minisink Valley Historical Society.

Two Shohola Glen Gravity Railroad passenger cars just as they were about to depart in June 1902. Photo courtesy of Minisink Valley Historical Society.

Reaching the cliff, the road turns Glen-ward, and follows the ledge to the creek, opposite the old mill at the Glen entrance. On the return trip the road climbs the cliff until an elevation of 100 feet is reached, from which the cars speed back to the starting point at the station.

The trip to and from the Glen by this novel means is a thrilling ride of two miles. There are no locomotive cinders, no smoke, no dust, for the elegant cars are run without locomotives, by the same system of inclined planes and gravitation that has made the switch-back roads of the Pennsylvania coal fields so popular and famous.—*Summer Homes and Rambles, N.Y., L.E. & W.R.R., 1886.*

(ages 2–11): Anna Mae, Truman, Jennie Louisa, James Garfield, and little Martin David Leavenworth.

It must have been very challenging for Great-Grandma Maria, as little Martin developed either scarlet fever or measles with an extremely high fever when he was a baby. His mental development was arrested at 4 or 5 years old.

One of the threads that goes through the Sherman S. Leavenworth story is the family's care and concern for Martin D. Leavenworth who grew to be very tall and lived into his 80s.

Sergeants and Clarks
The Leavenworth neighbor Ethel Sergeant died in 1884. Ethel was the husband of Lettie Gardner and son of Stephen and Anna Penney Sergeant. In September the following year (1885), neighbor George Clark died. George was the husband of Harriet, son of Wilmot and Mary Van Auken Clark, and father of Clarissa Clark who would marry Frank Sergeant.

John and Amelia Leavenworth
John and Amelia Leavenworth and their daughters Florence, 3, and Charlotte (Lottie), 1, lived in Colorado in 1886. John was a miner. At some point, John and Amelia lived in a crude log cabin by Fish Creek in Dolores County, a gorgeous area surrounded by high mountains. We'll talk more about the family in Chapter 5.

Mary Frances Bradley Scott
In September 1886 Amelia Leavenworth's sister (also Isaac and Joanna Brown Bradley's daughter) Mary Frances Bradley married George Scott of Otisville, New York.

George and Mary F. Bradley Scott's daughter Lottie Waller Scott was born the following September (1887). Lottie would marry William Meyers. Lottie and William's son William Meyers Jr. would marry a daughter of Garfield Leavenworth.

Viola Bradley Hazen
In September 1887 Viola Bradley married Abel Hazen. The Hazens would have a boarding house, Laurel Cottage, near Washington Lake.

Sadly, at the end of the following year, Viola Hazen's sister Mary Scott became a widow when George Scott died. Their daughter Lottie Scott was 1. Mary would later marry Charles F. Myers.

Isaac Sergeant Finally Marries
Finally on September 26, 1888, Isaac Sergeant, age 50, married Elizabeth (Libbie) B. Persbacher, age 30, of Shohola. The witnesses were Valentine J. Persbacher

Kilgour's Shohola Glen

The beautiful Shohola Depot trimmed in gingerbread, welcomed thousands of visitors per day to the Shohola Glen Resort and the Shohola area.

From 1882 until 1907 the Erie Railroad ran excursion trains from New York City and Scranton, Pennsylvania, to Shohola Glen—the original of the modern theme parks.

In lower Shohola Glen, Kilgour constructed a large lake, pavilions, galleries, amusement rides including a carousel, a huge dancing and roller-skating platform under the Shohola Viaduct on the Erie Railroad, and a large dining hall and kitchen...

In the upper glen he constructed paths and rustic bridges across the Shohola Creek and through out the park to showcase the natural beauty of the Glen.

Pools of water and formations named Cascade Cavern, Bell Rock, Devil's Pass, Hell Gate, Terror Grotto, Satan's Nose, and The Spirit of Dark Waters, were some of the names given to these places of natural beauty...

The park was lighted by colored electric lights, lanterns and electric torches with power being generated on site from a turbine in the old mill.—*shohola.org.*

High Bridge across Shohola Creek was part of the Shohola Glen rustic walking attractions in the area of the gorge upstream of Twin Lakes Road, a few hundred feet from the old mill and falls.—George J. Fluhr, Historian for Pike County, Pennsylvania. Postcard courtesy of Katherine Calkin Traxler.

Isaac Sergeant and Elizabeth (Libbie) Persbacher. Photos courtesy of Chuck Myers.

Clarissa Clark Sergeant. Photo courtesy of Cynthia Leavenworth Bellinger.

Frank Sergeant. Photo courtesy of Cynthia Leavenworth Bellinger.

and Katie Campbell who were married in December that year. The preacher for both weddings was Rev. H. Litts. Elizabeth's (and most likely Valentine's) parents were Jacob Persbacher and Catherine Kreiter. It is possible that the Jacob Perschbacher who built the brick viaduct over the Shohola Creek was a relative of Libbie.

Isaac Sergeant, a carpenter, was a member, deacon, and Sunday School Superintendent at the Eldred Congregational Church for a long time.

Isaac Sergeant also held various offices in the Town of Highland.

Isaac and Libbie Sergeant would have a daughter Minnie Sergeant who would marry Archibald Abel Myers, son of Abel and Maria Hankins Myers. Archie and Minnie would have a son Chuck Myers, a good friend of my parents.

Frank Sergeant Marries Clarissa

In June 1888 Frank Sergeant married Clarissa Clark at the Eldred Congregational Church. Frank was the son of Alvah and Phebe Owen Sergeant, and nephew of Isaac Sergeant.

Clarissa's mother Harriet Covert Clark, widow of George Clark, died in 1889 in Eldred, at age 58.

Elizabeth Hoatson Clark

George and Harriet Covert Clark's son George Malcome Clark died the same year as his mother. George Malcome Clark had married Elizabeth Hoatson in 1888. Their daughter Georgia Clark was born 6 months after George M. Clark had died.

Within a year Elizabeth Hoatson Clark had been married, had a child, and been widowed. Elizabeth would later marry Charles Wilson, when he was a widower with 2 children. Georgia Clark would become the second wife of Walter Styles.

Edith May Palmer

A Leavenworth cousin Edith May Palmer, daughter of Henry and Harriet Leavenworth Palmer and granddaughter of Buckley Leavenworth, married Albert Ewart, December 25, 1888. Albert and his twin brother had been born in England.

Jean Charles Rouillon

In 1888 Jean Charles Rouillon, a baker, and Blanche Olga

Malinge, future grandparents of Gisele Rouillon, lived in France. Gisele would marry James R. Leavenworth, a future son of Garfield Leavenworth.

Jean Charles Rouillon had been in the French Territorial Army for five years. After Prussia (Germany) took Alsace-Lorraine in the Franco-Prussian War of the 1870s, France had started a soldier school. Each French soldier was to be enrolled for five years.

In September 1888 Jean Charles Rouillon completed the school and retired to Charsonville, France.

Charlotte Elizabeth Leavenworth
In July 1889 Jennie Louisa Leavenworth had a new sister, Charlotte Elizabeth Leavenworth. Charlotte would be a teacher for several generations of children in Eldred, including her own nephews and nieces (my father being one of them), and grandnephews and grandnieces.

Ella Phoebe Sergeant
Ella Phoebe Sergeant, daughter of Frank Roberts and Clarissa Clark Sergeant, was born at the end of 1889. Ella's grandfather was Alvah Sergeant and her great-great-great-grandfather was Rev. Isaac Sergeant.

Ella Phoebe Sergeant would marry Garfield Leavenworth (born in 1882). Ella's diary entries from 1935 to 1950 add much to the telling of this story in Book 3.

Town of Highland Schoolhouses
Barryville, Yulan, and Eldred school districts each had a one-room schoolhouse.

My Austin great-aunts complained bitterly about the Eldred schoolhouse in the 1870s. Eventually a new one must have been built to replace it. The new

Ella Phoebe Sergeant, future wife of Garfield Leavenworth. Photo courtesy of her granddaughter, Cynthia Leavenworth Bellinger.

schoolhouse would later become the Town of Highland's office building.

Lou Kloss told what it was like to go to school in the 1880s.

I had little time for school as I had to take care of the cattle. We had to leave home at 7:40 to walk the nearly 4 miles to school, down several big hills. When at last we reached town, we had about 6 minutes walk up a long hill to the top where stood the schoolhouse.

We were mostly on time and seldom missed while those that lived 5 or 10 minutes away were late many times and in bad weather didn't show up at all.

There were about 35 pupils in our school when I started. The teacher taught all the classes from primary to the higher mathematics, calling up each class with a little desk bell. Some of the classes contained 12 or 15 pupils and some only 1 or 2.

The boys played baseball games at recess and at noon, and a game played with two batters and two pitchers. When they hit the ball the batters changed places. If somebody caught the

Albert and Edith Palmer Ewart. Edith was the daughter of Henry and Harriet Leavenworth Palmer. Photo courtesy of Edythe King Westerfield.

ball, the batter had to exchange places with that one.

We also played "keely over." The ball was tossed over the schoolhouse and the side that caught it ran to the other side and tried to hit someone with the ball. If he hit one, that one belonged to the other side, till all were on one

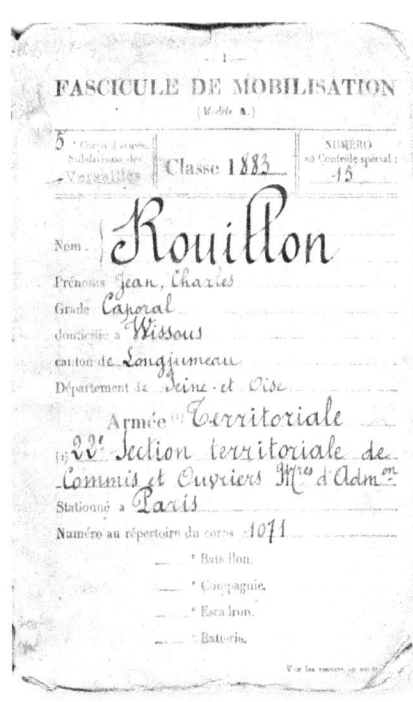

French Territorial book of Jean Charles Rouillon. Photo courtesy of Gisele Rouillon Leavenworth.

Clark and Bogert Families

There was another Clark family in town. They were related to Isaac Bradley's wife Joanna Brown, and others mentioned in this book.

Joanna Brown Bradley's mother Mary or Mercy Harding Brown had married George Case Clark when her husband and Joanna's father Silas Brown died.

George Case Clark and Mercy Harding Brown had a son, John Henry Clark.

In July 1887 John Henry Clark, a lumberer/sawyer, married Carrie Etta Bogert, daughter of John and Amanda Hogencamp Bogert.

Carrie's father John Bogert was born in Holland. The family lived on a farm at Little Egypt between Youngsville and White Sulphur Springs in New York.

John sold milk in cans with the initials J.B. John's wife and Carrie's mother was Amanda Hogencamp. John and Amanda Bogert had 9 children between the years 1861 and 1880.

George Case Clark was the son of Thomas W. Clark and Phebe Hazen Clark Myers.

Thomas W. Clark had died young, and Phebe married Moses Dewitt Myers.

One of Moses and Phebe Hazen Clark Myers' sons was Abel Sprague Myers who plays a part in this story.

John Henry Clark and his wife Carrie Bogert would have a son Ernest J. Clark who would marry Eunice Hallock. Ernest and Eunice would be the parents of Stella Clark, future wife of Clinton, son of Garfield Leavenworth.

George Case Clark died at Methol, Delaware County, New York, April 27, 1890.

John Henry Clark, son of George Case Clark and Mercy Harding Brown Clark. Photo courtesy of Emily Knecht Hallock.

George Case Clark was the son of Thomas W. Clark and Phebe Hazen Clark Myers. George C. Clark was the great-grandfather of Stella Clark Leavenworth. Photo courtesy of Emily Knecht Hallock.

John Henry Clark and Carrie Bogert Clark. Photo courtesy of Emily Knecht Hallock.

John Bogert, and his wife Amanda Hogencamp, parents of Carrie Bogert Clark. Photo courtesy of Emily Knecht Hallock.

side and they won. All the school children, also the teacher played.

They also played a game that was called "Deer." We would scatter through the woods, and two boys as hunters would have to catch us. Sometimes we would be late getting back to school, having gone too far into the woods and we had to stay in for recess.

The schoolroom was a one-room affair with a large pot stove in the middle. When the weather was very cold we would all huddle around the stove as it was too cold very far away from it.

The times that we got very wet feet, the teacher would let us sit by the stove till the socks and shoes were nearly dry. But they were not dry altogether. When we went home sometimes we would walk down through deep slush and had on leather shoes, and stockings were soaked. However, we had comparatively little sickness.

I left school a year before my younger brother went to school. About a half mile up from the school stood the monument of the battleground of Minisink Ford. And a mile from the school is York Lake, a very nice sheet of water about a mile long by a mile wide.

Where more children are together, there is always a pest to make it miserable for someone, and so it was here. A fellow by name of George Wilket used to wait for us and get behind and poke us with an umbrella or a stick, as he was several years older and we were afraid to do anything to him. He would keep this up for the several miles that we would be together.

We used to hide till he was past and then go home; or if we were ahead we would run nearly all the way till we came to our own road where he branched off. But quite often he would hide and jump out at us as we went by. Sometime later his family moved to Port Jervis and we were relieved.

While there was lumbering or bluestone being drawn down the hills on bobsleds, we could often get rides most of the way home.

But when there was no such business, we had to break our own paths all the way to town and sometimes all the way back home in the evening—sometimes through a foot or more of snow.

Sometimes there was an inch of crust on the snow and it nearly held our weight. But just as we put all the weight on it, down we went through and we had to walk to town that way.

There were generally 3 or 4 of us and each would take turns at walking ahead and that way give the rest a chance to take it easier.

When we came to what we called the Irishtown Road, 3 or 4 of the Smith boys quite often met us and we went down to school together, and a girl and boy of another family; for a year or two that made the going better.

Quite often it was zero weather and we had some job to keep warm. The first winter I wore rubber and leather boots and my feet were nearly frozen. It sometimes took my mother 10 minutes to get the leather boots off my feet, they were frozen stiff and on so tight.

Next year I got felt boots and everything was hunky dory; not so stylish maybe, but at least comfortable. Even in the town kids grinned at us.
—Lou Kloss Memoirs.

In Chapter 5 we continue our

> ## Homes in the Mountains
>
> The summer cottages, hotels and boarding houses thickly planted on the mountain slopes and by the lakes and living streams of Sullivan, Delaware, and Western Ulster Counties, are now tenanted by a larger throng of city visitors than ever before.
>
> …Sullivan County alone offered accommodations at the opening of this season for 8,000 guests, against 6,500 last year, and as a rule every available place of entertainment is filled with New York, Brooklyn, and Newark guests.
>
> Taking together Sullivan, Delaware, and the adjoining regions in Ulster west of the Catskills, the number of visitors now being entertained will exceed 15,000…
>
> In the rugged, picturesque, and healthful highland region in question, which has a mean altitude of 1,500 feet above sea level, many city people of means have built for themselves handsome country seats or cozy cottages for Summer abodes.
>
> Perhaps the most magnificent and costly of these country homes are those owned by Mr. George R. MacKenzie, President of the Singer Sewing Machine Company, and Mr. William F. Proctor, Treasurer of the same company, both situated in the Town of Lumberland in Sullivan County.
>
> In the same town, Mr. Leon DeVenoge, importer of New York, has a handsome Summer mansion and an estate of 2,000 acres…
> —The New York Times, "Some of the People Summering in the Catskills," Middletown, N.Y., *August 11, 1888*.

Eldred Schoolhouse. Photo courtesy of Chuck Myers.

visit with Highland's boarding houses, the Leavenworth family who lived on Eldred's west side, and friends, relatives, and neighbors in the Town of Highland from 1890 to 1900.

At some point a number of Sullivan County boarding houses began to discriminate against Jewish people. Fliers had such comments as: "Positively no Hebrews received," "No Hebrews entertained," or "Gentiles only."

The reasoning behind this intolerance is unknown. The two boarding houses that I found in the Town of Highland with anti-Semitic statements were from 1900 or later. In response to the ban, the Jewish people created their own resorts.

The next chapter starts back around 1883. We visit Henry and Mary Ann Austin, their children and relatives through the many letters that have been saved.

There is much discord in the Austin family over the Austin homestead home and lands which seems to change ownership often. Henry and Mary Ann had sold 100 acres *once owned and occupied by Augustus A. Austin and subsequently by William H. Austin,* to their son, Ell, in Kansas. At some point acreage was also sold or given to Dory Austin, who later sold at least some of it.

School in Yulan. Postcard courtesy of Helen Hensel Oset.

Town of Highland students around 1890. Top row: the tall girl with the arrow pointing to her head was Bertha Boyd, later, Bertha Wilson. The girl next to her was Belle Boyd, but her photo is torn out. The girl in front of the teacher, Mr. Merritt, was Norah Bradley, later, Norah Avery. The first boy in the second row from the bottom was Charles Myers, son of George W.T. and Martha Mills Myers. The boy in the middle of the same row with the check on his shirt was Garfield Leavenworth. Behind him on the right may be Jennie Leavenworth, his sister, my grandmother. Photo courtesy of Cynthia Leavenworth Bellinger.

Chapter 4
Paths Diverge
The Austins of Highland, 1883–1889

We meet and part the world is wide,
*   We journey onward side by side.*
A little while, and then again
*   Our paths diverge—a little pain*
A silent yearning of the heart
*   For what has grown of life a part.*
A shadow passing o'er the sun,
*   Then gone, and light again has come.*
We meet and part, and then forget;
*   And life holds blessings for us yet.*
—Hester Freeman, friend of Aida Austin.

Horse at home on the Austin farm. Photo courtesy of Mary Briggs Austin.

Henry and Mary Ann Austin's children—Maria, Ell, Lon, Aida, and Mort Austin—spent the 1880s in either New York City, Kansas, California, or school, but they would be back at the Austin home and farm in Eldred by 1889.

In mid-August 1881 my grandfather Mort Austin, age 16, had gone to Kansas to work for his brother Ell Austin. Mort was back in Eldred by December 1882.

In the winter of 1883–1884, Mort again left for Kansas to work for his brother Ell who ran Henry Parmenter's farm in Saline County, Kansas. Before Mort left for Kansas, he had family and friends sign his autograph book.

At one time Lon Austin also worked for Ell on the Parmenter farm. Lon had also worked in California, but was probably in Eldred sometime in 1883. Then for a few years, Lon lived and worked in New York City. Many of the letters Lon received were from friends he had made out west.

Aida Austin would start classes to be a teacher in the fall of 1884. Aida also had an autograph book.

Mort and Aida's autograph entries are included in this chapter, as are letters to and from Mort, Ell, Lon, and Aida, and their parents Henry and Mary Ann Austin.

George Lovee, Brookside, N.J., to Lon Austin
April 29, 1883
Dear Friend [Lon],
*   Snowing here today. We are having a varry late spring; just sowing oats when it is time they were up. I am well as usual.*
*   You told me that you thought a fellow was better off with a mate than he was alone, but I am alone yet and will be for sometime yet and will let you know when it happens and have you on hand.*
*   Your friend, George A. Lovee*

Mort Austin (right) in Kansas. "Mort again left for Kansas to work for his brother Ell who ran Henry Parmenter's farm in Saline County, Kansas." Photo courtesy of Mary Briggs Austin.

Emily Augustus Parmenter who married James Eldred Austin in Solomon City, Kansas, July 1883. Photo courtesy of Katherine Calkin Traxler.

The Parmenters in Kansas

Out in Kansas, Ell Austin worked on the large farm owned by Henry Parmenter Sr., a widower from Rhode Island.

In 1880 the Parmenter Family: Henry Sr., 70; Sarah Sophronia Parmenter, 47; Emily A. Parmenter Slocum, 31, her son Henry Earl Slocum, 7; Henry and Effie Parmenter Jr.; and John Earl and Annie Parmenter, had been in Kansas around 5 years.

Henry Parmenter Sr. owned over 200 acres on the Smoky Hill River, and a number of lots in Solomon City, Saline County, Kansas. In 1880 the Parmenters lived in Dayton, Kansas, about 3 miles from Solomon City, Kansas, where the Austin brothers' sister Edith Emogene Austin had died in 1879.

Jas. E. Austin, Solomon City, Kans., to Lon Austin
June 24, 1883
Dear Brother Lon,
   I have got 85 acres of a good corn as I ever saw. It is too high to cultivate and I have got 25 acres of pretty farm corn, but I had to plant the most of it so it is not as large as the other field of corn.
   I expect that you will have a sister-in-law about the middle of July unless some unforeseen thing prevents me from getting a wife, for I intend to get married the 10th of July.
   But as there is many a "slip betwixt cup and the lip" you must never count on a bird until we have her caged.
   If you can raise the money, I would like to have that $25.00 I sent you, as I will need all the money I can raise as I have to pay a man $20 per month. My help has cost me over $100 so far, and my pocket book is getting rather thin, but if I can get in what money I have, I will be all right.
   Hoping to hear from you soon.
   Your aff. brother,
   Jas. E. Austin

Ell (James Eldred) Austin did marry Emily Augustus Parmenter on July 10, 1883, in Solomon City, Kansas.

Congregational Church in Eldred

Back in Eldred in 1883, there seems to have been one of the many changeovers of pastors at the Congregational Church. Rev. Ed W. Fisher, who had been pastor at the Eldred Congregational Church since 1880, left under unhappy circumstances. There were several friendly, lengthy letters to Aida Austin from Lucy (L.F.) Fisher, wife of Rev. Fisher, in my mother's letter collection.

Lucy Fisher, Fort Lee, N.J., to Aida Austin, Eldred
August 18, 1883
Dear Friend Aida,
   I suppose your Mother has left

New York before this, so I will not be able to see her. Tell Lon I am anxiously waiting for his picture.

And now my dear girl, how do you all do in Eldred? Are you all on a move as usual and how does your church flourish in the ministry and how did your fair come off 4th of July? I suppose the Ladies' Aid Society feels quite rich now. I hope they do.

Please remember me to Mrs. David Hickok and tell her I have thought of her 50 times since I am here and at her request I will write her when we get settled in our western home.

Aunt Sarah says tell Alonzo that she wishes to be held in fond remembrance as he was the only young gentleman that took her out riding while at Eldred.

Now Aida, you must excuse this scribbling as the baby and I are occupying one chair and I can scarcely write, he wiggles so.

I am glad you are going on a journey west. Is Mort agoing with you or are you going alone.

Let me know when you intend to start and perhaps I can see you off at the depot. Don't forget your picture. When you get west, I hope you will write me then at Ohio.

My love to all and a share for yourself. Your loving friend,
L.F. Fisher

Henry Parmenter's Will
In November in Kansas, Henry Parmenter Sr. died. His will divided his property and belongings among his children and grandchildren.

The Smoky Hill River property of 220 acres went to his daughters, Sarah Sophronia Parmenter and Emily Augusta Austin. The large piece of property meant paying taxes, which would at one point put Ell in a bit of a financial bind.

Photo from 1860–1870 shows cattle fording the Smoky Hill River at Ellsworth, Kansas, on the old Sante Fe crossing, 508 miles west of St. Louis, Missouri. When Henry Parmenter died, his 220 acres on the Smoky Hill River went to his two daughters. Photo: Alexander Gardner, Library of Congress, Prints and Photographs Division: LC-US262-8087.

William Hallock, Raftsman
It's been some time since the Hallock family has been mentioned. In 1883 William Hallock died at the age of 70. He was the son of Thomas W. and Julia Van Tuyl Hallock, brother of Oliver Blizzard Hallock, and father of Daniel Hallock (mentioned later in this chapter). William Hallock had been a raftsman on the Delaware River.

One spring day, William's raft became grounded. He and his helpers worked in the cold water all day and part of the night to pry it loose.

Very unfortunately, Mr. Hallock caught a cold which settled in his eyes. The inflammation became so severe that the eyeballs swelled and bursted and he was blind for 25 years.—Republican Watchman, March 30, 1923, p. 2.

James Eldred (Ell) Austin. Photo courtesy of Katherine Calkin Traxler.

George Lovee, Brookside, N.J., to Alonzo (Lon) Austin
December 18, 1883
Dear Sir,

I am now in a store here for a short time. While charging a young man with some tobacco by the same name as your first name is, I charged it to you.

My boss wanted to know who Alonzo Austin was. I asked him

Mort Austin's Autograph Book

In the winter of 1883–1884, Mort Austin again left for Kansas to work for his brother Ell who ran Henry Parmenter's farm in Saline County, Kansas. Before Mort left, he had family and friends sign his autograph book. The original scans start on page 453.

Friend Mortimore,
Be not overcome of evil
but overcome evil with good.
    Charles C.P. Eldred [uncle]
    Eldred, Feb. 6, 1884

To Charles,
Remember thy Creator is the earnest wish of your friend.
    Mrs. A.S. Myers, Eldred, N.Y.

    Edwin V. Myers [friend]
    Eldred, February 6, 1884

Cousin Mortie,
Bring a willing sacrifice
Thy soul to Jesus' feet;
Stand in him, in him alone,
All glorious and complete
    Rebecca C. Eldred [cousin]
    February 6, 1884

Always your friend.
    James W. Sergeant
    Feb. 6, 1884

Mary F. Bradley, Eldred, New York

From a friend, Lottie Bradley
    Eldred, January 6, 1884

Bertha S.S. Collins
    Staten Is. N.Y., August 3, 1885

To a Friend
When the golden sun is setting
And in far off lands you be
When of distant friends you
    are thinking,
Will you sometimes think of me.
    Elbert Clark [cousin]
    January 30th, 1884

Mortie,
May you ever happy be
Sometimes will you think of me.
    Robbie Clark [cousin]
    Eldred, Jan. 30 , 1984

To my Friend,
Fear God and keep his Commandments for this is the whole duty of man.
    Mrs. O.P. Schoonover
    Eldred, February 3, 1884

Mortimer,
Remember now thy Creator in the days of thy youth.
    O.P. Schoonover
    Eldred, February, 3, 1884

    Charles F. Calkin [cousin]
    Barryville, February 5, 1884

Reputation is what people think of us. Character is what God and Angels know we are.
    Lillie Calkin [cousin]
    Barryville, February 5, 1884

To My Son,
Whate'er you have to do my boy,
Be sure you do it right;
If life is but a battle boy,
Be faithful in the fight.
With high resolve and holy,
With purpose firm and true
Let us go forth with meekness,
God's will and work to do.
    W.H. Austin
    Eldred, Feb. 2, 1884

My Dear Son,
Remember your Creator in the days of your youth.
Seek out ways of wisdom and truth.
Earthly pleasures my son bring us but pain
Then my Child see heavenly joys to gain.
May God watch over you on your journey
To Kansas and keep you from evil through life
Is the prayer of your Mother.
    Mary A. Austin
    Eldred, Feb. 2, 1884

Onward and upward be thy motto.
    Jas. E. Austin [brother]
    Solomon, Kansas, July 13, 1884

In that Holy Book, God's Album
May thy name be penned with care
And may all who here have written
Write their names forever there.
    Emmie [sister-in-law]
    Solomon, Kansas, July 13, 1884

Mortie, be faithful and write to us let us know often.
    Irvin Clark [uncle]
    February the 1, 1894

Long may you live
Happy may you be
When you get married
Come and see me.
    Laura Clark [Aunt]
    Eldred, Jan. 31, 1884

Cover of Mort Austin's autograph book. Book courtesy of Mary Briggs Austin.

what he wanted to know for. He said I charged you with some tobacco. They laughed at me a great deal, but it has been a long time since I heard from you.

I am a married man now. I expect you are too, but whether you are or not, please come down and see me (will you). I would like to see you varry much. It won't cost you a cent to stay here.

Customers is coming in so fast I will have to stop. Hoping to hear from you soon. I am yours respt.,
George A. Lovee

Lucy Fisher, Sand Hollow, Ohio, to Aida Austin
December 30, 1883
My Dear Ida [Aida Austin],

I was real glad to hear from you and about your church and your visit at the parsonage.

Well, I am real glad they have such a live man doing such a grand work in Eldred, but I am real sorry for Ida. I wish you could come and see me as you used to.

Had a letter from your dear cousin Becca [daughter of C.C.P. Eldred] and enclosed was one from Mrs. Mapes [Becca's sister Polly V. Eldred Mapes].

How is Lon and Mort? E.W. [Mrs. Fisher's husband] is away or he would have a message to send, I know. How is Fan [the Austin horse]? I wrote to Mrs. Hickok some time ago. Haven't heard from her yet.

Love to all, L.F. Fisher

Jacob Clouse and Emma Wagner
In January 1884 Jacob Clouse of Barryville married Emma Wagner of Eldred. John E. Perine was the minister. Herman Rixton and Aida Austin were the witnesses. The Clouse wedding certificate was found in the Barryville restaurant called Clouse's in the 1920s.

Marriage certificate for Jacob Clouse and Emma Wagner, January 7, 1884. Aida Austin was one of the witnesses. Original certificate courtesy of Christina Watts.

William and Mary Hickok Stidd
In March 1884 Aida was in New York City and received the following letter from her father. The Stidd Family mentioned was probably William and Mary Hickok Stidd, relatives of Mary Ann Austin, whose mother was Hannah Hickok Eldred.

W.H. (Henry) Austin, Eldred, to Aida Austin
March 9, 1884
Dear Daughter,

Your Mother wants me to write to you to let you know we received your kind letter. We was vary glad you was not detained in Port Jervis for it would have been vary disagreeable for you to have had to wait for the 4 o'clock train after being up all night.

I was into Stidds to dinner that day and they was very much pleased with our visit. They talk a great deal about the piece you spoke that night and praised it vary much.

I expect we will have to go up to Irv's some night this week. I wish you could be along to William Hickock's next week.

I think I shall quit surprising folks then.

Lon had a letter from Mort Saturday. He has been sick with the mumps, but is getter better. He said Eldred [Ell] would start for Sullivan, Monday, March 10th. Some around here think Mort went some ways to get the mumps.

I don't suppose you care much about politics, but I shall have to tell you how it went in this Town. There was 203 votes polled. Oliver Calkin got 103; T. Gray, 42 votes; C. Frace, 58 votes. Oliver got 3 votes more than both other candidates. So you see, A. Myers don't run this town yet.

Mother says she will wait until Eldred comes home before she sends you the sack and handkerchief.

Let's hear from you soon. Hoping this will find you well as it leaves us. I will close with much Love from your loving Father,
W.H. Austin

Abel S. Myers
A. Myers was Abel S. Myers who had a store in Eldred. His son

Edwin V. Myers was a good friend of Mort Austin. Abel and Maria Hankins Myers had three children in 1884: Jackson, Lulu, and Cleta.

Austin Land Document, 1884
An Austin land document from March 20, 1884, states that James E. Austin sold 100 acres of land in Eldred back to his parents for $500. It was signed by John W. Johnston.

Aida Austin, N.Y.C., to W.H. (Henry) Austin, Eldred
March 24, 1884
Dear Father,
Sunday, I went down to Willett Street Church in the morning to Sunday School and preaching; took dinner with Ida and went to Sunday School with her in the afternoon, and stayed all night with Maria.
Little Tom has quite a bad cold and has had to stay out of school a day or two, but is getting better. He is doing so nicely in school and likes his teacher very much. She lets him be monitor and keep the key to the closet where they keep the books and slates. So every morning he trots off to school alone as early as he can so as to have plenty of time to clean the slates and get the closet in order.
Little Ida [Clinton] is putting her dolls to sleep. She asked me a few minutes ago who I was writing to and I told her Uncle Henry. Then she wanted me to ask you if you would come down to see her. She says she is going up to the country again next summer to see the chickens.
Tommy says he must see his five pups this summer. He wants to know if old Jack is as high as the table and says he is going to harness him up to his wagon.

Ida Clinton, daughter of Henry and Net Austin Clinton. "Little Ida [Clinton] is putting her dolls to sleep." Photo courtesy of Katherine Calkin Traxler.

I am going to try to get in Brunele. I think it will be so much easier than Ridleys and I will have more time to study so I can be better prepared for school in the fall if it is so I can go.
I remain your loving daughter, Aida

There seems to be a family effort to get money to Aida so she could further her education.

Aida Austin, N.Y.C., to Lon Austin, Eldred
March 31, 1884
Dear brother Lon,
Ell says if father lets me have the $200 that you owe him, that he will raise me the money. So if you will make out the note in Ell's name (that is if father will do it and he told Ell he would), why I can pay it back to father when I get through school and you can pay it to Ell. It will give you so much more time before you have to pay.

I suppose that father can have your note made over to me, then it can be fixed for Ell and he will pay me the money and hold your note.
Now don't say to yourself, "I can do it in a day," and leave it undone until it is too late for me to get the money.
Hoping to hear from you this week, I remain,
Your loving sister, Aida

W.H. (Henry) Austin, Eldred, to Aida Austin, N.Y.C.
April 2, 1884
Dear Daughter Aida,
I have given up coming to the city until spring. So I will write to let you know that I will have $100 for you to commence going to school on this fall.
Eldred said if I would give you an order on him the first of September, he would send it to you and what Lon owes me. So you must not give up going to school. I will see that you have money enough to put you to school two years and I want you to go.
Little Tommy's pup is doing first rate. Tell little Ida I would like to see her vary much. Tell her I have got a kiss for her whenever I see her.
If my health will permit, I expect to work for Dr. DeVenoge this summer.
I wrote to M.B Austin [his nephew]. If he has not got my letter I wish you would tell him to send me how much I owe him and I will send a check to him as I want to pay it now while I am able.
Your mother says she will write to you this week. Take it easy and study all you can.
With much love, from your loving Father,
W.H. Austin

Ell Austin, Solomon City, Kans., to W.H. (Henry) Austin, Eldred
April 13, 1884
Dear Father,
   I will try and answer your very welcome letter. We are all quite well and hope these few lines will find you the same.
   I expect I will be able to pay you $400 of that mortgage in June and maybe all of it. I want to pay it as soon as possible and get the place clear.
   About that money you are going to let Aida have. I think you had better get Lon to make out a note to Aida for $100, and you endorse it on the chattel mortgage.
   If Lon don't want to give his note that way, why just give Aida an order on me and I will send her the money. I wish you would either get Lon's note to Aida or give her an order on me as soon as possible so I can make my arrangements according.
   As for A.S. Myers, I do not care a straw about him and he might as well talk to the wind about that money I owed him as to talk to me, for it would do just as much good.
   You say you are not behind Kansas in planting, but I believe you will be behind in the crops coming up.
   We are having very nice weather now, but the spring is very backwards. I intend to plant corn this week.
   You did not say if you would send them trees or not. We want to plant the birches in the cemetery [where Emma Austin was buried], and we do not know of any place else where we can get birch. If you will send them, I will pay you for your trouble.
   Hoping to hear from you soon.
   Your Aff. son,
   James E. Austin

Abel Sprague Myers Store

A.S. Myers statement to William Henry Austin, courtesy of Katherine Calkin Traxler.

Abel Sprague Myers. Photo courtesy of Chuck Myers.

Eldred, N.Y., May 14, 1882
Mr. W.H. Austin
Dear Sir:
   Will you be kind enough to give your name on this paper? If you will, I will take it as a fave: your other papers is all paid.
   With respects,
   A.S. Myers

Eldred, N.Y., July 1, 1882
Mr. W.H. Austin
Sir,
   As I am short in money to pay bill, please do all you can for me on this bill.
   With respects,
   A.S. Myers

Ell Austin, Solomon City, Kans., to Wm. Henry Austin, Eldred
April 30, 1884
Dear Father,
   I will try and write a few lines in answer to your very welcome letter. I suppose the first thing on programme is to tell you that you are now a grandfather of a bouncing little girl born on April 25.
   I received those trees all right and am much obliged and if you will tell me what your trouble is, I will pay you for the same.
   I did think I would pay you in June, but I have got to buy a bull and it is going to cost me more than I thought it would. It will cost me close on to $500 therefore I don't think I can pay you.
   We are having a very backward spring so far. I am nearly half done planting corn.
   We have had too much rain that it is slow work farming this spring. The wheat and oats look fine now and promise to be a big crop.
   Write soon to your aff. son,
   J.E. Austin

Lillie (Lydia Earl) Austin was the "bouncing little girl" of Ell and Emily Parmenter Austin. Photo courtesy of Katherine Calkin Traxler, granddaughter.

Lydia (Lillie) Earl Austin
Mort Austin wrote *(see letter p. 456)* the following letter to his brother Lon. "The bouncing little girl," and "The long looked for Austin," was Lydia (Lillie) Earl Austin, daughter of Ell and Emily Parmenter Austin, born April 25, 1884. It would be 15 years before Henry and Mary Ann Austin had another grandchild. Only their sons Ell and Mort Austin married and had children.

Mort Austin, Solomon City, Kans., to A.A. Austin, Eldred
Sunday, May 11, 1884
Dear Brother Lon,
   I was glad to hear from you, but I think you are too slow about answering my letters. If you don't write sooner next time, I will frig you in the ear with a stick.
   It is quite lonesome here after the good times we had last winter. I never enjoyed myself better in my life.
   So I have lost my dear Carrie. Well, bid her a finest farewell. Tell her for me that I am real glad to hear that she thinks so much of the bootblack and I wish her much joy and shall be happy to hear of her wedding for it would be a wedding in high life, no doubt of it. Tell her not to forget to send me a piece of cake. I presume you know how bad I feel over losing Carrie.
   Well Lon, the long looked for Austin arrived here, two weeks ago, Friday night. It is Miss Lillie Austin. Well, how does Uncle Lon sound? Don't you feel quite proud at being uncle? Ell thinks that their baby is just right. He got it a nice carriage.
   We have got corn up.
   Love to all.
   Yours truly,
   Mort

   In the next letter W.D. Muche updated his friend Lon Austin about the people Lon knew when he worked in Cuffey Cove, California. *Erysipelas* mentioned in Mr. Muche's letter was an acute bacterial skin infection.

W.D. Muche, Cuffey Cove, Calif., to Lon Austin, Eldred
August 9, 1884
Dear Friend,
   Your very welcome letter of July 24, came to hand. My wife's health is far better than when you left here. After you left she had a severe attack of the erysipelas, but she came through all right.
   I have a piece of timberland 1-1/2 miles from Abe's landing that I live on. Got about 10,000 (2×2 in.×4 ft. long) stakes made.
   Mr. Viland, Grant, and Warel and other failures of N.Y. City has affected us here quite as much as the East. There will not be much love until after the election. I think then times will be better, at least I hope so.
   My all here is depending upon the timber biz. If times get good, I would like to have you work for me. I would give you a job if I had one for anybody about.
   The school's board is from $16 to $20 for month; salaries from $60 to $80 for month. If you want I will see the Trustees and see if I can get this school for your sister and if anything starts up in the Timber Biz, I will let you know.
   If your sister should conclude to come out, I will do what I can to get her a school.
   Now for what little news I can think of. Jim Murphy married Mrs. Howard the July after you left. They lived together five weeks. Murphy left for parts unknown. She has applied for another divorce which will make four. I suppose she has another

man spotted.

My dear friend, I received one letter from you over two years ago, commenced a letter to you, soon after I was taken sick. My wife joins in sending our kindest regards to you.

W.D. Muche

Helena Gillespie's Letters

We meet Helena Gillespie in this next letter. The Gillespie family lived in New York City when Lon and Aida met them. This first letter is from Helena to Aida. Helena's other letters were addressed to Lon.

Helena Gillespie, Sing Sing, N.Y., to Aida Austin

August 11, 1884
Dear Miss Austin,

It was very dull here until the 5th when the Camp Meeting commenced. Since then I have not been at home except at meal times. I sing in the choir and will have to hurry now to get there in time.

The weather here is very changeable. We cannot seem to get an opportunity to wear light dresses. It was pouring all night and is rather chilly this morning.

Did you feel the earthquake at Eldred yesterday? Mamma and I were in our room dressing for the afternoon when it occurred. We thought some of the children were dancing in the attic, and our peace of mind was not at all disturbed. But when we descended, we found that the rest of the folks were congregated in the kitchen with very anxious faces.

Write Soon. Sincerely,
Helena Gillespie

Marietta West Eldred Hoatson

You may remember that George W. Eldred (son of C.C.P. and Effa Eldred) died after a tumble from a roof. After George's death in 1872, his widow Marietta West and their youngest son George Eldred lived with her parents Samuel and Mary West, and her brother Theodore West.

In 1884 Theodore and Phebe West had been married 3 years.

In fall 1884 Marietta West Eldred married Samuel D. Hoatson, a widower. Samuel Hoatson, born in Scotland, had four children from his first marriage. His daughters, Elizabeth and Mary would have a connection with the Austin family.

Elizabeth Hoatson Clark's daughter (from her first marriage) Georgia Clark would be the second wife of Walter Styles, whose first wife was Henrietta Austin.

Mary Hoatson would marry John Mortimer Austin, the son of Cousin Mortimer Bruce Austin.

Aida Austin Attends State Normal School in Oswego, New York

In September 1884 Aida Austin started classes to become a teacher at the State Normal School in Oswego, New York.

1873 photo of North Santa Fe Avenue in Salina, Kansas, located about 15 miles southwest of Solomon City, Kansas. Postcard in the collection of Katherine Calkin Traxler.

Lucy Fisher, Sand Hollow, Ohio, to Aida Austin, Oswego, N.Y.

September 21, 1884
My Dear Aida,

We were real glad to hear you were attending school. How long have you been there? How are you getting along and all your folks doing?

I supposed Eldred had found a perfect man when Mr. Perine [the preacher who came after Mr. Fisher] came there. I thought the worst man ever as had left the place there certainly would arrive a perfect one. Now he is done. Who will be the next I wonder? Such is this life. We all keep well.

Keep thy heart with all diligence for out of it are the issues of life.

Your loving friend,
L.F. Fisher

The following letter from Ida Belle Austin Brown to her cousin Aida Austin mentioned their cousin Linnie (Olinda) Austin (daughter of Alonzo Eugene and Belle Austin) who married Joseph Garrish Ayers in 1884. Ida's sisters were Net Clinton, Tina Laing, Rand Paton, and Ida's niece was Ida Clinton.

State Normal School, Oswego, N.Y., where Aida Austin went to college to be a teacher. Photo in the collection of Mary Briggs Austin.

Ida Belle Brown, N.Y.C., to Aida Austin, Oswego, N.Y.
January 4, 1885
Dear Coz. Ide,

Jennie and I have just returned from Eldred having spent the holidays at your home. We both thought and spoke of you many times and wished you might have been with us. We quite missed our usual wrangles over "attributes," "relative pronouns," "conjunctive adverbs," and such like and such like and that "The sun is shining" was not questioned once during our stay.

I suppose you are still discussing the above interesting subjects but without our valuable assistance.

I understand you like your school very well and are progressing finely. The only thing for you to do now is to "keep a shark stick eye" on your health and not let that suffer.

It must be considerable of a strain to keep right to work from September to June without any intermission. But the time rolls by very rapidly and then you will enjoy your freedom all the more.

I visited Emmet Young's school at New Rochelle last Thanksgiving day. It is a splendid one, I assure you. Hattie is one of his assistants. I do not think you would have any trouble in procuring a situation there,

Ida Clinton. "Nettie's Ida is as cute as ever and just too old fashioned for anything." Photo courtesy of Katherine Calkin Traxler.

without an extra examination. Emmet has a great deal of influence and is very pleasant. Hattie came home with me and stayed all night. I do not like her quite as well as Lou.

I suppose you have already heard that Linnie [Olinda Austin Ayers] has been here visiting. She is spending the winter with her husband's people in New Hampshire. Tina is again in Chicago.

All the rest of the friends here are quite well. Tommy is grown a great boy and is quite a speaker. He recited two pieces at the Christmas entertainment. Nettie's Ida is as cute as ever and just too old fashioned for anything. All of Rand's chicks are well.

I suppose you have made quite a number of pleased friends and acquaintances and that you feel quite at home in your school, by this time.

As I sat here tonight, I all at once made up my mind to scribble you a few lines that you might know that I had not forgotten you and that you have my best wishes for a very prosperous and happy new year and many returns of the same. And now I will close with Rip Van Winkle's toast.

I manage to keep track of you through Mort and Aunt Mary. Here's to your health and all your family, etc. What more can be said except, adieu.
Very truly yours,
Love, Ida

Aida Austin, Oswego, N.Y., to W.H. (Henry) Austin, Eldred
February 26, 1885
Dear Father,

I have received the money from Eldred.

Your kind and welcome letter was received some time ago, but

I have not had time to answer it before, being kept so very busy with my lessons which are much harder this term than last.

We are not going to have finals this term, so it will all depend upon our class work and our impromptus whether we pass from our subjects or not.

I am getting along pretty well so far, but begin to feel rather tired, and shall not be sorry to see the first of June.

I had a letter from Lon a few days ago. He tells me that he thinks the trouble between Mr. Perine and the Church will end in a law suit.

It seems strange they will act so foolish. I should think that by this time, they could see it would be better to leave him alone.

Those verses were splendid, especially that one about the Governor.

How is mother? Does she keep well this winter? I would write you more about the school and my work, but my head is aching quite badly and I am very tired and sleepy.

With love to all, I remain your loving daughter,
Aida

Oswego Movement

The *Oswego Movement* was a teaching method based on the ideas of Johann Pestalozzi (1746–1827). Pestalozzi's educational philosophy had a major influence on the Prussian elementary school system and the American educational system.

Pestalozzi's "object teaching" method of instruction had a big impact in the U.S. largely due to the efforts of Dr. Edward A. Sheldon.

Dr. Sheldon founded the Oswego Primary Teacher's Training School in May 1861 to prepare future educators to teach based on Pestalozzi's ideas. Oswego Normal School became the center of Pestalozzi education in the U.S. Future normal schools adopted the Oswego plan and influenced the whole educational system.

Some 100 years later when I took education classes in college, many of the following ideas were still taught.

Some of Pestalozzi's Principles:
1. Education is the unfolding of natural powers and faculties latent in every person.
2. The purpose of education is for the social regeneration of humanity. Society is improved by individuals who achieve their full potential.
3. Elementary curriculum added geography, science (through the study of nature, drawing and music).
4. Education should be child centered, direct experience (don't teach by words or books; nature can teach child better); and simplified subjects, so that the child proceeds from concrete to abstract.
5. "Thinking love" when handling children. Restrictive measures limit teacher-pupil relationship and prevent the natural development of children.—*oswego.edu; cals.ncsu.edu.*

Dr. Edward Austin Sheldon was the founder and first principal of Oswego Normal School. Photo in the Austin Collection.

The Schoonover Family in Orange County, New York

By 1885 Uncle Perry, Aunt Mary Murray Parker Schoonover, Emily, and Rowlee had moved to Orange County, New York, to help out Mary's father, George W. Murray. Possibly Mary's children from her first marriage, Laura, Kate, and George Parker, also went with them. Many years later, when Rowlee moved back to Eldred, he wrote this about their move:

It seems so funny that I can set in our house and look out on the old foundation where I lived until I was 12 years old and the apple trees that I remembered my father set out when they was not larger than my finger and they are now as large as my body.

We had to move from Sullivan to Orange Co. to get Grandpa Murray straightened out.

Pa [Perry Schoonover] went to work at the carpentry trade, but Granddad Murray had a general store and a lot of bad debt. Pa tried to tell him not to let anyone have any more without the money.

Pa could adapt himself to most any conditions, so he went to work to get Grandpa Murray's books in some kind of shape.
—Daniel Rowlee Schoonover.

Laura Parker Marries John Britt

Rowlee's half sister Laura Parker married John Britt around 1885. John Britt's parents were from Ireland and had settled in Kingston, New York.

I know that Laura fell in love with John Britt (a dark-haired, blue-eyed charmer) and that they had a parlor wedding and went to Brooklyn to "set up housekeeping" as it was called, in

John Britt, husband of Laura Parker Britt. "Laura fell in love with John Britt, a dark-haired, blue-eyed charmer." Photo courtesy of Richard James.

Laura Parker Britt, wife of John Britt with one of their children. Photo courtesy of Barbara Kate James Stowell.

one of the new flats for rent...
His trade was marble cutting which necessitated short trips to where the marble was.—Norma Wood James, granddaughter.

Since John Britt was a stonecutter, he went where the quarries were for work so he was often away from home.

John and Laura Parker Britt had 5 children. The 3 that lived (Kitty, Ada, and William Britt) are part of this story.

It was in 1885, that Alonzo Eugene and Isabelle Austin's daughter Henrietta Styles and her husband Walter Styles (mentioned in Chapter 2) moved from Alaska, back to New York.

Out in Kansas, in March 1885 Ell Austin adopted his wife Emily's son. Henry Earl Slocum, 12, was legally Henry Earl Austin. He would write a note in Aida's Autograph Book.

Aida Austin, Oswego, N.Y., to Lon Austin, Eldred
June 6, 1885
Dear Brother Lon,
Will you please meet me at Lackawaxen next Wednesday, June 10, at 6:44 p.m.? I can not go to Shohola as there is no train on the "Erie" which connects with the "Delaware" train and stops there. So I will have to get off at Lackawaxen.
Your loving sister, Aida

From the following letter it seems my grandfather Mort had left Kansas sometime in 1885.

J.E. (Ell) Austin, Solomon City, Kans., to Lon Austin, Eldred
July 22, 1885
Dear Brother Lon,
I suppose you are through haying by this time. And how are you making it farming?
What is Mort doing and has he got his team paid for? I have not heard from him for some time.
I don't believe you can get a money order there, but if you can, you can send it anywhere they

Kingsford's Oswego Pure and Silver Gloss Starch ad in Erie Railway's 1881 Summer Excursion Routes booklet.

will give it for. Hoping to hear from you soon.
I remain your aff. brother,
J.E. Austin

Aida Austin, Oswego, N.Y., to Her Brother
November 1, 1885
Dear Brother,
I received the money all right.
Mr. Poucher was at the Welland [the college dormitory] yesterday afternoon to collect, but I did not give him the money as it was not enough to make another full month's payment. But he will most probably be here again next week and I can pay him then. So please be sure and send me some more money as soon as you receive this letter.
I had a letter from Maria Friday. She says they are going to have a donation at our house soon for Mr. Perine. I wish I could be there, but I suppose it is no use wishing. I suppose things are going on as usual at home.
We had a party here last night, but I was so busy that I did not go down. My roommate said they had a very good time.
Have you seen Becca [Eldred, her cousin] lately and what is she

doing? I saw her while I was in the City. She did not seem to feel very badly about going blind. I thought she would most probably make a great time and was quite surprised to see her so calm.

Your loving sister, Aida

Cousin Addie Austin Thompson's son Gussie was around 12 years old when he wrote the following letter to Mary Ann Eldred Austin, his great aunt.

Gussie Thompson, N.Y.C., to Mary Ann Austin
December 31, 1885
Dear Aunt Mary,
Tom [his brother] went down to Aunt Nett's yesterday and I am alone with Mama [Addie]. She is not very well and wanted me to write for her to let you know that we have not forgotten you.
We often think of you and wish we could see you. Mama wants to know when you are going to be ready to come down. She sends lots of love and says she will send you the money for your fare whenever you will come. Grandma [Mary Ann's sister, Maria] sends her love and hopes you will come down as soon as you can.
Hoping this will find you all well and wishing you all a Happy New Year with much love.
I am ever your affectionate nephew,
A. Austin Thompson [Gussie]

The Bosch, Horton, and Hallock Families Near Hagan Pond
The Bosch, Horton, and one of the Hallock families lived near Hagan Pond (Highland Lake), northeast of the Austins.

There is a handwritten land deed to Daniel Hallock from William H. Austin and Mary Ann his wife dated April 8, 1886.

Possibly the John Horton residence on Hagan Pond (Highland Lake), about 1886. Photo courtesy of William E. Horton.

Dan Hallock was the son of William and Mary Hallock, and grandson of Thomas W. and Julia Van Tuyl Hallock.

Dan was about 50 in 1888. There are a number of stories about Dan Hallock *(see p. 103).* He was a hunter, a guide, and a farmer. He was listed as a saloon keeper in one of the censuses, and had a boarding house.

In 1883 Daniel Hallock and his wife Elvira Horton adopted 3-year-old Jane Mary Murns, whose mother had died. Jennie May Hallock, as Daniel and Elvira called her, always considered the Hallocks her family.

Some of Daniel Hallock's land later went to Herman and Mary E. Horton Bosch (who were not born yet). They would be very helpful to Aida Austin in the 1940s.

Herman Bosch would be born to Heinrich Wilhelm and Mary Maier Bosch, who we talked about in the last chapter. Mary Elvira Horton would be the daughter of

The John Horton family lived on Highland Lake. Photo courtesy of William E. Horton.

John and Anne Elizabeth Stanton Horton. John Horton was a brother to Elvira Hallock, Daniel Hallock's wife.

Mort Austin, Eldred, to Lon Austin
May 16, 1886
Dear Brother Lon,

Your ever kind and welcome letter came to hand last night and found when I opened it $12.00, which I am very much obliged to you for. I will give Mr. Darling the $10 just as soon as I see him. He will be here tomorrow I guess.

We are having very rainy weather here, so much so that I can't get my corn planted. But I suppose it will do no good to worry about it, for I will do as you said, die brave. But sometimes a brave death is a hard one.

I suppose you have given your heart away to some of them pretty girls by this time. I don't see how you can tell which one you like best where there are so many. I think I would love them all. Or do you go to see one each night in the week.

Have you heard of my driving old hen out of here some time ago? I guess I didn't tell you in my other letter. She got so the devil could not live with her, so I drove her off, but she was not gone long before she broke her leg and she is here again. I guess I will get a housekeeper of my own and then she will have to get. What do you think of that? Is it a good idea? Aida is at the River [Barryville] visiting. I have got to go after her tonight. I have just finished writing to Ell.

I am real glad you like your place. I shall look for you this summer. The $2.00 you sent me, I am a thousand times obliged to you, but I don't feel like keeping it as I am owing you. So please find enclosed $2.00. I thank you very much indeed for your kindness.

Please send your letters to Eldred P.O. We get our mail there.

I remain as ever, Mort

Helena Gillespie Writes to Lon Austin
Helena Gillespie lived at 221-14th St., Brooklyn, New York, and wrote to Mr. A.A. (Lon) Austin who lived at either the Car Stables at 839 Nostrand Ave., Brooklyn; with his cousin Ida Clinton at 290 E. Broadway, N.Y.; or at 713 Prospect Place, Brooklyn. The next letter from Helena to Lon was signed, Nell, a nickname for Helena.

Nell Gillespie, Brooklyn, N.Y., to Lon Austin, Brooklyn, N.Y.
June 28, 1886
Dear Friend,

Was sorry you could not come over yesterday, especially after I went to the trouble of putting on my best "bib and tucker."

Do you mean that you are not going to call to say good bye? You know that I start on Saturday at 2 p.m. If you can find an opportunity, run over before then; if not probably you can call before I start for the Catskills which will be on the 14th.

Halfway Brook Road near Barryville. "Aida's at the River [Barryville] visiting." Photo in the Defeo Collection, courtesy of Kevin Marrinan.

Dan Hallock, Hunter and Guide

Dan Hallock, noted hunter and guide. Highland Lake, Eldred, Sullivan Co., N.Y. Postcard courtesy of Carolyn Hallock Clark.

In his early days [Dan] attended lock on the D&H Canal, but gave it up to go back to his farm and the sport life of the woods. He loved to hunt and fish and guide sportsmen in the game country.

His brother Stephen of Monticello and he were among the most noted hunters of the Highland township, and it was most interesting to hear him tell of his bear and deer hunting.

They never went into the woods without a gun. One evening after supper he went out after chestnuts. He had just nicely climbed into the chestnut tree when along came a bear. He got a whiff of Daniel in the tree and wheeled to backtrack. Dan slid down the tree, grabbed his gun and fired.

His eye was too quick and his aim too good even at long range to allow a bear to get away, but the bear continued to run on as though nothing unusual had happened.

The rifleman was pretty sure he had hit him and proceeded to investigate. He followed him for some distance, but the dusk of evening deepened and he gave up the quest.

The next morning he found the old fellow in the edge of the woods only a few rods from the chestnut tree. He had looked for him the night before in every place but the right place.

That fall he was hunting in the vicinity of Mongaup Falls with his famous hound. Everyone in Highland knew Dan's dog.

Just back of the falls a buck came into the opening and he fired. The buck fell and Daniel rushed up to cut its throat, but the ball had only grazed the backbone of the buck and knocked it down, and when it saw Daniel coming it got up and showed fight, and it did fight.

It tore Dan's shirt clean from his body, ripped his pants until they hung by their waistbands, and lacerated and tore his flesh scandalously. He was about winded, tired out and ready to give up when he heard the cry of his dog, which appeared just in time to save his life.

Between the dog and himself they succeeded in killing the buck, which weighed 150 pounds.

Daniel went home partly naked. With his knife he whittled some pins and repaired his pants the best he could, but he couldn't patch his cuts and bruises.—Republican Watchman, March 30, 1923, p.2.

Hunters at Highland Lake. Photo courtesy of the Bosch Family.

I trust you will have a fine day for your excursion; remember me to the folks at Eldred, and don't try to cut Mort out.
  Sincerely, Nell
  P.S. Are you still sleepy?

Nell Gillespie, Brooklyn, N.Y., to Lon Austin, Brooklyn, N.Y.
July 2, 1886
Dear Friend,
  Your letter received last night.
  Can only write you a few lines as my new class is not quite tame yet and needs watching all the time or they will cut up high.
  Will be greatly pleased to see you this evening.
  Good bye until then.
  Yours etc., Nell

Salina, Kansas, located 17 miles southwest of Solomon City, Kansas, where Ell Austin and his family lived. Postcard in the collection of Katherine Calkin Traxler.

Nell Gillespie, Sing Sing, N.Y., to Lon Austin, Brooklyn, N.Y.
July 19, 1886
Dear Friend,
You remember I promised to write when at the Catskills. By the address you can see I haven't reached there yet. We all came here on the 3rd. Papa and sister returned the following Tuesday morning. I remained until Friday, went home for a few days, took my trunk with me and am here since.

During the first two days I was at Sing Sing, I felt very poorly. Papa noticed it, and forbade my going to the Catskills. I called on the doctor and he advised me to remain here. It was with considerable reluctance that I consented to inform the girls that I was not going.

"What can't be cured, must be endured," so I have been trying to make the best of it ever since.

If you were here, I know what you would say, "Don't you care."

I will have to console myself with this, and with the thought that on August 2nd we leave here for the sea shore.

On Monday July 5th, Mr. Smith came here, just as we were seated at the dinner table. In the afternoon we all went to a horse race.

On our return Mr. Smith took two pictures of the house with the folks on the veranda, then we started for the campground. He started for home on Tuesday morning with Papa and Sister.

I hope you have had a very pleasant time at Eldred. I am first rate now. No more doctors for me.
Good bye,
Your friend Nellie

Ell Austin, Solomon City, Kans., to W.H. (Henry) Austin
July 28, 1886
Dear Father,
I wrote to you about a week ago. Since then I have been to a sale of cattle and they went so cheap that I thought I would write again to you about that money I owe you.

I will explain what my intentions are. We have rented this place for 5 years and am going to let him have some cattle on shares.

We are going to go to Florida to live. The place we want to buy costs $1,500. We have not got the money to buy it unless we sell our stock. At the present price of cattle, I don't like to sell, for cattle are bound to be high next year.

In nearly all the range country west of here, it has been so dry this year that there is no feed. Cattle are dying of starvation. Ranch men put their cattle on the market and have glutted the market.

Hay won't make half a crop in Kansas, and we have a poor prospect for corn. Therefore, feed will be scarce and high. So you can see why stock cattle are low. So many cattle are dying on the

Aida's Autograph Book

"Go forth thou little volume
I leave thee to they fate:
To love and friendship truly
Thy leaves I dedicate."

We are all placed here to do something. It is for us and not for others to find out what that something is; and then, with all the energy of which we are capable, honestly and prayerfully to be about our business.
    Emmie [Parmenter Austin, sister-in-law.]

Aunt Aida,
May happiness ever be thy lot,
Wherever thou shalt be;
And joy and pleasure light the spot
That may be home to thee.
    Your affectionate nephew,
    Earl Austin,
    Eldred,
    February 2nd, 1887

Do not believe that happiness makes us selfish; it is a treason to the sweetest gift of life. It is when it has deserted us, that it grows hard to keep all the better things from dying in the blight.
    Semper Eidem.
    Ida Belle [cousin]
    New York, May 30, 1887

Let joy or ease, let affluence or content
And the gay conscience of a life well spent
Calm every thought, in spirit every grace,
Glow on thy heart and smile upon thy face. Semper fidelis.
    Cousin Addie,
    New York, June 27, 1887.

The gem cannot be polished without friction, nor man perfect without adversity.
    Your loving cousin,
    Mary E. Paton

When the name that I write here is dim on the page
And the leaves of your album are yellow with age,
Still think of me kindly and do not forget
That, wherever I am, I remember you yet.
Sincerely your friend,
    Gertrude Bellew, New Milford, Pa.
    Oswego Normal School,
    Jan. 17, 1886

In compliance with your request, with pleasure do I sign myself.
    Very sincerely,
    Your friend,
    Geo. W. Braisted, Oct. 6, 1887

May your life have just enough shadow
To temper the glare of the sun.
    Your friend, Laura Braisted,
    New York, October 16, 1887

"An Idler is a watch that needs both hands,
As useless if it goes as if it stands."
—by Cowper.
    Bertha E. Berbert [classmate]
    Welland, Sept. 28, 1888

We meet and part the world is wide,
    We journey onward side by side
A little while, and then again
    Our paths diverge; a little pain
A silent yearning of the heart
    For what has grown of life a part.
A shadow passing o'er the sun,
    Then gone, and light again has come.
We meet and part, and then forget;
    And life holds blessings for us yet.
    Mary Ellermeyer [classmate]
    Kittanning, PA
    Welland, January 3, 1889

These few lines to you are tendered
    By a friend sincere and true;
Hoping but to be remembered,
    When I'm far away from you.
    Yours truly, William F. Braisted
    New York, Oct. 11, 1887

Autograph book of Aida Austin, courtesy of Melva Austin Barney.

Page in Aida's Autograph Book (see p. 458 for more of the original pages).

range that they are bound to be higher next year.

Now I will make you an offer. I am willing to renew the mortgage on the place or I will give you my note for 3 years for $500 at 8 per cent or I will give you my notes for $100 for one year; one for $200 payable in two years; and one for $200 payable in three years; all bearing 8 per cent interest. My wife will go security on them, and she is worth somewhere from $7,000 to $9,000.

Our health is poor here and we are bound to leave here. You may think it very strange for me to go to Florida, but I believe it is a good country. I never told just what I thought about Florida. When I got back from there, I made up my mind to go again some time and now I am going.

If you have not bought Kelso out yet, I think you had better not be in a hurry to, but come to Florida this winter and make us a visit and see [end of letter].

Helena Gillespie, Atlanticville, N.Y., to Lon Austin, Brooklyn, N.Y.
August 4, 1886
Dear Friend,

I delayed writing until our removal. We are six and not one of us owns a bottle of ink, so I will be obliged to use shoe blacking to direct the letter.

It is delightful here. We are more than satisfied in every particular, except in the number of mosquitoes.

Mr. Squires the hotel keeper took two of the girls and myself yesterday for a 5 mile drive; the wagon is similar to the "soap box" only it is two seated.

The place is almost beyond description. I took one of the girls out twice yesterday. The girls have just gone in the yacht for a 20 minute sail; have taken their bathing suits, and are going in the surf. The beach reminds you of Coney Island.

There are 60 boarders here. Everything is just grand. I had but one letter from Ida [Lon's Cousin] this summer and have not answered that; she is in Chicago just a week and expects to come here with her sister Addie and little Tom for a while.

Mr. Smith started July 9th for the West. I guess you know all now, so good bye.

Your true friend, Helena

Helena Gillespie, Brooklyn, N.Y., to Lon Austin, New York House
September 8, 1886
Dear Friend,

If you went home on the excursion train today, you are probably returning at present or else have decided to remain until tomorrow.

Ida must be at Eldred about this time. I remained at Atlanticville only 4 weeks and as our party left on the 30th, your letter reached Atlanticville 2 days after I left. After a great deal of wandering around, it finally reached me.

Papa is feeling much better. Mamma is still in Sing Sing. Sister is preparing for bed, although it is only 9 o'clock and I am losing my sunburn and a few pounds already.

On Sunday night I managed to get up a very sore throat, what do you think of that so soon?

I was obliged to pay a visit yesterday at 10 a.m. to the MD. He said my tonsils were ulcerated and gave me some paint and a brush to daub them with tonight.

I feel so very much better that I promised to accompany my sister to Union Hill in the morning if the weather is favorable.

Mr. Smith has not returned yet, and is not expected until the 20th of this month.

The lamp is almost out and I am too lazy to fill it. There now, I have told you all, so Good-night,
Sincerely,
Helena Gillespie

Helena Gillespie, Brooklyn, N.Y., to Lon Austin
September 20, 1886
Dear Friend,

I am glad you are having such a good time, and you have not had much occasion to complain of the weather.

You say, "Mort will be married during the holidays." It is very considerate of him to wait until Ida and I can attend, as I played the part of spectator so nicely in the left handed wedding, I ought not to refuse to do as much at this one, especially as this bride elect is sister to the other one.

You know the style nowadays is to rehearse the whole affair a few times before it comes off. By so doing folks avoid all laughable mistakes.

I trust you enjoyed yourself at White Lake. If you profited by last years experience, you had no trouble in procuring food.

How would you like to be groomsman at my wedding?

Mr. Smith arrived from the West last Sunday. He called at the house last night. It was too bad he selected Friday night, for that is my evening for attending class meeting. However, I excused myself and went. Duty comes before pleasure and beside my sister was equal to the task of entertaining him.

There now. I have told you all the news, so will close.
Ever your friend,
Helena Gillespie

Helena Gillespie, in School, to Lon Austin, N.Y.C.

October 8, 1886
Dear Friend,

Your letter received at 5 p.m. on Wednesday. You see it was entirely out of the question for me to get a note to you in time.

However will be pleased to see you Sunday afternoon at the house. Trusting this will reach you in season.

I remain, Yours in great haste,
Helena S. Gillespie

Aida Austin, Eldred, to Lon Austin, Brooklyn, N.Y.

October 25, 1886
Dear Brother,

As usual I failed to keep my word and neglected to write to you last week as I promised, but I really have been very busy.

We have been whitewashing and painting so as to have the house look a little respectful or respectable. I don't know which it will be yet, and we are nearly through or at least have the greater part of the work accomplished and I must say that the rooms look real purty, too.

But I suppose you would rather hear something about the tigers, animals, and snakes, or (to use more respectful terms) the inhabitants of Eldred and its suburbs. Well they are all flourishing and appear to be real happy, too.

Maria and I walked up from church yesterday morning with Alice, Dr. and "Sweet Smiles." She (S.S.), has been attending the Institute at Liberty and is in "high glee" swing, I suppose to the fact that she held the position of organist.

I do not remember whether I told you in my note or not that Maria, Mort, and myself, had spent an evening at Collins'

Front of the Austin home in Eldred, New York. Photo courtesy of Mary Briggs Austin.

since you went back, but such is the case.

Friday morning (during the week following your departure) Sweet Smiles came down and made Maria and I promise that we and Mort would spend that evening at her house. We had hard work to induce Mort to go with us. He said that if you had been home, he would not have had an invitation; but whether this was really the cause of his hesitation, or whether it was fear of a lecture from Miss G. I do not know. However, whichever it was, we at last persuaded him to go with us.

We were the only ones there excepting Mr. Twitchell (the teacher here), but we had a real good time talking and playing dominoes and "going to Jerusalem."

Mr. Twitchell has been attending the Albany Normal, so he and I had quite a chat about our schools. I had never met him before to speak to him and I had an idea that I would not like him; but he is ever so much nicer than his brother John and I do like him quite well. My first impressions however, are seldom the same as those formed by a better acquaintance, and they may prove to be quite as disagreeable as, if not more so than his brother.

Mort and I were out to Monticello last Tuesday. The weather was fair and we had a very pleasant drive as well as a pleasant sociable chat with Mrs. Brown, the lady with whom we took dinner.

We started at 7 in the morning and went by DeVenoge's. We came back by White Lake and reached home about nine o'clock.

Dora West is married, but we did not stop to wish her "God speed" in her matrimonial life, as we were in a hurry to get home; but Mort was out to the Lake the following Thursday and had the opportunity of congratulating his "old love."

Father is going to stay home this week to harvest his rutabagas, cabbages and "sich like;" but I suppose Mort has told all about the farm affairs.

When you see Net, tell her everything is flourishing here. I will write to her as soon as I have time.

There are enough mistakes and enough bad writing now in this letter to send an Oswego

West 1st St., Oswego, New York. Photo from album of Aida Austin, courtesy of Mary Briggs Austin.

Normalite to prison for 20 years, but I have had to scribble it in about two jerks of a lamb's tail.

Let me know as soon as you can and if you don't receive it, why you tell the postman you want the letter that has in it news about Sweet Smiles.

Burn this as soon as you have perused it and tell me when you write that you have done so, for if this letter is ever brought in to court against me I shall have to perjure myself and swear I never wrote it.

Ever your loving sister,
Aida

James K. Gardner and Ella Breen
In November James K. Gardner and Ella Breen, both of Barryville, were married by Rev. H. Litts. James K. Gardner was the son of Stephen and Louisa Gardner, and grandson of James K. and Eliza K. Gardner. James Eldred was his great-grandfather. James K. and Ella Breen Gardner would be the parents of Edna Gardner.

Aida Austin, Oswego, N.Y., to Lon Austin, Eldred
November 16, 1886
Dear Brother,
Instead of going to church I am staying at home in order to answer your letter as I shall not have time to this week.

How I wish I could have been there to the donation Thursday evening. Were there any up from Barryville, or any over from Denton? I suppose Aunt Effie and Becca are horrified, aren't they? When is Becca going to Polly's [Becca's sister]?

There are a great many new girls here this term and some of them are pretty lively. Either Miss Cooper or Miss Myers is up after some of them nearly every night.

Friday evening Miss Hall, Miss Bellew, and I were all sitting here quietly when we heard a scream in the hall and of course rushed out to see what was the matter.

Some of the girls on the next floor had dressed a broom stick in some old clothes and an old hat and brought it up to Miss Walsh's door to frighten her, but one of the other girls on this floor happened to be passing through the hall and of course screamed when she saw it. But you could not blame her for it really did look like Satan himself.

Well, all the girls rushed out to see what was the matter and one, a real comical tall thin girl, grabbed the dressed broomstick in her arms and started on a mad waltz down the hall.

She got just opposite the stairs as Miss Cooper's head appeared above the banisters and such a scampering and noise as there was. Each girl flying for her room and Miss Cooper calling, "Come back girls, come back."

The two girls that brought the figure up rushed into our room and so escaped Miss Cooper. So the girls that happened to be nearest the stair were the ones that got the scolding. And I guess it was no light scolding for they have been very quiet both yesterday and today.

Please let me know if you send the money by express, so that it will not get lost.

Love to all. I remain your loving sister, Aida

Nell Gillespie, Brooklyn, N.Y. to Lon Austin, N.Y.C.
November 26, 1886
Dear Friend,
Yours received. Will be pleased to accompany you to Beecher's and will expect you at my house in the afternoon. Remember you have no watch to hunt for now.

I was very sorry to learn that you reached home so late, we will have to see that it does not occur again. There now, I will have to close, am going to class meeting and will put this in the post office on my way.

Good night. Ever your friend,
Nellie Gillespie

Aida Austin, Eldred, to Lon Austin, N.Y.C.
December 1, 1886
Dear Brother,
Mort and I have been to Collins' again to spend the evening, and spent a very pleasant evening and did not get home until about 1 o'clock.

Father has been home since

Saturday with the pink eye, and I don't think he will get back to work this week, although his eyes are a great deal better and he has gone to Barryville today.

Mother says she told Maria that Isaac Sergeant was married, but Aunt Eliza was telling me that it is not true that he is married. Some of the boys around Barryville started the story. [Aunt Eliza was correct. They married in 1888. See Chapter 3.]

By the way, tell Net that we have had a very "nawce" [nice] visit from Aunt Eliza. She came up Monday afternoon and we took her down to Aunt Effie's this morning. Myers Gardner came up for her this afternoon and took her home.

Mort says to tell you that he will write to you soon and would have written to you before, but has been so busy drawing coal for Bolton and besides this, he has had the pink eye.

Fanny and Black Hawk are doing splendidly. Blackhawk is fat as a pig and takes the world as easy as ever.

"Doc" Kelso is sick; and Rob came home this afternoon. I stood in the window and watched him go by.

Ell has not come yet and we have not heard from him since Maria went back. Tell Maria I will try to write to her soon.

Mort says you had better stay where you are instead of going to California and I think so too.

Love to all.

Yours in haste, Aida

Rob Kelso had written Aida some endearing letters from Kansas in 1878. I wonder what Aida was thinking when she watched him go by.

Mort Austin, Eldred, to Lon Austin, N.Y.C.

Sunday, December 12, 1886
Dear Brother Lon,

Please excuse haste for I have a book to read. As I was thinking about writing, I was blessed with the wonderful pink eye which has been a very common complaint here at the present time. Maria didn't catch it yet, did she?

I have had but one sleigh ride this winter. We have had quite some snow, but not much sleighing.

I have more leisure time now. I think you ought to bring your intended bride up and spend holidays with me, if I keep the house. I suppose Ell will be here this week sometime. Then I will know what I am going to do. There will not be a wedding, but we can have a good time all the same. Maybe Cousin Ida will come, too.

I have made up my mind to live an old bachelor the rest of my days. Don't you think I would make a good one? But I think you would do well to take Nell, for I guess she is a real good girl and I think you would be better off with a good wife than single.

I am not giving you lately but facts as I see them. I am in a hurry for Ell to get home so I will know what I am going at. If I don't work the place another year, I am going to sell my horse and go west somewhere and seek my fortune. I never shall return until I have got what money I need to take me through this world.

I guess we could sell our horses to Mr. Bolton for his team is nearly played out. If I should sell my horse, do you want me to sell Flora with her, if I can get you $200 for her? I think I can for she is looking real good. I don't know what I will do until Ell comes.

Things are going on the same as usual. No one hurt, but plenty

Groceries, 1886

C.M. Austin Grocery Book

1 barrel flour	$6.50
10# sugar	.70
1 broom	.35
10# sugar	.70
1 barrel flour	6.50
10 pounds sugar	.85
100 pounds meal	1.35
1/4 barrel flour	1.60
2# coffee	.50
5-3/4 yards shirting	.63
6 yards shirting	.72
1 rake	.25
750 hoops	3.375
850 hoops	3.825
1,000 hoops	4.50
1,200 hoops	5.40

of quarreling. Aida and Dory have gone to church and the rest to bed, so all is quiet. This is the second Sunday night I have spent at home for some time. Well be a real good boy and write very soon.

Give my love to all the folks by all means, to Sister Nell, and don't forget, I should like to see you and your intended if it is so you could come.

As ever, your Brother Mort

Nell Gillespie, Brooklyn, N.Y., to Lon Austin, N.Y.C.

December 15, 1886
Dear Friend,

I suppose you have been thinking what a mean old thing Nell is, not even to write when she knows I am wounded. Never mind, I'll forgive you for such thoughts, especially as you are not to blame, but if I had a hold of your postman, he should have a good shaking.

The Halfway Brook stage headed towards Barryville on Brook Road beside Halfway Brook. "Mort may go to Barryville soon." Postcard courtesy of Chuck Myers.

On Friday afternoon I wrote two letters, one to you, and one to Miss Renne. Ida handed me two stamps for them. Directly opposite Ridley's, one of the stamps fell to the ground, and the streets being wet was sufficiently moistened to put it on the letter, yours being the uppermost one.

I put it on, but even if it fell off I should think they would have delivered the letter and collected again at the house; however we will both have to forgive the postman this time and both may thank Ida for clearing up what might have caused a misunderstanding.

I believe you are feeling much better and I am glad to hear it. It is advisable to take good care of yourself and steer clear of such fierce animals.

If you intend to go to Mort's wedding, I would advise you to hurry up and get well, or he will have to hunt up another best man.

How are they all at Eldred? Haven't you some news to tell?
Good-night, Ever your friend,
Helena S. Gillespie

Helena Gillespie, Brooklyn, N.Y., to Lon Austin, N.Y.C.
December 18, 1886
Dear Friend,
I received both your letters and was pleased to learn that you were on the convalescent list. You have cause to feel thankful that you escaped without a broken bone.

I will look for you tomorrow (Sunday) afternoon. Mr. Smith will probably be here, but don't you care, sister can go with him to church, and we can go together. I will expect you tomorrow.
Your true friend,
Helena Gillespie

Ell Austin's Family Moves Back to Eldred
Ell, Emma, Henry, and Lillie Austin arrived in Eldred on December 25, 1886. Emma's sister Sarah Sophronia Parmenter seems to have moved with them from Kansas.

Nell Gillespie, Brooklyn, N.Y., to Lon Austin, Brooklyn, N.Y.
January 11, 1887
Dear Friend,
Your letter reached me on Saturday eve. As you intended calling the first part of this week, I did not think it necessary to write.

I looked for you last night and tonight also, and as you failed to put in an appearance, thought I would write and let you know that I have an engagement for every other evening this week.

If we did not expect company on next Sunday, I should have liked you to call, but we will look for some folks from New York on that day.

If next Monday evening will be convenient for you, I would be pleased to see you.

I hope you like your new place and will have no occasion to regret leaving the other.

So Mort and Georgie have come to a settlement at last. Well whatever happens is best. This will be a subject for conversation when we meet.

Good night. Your true friend,
Helena Gillespie

Aida Austin, Eldred, to Lon Austin, Brooklyn, N.Y.
January 11, 1887
Dear Brother,
You must have thought I had run away with the $5 which you sent for your boots. I wrote you a few lines as soon as I saw Gus after receiving your letter.

I was going to send you the money, but Mort said he thought you would surely be home sometime during the holidays and that I better keep the money for you until then so it would not get lost. Mort will take the money to Ira Austin as soon as he can. He says the bill is $8.50, so instead of sending the $5 back, I will give it to Mort and let him pay the whole bill, unless you want the money and would rather wait. If so, let me know as soon as you can, for Mort may go to Barryville soon.

I think I will wait until next fall to go back to school, for I have some hopes of getting this school this summer and I would rather teach a term before I go back; and besides, Father has promised that he will help me then.

I think I will go down to Net's a while, if she wants me, after Maria leaves, and then we can see what we can do. I suppose Mort has told you about Georgie. I will close as I want to write a few lines to Maria.

Your loving sister, Aida

Mort Austin, Eldred, to Lon Austin, Brooklyn, N.Y.
January 24, 1887
Dear Brother Lon,

Your ever welcome letter came to hand some little time ago.

Ell has been home a month tomorrow. He brought a horse, 2 head of cattle, some chickens, and ducks.

I am quite busy and do not have much time to write. We are having plenty of snow and very cold weather.

I met the Rev. John E. Perine. He could hardly speak to me. They turn the cold shoulder, but I don't care for I think I have come off lucky. I guess the old folks will find out they can't catch me as they did Will.

I don't think Mother likes the way things has turned out. Are you still going with Nell? She is a nice girl and you had better hitch yourself up with her for a man can't always find a good mate.

Kelsos are very friendly now. What do you say if I run off with Sweet Smiles—just for awhile.

Do you intend to stay where you are? When do you think you will be up? Good night old boy. Take good care of Nell and remember me to her.
By By, Mort

Aida Austin, Eldred, to Lon Austin, Brooklyn, N.Y.
January 28, 1887
Dear Brother,

I wrote sometime ago and said that I thought it best to wait until next fall to go back to school, but I expected then to have this school this summer.

I had a note from Jim Boyd the day before yesterday and he says that there was one person who spoke to him for the school before father did and that he will have to let that person have it this summer, but that I can have it next year if he is trustee, as father was the second one to speak to him about it.

He says he will keep a lady teacher 40 weeks each year and not hire a man teacher again. I am sure he will be trustee next year and so I am sure of the school, and would like to go back to school this spring term if I can.

Mother is at Barryville and will be home tomorrow or Sunday. She is going to see if Lou Stidd or anyone else intends to buy an organ and if so I am going to try to sell them mine. If I can do this, and get about $50 for it, and you can let me have $10 a month, why I can get through the term alright I think. There may be a little more expense but it will not be over $3 or $4.

If I can not sell the organ, do you think you could raise the $50 now, and the $10 a month after? If you can, and I get the school next year, I will pay it back then and also all the other money you have let me have.

You see if I only get through school and obtain a good position, why I will be much better off myself and can help the rest too.

If I go I will have to start just 2 weeks from today. You can let me know soon what you think best about it. If you have made arrangements to take a house in Brooklyn, I will come there instead of going back to school. Please write as soon as you can and let me know.

Don't say anything about my having the school to Nell, if you think she would tell Cousin Ida. I think it is best to keep our affairs to ourselves and then no one can interfere.

Ever your loving sister, Aida

Addie Austin Thompson, N.Y.C., to Mary Ann Austin
January 31, 1887
Dear Aunt Mary,

I was so pleased to receive your letter. I have threatened to write you, but have been sick a good bit and could not seem to get at it.

I am so sorry you have been so sick. When Lon's letter came, I was worried enough I tell you for fear I might never see you again and was so rejoiced to see the dear familiar writing again and hope to see your dear face again ere long.

We have had very warm weather most of the winter until these last two weeks. 'Pears like as though winter has just "sot" in.

Tell my cousin Alonzo when he writes again to not be so stingy of his words, but to write me a letter.

Guss [Addie's son] has been teasing me for the last three or four days to write to you. Aunt Polly (Addie's husband's sister) is staying with us this winter. I suppose she will be here until May probably.

Ida Paton [Addie's niece, daughter of Archie and Rand Austin Paton] is here also. She

West Fifth Street, Oswego, New York. Photo from album of Aida Austin, courtesy of Mary Briggs Austin.

is attending the Conservatory of Music. Do not know how long she will remain, but between you and I, hope it will not be for any great length of time. She has been here now over 6 weeks.

This is the fourth pen I have tried and each one is worse than the last.

Now hurry up and get well and strong enough to come down dear. Maybe Lon will come with you.

Addie

**Aida Austin, Eldred,
to Lon Austin, Brooklyn, N.Y.**
February 2, 1887
Dear Brother,

I received your note last night. I think I will go to the City Saturday if I can. I will have to get the fare from you as Father will not be home until Saturday night and I am afraid he will not have the money now. I think he will let me have the $10 in a month or two.

Hoping to see you soon, I remain your loving sister, Aida

**Aida Austin, Oswego, N.Y.,
to Lon Austin, Brooklyn, N.Y.**
February 12, 1887
Dear Brother,

I was to church this morning, but I am going to stay in my own room tonight and write letters, for it is not likely that I will have much spare time during the week.

I arrived here safe and sound yesterday morning; came right to the Welland and then went to the school building with Lucy for my books and classification; but there were such a number of students that I was not able to procure either my classification or books until afternoon.

Mr. Poucher was here yesterday afternoon collecting, and I paid him $38 instead of $40 as I intended, because I did not have quite enough change left to get my notebooks.

Mr. Poucher booked me for 29, my old room. I'm real glad for I like it better than any other room in the house. I thought Mr. Poucher must have forgotten to keep me a room when I was registering yesterday afternoon. "Why Aida, Do you think I would forget you?" Then he told me I could have 29. Now isn't that just splendid? It is on the fourth floor and my board will be $73 this term instead of $76.

I have just sent Ell's $2 to him, but did not send mother's.

Everything looks natural and there are a number of the old girls here yet, so I have not been very lonesome or homesick.

I got slightly acquainted with Miss Clark. She seems like a real sweet girl. The teachers all seem to remember me and are very pleasant and kind.

I must write a few lines to Maria tonight. I suppose she is at Net's yet.

Don't forget to write soon.
Your loving sister, Aida

**Aida Austin, Oswego, N.Y.,
to Lon Austin, Brooklyn, N.Y.**
February 17, 1887
Dear Brother,

Can you send me $5? It seems too bad to have to have money so soon, but I don't see how I can help it. We have got to have a couple of books in two of our classes, which are not in the library, and so we will of course, have to buy them ourselves.

If I had known about it sooner, I would have kept the $2 I sent to Ell; but you see I thought that I had everything I should have to have and that there would not be any extra expense until near the end of the term.

It will not take all of $5, but I have only a few pennies left, and I hate to be without a little money. Still if it is going to put you out too much, don't you send over $4.

Now Lon I want you to mind what I tell you, because it is not necessary that I have anymore than enough for the books, and if anything happened, so that I should positively have to have some, why you know I could draw a little back from what I paid Mr. Poucher.

The work which I am doing in methods is very much harder and far more tedious than any work which I have yet had in the school.

I shall be very glad when the term is over if I am only safely through with all my subjects.

With much love, I am your ever loving and grateful sister,
Aida

**Aida Austin, Oswego, N.Y.,
to Lon Austin, Brooklyn, N.Y.**
April 10, 1887
Dear Brother,

I will leave here tomorrow morning 11 a.m. and will be in Hoboken at 8:50. Will you please meet me there if you can?

If you can not come or if I miss you there, I will go right up to cousin Net's and then you can stop there for me, if you come.
Ever your loving sister,
Aida

**Aida Austin, Oswego, N.Y.,
to Lon Austin, Brooklyn, N.Y.**
April 17, 1887
My Dear Brother,

I am still improving very fast and the doctor says I may sit up tomorrow. I have had very good care and everyone has been very kind. I have been living on beef tea, but now I have anything I want. Mrs. Shelly, the housekeeper, fixed me a lovely piece of toast this morning, just like mother fixes it and it tasted so good I ate a whole slice.

Today noon they sent me up chicken, mashed potatoes, a dish of corn, tea bread and butter and a dish of ice cream. Of course, I could not eat so very much of

Welland Hall where Aida stayed when she went to college at Oswego, New York. Welland was a girl's dormitory from 1867 to 1918. Postcard in the collection of Mary Briggs Austin.

it, but you can see that I have everything and more than I want.

Wednesday: I received your kind letter today. I am still gaining and was outdoors a little while this afternoon.

I think perhaps I had better not stay the rest of the term for I am afraid I shall not be able to make up what I have lost. I will see what I can do and let you know soon.

Father has not sent the money yet. I will let you know as soon as he does. Ever your loving sister,
Aida

**Aida Austin, Oswego, N.Y.,
to Lon Austin, Brooklyn, N.Y.**
April 27, 1887
Dear Brother,

I have received both your letters with $5 in each of them. I will write tomorrow I am sure.

Don't worry. Are Mother and Maria well? Love to all,
Your loving sister,
Aida

Gus Osier mentioned in the following letter and again in letters from 1888, was a family friend.

**Mort Austin, Eldred,
to Lon Austin, Brooklyn, N.Y.**
May 8, 1887
Dear Brother,

Your very welcome letter came to hand Thursday. I sent the money down to Quick by Gus Osier, so I trust it will be all right. I did not like to send it by mail for he might claim he did not get it. I told Osier to get a receipt and give it to me. I will send it to you.

We are quite busy, so I could not go to the River [Barryville]. I have been working out and did not have time to answer as soon as I received your letter.

The spring is quite late and very rainy. We sowed a few oats Friday, but it rained very hard yesterday so it will be a long time before we can plow again. The grass and rye is looking so fine like.

I don't know when the excursion trains run. I would like to see you as soon as you can come up and see what you think we had better do with the horses. I have been offered $225 for Fan. I don't care to sell yet. If I could stay here, money can't buy her. And I think they ought to be kept together.

I don't think I will stay here

Sarah Sophronia Parmenter, sister to Emily Parmenter Austin. Photo courtesy of Katherine Calkin Traxler.

longer than the first of January. My year will be up then.

Father says to tell Aida that he can get $60 for her organ if she wants to sell it. The fellow will pay $5 a month till it is paid for and father will give the money to her and will be responsible for the pay. He wants to know this week.

Tell Aida I can't get to New York, but for her to come here right away and to let me know what day and I will meet her at the train. And you do the same when you get ready to come.

Tell mother I have not forgotten her, but will try to write soon. I am in a hurry now.

Well, Lon be a good boy, and excuse haste. I hope to see you soon. Black Hawk is doing nicely and sends his love to you.

I close. By By, Mort

Helena Gillespie, Brooklyn, N.Y., to Lon Austin, Brooklyn, N.Y.
May 10, 1887

Dear Friend,
Was pleased to hear from you. As I have refused 2 other invitations for tomorrow night, it would be hardly fair to have you call. We rehearse for the Choral Union every Tuesday and Thursday and as I intend going to a sociable on Thursday Eve after the Choral Union, I have decided to remain at home and make some alterations on my silk suit.

Now there don't say "vanity of vanities." As you have left it with me to settle on any other evening I should prefer, I will reserve next Monday, the 16th for you.

I must close now; will post this on my way to the Union. Yours very hastily,
Helena Gillespie

The Austin Homestead
This next letter indicates that Ell and his family (and sister-in-law Sophronia) lived at the Austin Homestead.

There seems to be an undercurrent of discontent, possibly related to money. Perhaps Ell was caught up in a financial situation with both a mortgage on the Austin place and taxes to pay on the land in Kansas that was deeded to his wife and sister-in-law.

Mort Austin's engagement to the preacher's daughter (whether genuine or not) had been broken off, according to this next letter.

Mort Austin, Eldred, to Lon Austin, Brooklyn, N.Y.
June 5, 1887
Dear Brother Lon,
I have been real busy through the week and feel quite tired Sundays. The horses are standing the work first rate and are looking fine like. I let Flora out today a little while to pick some grass.

Ell won't let me let Fan out because she runs all over. So today, Flora jumped over into his garden and landed down, rolled and got up, and the way she did run was laughable, but I got her out by the time Ell got out of the house with his hire standing straight. I laughed. I could not help it. So now Miss Flora will have to stay in the stable.

His [Ell's] wife and sister-in-law thinks I ought to have them broke better. She said Eldred had his horses broke after I left there, so he could let them loose any where and he would have these broke if he had been driving them as long as I have. Well, I think he would, for one foot would be in the grave and the other one all but, if he drove them long.

How soon will you be up? Ell wants me to take the place for 5 years. I hope to see you soon, then we can talk it over. But I hardly think I will stay here. I don't know yet for sure what I will do.

How is Aida? Is she well now? Tell her I am in a hurry to see her.

Old Prine is talking quite strange of suing me for breach of promise, so I hear, and it came straight this time. She has gone off to sell his horse to get the money. They are a living set if what I hear is true.

Georgie is not the girl I thought she was. I would marry the devil before I would her. Now they can sue just as soon as they like. I think I can win the suit. But I don't believe they dare do it. It is all talk, I guess.

It is getting late so I will have to close. Please write soon. Give my love to all.

As ever, your brother,
Mort

Wm. Linimous, N.Y.C., to Mr. A.A. (Lon) Austin, Brooklyn, N.Y.

*July 20, 1887
Dear Sir:*

I herewith enclose you a postal order for 25 cents and am most truly grateful to you for your kindness and may you always be as fortunate in finding as good a friend in times of necessity.

The ant was small, but the spirit was same as if much larger and a very commendable one.

Thank you again for your kindness. I care not to get caught that way again.

*Believe me sir, your friend,
Wm. A. Linimous
Henry & Nathan Russell & Day
Wholesale Dealers in Glassware, Kerosene Lamps and Crockery*

**Mort Austin, Eldred,
to Lon Austin, Brooklyn, N.Y.**
*July 23, 1887
Dear Brother,*

I saw the Count. He will not sell his place. I will see what we can do about a place on some pond. Father thinks we can buy a piece of land of Maney.

We are so busy just now. I will try it out to the lake just as soon as we get through with the haying. We would have been through today only for so much rainy weather.

I guess we had better get Clark's place for a while, for I can't stand it here.

They made out their note for me, but made it out so it was not good. I just told him I wanted a note that was good so I don't know but what I will loose the $200 yet before I get through. They are the most dishonest folks I ever saw. I will mail Ell if he don't give me a good note. He will cheat mother out of everything if he can.

I think we will move the furniture up to Aunt Laura's place if mother will let us and live there for it is not safe to have Black Hawk here. I will write you more about it very soon. I will close for this time.

Your Brother Mort

The above letter indicates the Austin family (or some of them) were looking for land or a different place to live, possibly the Irvin Clark place. They seem to be considering taking in boarders in this next letter.

**Aida Austin, Eldred,
to Lon Austin, Brooklyn, N.Y.**
*July 27, 1887
Dear Brother,*

Mort and father were out to Bethel, Monday, to see about a wagon. They can not possibly get one before the last of next month and that will be too late.

Mort wants to know if you will go in with him in taking Irv's place and get him on the cars there. That is if mother will let us have the furniture.

He will take the shoes off the horse and put them to pasture and father, Dory, and I will stay there. Then next summer, Mort will go to caring boarders.

He thinks Ell will cheat him out of everything and I am afraid he will. I am sure he will if it is so he can. Ell says he will buy mother's furniture if she will sell reasonable, but he will only give her his note. If he and Emma put everything in Shorona's hands, then none of their notes will be worth a cent.

Write just as soon as you can and let us know what you and mother will do. Mort can settle up with Ell the last of the week and tell him about the furniture if mother lets us take it.

If we don't go to Irv's place, Mort is going to sell his horse and wants to know if he shall

Henry Ladore (Dory) Austin. Photo in the Austin Collection.

sell yours too. You will get this tomorrow and if you write right back, we will get your letter Friday.

We are looking for Mother today and I hope she comes so we can have something settled. I would go down to Lil's and Kate's awhile, but I don't like to leave things now the way it is.

Dory is going to work for Middaugh a month. Emma [Ell's wife] told Dory the other day she wanted to give him a little advice—if he said anything to hurt Eldred's character, they would sue him. Dory told her that Ell had not done by him as he had promised and that he would swear that he would not believe Ell under oath.

If mother comes today will let you know just how things are settled. I hope we go to Irv's place and we will have just a lovely time when you come up this fall.

How soon does Maria think she can come?

C.C.P. and Effa Eldred's house is on the right. This postcard of Eldred, looking west, seems to have been taken in the early 1900s. Photo courtesy of Chuck Myers.

*Be sure and write tomorrow.
Your loving sister,
Aida*

Challenging times for the Austin family, it seems. From the above letter, it sounds as if Ell now owned the Austin property and that some of the others were going to live in the Clark home. Ell's siblings were not very happy with him. In later years, Mort and Ell were on quite good terms, so things must have worked out eventually.

Mary Ann Austin's brother Charles C.P. Eldred was also experiencing some financial difficulty. C.C.P. and Effa Eldred's daughter Maria A. Kendall had died in 1884. C.C.P. and Effa had cared for their grandchildren, Nellie and Charles Kendall. C.C.P. Eldred wrote a letter to his son-in-law, Charles Kendall, kindly asking for Charles to pay his bill (letter from *The Eldred Family,* pp. 50, 51).

**C.C.P. Eldred, Eldred,
to Mr. Charles Kendall**
*August 17, 1887
Dear Sir:
We are all reasonable well. Egbert and Polly [Mapes, another daughter] has been up to see us from Philadelphia and Egbert went back the 15th, and Polly will stay with us a few days yet.*

Our crops will not be very abundant this year. I think we will have hay and other fodder enough to get through the winter or we will live with what little stock we have and potatoes enough for family use.

The other necessaries of life we'll have to buy and not anything to sell to buy them with. And I am somewhat in debt and not any means under my control to meet my obligations and am not able to do much work.

*I will give you a statement of my account with you.
Mortgage on farm: $200
Note due of: $40
Hired help: about $80
Grain bill: $22; Total: $342*

All now due and must be paid by October 1 next with interest and no funds on hand to meet it.

You see that I have made out your bill to June 30, 1887. Now if you have any means to pay it, it will come in very acceptable.

My wife and me have got to be well advanced in years and there must be a change in my family before a great while. Which of us will pass over the river of death first is not for us to say.

But I thought if you could remit to me the $400 during the next month it would pay my debts and leave me a very small margin to help through the coming winter and that I make no more bills against your boy Charles while he stayed with us and that might be as long as my family held together as now is or as long as you think proper to leave him with us.

*But when wife or me passes away will be very likely to make a change in my family. Of course, you know more about that than I do. You will please let me hear from you on the receipt of this.
C.C.P. Eldred*

James (Ell) Austin, Solomon City, Kans., to Wm. H. Austin
*September 7, 1887
Dear Father,
I received a letter from Lon today. He says you are hurrying him on that note he gave you. I suppose you are aware that you gave us an extension of time (as our option I hold the letter stating it). And that time has not expired.*

If you had wanted the money before it was due, you had ought to give a longer notice. I will hurry Lon up a little and get the money for you as soon as convenient.

*As for collecting the note before the extended time has expired, it is impossible. I should hate to have any fuss but business is business and I must treat it as such where I am connected with it. Hoping that you will get along quietly, I remain, Your Aff. son,
Jas. E. Austin*

**Aida Austin, Eldred,
to Lon Austin, Brooklyn, N.Y.**
December 21, 1887

Schoolhouse Blizzard January, 1888

The second week of January 1888, an unexpected blizzard hit the Plains states. It had snowed on the Northern and Central Plains, January 5 and 6. The next four days had been terribly cold.

When the temperatures increased from 20 to 40 degrees the morning of January 12, people in the area thought it safe to leave their homes for town, school, or just be outside.

But the weather played a cruel joke. An Arctic cold front collided with warm moisture from the Gulf of Mexico. The temperature dropped over 50 degrees, to 20 below zero.

High winds and heavy snow accompanied the fast moving storm that first hit Montana early January 12. It swept through the Dakota Territory and reached Lincoln, Nebraska at 3 p.m.

Many school children were caught in the blizzard. There were 235 people who died.—*wikipedia.org*.

The story of the *Schoolhouse Blizzard*, as it has been called, made such an impression on my maternal grandmother Myrtie Crabtree Briggs (born in 1891 in Nebraska) that it was one of the stories she repeated to her children and grandchildren.

Part of Grandma Myrtie's story was about a school teacher who had gotten her students to safety by having them hold on to a rope.

Dear Brother,
Your letter with the money was received last night.
Father says to tell mother not to take the $500 or make any settlement about it until she hears from him. I will write to Charley Stage for him today and find out about the papers and if they are all right. Father says he will see to it right away.
Aunt Laura, Rob, and Ellsworth came up Saturday night. Ellsworth went back yesterday and Aunt Laura and Rob are going back this morning.
Don't let mother take the $500 if you can help it.
In haste, Your loving sister,
Aida

Higginson, Crabtree, and Briggs Families in Nebraska, 1888

Ida Higginson, future wife of John Crabtree and mother of Myrtie, was a school teacher in Nebraska in 1888. Ida and her family were homesteaders. Ida Higginson would marry John Crabtree at the end of 1890. John Crabtree and his family were also homesteading in Nebraska.

Clinton Briggs and Marium Indianola Clark, parents of Irwin Briggs, Myrtie's future husband, still lived in Indiana. Clinton and Marium were married in January 1889, and would soon be homesteading in Nebraska, too.

It would be 1935 before Irwin and Myrtie Crabtree Briggs and their family arrived in Barryville, Town of Highland, New York.

Aida Austin, Eldred, to Lon Austin, Brooklyn, N.Y.
February 26, 1888
Dear Brother,
Mort says there is no use trying to do anything with so little capital, as it would only be a failure and I do not see how we could get along with so little to start with. So I think we will have to give up the plan entirely and try something else.
In haste, your loving sister,
Aida

Lucy Fisher, Sand Hollow, Ohio, to Aida Austin, Eldred
March 7, 1888
My Dear Aida,

Ida Higginson, the future Mrs. Crabtree, was a school teacher in Nebraska in 1888. Photo courtesy Mary Briggs Austin.

John Lewis Crabtree. John and his family homesteaded in Nebraska. Photo courtesy Mary Briggs Austin.

I am very sorry indeed to hear your minister has got to leave again. That makes the third one since we've been here. I had a letter from Lizzie MacKenzie,

Blizzard, March 14, 1888, Brooklyn, New York. Photo courtesy of the National Oceanic and Atmospheric Administration, U.S. Department of Commerce.

Glen Spey, and she told me he could not stay, but Mr. Criegan said he had a man in view that would suit that field.

How large a family has Mr. Hamilton? I feel very sorry for him. We have heard nothing but good report from him and his work. I thought the church would get along better since C. Hickok was out, but it's no better than when we were there, is it?

How are all your folks getting along? Remember us kindly please to your father and mother. When I am oft alone, I think about Eldred, some pleasant and happy days and some as unpleasant, sorrowful as I ever spent in all my life, but they are all gone, never to return anymore and the good Lord knoweth them all.

Now my dear girl, do tell me where they are going to build their new parsonage. I would love to take a peep on the hill if I could and see if it looks like home.

E.W. Fisher [her husband] and Rebecca [Eldred] have been corresponding since we have been here. I did a while with Mrs. Mapes, but not for a year or more.

Four years last fall since we came here. How the time does fly and bring changes to us all wherever we are. Does Anna and Mary Wilson live there yet?

We have had no sleighing this winter, but if mud was snow, we could have plenty and it would last until the month of June.

Good night and don't forget your true friend,
L.F. Fisher

The Great Blizzard of 1888
In March 1888 there was a terrible winter storm on the east coast. It was so bad that it was remembered by an Eldred neighbor, Tom Collins, in a letter to my grandfather Mort Austin in 1908:

It was like the storm we had in '88. You remember it snowed all day and night and oh, the wind how it did blow—raise the hair off your head.—T.K. Collins.

The Great Blizzard of 1888 or the Great White Hurricane, as the snowstorm was called, dumped 40 to 50 inches of snow on parts of New Jersey, New York, Massachusetts, and Connecticut. It paralyzed the East coast from Virginia into the Atlantic provinces of Canada.

Winds were recorded at 40 miles per hour with gusts from 54 to 80 miles per hour. Snowdrifts were 30 to 40 feet with the highest drift recorded as 52-foot snowdrifts.

The storm, which started March 12 after midnight, was preceded by mild weather with heavy rains. As the temperature dropped, the rain turned to snow, and the storm continued for a day and a half.

Albany, New York, recorded 48 inches of snow and New York City recorded 22 inches.

Over 200 ships were grounded or wrecked. Travel by roads or railroads was impossible.

Property was damaged or lost due to fire because fire trucks were immobilized. The melting snow later caused severe flooding. Over 400 people died from the storm and the ensuing cold, including 200 from New York City.

Because the storm disabled the telegraph infrastructure for days, the telegraph and telephone lines began to be placed underground.—*wikipedia.org.*

Both Lou Kloss and Rowlee Schoonover wrote about the Great Blizzard in their memoirs.

On March 1, 1888, on a Sunday evening, we three, mother, baby brother Will, and I, had been on a visit to our neighbors, the Kestlers. And as we were brought home by several of the neighbor's boys, there was snow on the ground to about 3 inches and was snowing heavily.

Great big snowflakes came down, and the next morning it was howling and whistling a gale, and snowing to beat the band, and it kept this up for 3 days, and it wasn't till the third day that the neighbor "broke the road," as the saying is in the country when they make a path through the snow.

The snow was 4 feet deep and we could barely see the man's oxen. He went as far as the entrance to our stable and turned back as that was all the oxen could stand. He said it took him half a day to get to our place.

We didn't get to the town for a week and father said later that they were tied up in New York the same way.

The wind blew the snow around all day for 3 days, and it was sometimes in billows 10 to 20 feet high, blowing back and forth, and piled up drifts 10 to 15 feet high.

Some of the snow was still lying in the fence corners late in May. It took mother and me half a day to shovel a path to the barn, and it drifted shut behind me nearly as fast as I could shovel it out. And it took nearly the same time to shovel a path to the spring across the road.—Lou Kloss Memoirs.

Blizzard, March 1888, 45th Street and Grand Central Depot, New York. Photo courtesy of the National Oceanic and Atmospheric Administration, U.S. Department of Commerce.

We lived in Orange County in the winter of the '88 blizzard, and that was something to remember.

For on Sunday night March 12, 1888, it rained and snowed and was very cold. Monday morning was very cold. Everywhere you looked the ground was piled high with drifts and mountains of snow. You could not see any of the lower floor windows. I slid down the snow banks from the second story window.

There was a Presbyterian Minister came to town the previous Friday which was a very nice day. And they was very much delighted with the climate up north for they had come from Kentucky and the children had never seen any snow.

Well, when we got up that Monday morning and saw how things was, the first thing Ma said, "Bub, as soon as you get your overalls and boots on, you better go over to see how those new folks are faring," for they only lived just across the road from our house.

So when I got everything tied down, I slid out the second story window down to the road and scrambled over the banks and got in the front yard. But when I got to the stoop, there was just a small hole next to the edge of the porch roof. So I slid down on the porch and at last got the front door opened in the living room.

I do not want to see any more dejected people than that family was. They was all crying and there was no small children among them. They had a little fire in the fireplace that would not keep a canary warm and was just about ready to cash in.

So when they saw me come tumbling in, they sure was happy. I went out to the woodshed which was all enclosed and got some wood and started a fire in two stoves and got the tea kettle going. You never saw a more happy family in your life.

I went back home and told Ma. She said I hope they got something in the house to eat and drink. So she fixed up a lunch of toast and fried eggs, and a jug full of coffee, and I made the second trip over the snow banks and they was the most grateful people that I ever remember seeing in my whole life.

The blizzard was so bad that it was 4 days before anyone could get out. We lived 8 miles from Middletown which was the source of supplies for our neighborhood and was where all the farmers had to go to deliver their milk. So everybody had to turn out and shovel snow. There was places for 1/4 mile that was tunneled through.

I remember Ma said, "Bub, suppose you go over to Phil Vans and get some milk."

I said, "I'll try."

So I started out and went up behind the church where the snow had blown away and got on top of a rail fence and fell. At last I got over to Phil's. Mrs. Van did not want me to start home, but I said I could make it.

I had the milk in a pail with a cover on tight for that was the time milk bottles had not been invented and when I got home, I was just in time to catch Pa starting out to look for me. He had made the attempt before.

At that time, the men wore big bowler hats and he stuck his head out the door and a gust came along and it was good bye hat. And when we found it after the snow had gone, it was 1/2 mile below the house in a pond hole.

When I met him on his second try, he had a scarf tied around his head and ears and that was the only time I ever knew Pa to cover up his ears.

Now I guess you have got enough of the '88 blizzard, but do not let anyone tell you there has been anything like it up to 1947.—Daniel Rowlee Schoonover.

A letter to Lon Austin also talked about the Blizzard of '88.

Thomas Brady, Brooklyn, N.Y. to Albert (Lon) Austin, Eldred
April 5, 1888
Friend Albert,
I tell you, we had a hard time of it through the storm. The road was stopped for 3 days.

The company sent for all the men to come down to Park Ave. to shovel snow.

Well we went to work for about 1 hour when someone told us B.C.R.R. Co. was paying 40 cents an hour and of course that caused a tie up right away in the shovels, for they were only paying us 20.

Then we appointed a committee and sent them in the office to see the President and they came out with 30 cents an hour for us and after we found out that B.C.R.R. was only paying 20 cents an hour.

I hope you will come and see me and I will have a nice girl for you. Wishing you happy times.
Your Faithful Friend,
Thos. F. Brady

Rowlee Schoonover, Blacksmith
In 1888 Rowlee Schoonover was 16, and wanted to learn the blacksmith trade.

But there was nothing that could satisfy me but to learn the trade. So Mother gave in and so did Pa, with reservations. If I was bound to learn that trade, I must learn it all for he did not want any half way mechanics in his family.

So I went down to see Bill Cortright and asked him if he would take me on as an apprentice. That was the Spring of 1888, and I was 16 years old. He told me he thought I was not strong enough to stand it.

I told him I thought I could stand it. So he said, "There is a keg of horseshoes over there and if you can shoulder that keg, I will make a bargain with you with your folks' consent."

So I went over and tipped the keg over, rolled it up on my knees and got my arm around it and got it on my shoulder. So that was settled right there.

The family had moved to Brooklyn and was having pretty tough sledding to get along, so Ma wanted me to come home and help out. Kate [Parker, his half sister] and Em [his sister] was trying to keep the home together. So I asked to go home for a visit.

Well, when I got home, I could understand that they was having a pretty hard time getting along, so I made up my mind to stay and get a job and that was no easy thing in them days for that was before Brooklyn was consolidated with New York and everything was handled by Politicians and all you had to do was go down to Castle Gardens and get any kind of help you wanted.

Of course I looked for a job of horseshoer. We had a good friend of the family who told me to come to his place the next morning and he would take me down to Nostrand Ave. Car Barns and I would have no trouble at all.

Well we went down and they took my name and said they would send for me in a few days (the few days is going yet). I went to work for Mr. Shadlot in 1890.
—Daniel Rowlee Schoonover.

The next letter indicates Ell went back to Solomon City, Kansas, and the Parmenter farm—perhaps to settle the Parmenter Estate.

Ell's wife Emma, her sister Sarah Sophronia, son Henry Earl, and little Lillie, stayed in Eldred to take care of the farm.

Emma's very detailed letters of what she did on the farm while Ell was gone, show the hard work and thought that went into farming.

The letters are addressed to Mr. J.E. Austin in care of Henry Parmenter, Emma's brother, in

Casey at the Bat

Baseball would become a very important sport in Highland and the nearby towns.

Casey at the Bat, written by Ernest Thayer, and first published June 3, 1888, in the *San Francisco Examiner*, was a poem in my father, Art Austin's eclectic assortment. I have fond memories of Dad quoting all of the verses from memory.

The Outlook wasn't brilliant for the Mudville nine that day:
The score stood four to two, with but one inning more to play.
And then when Cooney died at first, and Barrows did the same,
A sickly silence fell upon the patrons of the game.

A straggling few got up to go in deep despair. The rest
Clung to that hope which springs eternal in the human breast;
They thought, if only Casey could get but a whack at that
We'd put up even money, now, with Casey at the bat.

But Flynn preceded Casey, as did also Jimmy Blake,
And the former was a lulu and the latter was a cake;
So upon that stricken multitude grim melancholy sat,
For there seemed but little chance of Casey's getting to the bat.

But Flynn let drive a single, to the wonderment of all,
And Blake, the much despised, tore the cover off the ball;
And when the dust had lifted, and the men saw what had occurred,
There was Jimmy safe at second and Flynn a-hugging third.

Then from 5,000 throats and more there rose a lusty yell;
It rumbled through the valley, it rattled in the dell;
It knocked upon the mountain and recoiled upon the flat,
For Casey, mighty Casey, was advancing to the bat.

There was ease in Casey's manner as he stepped into his place;
There was pride in Casey's bearing and a smile on Casey's face.
And when, responding to the cheers, he lightly doffed his hat,
No stranger in the crowd could doubt 'twas Casey at the bat.

Ten thousand eyes were on him as he rubbed his hands with dirt;
Five thousand tongues applauded when he wiped them on his shirt.
Then while the writhing pitcher ground the ball into his hip,
Defiance gleamed in Casey's eye, a sneer curled Casey's lip.

And now the leather-covered sphere came hurtling through the air,
And Casey stood a-watching it in haughty grandeur there.
Close by the sturdy batsman the ball unheeded sped
"That ain't my style," said Casey. "Strike one," the umpire said.

From the benches, black with people, there went up a muffled roar,
Like the beating of the storm waves on a stern and distant shore.
"Kill him! Kill the umpire!" shouted someone on the stand;
And its likely they'd a-killed him had not Casey raised his hand.

With a smile of Christian charity great Casey's visage shone;
He stilled the rising tumult; he bade the game go on;
He signaled to the pitcher, and once more the spheroid flew;
But Casey still ignored it, and the umpire said, "Strike two."

"Fraud!" cried the maddened thousands, and echo answered fraud;
But one scornful look from Casey and the audience was awed.
They saw his face grow stern and cold, they saw his muscles strain,
And they knew that Casey wouldn't let that ball go by again.

The sneer is gone from Casey's lip, his teeth are clenched in hate;
He pounds with cruel violence his bat upon the plate.
And now the pitcher holds the ball, and now he lets it go,
And now the air is shattered by the force of Casey's blow.

Oh, somewhere in this favored land the sun is shining bright;
The band is playing somewhere, and somewhere hearts are light,
And somewhere men are laughing, and somewhere children shout;
But there is no joy in Mudville— mighty Casey has struck out.
—Ernest Thayer.

Solomon City, Kansas.

Emma's letters to Ell indicate they had a strong marriage. So it was surprising that in later years Ell and Em divorced. But these letters of 1888 were written during happier times of marriage.

Emma Austin, Eldred, to J. Eldred Austin, Solomon City, Kans.
October 21, 1888
Dear Eldred,
 Another Sunday has come around. How long it seems since you went away. Lillie [4 years old] says it seems like 29 weeks.
 I received both of your postals and letter and suppose you have mine. When I got your first card I got a letter for you from Day. He said he would have written

The Village Post Office at Barryville (also called the River). "Thursday I had to send Earl to the River again." —Emma Parmenter Austin. Postcard courtesy of Kevin Marrinan.

before but Henry [her brother in Kansas] said you were coming out there this fall. That he was going to start for Michigan the next day (the 13th) to try and raise some money.

I should say Effie [Henry Parenter's wife] did give you a surprise. What was the reason they did not tell us of it? I don't wonder Henry has the rheumatism.

Does it seem good to you to get back to the old place? Which is best, here or there? Have you any idea how much longer it will take you?

We have had but one whole pleasant day. That was Monday. I walked to Barryville in the morning and came back with Earl [her son]. Thursday I had to send Earl to the River [Barryville] again. The rest of the time he has been doing little things—cleaning the hen house, fixing poles, mangers, doors to the barn, etc.

Sophronia has been crippled up all the week with rheumatism. She could scarcely move or breathe without crying out. She is some better now but still bad.

Yesterday morning the sun shone brightly so I hurried and done my washing in the morning. After dinner Earl and I went to work on that apple tree in the lane. Daily came for his Tuesday. He took 8 bu., 1 pk., and paid $1.

We worked hard till chore time. It was raw and chilly with an occasional sprinkle. We gathered I should think 10 bushels and it looks as if there are as many more on the tree.

Today is very disagreeable. The thermometer stands at 34 and the wind goes right through a body.

Thursday morning Lillie was threatened with the croup. She was breathing badly so I got up at half past 2 and made the fires. At 10 minutes of 3, I roused her enough to give her some Piso and grease her throat.

The fires bothered me so I did not get any water hot till half past 4. By that time she was badly choked and barked terribly. I took a fruit can and filled it nearly full of boiling water and put in a goodly supply of turpentine and put it on the cricket by the bureau.

She was asleep all this time so I did not wake her. By and by she began to breather easier and by 7 o'clock she could cough it loose. You can imagine my relief.

It seems to me as though the animals were eating a great deal of hay but I don't know. They all eat it up clean except Collins' cow who tosses part of it out with her horns under her feet.

Flossie jumps all the fences, so we will have to keep her in. She has been having turnip tops, but they are gone so I suppose we will have to give her hay.

The Collins' cow gets the same feed as the others now. We have not weighed her milk lately but at one time she had gained 2.5 lbs. K.M. eats her feed all right now.

The Canfield cow has been down here twice since you went away. She is a nuisance. She puts the mischief into our cattle. The first time she led them up the road at full gallop (at night) into the woods.

Whitey seemed possessed and we could scarcely get her into the stable. The next time she came, the lane gate was open and she went up on the hill. I went and shut the gate so she wouldn't get to the other cattle. By and by she came back and waited at the gate. The others saw her and wanted to get to her.

Dory came along and without saying a word to anyone, opened the gate and let her out and drove her home. I knew he had no business to, but I wanted no words with him without your sanction so said nothing. As soon as the cattle were turned out into the road, Whitey ran way to the schoolhouse.

Thursday Dory came to the door and said Lon sent him for the sieves; that Tom [Collins] told Lon that he told you when you got through with them to bring them back. I knew that did not sound like him, so I told him if he brought me an order from Mr. or Mrs. Collins they could have them, not unless.

Yesterday I sold Mr. Osier 19 dozen eggs at .25. Your school tax is due Wednesday. It amounts to $2.65. Between us we can meet it. I have the receipt for your state loan interest.

Earl works hard and gets very tired. He has scarcely a minute he can call his own. I do not know when he can do much outdoors work. The weather is so unfavorable.

People haven't all their potatoes dug and can't and they are rotting badly.

We will all of us be glad when you come home. This responsibility is pretty heavy on my shoulders and I will be glad to shift it onto yours. I don't want it to make you leave there any sooner than you otherwise would.

Take good care of yourself for if anything should happen to you, I don't know what I should do. I feel that our lives are too short to have anything but perfect love and faith in one another.

Earl can not get his apples ground. Mr. Barnes is the only man that grinds this year.

Lillie has written her letter. She says she has written so much she could not tell me what she wrote. She says, "Do you suppose Papa will answer my letter?"

I hope by the time you get this you will know about how much longer you have got to stay. The papers think the yellow fever will not be entirely done away with till the last of next month. So be sure

Suspension bridge from Shohola, Pennsylvania, to Barryville, New York. "We took Mame and tied up at Gus's and walked to Shohola to send you a telegram." Postcard from Defeo Collection, courtesy of Kevin Marrinan.

and not go till all danger is over and if you can't wait that long, you had better not go at all.

With much love to my dear husband, I will bid you good night.

Yours lovingly, Emmie

October 29, 1888
Dear Eldred,
So yesterday we took Mame and tied up at Gus's and walked to Shohola to send you a telegram. I waited for an answer till after 3 o'clock. Then as I thought Earl would be late with his chores we left word to send it up by mail.

It commenced to rain. When it slackened we started. We had gone but a little way before down it came again. We were smart enough to leave the umbrella in the buggy so by the time we reached Gus's we were a sorry looking pair.

It turned suddenly cold with a little snow mixed with the rain and we had to face it. We put our feet into warm water just as soon as we got home and had some warm drink expecting both of us would have bad colds today, but we came out all right.

This afternoon Mr. Sanders brought your answering telegram and I got your letter of the 25th.

Don't you think it would be risky to let Harve Watts have the place. He used to drink didn't he? He may again and burn everything up. Doesn't he smoke? As for the loan, if you

The Parker house built and owned by James Y. Parker was near the center of Eldred. "The Parker calf broke the west side of the hen yard down and as fast as we fixed it, she would jump on it." Photo courtesy of Christena Stevens Myers, granddaughter of James Y. Parker.

can get it from the right parties, I don't suppose you could do much better. I told you I expected you would have to pay 10% commission. Be sure and get enough to cover everything.

We haven't had but about half a dozen pleasant days since you have been gone and Earl has had to work accordingly.

After you left, the apples, cabbages, onions, and turnips in the garden were got in, and potatoes sorted and put in cellar. There were 5 bushels in the pile by the door.

I go up with Earl every night to see that everything is all right and most always do the feeding.

When we cut K.M.'s feed down to half, she began to eat better. The Collins' cow gets the same feed as Dutchy and others and eats her hay good now. She gave 6 pounds of milk tonight. K.M. gave 8, which is 1 pound more than she gave when you left off keeping account. Whitey gave 6 pounds which is 3 pounds less. I don't think she has done so well since she got so wild for the Canfield cow.

I told Lon of her when he came for Black Hawk. He said he would keep her home. Gus owes us 100 meal.

The Collins' cow I think is beginning to look a great deal better. She likes her feed.

Earl got the manure on the east back furrow in the garden and plowed that. Has nearly enough on the north, will then plow that. He has to do a little at a time as it keeps raining.

Gus says he will take the roosters sometime. I have said nothing to him about K.M. as he has had an attack of rheumatism and could scarcely crawl.

The Parker calf broke the west side of the hen yard down and as fast as we fixed it she would jump on it. She has got the other calves so that now they jump the slab fence anywhere. She won't drink milk but gets into the hen house every chance she can and drinks their buttermilk. We have to keep the door shut and let the hens out the window.

We let Dot run on the hill and in the orchard back of the barn. We could let her in around the house only she could go way to the rye lot.

Uncle Jesse has chopped wood for us 2 days—almost 2 cords. He says there is enough to last till the holidays. We owe him.

You never saw anyone so pleased as Lillie was with her letter. She said, "I am so happy. I never was so happy in all my life. I have got a letter all my own." We have had to read it to her about a dozen times. She has heard it so often that she can read nearly all of it herself.

Lillie has written you a letter [small page with scribbles to "Dear Papa"], and wants to know when you are coming home.

I shall be glad when you get your business done out there and get home for I miss you so much. If you get home safely we won't be parted again very soon if I have anything to say about it.

Your loving Emmie

November 9, 1888
Dear Eldred,

You surely have had a very busy time. Did Day really mortgage your cattle. If he did he was a rascal truly. Day will have to pay Brinks' note won't he.

Gus was here this afternoon and brought me 300 of meal. That will last till you come home, if you don't stay too long. I told him to bring me 200 of bran.

Gus said he didn't remember exactly K.M.'s weight but thought it was about 550 pounds. He said your price was .06-1/2.

He did not take the hide till today which is one day over a week since he took the meat. D. Hallock salted it but yet it smelt some. I think if it is spoilt, Gus is *the one that ought to lose it for he promised to take it the next day.*

I sold the head to D. Hallock for .25. He said that was the customary price. That will make her bring just $36 without the hide. That won't be as much as you expected, will it? Gus thought it was a big price.

I am sorry to hear that Henry [Emma's brother] is sick. Florence had the erysipelas in the eye years ago and she cured it by applying a cranberry poultice. I think Henry had better try it. I think Effie [Henry's wife] must be glad you are there to take care of the cows.

How do you like store keeping? Are you getting your hand in ready to start one of your own?

Lillie wants me to tell you about her letter right away. In it she says "I thank you very much for my pictures and letters. I wish you would tell me when you are coming home, if you know won't you dear Papa?"

When you get ready to start let us know and if it is a fair day we will meet you at the gate or I will come down the road to meet you.

About the money, we think $500 a piece [for Emma and her sister] will do us. We may not want to use it this winter, but if we don't get it now we can't till the mortgage expires.

The yellow fever has sickened me of Florida. It is at Gainesville; also at Enterprise.

I have Washington Territory on the brain now. Henry Earl says the climate is fine and thinks the Territory has a bright future before it. He says a town lot at Seattle, containing 5,000 square feet, worth now about $50, will soon be worth quite a large sum. There is where the Navy Yard is to be placed.

I think some of having H. Earl invest some of my money in town lots. Then when the mortgage expires I may have something to pay it with.

There is one thing sure, I am never going to go away from you, for any length of time to stay if I can help it. (If you will have me.) If you come home safely you and I must spend the rest of our days together.

If the place can't be sold now, don't you think it would be well to put it into someone's hands to sell.

When it does not rain, we turn Flossie out and she stays around the house. If we turned Dot on the rye lot she would go too and be apt to break the fences down.

The cattle I think are looking well. The Collins' cow has picked up a good deal I think. This morning Dutchy gave 10 pounds, Texina, 7-1/2, Whitey and Collins, 6. Collins gave 7 lbs. last night. Plato looks well and feels good.

Your loving Emmie

Henry Parmenter Jr., brother of Emma Austin. Photo courtesy of Katherine Calkin Traxler.

This next letter indicates Aida was still attending Oswego Normal School.

Aida Austin, Oswego, N.Y. to Dr. Sheldon, Oswego, N.Y.
November 12, 1888
Dr. Sheldon
Dear Sir,
I was absent from exercises Friday by your permission.
Yours respectfully,
Aida Austin

Emma Austin, Eldred, to J. Eldred (Ell) Austin, Solomon City, Kans.
November 25, 1888
Dear Eldred,
I sent you the deeds a week ago Saturday.
I bought my feed of Sharp for $1.15 for meal and $1 for bran; freight, $1, drawing, $1.50, returning bags, .25. I told Sharp you would settle with him. I paid the rest.

I went to Ozenbaugh and bought the coal. Daily is to bring it tomorrow. I went to A.S. Myers and paid his bill. He charged no interest and gave me a receipt. Your father was the only one in the store beside when I paid him.

Gus said he sent you back Brinks' note. Did you get it? I asked him how our accounts stood. He said he owed me about .58 beside the hide.

Since then I have bought 3 gallons of oil. I gave him a good talking to about the hide. I don't know what he intends to do.

We are counting the days till you come home. Your board bill must amount to something by this time. Have you got your corn husked yet?

Today we had our first snow storm. It commenced about noon and about two inches fell by 6 o'clock. It is still snowing. We turned the cattle in the middle of the afternoon also the calves. The snow turned to sleet in the night but this morning it is raining.

The Old Cider Mill above Eldred, New York. "...all but the cider apples which are spoiling badly." Postcard courtesy of Mary Briggs Austin.

Lillie has a bad cold in her head. I think it is working down on her lungs. She came near having the croup this morning about daybreak, but I think I checked it with the turpentine and hot water. I think she caught cold while we were picking over the apples. We got them down cellar last week, all but the cider apples, which are spoiling badly.

Whose hand do you think we had better put the place in to sell. S. thinks we had better sell if we can't get more than $15,000.

Earl says he wished your next letter would tell him to meet you at the depot, but we can't expect that yet. Have you been to John's [Emma's brother] yet? How are you making out about the title to the place?

Kelso [in Eldred] is building a store on the corner opposite Beaumonts. I don't suppose he will have the Office another term. He is wild to go to Washington Territory. He thinks he would get rich in a short time. He wants to sell his place badly.

Nov. 26th: I was glad to get yours of 21st this afternoon. I was afraid you might have got hurt in dehorning cattle.

It has rained all day and everything is all slush. It makes nasty walking. Lillie I think is considerably better tonight.

Don't you worry about things at home. We are getting along very well for two greenhorns. I put the bees in the house sometime ago and have given them some of the dark comb with honey but they don't eat it very good. I think they would eat the honey sooner than candy.

The calves all ate their bran tonight. It was so bad both overhead and underfoot today that we gave them all some hay.

Do you think you will be home by the 20th? I think your father will try and have Mom sue you, but he is so afraid of the law I don't know as he would. He probably got your letter tonight. I hope he won't sue me for I don't want to go to court. I hope you can pay everybody when you come home so no one can bother you. Be sure and get enough.

Write as often as you can to you loving but waiting wife,
Emmie

December 2, 1888
Dear Eldred,
Notice was served on me that your father held your note to Mort. Not knowing what he might do next and being ignorant of the law, I went to see Mr. Whitney, this afternoon as he is away all the week.

Mr. Whitney says the notice was simply to hold me as an endorser. He thinks your father will let it rest there till you come home, as if he pushed it now in your absence, it would bring down the disapproval of the whole community upon him. It would be too bare-faced a thing for him to do. He thinks your father cares too much for his reputation to do it.

He cannot serve a summons on me till Tuesday and he has got to serve one on you at the same time. So he can do nothing till you come home.

I do not think I had better telegraph you as I may hear favorable from Jere [her brother] and a dispatch to Kansas costs so much (.75). If I get it from Jere, I will telegraph then, "All's well."

Mr. Whitney says I need not be the least uneasy as he thinks he can fix it all right till you come home. He feels sure your father will do nothing. Which is more faith than I have.

Mr. Whitney told me that the reason you lost the trusteeship of the school was out of no personal feeling toward you, but the people had made up their minds they wouldn't have Minnie for a teacher again. They knew you would employ her and Daily wouldn't. I asked why she wasn't liked, but they wouldn't tell me. He said this was told him by parties that knew. He thinks when the financial matters are settled between you and your folks, you will be friends once more.

Now don't worry. I don't feel uneasy. The most I minded was having to answer the summons, but Mr. W. will relieve me of that.

Your loving Emmie

December 9, 1888
Dear Eldred,

I am glad to hear there is some prospect of your getting home before long. The waiting has been long and wearisome. I got S.J. Gardner to cash my draft. He had to send to Port Jervis and the expressage cost me .35.

On the 6th, I received an envelope addressed to me from your father to both of us. It was requesting us to meet him at Myers's store yesterday afternoon at 2 p.m. to make arrangements about settling the note or he would take the proper course to collect the same.

If I hadn't had the money, I should have taken no notice of him, but I didn't want to keep it in the house, so went down. I did not get there till 3. He was not there, nor had he been there.

Myers offered to send for him. I told him that he made the appointment, if he didn't choose to keep it, he didn't need to. I think he was curious to know what it was about for presently, he slipped out and told him and then got back to his desk before your father came in.

He said, "You want to see me?" in a sort of insolent way.

I said, "I thought you wanted to see me. You sent me a note to that effect."

He looked this way and that and then said, "I want you to pay that note." I asked the amount. Presently he said, "Now if it is going to discommode you to pay the whole of it just now, why—"

I interrupted him with, "It is not going to discommode me in the least." Finally I paid him and got the note.

I got a cord of wood (oak) from Gussie Myers—all the largest pieces were split. Earl split the rest easily in a short time.

Santa Fe Avenue in Salina, Kansas, looking south from the National Hotel roof. Photo courtesy of Katherine Calkin Traxler.

Emma Austin's brother's store in Kansas. "I do not think I had better telegraph you as I may hear favorable from Jere [her brother] and a dispatch to Kansas costs so much (.75)." Stereograph card courtesy of Katherine Calkin Traxler.

When you send the papers, be sure and tell me what to do.

The more I see of this people here, the less I like to stay here. I had a time with old man Clark.

Will you lose anything through Day? Was his share of the cattle mortgaged or did you get possession of them? Have you paid the taxes?

I see Jay Gould has raised the rate on the R.R. Your fare will be

A young Gus Myers near the Myers' barn. "I got a cord of wood (oak) from Gussie Myers." The rock on the right is in many of the outside photos and still in that location. Photo courtesy of Stuart and Geraldine Mills Russell.

apt to be more than when you went out.

I wrote to Root about the bees. He said to feed candy instead of the honey and that the reason why they didn't eat the honey, they were too cold. They must be put in a cellar or packed with chaff. There have been about a double handful died since putting them in the little room.

Let me know when you are going to start for home. We will all be so glad to have you back again.

Write again soon to your loving Emma

December 9, 1888
Dear Papa,

I thought I would write and tell you a little how things are getting along. I have not got all of the things done that you laid out for me to do for it has been bad weather. It snowed last night about 2 inches deep.

Mr. Clark came up here the other day and bought 2-1/2 bushels of apples. We measured them out in the tin measure and I took them down for him. The next day he came up and said that they did not hold out. He said that he put them into a flour barrel and it lacked 7 inches of being full.

So he went up to A.S. Myers and measured out a half bushel and it filled it level full.

That made him mad and he thought we were trying to cheat him. So he came up, told Mama that they did not hold.

I went up to the barn and got the other measure and they did not vary but very little. He did not understand how that could be, so we took our measure down and compared it with Myers and it held more than his did. Then we measured the whole of them and it lacked about a half a peck. But he thought a peck would be about right, so mama thought she would let it go at that.

I have got about everything done that I can do now and I think I will go to school tomorrow. I will be glad when you come home. Mama said she will be glad too, so she won't have to run all over the country and I think there will be a glad house all round. Mama said you would have to be our Christmas present.

With love from your boy, Earl

December 13, 1888
Dear Eldred,

We received the papers night before last. Mr. Whitney is not a N.P., but said he always did such work for W. Johnson. So he came over in the afternoon and wrote the letter for me. Charged $1.00. As it is to be recorded out of the county, he said I must send it to Monticello and have the county clerk's certificate attached to it.

I shall send it there this morning. I will then forward it to you when it is returned. So try and be all ready to start when you get it, for I want my boy home again.

I hope you will not have any trouble getting Day off the place. You had better have the ones that take the place understand that if we have a chance to sell, we are going to.

Lillie had one of her bad turns yesterday. She is better this morning.

Yours lovingly, Emmie

Ell Austin Arrives in Eldred

Finally on December 13, 1888, Ell arrived at his home in Eldred. It had taken some time to track down the owners of a couple deeds in order to resolve Henry Parmenter's estate, as well as the other business matters Ell seemed to have taken care of.

There were no unsettled claims against Henry Parmenter Sr. according to a December 24, 1888 document signed by Henry Parmenter Jr. and James E. Austin.

Lon Austin, Eldred, to His Sister
December 20, 1888
Dear Sister,

I have been busy making hoops and they are having a series of meeting in the Congregational Church.

Mr. Willcox, their minister gave a discourse each night of last week on "Pilgrim Progress," which was quite interesting. Consequently I attended each night. Therefore I neglected to answer your letter, but as I was good for a whole week you will pardon the neglect.

Ell has returned at last. He arrived a week ago, but he does not show up much. I have not seen him since he returned. I don't believe he brought back much money with him.

Are you going round by New York or not when you come home, for I want you to get me something if you do.

Let me know if you need some money. I suppose you will be home in about two weeks. I hope you are keeping well.

Minnie Kelso and Tom Collins were home during the holidays. Emma Collins is going to New York Saturday to live.

It is nearly church time, so I will have to close.

Your aff. brother, Lon

Maria Austin, N.Y.C., to Aida Austin
December 25, 1888
Dear Sister Aida,

Christmas has come and I am going to lay everything aside for a little while and write to you. Ida is playing the piano and I much more like dancing than writing.

Well, I didn't spend all Thanksgiving eating as you did. But you may think I spent it worse when I tell you I was reading "Mignon." I think Mignon perfectly hideous, but I blame her husband more than I do her. Although he was a splendid man, no woman could love nor respect him. I had no patience with him. But I was just in love with Leo and Olga. I am so glad they are married for they are just lovely. You had oughta read the book.

The tall man and the short man are boarding at Net's. I haven't seen her yet. Ida goes to Philadelphia tomorrow to spend the week.

Dear little Tom is getting along splendid in school and at home everybody loves him, even other children in the street.

My pencil is only about an inch long and my hand is tired of

Johnstown Flood

Remnants of a house in the Johnstown Flood, 1889. Photo: Library of Congress, Prints and Photographs Division: LC-USZ62-60957.

On May 31, 1889, the United States had the worst flood in the 19th century. The Johnstown Flood (The Great Flood of 1889) took place in Johnstown, Pennsylvania, some 300 miles southwest of Eldred, New York.

There had been an extremely heavy rainfall, causing the South Fork Dam (14 miles upstream of Johnstown) to fail, releasing 20 million tons of water.

Over 2,200 people were killed, including 99 entire families. Four square miles of Johnstown were completely destroyed. Property damage was $17 million; and the clean up took years.

It took 7 days and nights to replace the huge stone railroad viaduct that had almost disappeared in the flood.

By June 2 the Pennsylvania Railroad was able to provide service from Pittsburgh, bringing food, clothing, medicine, and other necessities to the disaster area.

Clara Barton, who led the American Red Cross in its relief effort, was in the area for over 5 months.

Help for the flood victims came from all over the U.S. and 18 foreign countries. There were up to 7,000 relief workers.

—*wikipedia.org.*

Teacher of the third grade certificate for Aida A. Austin of Eldred, March 15, 1889. Aida's highest score of 95 was in Orthography (spelling) and reading. Courtesy of Katherine Calkin Traxler.

holding it so I will stop writing.
Ever your loving sister,
Maria

Ell Austin Buys a Cow
January 15, 1889
Received of J.E. Austin, $17 payment in full for one cow.
   Emma Collins

Aida Austin Receives Her Teaching Certificate
On March 16, 1889, Aida Austin was licensed to teach school in District No. 4 in the Town of Highland for 6 months.

Invitation from Sunny Slope Cottage, Eldred, to Lon Austin
September 1889
Mr. L. Austin,
   You are cordially invited to attend a bean-bag party given by the Misses Cobb of Eldred on Wed. September 18, 1889.
   E. Mabelle & J. Florence Cobb

Lon and possibly others in his family had bought land and were going to build a house according to this next letter from Tom Collins, a former neighbor in Eldred.

Tom Collins, Mount Vernon, N.Y., to Lon Austin
October 19, 1889
Friend Lon,
   I received your letter with the money all right and am very much obliged to you. I handed it right over as soon as I got it.
   Now you want to know if I will sell any of my lumber. I don't want to sell any of it. I want all of it for future use.
   There has been 3 parties that wanted to buy it of me, but I told them that I did not want to sell it. I don't want to sell any kind of wood off my place to anyone as I expect to go back there and work my home.
   We have just heard that you have bought some land and expect to build a house. Well I am glad to hear of it. Lon, don't go in debt for it. This is my advice to everyone that is commencing in life. I hope you will do well.
   I will now close with kind regards to all the family.
   I am as ever your friend,
   T.K. Collins

There was a list of signatures from a church organization, around 1889, in my great-grandpa Henry Austin's 1872 Cartage book. The scans of the signatures can be seen in the Appendix, page 452.

1889 Church Signatures
Wm. A. Kyte
E.B. Wilson
E. Hardcastle
James W. Sergeant
A.J. Ingram
R.C. Eldred
H.L. Austin
Pvt. Sergeant
James Eldred Jr.
A.A. Austin
Minnie C. Kelso
James Boyd
J. Boyd
E.E. Smith
C.M. Austin
Mr. Stephen Carmichael
Aida A. Austin
Alice C. Kelso
Annie M. Leavenworth
Bertie Kyte
John P. Bradley
Frank Clayton
Charley Kendall
Lulu E. Beck

In Chapter 6 we will talk more about the Austin family in the 1890s, and we'll find out why Helena's letters to Lon have stopped.

Chapter 5 talks about the Leavenworth family, some townsfolk, and boarding houses in the Town of Highland by 1900.

Chapter 5
Sublime Scenery
Highland Boarding Houses, 1890–1900

Few of the hundreds of people who summer at White Lake and the many charming spots in its vicinity know that within a few miles of them are numberless treats in the way of sublime scenery:

Beautiful glens with their gorgeous waterfalls, trout streams, lakes, beautiful lakes, and numerous groves where picnicking could be indulged in without the many misfortunes which are wont to attend these attempts at frivolity.

Things beautiful and interesting are constantly appearing, too numerous to recall here.—Charles E. Proctor.

Sublime scenery beckoned summer visitors to boarding houses and hotels in the hamlets of Highland and other villages along the Delaware River as the 19th Century came to a close.

The 1890s would see the decline of the D&H Canal which had been responsible for the growth of the area since 1828. Trains, which transported passengers and goods such as petroleum, livestock, lumber, and dairy products, were not so limited by winter weather, droughts, and floods.

Summer tourists and boarding houses would flourish into the 1960s.

If the boarding house was not on a lake, or stream, there was one not far away. Visitors to picturesque Highland's boarding houses (summer homes) in Barryville, Eldred, Venoge, or Yulan would have a healthy, enjoyable vacation—just as advertised in both newspapers and railway booklets.

Meals would be made from fresh farm ingredients—milk, butter, eggs, and produce. Farms were close by, and many of the proprietors were also farmers. The many apple trees meant there would be cider to look forward to in the fall.

Whether you stayed at Bodine's and enjoyed French gourmet cooking, or at a home that featured typical local fare (like the Leavenworth's), you could plan on excellent meals.

The sportsman could hunt for deer, bear (sometimes), rabbit, and wild pigeons; or fish for trout, perch, pickerel, and bass. Hunting dogs were available for a fee. Some places had horse stables.

Boarding House Activities
There was boating (canoes were popular) and swimming (bathing). Some places offered archery, croquet, dancing, bowling, lawn tennis, or perhaps a piano for guests to play.

Picnic grounds and sometimes

The Bluff which looked down over the Delaware River and Erie Railroad was a favorite site to visit. Postcard courtesy of Kevin Marrinan.

View from the Bluff showing the Delaware River and billows of smoke from a train going down the track. Photo by Mary Marrinan, courtesy of Kevin Marrinan.

View from the back of the Congregational Church in Barryville with the Barryville-Shohola Bridge in the distance. Photo courtesy of Minisink Valley Historical Society.

a playground for children were available. Arrangements could be made to visit other points of interest—complete with a picnic lunch.

Shohola Glen was one place to visit. Or maybe a trip to Port Jervis with a stop near the Hawk's Nest for a view of the Delaware River.

The Bluff which also looked down over the Delaware River and across to the Erie Railroad was another favorite site to visit. There vacationers carved their initials into the shale, took photos, or smooched. If you weren't from the area, a guide from the resort would help you locate the hard-to-find Bluff.

Hayrides, ice cream socials, church bazaars, dances, plays, and town fairs were other events for the summer guests.

Meet Us at Shohola Station

Vacationers to the Town of Highland would write or telegraph the proprietor of the summer home of their choice as to when they would arrive. The guests would be met at the Shohola train station in Pennsylvania across the Delaware River from Barryville. This was one of the ways Truman Leavenworth helped out at Echo Hill Farm House. My grandfather Mort Austin met guests at Shohola for over 30 years to take them to his boarding house.

At different times I would drive the ox team down to get the boarders, but the 7 miles was too much for them in hot weather.
At Shohola the wagons, carriages, and other kinds of vehicles came to get the summer boarders for miles around.
—*Lou Kloss Memoirs.*

There were times when it cost more to take the buggies across the bridge than to walk. Then the horse and buggies lined up along River Road on the New York side.

Someone was sent over the bridge to the Shohola Station to carry the luggage and to let the guests know where the carriage or wagon was waiting. The summer visitors walked across the bridge, and the driver took them to their destination.

The Town of Highland's boarding houses were up to 7 miles away from the Shohola Depot. We'll visit the summer homes in Eldred and Venoge (4–7 miles to the northeast) later in this chapter.

The Barryville-Shohola Bridge and the Spring House
The Barryville-Shohola suspension bridge ended (or started) in Barryville near Stephen St. John Gardner's property and George Layman's Spring House on River Road.

You may remember from

A group stopped along the Hawk's Nest Road for a photo. The Delaware River is in the background. Photo courtesy of Minsink Valley Historical Society.

Guests playing lawn tennis at the Greig home. Photo in the collection of Ed Grotecloss, courtesy of Kevin Marrinan.

The Spring House on the left was owned by George Layman in 1900. "Mr. Layman employs it for summer boarding and entertainment of travelers." The Barryville-Shohola Suspension Bridge on the right. Postcard in Defeo Collection, courtesy of Kevin Marrinan.

A grandson of the Toasperns with his dog. Maple Grove Farm is on the left. Photo courtesy of Bill Ihlo.

Maple Grove Farm first owned by Henry Christian and Ida Heyen Toaspern. Postcard courtesy of Larry Stern.

Chapter 1, that Stephen St. John Gardner owned the larger part of the Barryville-Shohola Bridge, because he was able to purchase the rights from Chauncey Thomas's heirs.

During the last preceding summer and fall [1900], Stephen St. John Gardner renovated the structure [bridge] generally, added additional cables; laid a new floor, supplied new stringers, erected a new and improved railing and the bridge is now a safe passageway and a good source of income…

[Nearby] is the beautiful and valuable house buildings and premises of George Layman.

Mr. Layman has enlarged the house, improved and beautified the grounds and now presents a premises that, for its location and attractiveness, may vie with any in the land. He employs it for summer boarding and entertainment of travelers and the comfortable entertainment and moderate charges combined, insures a general custom to his place.—Johnston, pp. 351–3.

George, his wife Mary Doolittle, his mother Mary Layman, and two nephews, Chester and George Doolittle lived in the Spring House.

River Road by the Spring House connected with Barryville-Yulan Road, which went west, then curved north to Yulan about 3 miles away.

Toaspern Family

On its way to Yulan, the Barryville-Yulan Road passed Corkscrew Road which went to the boarding house of the Toaspern Family where Henry Christian (Chris), Ida, Arthur, and Walter Toaspern lived. The house would later be called Maple Grove Farm.

Meta Toaspern married John Lass. In 1900 they had three children: Jay, Charles, and baby Helen Lass.

In 1900 Arthur Toaspern was 15, and Walter was 8. Walt walked to the Barryville schoolhouse which we will mention when we travel Brook Road north to Eldred.

Boarding Houses Near Yulan
By 1900 there were a few other boarding houses in the area between Barryville and Yulan.

William and Margaret Wolfe were the proprietors of Mount Pleasant. Herman and Belle Barber ran Mountain Farm House.

Fredrick Peterson and his two children Erick and Matilda (all from Sweden) had a boarding house.

Andrew and Sophia Peterson, also from Sweden, had a boarding house. Their daughters Anna and Matilda, and two boarders, Anna Prange and Anna Redding lived with them.

One of the Peterson Houses was near the Yulan Schoolhouse.

Fred and Mary Metzger's bowling alley was north of Yulan. It had a dance hall on the second floor. Fred, a saloon keeper, and Mary also had a boarding house.

John and Matilda Metzger had a boarding house in the Yulan area. They had been married 46 years. Their daughters Matilda and Harriet helped out.

Theodore West farmed. He and his wife Phebe lived north of Yulan near Beaver Brook Mill Pond. In 1895 they advertised for boarders for their West Farm *(see p. 159)*.

Airport Road
At Yulan, the Barryville-Yulan Road changed names. The road around Washington Lake will be referred to as Airport Road, its current name, because the name has changed several times.

Airport Road went along the northwest side of Washington Lake, passed the Bradley and Leavenworth homes (which we will talk about soon), zig-zagged

Fred and Mary Metzger's bowling alley and dance hall, north of Yulan Corners. Photo courtesy of Helen Hensel Oset.

View on Eldred-Yulan Road heading towards Eldred from Yulan. Bodine Lake is on the left and Bodine's Cottage would have been on the right. Photo from Helen Hensel Oset.

The Waning Season at Yulan, 1894

The Last Dance the Jolliest One of the Summer
The season drawing to a close has been the most successful ever known in this section of Sullivan County, and the boarding house keepers are correspondingly happy.

Washington Lake is the center of attraction for the boarders in this neighborhood, and its mirror-like surface is dotted daily with merry rowing parties and the more sober fishermen luring from the depths the pickerel and black bass.

Last Wednesday evening at Prang's Lake View Farm House was given what will probably prove to be the last barn dance of the season and it was pronounced by all to be the jolliest. The barn was prettily decorated with autumn foliage, sumach and golden rod, but these were far outshone by the bevy of pretty girls…

Refreshments were served after the dance. The music was by Professor Kinley.—Brooklyn Daily Eagle, *September 9, 1894.*

Cold Spring Farm Boarding House owned by Milton Crandall was west of Beaver Brook Road, off of Irishtown Road. Postcard courtesy of Kevin Marrinan.

At the River (as Barryville was sometimes still called) there was a sawmill and gristmill. Postcard from the Defeo Collection, courtesy of Kevin Marrinan.

Joseph and Juliana Maier's Pine Grove Farm on Crawford Road. This second home replaced the first one which burnt down in the early 1900s. Photo courtesy of the Bosch Family.

a bit, and connected with Eldred-Yulan Road just west of Eldred Corners.

Eldred-Yulan Road

At Yulan Corners, Eldred-Yulan Road went east along the south side of Bodine Lake, continued northeast past Crawford Road, turned right, and connected with Proctor Road at Eldred Corners.

Justin, 74, and Adele Bodine still had Little Pond Cottage on Bodine Lake in 1900. At some point, Justin's son Henry began running Bodine's Cottages.

Crandall, Kloss, and Wolff Families

Beaver Brook Road went northwest from Yulan Corners and curved north as it passed Woods and Irishtown Roads. Just off Irishtown Road was Cold Spring Farm (advertised in 1897) owned by Milton and Martha Crandall. Milton had hand dug wells and had run a pipe from the spring to the house.

The family of Lou Kloss, whose *Memoirs* have provided a good idea of life during the years that this story takes place, lived in Tusten. In 1900 Lou and his parents Ernest and Emma Kloss had been in the United States for 20 years. Lou's siblings, Willie, Karl, and Frieda, and his grandmother Fredericke Wolf lived with them.

Frieda Kloss, Lou's sister, would marry Carl Wolff, son of Charles and Janette Wolff.

Charles and Janette Wolff's 5 children, Carl, Frank, Agnes, Albert, Norman, and a servant, Lorna Wood, lived in their home, in 1900.

There were at least two Wolff families (with 3 different spellings) that had boarding houses. The relationship between these Wolff families is unknown.

There were other boarding houses in or near Barryville. Steven Wormuth was a boarding house keeper. So were Fredrick and Margery Schwab, and Horace Twitchell. The Schwabs had a young daughter and a servant.

The Families on Crawford Road
The Maier and Myers boarding houses were on Crawford Road, about 2 miles north of Barryville.

Cemetery Road (Mail Road) went north from Barryville, passed Montoza (Barryville) Cemetery (created by Stephen St. John Gardner, Oliver Calkin, and John W. Johnston in 1884), and connected to Crawford Road.

Joseph and Juliana Maier, who we talked about in Chapter 3, ran Pine Grove Farm on Crawford Road. Their children Julius and Anna lived with them. Daughter Mary Maier was married to Wilhelm Bosch and lived near Highland Lake.

The Fred Myers Boarding House was also on Crawford Road. In 1894 Charles Fred Myers, a widower, married Mary Frances Bradley Scott, a widow.

Fred had 3 children: Della, Charles Fred, and Harvey Myers from his first marriage; and Mary had a daughter, Lottie Scott. Fred and Mary would have four children including daughter Ada, the mother of Berniece Wells Haas.

Fred Myers Farm House was 3 miles from the Shohola Station at an elevation of 1,800 feet.

Can accommodate 25 guests comfortably; Rooms large, airy, clean and well furnished; Table supplied with fresh products of the farm; Wide porch all around the house; Plenty of shade, piano, good livery, daily mails;

Fred Myers Farm House on Crawford Road. Photo courtesy of Christena Stevens Myers.

Ira Austin's home. Ira and Minerva Drake Austin lived in their old house east of Halfway Brook and south of the Barryville Schoolhouse. Photo courtesy of Christina Watts.

Postcard of the Old Mill Dam. The Village Blacksmith Shop (right) was owned by Ira M. Austin. The house and three-story barn on the left (obscured by trees and hard to see) was owned by Irving Quick. The Old Mill Dam was used for water power to run the gristmill and sawmill. Information and photo comment from Austin Smith, historian. Courtesy of the Town of Highland.

1900 photo of Cemetery Road (which is now called Mail Road). The high bridge goes over the canal. From the left is James Gardner's house and the Atkins' house. On right, the first building was probably a canal barn, next Oliver Calkin's house. Information from Austin Smith, historian. Courtesy of the Town of Highland.

Street view of Barryville. From the left, Sue Gardner's candy store, Bernard Thiesen's butcher shop, John Schumacher's Hotel (which became Clouse's Casino, which became the Riviera Movie Theater), and the gristmill built in 1895. The Canal Store and Post Office are at the end on the right. Photo courtesy of Kevin Marrinan. Information from Austin Smith, historian. Courtesy of the Town of Highland.

View down the Delaware River and lower part of Barryville, New York. The Canal Store is on the right. A Mrs. Hill owned the building to the left. It was later bought by F.J. Clouse and would be Clouse's Casino, and later Reber's. The road in front of the store and the Hill house was the canal towpath with the remains of the D&H Canal on its left. Photo courtesy of Kevin Marrinan. Information from Austin Smith, historian. Courtesy of the Town of Highland.

Conveyance to and from Shohola Depot, 75 cents each way. Trunks extra; Trains leave Jersey City 9:15 a.m. and 3 p.m.—Fred Myers Farm House.

The Crawford family also lived on Crawford Road. Jennie Crawford's letters, which we will read in Chapter 7, mention the Maier and Fred Myers families, Lottie Scott, and the children of Abel and Maria Hankins Myers.

In 1900 Jennie, 19, lived with her parents Alfred and Melvina Crawford and grandfather Andrew Crawford, 84. Joel and Maud Crawford, possibly her uncle and aunt, had been married 5 years.

The Village of Barryville and Some of its Townspeople

At the River (as Barryville was sometimes still called) there was a sawmill, gristmill, canal store, shops, hotel, and Post Office. The Old Mill Dam was used for water power to run the gristmill and sawmill.

Sue Gardner, daughter of James E. and Rebecca Gardner, ran a candy store. Bernard Thiese had a butcher shop. John Schumacher's Hotel would become one of the Clouse Casinos.

The Baptist Church was on River Road to the west of the Gristmill Pond. Union Church (originally the Congregational Church) was set on a hill behind the Mill Pond.

Irving Quick's house and three-story barn were near the blacksmith shop owned by Ira M. Austin.

Ira and Minerva Drake Austin's house, east of Halfway Brook and south of the Barryville Schoolhouse on Austin Road, was advertised in the 1890 Erie Railway's *Summer Homes*. Ira and Minerva's children (ages 8–33):

Barryville, New York, circa 1900

In 1900 Charles M. and Lottie Bradley Colville and their newborn daughter Ruth lived in Barryville. Charles was a farmer. Lottie was a daughter of Isaac and Joanna Bradley. We learn a bit more about the Colville family through letters Ruth writes in 1918, to my uncle McKinley Austin.

Samuel and Elizabeth Hulse's son Chester was a friend of Rowlee Schoonover. Mary Eaton, a servant, and Mr. Decker, 57, boarded with them.

Marie DeKnetel taught music. George and Julia Eckhart had 2 children, Albert and Lillie.

August and Anna Clouse had 3 children: Katie, Freddie, and Clarence. August was a master carpenter. We will read about him in a later chapter.

Samuel Rusby was a pastor. He and his wife Carrie had 6 children.

Gilbert and Mary Nelson had been married 30 years. Gilbert was a mail carrier. Their daughter Minnie, 26, would attend the Methodist Church in the 1930s when Irwin Briggs was the preacher. (The Gilbert Nelson family was not related to the Robert Nelson family who would later live nearby.)

Brothers John and George Steel were both butchers.

Menzo Quick was a General Merchant; James Quick was a foreman with the D&H Canal company; Charles Nelson was a railroad laborer.

Mary Rixton, 68, lived with her son Henry who was a hotel keeper. Oliver Cory was a house painter. James Ozenbaugh was a salesman. John Fox from Pennsylvania was a collar maker.

The Gardner and Calkin families in Barryville were related to Eliza Eldred Gardner, daughter of James and Polly V. Eldred, who settled in late 1815, in what became Eldred.

Eliza Gardner, 89, had been a widow since 1860. She lived with her son Stephen St. John Gardner

The village of Barryville. On the far right is the Union Church, next in the foreground is the gristmill, then the Schumacher Hotel and horse shed; last on the left, the Baptist Church. Photo courtesy of the Town of Highland.

Older map of Barryville. J. Kerr's (John Kerr) property in the right hand corner was where the William Kerr family lived. To their left was the D&H Office which the Peltons bought. North of J. Kerr was the Ira Austin house. The school was below J.H. Quick. The Baptist church was right of N.B. Johnston, in the dark section. Map courtesy of Minisink Valley Historical Society.

and his family. Stephen had been married to his second wife Maggie Terns for 20 years. His daughter Katie and his brother-in-law John Terns, 72, lived with them. Stephen's son Myers Gardner and his wife Annie Long were in California. Myers was a bookkeeper for a lumber firm in Stockton.

Stephen and his son James K. Gardner ran the store in Shohola next to the Shohola Glen House. James K. sold coal and lumber.

James K. (namesake of his grandfather) and Ella Breen Gardner's daughter Edna, 9, would be the organist at my parents wedding.

Edna's twin sister had died young.

Ella Breen Gardner was a sister to Meda Breen Tether, wife of Walter Tether. The Tethers also had a house in Barryville.

Maria Calkin was Eliza Gardner's daughter. Oliver, a farmer, and Maria Calkin's children: James Calkin, a telegraph lineman; Charles F. Calkin, a gristmill worker; and Maria (Lilly?) lived with them.

Eliza's son James E. Gardner and his wife Rebecca Rider were in Brooklyn where James E. ran a grocery store in 1900. Susan Gardner was their daughter.

On the left is Abel Myers' store near the southeast corner of Eldred, then the Parker House and barn. Photo courtesy of Christena Stevens Myers.

Little Emily Parker with her parents James Y. Parker and Emily Payne, and her brother William. Photo courtesy of Christena Stevens Myers, daughter of Emily Parker Stevens.

Nellie, Minnie, Frank, Mabel, Lou, and Ralph Waldo Austin. Sears, a laborer, lived with them.

Ira and Minerva's daughter Mabel would marry Ed Smith. Their son Austin Smith (not related to me) would be the Town of Highland Historian.

William Kerr, his wife Mary (from Ireland), their young daughters, Margaret and Jessie, and his parents John and Mary Kerr lived a couple of lots south of Ira Austin, near the D&H Canal Office *(see J. Kerr on map, p. 139)*.

John and James Kerr had bought the house and lot from John W. Johnston for $1,900 in 1873. Johnston's mother had lived in the small house with her son Napoleon. When Napoleon got in a financial bind, his brother John W. Johnston bought the property.

They [the Kerrs] used the old house for a time and then erected the present building and made other improvements.
—*Johnston, p. 324.*

The lot William Kerr and his family lived on in Barryville, was next to the Pelton Soda Bottle Factory, which we will talk about at the end of this chapter.

The original Kerr homestead in Lumberland would become John and Katie Kerr's boarding house called Old House at Home in 1907, and later, Torwood Farm.

In 1899 John H. Kerr married Miss Katie E. Greening. They were the parents of Charles Kerr, my parents' friend.

Visiting Boarding Houses in Eldred and Venoge

The area around Highland Lake was called Venoge from 1897 to 1911. Visitors to the Eldred and Venoge Boarding Houses would meet the driver at the Barryville-

Shohola Bridge and River Road. The driver would head east from the bridge, pass Mail Road, make a gradual curve to the northeast around Mill Pond with the grain and sawmills, and head north to Eldred on Brook Road. On the way they would pass the road that went to the Barryville Schoolhouse and Ira Austin's house.

Families Near Eldred Corners
Brook Road paralleled Halfway Brook for about 3 miles to the place that Blind Pond and Halfway Brooks met and formed a land triangle with Proctor Road on the northeast. This was where the James Eldred Family had settled (at the end of 1815) in an old log cabin and a nearby sawmill. Some people we have met lived, or would live in this area.

We first met the Crandall family in the Town of Bethel. David and Robert Crandall would each have a home near the old Eldred house and sawmill. Milton had Cold Spring Farm that we talked about earlier.

East of Eldred Corners was the first Parker Hotel owned by the Autenrieth family around 1900. Notice Emily Parker's house she had built with her tip money. Photo courtesy of Chuck Myers.

The Crandall brothers' mother, Betsy, was a widow and lived with Robert and his wife Nellie Simpson, a very good friend of my grandmother Jennie Austin.

David Crandall's son George would marry Jennie Crawford. At some point they would own the James Eldred home built about 1830 that had replaced the original loghouse.

Close to the center of Eldred near the southeast corner was the second hotel that James Y. Parker built. In 1892, sixteen years after their last child Adelaide had been born, James and Emily Payne Parker had a delightful surprise— a daughter, Emily Parker, future mother of Teenie Stevens Myers.

William H. Wilson's store at the northeast corner in Eldred. Next door was the Autenrieth Hotel. Photo courtesy of Cynthia Leavenworth Bellinger.

Abel S. and Maria Hankins Myers home, Orchard Terrace, which later was used as a schoolhouse. Photo courtesy of Chuck Myers, grandson of Abel and Maria Hankins Myers.

Eldred Methodist Church with steeple (added around 1900) and wagon barn. Photo courtesy of Chuck Myers.

One room of the Parker Hotel was often the Eldred Post Office. My father would work there for a few years in the 1930s when Emily Parker Stevens was Postmaster.

James Y. and Emily Parker's son William Parker and his wife Victoria had a son James Y. Parker.

Behind the Parker Hotel was Orchard Terrace, the home of Abel S. and Maria Hankins Myers. It was advertised in 1900 as a boarding house. Orchard Terrace would later be used as a school.

Abel Myers was a farmer and lumberman. His store was north of the second Parker Hotel near Eldred's southeast corner. Abel and Maria Hankins Myers' children, Jackson, Lulu, Cleta, Archibald, Norman, and Lila, play a part in this story.

On Eldred's northeast corner, William H. Wilson had a general merchandise store. East of the Wilson store was the first Hotel that James Y. Parker had built.

James Parker had sold that hotel to the Autenrieths whose daughter Caroline Autenrieth was born in 1896 in Eldred.

Caroline Autenrieth was one of the students of Anna Leavenworth, shown in the photo at the end of Chapter 7. Caroline Autenrieth would marry James Cash Penney of the J.C. Penney Company.

Starting at Eldred Corners, Proctor Road went southeast past the Wilson store and the Autenrieth Hotel on the north, and the Eldred schoolhouse and Congregational Church on the south. It continued on to boarding houses on the east side of Eldred and Venoge near Highland Lake, which we will soon visit.

Families who Lived West of Eldred

Eldred-Yulan Road went northwest from the center of Eldred to homes on Eldred's west side, not

Charles Wilson's sawmill on Clark Road. Charles Wilson was a brother to William H. Wilson. Photo courtesy of Chuck Myers.

The Slonek house on top of the hill and lumber from William Wait's sawmill at the bottom. Photo courtesy of Christena Stevens Myers.

far from Washington Lake.

Starting at Eldred Corners, Eldred-Yulan Road went past a building (called Eldred Inn at one time) which was possibly built by Charles Wilson around 1900. Next, on the right hand side, was the Methodist Church with its wagon barn, Blind Pond Brook, and then Clark Road.

On Clark Road was the sawmill of Charles Wilson, a lumberman and brother of William Wilson. The Charles Wilson home was closer to Board Road (the road which headed towards Bethel from Eldred Corners). Charles's first wife Christina Mills Wilson died in 1895, leaving Charles with two young children, Arthur and Julia Wilson.

In 1898 Charles Wilson married Elizabeth Hoatson Clark. You may remember that Elizabeth Hoatson Clark was a bride, mother, and widow in one year. Elizabeth's daughter was Georgia Clark. Charles and William's father Edward Wilson lived with Charles and Elizabeth and their children.

Opposite Clark Road was the sawmill of William Wait. One of the many postcards of Eldred shows the Slonek home at the top of the hill and lumber from William Wait's sawmill at the bottom of the hill.

The original home of Felix Kyte was after Clark Road, on the northwest side of Eldred-Yulan Road. William and Mary Alice Whitney Kyte, and their children, Herbert, Mary A., and Felix lived there.

Harry Wormuth who would marry Mary A. Kyte, would also have a sawmill on Clark Road, north of Charles Wilson's Mill.

Shortly after Clark Road came a Y in the road. The property between the roads was later called

Felix Kyte Descendants

William Henry Kyte, son of Rev. Felix and Eliza Greiger Kyte and husband of Mary Alice Whitney, died in Eldred, in 1896.

Mary Alice Whitney Kyte's mother was a daughter of Edward and Elizabeth Tether.

William and Mary Alice Kyte's daughter, Mary A. Kyte, would marry Harry Wormuth. Aida Austin would write in her 1940s diary about Mary Wormuth, Felix Kyte's granddaughter.

Eliza Greiger Kyte, wife of Felix Kyte, died in Goshen, New York, January 21, 1898. 2 Timothy 4:8 is written on Mrs. Kyte's tombstone.

Henceforth there is laid up for me a crown of righteousness, which the Lord, the righteous judge, shall give me at that day: and not to me only, but unto all them also that love his appearing.—2 Timothy 4:8

Ada Cortright and Mary Kyte, daughter of William H. and Mary A. Whitney Kyte. Photo courtesy of Cynthia Leavenworth Bellinger.

Frank Crouch Kyte was born in 1897 in Illinois to Charles Colony and Elizabeth Bliss Kyte. Charles Colony Kyte, grandson of Felix and Eliza Greiger Kyte, was a postal clerk for the Railroad in Alton, Illinois, and most unfortunately "was killed by the cars," in 1899.

Eldred-Yulan Road went to the left, passed Crawford Road, and went to Yulan. To the right is Airport Road that went past the Leavenworth and Bradley homesteads and Washington Lake, and eventually went to Yulan. The property in the middle was later called Becker's Woods and plays a part in my Austin grandparents' lives in 1935. Photo courtesy of Chuck Myers.

The Leavenworth Echo Hill Farm House around 1896. From the left: Garfield, Sherman S., Maria, Christina, Charlotte, and Truman. Photo courtesy of Cynthia Leavenworth Bellinger.

Maria Myers Leavenworth with their dog, Old Don. She was a gracious, gentle lady that thought the best about people. Sherman S. Leavenworth was a real gentleman, though you would know if he was upset with you. Photos courtesy of Cynthia Leavenworth Bellinger.

Becker's Woods and plays a part in my Austin grandparents' lives.

At the Y, the Eldred-Yulan road turned to the left and headed slightly southwest toward Yulan as it passed Crawford Road.

The right leg of the Y (called Leavenworth Road at one time) continued as Airport Road.

The Leavenworth Family
My Leavenworth relatives lived on Airport Road. Perhaps the Leavenworth Homestead became the boarding house, Echo Hill Farm House, closer to 1900. It would be interesting to know where the name Echo Hill originated.

In 1894 Sherman Buckley Leavenworth had been widowed for two years. He lived with his son Sherman S., Sherman's wife Maria Myers, their children, Anna Mae, 19, Truman, 16, Jennie, 14, Garfield, 12, Martin David, 10, Charlotte, 5, and baby Christina Hayes Leavenworth.

Christina was named after her great-grandmother Christina Hayes Ingram. Christina's future husband Anthony Hirsch lived in Hungary in 1894.

A gracious, gentle lady, Maria Leavenworth thought the best about people. She told Christina not to be judgmental about the pipe smoking of the Spanish or Cuban housekeeper (possibly "Aunt Becky") of Gus Myers (Maria's brother), but to see it as a cultural difference.

Sherman S. Leavenworth was a real gentleman, though apparently you would know if he was upset with you. Sherman S. still farmed like many of the other Boarding House owners.

Anna Leavenworth, the oldest, seems to have taught at both the Yulan and Eldred schoolhouses (during different years). It was Truman's job to get the summer boarders from Shohola as well as take them for outings. In 1894 Jennie and Garfield were probably in school. Garfield and Martin also helped on the farm.

When Garfield was young he could walk to town and never touch the ground by hopping from downed hemlock tree to hemlock tree that had been left on the ground after the bark was stripped for tanning.

In the fall, Garfield hunted partridges. It was easier then because the partridges got drunk on the thorn apples. Garfield would get 10 cents for each

Echo Hill Farm House.

RULES AND REGULATIONS.

1. When rooms are vacated, lights must be put out.
2. Children must not meddle with piano unless capable of playing.
3. No dancing or card playing allowed on Sunday.
4. No towels taken from rooms.
5. Doors close at 11 p. m.
6. No spoons or glasses taken from dining-room.
7. Proprietor will not be responsible for valuables left in rooms.
8. Guests are requested to throw all waste paper in baskets.

MEAL HOURS:

First call .... 7:00 a. m.
Breakfast .... 8:00 a. m.
Dinner ....12:30 p. m.
Supper .... 6:00 p. m.

To GUESTS.—The above rules are formulated with the intention of making everything as agreeable as possible for all, and a strict adherence to them will be found conducive to that end.

S. S. LEAVENWORTH, Proprietor.

Rules for guests of Echo Hill Farm House. Courtesy of Kevin Marrinan.

Maria and Christina (left) and Sherman S. Leavenworth (right) watch Truman Leavenworth (left) sipping cider from the keg with his friend Clarence Sergeant. Photo courtesy of Cynthia Leavenworth Bellinger.

Truman Leavenworth gave boarders from Echo Hills Farm House tours around Eldred and Yulan. Photo courtesy of Cynthia Leavenworth Bellinger.

Charlotte and Christina Leavenworth. Photo courtesy of Cynthia Leavenworth Bellinger.

Haying on the Leavenworth property, in later years. Garfield Leavenworth is standing in front of the hay wagon and Sherman S., his father is on the right, standing behind the pile of hay on the ground. Photo courtesy of Cynthia Leavenworth Bellinger.

Four generations: Edith Palmer Ewart, Harriet Leavenworth Palmer, Sherman Buckley Leavenworth, and Victor Ewart. Photo courtesy of Cynthia Leavenworth Bellinger.

Top row: Harriet Leavenworth Palmer, her husband Henry Palmer. Second row, 3rd from the left: Edith Palmer Ewart, Elliot Ewart, Albert Ewart holding Millie (Pamela); Willard and Victor Ewart in the bottom row. Photo courtesy of Cynthia Leavenworth Bellinger.

partridge he shot.

Sherman S. Leavenworth had a list of rules and the time meals were served printed out for their guests at Echo Hill Farm House.

Echo Hill Farm House Rules
1. When rooms are vacated, lights must be put out.
2. Children must not meddle with piano unless capable of playing.
3. No dancing or card playing allowed on Sunday.
4. No towels taken from rooms.
5. Doors close at 11 p.m.
6. No spoons or glasses taken from dining room.
7. Proprietor will not be responsible for valuables left in rooms.
8. Guests are requested to throw all waste paper in baskets.

With the intention of making everything as agreeable as possible for all, and a strict adherence to them will be found conducive to that end.
—S.S. Leavenworth, Proprietor.

Sherman Buckley Leavenworth
Buckley deeded his land to his son Sherman S. Leavenworth in December 1893. The document stipulated that Sherman S. would pay his sister Harriet Leavenworth Palmer $500 from the profits of the Leavenworth property within 18 months of Buckley's death.

In 1895, at the age of 86, my great-great-grandfather Sherman Buckley Leavenworth died.

Mr. Sherman Buckley Leavenworth, one of the most highly respected citizens of Eldred, Sullivan County, died at his home in that place, at 3:30 o'clock this morning.

Several years ago he sustained a stroke of paralysis, which was followed at various interval, by lighter strokes, which ultimately ended in his death.

Mr. Leavenworth was born in Connecticut and was 86 years of age, 60 years of which he resided in Eldred.

Upon coming to Eldred, he purchased a tract of land, in the clearing of which he immediately engaged. From this land and the improvements made on it by clearing it, he developed one of the most productive farms in that whole district, which consists of about 150 acres.

About 45 years ago he was converted to the Methodist Episcopal Church and 20 years ago joined the Congregational Church at Eldred, of which he was a member at the time of his death.

Three of Mr. Leavenworth's son's served in the war of the Rebellion; Hezekiah, who contracted a disease while in the service, and returned home and died shortly afterwards at Eldred; Atwell who died during the third year of the war and was buried

Old Oak Tree at Kaese's in Yulan, New York. Scene looking out the window of the Kaese home. Washington Lake is in the background. Postcard courtesy of Kevin Marrinan.

daughter Edith and her husband Albert Ewart had 5 children: Victor, Willard, Elliott, and Pamela (Millie) Tippling, and Rolland (born in 1901).

Harriet Palmer had apparently insisted that Albert and Edith name their daughter Harriet after her. Neither Edith nor Albert wanted that name. Albert came to the rescue with the suggestion to name the new little one after his mother—Pamela Tippling Ewart. Pamela Ewart, it turns out, did not like her name, and went by Millie Ewart.

Later in this chapter we'll talk about Buckley's son John Leavenworth and his wife Amelia Bradley who lived in Colorado.

in South Carolina, and Sherman, now residing at Eldred.

He is survived by two sons, Sherman S., at home with whom he resided and John of Denver, also by one daughter, Mrs. Harriet E. Palmer, wife of Mr. H.W. Palmer of Port Jervis.

The funeral will take place from his late residence at 3 o'clock on Friday afternoon. Interment at Eldred.
—The Evening Gazette, *Port Jervis, N.Y., April 3, 1895.*

Henry and Harriet Palmer Family
Henry and Harriet Leavenworth Palmer had been married for 41 years by 1900. They lived in Port Jervis, on 7 Spring Street. In October, Henry Palmer died.

Nothing is known of Henry and Harriet Palmer's son James. In 1900 Harry C. Palmer and his wife Lydia lived in Benton Harbor, Michigan. Lydia had a young daughter, Florence Reprogel from her first marriage.

Henry and Harriet Palmer's

Isaac and Joanna Bradley Family
Amelia's parents Isaac M. and Joanna Brown Bradley lived between the Leavenworths and the top of Washington Lake. In the 1890s Isaac and Joanna still ran the Bradley Boarding House. Isaac was still listed as a farmer. His half brother John Bradley was a farm laborer. Edna Goss was a servant.

Joanna's mother Mercy Harding Brown Clark (widow of George Case Clark) died around 1895 in Eldred. Mercy was also the

Isaac Bradley Boarding House. In the 1890s Isaac and Joanna still ran the Bradley Boarding House. Photo courtesy of William E. Horton.

Laurel Cottage, the Boarding House of Abel and Viola Bradley Hazen. Postcard courtesy of Larry Stern.

Joseph and Anne Tether at Washington Lake House, 1907. Postcard courtesy of Ivan J. and Jana Tether.

Joseph and Anne Tether's Washington Lake House. Photo courtesy of Helen Hensel Oset.

mother of John Henry Clark.

Most of the Bradley children were married by 1900, and are part of this story. Several of them had boarding houses. Fred and Mary Bradley Scott Myers (already mentioned) had Myers Boarding House on Crawford Road.

Around 1894, Erwin (Ernie) Avery, 16, started working at the Bradley farm. Ernie also was a lumberman. A few years before his death, recalled to me 8 or 9 properties in the area where he cut timber in his early years.
—William Erwin Horton, grandson.

In December 1900 Erwin David Avery married Norah Bradley. They ran a laundry in White Lake. Erwin and Norah would eventually run the Bradley Boarding House.

In 1900 Atwell Bradley was listed as single and a saloon keeper. He married Wilhelmena Clemens soon afterwards. She died in 1902, shortly after their son Clifford Bradley was born.

Viola Bradley had married Abel Hazen. The Hazens' Laurel

Tether's Washington Beach Hotel in Yulan. Postcard courtesy of Kevin Marrinan.

Racine's West Shore Cottage on Washington Lake would one day belong to the Cantwells. Postcard courtesy of Kevin Marrinan.

Oakdene owned by William and Phoebe Middaugh Owen. Photo in the Defeo Collection courtesy of Kevin Marrinan.

Cottage near the southeast tail of Washington Lake was advertised in the newspaper starting in 1893. Three years later their daughter Mabel Hazen was born.

This may be a photo of Elizabeth Tether Owen. Elizabeth was the sister of Joseph Tether, wife of Robert Owen and mother of Mabel, William, and Frank Owen. Photo is courtesy of Melva Austin Barney.

The Hazens were neighbors of the Tether family. In 1896 Isaac Newton Bradley married Jessie Tether, daughter of Joseph and Anne Tether, who lived on the east side of Washington Lake.

Joseph and Anne Tether

Joseph and Anne Tether owned Washington Lake House. Their daughter Lucy Tether was married to Joseph Rixton. Their son Walter Tether had married Meda Breen.

Walter and Meda had a place in Barryville where Walter was a blacksmith, according to the 1900 census. Walter and Meda would later run the Washington Beach Hotel, which seems to have been built in the early 1900s at the north end of Joseph's property, on the east side of Washington Lake.

The Washington Lake House was nearer the tail and closer to the Hazen property. There is an endearing postcard photo of Joseph and Anne Tether from 1907 on p. 149.

Other Boarding Houses On or Near Washington Lake by 1900

Airport Road went on the northwest side of Washington Lake. Lake View Farm House was between the road and lake. Edward Prange ran the home until at least 1894. It may be the home that Alfred and Sophia Kaese owned by the early 1900s.

West Shore Cottage was south of Lake View Farm House and was run by Charles Racine (at least through 1899). T.W. Racine seems to be the next proprietor. West Shore Cottage and several nearby houses become Cantwells' West Shore Lodge in Book 3.

Airport Road intersected Washington Lake Road on its way to Yulan. There to the southeast was Oakdene, a lovely boarding house owned by William and Phoebe Middaugh Owen. Oakdene was advertised in 1900.

Phoebe Owen was the daughter of Dennis and Sarah Maria Myers Middaugh. Dennis, a Civil War veteran, died in 1887, and Sarah Maria Middaugh lived in the area.

William and Phoebe Owen, their young children, Basil, Etta, and baby Pearl; William's widowed mother Elizabeth Tether Owen; Florence Owen, a niece; Chester Middaugh, a brother-in-law; and Dorie Webber, a servant, lived at the Owen Boarding House.

The Greig and Beck Families

Back at Eldred Corners, and to the north, were two other major boarding houses: Robert and Kate Greig's House and Seven Oaks owned by George and Elizabeth Beck. Both families were from England and were listed on the Beers 1870 map.

The massive Greig home built in the early 1890s, was south of Mill/Stege's Pond and

Road. Robert, Kate, Isabelle, and Bennett Greig lived in the huge Greig House. Robert's sister Jane, his sister-in-law Julia and her daughter lived there also.

The Greigs owned over 100,000 acres in Highland, Lumberland, Tusten, and Bethel. They bought the land in lots of 400 acres or larger for the water rights because they believed steam power was the wave of the future.—Ed Grotecloss as told to Kevin Marrinan.

Ed Grotecloss III, who we will meet in Book 3, is the son of Isabelle Greig who inherited the Greig home from her parents, Robert and Kate Greig.

Robert's brothers Thomas and Bennett Greig wanted to create a high class hunting and fishing club on Mill Pond (later called Stege's Pond). They had rice growing on the upper end of the pond to benefit the large population of wild ducks.

Thomas Greig died in 1886, a few months after completing the stone wall to the west of Mill/Stege's Pond and the lovely stone arched bridge with the water falls at the south end of the pond. The stone wall was later the entrance to the Seven Oaks Estate.

Seven Oaks Boarding House

Seven Oaks, owned by George and Elizabeth Beck, was another huge, beautiful boarding house. It was set back some distance north of Mill/Stege Road and west of Mill/Stege's Pond. It was north of the Greig Home. The stone entrance to Seven Oaks that Thomas Greig built is still there today.

Seven Oaks has Piazzas, Lawn, Shrubbery, Orchards, a swift running brook, garden, cows, and

The impressive boarding house owned by the Greig Family. Photo courtesy of Ed Grotecloss and Kevin Marrinan.

The wall built by Thomas Greig. It was later the entrance to the Seven Oaks Estate. Photo courtesy of Ed Grotecloss and Kevin Marrinan.

Front of the Seven Oaks brochure, courtesy of Ed Grotecloss and Kevin Marrinan. Seven Oaks (insert on left) is shown in the middle in the distance; the Greig home is on the right.

1894 Sullivan County's Shawangunks

Sullivan County has of late years almost been annexed to Brooklyn, so large is the Brooklyn exodus which sets in each year with the heat of summer for the crests of the Shawangunks and the picturesque valleys beside the sparkling Sullivan County streams…

Sullivan County is near and accessible. It gives mountain air, freedom, good fishing and charming rural drives at reasonable rates. Brooklyn men of moderate incomes can establish their families in a farm house there for the summer, visit them over Sundays and for their own vacations about as cheap as they could stay at home, and without the fatigue or annoyance of long railroad journeys.

The railroads have been important factors in bringing this region into popularity [with their] admirable volumes on *Summer Homes* along their lines…Another cause of popularity is the excellence of the farm board offered…

Dr. Bowdish Writes: "…Let me urge business men, bankers, brokers, merchants, mechanics and ministers, wearied in body and worried in mind, to halt. Rest, and try this trip. Get the health that will surely come to you in this mountain summerland."

At Eldred: the Twin Lake House, the DeVenoge Mountain House, C.M. Austin & Co.'s Mountain Grove House, John Wait's, and Mrs. Rebecca C. Eldred's boarding houses…
—Brooklyn Daily Eagle, *1894.*

Some People in Nearby Lumberland

Some of the people in our story were listed in Lumberland in the 1900 Census.

James and Adeline MacIntyre had 7 children a few months old to age 15—including Elizabeth (Bessie) who would marry Alfred Hill. Alfred and Bessie Hill are part of this story.

George and Charlotte Maney had six children and he was a farmer.

Joseph and Lucinda Quick's son, Napoleon B. and his wife Fannie White, lived with them. Napoleon and Fannie White Quick would be the parents of Blanche Quick who would marry Herman Worzel. Herman and Blanche would be the parents of Ruth Worzel, future wife of Chuck Myers, both good friends of my mother Mary Briggs Austin. Napoleon and Fannie were very kind people, according to my mother.

poultry. It is 6 miles from Shohola and accommodates 25 guests in large, well furnished rooms.

There is about a mile of woodland walks on the premises with Mountain Laurels, rugged rocks, and occasional giant original pines—a healthful retreat at 1,800 feet.

There are several nearby lakes, other points of interest, and fair bicycle roads.

The village of Eldred is 3/4 mile from the house, and has 2 churches, stores, a post office, and a livery.

Good plain food, pure air and water.—Mrs. Geo. Beck, Seven Oaks Brochure.

Boarding Houses Near Highland Lake, Venoge, New York
Vacationers to Houses near Highland Lake would turn right at Eldred Corners and head southeast on Proctor Road. A short distance away, past the bridge over Halfway Brook, was a Y in the road.

The left branch, Highland Lake Road, went to boarding houses in the hamlet called Venoge (1897–1911). Proctor Road continued southeast past the Mountain Grove House of the Austin's on its way towards Glen Spey.

The Bosch Family and the Lake House
Wilhelm and Mary Maier Bosch had a boarding house called The Lake House on Hartung Road, northwest of Highland Lake.

In the early 1890s Wilhelm built the Lake House, a smaller residence, and a barn for their 2 cows, horse, pig, and chickens. Lake House would later be called Green Acres and then Green Meadows.

Most of the lumber was said to have been hauled up to Highland Lake via Shohola from demolished buildings in New York City. Notice from the old photographs that even when the buildings were newly built, they did not look new. Other buildings and guest cottages were added over the years.

For lake access, a boathouse and docks were constructed. Wilhelm dug a boat canal using a mule and a plow.—Ken Bosch, great-grandson of Wilhelm Bosch.

We had dug a well where we got water for our use. Also for the cattle we carried the water to the barn in the winter for the animals because it was too slippery and they would fall on the ice.

We had a dozen apple trees and we always had lots of apples to eat. Also, a big Bartlett pear tree and a larger cherry tree, black cherries and one red cherry tree, one crab apple tree, and two large grape vines, and they was loaded every year. Plenty of

The Bosch Lake House, 1900

The Lake House in the Heart of the Sullivan County Hills

The Lake House stands on high ground, overlooking the beautiful Highland Lake from the north, about 250 yards away. The lake is one and one-half miles long and one mile wide; is surrounded by a heavy growth of timber and abounds in several kinds of fish.

The house is new, contains 27 rooms, and has accommodations for 50 guests. The rooms are airy and comfortable. The parlor is supplied with a piano for the accommodation of guests.

The Lake House is 7 miles from Shohola by carriage over a beautiful road. Livery accommodations are reasonable. All guests are promptly met at Shohola Station when notified. Transportation: 75¢. Trunks 25¢.

Parties who wish a quiet healthful resort are sure to find it at this house. There are other boarding houses and lakes nearby, affording plenty of attractions and amusements to all who desire to avail themselves in that direction; and a good time and lots of sport can be assured.

Fresh vegetables from the garden. Fresh eggs, milk, and the best of meats are supplied, and prices are reasonable. Mail daily and telephone nearby.

Board $6 to $8 per week. Children under 10 years half price. Wilhelm Bosch, Prop.—*Lake House Flyer.*

Boarders at the Lake House built and owned by the Wilhelm Bosch Family. Photo courtesy of the Bosch Family.

Mary Maier Bosch, wife of Heinrich Wilhelm Bosch. Photo courtesy of the Bosch Family.

Heinrich Wilhelm Bosch, husband of Mary Maier. Photo courtesy of the Bosch Family.

grape jelly for the winter or year around.

Pop also had 5 acres of garden and most of it red and yellow onions. Herman and I had to weed them. Some big piles of weeds.

But one year Gus Myers put a dam in the lake's outlet and raised the lake too high and flooded the onion field, so no more onions to weed.

We planted hay on the onion patch. How big the hay got. The Dailey boys always cut the hay for my father, and piled it all up for the winter. Pop sold some of it to the neighbors.

Herman and I used to go to Mud Pond and pick cranberries in the fall. There was loads of them. We picked 2 and 3 big feed bags full in a day. We got them home with the horse and wagon. Then we ran them through the fan mill to blow the chaff and leaves out. Pop sold them in Port Jervis.

—Ed Bosch, son of Wilhelm and Mary Maier Bosch.

Venoge Post Office. Venoge was renamed Highland Lake in December 1911. Photo courtesy of the Proctor Family.

In 1900, the Bosch children were: Wilhelmina, 24, Charlie, 18, Lulu, 14, Herman, 10, Edward, 9, Ralph, 6, Menzo, 4, and Tillie, 2.

Town of Highland Postmasters

Barryville Postmasters
James A. Ozenbaugh 08/24/1885
Menzo Quick 09/12/1889
James A. Ozenbaugh 11/24/1893
Menzo Quick Postmaster.. 04/23/1897

Eldred Postmasters
Robert Kelso 12/23/1885
Abel S. Myers 5/01/1889
Moses B. Eaton 11/24/1893
Isaac M. Bradley 1/18/1896
Charles W. Wilson 8/27/1897

Yulan Postmasters
The first Postmaster: John Metzger Sr.
James A. Ozenbaugh 8/24/1885
Menzo Quick 9/12/1889
James A. Ozenbaugh 11/24/1893
Menzo Quick 4/23/1897

Venoge Postmasters
James Boyd 6/18/1897
Venoge became Highland Lake on 12/4/1911.

To help augment his income, Wilhelm traveled (first with a large backpack, later a wagon) the countryside far and wide, selling everything from household goods, fruit trees, wallpaper, and his famous "medications" from his wagon.

My father and other family members described Wilhelm's making "pills" from flour and sugar using a pill press. The pills were reported to be efficacious for a wide range of ailments.

Wilhelm was well known for his skill with a story and his salesmanship. He had the ability to deflect the wrath of a customer dissatisfied with a defective or inadequate item purchased at one of his prior visits.

He would disarm them by saying, "You had that trouble too? So did I! Let me show what I have now."

The children worked at the boarding house cleaning, washing dishes, tending the vegetable gardens, cutting hay, caring for the animals, etc.

Unfortunately Wilhelm repeatedly squandered much of the family resources on periodic binges, or "toots." He might be gone a week or more before he returned home.—Ken Bosch, great-grandson of Wilhelm Bosch.

The Horton Family

John and Anne E. Stanton Horton were probably country neighbors of the Bosch family. John Horton was a teamster. The Horton children in 1900: Walter, Carrie, Edith, Mabel, John, Maud, Ernest, and baby Mary Elvira Horton.

Mary Elvira Horton, whose aunt Elvira Horton was the wife of Daniel Hallock, would marry Herman Bosch.

Walter Horton would marry a daughter of Abel and Maria Myers. William Horton and his wife Catherine Sutherland would have a son Charles who would marry Beatrice Avery, a granddaughter of Isaac and Joanna Brown Bradley.

Daniel and Steve Hallock

Daniel Hallock, 61, a saloon keeper, his wife Elvira Horton, their daughter Jane (Jennie), 17, and Daniel's sister Martha, lived at *Highland Lake Grove*, a boarding house on Highland Lake.

Rowlee Schoonover told some stories about Daniel Hallock and his brother Steve.

There was an old fellow who used to live on the road to Highland Lake, which was called at that time Hagan Pond, but when the city folk commenced to come up, the name was not high brow enough and they changed it to Highland Lake.

Well, this old man had an old scow for a boat and would not let anyone use it. He had it chained to a ring in a rock near Dan Hallock's landing. Old Dan was half blind and made himself totally when us boys came up to take old Allen's boat out to go fishing.

We used to take a plank, roll the rock chain and lock up on the rear seat, and take the old scow out and fish. When we got through, we dropped the rock in the same hole and the old fellow would not be any wiser for he did not do very much fishing. When he found out we had used the boat, he took it out and sunk it.

I must tell you about Steve Hallock. He was one of them innocent looking men that never knew anything, and would say yes to anything you would say.

There is a place up on Highland Lake they call Tom Quick's Cave. And as the legend runs, old Tom Quick used to live there and he was somewhat of a bad man and an Indian hunter and they had all kind of stories about his doings.

It was about the time that the first city people commenced to come up in Sullivan County to board in summer and they all wanted to go to Tom Quick's cave.

So someone told them to see Steve Hallock and he would take them to the cave. But he told them there was a hole that went back in the cave that no one but him had ever been back in, and he knew there must be a number of things in there for he found an old gun, but he got so scared when he found that gun he got right out. But he intended to go back some day and see what he could find.

So the boarders wanted to make an appointment with him to see him go in. So Steve got some old flint lock muskets from his friends (for there was plenty of them those days around the country), and got a horseshoer's rasp and rasped the stocks down and put acid on the iron works and went up to the cave and planted them inside with some old boots and knives. He met

Boarding Houses, 1890 to 1894

Bradley Farm Boarding House, Eldred
Isaac M. Bradley, Proprietor
6 miles from Shohola. Conveyance, $1; 5 single, 12 double rooms; adults $6 to $8; children $4 to $5; servants $5 to $6; $1.50 per day; discount for season. Centre of trout, perch, and pickerel fishing; boats free; deer hounds and setters furnished; croquet grounds; headquarters for sportsmen; guides at hand; pine shade; 100 feet of piazza. Reference, Mr. James Smith, Cashier, Astor House, New York City.—Farmer, L.P., Picturesque Erie Summer Homes, *N.Y., L.E., & W. R.R., 1890.*

Wm. Hickok, Barryville
1 mile. 5 single and 6 double rooms; $6 per week; $1.50 per day; discount for season. Livery; good fishing.—Farmer, L.P., Picturesque Erie Summer Homes, *N.Y., L.E., & W. R.R., 1890.*

Ira M. Austin, Barryville
1 mile; 5 single, 3 double rooms; adults, $6; children, $3; servants, $5; $1 per day. Good livery and fishing; boats free.—Farmer, L.P., Picturesque Erie Summer Homes, *N.Y., L.E., & W. R.R., 1890.*

Lake View House, Highland Lake
Boarders wanted for September and October; fine locally; good fishing and hunting; terms moderate. For particulars address Myers, Mills & Co.—Brooklyn Daily Eagle, *September 4, 1892. Postcard courtesy of Larry Stern.*

Laurel Cottage, Yulan
Country board at Washington Lake; elevation 1,800 feet; no malaria; four miles from Shohola Glen; good fishing; boating and bathing; shady walks and pleasant drives; table well supplied with fresh milk, eggs, chickens and vegetables; carriage to take parties out riding; boats free to guests; terms $5 to $6 per week; children under 10 years of age, half price. For circular address: A.A. Hazen, Yulan.—New York Sun, *August 27, 1893. Postcard courtesy of Larry Stern.*

Highland Cottage, Yulan
Highest point on Washington Lake, boating, bathing, fishing, gunning; 4.5 miles from Shohola, Pa., $6 to $7; beautiful scenery; nice drives. Henry E. Wilke.—New York Sun, *August 27, 1893.*

Twin Lake House, Eldred
A select family house; elevation 1,700 feet; highest healthiest summer resort; beautiful pine groves, lake, boating, bathing, fishing, excellent cuisine. Accommodates 100 guests. Terms: $8 to $10 per week. W.H.C. Onderdonk. —Brooklyn Daily Eagle, *May 20, 1894.*

George W.T. and Martha Mills Myers' Lake View House on Highland Lake. Postcard courtesy of Stuart and Geraldine Mills Russell.

the party and crawled back in the hole and kept hollering back through his hands to give the sound effect, for the hole does not run more than 10 feet.

He stayed there for a while, then yelled out that he had found a lot of stuff and came out with two old guns. He sold them for $10 each, but he told them there was a large room in there with a lot of other stuff and he would go back another day if they wanted, and bring out some more. He worked that racket all summer until someone put them wise.
—Daniel Rowlee Schoonover.

The Ark, a floating ice cream store with sayings written on the building, was another tourist attraction on Highland Lake.

Mills, Myers, and Boyd Houses
In 1900 George and Elizabeth Gillespie Mills ran the original boarding house of his parents, Alexander and Margaret Gillies Mills. George Mills was also a farmer. His father Alexander, a

George W.T. Myers and Martha Mills Myers sitting in front of their lovely Lake View House. Sons Charles C. and Martin D. Myers standing. Photo taken at Lake View before 1900, courtesy of Christena Stevens Myers.

Agnes Darling, a granddaughter of Jane Ann Myers. Photo courtesy of Cynthia Leavenworth Bellinger.

carpenter, died in 1900.

George and Elizabeth Mills' children in 1900: Belle, James G., Agnes, and baby Alexander.

Little Alexander would one day be the proprietor of the Spring House in Barryville.

James Mills would marry Sophia Stellwagen and one day own Jane Ann Myers's boarding house. James, Sophia, and their children Geraldine and Kenneth Mills play a part in Book 3.

The families of Martha Myers and Margaret Boyd (sisters of George Mills) had boarding houses near Highland Lake.

James and Margaret Boyd, proprietors of Piermont Hotel, had 10 children ages 4 to 22, in 1900. Their daughter Isabelle Boyd would marry Henry Asendorf.

The Boyd house was near the large, long, lovely Lake View House, a boarding house on Highland Lake owned by George W.T. and Martha Mills Myers.

George W.T. and his wife Martha had two sons, Charles C. and Martin D. Myers, and a hired man, Patrick G.

Jane Ann Myers Dies

In 1896 George W.T. Myers's mother Jane Ann Van Pelt Webb Myers died at age 80. Jane Ann Myers was also the mother of Gus Myers, Maria Myers Leavenworth, and Lottie Myers Darling.

Charles and Lottie Myers Darling lived near Binghamton, New York. Agnes, Ida, and Edith Darling were their daughters.

After his mother died, Gus ran the Myers Boarding House which was across the road from Highland Lake near Collins Road. Edith Masvidal, a widow, was housekeeper. Louis Basque from France was the hired man. Edith's sister-in-law Rebecca may have been pipe smoking 'Aunt Becky.'

George Mills Boarding House near Highland Lake. In 1900 George and Elizabeth Gillespie Mills ran the original Mills boarding house. Photo courtesy of Katherine Calkin Traxler.

"Smile and the world smiles with you; weep and you cry alone," was one of the sayings written on a tourist attraction called "The Ark" in Venoge, New York. Postcard courtesy of the Bosch Family.

Dr. and Mrs. DeVenoge

Dr. DeVenoge had owned much of the land around Round Pond (Lake DeVenoge) and had run a boarding house which was advertised as Mountain Lake House in the 1890s. Both Dr. DeVenoge and his wife Caroline died in the late 1890s. Their daughter Mary DeVenoge Miller and her husband ran a boarding house in 1900.

The Proctor Family

The Proctor family in nearby Lumberland included Charles E. Proctor, an artist, who had written a travelogue about the area and included his visit to the boarding house of Jane Ann Myers.

Jane Ann Myers Boarding House near Highland Lake. Photo courtesy of Mary Briggs Austin.

Gus Myers was a country neighbor of the Austins. He was the son of Jane Ann Myers, and uncle to the Leavenworth children. Photo courtesy of Stuart and Geraldine Mills Russell.

India Shawls

We have very fine Valley Cashmere Shawls at $100.00, and from that price up to $400.00 and $500 for extra fine grade.

Also India Mountain Cashmere Shawls at $25.00 These prices are about 1/3 what they sold for a few years ago. Lord & Taylor, Broadway at Twentieth Street, N.Y.—*1890 ad.*

There are some people that lived elsewhere in the 1890s who had or would have a connection to the Town of Highland.

John and Amelia Leavenworth
John and Amelia Bradley Leavenworth lived out west in Colorado. Their oldest daughter Florence died of typhoid at the age of 7 in October 1890. Their daughter Ida May, born in 1895, joined Charlotte (Lottie), 10.

John and Amelia lived near Fish Creek in Dolores County, Colorado, in 1896. The nearest neighbor lived about 3 miles away.

In March 1896 Hazel Alice Leavenworth was born in a drafty log cabin on a ranch near Fish Creek. Hazel would live a very full life for 102 years.

Fish Creek and the homestead are in a valley between steep mountains. John Leavenworth founded the ranch. It was virgin land and never homesteaded or bought.

Finally in the 1970s I had the chance to go there. My mother Hazel's half-brother Charlie was our guide. We drove up and up the north fork of the Dolores River to Fish Creek, now on park land. It is a rapidly moving stream fed by melting snow. We drove over on Charley Gregory Bridge, a substantial log bridge, in a rented 4-wheel drive onto the grassy fields, following the river. Shortly the ruins appeared, just inside the park grounds.

We walked toward the headwaters where the old irrigation canal was sourced, and along the low berm remaining. John had hand dug a mile-long irrigation canal diverting some of the waters. It was still there.

Fish Creek really moves water, and it does have boulders. My mother [Hazel] told me that once Amelia gave her a severe spanking for crossing it on a log.

The log cabin he had built was razed by the rangers as a drug den. I picked up some shards of the old iron stove, some chimney bricks he had chiseled out of local stone, and a large blackened hearthstone I could hardly carry.

Due West from Dunton about 6 miles is a large dome-shaped mountain. My father told me it lies at the back of the ranch. Streams on its east and west side join to form a single channel running south-southwest; the whole looks like a 'Y'. The stem of the 'Y' was the ranch.

Dunton Hot Springs was the nearest town and figures in the family history.

John Leavenworth abandoned his wife Amelia Bradley from Eldred, perhaps on her invitation. She was left to cope with her family on a small ranch with a short growing season 4,000 feet up in the mountains of Dolores County, Colorado.—Gerald Koenig.

Boarding Houses, 1895 to 1898

Crest Hill Cottage, Barryville
1-1/2 miles from Shohola Station; Health resort; elevation 1,600 feet. Superior rooms and board. Send for circular. Mrs. Greig.—Brooklyn Daily Eagle, *June 23, 1895.*

Highland Cottage, Yulan
On Washington Lake; near Shohola Glen, on Erie R.R.; elevation 2,000 feet; boating bathing, fishing; beautiful scenery; overlooking 15 miles; fine drives and good bicycle roads; terms $6 to $7. A.E. Grove.—Brooklyn Daily Eagle, *June 23, 1895.*

West Farm, Yulan
Pleasant location; high altitude; good table; pure spring water; airy rooms; boating, fishing and bathing; four miles from Shohola Glen, Pa. Theodore West.—Brooklyn Daily Eagle, *June 23, 1895. Postcard courtesy of Larry Stern.*

Mount Pleasant House, Barryville
Large cool rooms; plenty shade; pine grove; adults $5 to 6 per week; children according to age. Send for circular. Wm. Wolfe.—Brooklyn Daily Eagle, *July 5, 1896. Postcard courtesy of Larry Stern.*

Pine Grove Farm, Box 41, Eldred
Boats free; fresh milk, butter and eggs; good livery; [Maier].—New York World, *June 16, 1897.*

Cold Spring Farm, Yulan
Will accommodate few families; $5 per week; plenty of milk, butter, eggs, vegetables from farm; lake 3/4 mile from house; boats free; good roads, shade, pine groves; elevation 2,00 feet; no malaria. Circular Eagle Bureau. M.E. Crandall, Yulan.—Brooklyn Daily Eagle, *July 25, 1897.*

Highland Cottage, Yulan
Near Shohola Glen; elevation 2,000 feet; boating, bathing, fishing, bowling alleys; terms $6 to $8. Circulars at Eagle Bureau. A.E. Grove. Brooklyn Daily Eagle, *June 21, 1897.*

Mountain Lake House, Venoge
Altitude 2,000 feet; finest place in Sullivan County; good table; bathing, boating, fishing; terms $7 to $8; Write for booklet. Address above.—Brooklyn Daily Eagle, *June 12, 1898.*

Highland Cottage, Yulan
Near Shohola Glen; on Washington Lake, elevation 2,000 feet; boating; bathing, fishing; beautiful scenery; fine drives; bowling alleys; terms $6 to $8. Dalton & Corey.—Brooklyn Daily Eagle, *August 20, 1898.*

Dolores River near Fish Creek and Dunton, Colorado, where John and Amelia Leavenworth and their daughters lived. Photo courtesy of Louisa Gray LeSatz.

Mine shaft in Rico, Colorado. Photo courtesy of Louisa Gray LeSatz.

John, Ida, and Myrtie Crabtree. Myrtie would marry Irwin Briggs. Photo courtesy of Mary Briggs Austin.

Amelia married rancher Charles Eber Gregory when Hazel was 3. In 1900 Eber and Amelia Gregory and Amelia's children, Lottie, 16, Ida, 6, and Hazel, 4, lived in the gold mining town of Rico, Dolores County, Colorado.

In 1900 John Leavenworth was an ore miner in Telluride, Colorado, 28 miles north of Rico. He was listed as divorced and lodged with a number of other boarders in the area. (There are several stories told about how John and Amelia's marriage ended.)

Crabtree and Briggs Families

My maternal grandmother Amanda Myrtie Crabtree lived with her parents John and Ida Higginson Crabtree in South Dakota. In 1891 Grandma Myrtie was born in a sod house in Nebraska. Shortly after her birth, the Crabtree family moved to the new town of Bonesteel, South Dakota. They lived there a few years and then moved to Mondamin, Iowa. The family returned to Nebraska when Myrtie was in her teens.

Irwin Briggs, Myrtie Crabtree's future husband, was born in Indiana. When Irwin was about a year old, he and his mother Marium Indianola Clark Briggs took the train to Ainsworth, Nebraska, where his father Clinton L. Briggs and grandfather James T. Briggs had a homestead.

It would be the 1930s before Myrtie, her husband Irwin Briggs, and their family arrived in the Town of Highland. Irwin would be the Methodist pastor for the Pond Eddy, Barryville, and Eldred Methodist Churches.

Lair and Rouillon Families in Paris, France

Several thousand miles from Eldred, Jeanne Marguerite Marie Lair was born in Paris, France. Jeanne would be the mother of Gisele Rouillon who would marry a son of Garfield Leavenworth. Jeanne's parents Albert Auguste Henri Lair and Armandine Aimee Dubos both died when she was young.

My mother was raised in a convent, where she did a lot of embroidery on pillowcases and sheets, according to my dad.
—*Gisele Rouillon Leavenworth.*

Jeanne Lair's future husband Cyrus Albert Rouillon, son of Blanche Malinge and Jean Rouillon (a baker), was born in Wissous, France, in June 1896.

Oliver B. and Emma Schwab Hallock

We met Oliver Blizzard Hallock and his wife Emma Amelia Schwab in, *The Mill on Halfway Brook*. Oliver and Emma had 3 children, but only Samuel Jesse Hallock lived to adulthood.

In 1896 Samuel J. Hallock married Anna May Buchanan at his home in Hillside, Lumberland. Samuel and Anna were the parents of one daughter, Eunice Hallock, and 9 sons.

Eunice would marry Ernest J. Clark, son of John H. Clark and Carrie Bogert. Eunice and Ernest would be the parents of Stella Clark who would marry a son of Garfield Leavenworth.

Two of Samuel and Anna May Hallock's sons are a part of this story. Raymond S. Hallock would be the father of Doug Hallock, husband of Emily Knecht Hallock. Oliver Lewis Hallock was the ancestor of Carolyn Hallock Clark.

In 1896 Oliver Blizzard Hallock died. Emma Schwab Hallock, an expert oil painter, later married Chris Hallenbeck.

A large group of Hallocks settled in the area above Handsome Eddy (sometimes called Hillside). Emily Knecht Hallock told two stories about the families she heard in September 1968 from "Aunt Lib Bloom."

William Hallock, brother of Oliver Blizzard (and father of Daniel Hallock the hunting guide), was blind from a rafting accident *(see p. 91)*.

William Hallock and a small boy were fishing on a lake or river. When the boat overturned, he instructed the boy to get on his back and direct him to shore, which the boy did. Though blind, William still managed to save their lives using the boy's sight for his own.

Many women in the family were named *Mary*. To keep them straight, the husband's name was added. So, for example: William Hallock's wife (Mary Brodt) was called Aunt *Mary-Bill*.

Oliver Blizzard Hallock (1834–1896). Photo courtesy of Emily Knecht Hallock.

Emma Amelia Schwab Hallock Hallenbeck (1852–1926). Photo courtesy of Emily Knecht Hallock.

Anna May Buchanan. Photo courtesy of Emily Knecht Hallock.

Samuel Jesse Hallock. Photo courtesy of Emily Knecht Hallock.

Another brother of Oliver B. and William Hallock, Daniel Van Tuyl Hallock, and his wife, Mary Alice Rider (Aunt *Mary-Dan*, perhaps), had 4 children. Dan and Mary Rider Hallock's daughter Annie married Archibald Pine. In 1900 Mary Alice Rider Hallock, a widow, lived with her 2 daughters and mother, Susan Van Tuyl Rider McPhillemy, also a widow.

Pond Eddy sometime after the fall of the 1898 season when the D&H Canal ceased operation. Photo courtesy of the Minisink Valley Historical Society.

Leavenworth Family, 1900

Back in Eldred, the 1900 Census listed Sherman S. and Maria Leavenworth's family: Anna was a school teacher; Truman, James Garfield, and Martin D. were farm laborers; the two youngest, Charlotte, 10, and Christina, 6, were in school. Where was their daughter Jennie? We'll find out in the next chapter.

Demise of the D&H Canal

The D&H Canal, which for 50 years had been responsible for much of the growth in commerce and population along the Upper Delaware River, came to a close at the end of the fall 1898 season.

The D&H Canal became the Delaware and Hudson Company.

In the autumn of 1898, the D&H Canal Company announced the closing of the canal at the close of the navigation season. —Johnston, p. 125.

Around 1898, the canal company was rebuilding the bridge across the Delaware River at Lackawaxen and Minisink Ford. By spring it was ready for the boats, but that was the last time that it was used as a canal.

All the men lost their jobs— the men that had operated the locks and the 150 Italians that came up every year to quarry rocks out of the side hill for the fill to fortify the spillway at the dam.

The canal company offered land cheap to the people living along it. There had been rumors that there would be a railroad built on it, but it never did as the Erie alongside it could handle all the business. The railroad could bring the coal down in 7 hours while it took a canal boat several days. So went another industry. —Lou Kloss Memoirs.

The [Roebling] aqueduct was then converted to a private toll bridge. Eventually, the towpaths were sawn off and the wooden trunk walls were dismantled. The protective icebreakers were not maintained and were destroyed by the river over time.—www.nps.gov/upde/historyculture/roeblingbridge.htm

Holbert Property

In October 1898 Frederick and Mary Holbert paid the Canal $300 for the 3 acre farm with house and barn that they had been renting. The Holbert property, just south of where the Lackawaxen River joined the Delaware River (in Pennsylvania), would be owned by author Zane Grey in a few years.

Mr. Grey had gone to dental school on a baseball scholarship, and in 1898 had his own dental practice in New York City. He and his brother Romer Grey enjoyed exploring, fishing, and hunting in the "really wild country" near Lackawaxen, Pennsylvania.

Decline of Bluestone

In 1899, a serious blow was dealt to the bluestone industry by the introduction into the United States of the rotary kiln for making Portland Cement. Because it was cheaper and easier to obtain and transport, cement began to replace bluestone for sidewalks. Through the twentieth century all the uses of bluestone declined rapidly.—*Fluhr, George, J., Quarries, Kilgour, and Pike County, Pennsylvania, 1984, p. 18.*

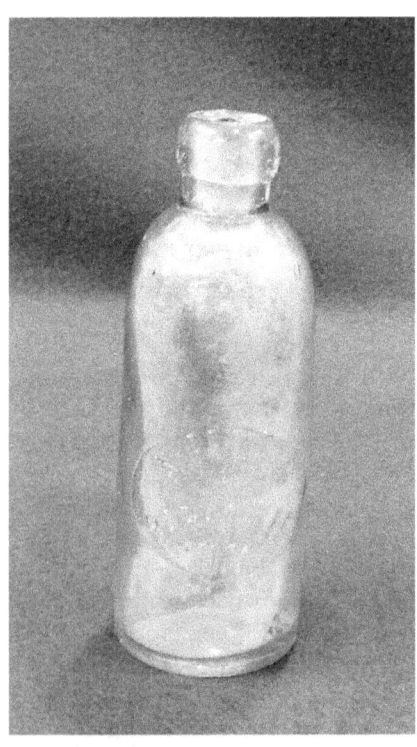

Soda bottle from the Pelton Soda Bottle Factory. From the collection of Kevin Marrinan.

Pelton Soda Bottle Factory
Less than five miles east of Zane Grey's future property was an old D&H Canal office building in Barryville that Asher and Carrie Pelton had turned into a Soda Factory. The William Kerr family lived next door to the factory.

Directly opposite this [Kerr] house, on the westerly side of the canal and beside the tow path, is the spacious dwelling house once of the Canal Company, and quite recently sold to a man named Pelton. It stands midway and opposite lock No. 71 [lock numbers have since changed], and on the side of the original lock house...

It was erected in 1869 as a residence for the superintending foreman of the company and as a stopping place for the higher dignitaries connected with the company...It was inhabited by James H. Quick until sold to Pelton...It is rather a desirable place.—Johnston, p. 324.

In 1900 Asher Pelton was a carpenter. He and Carrie had two sons: Edward and Howard, who were day laborers.

An October 4, 1900 land deed stated that Carrie Pelton, Ashur's wife, bought the property from the D&H Canal Co. for $1,000.

In 1836 that property (one boundary of which was "along a line of white pine trees") had been sold to the D&H Canal Company by Robert and Phebe Johnston. James Eldred was the commissioner at the time.

The Pelton Company made their own bottles and filled them with their own soda and shipped them on the canal to the city.

The next chapter follows the Austin family on the east side of Eldred, through the 1890s.

Some Gardner and Sergeant Families

Hazel and Ella Phoebe Sergeant, daughters of Frank and Clarissa Clark Sergeant. Photo courtesy of Cynthia Leavenworth Bellinger.

You will remember that the Sergeant families originally lived near the Leavenworths of Eldred.

In 1896 Hazel Ruth was born to Frank and Clarissa Clark Sergeant. Hazel's sister Ella Phoebe would marry Garfield Leavenworth, son of Sherman S. Leavenworth.

Isaac and Elizabeth Persbacher Sergeant's daughter Minnie Ethel was 6 in 1896. Little Minnie would be the wife of Archibald Myers son of Abel S. and Maria Hankins Myers.

Isaac Sergeant's mother Lettie Gardner Sergeant (widow of Ethel Sergeant) died in March 1892 at age 84. Lettie, daughter of Sears and Mary Keen Gardner, had been born in Pond Eddy.

Lettie's youngest sibling, Eliza Gardner Young, was also born in Pond Eddy. Eliza lived in Philadelphia, Pennsylvania, and was an ancestor of the Maudsleys who are friends of my family.

Mary A. Greiger Gardner, widow of Sears Robert Gardner, died in 1898. Sears R. Gardner was the brother of Lettie Sergeant and Eliza Young. Mary A. Greiger Gardner was a relative of Elizabeth Greiger Kyte.

Lettie Sergeant's son Alvah Sergeant (brother of Isaac) died in Eldred in 1897. Alvah was survived by his wife Phebe Owen Sergeant, 7 children, 27 grandchildren, 2 great-grandchildren, 2 brothers, and 2 sisters.

Phebe Owen Sergeant then lived with her son and his wife, Morgan and Lettie Sergeant. Morgan was a laborer.

Bertha M. Hill, a granddaughter of Alvah and Phebe Owen Sergeant, was born in 1898. Bertha's parents were Thomas and Alice Sergeant Hill. Bertha would marry a descendant of C.C.P. and Effie VanTuyl Eldred.

William and Jane Sergeant Livingston had 7 children.

Gladys Hill, daughter of John and Esther Grinnell Hill, was born in 1900. John Hill was a Sergeant descendant.

Frank and Alma Sergeant Kelley's children: Everett, Raola, and Leila.

Minnie Sergeant, daughter of Isaac and Elizabeth Persbacher Sergeant. Photo courtesy of Chuck Myers, Minnie's son.

Roebling Aqueduct Converted to Toll Bridge

Roebling Bridge. The aqueduct was converted to a private toll bridge. The towpaths were sawn off; the wooden trunk walls dismantled. Photo: Library of Congress, Prints and Photographs Division; Historic Engineering Record: HAER PA, 52 LACK,1-11.

Roebling Bridge. Photo: Library of Congress: HAER PA,52 LACK,1-9.

In 1898 the last boat moved over the waterway [Aqueduct] and the following year the physical plant of the system was liquidated.

Of the four suspension aqueducts that Roebling designed as part of the major enlargement operation, only the Delaware had any apparent adaptive usefulness. The spans over the Lackawaxen, Neversink, and Roundout were all simply abandoned and eventually demolished.

The Delaware Aqueduct was purchased privately and converted into a highway bridge. The tow paths were sawn off, a low railing was run along the downstream side of the trunk floor to provide a separated pedestrian walk, a toll house was built at the New York end, and some grading was done at each end for accommodation to the existing roads...

The first private owner was Charles Spruks, a Scranton lumber dealer, who specialized in the heavy timbers used as supports in the area's coal mines. His principal timber lands being in Sullivan County, N.Y., he purchased the aqueduct primarily to afford a simple means of getting the logs across the Delaware to the railroad in Lackawaxen. The collection of tolls from common road traffic was actually a side line.—From Edward H. Huber, Scranton; Roebling Bridge, HAER No. PA-1, 52, LACK; page 7.

Roebling Bridge. Photo: Library of Congress: HAER PA, 52, LACK,1-8.

One of the supports for the Roebling Bridge. Photo: Library of Congress: HAER PA, 52 LACK,1-6.

Chapter 6
An Old Bachelor
The Austins of Highland, 1890–1900

I have made up my mind to live an old bachelor the rest of my days. Don't you think I would make a good one?
  But I think you would do well to take Nell for I guess she is a real good girl and I think you would be better off with a good wife than single.—Mort Austin's letter to his brother Lon.

Jennie Louisa Leavenworth would change Mort's mind about being a bachelor. Photo courtesy of Cynthia Leavenworth Bellinger.

Charles Mortimer (Mort) Austin's advice to his brother Albert Alonzo (Lon) Austin did not work out well for Lon. Nor did Mort take his own advice, fortunately for me.

Mort and Lon had each had romantic relationships and even wedding plans, according to several of the letters. But in 1890 they were both still bachelors.

Mort and Lon always enjoyed a good debate. Others might have thought them antagonistic toward each other, but they were not. They just loved to spar with words.

Both Lon and Mort had Exhorter's Licenses which were given to lay preachers.

Lon drank whiskey and smoked cigars. Mort did not. So Lon called Mort "the good boy."

Temperance instruction seemed to be of importance in past years. Church congregations would have debates to persuade parishioners not to drink.

On one occasion no one would take the pro side of evil alcohol. So Mort Austin, a non drinker, touted the benefits of alcoholic beverages, and won the debate. People in the church were mad at him for years.

In 1890 Lon was 33, and Mort was 25. At the end of the year, Mort started seminary in New Jersey. Through much of the 1890s Lon worked for William F. Proctor at his Lochada summer home and property. Lon was listed as a farm manager in the Lumberland 1900 Census.

Henry and Mary Ann Austin's Family and Boarding House
Henry and Mary Ann Austin's Mountain Grove House on Proctor Road was completed by 1894, so Mort Austin & Co. then advertised for boarders.

In 1891 Aida Austin taught school in Phillipsport, New York. Maria, initially in New York City, would help at the boarding house as did all the children at different times.

There is very little recorded information in the 1890s on Mort and Lon's brother Ell and his family. Ell, Emma, Lillie, and probably, Henry Earl and Emma's sister Sophronia Parmenter lived in Bethel. A disagreement between Ell and his mother and sister Aida

Proctor Road to Glen Spey around 1900. The school is in the center of the photograph. It was built with the help of George Ross MacKenzie, and is currently the Lumberland Town Hall. Photo courtesy of the Proctor Family.

was severe enough that both Mary Ann and Aida went to see a lawyer.

In January Annie Collins, at one time an Austin neighbor, wrote to Mary Ann Austin. Annie was a sister to Tom and Robert Collins. Bertie (or Bertha Collins) was the daughter of Robert, a Methodist minister.

Annie Collins, Bloomfield, N.J., to Mary Ann Austin
January 5, 1890
Dear Mrs. Austin,

Your very welcome letter was received over a week ago.

I thank you very much for your kind invitation to come and see you. I will be unable to accept this winter, but in the Spring, will try to do so before I go out to Chicago.

For over a week I have been at Robert's who is stationed at Bloomfield. Bertie is home on her vacation from the Seminary at Hackettstown and I have been helping the dressmaker make some clothes for her. She goes back to school tomorrow.

They are all well at South Orange excepting they have colds, and everybody is having them. Bertie and Emma have been quite sick, but both are better now.

Sometime when I'm in New York, I will go see Maria since you have given me her address.

Have you had the new disease yet, "La Grippe [an influenza pandemic]?" Everybody is having it and in some cases it proves fatal.

I think you had better get ready and go out West with me. Don't you?

I wish for you a Happy and Prosperous New Year. As ever,
Your loving Annie

In January 1890 Irvin and Laura Austin Clark's second grandchild Lillie Clark was born in Pennsylvania to Elbert Clark and his wife. Lillie's brother Frank Clark was 2 years old.

The Eldred and Austin relatives we first met in *The Mill on Halfway Brook* have become elderly and several of them died in 1890.

Charles Cotesworth Pickney (C.C.P.) Eldred Dies
In March 1890 Uncle C.C.P. Eldred, the brother of Mary Ann Eldred Austin, Eliza Eldred Gardner, and Maria Eldred Austin, died. Charles Cotesworth Pinckney Eldred was 7 when he arrived in Lumberland with his family at the end of 1815. They had settled in an old log cabin with a sawmill near Halfway Brook.

C.C.P. Eldred had joined the Congregational Church of Lumberland in March 1824. He was very active in the work of the church and served as a deacon from 1849 until his death in 1890.

C.C.P. had also been Postmaster of Eldred for a number of years. He was responsible for renaming Halfway Brook Village when the U.S. Post Office required a shorter name. So the charming, much preferred (to me, anyway) name of Halfway Brook Village became

1890s Descendants of James and Polly V. Mulford Eldred

Abraham Mulford Eldred Descendants

Mulford Eldred had died young. His widow Elizabeth Wheeler Eldred Travis died in 1894.

She was a good woman in sickness and had a great many friends.—The Wayne Independent, *May 16, 1894.*

Mulford and Elizabeth Eldred's son Frank (Benjamin Franklin) Eldred was a supervisor for Damascus Township, Pennsylvania, in 1895. That year Frank's wife Almira Barnes died. Frank then married Margaret Rutledge, a widow, in Honesdale.

Around 1899 Frank Eldred visited his sister Amelia Eldred Hancy who he had not seen for 35 years. Some descendants of Frank Eldred's sons, John F. Eldred and Lewis LaForde Eldred, are a part of this story.

John Franklin Eldred ran his father's farm until April 1900. John was a woodcutter and bought 78 acres in West Damascus, Pennsylvania. He and his wife Minnie Sears would have 11 children, including Orvis R. Eldred, father of Richard O. Eldred.

Judson Eldred, son of Frank and Almira Barnes Eldred, ran his father's farm after April 1900, and bought it in 1902. Judson married Emily Dunlop.

Lewis Laforde, the youngest child of Frank and Almira Eldred, would marry Cora Sisson.

In March 1899 Clara Eldred Theadore (daughter of Frank and Almira Eldred) wrote her sister that her brothers Lewis and Judson were staying with her and were lumbering for a Mr. Leighton. Lewis and Judson were cutting wood and John was driving a team.

C.C.P Eldred Descendants

C.C.P and Effa Van Tuyl Eldred's son George W. Eldred had died at the age of 35 because of a fall off the roof. George's wife Marietta West Eldred later married Samuel Hoatson.

George and Marietta's sons, James and Herbert Lincoln Eldred, lived with their grandparents, C.C.P. and Effa Eldred. Herbert L. Eldred and his wife Eliza Coleman Post would most likely live in his Eldred grandparents' home. Herbert was a carpenter, a Justice of the Peace for 30 years, a member of the Highland Town Board, and a member of the Eldred Congregational Church. Several of Herbert and Eliza Eldred's children play a part in the story.

C.C.P. and Effa's grandson James Eldred (Herbert's brother) at one time worked on the Gravity Railroad in Honesdale, Pennsylvania.

James married Elizabeth Hardcastle. Their daughter Elizabeth J. Eldred would marry George Dunlap. James and Elizabeth Eldred's other daughter, Cora Hardcastle Eldred, would marry a descendant of Zophar and Sarah Eldred Carmichael and would be instrumental in collecting Eldred Family information.
—*Information from Richard O. Eldred's,* The Eldred Family.

Eldred, named after C.C.P. Eldred's father, James Eldred, or named after C.C.P. himself —both stories are told.

In March, Charles C.C.P. Eldred died at his Eldred home after a three week illness. He was buried the following Wednesday in Highland Cemetery in Eldred.
—The Port Jervis Union, *March 12, 1890.*

He [C.C.P. Eldred] was an honest industrious man of most excellent qualities which made him a great favorite in the community in which he lived.
—The Evening Gazette, *March 10, 1890.*

Mary Ann Eldred Austin, my great-grandmother. Photo courtesy of Mary Briggs Austin.

Mort Austin on the right. Photo courtesy of Mary Briggs Austin.

Mr. C.C.P. Eldred died Sunday morning, February 9. He was of long and faithful standing of the Congregational Church. One by one the old pillars of the church are falling down. Ah, who will take their places?—Austin family notebook.

In May, C.C.P. Eldred's grandson George Washington Eldred Jr., 18, son of Marietta West Eldred Hoatson, drowned in the Delaware and Hudson Canal at High Falls, New York. (George W. Eldred, his father, had died in 1872.)—The Evening Gazette, May 19, 1890.

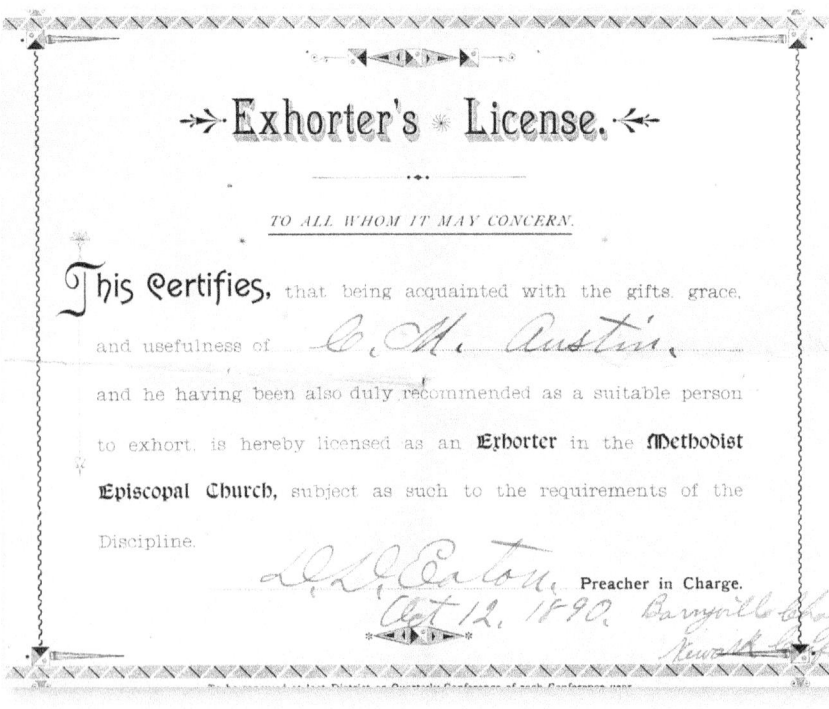

Mort's Methodist Exhorter's License, 1890. Certificate courtesy of Mary Briggs Austin.

Augustus and Phebe Maria Austin
In August Uncle Augustus Austin, husband of Aunt Maria Eldred Austin, died. Augustus was a brother to Henry Austin and Laura Austin Clark.

Augustus seems to have been the first of Ralph and Fanny Knapp Austin's children to live in what was then Lumberland. He was in Lumberland by 1834, the year he joined the Congregational Church and married Phebe Maria Eldred.

Died on Monday morning, August 4, Augustus A. Austin, in the 81st year of his age. Relatives and friends are respectfully invited to attend the funeral services at his late residence, 111 East 82nd St., on Tuesday evening at half-past seven o'clock. Interment at Paterson, N.J., on Wednesday morning.—New York Herald, August 5, 1890.

At the end of September, Augustus's widow Aunt Maria Eldred Austin died. She was the sister of Mary Ann Eldred Austin and Eliza Eldred Gardner.

Phebe Maria Eldred Austin was born in January 1816 in Lumberland in the cabin near Halfway Brook—10 days after her parents James and Polly Eldred had arrived from their home in Orange County, New York.

On Tuesday, September 30, Phoebe M., widow of Augustus A. Austin, in her 75th year. Funeral services at her late residence, 111 East 82d St., this evening at 8 o'clock.—The New York Times, New York City, 1890.

Centenary Collegiate Institute, Hackettstown, New Jersey
In October 1890, Mort Austin received an acceptance letter from

Centenary Collegiate Institute, a seminary in Hackettstown, New Jersey. Centenary was founded by the Newark Methodist Episcopal Church in 1867. It was built at a cost of $200,000. George H. Whitney, D.D., was president from 1869 to 1895. In September 1884 the tuition and board was $275 for 36 weeks.

Geo. Whitney, Hackettstown, N.J., to Mort Austin, Eldred
October 20, 1890
Dear C. M. Austin:
My Dear Sir:
  Your favor is rec. We shall be glad to have you come on the 3rd of Dec., the day of our term opening.
  I enter your name for that time, we shall be glad to do what we can for you.
  Sincerely yours,
  Geo. H. Whitney, President
  Centenary Collegiate Institute

  He [Mort Austin] studied to be a minister, but only went one year. I know he took Greek and also studied "Milton's Paradise Lost." C. Soule Bok was a Chinese doctor he knew at school."
—Robert Austin, son.

  The letters of C. Soule Bok from the Austin Archive are included in this chapter.

Archie Paton Dies
In November Archie Paton, husband of Cousin Rand Austin Paton, died. 1890 must have been a difficult year for Rand as both her parents and her husband died. Only her son Archie and daughter Ida were still living.

  On Saturday November 1st, 1890, Archibald H. Paton, Beloved husband of Miranda A. Paton, age 46 years.
  Friends and relatives are respectfully invited to attend the funeral on Tuesday Nov. 4th, 1890, from his late residence No. 17 Hamburgh Ave. at 2 o'clock p.m. Interment at Cedar Lawn.

Austin Land, Taxes, and Ledgers
On November 13 Charles M. (Mort) Austin bought 9-1/2 acres from his brother Lon for $225. This seems to be the property that Mountain Grove House would be

Letter from George W. Whitney, the president of Centenary Collegiate College in Hackettstown, New Jersey, to Mort Austin. Letter courtesy of Mary Briggs Austin.

Labor Costs in Eldred

It was hard earning a living in Eldred as a number of Mort and Lon's friends indicated in their letters. One of the Austin Grocery Books included the rates they charged for work done in April through July 1890, when Henry Austin was 66 years old. Perhaps Mort, Lon, and Henry Ladore (Dory) helped with the work.

Rates charged:
8 hours with a horse	$1.60
1 whole day with a horse	$2.00
1 day of work (no horse)	$1.00
1/2 day of work (no horse)	$.50

Centenary Collegiate Institute on an 1891 envelope, courtesy of Mary Briggs Austin.

on, near the junction of Highland Lake and Proctor Roads. This land changes hands often, perhaps depending on who had money.

There are records of the taxes Ell Austin paid on 180 acres by Smoky Hill River in Kansas each December in the 1890s. In 1890 Ell paid $45.42 for the property which was valued at $1,370.

The December 1890 and January and February 1891 entries in the Austin work ledger indicated that William Henry Austin helped out his neighbor and sister-in-law, Effa Eldred, after her husband C.C.P. had died.

Lon Austin rented from Walter Styles in 1891. Walter was married to Henrietta Austin, Cousin Alonzo Eugene Austin's daughter. At some point Alonzo Eugene Austin became the owner of most of the 260 acres originally owned by Augustus and/or Henry Austin.

Alonzo Eugene Austin and his wife Belle Camp were in Alaska, but return by the end of this chapter. Alonzo Eugene Austin Jr. was at Tilton Seminary in New Hampshire, and later went to Columbia College where he got his M.D.

The letters in previous chapters indicated that Mort's father Henry Austin had been hard on Mort and the Austin home had not been a happy one. In this first letter from college, Mort seems hopeful of a change in his father. The Congregational Church record states that William Henry Austin became a member in 1890, and was later a trustee.

Mort Austin, Hackettstown, N.J., to Lon Austin, Eldred
*Winter 1891
Dear Brother,
I hope you will not think I did not appreciate your very kind letter by my long delay in answering, for I have made 3 or 4 faithful attempts to answer it.
I have been very busy since my return to H. [Hackettstown]. I have taken up a Bible study which requires two hours study each day and we have to go to class on Saturday afternoon.
I am very glad to learn that the Lord is pouring out his blessing on the people at Eldred. It also gave me great joy to know that the family altar [Bible reading and prayer time] has been erected for I think there is so much strength derived from it. It must be a very different home now. I trust every thing will be sunshine and happiness.
I have much I would like to say on this subject, but time will not permit. I do most earnestly thank God for His watchful care over us and my prayer is that our kind and loving Father in heaven will take care of us as a family and bring us safely through this life that we may meet each other where parting will never come.
I saw Bertha a few days ago. I was in the kitchen getting something for one of the boys that was sick and she came in, so we came face to face. I think we were both some what confused. I spoke to her, asked how her folks were, and gave her my folks' best regards. Mr. Collins has been sick and also Bertie.
How are you making out with your house? Is little Jimmy well and the other horses?
Remember me to all my friends, especially Miss Norah.
I remain as ever,
Mort*

Mort Austin, Hackettstown, N.J., to Lon Austin, Eldred
*January 14, 1891
Dear Brother,
I was real glad to hear from you. I have recited my last lesson for today. So we will have a little time to do as we like before supper time.
I will write you a few lines in answer to your ever welcome letter. Bertie Collins will not be back here this year.
I think I learn to trust God more and more every day I am*

here. I am getting along quite well with my studies now, but of course, I have to work hard to get them, and the worst of all is I will have to write a composition next week. I dread that the most.

Do you think you will be able to get ready for boarders next summer? And how are you getting along with your house? I hope you will have good luck.

The weather here is almost like spring. The snow is all gone. I suppose you have plenty of snow at Eldred.

I have not heard from mother, have you?

I wish you would remember me to Brother Boyd when you see him, and tell him I will write to him before long.

I am quite well. I do not have time to get lonesome, but I get very tired and will be glad when my school days are over.

If I didn't feel that God had a work for me to do, I think my days at school would be short. But I must be reconciled to do God's will. I tell you some of the fellows feel very discouraged. I don't mind it like some of them do.

I hope you will write very soon and tell me all the news.

Tell father I will write to him soon. Please excuse haste.

With love to all, I close,
C.M. Austin

Mort Austin, Hackettstown, N.J., to Lon Austin, Eldred
February 8, 1891
My dear Brother Lon,

I have been staying with a friend this week that is rooming on the second floor. So I will not have to sweep my room this Saturday.

I find that to accomplish our aims in life we must stick to it, although the way may be rough and dark, "Let us be sure we are right, and then go ahead."

I am glad you are going to join the Methodist Church, for I feel the Lord has a work for you to do there. I am sure you will grow in grace faster, in the Methodist Church, than in the other one.

I think Walter [Styles] is very reasonable in his charge for the house. I suppose he will let you have a garden and the use of the lake. I do believe the Lord will bless you in your business and it looks as if you will get along good. But in the hour of prosperity, forget not the Lord who is the giver.

I wish you would tell father I have not forgotten him, but will try and write him a few lines.

Give my love to Brother Boyd. Is he going to do anything?
Mort

Mary Ann Austin, to Lon Austin, Eldred
April 26, 1891
My Dear Son,

Something has occurred that I change my mind. I can't come home till Saturday. I thought if I was alive, I should go Wednesday. Nothing but sickness or death will hinder me from coming, unless it rains Saturday.

Will you write when you get this and let me know if you or Mort can take me to Monticello one day next week—that is the first week in May. You need not mention my going to Monticello.

I hear you have given up the place to Lon. I hope you have not been so unwise. I am anxious to see you all.

Don't fail to answer. I will certainly come Saturday unless it rains hard.

Much love to you all.
Your ever loving Mother

Austin Land Changes Owners
The above letter may indicate that Alonzo (Lon) Eugene Austin had bought the Austin homestead. It is not known if Alonzo Eugene Austin Sr. (in Alaska) or his son Alonzo Jr. bought it.

Also, Mary Ann may have been in Monticello to see F.F. Bush (a lawyer), as had Aida, as shown in this next letter. The reason mother and daughter went to see an attorney seems to be connected to Ell (James E. Austin) and the Austin homestead.

The Austin land deeds are confusing as to who owns what land and when it was sold. It seems from several deeds that Ell Austin may have gotten himself into a financial bind having to pay taxes on the property in Kansas as well as on property in Eldred.

School tax of 80 cents paid by Mort Austin. Check courtesy of Mary Briggs Austin.

F.F. Bush, Monticello, N.Y., to Aida Austin
July 18, 1891
Miss Austin,

Your letter of the 15th is just at hand. I suppose you paid the costs and the $2 to the justice. I do not think you need have any fears as to the result of your case.

As to the matter of paying me. You gave me $5.00 retainer and we will let the matter stand until we see what results we get. I expect to collect enough from James E. to pay me. If I do not, I will allow you to pay me.

Very respectfully, F.F. Bush
Attorney and counsellor

Mort Austin, Hackettstown, N.J., to Aida Austin, Phillipsport, N.Y.
September 9, 1891
My dear Sister,

I left home on Tuesday morning, reached Mr. Collins in the afternoon, remained there till morning. Then Bertie and I started for Hackettstown; Arrived here 10:30. I had a real good time at Mr. Collins. Bloomfield is a very nice place.

I feel I have got a good fellow to room with and a nice room on the first floor.

The way looks brighter than ever before. I think I will be able to do good work this time. I could not get time to write to you at home. I was very glad to hear you like your school so well. I am well, but quite busy getting my room in order.

With much love I close. As ever your loving brother,
Mort

Mort Austin, Hackettstown, N.J., to Lon Austin, Eldred
September 20, 1891
Dear Brother,

I was real glad to hear that Flora [their horse] has recovered from her sickness! But more than sorry to learn of poor little Jimmy's illness. I hope he gets well, for he will make a fine horse.

You must feel almost discouraged. Well Lon, it does seem very strange the way things goes at times. But surely, all will be well, if we continue to trust in the Lord.

I have been real sick for a few days, but am feeling somewhat better today.

The weather here is very hot. I am getting along real well with my studies. I do not feel able to write much today.

Give my best regards to the Bradleys, and remember me to Beck's folks, also to Boyds. Be sure to write soon, and tell how Jimmy is and how you are getting along. With love to all I close.
Your loving brother, Mort

Aida Austin, Phillipsport, N.Y., to Lon Austin, Eldred
September 21, 1891
Dear Brother [Lon],

I was sick all day yesterday and the day before with a sore throat. Was able to teach today, although, I do not feel very well yet. I have not written to Mort yet.

I wish you would tell Maria to finish my dresses as soon as she can for I need them very much.

Hope you will write soon and tell me all the Eldred news.
Your loving sister,
Aida

Mort Austin, Hackettstown, N.J., to Aida Austin, Phillipsport, N.Y.
October 26, 1891
Dear Sister,

Saturdays are the only days we have any spare time and so little then we hardly know it, for in the morning we have to clean up our room, take a bath, and get part of our lessons out for Monday.

I will be glad when Christmas comes and the examination is over and I can get home for a few days to see you all. To tell you the truth I did feel a little homesick when I received your letter that you had been home.

I told you that I would tell you all about why I did not go and talk to her, but I think I had better wait till I see you. Then I can tell you better.

I do not think you had better write to her, for she will think I got you to do it. I thank you for mailing that letter for me. Saturday she went home. I do not know when she will be back, so it is hard to tell when she will get the letter.

I tell you Aida, there are many very strange people in the world. But I find I have no time to worry or to think about the girls. For God has a particular work for me to do, that I am sure, and I feel I must improve every opportunity I have.

Sometimes the way is very dark and it is only by the grace of God I am able to get along. I am firmly trusting in the Lord and though friends forsake me, Jesus is mine and with my soul, all is well.

I am very sorry about one or two things that have happened. But I feel I have done what God would have me do.

I wish I could see you and have a good talk. I am getting along very well with all of my studies. I have not taken writing yet because I have not the time.

You could write to Miss Johnston if you think best and ask her and Bertie up Christmas. But do as you think best. I shall not care anything more about it.

How do you get along with

The main building on Ellis Island around 1905. From 1892 to 1954 over 12 million immigrants entered the United States through Ellis Island. Photo: Library of Congress, Prints and Photographs Division: Detroit Publishing Co., LC-D4-18676.

your school and do you like it as well as the one last year?

I hope you are well. Write very soon to your loving brother,
C.M. Austin

Lon Austin, Eldred, to Aida Austin, Phillipsport, N.Y.
October 26, 1891
Dear Sister,
Why don't you write? We have not heard from you since you went back. We begin to fear something is the matter.
It is so late I can't write tonight. Besides there is not much to write about. Do write soon.
In haste, your loving brother,
Lon

Tax Receipt, Eldred
November 18, 1891
Received of Ida Austin
The Sum of Seven Cents
For School Taxes.
School District 4; Lot 22
S.E. Carmichael, Collector

George Whitney, Hackettstown, N.J., to Mort Austin, Eldred
December 8, 1891
Dear C.M. Austin,
The registered letter came, and I credited the $40 in it to your account. Here is the receipt.
I trust you are well by this time, and that you will soon be back again among us.
With kind regards,
Geo. H. Whitney, President
Centenary College Institute

Ellis Island Opens
January 1892
On January 1, 1892, the U.S. Immigration Station on Ellis Island at the mouth of the Hudson River in New York Harbor opened. Previously, the states were responsible for immigrants.

The first structure on Ellis Island burned down in 1897. A new building opened in late 1900. Over 12 million immigrants had entered the U.S. through Ellis Island when it closed in 1954.

George Ross MacKenzie Dies
George Ross MacKenzie died in 1892, three years after he had retired as President of Singer Manufacturing Company. Mr. MacKenzie and his family were summer residents in Lumberland, on their 3,000 acre estate. Mr. MacKenzie had built a school, church, orphanage, and cemetery in Glen Spey (originally called South Lebanon).

Bramble Brae, one of the MacKenzie Mansions in Glen Spey, Town of Lumberland, New York. Photo courtesy of Frank V Schwarz.

The Erie Railroad Depot in Port Jervis, New York, opened their new station on February 2, 1892. This postcard from 1907 was addressed to Jennie Austin, and is in the collection of Mary Briggs Austin.

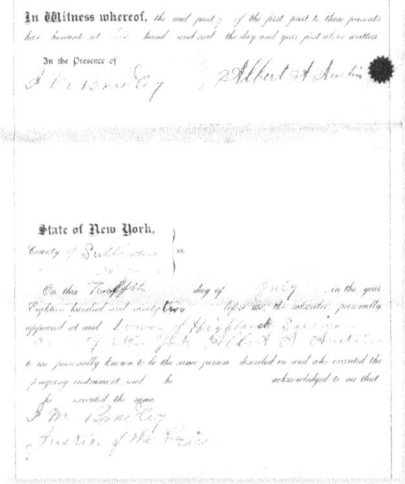

1892 Deed of Albert A. Austin (Lon) signed by I. M. Bradley, courtesy of Mary Briggs Austin.

A summer mansion was built for most of his children upon his death in 1892. Among the mansion names were, Windy Knoll, Woldcroft, Bel-Air, Ardmore, Burn Brae, Thornliebank, Bramble Brae and of course his, The Homestead. —Frank V Schwarz.

Mort Austin, Hackettstown, N.J. to Lon Austin, Eldred
January 4, 1892
Dear Brother,
  Well I am once more in my old room at the H. I arrived here about 7 o'clock, safe and sound. I did not go to New York. I suppose you are at church while I am writing.
  I am quite tired, so I will just write a few lines to let you know that all is well.
  Trusting that you will write very soon and with love to all, I remain as ever,
  Your loving brother,
  Mort

Mort completed a year of college. The above letter was the last college letter in the Austin Collection. Perhaps Mort left for health and/or financial reasons.

Erie Railroad Depot Opens
The Erie Railroad Depot in Port Jervis, New York, opened their new station on February 2, 1892.

Eldred, May 2, 1892
Received from Mortimer Austin:
The sum of 80/100 dollars for School Board Tax for 1891, $.80.
  S.E. Carmichael, Collector

James Moffatt, Poughkeepsie, N.Y., to Mort Austin, Eldred
May 14, 1892
My dear Austin [Mort],
  Well old boy, I am up here in Poughkeepsie at Eastman College, and I find it is very different from H. Town. We have about 400 students from almost every state and country.
  I have to study here more than I did at C.C.S. We are at it about 8 or 10 hours per day. The course here is thorough and hard.
  My dear Austin, I often think a great deal about you—your actions and honest words impressed me very greatly, and it is yours and others' Christian characters that stimulates to live a better life. I would like to see you very much at least once more.
  Do you ever hear from Bok? If you do, send him my best regards. I always liked Bok, he was a genuine fellow.
  Write me soon Austin. Your friend and chum, James Moffatt

F.F. Bush, Monticello, N.Y., to Aida Austin, Eldred
June 24, 1892
Miss Austin:
  I wrote you yesterday about your case. There is one thing that I want to tell you so that you can guard against it.
  There is no doubt but you sincerely think that James E. changed some of those letters—and wrote or had some of them written, and that he swore falsely in regard to them, but you must not say so to anyone for if you do he will very likely bring another

General Electric

General Electric was created in 1892, when Edison General Electric (Thomas Edison) and the Thomson-Houston Company (Charles A. Coffin) merged.—wikipedia.org.

action against you for slander, and give you a vast amount of trouble. If you are absolutely right about it, you would have great trouble to prove that he did so, and probably could not prove it, and then he would get a very big judgment that would trouble you all your life.

Take my advice and say nothing to anybody about the matter. The action will be dropped—and your mother's matters will be cleared up with him—and it is better to not say anything that will make you any more trouble.

*Very Respectfully,
F.F. Bush,
Attorney & Counsellor*

F.F. Bush, Monticello, N.Y., to Mary Ann Austin, Eldred
July 25, 1892
Mrs. Austin:
Both cases—yours and Aida's were settled Saturday. I enclose check for $550.00.
All costs and expenses including my services in both cases are paid in full.
Very truly yours,
F.F. Bush
Attorney & Counsellor

Austin Land Deeds and Ledgers
In July 1892 there was an Austin Deed document that indicates Lon bought property from his dad, Mort, and Aida.

A mortgage was signed between Albert A. Austin of the first part and Aida A. Austin, Charles M. Austin, and William H. Austin of the second part for $700. It was for 9-1/2 acres in Lot 21. I.M. Bradley, the Justice of the Peace, signed the document.

There are a number of grocery/work ledgers of the Austin family in my mother's collection. Some of the items mentioned in the 1892 booklet indicated that the Austins were doing some construction (*see 1892 Groceries, p. 175*). A couple letters have also alluded to a new place.

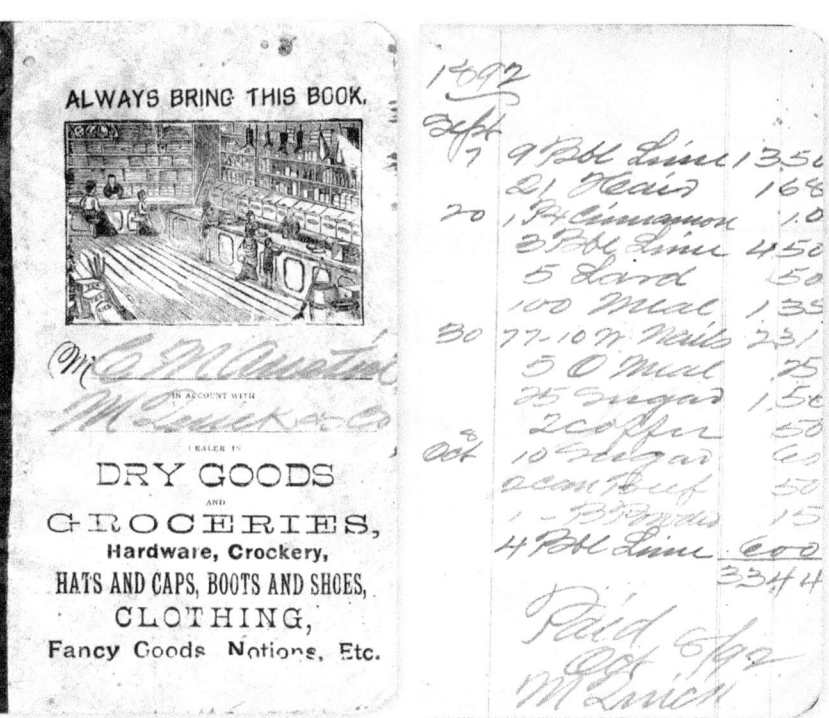

1892 Dry Goods, Groceries, etc.

C.M. Austin in account with M. Quick and Co., Dealer in Dry Goods and Groceries, Hardware, Crockery, Hats and Caps, Boots and Shoes, Clothing, Fancy Goods, Notions, Etc. Grocery book courtesy of Mary Briggs Austin.

Building supplies
35# hammer	2.80
3 cans paint	.75
30 gal. paint	42.00
1 boot oil	.10
5 L. nails	.75
1 bbl. lime	1.50
4 bbl. lime	6.00
5 bbl. lime	7.50
3-1/2 plaster Paris	.35
5 gallon b. oil	3.25
2 cans shellac	2.00
35 Bricks	.35
10-4D nails	.40
77-10W nails	2.31
5 gall. b. oil	3.25
1 w. hand oil	.60
1 turpentine	.60
3 cans paint	.75

Food staples
1 b. powder	.15
3 b. powder	.25
2 cans beef	.50
1 can beef	.25
5# butter	1.25
3 cake	.37
4 cinnamon	.10
2 coffee	.50
2 coffee	.60
2 doz. eggs	.40
4 ginger	.05
5# lard	.50
100 meal	1.35
50 meal	.25
4 mustard	.10
25 sugar	1.50
10 sugar	.60
1 tea	.50

In October 1892 Effa Van Tuyl Eldred died, two years after her husband C.C.P. Eldred. Effa was buried beside her husband in the old Eldred Cemetery.

Mountain Grove House may have been a boarding house by 1893. Postcard in the collection of Mary Briggs Austin.

Panic of 1893

The Panic of 1893 was a serious economic depression similar to the Panic of 1873 and the worst depression in the U.S. until the Great Depression.

The panic was caused by railroad overbuilding and shaky railroad financing which set off a series of bank failures. Along with market overbuilding and a railroad bubble was a run on the gold supply and a policy of using both gold and silver metals as a peg for the U.S. Dollar value.—*wikipedia.org.*

Nancy Wallace, Phillipsport, N.Y., to Aida Austin, Eldred
November 29, 1892
Dear Friend,

I thought I would write you a few lines today and let you know we had a very hard snowstorm yesterday.

Do you like your school this winter any better than you did last?

We are going to have singing school here this winter.

Old Mr. Halstead is dead and was buried Sunday. He got cold sitting on the ground while the cow was eating.

Ella Graham, Amber Graham's wife, has congestion of the brain and the doctor says she can't get well. Ida Tice is home and sick with neuralgia.

Tommy took Louie and I for a ride last Friday. He was asking about you.

Have you got your house done yet? Have you had much snow up there yet? Can't you come up for the week between Christmas and New Years?

Have you seen the comet yet? I think I have.

What do you think of the election? I think it was a regular cheat. I suppose we will have to starve for four years now.

Be sure to come down Christmas.

Yours truly,
Nancy Wallace

Mount Grove House
The next letters indicate that the Austin Mountain Grove House may have been ready for boarders.

C.C.P. Eldred's Will

C.C.P. Eldred's will dated 1882, was probated on October 4, 1892:
- 15% to his son James D. Eldred
- 15% to daughter Polly E. Mapes
- 30% to daughter Rebecca Eldred
- 5% each to his grandchildren: James Eldred, Herbert L. Eldred, George W. Eldred, Nellie E. Kendall, Charles E. Mapes
- 10% to trustees of the Congregational Church of Eldred.

—*Eldred, p. 38.*

Mrs. Moss, Chicago, Ill., to Aida Austin, Eldred
January 6, 1893
My dear Aida,

Emma received your letter sometime ago and as Willie's Napkin Ring you spoke of sending has not yet arrived, I thought best to mail you so it can be traced if it was registered.

Willie has been having croup again but is better. We have all had colds. Mr. Collins has been in California for over a month, but we expect him home tomorrow morning.

We were so glad to hear from you, but sorry you were not feeling well; trust you are better. Will write you again as soon as the ring comes.

Hastily yours, wish love to all,
Mrs. F.G. Moss

March 5, 1893
My dear Aida,

We shall come to you and leave Chicago by the first of May, if not sooner, as we are to give up our house and store our goods until our return in August.

Is the plastering perfectly dry?

Willie seems so susceptible to colds that I was a little anxious on his account.

I know you will arrange so we will be perfectly comfortable from past experience. I thought we had better have a room where we could have a stove so that we might have fire on cool or damp days.

I am having a very lame back at present, but I hope to feel better soon.

Hope you all continue well. Is Miss Maria at home this winter?

Will write you again as soon as I know positively our plans.

Heartily Yours, With love,
Mrs. F.G. Moss

April 7, 1893
My dear Aida,

I fear you will think me a very poor correspondent. I have been sick in bed with inflammatory rheumatism for nearly 3 weeks and it has knocked all our plans to pieces for I shall not be able to go away from home this Summer. I have to keep near my physician.

I am able to sit up a few hours at a time but with difficulty. The children are so disappointed at not being able to come to Sullivan. Willie can't see why we can't go.

I trust it will not disarrange your plans, our not coming.

Hoping to hear from you then, if not sooner. I will close as I cannot write very well lying in bed when two of my finger joints are sore.

Kind regards to all and best love to your dear self from Willie and all. Lovingly yours,
Cora F. Moss

Nancy Wallace, Phillipsport, N.Y., to Aida Austin, Eldred
May 2, 1893
Dear Friend,

New York Herald Building

New York Herald building around 1895. Photo by J.S. Johnston. Photo: Library of Congress: LC-USZ62-68731.

The *New York Herald* Headquarters at Broadway and 34th Street was designed by McKim, Mead, & White in 1890. The building was completed by 1895.

James Gordon Bennett Sr. had founded the *Herald* in 1835. His son, James Bennett Jr. took over when James Sr. died in 1872.

The building was a Renaissance Revival building, designed after Fra Giacondo'd Palazzo del Consiglio in Verona. It was demolished in 1921.

Pneumatic tubes, speaking tubes, and a telephone system connected the offices. On the roof along with about 24 bronze owls with blinking eyes (electric lights), was a flock of carrier pigeons who brought the latest distant news events.

The *New York Herald* under James Bennett Jr. financed Henry Stanley's expedition to Africa to find David Livingston.

New York's Herald Square was named after the *New York Herald* newspaper. Times Square, named after *The New York Times* (the *Herald*'s rival), is north of Herald Square.

The *New York Tribune* acquired the *New York Herald* after Bennett Jr.'s death in 1924, and created the *New York Herald Tribune*.
—wikipedia.org., nytimes.com.

I haven't taken time to answer your letter because nearly all of the family have been sick. Aunt Emma is sick now and we have Eva down here. I am getting along nicely in school now, but I will never go back after June.

Did your brother scold you very much when you got home? I suppose your school will soon be out. We only have six weeks more. I am glad.

Has Miss Leavenworth's school closed yet? There is no school down where you taught. May Masterson has the consumption and they can't find another teacher. We have Singing School yet and we are going to have a concert the 30th of May.

Can't you and your brother come down to it? Remember me to your brother. Your Friend,
Nancy Wallace

Main Street looking North to Eldred. The Parker Hotel is on the right. William H. Wilson's Store is in the center of photo. Postcard in the Austin Collection.

C.S. Bok, Hackettstown, N.J., to Mort Austin, Eldred
June 11, 1894
My dear Friend,
Enclosed kindly find eight of your pictures and I kept the other four and did with them accordingly what you told me. I have also seen Dr. Whitney about your bill, but he told me that he will not charge anything this time.
Hoping you will keep well and be successful in your business. Kindly remember me to your partner.
I am your friend, C.S. Bok
30 East 7th St., N.Y.

Perhaps Mort's business referred to by Mr. Bok, was the Mountain Grove House. An ad for the house appeared in the summer 1894 newspaper, with the contact name, C.M. Austin & Co.

Mountain Grove House Ad
New house; cool rooms; good board; elevation 1,400 feet; fishing and boating. For particulars apply to C.M. Austin & Co., Eldred, N.Y.—Brooklyn Daily Eagle, *June 4, 1894.*

Chas. Metzger, Tannersville, N.Y., to Mort Austin, Eldred
January 18, 1895

Dear Friend Mort,
I heard the other day that you was in winter quarters so I have concluded to drop you a few lines. I suppose you saw Rob before you left Eldred and heard all about our trip to New York.
I have been working for the last 8 days and I guess I am good for all winter. We only get in 8 hours a day, but $10.80 is better than a snow bank each Saturday night. Talking of snow, we only have a couple of inches. It acts as if we were going to have a thaw.
Well, January is more than half gone and soon Spring will be here again, and you and I are not in the West yet. I am getting the fever again (quite bad) and if work plays out here in the Spring, I expect to make a break.
There is certainly no use to go back to Eldred looking for a job. I feel sure that we will fetch up out there yet don't you?
Hoping to hear from you soon.
I am your sincere friend,
Chas. C.R. Metzger

Charles Metzger, The Minisink House, Eldred, to Mort Austin
January 27, 1895
Dear Friend Mort,
Glad to hear that you are managing to keep contented. One thing is settled in my mind and that is to leave Eldred. I think it will be better for me every way. When a young man leaves his native town, he is then thrown on his own resources and put to his best mettle. No one remembers when you went to school and keeps thinking you are still a Boy.
I've been trying to keep busy a little by cutting fire wood, but this snow is so deep in the woods that it's rather up hill work. I used to go skating last month sometimes, but of late the snow has covered the ice for good.
While I am on the subject, Mort, unless I strike something before that, I will be right with you to travel till we can strike a favorable position. I think the spring is the best time to go only we ought to get started midling early, Providence permitting.
I will try and get up to see you next month and then we can talk matters over. Someone is trying hard to get me a job up in the Catskills, but I have some doubt of their succeeding.
But if nothing unforeseen occurs, the indications are that you and I may still take that overland trip. George Beck was last heard from out in Missouri, so he is well on his way to Alaska. He promised to write to me as soon as he conveniently could.
I see your folks nearly every day. Lon has been assisting Mr. Reese in his meetings sometimes.
There have been no social gathers since Jan. 1st, but there is to be an oyster supper at I.M. Bradleys on February 5th.
Trusting to hear from you soon. I am as ever your sincere friend,
Chas. C.R. Metzger

Red Men's Hall
Both Barryville and Eldred had

a Red Men's Hall. The Red Men Order traced its roots to 1765 and the Sons of Liberty, known for its Boston Tea Party. The Sons of Liberty became the Society of Red Men, and later, the Improved Order of Red Men.

Barryville's chapter of the Red Men was formed in 1888. They had a Hall near the Delaware River in 1894.

In 1888 Maria H. Myers sold the property for Red Men's Hall in Eldred to the Red Men Trustees of No. 44: Hiram Daley, Frank Kelly, and William H. Austin.

Many of the town's men belonged to the Red Men Order, including my great-grandfathers, Sherman S. Leavenworth and Henry Austin, my grandfather Mort Austin, and Abel S. Sprague.

Daniel Hallock was a member until November 8, 1889, when A.S. Myers accused Dan of "conduct unbecoming a Red Man."

Abel (himself perhaps not blameless) accused Dan of saying several untruths including that Abel "was a member of a ring that was not as good as thieves and robbers."

Edwin V. Myers and Mabel Owen
Red Men's Hall was a social center for the community and a number of events were held there. It was at the Red Men's Hall in Eldred that Abel's son Edwin Van Schoick Myers met pretty Mabel Louise Owen and knew she was the one for him. Mabel was the daughter of Robert and Elizabeth Tether Owen.

Looking south from Eldred Corners towards Barryville on Brook Road. From the left was the corner of William Wilson's grocery store, then possibly Abel Myers store, the Parker Hotel, and in the center the Red Men's Hall (with a bell tower). Postcard in Austin Collection.

My grandpa, Edwin Myers, was attending a social function at Red Men's Hall with one of his not-too-well regarded circle of friends. My grandma-to-be [Mabel Owen] came in and Grandpa asked his friend who the girl was who came with his sister.

The friend replied that it was his youngest sister Mabel. Grandpa asked him to introduce him and was told, "Certainly not! I would never introduce one of my friends to my sister!"

Someone else was more accommodating. There were ups and downs with family disapproval and misgivings, but Grandpa Edwin worked hard at proving who he really was. (They were allowed very limited association. Mabel's mother, Elizabeth Tether Owen was a very proper English lady.)

Some three years later, after he had worked at Proctor's while building a house and barn and getting a farm and carting business functional, permission was granted. The rest is history.
—Melva Austin Barney.

In October 1895 Mort Austin's good friend Edwin Myers married Mabel Louise Owen.

In 1900 Edwin and Mabel Owen Myers' son Raymond Myers was born. (Their first two children died young.) Edwin and Mabel would be the parents of my favorite (but only) Austin aunt, Gladys Myers. Gladys would marry Charles Raymond Austin, the son of Mort and Jennie Austin.

Parker and Schoonover Families
We haven't heard much about the Parker/Schoonover family lately.

In the 1880s Oliver and Mary Murray Parker Schoonover and their children Rowlee and Emily

Pretty Mabel Owen Myers, wife of Edwin V. Myers; the other grandmother of my Austin cousins. Photo courtesy of Joan Austin Geier.

The couple on the right are Daniel Rowlee Schoonover and Emily Banner at Shohola Glen. Photo courtesy of John Hull.

had moved to Orange County, New York, to help Mary's father George Washington Murray out of financial trouble with his store. Then the family had moved to Brooklyn.

Rowlee had apprenticed as a blacksmith, and in 1900 he started work as a helper at Shadbolt Co.

One morning I saw an ad for blacksmith and helpers wanted at the Shadbolt Mfg. Co., Flushing Ave. and Cumberland St., Brooklyn. I was a little afraid I could not handle the blacksmith trade so I took a job as helper.

They put me to helping a big Dutchman named Miller with another helper on the same fire. The helper's wages was 9 and 10 dollars a week, 10 hours a day, 60 hours a week.

They put me on with an old man (about 75) who told the boss that they might give me a fire, that I was better than half of the men they had.

They had an order for a big tree truck from the State of Maine and the two back wheels was 8 feet high and the tires was 8 inches wide by 1-1/2 inches thick. The iron had to be special rolled. It came in 30 feet lengths and was very expensive.

Doile who was in charge, liked his drink and he had burnt a big piece out of one side and that meant curtains for him.

Shadbolt whistled for me, "Can you put a piece in this tire?"

I was scared, I must admit, but I said, "Yes, if you let me have what help I want."

He said, "Take every man in the shop, if you want."

So I picked out Otto Markline, a Russian Jew and a very good man. I gave him a piece about 3 feet long. It weighed about 200 pounds. We had very good luck, welded on the piece, let it cool, and bent it. Everything came out all OK. From that time on I got a first fire and did nothing but new work.

In 1892 Oliver and Mary Schoonover, her daughter Kate Parker, and father George W. Murray lived in Brooklyn. (Mr. Murray died the next year.) Emily Schoonover lived in the same building. Emily may have married Will Waidler in the early 1890s.

Around 1895 Mary's daughter Laura Parker Britt died in childbirth leaving three young children: Kitty, Ada, and William Britt. Laura's sister Kate Parker and half sister Emily Schoonover Waidler helped to raise Kitty and Ada Britt.

Aunt Kate and her half sister

Boarding House Ads in 1894

DeVenoge Mountain House and Mountain Grove House newspaper ads. —*Brooklyn Daily Eagle, June 4, 1894.*

[Newspaper advertisements:]

DE VENAGE MOUNTAIN HOUSE, ELDRED, Sullivan County, N. Y. This house is situated 1,710 feet above tide water; fishing, bathing, boating, tennis grounds; dancing hall; bowling alley; billiards; accommodates 200; send for circulars. WILLIAM TAETLROW, Proprietor or Eagle Summer Resort Bureau.

MONTICELLO, SULLIVAN CO., N. Y. TERRACE COTTAGE NOW OPEN. Situated on high ground, commanding a fine view of Shawangunk and other mountains. Large piazza. Fresh vegetables from home garden. Good hunting and fishing near. For terms address Mrs. STEEDMAN, Box 60.

SUMMER BOARD ON FARM NEAR LIBERTY FALLS; house and furniture entirely new; all modern improvements; bathroom, with hot and cold water; shade trees; large piazza; fresh vegetables; good fishing; everything first class; terms moderate. Apply to M. J. PAINE, LIBERTY FALLS, Sullivan County, N. Y.

LAKE SIDE HOUSE. AMONG THE LAKES AND MOUNTAINS OF SULLIVAN COUNTY. Address J. P. CALLBREATH, WHITE LAKE, N. Y.

HOBBY VILLA, LARGE ROOMS; FREE transportation from and to depot; high elevation; good livery; terms $5 to $7 per week; cottage of 7 rooms, partly furnished, to let for season. Apply to M. E. HOBBY, DIVINE CORNERS, Sullivan County, N. Y.

MITCHELL HOUSE, MONTICELLO, SULLIVAN COUNTY, N. Y. Family hotel; first class table; large rooms; pleasant location; surrounded with lawns and croquet grounds; good fishing and driving; five minutes from station; rates from $12 to $18.

MOUNTAIN GROVE HOUSE. New house; cool rooms; good board; elevation 1,400 feet; fishing and boating. For particulars apply to C. M. AUSTIN & CO., ELDRED, Sullivan County, N. Y.

Em helped raise Laura Parker Britt's daughters when Laura died young. Laura and John Britt's son Will was raised by his dad who settled in Port Jervis.—Richard James, grandson of Ada Britt.

Daniel R. Schoonover married Emily Banner on March 17, 1896. They got married when on a date and did not tell Mrs. Banner (Emily's mother) right away.—John Hull, great-grandson.

Rowlee had met Emily Banner at an Epworth (Methodist) League party that he went to with his sister. They dated about 3 years.

We just got on the L-train on March 17, 1896, on her birthday—went up to East New York, and was married by the Rev. Baker of the first Baptist Church.

Em's old lady did not care any too much for me when she found out that I was a blacksmith. When she found out that we was married, she was fit to be tied. (We became good friends and in after years she came to live with us.)

In them days the tires on bikes was the Dunlap and they had an inner tube in and they laced up the same as a shoe with a corset lace. When they fixed the tube, it was too much trouble to lace the whole tire so they skipped every other hole.

One time I was riding behind Irv and I saw a little blubber commence out of his hind tire and it kept getting bigger and bigger. Pretty soon it got so big it would not go through the frame and before I could stop him, "Bang" went the tube.

Well we took it off and unlaced

Kate Parker was the aunt who helped raise Kitty and Ada Britt when their mother Laura Parker Britt died young. Photo courtesy of Richard James.

Ada, William, and Kitty Britt, children of Laura Parker Britt, who died young. Photo courtesy of Richard James.

National Prohibition Candidates 1896

FOR PRESIDENT, JOSHUA LEVERING, of Baltimore, Md.

HONOR GOD, PROTECT HOME, DEFEND NATIVE LAND,

By voting against the RUM POWER, which is now DEFENDED by the Democratic and Republican parties, by means of tax and license laws.

FOR VICE PRESIDENT, HALE JOHNSON, of Newton, Ill.

BIOGRAPHICAL SKETCHES.

JOSHUA LEVERING, the Prohibition candidate for President, is a native of Baltimore, Maryland, and is 51 years of age. He is one of the most successful business men in that city, and highly respected by all good citizens. He has been an active and consistent member of the Baptist Church, and superintendent of their Sabbath school, for many years; also president of the Y. M. C. A. of Baltimore, a strong supporter of christian education and of home and foreign missions. Until 1884 he was an Independent Democrat. He that year voted the National Prohibition ticket, and has been an active Prohibitionist ever since. He is a good and true business man, one who would fill the Presidential chair with honor and ability, and should have the support of every man who is opposed to the saloon.

HALE JOHNSON, the Prohibition candidate for Vice President, is a native of Montgomery Co., Indiana, and is aged 49 years. His home is now in Newton, Ill. In 1861 he enlisted in the 135th Indiana Volunteers, and served through the war. He is a lawyer and an active and consistent christian, a member of the Christian or Disciple Church, a highly respected citizen, a Past Commander in the G. A. R. and a Colonel of the Veteran Commandery. He was a delegate to the National Republican Convention at Chicago in 1884, and became disgusted with their refusal to insert a prohibition plank in their platform. He then left said party and has since supported the National Prohibition party. No better or more loyal man could be put up as a candidate for Vice President.

NATIONAL PROHIBITION PLATFORM.

We, the members of the Prohibition Party, in National Convention assembled, renewing our acknowledgment of allegiance to Almighty God as the rightful Ruler of the Universe, lay down the following as our declaration of political purpose:

THE PROHIBITION PARTY, in National Convention assembled, declares its conviction that the manufacture, exportation, importation and sale of alcoholic beverages has produced such social, commercial, industrial and political wrongs, and is now so threatening the perpetuity of all our social and political institutions, that the suppression of the same by a national party organized therefor is the greatest object to be accomplished by the voters of our country, and is of such importance as that it, of right, ought to control the political action of all our patriotic citizens until such suppression is accomplished.

The urgency of this cause demands the union without further delay of all citizens who desire the prohibition of the liquor traffic; therefore,

Resolved, That we favor the legal prohibition, by state and national legislation, of the manufacture, importation, exportation, and interstate transportation and sale of alcoholic beverages; that we declare our purpose to organize and unite all the friends of prohibition into one party, and in order to accomplish this end we deem it but right to leave every Prohibitionist the freedom of his own convictions upon all other political questions, and trust our representatives to take such action upon other political questions as the change occasioned by prohibition, and the welfare of the whole people, shall demand.

Flier for the National Prohibition Candidates of 1896, courtesy of Melva Austin Barney.

it and packed it full of grass and laced it up, but we did not have lace enough. So I took one of my shoe strings and finished the job and at last we got home.

I remember everybody went bike crazy. There was a feller on Broadway who had a bike shop and he worked night and day so I used to help him string wheels and he let me use his tools and I made myself a wheel and everybody wanted a light wheel.

When I finished my wheel, it weighed 18 pounds. I had it all nickel-plated and it was the envy of all the club for I had joined the Bushwick Wheelman. The clubhouse was on Lexington Ave. near Broadway.

The day they opened the bike path to Coney Island was a holiday and there was thousands of wheels on the path. There was all kinds of smashups. I know I carried a wheel string around my neck from Coney to the club.

You may talk about the craze about autos, but it could not compare with the craze of the bike. Everyone had one. We had five in our house. First I bought one and George got one, then your aunt Kate got one and about that time I got married to your mother and she demanded one and it was not long before she wanted a tandem.

So we had 5 wheels in our house. Your mother bought a divided skirt and went around to call on her mother with her wheel to show her what her husband had bought her. Her mother shut the door in her face and told Emily that when she could dress like a lady, she could come in.

Well, when we got married, I was making $15.00 a week and I gave the minister $5.00 and we had the sum of $2.50 between us, so Em went to work. She had a job at $12 a week which was very good wages at that time. But the boss said something that did not set right, and she up and quit.

So I went home and told my folks and Pa said, "Bub, that is no way to live. Bring your wife home here. We will get along someway."

I brought Em over to our house and her and Ma hit it off fine and then we moved to another place on Shepard Ave., and that is where you was born.
—Daniel Rowlee Schoonover to his daughter Justina.

At the turn of the century, Perry and Mary Schoonover still lived in Brooklyn with Mary's children, George and Kate Parker.

Irvin Clark Family in Eldred

Back in Eldred sometime after 1895, Elbert Clark (divorced) and

1896 News

Gold was discovered in the Yukon, Utah became a state, and Hawaii was annexed.

his five children: Frank, Lillie, Florence, Irving, and Hazel Clark, lived with his parents, Irvin and Laura Austin Clark, and brother Robert. Irvin was a mail carrier.

L. Young, New Rochelle, N.Y., to Aida Austin, Eldred
May 25, 1896
My dear Aida,

I received your letter of the 17th. I am glad you have so good a lookout for summer boarders. Who are they? Ladies or gentlemen and are they real nice?

I am thinking some of going west; if I do not go west you will probably see me at your place in July. You need not save a room for me because I am not sure enough for that.

I would like to help you fix up your house. I like that work if I am not all tired out.

I am so glad your mother is able to be around. Is Maria with Lon now? Remember me to them. Has Dory work yet?

I expect Aida, you will see me in July. I wish school was over for this year and always for me. I am sick of it tonight. Remember me to all your folks.
Lovingly, L. Young

C.S. Bok, N.Y.C., to Mort Austin, Eldred
August 10, 1896
My dear old Fellow,

Have you anything to fill up a feller's belly and his friend's (gentleman) and a place to sleep at night; and let me know whether you are home? My friend, a Chinese like myself, will pay six dollars a week. Kindly let me know on returned mail.
Truly yours, C. Soule Bok

September 5, 1896
My dear Mort,

I send you today some new tea which I think will meet the taste of most of the American people. So I want you to try it to see whether your opinion is coincident with mine. Though it is a better tea than those we have had, yet I can get this at the same price.

I also sent you some Chinese Lichee nuts and some sweet meat that you may have something to entertain the people in the house. Next Tuesday, I shall go home, that is to East Orange, N.J., to stay over night with my people, whom you saw in the 14th St., the time when you were with me; then I shall go on the next day to Hackettstown with my friend Vincent.

How I wish that you can arrange to go too, that we may have a good old time together in C.C.I. for two or three days.

I may go to Orange to live after my return from H'town. I don't think I had better write to Bella, but you will be kind enough to tell her for me the reason we did not go up last Saturday night when you see her, and also remember me

Mott Street in Chinatown, New York City, where Mr. Soule Bok, Mort's friend from Centenary College, lived at one time. Postcard courtesy of Mary Briggs Austin.

to Mr. Boyd. Your old friend,
C. Soule Bok

Charles Metzger, Catskills, N.Y., to Mort Austin, Eldred
November 1896
Well Mort! Old Sport,

I am glad to know that you are still alive, and rejoicing in our Republican Victory.

You are going to put yet another winter at Eldred are you? Well probably, it's wise not to make a break right in the teeth of winter. But for land sake, pull out of there next spring, or you will get grated there for good yet.

Since my return from that little trip to Eldred, I have earned over $150. Where could I have

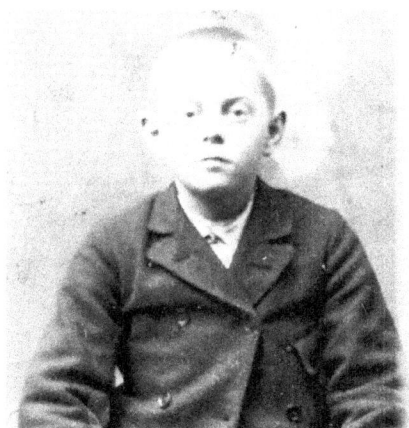

Frank Clark, grandson of Irvin and Laura and Austin Clark. Photo courtesy of Melva Austin Barney.

View towards Barryville from the center of Eldred. The Parker House (often also the Post Office) is second on the left; then the Parker barn. Photo courtesy of Christena Stevens Myers.

done that in Eldred during Sept. and Oct.? I did not loose a day. I even worked all of Election day (I didn't forget to vote though.)

You ask (1st) am I going to remain here this winter? (2nd) am I coming to Eldred?

Well, 1st if I can get enough work to make expenses, I am going to stay. (2nd) I am not going to Eldred in any event, as there is nothing there for me except vexation and you know that I have had my share of that.

If I get laid off I am not sure yet where I will go, but I don't intend to lay still unless I am compelled to.

So there are to be two new houses at Eldred are there? I am glad to hear that. I suppose that when I see that Town, I will hardly know it.

Hoping that you are in good health and spirits. And to hear from you in the near future.
　　Your old friend,
　　Chas. C.R. Metzger

Edward MacKenzie, Jersey City, N.J., to Lon Austin, Glen Spey
November 27, 1896
Dear Sir:

Your letter of the 23rd received. I regret very much to say that I will not be able to come up on Sunday as you suggested, as Mrs. MacKenzie is not feeling very well and I do not want to be away over night.

As for the purchasing of the Christmas goods, I would much rather have you take the matter in hand yourself.

If I can be of any use to you otherwise, inform me at once.

Hoping you have success in your work. I remain, Very Truly Yours,
　　Edw. E. MacKenzie
　　Office: 520 Jersey Avenue

Oliver Smith, Solomon, Kans., to Lon Austin, Glen Spey
December 2, 1896
Dear Sir,

Your enclosed express money order for $16.64 received.

My mother is still living and this money will come in very good indeed. Have had a good many years of crop failures.

Many thanks. The Lord must have been speaking to you. Glory to His name.
　　Yours very respectfully,
　　Oliver Smith

Ell and Emma Austin's son Henry Earl Austin married Sarah Jane LeRoy on December 30, 1896, in Jeffersonville, New York.

C.S. Bok, N.Y.C., to Mort Austin, Eldred
December 31, 1896
My dear old Friend,

I wish you were here, instead of your letters, while I am having my vacation, so as to have a good

Bertha Collins is third from the left. Photo courtesy of Mary Briggs Austin.

old C.C.I. time and talk over some of the things which we did and may do and go to see our friend, Styles.

By the way, will you be kind enough to send me Mr. Styles' address, as I have lost the one they gave me last summer. Please remember me to Dr. Austin and wish him a very happy New Year.

About 7 or 8 weeks ago I met, in Fifth Ave., a young lady friend of yours whose name I will let you make a guess. She was looking well and was on her way to call upon a friend.

Hoping you are well and happy and up to all of the fishing tricks and hope to hear from you not for long will be an invitation to your wedding to start in the blessed year of 1897. Wishing you a great many New Years.

I am ever your friend,
C.S. Bok

Bertha Collins, Port Jervis, N.Y., to Lon Austin, Mt. Grove House
January 26, 1897
Dear Lon:

Last Thursday, while Mamma was in New York, Papa and I were much surprised to receive a barrel of apples and the butter enclosed from you.

Please accept our thanks for the apples and as to the butter, there is none too much for we can use it all and after using it, will weigh the crock and then Papa will send you a check.

The apples came just at the right time, for we were getting down to the last of what we had.

The presiding elder has been with us since Sunday. Papa informed the official men that he rather expects to leave here in April, so if he does, that will mean a new home for us.

Yesterday and today have been very cold here. Can't imagine

Bronx Park and Zoo

In 1891, 250 acres were set aside for a New York Botanical Garden out of the 640 acres acquired for the Bronx Park around 1888.

Nathaniel and Elizabeth Britton Lord, whose ideas inspired the park and conservatory, were influenced when they visited the Royal Botanical Garden at Kew in London.

The Conservatory, built mostly of steel, cast iron, wood, and glass, was designed by the Lord and Burnham Company, the premier glasshouse design and fabrication firm of the time.

Construction (from 1899–1902) cost $177,000. The Zoo opened in November 1899, with 843 animals in 22 exhibits.

—wikipedia.org.

The Conservatory, Bronx Park, 1906. It was eventually renamed the Bronx Zoo. Photo: Library of Congress, Prints and Photographs Division: Detroit Publishing Co., LC-D4-19579.

The Conservatory, Bronx Park, New York. Postcard in the collection of Mary Briggs Austin.

Riding an Indian Elephant at the New York Zoological Park. Postcard in the collection of Mary Briggs Austin.

Buffalo herd at the New York Zoological Park. Postcard in the collection of Mary Briggs Austin.

Jennie Louisa Leavenworth married Charles Mortimer Austin. Photo courtesy of Mary Briggs Austin.

Charles Mortimer Austin married Jennie Louisa Leavenworth. Photo courtesy of Katherine Calkin Traxler.

what it must be up in Sullivan.

Remember me to all. If you are in Port Jervis at any time, come in to see us. Again, thank you for your kindness.

Very sincerely,
Bertha S.S. Collins

The following unsigned letter to Mary Ann Austin seems to be from one of the Eldred-Austin cousins, Net, Rand, or Addie (probably Addie). Polly Vanorsdol Eldred Mapes (mentioned in the letter) died of heart disease at her home in Philadelphia in May 1897. She was the daughter of C.C.P. and Effa Van Tuyl Eldred.

To Mary Ann Austin
April 10, 1897
Dear Aunt Mary,

Your dear letter gladly received. Yes dear! You waited so long I had heard all the news. Willie Kyte's death, Alvy Sergeant's cancer, Isaac's illness, ground broken for the new mansion and studio on the hill [possibly Walter and Henrietta Austin Styles's home], proposed return of the Alaska delegation, George Beck's marriage, etc.!

Ida received a letter from Polly Mapes saying that Rebecca had started (by easy stages) for home. She intended to stop on the way to visit her friends. I suppose they are as numerous as the sands of the desert or leaves of the forest. She will probably arrive in time to ride home on the first trolley car that runs between Barryville and Eldred!! Hoop La!!

Ida had a letter from Tina a short time ago. She was not very well, having just recovered from an attack of grippe, which had left her with Catarrh of the stomach that is pretty bad, I think. She does not say anything about coming home. I wish she would come. I should like to see her very much.

I received a letter from Aunt Julia Austin [widow of James Austin] a week or two ago. She and her sister Mamie are living at Golden's Bridge, Westchester County. They are keeping house. I had not heard from them for six years and was very glad to hear from them once more.

Yes, that was very sad for Annie C. to lose her husband, poor girl! She has had her share of trouble.

You wrote that Maria had gone back of Proctor's. Has she given up the idea of running the boarding house this summer? I hope you have all got rid of your colds.

**Bertha Collins, Tottenville, N.Y., to Lon Austin,
Mountain Grove House, Eldred**
May 23, 1897
My dear Lon,

It was a great disappointment that we were unable to come up and see you all before our departure from Port Jervis, but owing to our being busy, we had to forego the pleasure.

We had expected you and Mort would drive down and we could then have given you the crock and butter pail which belong to you, but since you did not come, we took them into the house next to ours and left them with Mrs. Ingram to keep until you call for them. So they are there awaiting your coming.

I've been terribly homesick for Port Jervis and the mountains, for this place is entirely different, but I'll get used to it, and then we are near New York.

We have a very pleasant home, nice large yard and a garden, very nice church, fine pipe organ, and good music.

The people are pleasant. After we know them, I think we'll like them. They have done much in the house for us and have shown their goodwill in many ways.

Sometime when you or Mort or the girls are in New York City, just take a little trip down to Staten Island. It's only an hour's ride.

Remember us all to all the family. We will hope to meet again in dear old Sullivan some future day. You received Papa's last check, did you not?

Very sincerely,
Bertha S.S. Collins

Charles Mortimer Austin Marries Jennie Louisa Leavenworth

In the hamlet of Eldred everyone knew everyone—whether they lived on the east or west side of the village.

Mort Austin's Uncle Irv, Aunt Laura Austin Clark, two of their sons, and some grandchildren lived on Clark Road north of the Leavenworth home.

Jennie Leavenworth's uncle Gus Myers ran the Myers Boarding House northeast of the Austin's Mountain Grove House and near Highland Lake.

Jennie's uncle George and aunt Martha Mills Myers and their sons (cousins Charles and Martin D. Myers) lived on the east side of Highland Lake.

Seems Grandma and Grandpa Austin must have known each other for all their lives. The Austins lived on the hill at one side of town, the Leavenworth's on other.

Evidently Grandpa was calling on a lady who became Mrs. Avery who lived beyond Leavenworths.

In later years Mrs. Avery, at a church social, said to Grandma Austin, "Mort used to go right by your house coming to see me."

Grandma said, "But then he stopped once and never went past again."

Guess that was the start, but seems they knew or at least knew of each other forever.
—Melva Austin Barney.

In October 1897 Charles M. Austin, 32, married Jennie L. Leavenworth, 17. Actually, they eloped.

Big doings was not the Austin style. Seems that Great-Grandma Maria Myers Leavenworth [Jennie's mother] wanted a larger affair and they decided not to argue about it.

They didn't have a lot of money ahead and wanted to get on with establishing themselves with what they had. Great-Grandma Maria seems to have thought Jennie was pretty young to just step out, as well.—Melva Austin Barney, granddaughter.

Quite understandably, Maria Myers Leavenworth (normally a quiet, gentle person), gave Mort a major scolding.

Wedding Certificate for Mort and Jennie Leavenworth Austin, signed by Samuel and Carrie Rusby. Certificate courtesy of Mary Briggs Austin.

Lochada, summer home of William F. Proctor and his family. Photo courtesy of the Proctor Family.

William F. Proctor. Photo courtesy of the Proctor Family.

"I'll never do that again," Mort said in a typical Austin response.

Grandma and Grandpa Austin purchased their first home and boarding house when they first married. It was on Collins Road, on the way to Highland Lake Road. They called it the Collins Place, though as a boarding house it was known as, The Homestead Cottage.—Melva Austin Barney.

Bertha Collins, Tottenville, N.Y., to Mort Austin, Eldred
October 1897
My dear Mort,
　Having just heard of your marriage, we wish to extend our heartiest congratulation to you and your wife. Such an occurrence is an important one and we wish for you both many happy years spent together.
　We spent Christmas day in Irvington during the morning. Uncle Joe had the colts brought down to the house for us to see. They looked handsome in their new harness and new plaid blankets. Mamma remarked then that she "did wish Mort could see those dear horses."
　Now you will have to bring Jennie to see us. When you do come, we all will be most pleased to entertain you in Tottenville, and thus try, in a measure to show our appreciation for your many kindnesses to us one and all.
　Give my love and best wishes to Mrs. Austin. May you both have a joyous married life!
　Always your sincere friend,
　Bertha S.S. Collins

Lon Austin and Mr. Proctor
As mentioned at the beginning of the chapter, Uncle Lon (A.A. Austin) managed some Lochada property for the Proctors in the 1880s. Lochada, the Proctor's home, overlooked Loch Ada (Haggai's Pond). Their English Tudor residence had been designed by H.J. Hardenbergh, also responsible for the design of the Waldorf-Astoria.

William F. Proctor fishing with a friend on Loch Ada. Photo courtesy of the Proctor Family.

I have read that Uncle Lon herded some 80 cows. In Melva Austin Barney's collection were several letters to Lon Austin from Proctor family members. The two letters in this chapter from William Fash Proctor indicate something was wrong with the butter that Lon was in charge of.

W.F. Proctor, 149 Broadway, N.Y.C., Singer Manufacturing Co., to Mr. A.A. Austin
December 8, 1897
Dear Sir:

The butter sent to Albany lately has not been good. If there is anything wrong with the tool you have for making it, let me know and I will furnish anything required. If it is not possible to make good butter, then is no use of buying parts and paying express charges for what cannot be used. I think it is quite likely that you have trusted it to some one else, as you know how to do it yourself.
Yours truly,
W.F. Proctor

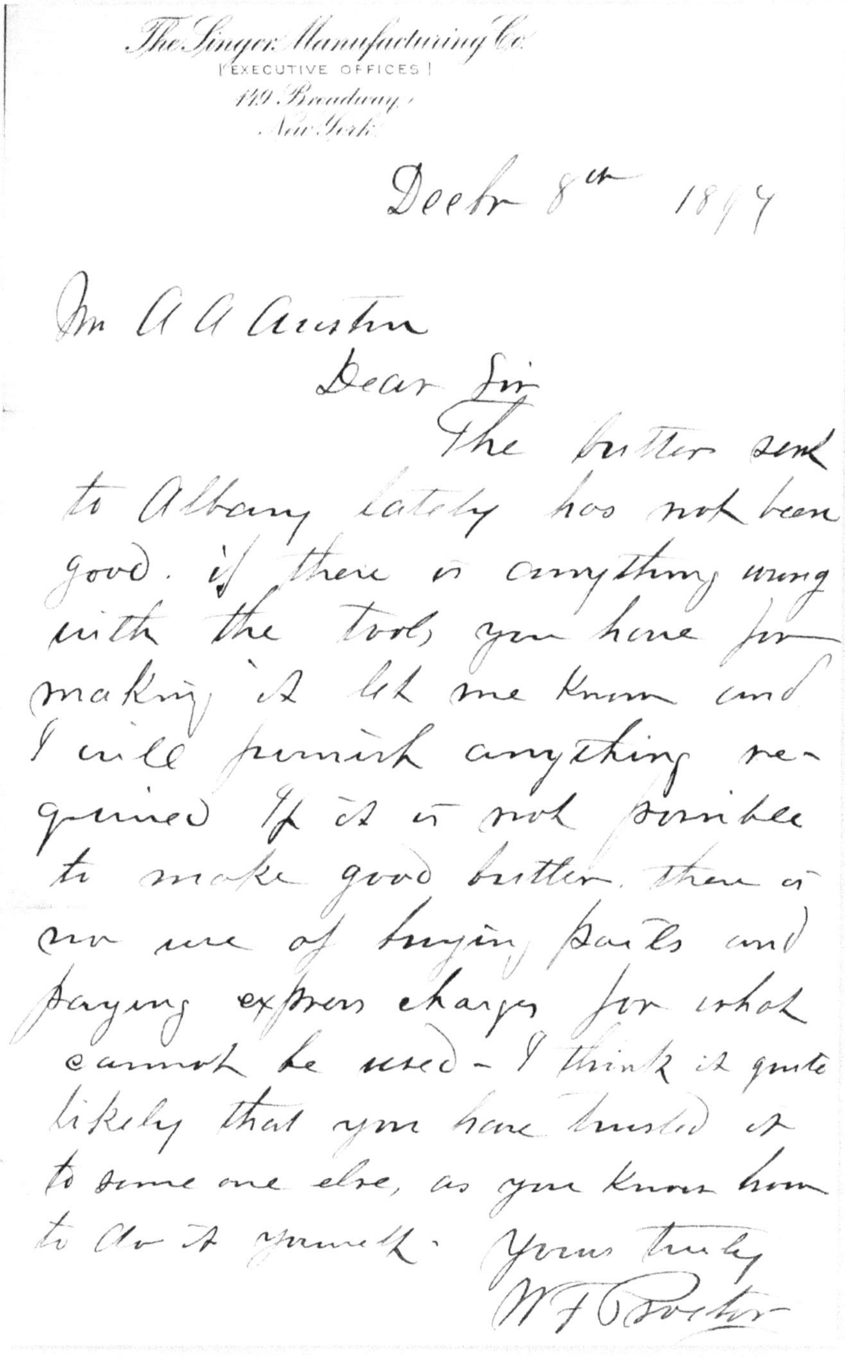

December 15, 1897
Dear Sir,

I am in receipt of your jams of the 11th and 13th.

There is no doubt at all that the facilities you have for keeping milk and cream and for making good butter are far from what they should be, more especially in winter. I will look into that separator business and see if I can get one. In the mean time, do the best you can with what you have.

You can use your own discretion about the hay horses. There are plenty of useless horses on the place in that [without] getting any more.

I enclose my check to order of J. Howlett Collector of $91.27 for school tax, which you will please get a receipt for and send me. The taxes have not been so low since the new schoolhouse was built. Last year it was $155 and the year before $125, but I suppose the amount you gave me for this year is correct.

We had a very rainy day yesterday and think probably it was the same with you.

Letter from W. F. Proctor to Lon Austin, 1897. Letter in the collection of Melva Austin Barney.

Yours truly,
W.F. Proctor

Robert Collins to Newlyweds, Mort and Jennie Austin, Eldred
December 31, 1897
Aunt Annie and M. Johnston were here when the news reached us [Mort and Jennie's marriage]. They wished me to extend their

Park Row Building

Park Row Building, 21 Park Row, 1912. Photo: Library of Congress, Prints and Photographs Division: Irving Underhill, LC-USZ62-127126.

A post card of the Park Row building was sent to Mort and Jennie Austin.

New York City's Park Row is located in the Financial District of the Manhattan borough.

The building at 15 Park Row, was one of the first buildings to be called a skyscraper. At 391 feet high, the Park Row building was the tallest office building in the world from 1899 when it was completed, until 1908 when the Singer Building was built.

William M. Ivins, lawyer and judge advocate general for New York State, was the builder. The skyscraper, first called Ivins Syndicate Building, had 26 full floors and two 3-story cupolas.

The base of the building covered about 15,000 square feet. Some 3,900 Georgia spruce piles were driven into wet sand and topped by granite blocks for its foundation.

The structure contains about 8,000 tons of steel and 12,000 tons of other materials, mainly brick and terra cotta.

The $2,400,000 building had 950 separate offices for up to 4 people per office.—wikipedia.org.

congratulations and hopes for a very happy New Year. Nearly all of our "summer party" are represented in this little note.
  R.S.S. Collins

Bertha Collins, Port Jervis, N.Y., to Lon Austin
January 14, 1898
My dear Lon,
  We are in need of more butter. Will you please send or bring us a pail at your earliest convenience.
  Was sorry that I could not accept your invitation for the holidays, but between duties at home and all of us being half sick with colds, I could not get away.
  Papa and Mamma have both been quite sick, but are better now and able to be out as usual.
  We are holding services in the church every evening. Some minster preaches and the interest is very good.
  Hoping that you will soon be able to supply our needs, and with best regards to all the family, I am very sincerely,
  Bertha S.S. Collins

In April Mort and Jennie Austin were invited to the extravagant wedding of Alonzo Eugene Austin Jr., son of Mort's cousin, Rev. A.E. Austin. Rev. Austin assisted Dr. Hall, the bride's father, in performing the ceremony.

Alonzo Eugene Austin Jr. Marries Sara Frances Hall

Dr. and Mrs. Edward Hall request the honour of your presence at the marriage of their daughter
Sara Frances
to
Alonzo Eugene Austin Jr.
Tuesday Eve., April 26, 1898
at 8 o'clock p.m.
5th Ave. Presbyterian Church

CHAPTER 6: AN OLD BACHELOR, 1890–1900 • 191

U.S.S. Maine

The U.S.S. Maine exploded in 1898 and the Spanish American War started—but ended with the 1898 Treaty of Paris. Col. Theodore Roosevelt and his Rough Riders gained fame for their "capture of San Juan Hill."—wikipedia.org.

5th Ave. and 55th Street
New York City, New York

Revolutionary times were recalled in the presence of two little pages, Joseph Garrish Ayers and Charles Haines Ayers, the bridegroom's nephews, in purple coats, powdered wigs, and satin breeches.

The Chinese Consul in this city, Chung Pao Hsi and his suite, were among the guests of honor. Mr. Chung is an acquaintance of Miss Charlotte Chambers Hall, the bride's sister, who was maid of honor.

The chancel was adorned with lilies and palms...The bride wore white satin, a tulle veil caught with orange blossoms, and carried white lilacs and sweet peas.

Seats near the main aisle had been reserved for the Orientals, but they were ushered by mistake into the gallery by their interpreter, and when it was suggested that they change their seats, he explained that Consul Chung would consider himself insulted at the proposition.—The New York Times, *April 27, 1898.*

Olinda (Linnie) Austin Ayers and her sons Joseph and Charles Ayers. "Joseph Garrish Ayers and Charles Haines Ayers, the bridegroom's nephews, in purple coats, powdered wigs, and satin breeches." Photo courtesy of Katherine Calkin Traxler.

Alonzo Eugene and Belle Camp Austin Return from Alaska

Sometime in 1898, Alonzo Eugene Austin Jr.'s parents Alonzo Eugene and Isabelle Camp Austin returned from Alaska, where they had been Presbyterian missionaries.

Alonzo Sr. and Belle Austin's daughter Henrietta was married (for a little longer) to Walter Styles whose home (referred to in an earlier letter) was being built on the southeast side of Proctor Road, before Collins Road.

Alonzo and Belle's other daughter Olinda was married to Joseph Ayers. Olinda (Linnie) and Joseph's sons, Joseph G. and Charles H. Ayers, were the pages in Alonzo Austin Jr.'s wedding.

We will hear more of Dr. Austin (Alonzo Eugene Jr.) and his visits to Eldred in the 1940s in the diary of Aida Austin. Dr. Austin at some point became the owner of the original Austin property, where Aida and Lon would live.

Bertha Collins. Photo courtesy of Mary Briggs Austin.

1896 Cures

Paine's Celery Compound
It is not that rheumatism, neuralgia, insomnia, and kidney troubles are hard to cure. Paine's Celery Compound has made a host of sufferers well.

Thousands of lives that are now fast wearing out would be prolonged if *Paine's Celery Compound* were in each instance used to stop those ominous pains over the kidneys, to build up the rundown nervous strength, and cure permanently those more and more frequently occurring attacks of headache and indigestion.

Here is a recent testimonial from the wife of U.S. Senator E. F. Warren:

I was persuaded to try your "Paine's Celery Compound" in the early spring, when in a very run-down condition. The duties devolving upon the wife of an official in public life are naturally very exhausting, and I was tired out and nervous when I commenced using the remedy. I take pleasure in testifying to the great benefit I received from its use, and can truthfully say that I am in almost perfect health again.

Fellow's Syrup
When the system is run down through overwork, loss of sleep or from poor food assimilation, the nervous system is affected.

To help overcome nervous upsets try *Fellows' Syrup of Hypophosphires*. *Fellows* contains iron and other essential minerals needed to correct a run down condition.

By stimulating appetite and aiding digestion, *Fellows* helps you derive full benefit from your daily meals. Ask your druggist for a bottle of *Fellows' Syrup* today. Discover for yourself the help it may bring you.

Don't be a Nagger!
Let Fellow's Syrup help you

—Birmingham State Herald, September 19, 1896.

Hattie Dana, N.Y.C., to Jennie Austin, Eldred
June 6, 1898
Dear Jennie,

Lon was here all afternoon nearly 2 weeks ago to deliver a message that you and Mort sent (so he said). Now Russell and I appreciate your kindness in wanting us at your home this summer and should we go away, no place would we go sooner than there.

I expect an arrival next month so will be unable to go away at all unless it should be in September and that is hardly possible.

I thought I ought to write and tell you as someone else might take the room you were keeping for us. I'm sorry to keep the children here all summer. We have been housekeeping here two months tomorrow and we have a very cozy little place although I miss Mama very much.

I should have written before but have been alone getting settled until a week ago when Katie came with me, so we have been very busy.

Thanking you for thinking of us with kindest remembrances from Russell and myself to you and Mort. Very sincerely,
Hattie S. Dana

T.G. Metzger, Yulan, N.Y., to C.M. (Mort) Austin
June 13, 1898
Dear Sir:

As per apportionment of Town Board of 6/11, you will place 20 days labor of D&H time on your warrant and issue a call on James Quick of Barryville for the number of men you may deem necessary to perform that amount of labor to advantage.

They must not be allowed to start in earlier than 7 a.m., but may have the privilege of working 10 hours per day.

By all means, watch these men closely in order to get full value.
Respectfully, T.G. Metzger, Commissioner of Highland

Justina Schoonover Born
In August 1898 Justina Schoonover, daughter of Daniel Rowlee and Emily Banner Schoonover, was born. Rowlee and Emily were living with his folks, Kate Parker, and George Parker.

Well, we did not have to wait long before we found there was not room for a baby around where there were two old people and an old maid and old bachelor. So we made up our minds to start keeping house.

So Em found a nice place down on Harmon St. for $9 a month, first floor 4 rooms, and we went on our own.

The next thing I knew we was going to have another. So we moved back to E. New York on Ridgewood Ave. Then Ethel was born. So we stayed there for a while. We had a first floor in a two family house for $14 a month and the last I heard the same floor was renting for $89. So you can not blame me if I think the horse and buggy days was as good as we have now.—Daniel Rowlee Schoonover.

Addie Thompson, Fair Haven, to Mary Ann Austin, Eldred
September 5, 1898
My dear Aunt Mary,

I have been writing to Ida and feel very tired or lazy. I hardly know which, but one complaint is about as bad as another, don't you think so? But anyway, I am going to write to you or perish in the attempt and I am not going to say one word about the weather for that subject has become about exhausted and you know all about it yourself.

I do not think we have ever felt the heat so much here as this summer. Poor Polly [her husband Tom's sister] has been nearly broiled in the kitchen, but she keeps most as fat and quite as jolly as ever, only when she is so tired, she can hardly speak.

The boarders are beginning to leave and I suppose the weather will soon begin to get cooler and I will have to begin to leave for home. I hope I will be able to come up and see you this Fall, but I do not know what I can do as I cannot leave the house to the tender mercies of a servant girl. And Polly always likes to stay down as long as she can. I think you will have to come down and see me after I get home and get settled up again.

Julia wrote me a week or two ago that you only had seven boarders. I hope Maria has been more successful than last year. Tell her we do not intend to let her board Harry for three dollars per week, but will manage to pay a little more if it takes our bottom dollar. Do you think Harry is improving or that he really has consumption? I have not seen him for a long time and he looked not well then, but I must not write anymore. It is time for supper.

I hope this will find you all well and that you will write me as often as you can. I do want to see you. With love and kind wishes to you and all the best.

I am your affectionate
Addie

The Piermont Hotel owned by the Boyd family. Photo courtesy of Larry Stern.

F.F. Bush, Port Jervis, N.Y., to A.A. (Lon) Austin, Eldred
October 4, 1898
Dear Sir,
Received your $60.00 interest on the mortgage.
F.F. Bush

The Austins received an invitation to the marriage of William H. Wilson and Bertha Boyd. Bertha's parents, James and Margaret Mills Boyd, were proprietors of Piermont Hotel, near Highland Lake. William Wilson was the owner of the Wilson store at the center of Eldred.

William H. Wilson Marries Bertha Boyd

Mr. and Mrs. James Boyd
invite you to be present at the
marriage of their daughter
Bertha Emily
to
William H. Wilson
Wednesday evening,
October 19, 1898, at 8 o'clock,
Piermont Cottage,
Venoge, New York

Addie Thompson, N.Y.C., to Mary Ann Austin
November 24, 1898
Dear Aunt Mary,
At last I seat myself to scribble a few lines to you. It is snowing quite hard now. We expected company today, but it has snowed so nobody came and we ate our Thanksgiving dinner alone.

I don't see why you did not get in that barrel and come down. We would have been very glad to see you. It seems as if I would never be able to get up to see you, try as I will.

The winter has sot in very early this year. I hate to see so much snow fall before Christmas. The winter seems so much longer when we have snow so early.

Mr. and Mrs. James Boyd
invite you to be present at the marriage
of their daughter
Bertha Emily,
to
William H. Wilson,
Wednesday evening, October nineteenth,
eighteen hundred and ninety-eight,
at eight o'clock,
Piermont Cottage,
Venoge, New York.

Wedding announcement for William H. Wilson and Bertha Boyd, sent to the Austin family. Courtesy of Melva Austin Barney.

Austin Groceries and Work Records

1899 Grocery Book courtesy of Mary Briggs Austin.

C.M. Austin in account with Stephen S.J. Gardner, Dealer in Choice beef, Mutton, Lamb, Veal, Pork, Hams, Bacon, Corned Beef, Tongues, Etc. Poultry and Game in Season. Goods promptly delivered.

Groceries 1899
1 chip beef	.25
2 cans cocoa	.50
1 coffee	.20
1 corn	.25
1 dish	.25
1 pk. flour	1.40
8.5# ham	1.02
11-3/4# ham	1.53
4 lamps complete	1.00
100 meal	1.05
2 maple syrup	.24
5 bu. oats	2.25
1 overalls	.50
1 dozen plates	.90
4 sheets	2.20
1 shoes	2.00
1 soda	.08
1 stew kettle	.50
5# sugar	.30
1 sun tea	.50
3 tablespoons	.20
1 yeast	.05

1897 Work for A.A. Austin
3 hours with horse	.60
4 hours with horse	.80
half day with horse	1.00
6 hours with horse	1.20
A load coal	1.00

1898 work for A.A. Austin
Feed	2.50
Hay, straw	2.50
Horse half day	.50
Horse 6 hours	.60
Horse 7 hours	.70
Horse one day	1.00
C.M.A. 4 hours	.50
C.M.A. 1/2 day	.625
Elbert 7 hours	.75
C.M.A. 8 hours	1.00
Elbert 9 hours	1.125
Rob Clark 1 day	1.25
Half day, me and horse	1.00
Horse and me 7 hrs.	1.40
With team 3.5 hours	1.05
Team 1/4 day	1.25
Team 3/4 day	2.25
Team one day	3.00
Lumber	18.00
Team half day	1.50

1898 Work for W.B. Styles
One trip to Shohola	1.25
Water from Shohola	.56
1 stove from Shohola	1.50
Road work	4.00

1899 Costs
Bridge toll	.40
Half day work	.625
A man to help	.70
Team 1/4 day	.75
7 hours	.875
Half day with horse	1.00
8 hours	1.00
1 day work	1.25
Half day with team	1.50
Team of 7 hours	2.10
Trunks from Shohola	1.00
Road work	3.00
One load from Shohola	1.50
To Shohola for chickens	1.00
Trunk from Shohola	1.00
Trim trees, planting	12.00

I have had a fearful cold on my lungs and a gathering in my head; have not got over it yet, although I am better, but the weather is so changeable every one seems to have colds. It is very cold tonight and looks very much like another snowstorm.

Do you want me to send you Paine's Celery Compound? [See sidebar on p. 192.] Our doc says that Greene's Newcure is much better than the compound and shall I send Marie some Fellow's Syrup? Or if there is anything else you want to have?

Harry wrote me you had been down to Barryville. How is Aunt Eliza? Mrs. Millspaugh died last Wednesday. She was in her 78th year, ten years younger than Aunt Eliza. She has not had as easy a life though. I think she was a lovely woman as I ever met. Did you receive a paper with the account of her death? I do not think Mr. Millspaugh will live very long as he was very feeble the last time I heard from him. He is several years older than she was.

How is brother Lon's side getting along? Harry told me that he strained it lifting or breaking stones. It's too bad for him to do such work I think.

I have not seen any of the girls since I came home from the country in September. Ida Clinton was here the week before Thanksgiving. All were well then.

How do you think Harry is getting along? His letter to "Pop" was more cheerful I thought than previous ones. Are you getting tired of having him there? Now tell me if you are and we will make different arrangements.

Tell Maria if there is anything else she wants for the dress or anything to write and I will send it to her.

How is Aida and Lon getting

Mortimer Mckinley Austin, son of Mort and Jennie Austin. Photo courtesy of the Austin Family.

along? I hear that Walter has been up to the "Austin house." How are the various members of the "Royal family" getting along? They have none of them called on dear Aunt Addie as yet. Did his "royal" Dr. Ayers arrive from abroad at the specified time?

But it is half past 11 and I am very tired and guess you are too. So I must say good night sweetheart and hope to hear from you very soon again.

Wishing you all a Merry Christmas and a Happy New Year. Ever your affec. Addie

Mortimer McKinley Austin Born
On January 5, 1899, grey-eyed, Mortimer McKinley, son of Mort and Jennie Leavenworth Austin, was born at the Leavenworth homestead where Jennie and her father had been born.

McKinley was the first of six children that Mort and Jennie would have. The Leavenworths and Austins loved children, so I imagine there was great excitement in both Jennie's and Mort's families.

McKinley's only other Austin cousin, Lillie (a favorite of all the cousins), was 15. She lived in Bethel, New York, with her parents, Ell and Emma Paramenter Austin, and her aunt Sophronia Parmenter. Her half brother Henry Austin and his wife Sadie and their children seem to have lived nearby.

Bertha Collins Marries Louis Noe
Mort and Jennie Austin received an invitation to the marriage of Bertha Collins in January.

Reverend and Mrs. Robert B. Collins invite you to be present at the marriage of their daughter Bertha Silvey Seymour to Mr. Louis Albert Noe on Wednesday, January 18, 1899 at half after 3 o'clock 176 Amboy Avenue Tottenville, New York

Church Members

1890s Eldred Congregational Church New Members
William H. Austin
Sarah E. Wormuth
Sadie DeSilva
Mary A. Kyte
Eliza C. Eldred

1896-1900 Joel F. Whitney, minister

1897 William H. Austin deacon in Congregational Church.

Oswego Daily October 31, 1899

Washington
President McKinley left Washington at eight o'clock this morning for Richmond, Va., where he will attend the launching of the torpedo boat Shubrick. Several members of the Cabinet were in the party. The weather was extremely inclement, a cold rain falling.

Hackettstown, New Jersey Seminary Building Burned
The Hackettstown Seminary building owned by the Newark conference of the Methodist Episcopal Church, was completely destroyed by fire this morning, entailing a loss of about $300,000, on which there in only $150,000 insurance. The structure was of brick, 250 feet long, 100 feet in width, and 6 stories in height. It was located in the outskirts of the town.

Two hundred students, half of them females, occupied rooms in the building. All escaped uninjured, but not more than a quarter of them were able to save their clothing and other belongings.

The janitor who had returned to the basement of the seminary about 12:30 o'clock this morning from a tour of inspection that occupied nearly an hour of his time, found the lower portion of the structure filled with smoke. When he reached the boiler room, he discovered it to be in flames. An alarm was sounded and the work of getting the students out begun.

Everything was done quietly and effectively as there were about 200 students, teachers and employees in the building and these are all accounted for…

The building is entirely ruined… It is assumed that the building will be reconstructed as soon as possible.

The Congregational Church of Eldred, built in 1835, had it's Centennial Celebration in 1899. Postcard (date unknown) courtesy of Charles Myers.

Rev. Joel F. Whitney, the Congregational Church Pastor who offered words of welcome. Photo courtesy of Mary Briggs Austin.

C.S. Bok, Brooklyn, N.Y., to Mort Austin, Eldred
March 11, 1899
My dear old Friend Mort,

I am so glad to hear from you. Let me congratulate you for doing so well in having a little son come to bless you. I suppose you think I have forgotten you, like some of your city friends. I was on the point to write you many a time and have thought of you often.

I had a very bad winter this year. About Christmas time last December I was taken down sick with the grip for two weeks and also had a relapse of it that renders me more or less ill ever since then. I am not entirely well yet. Hoping you, your wife and the kid are all well.

Thank you most heartily for your kind invitation to visit you next summer. Perhaps then I may have the other half of me as well as myself come to see you. Are you going to run a boarding house for the summer? I like to know of this and I may be able to tell some of my friends about it especially those who go away during the hot season.

It is now a very long while since I saw you last. I think it was the time when you brought the horses to Walker. Are you still in the old farm? My dear old man, how delighted would I be if I can see you now and talk together about everything both of the old times and of today.

It surprised me greatly when I heard of the marriage of Noe and B.C. (Bertha Collins). C.C.I. has sent out quite a number of fellows and girls, in two of a kind. I mean in pairs, hasn't it?

Please excuse this paper. It happens this is the only thing I have in the house and I don't want you to wait any longer until I get some paper, to hear from me.

Remember me kindly to your wife, and hug little McKinley for me. I am ever your friend,
C. Soule Bok

Congregational Church of Eldred's Centennial

The Congregational Church of Narrows Falls was started by Rev. Isaac Sergeant in August 1799, as mentioned in *The Mill on Halfway Brook*. One hundred years later the church was still in existence as the Congregational Church of Eldred.

Centennial services were held in the church built in 1835 when Felix Kyte was the pastor.

The first meeting was Friday, August 11, 1899, at 2 p.m.

The newspaper article,

A Century of Church Life in the *Tri-States Union,* was in my mother's wonderful collection. We have met a number of the people who were mentioned.

The Methodist Pastor Rev. S.O. Rusby read Psalm 84. Words of welcome were offered by the Congregational Pastor, Rev. Joel F. Whitney.

Children, including Minnie Sergeant, a descendant of Rev. Isaac Sergeant, read scripture. Minnie's father Isaac Sergeant was a deacon and Sunday School Superintendent.

Two of Rev. Felix Kyte's sons spoke. Felix J.S. Kyte told of the family's travels to the area in 1832. Rev. Joseph Kyte remembered the "roast beef" at the Covert's house in Glen Spey was "bear meat."

Jacob Stage, 93, remembered one of the first members, Deacon Ichabod Carmichael.

Stephen St. John Gardner spoke for his mother, now 88 years young. "If I were 30 years younger, I would walk up to Eldred, even in a storm, if I might see the same spirit of love there now that I saw in those early days."

Mr. Gardner spoke feelingly of his remembrance of those who used to worship here, picturing them as they sat so that we could almost see them again as they listened to the Word, sang God's praise and studied the Bible.

Deacon Edward Wilson, in his gentle way told the children, "I was 17 years old when I first went to Sunday School and learned that verse, 'God so loved the world.'"

Rev. A. Eugene Austin spoke with emotion. I remember dear old Felix Kyte. No storm or weariness kept him from doing

Wall Street

Wall Street, New York, 1895. The Old Trinity Church is in the center. Postcard in the collection of Mary Briggs Austin.

Wall Street in Lower Manhattan, New York City, was the first permanent home of the New York Stock Exchange. The street runs through the historical center of the Financial District.

The street name was derived from the 17th century when Wall Street formed the northern boundary of the New Amsterdam settlement. Later a stronger stockade was constructed. In 1685 surveyors laid out Wall Street along the lines of the original stockade. The British colonial government dismantled the wall in 1699.

In the late 18th century, there was a buttonwood tree at the foot of Wall Street under which traders and speculators gathered to trade informally. The traders formalized their association with the Buttonwood Agreement, in 1792. This was the origin of the New York Stock Exchange.

George Washington took the oath of office on the balcony of Federal Hall overlooking Wall Street on April 30, 1789. This was also the location of the passing of the Bill of Rights.

In 1889, the original stock report, *Customers' Afternoon Letter*, became *The Wall Street Journal*.

—wikipedia.org.

Others in the 1900 Census

Some Barryville townsfolk in 1900 are listed on page 139. Most of the folks listed here lived in the Town of Highland (or nearby) in 1900.

Joel F. Whitney was the preacher at the Congregational Church. His wife's name was Louisa.

James Hulse, 79, lived with his son John Hulse, John's wife Mary, and their children. Frederick Hulse, a stone cutter, and his wife Katherine had two children.

George Wait, a carpenter, and his wife Mary Mills had a son, Alexander. George Wait's brother William Wait had a sawmill on the west side of Eldred. William's wife was Carrie.

Abraham Rundle boarded with James D. and Frances Eldred. Walter and Maggie Dunlap had two sons, Charlie and George. George Davenport was a blacksmith.

Calvin S. LaBarr, a farmer in Beaver Brook, and his wife Elizabeth Rice had 5 children including Jacob Daniel who would marry Anna Hankins. Calvin S. LaBarr died in 1901.

John Twitchell, a farmer, and his wife Edith had two daughters. James Black helped out and they had a servant Anna Custer.

Sarah Maria Middaugh was the widow of Dennis Middaugh. Three of their children are part of this story: Stephen and Charlotte Middaugh Myers had 3 children: Stanley, Marie, and Kathryn Myers; Henrietta Middaugh was married to George LaBarr; and Chester Middaugh would marry Florence Hammond (who had immigrated from Wales). In 1900 Florence Hammond was a servant for Seele and Henrietta Crawford who had a young daughter, Anna.

Frank Ort, a shoemaker, and his wife Mary Crandall had 4 children: Frank, William, George, and Charlie. Mary Ort seems to be the midwife who would deliver the children of Garfield and Ella Sergeant Leavenworth.

Frank and Mary's son William Ort, a teamster, would marry Bertha LaBarr. Their daughter Eleanor would marry a grandson of Almond and Mary Lilley who lived in Pennsylvania. Almond may have been distantly related to the Lilley (Lilly) family listed in Lumberland's 1810 Census.

Alexander and Sarah Foster's son George Foster would marry Jennie Hallock. Jacob and Emma Clouse had been married 16 years. He was a day laborer. Martha Atkins, 75, lived with her two sons. Anna Cobb, 68, was a widow.

John Weber was sawyer in a mill. He and his wife Kate had 4 children.

Chauncey Van Auken was a carpenter. His mother Sarah, 74, lived with him.

Theodore and Phoebe West and their adopted son Charles West, 7, lived at their West Farm House. John and Mary Wolf's 4 children and his mother Catherine lived with them. William and Margaret Wolfe had a boarding house. They had 4 children.

Thomas, Sherman, Claudia, Emerson, and Ezra McBride were children of Sherman (a sawyer) and Eliza McBride.

George James Clark (who we will meet again in WWI) lived with his siblings and parents, Martin Dominick and Mary Costello Clark in New York City, where he had been born. Mary's father Alfred Costello photographed George around the turn of the century. Alfred had sold land to the Maiers on Crawford Road in 1875. Martin D. Clark died in September 1899.

George James Clark. Photo taken by his grandfather, Alfred Costello. Photo courtesy of Joe Arlt.

---

his duty to the uttermost. I used to see him getting off his saddle at my Grandfather Austin's almost too feeble to ride, and thought of him with wonder and boyish admiration. What a good man he must be. I have seen him walking by his horse that the weary animal might have rest.

There is dear old Aunt Eliza Gardner. You never go there but she speaks of God, strong in the faith and in her childlike trust in Him. How much I owe my mother. When far from home, I thought of her and that kept me in the hour of temptation.

There was a brief intermission with pictures and reminiscences of the former days. The pastor read a historical sketch, and dismissed the audience with a benediction after they sang, *Blest be the Tie that Binds*.

On Sunday (called the Sabbath) Rev. Joseph Kyte preached on Ephesians 5:35–27.

Mrs. Eliza Gardner, 88, the oldest surviving member of the

> ### Guests at the Centennial
>
> Barryville: Mr. and Mrs. Stephen St. John Gardner, Mr. Jacob Stage (93 years), Miss Lillie Calkin, Mr. and Mrs. Wm. H. Whitney, Rev. S.O. Rusby, Mr. and Mrs. Albert Stage, School Commissioner, John Twitchell.
>
> Glen Spey: Mrs. James Gillespie and daughter, Margaret.
>
> Goshen, N.Y.: Thomas Kyte, Miss Elizabeth Kyte.
>
> Brooklyn, N.Y.: Mr. and Mrs. Perine and Miss Jessie Bolton.
>
> Port Jervis: Merritt C. Speidel of the *Port Jervis Union*.
>
> Philadelphia, Pa.: Miss Rebecca C. Eldred.
>
> Boston, Mass.: Rev. Joseph Kyte
>
> New York City: Mrs. Hall, widow of the late Dr. Edward Hall. Dr. and Mrs. A. Eugene Austin and Miss Charlotte Chambers Hall.
>
> Jersey City, N.J.: Felix J.S. Kyte and Clarence Kyte.
>
> Sitka, Alaska: Rev. Alonzo Eugene Austin
>
> Deacons: Isaac Sergeant, William H. Austin, and Edward B. Wilson.
>
> Trustees included: Deacon Isaac Sergeant, Rev. A.E. Austin, and Deacon W.H. Austin.

church, was not present.

Jacob Stage, 93, the oldest person present, had been a member of the Congregational Church before he joined the Methodist Church. Jacob's wife Martha Carmichael had died in 1894. Jacob lived with his son at Handsome Eddy. The story of Martha's grandmother and the bear (found on p. 21 in *The Mill on Halfway Brook*) was told at the centennial.

Stories teeming with interest were told during the afternoon of the first log house, the first church meeting, thrilling adventures of forefathers with bears, wolves and panthers which made the younger generation almost wish they had lived in those days to encounter and pass through some of the thrilling vicissitudes with which our ancestor had to contend.

After a profitable afternoon the meeting closed by the singing of the centennial hymn.

On Sunday, a continuation of the centennial service was held.

Felix J.S. Kyte, Rev. Joseph Kyte, and Thomas and Miss Elizabeth Kyte, children of Rev. Felix Kyte, who was pastor of the church for 46 years, were present and were conspicuous speakers at the meeting.

The choir included: Deacon Isaac Sergeant, a great-grandson of Rev. I. Sergeant, the organizer of the church; Herbert N. Kyte, organist, a grandson of Rev. Felix Kyte, Miss Florence Grace Beck, Mr. and Mrs. Perine of Brooklyn, and Miss Jessie Bolton of Brooklyn, and Henry Ladore Austin.

Deacon Henry Austin has resided on the Austin homestead for over 60 years.

The motto from Psalms 115:1, "Not Unto Us, Not Unto Us, but Unto Thy Name," which adorned the walls, was chosen for the occasion by Miss Elizabeth Kyte.

George Lovee, Brookside, N.J., to Lon Austin, Eldred
December 22, 1899
Friend Alonzo,

I received your letter tonight. You don't know how surprised I was to hear from you. I have often thought that I would rite to

Lon Austin. Photo in the collection of the Austin Family.

you, but did not think you was at the same place.

You said in your letter you often thought you would take a run down to Brookside. Why don't you come? I would like to see you very much and talk over olden times in Kansas.

You wanted to know if I was married. Yes, 16 years ago. I have got 2 children, boy and girl, and have got a home and 6 acres of Land. (Oh, come and see.)

I lernt the mason trade and worked at it for 7 or 8 years, and then lernt the carpenter trade and am working at it now. I will have work all winter. We have a railroad through here to Morristown.

Tomorrow night I must go to Morrison to get some Christmas for the children.

Wishing you a Merry Christmas and a Happy New Year.
I remain your friend,
George A. Lovee

At the beginning of this chapter, Mort had advised Lon to marry Nell (Helena Gillespie). It seems that Lon did want to marry her, but as life goes sometimes, it did not work out.

Lon had several lady friends

Eldred, about 1900, looking west. The library is now where the barn is in the photograph. C.C.P. Eldred's home is on the right. The original Parker House and William H. Wilson's store are in the middle of the photo. Next seems to be the Methodist Church, still without its steeple. The Slonek home, on the left, is on the hill in the distance. Photo courtesy of the Proctor Family.

over the years. There were many letters of correspondence between Lon and a lady named Daisy from 1907 to 1911, but Daisy was not interested in marrying Lon.

Nell Gillespie (whose letters we read in an earlier chapter) seems to have been Lon's one true love.

Lon wrote the following poignant story regarding Nell Gillespie, in his own handwriting.

Why Lon and Nell Did Not Marry

There are many infallible proofs which I might give, but I will only give you one which comes under my observation. It was one of sacrifice.

Several years ago, I met a young lady in Brooklyn. For two years, I called frequently at her house. We were close friends,
there was none whom I esteemed more highly than her or in whose society I found more pleasure.

Another gentleman used to call at the same house, quite attentive to her only sister. The family all thought that she was the lady of his choice, but I knew better. The father of these girls had been a well-to-do merchant, but had just met with financial embarrassment.

The gentleman of whom I speak, had enough as to spare. He saw his opportunity and availed himself of it. He offered his hand and his home to the one whom I was keeping company with.

She did not love him. She told him so and she told me so. The pressing need of her father
seemed to demand the sacrifice resignedly. [Nell married the other man, out of a sense of duty to her father's request.]

I have never seen her since. Though she frequently asks my cousin to bring me over. Knowing my relations with her and fearing that I might pose a problem on their happiness, I would not go.

When I was to New York some days ago, my cousin asked if I was going to see Nell this time.

I said, "Yes, if you care to go." Twelve years have elapsed since last I met her and I thought there could be no harm in calling for a few minutes.

My cousin wrote that we would call on a certain day unless warned that we must not come. On the morning that we had planned to go, we received a note, "You must not come." She had recently lost father and mother. Now her children were lying upon beds of sickness.

In the next two chapters we learn more about Ell, Emma, and Lillie Austin in Bethel, New York, and some of the townsfolk of Eldred through the letters which Jennie Crawford wrote to Lillie, her very good friend. Jennie Crawford (later Crandall) lived on Crawford Road west of Eldred.

A number of excellent early 1900 photos (many were glass negatives), courtesy of the Proctor Family, are included in the next chapter.

New York City, 1900. Photo: Geo. P. Hall & Son. Library of Congress, Prints and Photographs Division: LC-USZ62-69028.

Chapter 7
Turn of the Century
1900-1905

Jobs in 1900: day laborer, railroad laborer, mason, pastor, hotel keeper, telegraph operator, dressmaker, blacksmith, butcher, hostler (takes care of guest's horses), teamster, merchant, farmer, carpenter, teacher, salesman, barber, stone cutter, house painter, servant, telegraph lineman, miller, stone cutter, weaver of carpets, mail carrier, sawyer, traveling salesman, wood carver, and housekeeper.
—1900 United States, Town of Highland Census.

Photo taken at the end of the year in 1899. The young ladies are unknown. Photo in the original collection of Lillie Austin Calkin, courtesy of Dot Calkin Hale and Katherine Calkin Traxler.

January 1, 1900—a new day, a new month, a new year, a new decade, a new century.

The 20th Century would bring many marvelous inventions that would soon be commonplace in everyday life including radio, television, cars, and airplanes. But lives would also be touched by natural disasters and two world wars. Change also came to many of the ways people made a living.

Gone were the days of reckless lumbering by large companies. Townsfolk—Mr. Wormuth, Mr. Wilson, Mr. Wait, and others had their own private mills. It would be 1927 before the Narrowsburg Lumber Company would be started. They would provide a number of jobs, and be responsible in their lumbering.

Boarding houses would continue to provide income for many Town of Highland families for at least 60 more years. New boarding houses would be built, some would change owners and names, and some would burn down.

Proctors still provided many people with employment. Katie Sidwell/Stege, who lived near Stege's Pond, would employ some residents for a time.

Some of the young ladies we have met taught at one of the nearby schoolhouses. Sometimes after teaching a short time, they attended a Normal School to further their teaching education.

Other jobs not mentioned, such as churning butter, haying, and cutting ice from the lake, were just part of everyday life.

Homestead Cottage
My grandfather Mort Austin was listed as a farm laborer in 1900. Mort, Jennie, and little McKinley Austin lived in a house on Collins Road. The Collins Place (as it was often called) was also Mort and Jennie's boarding house, Homestead Cottage. We will talk more about it in the next chapter.

The Collins family had been neighbors and friends of the Austins since the 1860s. The parents had died, but three of the children continued to keep in touch. Tom Collins and his

Herman Bosch (when he was older) and others cutting and harvesting ice blocks. "It has been quite a snow here tonight. I suppose you will soon be cutting ice."—Letter to Lon Austin. The photo is courtesy Victoria Kohler and Ken Bosch.

wife Emma Kelso lived nearby until they moved. Annie Collins may have lived with or near her brother Robert Collins who was a Methodist minister in New Jersey. Bertha Collins Noe, Robert's daughter, was mentioned in Chapter 6.

Mort Austin's parents Henry and Mary Ann Austin lived west of Collins Road. In 1900 Henry and Mary Ann had been married 50 years. They ran a boarding house (Mountain Grove House) with the help of their daughter Maria, and sometimes, Aida and Lon.

Lon Austin was a farm manager for Mr. Proctor. Aida was listed as a housekeeper, though she also taught school.

Little McKinley Austin visited his aunts Aida and Maria so often that in one census he was listed as living with them. Aida was very partial and attached to McKinley, which would cause some family conflict in the early 1920s.

Austin Land
Henry Austin's 9.5 acres that started where Highland Road and Proctor Road met seems to have gone from Henry and revolved between Lon, Mort, and Aida. In a 1900 land deed, Aida purchased Lon's one half interest for $100.

Dory Austin had conveyed 12 acres to Alonzo E. Austin in 1898.

In 1900 Rev. Alonzo Eugene and Isabella Austin lived on the original Austin homestead of 260 acres, east of Henry Austin's 9.5 acres.

Either Alonzo E. or his son Alonzo E. Austin Jr. had purchased it when Henry could no longer afford the payments.

Ell and Emma Austin's Family
Henry and Mary Ann's son Ell, his wife Emma, and their daughter Lillie, 16, lived in Bethel in 1900. Emma's sister Sophronia lived with them or nearby. Henry Earl Austin was married to Sadie Leroy and they had a son Ralph.

The Bosch Family, 1900
The Bosch family lived north of Mort and Jennie, northwest of Highland Lake. In 1900 Wilhelm and Mary Maier Bosch ran the Lake House.

Wilhelm and Mary had a busy household of 7 children (ages 2–24): Wilhelmina, Lulu, Herman,

Mortimer McKinley Austin. Photo in the Austin Family Collection.

Ed, Ralph, Menzo and Tillie *(see p. 204)*. Son Charlie Bosch was in the Army in Ft. Riley, Kansas. Herman Bosch and his future wife Mary Elvira Horton (a newborn) would be helpful to Aida Austin when she was older.

Arthur, Albany, N.Y., to Lon Austin, Eldred
January 12, 1900
Dear Friend Lon,
I take pleasure in writing you of my safe arrival in Albany again and feel very much more contented after my visit.

It has been very busy here and will be all the month taking inventory.

I received an invite to Addie G.'s wedding. Was surprised, but glad. How I would like to be there. Tell her that I want you to kiss her for me. I thought something was in the wind that Sunday I was there. She looked so supremely happy.

Write me all about it. Who was best man? I expect to send her a H.C.C. Lemonade Set.

It has been quite a snow here tonight. I suppose you will soon be cutting ice.

I am having a very pleasant time socially. Tonight was a great meeting at the first M.E. The church was packed. It holds about 3,000 people. They burned $32,000 worth of mortgages leaving all five churches in the city clear of debt. Bishop Warren's speech was fine.

Remember me to Mort and your sister. Hoping you are all well as this leaves me.

I remain your friend, Arthur

There are a few letters in the Austin Collection that indicate that Lon Austin and sometimes his brother Ell Austin helped people with a small financial gift.

Charlie Bosch (below the X) in the Army in 1900 at Fort Riley, Kansas. Photo courtesy of Ken Bosch, grandson.

Thank You Notes, Lebanon Springs, N.Y., to Mr. Austin
October 4, 1900
Dear Mr. Austin,
I am very sorry that we are compelled to take advantage of your kind offer and ask you for a little more help financially. Could you without any inconvenience let us have $25.00?

We have tried to get on without asking for it, but find it will take that much to put us through. If it is not convenient, do not hesitate to say so for we know you have your bills to meet.

Lewis sat up today for the first! We think he will now gain fast. We all feel so thankful that his life was spared. Marion and the children are well.

Please let us hear from you as soon as convenient.
Sincerely yours,
Tillie E. Buchanan

An unknown couple in Lumberland in the early 1900s. The woman is churning butter. Photo courtesy of the Proctor Family.

October 10, 1900
Dear Mr. Austin,
I cannot tell you how grateful I am to you for your kindness in helping us over this difficulty. Your letter containing the $25.00 just received and I can now meet our last bill and feel easy.
Again I want to thank you for your kindness and I hope we will soon be able to pay you.
We have had so much sickness the past two years, but the dear Lord has been so good through it all. This last illness of Mr. T., I feel has drawn us very close to him and I feel that his health is going to be better than it has been in a long time.
With very best wishes and many thanks. I am Your sincere friend,
Marvin B. Finchell

McKinley's New Brother

Little Mortimer McKinley Austin, or Mac as he came to be called, was almost 2 when his brother Charles Raymond Austin was born on December 6, 1900. Charles Raymond was born at the Collins Place.

People who still remembered Sherman Buckley Leavenworth, would often say how much little Raymond looked like his great-grandfather, Buck.

Eliza Eldred Gardner, 1810–1901

In January 1901 Eliza Eldred Gardner died at the age of 90. We first met Eliza Eldred in 1815, when she was 5. Eliza and her siblings had arrived with their parents James and Polly Eldred, and settled near Halfway Brook in what was then Lumberland. Eliza Eldred Gardner was Mary Ann Austin's half sister.

She [Eliza Eldred Gardner] was interested in the Sunday School, and many here who are now men and women will recall her tact and her loving ways of interesting and instructing children. Her interest in the church never grew less, and her work for it was not laid down until failing health and declining years made it necessary.

She was a faithful wife, a devoted mother, a helpful, sympathizing friend and neighbor. She died as she lived, loyal to her family, to her church, and to her Saviour.—Port Jervis Union Gazette, *January 23, 1901, Eldred, p. 40.*

Wilhelm Bosch family around 1900. Back left: Lulu, Wilhelmina (Minnie), Mary, and Wilhelm. Sitting on the porch Herman, Ed, Ralph, and Menzo. Photo courtesy of the Bosch Family.

In the old Eldred Cemetery, there is a huge memorial to Eliza Eldred Gardner and her husband James K. Gardner who had died in 1860. *(See p. 472 for information and a photo of the original stone sculpted by George Beck.)*

Mary Ann Austin, the only child of James Eldred and his second wife Hannah Hickok, was the last of James Eldred's children. Sarah Eldred Carmichael had died in 1882; Charles C.P. Eldred and Phoebe Maria Eldred Austin had died in 1890.

Jennie Crawford's Letters to Lillie
Lillie (Lydia) Austin and Jennie Crawford (later the wife of George Crandall) were always good friends. Lillie saved Jennie Crandall's newsy, lively letters— excerpts of which are in Chapters 7 and 8.

The Crawford family lived on Crawford Road and Jennie often mentioned nearby neighbors: the Maiers; Fred and Mary Bradley Myers and Lottie Scott; Jackson, Cleta, and Lulu Myers, children of Abel and Maria Hankins Myers; Raola Kelley; as well as others.

At the start of 1900, Lillie Austin was 16, and Jennie Crandall, 18. Both young ladies would take examinations to be teachers, and both would teach school. Jennie Crawford Crandall was well loved by the children in Eldred.

George and Jennie Crandall never had a family, but were Aunt Jennie and Uncle George to all of us kids in the neighborhood.
—Christena Stevens Myers.

George Crandall, son of David Crandall, seems to be a nephew to Robert Crandall who married Nellie Simpson in 1893. Nellie Crandall was a very good friend of

Four Boarding Houses, 1900

Shawangunks and Sullivan County
The rolling uplands and mountain country of Sullivan County make it one of the most healthful of all the eastern sections.

Crest Hill Cottage
The Crest Hill Cottage at Barryville is one and a half miles from Shohola station and is built on a hill in full view of the village of Barryville, the Delaware River, and the surrounding hills and valleys. There are accommodations for 40 people. In connection with the house is a farm on which are grown the vegetables for the table, and which supplies also the milk, eggs, and poultry. Mrs. T. Greig is the proprietor.

Orchard Terrace

Orchard Terrace owned by Abel S. Myers. Postcard courtesy of Larry Stern.

Orchard Terrace at Eldred is four miles from Shohola. The house has 165 feet of piazzas and there are 10 lakes within walking or driving distance, where boating and fishing may be had at any time. The house contains twenty rooms, and a tennis and croquet ground is provided. The farm supplies the vegetables and milk. The house is open all the year. A. S. Myers is the proprietor.

Highland Cottage
The Highland Cottage in the mountains of Sullivan County stands on the shore of Washington Lake 4-1/2 miles from Shohola Glen. The

View of Highland Cottage from Washington Lake. Postcard courtesy of Larry Stern.

post office is Yulan. The house has over 75 acres of lawn, shady ground and woods with a frontage of over 1,200 feet on Washington Lake. Since the last season, a new parlor, a large veranda running the full length of the hotel and 40 new rooms have been added.

Four bowling alleys together with an entertainment hall have also been added. The hotel will now accommodate 100 people. A.E. Grove is the proprietor.

Oakdene

Oakdene owned by William E. Owen. Photo courtesy of Larry Stern.

Oakdene owned by William E. Owen is situated such that there is a view of the country for miles around; the air is perfect, water pure and roads first class; cool forests are in close proximity to the house, affording opportunities to roam in its cool and healthful shade; house near Washington Lake; plenty of fish; good boating and bathing; four miles from Shohola station, on the Erie, and 1/4 mile to post office and telephone; mail daily; rooms are large and airy; accommodates from 35 to 40; bowling alleys and pavilion nearby. Rates $6 to $8 per week.—*Brooklyn Daily Eagle, June 17, 1900.*

View of Eldred from the east in the early 1900s. A.S. Myers owned the Orchard Terrace boarding house on the far left behind the Congregational Church. The house in the distance, past the Congregational Church, was originally owned by the Slonek family. The house on the right, past the bridge, was C.C.P. Eldred's. The Methodist Church in about the middle of the photo, is still without a steeple. Photo courtesy of Chuck Myers, grandson of A.S. Myers, and son of Archibald and Minnie Sergeant Myers.

my grandma Jennie Austin.

In this first letter, Jennie Crawford scolds Lillie Austin for even thinking about taking easier teacher examinations in Pennsylvania instead of the great state of New York. Jennie calls Lillie's dad, Jim (James E. Austin).

Jennie Crawford, Eldred, to Lillie Austin, Bethel
Saturday night, January 28, 1901

Close up of engraving on monument to Eliza Eldred Gardner who died in 1901 and her husband James K. Gardner who died in 1860. Photo courtesy of Cynthia Leavenworth Bellinger.

Dear Lillie,

The very idea of you trying Pike County [Pennsylvania] examinations.

If the person who teaches Bethel School has a certificate to teach, which she must have, she is certainly smarter than you who have failed to get one. If you pick up your books and start to school with the determination to learn, your Bethel School teacher can teach you.

I don't pretend to be smart for I have went to a good many school teachers and all could teach me a thousand things. And should I go to school for many years to come, they could still teach me, even right in our own country school.

I am very sure, should I live in Bethel I could learn of your Bethel school teachers; besides I am quite a good deal older than you and have been knocking about trying to acquire knowledge 17 months longer than you, and if you go to school right there in Bethel for 17 months more and study, I'll warrant you pass in your examination at the end of that period.

Would anyone leave our old Empire state for the Keystone? Wouldn't you be an Empire teacher rather than someone who has left our state and taken an easier examination and who receives smaller pay in a neighboring state?

There is more than one kind of heroism. It isn't always the man who can shoot a musket straightest that is the greatest hero.

Everyone has a chance to show true heroism. Sometimes it is to wash dishes; sometimes it is to take care of a sick relative and the boys call him "coward." But what about the home folk? Do they call him coward? No, indeed. He has been a hero; The world does not know it, but God does.

Now the way for you to be heroic is to pack up your books, march into Bethel Schoolhouse next Monday morning, and when you put your books on the desk, smolder the fire of conceit which is running your ambition, your morals, and all your inward self, and burning up the girl who can be noble and brave, and let yourself be able to see your folly.

Just remember that the laws of the Empire state are the best in the world. And that her schools are the best in the U.S. Now lets you and I try to be scholars and teachers that are worthy of belonging to it and let us strive to make her schools with what aid we can give, equal or better than those of Germany.

And again, burn up all your emotional love stories, let facts take the place of sentiment and hard work take the place of your useless dreaming.

George is laid up. He run a nail out of a scaffold into his foot.

The Lackawaxen Depot burned up either Thursday or Friday morning.

How is your mother? I do hope she is better.

I am getting quite thick with the folks downtown. Was to Crandalls to supper again Friday night. What would your daddy say to that? Should he know it?

I am getting so I use terrible grammar. I am just going to try and stop some of it. Raola Kelley has her seventh grade certificate.

I haven't driven the horse since you was out. They have used her every day.

Poor Mrs. Gardner is dead, isn't she?

I stayed to Lottie's all night Thursday. We got up at 10 o'clock this morning, all of us.

Write. Come out.
Your friend,
Jennie J. Crawford

Wm. Henry and Mary Ann Austin
By 1901 Henry and Mary Ann Austin had separated. Apparently they just couldn't get along. If you ask a male relative, it seems Mary Ann was at fault; a female member might say it was Henry's fault. Henry lived with Mort and his family. Mary Ann lived with Lon.

Mary Ann Austin's niece, Addie Austin Thompson, wrote her aunt Mary Ann the month after Eliza Gardner's death. (Eliza was also Addie's aunt, as Eliza and Addie's mother Maria Eldred Austin had been sisters.)

Addie Thompson, N.Y.C., to Mary Ann Austin
February 16, 1901
Dear Aunt Mary,
It's high time I should answer your New Year's letter which I was very glad to receive.

I would have written sooner, but had quite a sick spell, and then my eyes commenced to cut up and of course I could not write until they were better.

Yes, Lon did manage to tell me you were with him and I was very glad to hear it. I wish he would keep you there all the time. That is where you ought to be.

It is so comfortable I wish I could be wafted over there with you for a while! Wouldn't our tongues wag though!

I had a very narrow escape from coming to see you when Steve [Stephen St. John Gardner, Eliza's son] telegraphed on Tuesday that Aunt Eliza was dead and would be buried on Wednesday.

Tom and I talked it over and decided that I could not go alone and he could not leave.

But you were not there were you?

Yes, indeed, I remember the happy days up on the old farm and the washing and bleaching, Harriet C., Archie and the grasshopper, and Uncle C.
Addie

Mary Hickok Stidd, 1835–1901
Laura Austin Clark, 1834–1901
Two other relatives died in 1901. Mary Hickok Stidd, daughter of Uncle Justus and Aunt Polly Hickok, was buried in the old Eldred Cemetery. Justus Hickok was a brother to Hannah Hickok

A ride on the roads of Lumberland. Photo courtesy of the Proctor Family.

Eldred, the mother of Mary Ann Eldred Austin. The Hickok family had been in the area since 1811.

Henry Austin's sister Laura Austin Clark died in 1901, and was buried in the old Eldred Cemetery. Henry Austin was the only one left in his family.

Laura's husband Irvin died 4 years later. Irvin and Laura Austin Clark had had 7 children. Four of them died young. In Laura's memory book, shared by Katherine Calkin Traxler, were a number of poems; some were in memory of her children. The following is one of those poems but it is not known if she wrote it or copied it from another author.

Sweet little children thou has left us
Thou hast gone to heaven to bloom
There no pain nor death can enter
There no weeping ore the tomb.

They are gone, yes gone to heaven
Left this world so cold and drear
They are in the arms of Jesus
Left their parents lonely here.

Parents do not wish to call them
Back into this world again
They are free from pain and anguish
They will never die again.

But prepare to go and meet them
When these changing scenes are ore
There thou will meet they darling children
There where parting is no more.

There were two stanzas from *Land of the Blest* by Mrs. Abdy that were also written in Laura's memory book.

Dear Father I ask for my Mother in vain
Has she sought some far country her health to regain?
Has she left this cold climate of frost and of snow
For some warm sunny land whare the soft breezes blow?

Yes, yes gentle boy, thy loved mother is gone
To a climate whare sorrow and pain is unknown.

George Ellery, Parmenter Relative

There are some letters and photo postcards sent from a George Ellery to Ell, Emma, and Lillie Austin in Bethel. George Ellery was a musician and a distant cousin (on the Parmenter side) to Emma and Lillie Austin.

Places to stay 1900–1905

Lake Side Cottage
25 guests near water. $6. E.H. Moore.
—Brooklyn Daily Eagle, *June 17, 1900.*

Orchard Terrace, Eldred
4 miles Shohola; elevation 1,600 feet; beautiful balsamic and pine clad hills; broad plazas, hunting, fishing, boating; fine scenery; modern improvements. Booklet. A.S. Myers.
—Brooklyn Daily Eagle, *July 19, 1900.*

Pine Grove Farm, Eldred
Beautifully situated; good board from our own farm; circulars. Jos. Maier.
—New York World, *August 29, 1900.*

Highland Cottage, Yulan
On Washington Lake, Yulan; Capacity 100. Amusement Hall, bowling alley, boating, bathing; terms moderate. Booklet. R.C. Miller.—Brooklyn Daily Eagle, *June 29, 1902.*

Pine Grove Cottage, Yulan
Pleasant location. Ample shade. Plenty fruit, milk, eggs, and vegetables. Pleasant drives. Near lake and Post Office. F.B. Owen.—Brooklyn Daily Eagle, *June 28, 1903.*

West Farm
Pleasant location; boating, bathing; fresh eggs, milk and vegetables; good accommodations; homelike; terms $6 and $7; circulars. Theo. West.
—Brooklyn Daily Eagle, *July 20, 1902.*

Highland Cottage, Yulan
Capacity 150; amusement hall, bowling alley, boating bathing fishing terms moderate. Booklet. Grannan & Johnson.—Brooklyn Daily Eagle, *June 13, 1904.*

The Bradley House, Eldred
Accommodates 50; high location, grounds, beautifully shaded; near lake and amusements; raise own vegetables, milk, butter, chickens, and eggs fresh, best cuisine. I.M. Bradley, Eldred.—Brooklyn Daily Eagle, *April 23, 1905.*

Woodland Cottage, Barryville
Fine new modern house, handsomely decorated; open fireplace; large airy rooms; nicely situated; pine groves near house; stable accommodations; $8 and $10. C.M. Colville, Barryville.
—Brooklyn Daily Eagle, *April 23, 1905.*

Pine Grove Cottage owned by F.B. Owen. Postcard courtesy of Larry Stern.

Woodland Cottage owned by Charles Colville. Postcard courtesy of Larry Stern.

George Ellery, Hoosick Falls, N.Y., to Lillie Austin, Bethel
May 27, 1901

I'm to sing at Carnegie Hall on Wednesday night in New York City. With love to your mother and most humble respects to Sweet 16.

It is raining cows and sheep and all sorts of things and has been all day.

I am always sincerely,
Geo. V. Ellery

Jennie Crawford, Eldred, to Lillie Austin, Bethel
July 21, 1901
Dear Lillie,

George [Crandall] has been sick; has been to the doctors twice.

I did not pass in Arithmetic or Grammar or any other thing, but school law. And Lillie my dear, come bring my arithmetic and my grammar and we'll study.

I am sure I'll never go through in current topics and history. Bertha L. did not get through either.

I've got the toothache.

George was up yesterday. We went down to church and I didn't have a thing to wear so I had to keep my coat on to keep folks from seeing my worst.

Last week I was over to Yulan and twice to Eldred to get a gun fixed with Nancy in Shohola.

Will Parker has a lawsuit. Rev. Mr. Ray preaches a too plain sermon. Mrs. Wormuth has boarders. Let me know how your mother is. I will go to Monticello with you if you want, for anything.
Jennie Crawford

This next letter seems to indicate that Jennie Crawford had gotten a teaching job.

Jennie Crawford, Eldred, to Lillie Austin, Bethel
September 1901
Dear Lillie,

Be sure and come. I have a fine boarding place all except my room that is warm and a fine bed, but it is very small. There is no carpet only pieces but it is clean. I have no looking glass and a homemade wash stand and basin.

Will tell you all about the Thursday night you left me at Mills' when I see you.

I have 13 scholars with the exception of a few more. I have one boy who is a perfect devil and two which are terrors. Got along fine the first week.

I've got a cold. Everybody around Eldred is sick.

Yes, I got my certificate all OK.

I shall write to Perry and ask him to condemn the schoolhouse. It is full of bedbugs.

Hope your mother is well and Jim also. Thanks for the songs. [Lillie composed some songs.]

They say it is nearer to come through Fosterdale.

Be sure if you don't come Friday to tell mother so Dad will come.
Jennie Crawford

Photo of unidentified man courtesy of the Proctor Family.

Eldred-Austin Cousins, 1900

The children of Uncle Augustus and Aunt Maria Eldred Austin in 1900:

Rev. Alonzo Eugene and Isabella Camp Austin lived in Eldred. Their son Dr. Alonzo Eugene Austin at some point owned the old Austin homestead. Dr. Austin had been married 2 years to Sara Hall. Sara's sister, Charlotte Hall, was closely associated with her sister and brother-in-law. There are a few of her flowery letters to Mort and Jennie in this book.

Rev. Alonzo E. and Isabella Austin had 2 married daughters. Joseph G. and Olinda (Linnie) Austin Ayers had two sons, Joseph Garrish and Charles Haines Austin Ayers. Henrietta Austin was married to Walter Browning Styles. There would be a major situation in a few years partially because of Henrietta's disdain for her husband working in New York City.

Mortimer B. Austin and Mary Letitia Millspaugh lived in Middletown, New York, with their children: Mary Isabelle Austin was married to William Hurtin; Charles Augustus Austin, a tinsmith, was married to Mary Johnson; and John Mortimer Austin was a salesman at an art store. At some point John M. Austin moved to Eldred.

Henry and Net Austin Clinton lived in Kearny, New York, with their daughter Ida Clinton, the only one of their 3 children to live to adulthood.

Addie Austin Thompson still wrote letters to her Aunt Mary Ann Eldred Austin. Most likely, Addie and her husband Tom still lived in New York City.

Rand (Miranda) Austin Paton had been a widow for 10 years. She lived in New Jersey with her daughter Ida and son Archibald and his wife Mary Brown Paton.

It is unknown where Edward D. and Evaline Austin lived.

Tina Austin Laing had been a widow for at least 20 years.

James Eldred's Descendants, 1900

Abraham Mulford and Elizabeth Wheeler Eldred's Descendants
Frank (Benjamin Franklin) Eldred and his second wife Martha visited his sister Amelia Eldred Hancy in Cleveland, Ohio, in August 1902.

Amelia Hancy, daughter of Abraham Mulford and Elizabeth Wheeler Eldred, died of heart exhaustion in March of the next year. Her husband John Hancy died 4 years later. Amelia and John Hancy were both buried in Cleveland, Ohio.

John Franklin Eldred (son of Frank Eldred) and his family lived in West Damascus, Pennsylvania. John F. Eldred and his wife Minnie Sears had 11 children, including Orvis R. Eldred (born in 1909), father of Richard O. Eldred who wrote, The Eldred Family.

Frank Eldred's son Judson Eldred was a woodcutter at Methol, New York. Judson married Emily Ina Dunlop. In fall 1902 Judson bought his father's farm from his brother John Franklin Eldred.

Lewis Laforde Eldred (another son of Frank Eldred) worked as a woodcutter in Methol, New York. Lewis started working in Equinunk in 1901, and in October married Cora Sisson. Lewis Laforde and Cora Sisson Eldred would have 10 children. Martha Eldred Worzel is one of their granddaughters.

Zophar and Sarah Eldred Carmichael's Descendants
Egbert S. Puff, ex-Superintendent of the Poor of Orange County, died at Middletown, New York, from paralysis, in April 1900. Egbert was the husband of Eliza Carmichael, daughter of Zophar and Sarah Eldred Carmichael. Egbert, a Civil War Veteran, had lost an arm at Chancellorsville.

Decator and Phebe Linkletter Carmichael's son Floyd Decator Carmichael would marry Cora Hardcastle Eldred, granddaughter of George W. and Marietta West Eldred.

Leonard George Watson was 5 in 1900. He was the son of Lina Carmichael and her husband Frank Watson. Lina was the daughter of Zophar and Sarah's son Lewis Carmichael who lived in Iowa.

C.C.P. and Effa VanTuyl Eldred's Descendants
George W. Eldred, the son of C.C.P. and Effa Eldred, had died young. C.C.P. and Effa helped raise George W. and his wife Marietta West's sons, James and Herbert Lincoln Eldred.

James Eldred married Elizabeth Hardcastle. Their daughters were Elizabeth Justina and Cora Hardcastle Eldred.

In 1903 Herbert L. and Eliza Post Eldred had 6 children and lived in Eldred. Their daughter Bertha Frances would marry Norman Myers, son of Abel S. and Maria Hankins Myers; their son George Ely Eldred would marry Bertha Hill.
—Eldred, pp. 71, 96, 101, 103.

Frank (Benjamin Franklin) Eldred, son of Mulford and Elizabeth Wheeler Eldred. Photo courtesy of Richard O. Eldred, descendant of Frank Eldred's son, John Franklin Eldred.

Samuel Hoatson Dies
In Eldred in October 1901, Samuel D. Hoatson died of typhoid fever. Samuel was the second husband of Marietta West Eldred. Mr. Hoatson was the father of Elizabeth Hoatson Clark Wilson and Mary Hoatson who married John Mortimer Austin.

Jennie Crawford, Swamp Mills, N.Y., to Lillie Austin, Bethel
November 20, 1901
Dear Lillie,

How is your room? I have 3 rooms. One at Swamp Mills, one at home upstairs, and one at home downstairs.

My kids were nearly crazy over the colored crayons.

Let's see, in my room here I have a bed, a piece of carpet, a shelf, a chair, a stand, a lamp a satchel, a shoe box full of trash, two pair of shoes, a cape, 2 coats, a cap, one petticoat, a waiste, several photos, one bottle of turpentine, one bottle of carbolic, one bottle peppermint, a towel, a tin wash basin, a curling iron, a pin cushion, a brush, some pencils, a pen, 2 cakes of soap in a dish, one hand glass, a calendar, a watch, door, window, one undone curtain besides 5-2 cent stamps, 1 penny, a nickel, a 1 dollar bill, and a few envelopes.

I had potatoes, cabbage, beef roast, squirrel, rye and wheat bread, applesauce and tea for supper. Answer soon.

With love from your friend,
Jennie C.

Jennie Crawford, Swamp Mills, N.Y., to Lillie Austin, Bethel
December 1901
Dear Lillie,

I have a lovely cold and a stiff neck. It rained a little tonight coming home.

Sunday I went over to Edna's

with George and then down to church. I enjoyed myself very much.

Pa froze his nose going to Monticello. George froze his ears working in the woods. And you know, I froze my ears, where I don't know.

I hope your mother is well. Regards to Jim.
Your friend,
Jennie J. Crawford

Jennie Crawford, Swamp Mills, N.Y., to Lillie Austin, Bethel
December 4, 1901
Dear Lillie,

My goodness what a snow. I got my two calves soaked. Like a fool I forgot my leggings this morning.

Gladys's folks have company, Mr. Hankins from Tusten—some relative to Mrs. A.S. Myers.

Poor George was not feeling well Sunday. He looks better than he has in a good while. He was very nice Sunday.

Thanksgiving I had spare rib, cabbage, potatoes, chocolate cake, apple pie, pickles, cranberries and coffee.

I went in to see Olive Wormuth and downtown and skated 25 minutes. I went over to the store, had 5 invitations out beside yours and did not accept any.

At night went down to Bertha Wilsons and stayed till 12 o'clock at night on the ice. I've got the cart before the horse.

First Maggie, Tina, Bertha, Mrs. Abendroth, Will Wilson, Alex Wait, and I ate supper. Next we went to church, then to the gymnasium. After that on the ice and skated till half past 12.

I am sorry I cannot come.
Your friend, Jennie.

Congregational and Methodist Churches
In 1901 Edna Gardner, Archie

Two boys fishing, around 1900. Photo courtesy of the Proctor Family.

President McKinley Assassination

On September 6, 1901, President McKinley became the third United Sates President to be assassinated.

William McKinley Jr., a Civil War veteran, had become President in 1897. On September 5, 1901, President and Mrs. McKinley were at the Pan-American Exposition in Buffalo, New York, where he had delivered a speech on tariffs and foreign trade.

The next afternoon, the President greeted people at the Temple of Music. Leon Czolgosz was in line with a pistol concealed by a handkerchief. Leon fired twice. The second bullet went through the President's abdomen and lodged in the muscles of his back.

President McKinley was reported as being concerned about how they told his wife what happened. He also wanted Czolgosz protected from the angry crowd which was severely beating Czolgosz.

Ada Britt, 11, lived in Brooklyn with her Parker and Schoonover relatives in 1901. Ada was a few blocks from home when she heard people talking about President McKinley being shot in Buffalo. (It must have come over a telegraph.) She raced home to tell her grandmother Schoonover and Aunt Kate the news.—Richard James.

Eight days later, the President died from gangrene. His last words were, "It is God's way; His will be done, not ours." Vice President Theodore Roosevelt then became President. There was a 1903 photo of the Theodore Roosevelt family in the Austin memorabilia.
—wikipedia.org.

View of Eldred after 1900. The Autenrieth Hotel (the original Parker Hotel) is on the right. The schoolhouse is in the center. Eldred Methodist Church is in the distance on the left. It has a steeple, therefore the photo was taken sometime after 1900. Photo courtesy of Chuck Myers.

A. Myers (Chuck Myers's father), and Georgia Clark were received into membership at the Congregational Church. The following year, James K. Gardner, Charles Breen, George Layman, Mrs. Ami Quick, Phebe Drake, Mrs. Shotwell, and Gussie and Edith Davenport were also received into membership. Rev. W.J. Carter was pastor from 1900 to 1903.

Eldred's Methodist Church had been built in 1859. Sometime after 1900 a steeple was added. There was also a wagon shed beside the church for the use of members who drove some distance to church *(see p. 142)*.

The Methodist Church in Barryville was built in 1902. The parsonage at the Barryville Church was owned by both the Eldred and Barryville Methodist churches.

E.R. Kalbfus and Ira M. Austin of Barryville, along with James Boyd and my grandfather C.M. Austin of Eldred, were the original trustees of the property. Rev. S.O. Rusby was pastor from 1896 to 1901. Rev. F.L. Rhodes was pastor from 1901 to 1904.

The Methodist preacher who lived in the Barryville parsonage had the charge of the Barryville, Eldred, and Pond Eddy Methodist Churches.

In 1935 Irwin and Myrtie Crabtree Briggs (my mother's family) would live in the parsonage beside the Methodist Church. How incredible to have had a view of the Delaware River from the front of the house.

In 1902 Irwin Briggs lived in Nebraska where his father Clint homesteaded. Myrtie Crabtree and her family would soon leave their farm in Mondamin, Iowa, for Nebraska where Irwin and Myrtie eventually meet.

Oliver Perry Schoonover Dies
Back in New York, Uncle Perry Schoonover died at the age of 82, in 1902. He was buried in the old Eldred Cemetery.

Zane Grey's First Article Published
As mentioned in Chapter 5, Zane Grey and his brother Romer enjoyed visits to Lackawaxen, Pennsylvania, "the picturesque mountainous region where the forests abounded with game and the stream with fish."

One of those trips inspired Mr. Grey's first article, *A Day on the Delaware,* which was published in 1902.

Jennie Crawford, Swamp Mills, N.Y., to Lillie Austin, Bethel
February 7, 1902
Dear Lillie,
   Last Saturday night there were 30 of us skating up in Highland Lake. What a good time we had. I wished you were with us to enjoy it, too. I got home 25 minutes to 2. Sunday night I went skating up to Swamp Mills. Monday afternoon I saw Mr. Perry and State inspector Symes. Perry said you were sure of your third grade.
   Jennie J. Crawford

Jennie Crawford, Swamp Mills, N.Y., to Lillie Austin, Bethel
March 4, 1902
Dear Lillie,
   Start early. Get to the schoolhouse by 3 or before. We will need all the daylight there is. The roads are bad.
   Atwell Bradley's wife is very sick.
   Be sure and come Friday early. Jennie J. Crawford

Jennie Crawford's letter indicated that Atwell Bradley's wife Wilhelmena (Minnie) Clemens was very ill. Minnie, 27,

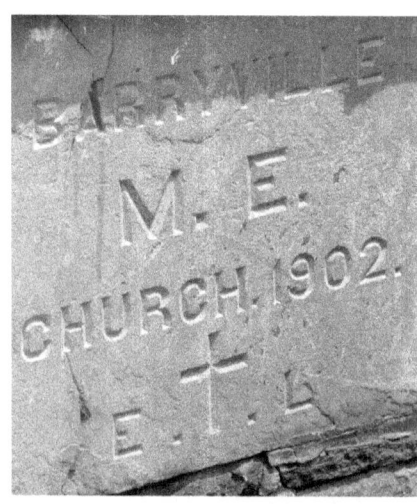

Barryville Methodist Church cornerstone. Photo: Gary Smith.

died on March 5, 1902, leaving Atwell a baby son, Clifford Bradley.

Minnie's mother Mrs. Anthony Clemens cared for baby Clifford at her home in Fremont, New York.

Jennie Crawford, Swamp Mills, N.Y., to Lillie Austin, Bethel
March 1902
Dear Lillie,

Too bad you've been sick. You ought to have known better.

Promise you won't tell. I've been to a dance.

Mrs. Tyler is teaching the kids a song for Arbor day. They do better than I ever thought they could.

We had an awful storm. The roads are awful.

With love,
Jennie Crawford

William F. Proctor Dies
William F. Proctor, owner of Lochada in Lumberland, died in April 1902. His son William Ross Proctor left his architecture practice in Pittsburgh and took charge of the Proctor Estate.

In the early 1900s, William R. Proctor built the lovely Brookwood Manor.

William Ross Proctor was married to Elizabeth Singer, the daughter of a prominent business man and steel magnate, William Henry Singer. (She was not related to Isaac Singer of the Singer Sewing Company).

William R. and Elizabeth Proctor had two children—Vouletti Theresa Proctor and William Ross Proctor Jr.

The Proctor family employed many of the townsfolk in the area. Uncle Lon Austin worked for the Proctors in the late 1890s and the early 1900s. There are several letters to Lon from Proctor family members in this chapter: one from William Ross Proctor,

Grocery Account Book, 1900–1906

Item	Price
1 can apricots	.25
1 baking powder	.20
1 can beef	.25
10# butter	2.50
2 lb. cake	.20
1 chicken	.65
1 box cinnamon	.10
3# cod	.10
1# coffee	.18 to .25
2 cocoa	.20 to .25
1 can corn	.10
1# cornstarch	.10
2 crackers	.18
1 dozen eggs	.12 to .25
50# flour	1.35 to 1.50
3# ginger snaps	.25
2# lard	.20
1 bottle lemon	.20
Van's lemon (1906)	.30
1 dozen lemons	.25
2 macaroni	.20
100 meal	1.20 to 1.35
3 milk	.30
1 oz. nutmeg	.10
3# oatmeal	.15
1 gal. oil	.14 to .15
1 pk. onions	.25
2# peaches	.30
1 can of pears or peas	each .12
2 plum puddings	.25
1 can plums	.25
1 peck potatoes	.40
2 pumpkin	.20
5# prunes	.50
1# raisins	.12
5# rice	.35 to .40
1 can salmon (1906)	.11
salt	.05 to .15
1# sugar	.06 to .05
2 tapioca	.20
1# tea	.50
1 tomato	.10
1 bot. vanilla	.10
2 qt. vinegar	.10
100# wheat	1.20
1 yeast	.05
6 glasses	.54
1 w. basin	.25
2 starch	.16
2 bot. blue	.10
1 sauce pan	.15
1 S. Brush	.20

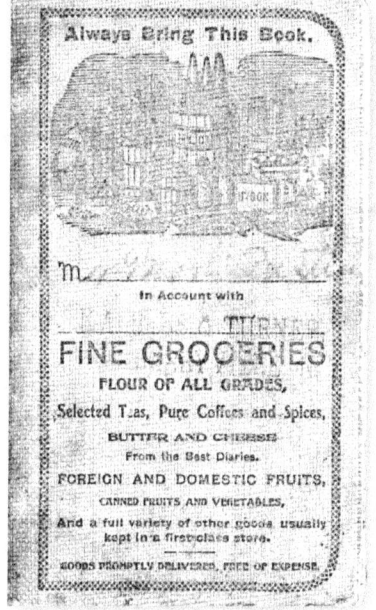

1900 Grocery booklet in the collection of Mary Briggs Austin.

Mr. Mort Austin in account with Mr. Turner. Fine Groceries, Flour of all grades, Selected Teas, Pure Coffees, and Spices, Butter and Cheeses From the Best Dairies. Foreign and Domestic Fruits, Canned fruits and vegetables. And a full variety of other goods usually kept in a first class store. Goods promptly delivered free of expense.

Item	Price
1 condition powder	.25
1/4 borax	.05
1 sapolio (soap)	.10
1 stove polish	.08
1 Castoria	.35
1 box pills	.25
1 salve	.25
1 cough med.	.25
1 expectorant	.50
med. bill (1906)	5.02
1 basket	.10
1 stove pipe	.45
1 axle grease	.25
1 matches	.05
1 axle grease	.10
6 fly paper	.15
1 cord of wood (1908)	1.00
20 yd. calico	1.40
4 spools cotton	.20
5 yd. flannel	1.50
pkg. needles, safety pins, each	.05
2 pr. socks	.20

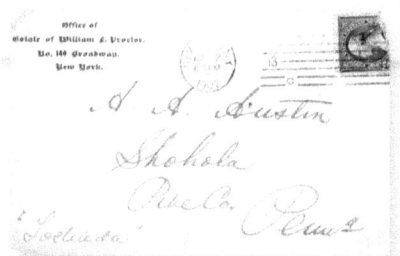

1902 letter and envelope from Wm. Ross Proctor to Lon Austin. Letter and envelope courtesy of Melva Austin Barney.

Elizabeth Singer Proctor, wife of William Ross Proctor, and mother of Vouletti T. Proctor. Photo courtesy of the Proctor Family.

William Ross Proctor, husband of Elizabeth Singer Proctor, and father of Vouletti T. Proctor. Photo courtesy of the Proctor Family.

two letters written by the wife of Charles E. Proctor (excerpts of whose *Travelogue* we have read), and one from young Vouletti T. Proctor.

Wm. R. Proctor, N.Y.C., to A.A. (Lon) Austin, Shohola, Penn.
May 2, 1902
My dear Lon,

I enclose cheque to your order for $589.75 for payment at Lochada for months of March and April. I have put Pine and Bouear down at $40 per month and if there is any difference, let me know. I have put Collins down at $2.25 per day which I believe is right. I also enclose cheque to order of Wm. Wait for $6.95 for shoeing.

As to grass seed, let Job have what he needs of it. If anything further is needed, address me at once. Please acknowledge receipt of cheque.
    Very Truly Yours,
    Wm. Ross Proctor

Jacob Stage Dies
Jacob Stage, who we first met in *The Mill on Halfway Brook*, died May 4, 1902. Jacob was 96 years old.

Margaret Terns Gardner Dies
Margaret J. Terns Gardner, second wife of Stephen St. John Gardner, died in August 1902. She was 63. Stephen and his son, James K. Gardner, operated the general store next to the Shohola Glen House across the Delaware River from their home in Barryville. James K. also sold coal and lumber.

Ida Brown, Highland Lake House, Lon Austin, Mountain Grove
Monday evening, summer 1902
Dear Lon,

I am very sorry I did not receive your note in time to

send you word that I had left Barryville.

I came here last Thursday and like it so well I shall probably remain through July. If it ever stops raining, I hope you will come over to see me. My love to Aunt Mary and Tom. Tell him to come over to see me, too. It is very pleasant here and we enjoy the boating very much.

With kindest regards and hoping to see you soon.

Your aff. cousin, Ida

Jennie Crawford, Eldred, to Lillie Austin, Bethel
August 6, 1902
Dear Lillie,

Will you come out for me or how will I get out to your place? Dad is so cross I would not dare to ask for the horse.

Examinations are the 14 and 15. Are you sure that grammar and drawing both come on the same day?

Tell your father to be sure and bring us 4 pounds of butter the next time he comes to Eldred. He can leave it to Wilson's and if I am not around we will leave the price there too. How much is it a pound?

Guess I've got the hay fever. I am going to see the Dr. today if my courage holds out. Jennie C.

Lillie Austin taught in School District No. 9, in the Town of Cochecton, in the 1902 to 1903 school year. There was a souvenir booklet that listed the names of 26 students.

The next letter may have been from a descendant of Zophar and Sarah Eldred Carmichael.

Maria O'Neil, Chicago, Ill., to L. Austin, Eldred
August 18, 1902
Dear cousin Lon,

Motoring by Loch Ada in a 1901 Winton Runabout. "You can make it go fast or slow, just as you wish, and start or stop when you please. It is easy of control and is operated on the hydro-carbon system. It costs about half a cent a mile to run it. Price $1,200."—Winton Motor Carriage ad. Photo courtesy of the Proctor Family.

The butter came this a.m. It is lovely. The first thing I did was to sit down and eat bread and butter till I felt like a pizzen pup.

We had corn for dinner and Mr. O'Neil said it was like old times to eat such butter.

Lizzie is up in Wisconsin. She has had bad weather most of the time. Today it is trying to warm up a little. Mr. O'Neil is making great calculations on our coming East in October. The only thing I think the time will be short to stay for me.

My daughter-in-law has been quite sick since I came home and the Grandma is now sick. It is very severe and an epidemic all through the nest and a great many deaths have been the result.

How is your mother and Maria, and Aida? I had such a pleasant time every place I went.

Have you had such cold weather there? We kept a fire all last week, so damp and then such a wind from off the lake.

Lou wrote me last week that she did not believe she would ever be able to work again. I feel so worried about her. Hattie has gone to Kentucky with her

Ida Austin Brown, an Eldred-Austin cousin. Photo courtesy of Melva Austin Barney.

children and says it is so very warm there.

Many thanks to you in your kindness to me while I was there at your place.

There is nothing as beautiful

Lillie Austin, teacher in Cochecton, school year 1902 to 1903. Photo courtesy of Katherine Calkin Traxler.

to me as a dutiful son to a Mother and your mother has such a one in you. Remember me to Eldred, Mort, and all the rest; Especially your mother and father.
 Write me when you have time. Remember me to Henrietta when you see her.
 Trusting we may see you soon, I am sincerely your cousin,
 Maria Young O'Neil

Girl picking berries. Photo courtesy of the Proctor Family.

Mrs. Chas. Proctor, Lakewood, N.J., to Lon Austin, Shohola, Pa.
October 23, 1902
Dear Lon,
 Will you send me as soon as possible, one barrel of assorted vegetables, one of apples and one of potatoes to the above address and oblige.
 Yours truly,
 (Mrs.) Chas. E. Proctor

Mary Ellery, Brooklyn, N.Y., to Lillie Austin, Mountain Rest Farm House, Cochecton Center, N.Y.
November 9, 1902
Miss Lillie Austin,
 Glad your mother has some one to help her and also glad that she can see you every week.
 I think you must have a very nice boarding place and that is such a good thing.
 I think June is very nice to go to training school and hope you may be able to do so.
 Yours affectionately,
 Mary J. Ellery

Mrs. Chas. Proctor, Lakewood, N.J., to Lon Austin, Shohola, Pa.
December 7, 1902
Dear Lon,
 Do not send butter oftener than once in two weeks. We can not use more. Also send another barrel of assorted vegetables and one of apples. I should prefer Baldwin or Greenings and only a few Ben Davies.
 Very truly yours,
 (Mrs.) Chas. E. Proctor

Mary Ellery, Brooklyn, N.Y., to Lillie Austin, Cochecton Center, N.Y.
February 1, 1903
My dear Lillie,
 I heard from Mrs. Collins a short time ago and she said she expected to go back to Eldred in the Spring.
 Does your school continue all the year (of course with the exception of vacation time) or is it only for the winter? I am glad you like it so well.
 With lots of love from us all, I am your affectionate fifth cousin,
 Mary J. Ellery

C.A. Gieselman, Los Angeles, Calif., to Lon Austin
February 15, 1903
Dear friend,
 Well you will see by this that I am in California. I have been here nearly a month and like it very well, especially in winter as it is nearly as pleasant as in summer.
 I came here from Denver, Colorado. I was here about six months. I don't know how long I will stay here, but at least as long as the weather is bad further north.
 Were you in Los Angeles when you were in California? There is no need of me writing and telling you about the place as you were out here 3 years ago, if my memory serves me right.
 I have had plenty of work ever since I left Glen Spey, so I don't get any chance to get in any mischief or to get homesick, but then you told me a fellow wouldn't get homesick after he had been away six months or more, so I guess I am not in anymore danger.
 I remain as ever,
 C.A. Gieselman

1903 Events

The year 1903 brought the *Great Train Robbery* movie, the formation of the Ford Motor Company, the first world series, the first Teddy Bear, and Helen Keller's, *The Story of my Life.*

Brookwood Farm

Brookwood was a 5,000 acre farm owned by William Ross Proctor.

The following information from The Story of Brookwood, *by Harold G. Gulliver, from,* The Field Illustrated, *October 1918, is courtesy of the Proctor Family.*

A visit to Brookwood Farm will prove a delightful journey. It is situated on the high ground of Sullivan County in the township of Lumberland, on the Delaware River, at an altitude of 1,400 feet above sea level. The railroad station is Shohola, Pennsylvania, about 100 miles from Jersey City on the Erie Railroad.

The post office is at Barryville, N.Y. It is in the foothill country, a region of rare natural scenic beauty. Great forests of pine, hemlock, oak and chestnut clothe the hills and the rolling pastures are thickly carpeted with rich grasses.

The entrance to the farm is a fine highway bordered picturesquely with shaggy hemlocks. There is mile after mile of well-kept roads which any community might be proud of.

The road entering the estate divides two spacious deer parks tightly fenced, where hundreds of deer feed on herbage and add to our meat supply.

The highway completely encircles a quiet lake 135 acres in extent, and on the shore of this lake behind terraced lawns stands the magnificent residence of the owner, Brookwood Manor.

At a distance of about a mile is the dairy plant, complete in every last detail. It is a model establishment of its kind, representing the last word in sanitation and labor saving, although there are no frills or unnecessary architectural embellishments.

The main building is 350 feet

The lovely Brookwood Estate. Photo courtesy of the Proctor Family.

long and there are accommodations for 150 head of mature animals. The exterior is all reinforced concrete with stucco and the walls and ceilings are done in plaster with white enamel finish.

The King system of ventilation is used and a steam pipe in the outtake ventilator stack facilitates the constant removal of foul air. Ample lofts provide storage for the forage crops of hay and a battery of hollow tile silos preserves the great corn harvest.

All buildings are light, airy, and warm. Inasmuch as the temperature at Barryville frequently goes from 20 to 30 degrees below zero in winter, it has been found advisable to install steam heat in the buildings.

Only enough heat is used to raise the temperature of the air to a point where the ventilating system functions properly. A moderate amount of heat keeps the air dry and circulating freely. Were it not for this, in the very cold weather moisture from the cattle's breath would gather and congeal on the walls and windows, resulting in a very unhealthy condition.

The calf barn, a separate building, is provided with a larger radiating surface and is a particularly well ventilated, and light building.

The milk is handled under conditions that insure scrupulous cleanliness and purity. No milker is allowed to enter the white tile dairy.

The milk from each cow is weighed and recorded, poured into a funnel connecting with a tube which passes through the wall into a receiving vat whence it passes into a clarifier and from there over a cooler.

It is bottled at a temperature of 45 degrees and kept on ice until delivered. There is a complete butter-making plant. When butter is made the milk passes from the receiving vat into the cream separator. Skimmed milk is fed to calves and the cream is placed in a combination pasteurizer and ripener. After pasteurizing a culture of lactic acid bacilli is added to the cream, after which it is held at a high temperature until the desired degree of acidity is attained. All cans, bottles and other utensils are thoroughly sterilized and cleansed in a special apparatus built for this purpose.

Spring House in Barryville, New York. Photo courtesy of Kathy Datys.

McKinley and Raymond's Brother

In April 1903 William Sherman Austin (my uncle Bill) joined his brothers McKinley and Raymond at the home of his parents, Mort and Jennie Austin. I imagine Uncle Bill was named after his grandfathers, Sherman S. Leavenworth and William H. Austin.

Grandma Jennie would be kept very busy running the boarding house, as well as caring for her boys. It would be eight years before her next child Elizabeth would be born.

John Mortimer Austin, son of Mortimer Bruce and Mary Letitia Austin, married Mary D. Hoatson in May 1903. They seem to have lived in Eldred at least a few years.

George Layman Dies June 1903

George F. Layman, proprietor of the Spring House at Barryville, died at about 5:30 o'clock this morning, after a long illness of Bright's disease. He was nearly 70 years of age. Mr. Layman was prominent in the Barryville section of Sullivan county, and for many years conducted the Spring House, of which he was the proprietor when he died.

He leaves a wife and two nephews, George and Chester Doolittle who resided with him.

Mary Layman may have had some financial difficulties after George's death. Three years later, Mary took a mortgage from the Elmendorfs for $3,500 for the Spring House.

Jennie Crawford wrote a newsy letter to Lillie Austin in July. She apparently was trying to pass the examinations to become a teacher in New York.

Jennie Crawford, Eldred, to Lillie Austin

July 18, 1903
Dear Lillie,

I failed in four, isn't that terrible? Well it's all in a lifetime.

Mother is feeding the dogs, we have only two. Grandmother doesn't feel very well today.

Maiers have quite a few boarders, but Fred's folks [Fred Myers] have only 3.

I am lonesome enough to die if the Lord would have me.

I have a new hat. It is black chiffon with a tucked silk crown striped white and gray with a bunch of almonds on it. It is not a bit gay, but I think it is nice.

Fred Myers has an increase of stock. It is a girl. Ray Kalbfus has an heir, male or female I don't know which. Also Walt Dunlap's folks.

How is your Mother? I saw your dad once when I was to Waits, but the other time I was asleep. You must be well blessed with clothes for the summer. I think that blue plaid is very pretty. All of it is nice, but I like that the best.

Edith Parker came up from Shohola with me yesterday and Lottie was with me too. Yes, and Raymond Beufve. So you see I didn't want for company.

Momma and I were to Barryville Tuesday. We stopped and seen Mary Eaton Hulse and her baby. The kid is nice, but Mary is as thin as a rail.

Grandmother is going to bed. Mom is rocking and Daddy lighting his pipe.

Yesterday I was to Yulan, Eldred, Barryville, and Shohola. I walked to Yulan and back.

Good by,
June Bug

Cartoon given to Lillie Austin February 14, 1903. Fair Lillie! He loves me, he loves me not. Your admirers, The Echo Hunting Club. Courtesy of Katherine Calkin Traxler.

The following note on a postcard was unsigned.

Barryville, New York
September 14, 1903
We are usually well. It is very dry. The forest is a fire. They have been fighting it for two weeks; have it under control now. They have no water to fight it with; can not save, only as they draw water 1/2 mile. Will write soon.

Toaspern Family
You may remember that the Toaspern family lived on Corkscrew Road on the way from Barryville to Yulan. Their boarding house was called Maple Grove Farm.

After reading about the Toasperns in the 1880 Census, it was fun to see a photo of Chris and Ida with 3 of their children: Meta Lass, Walter, and Arthur; and two grandchildren.

Great Pumpkin Flood 1903
In October 1903 the Delaware River flooded so severely that it was called the Great Pumpkin Flood—a reference to a severe 18th Century fall flooding where great numbers of pumpkins floated downstream.

Nearly 20 inches of rain fell on October 8th and 9th of that year [1903], and the Delaware crested on October 10th in a flood that destroyed several of the bridges spanning the river, including the Pond Eddy Bridge, wiped out the Erie Railroad's tracks in a number of places, and devastated homes and businesses in three states.

That 1903 flood and a similar, though not quite as destructive flood in March 1904, led some of the homeowners along the

A photo from 23rd Street, New York City. "How would you like to get into one of these big vehicles and ride all over New York? They pass this house every day. The trip costs one dollar. Merry Christmas!" Postcard from E.J.B. to McKinley Austin, courtesy of Mary Briggs Austin.

Delaware River in Barryville to take drastic action.—John Conway, Retrospect, Sullivan County Democrat, *October 8, 2010.*

Jennie Crawford to Lillie Austin
Possibly October 1903
Dear Lillie,
Crandall's folks have lost, house, wagons, sleighs and all such things. The flood carried them away.

Orts are in a bad plight. Worse off than any. Poor Mrs. Turner lost her wash house.

I could not get to my school in time to teach Monday.
You must answer. Love to all.
Jennie Crawford

A Fire at Pine Grove Farm
On October 9, 1903, Pine Grove Farm, the boarding house of Joseph and Juliana Maier on Crawford Road, burned down. Joseph set about to rebuild their home on a smaller scale.

The Toaspern Family in the early 1900s. Left, sitting: Ida, Meta Toaspern Lass with her little ones, and Chris Toaspern. In back: Walter and Arthur Toaspern. Photo courtesy of Bill Ihlo.

Several men did carpentry work for Joseph Maier that have been a part of this story: Frank, Morgan, and Alvie Sergeant; and John Hill. The rate range was $2 to $2.50 per day.

Mr. Maier wrote a number of letters for work and cost quotes and to order supplies, a few of which are included in this chapter.

Joseph and his son Julius kept meticulous records, which along with copies of their letters, were shared by the Bosch Family for this book. (Wilhelm Bosch's wife Mary was a Maier daughter.)

Aaron Montgomery Ward
Joseph Maier ordered some supplies from Montgomery Ward & Co. He wrote to them at the end of November with a concern.

Aaron Montgomery Ward, the originator of ordering goods by mail, had worked as a traveling salesman in rural areas for several years. Mr. Ward thought he could lower costs by cutting out the middle man and started his mail order business in 1872. Rural customers ordered by mail from a wide variety of merchandise and picked them up at the nearest train station.

Ward's catalog, known as the *Wish Book*, offered 10,000 items in 1883. Richard W. Sears offered some serious competition with his first general catalog in 1896. In 1875 Ward had offered a policy of "satisfaction guaranteed or your money back."—*wikipedia.org*.

That could be the reason for the letters that Joseph Maier wrote to the Montgomery Ward & Co. in 1903–4.

Joseph Maier, Eldred, to Montgomery Ward & Co., Chicago, Ill.
November 27, 1903
Order no. 19344
Dear Sirs:

I write you these few lines to let you know that the goods arrived safe, with the exception of the Sewing Machine which has not yet arrived at this writing; also the crank to the grindstone was not with the frame. Either you failed to pack same with frame or it got lost on the R.R.

Am very sorry it happened. I also want to remark to you that the freight charged on the grindstone and frame and saw and one box was $1.13 which I think is too much. If you think it is too much, I wish you would try to look this matter up and besides I will have some freight to pay on the machine which will make goods come rather high.

I intend to give you another order later on. By looking into this matter for me you will oblige me very much.

Truly yours, Joseph Maier

After the fire the Maiers had converted one of their out buildings into a temporary residence. The stove they had received did not have all of the necessary parts to burn wood, so Mr. Maier wrote the following letter to Menzo Quick who had a store in Barryville.

Joseph Maier, Eldred, to Menzo Quick, Barryville
December 10, 1903
Dear Sir:

I have got to complain to you in regards as to the stove. I see it was fixed for coal. I looked for the wood fixtures, but could not find any.

I did not at the time think to look if all the pipe was there, so yesterday, when I put the stove together, I found there were only 8 lengths of pipe and there should have been 9 altogether. The first length of pipe with damper is missing; then there are 4 pieces that belong to the wood fixtures; the first piece is the fire back; second the fire front and third the grate that goes on top of the rollers, and the box that projects out in the back of the firebox also.

We want a stove for wood as we do not burn coal. So you see we have a stove and cannot use it. So be so kind and send for these things as soon as you can and send them up when they come with the mail carrier and oblige.

Respectfully yours,
Joseph Maier

Joseph Maier, Eldred, to A. Robertson & Son; M. Hermann
December 28, 1903
Dear Sirs:

I herewith send you a bill for sash and frames and doors for you to give me your lowest cash figures on same, but give separate prices. All these to be second grade material 12 or 13. Sash check rail 4 lights 14 x 28 x 1-1/4. Give weight per window as I have

---

Popular Boarding Resorts in 1903

For Sullivan County
The Sunday World has the following list of boarding resorts in this county.

Popular with New York visitors are the following hotels and boarding houses: Washington Lake House at Yulan, Pine Grove Farm at Eldred, West Farm at Yulan, Myer's Farm House at Eldred, Minisink Farm at Eldred, Laurel Cottage on Washington Lake, Crest Hill Cottage at Barryville, The Arlington at Eldred, Orchard Terrace at Eldred, Oak Dene, Pine Grove Cottage, and Lake View Farm at Yulan.—*Republican Watchman, July 1903.*

Wright Brothers

At Kitty Hawk, North Carolina, on December 17, 1903, Wilbur Wright's fourth flight was 852 feet and lasted 59 seconds.—*wikipedia.org.*

the weights 16 or 18.
   Give price on one front door, two lights, frosted glass, circle top size 3 feet by 7 feet high, 2 inches thick; also I may make the frames myself, but I want to hear from you first. And please let me know how long.
   Respectfully yours,
   Joseph Maier

Joseph Maier, Eldred, to George Maney
December 29, 1903
Mr. George Maney,
Dear Sir,
   I write you these few lines to let you know that I can do better in Eldred and it is not so far to go after it, but I may want dry white pine lumber for casing. Will be over to see you just as soon as I hear from Binghamton and Deposit. Thanking you for your trouble, I remain
   Respectfully yours,
   Joseph Maier

Eliza Ann Gardner Young Dies
Eliza Ann Gardner Young died in December 1903, in Philadelphia. Eliza was the youngest child of Sears and Mary Keen Gardner who had settled in Pond Eddy around 1800. She was an ancestor of Louis Maudsley, a friend of my parents.

Joseph Maier, Eldred, to Andrew Paye
February 7, 1904
Dear Sir,
   Will you please give me a

Young girl and her father (identities unknown). Photos from the Proctor Collection.

price on 3,000 Shultz hard brick, the same kind I bought of you once before and the same kind you furnished W.F. Proctor a boat load. The price is to be delivered to Shohola. You pay the freight. I will draw them myself from Shohola. Give me your lowest cash price money ready when the brick arrives at Shohola. Also, how soon could you get these brick for me.
   The sooner the better. Let me know at once so I can give you the order if everything is OK, and oblige.
   Yours respectfully,
   Joseph Maier

1903 Photo of President Theodore Roosevelt's family in Mary Ann Austin's scrapbook. Photo courtesy of Melva Austin Barney.

Robert and Kate Greig

It's been a while since we talked about Robert and Kate Greig who had the huge, impressive boarding house near Mill/Stege's Pond. Robert and Kate's children Isabelle (Belle) and Bennett, and Robert's sister Jane lived with them. Belle would be the mother of Ed Grotecloss III.

Joseph Maier, Eldred, to Robert A. Greig, Esq.

February 15, 1904
Dear Sir,

I write to you to come back. I wanted to see you in regards to some dry white pine lumber.

I want to commence to build, but I cannot as I have no dry boards. Could you let me have 2 or 3 thousand feet? I want some wide boards for Cornish casing and face boards. Please let me know if I could get the lumber right away.

I will get Mr. Daily or if you like your sister to count the lumber for you. I want to take it to Mr. Daily to have it planed so I can use it at once. I could go up and get what I want and take it to the mill. Let me know what your lowest cash price is per M, and I will pay you at once as I cannot commence to build until I get dry lumber. So please be so kind as to answer this at once by return mail and oblige.

Yours Respectfully,
Joseph Maier

Joseph Maier, Eldred, to Montgomery Ward & Co., Chicago, Ill.

March 1, 1904
Dear Sirs:

Goods arrived safe, but I must complain. I suppose you think I am a regular crank as every order I get from you I have some complaint to make or find fault about something, but I cannot help it.

The one top screw that screws down the rollers on the Anchor brand Domestic Wash wringer is missing as there was only one wrapped up in paper that I could find. This is the name of the wringer you sent to me, although it is not the wringer I ordered.

I ordered Our Word Wringer No. 5700, but I will not kick about this as long as I get the top screw to the Anchor Brand Domestic wringer and the other article is one single tree strap. I have 3 of them and 4 hooks. No. of this article is 3235.

As far as I could see, the box was in good condition.

Hoping to hear from you soon,
I remain respectfully yours,
Joseph Maier

Julius Maier, Eldred, to Thomas Sidwell, Eldred

March 7, 1904
Dear Sir,

I was up to the Boyd place and had a look at the house, but I found same in a very bad condition.

The sills are all rotten, the rafters are warped, so that they

Unknown young girl holds a baby with a doll. Photo courtesy of the Proctor Family.

Joseph and Juliana Maier's New House

Joseph Maier kept records of the costs of rebuilding his boarding house. The cost of freight to Shohola, Pennsylvania, and the toll to go across the Barryville-Shohola Bridge was also added in. Mr. Maier first wrote for quotes on the cost.

Eldred, New York
December 21, 1903
Mr. Daily, Myers, Webber, Maney, Paye
Dear Sirs,

I herewith send you a bill for lumber on which I want you to give me your lowest cash price when it is delivered at my house. Give me a price per 1,000 feet, and how many 1,000 feet there are in this bill. Give me the number of feet in each stick and oblige.

This bill calls for yellow pine lumber. Price on same to be delivered at the house and what it would be at the mill if I decide to draw the lumber myself. Give your lowest price as this will be cash when the bill is sawed and drawn and how soon could you get this bill out for me? The sooner the better for me as I want to commence to build at once.

4 p. 8 × 8; 2-feet long
8 p. 8 × 8; 14-feet long
90 p. 2 × 8; 16-feet long
20 p. 2 × 8; 12-feet long
36 p. 2 × 6; 26-feet long
28 p. 2 × 5; 20-feet long
18 p. 2 × 5; 18-feet long
250 p. 2 × 4; 18-feet long
4,000 feet of sheathing

Respectfully yours,
Joseph Maier

Joseph Maier in 1921. Photo courtesy of the Bosch Family.

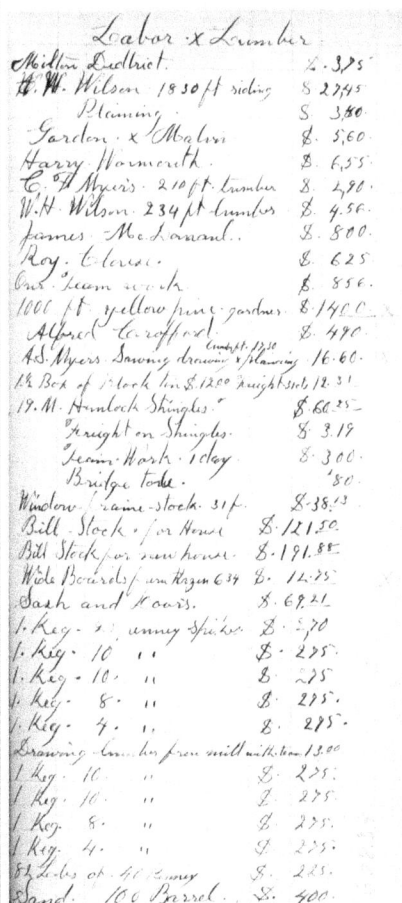
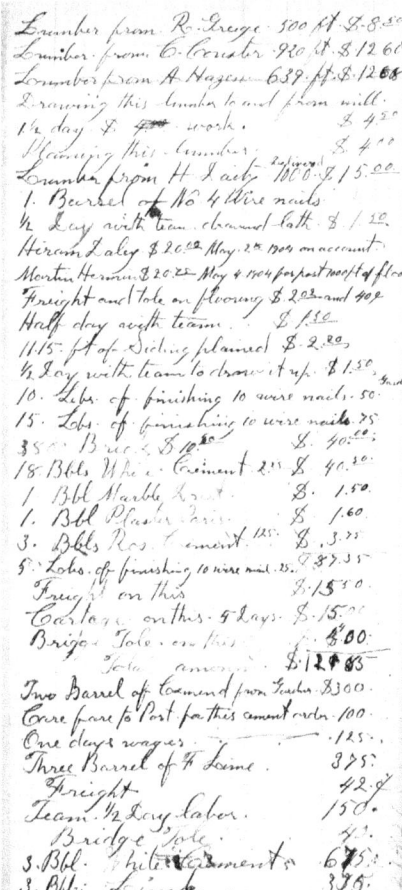

Juliana Maier, wife of Joseph Maier. Photo courtesy of the Bosch Family.

Two of Joseph Maier's records he kept while rebuilding his house. Courtesy of the Bosch Family.

Eldred's north corner around 1904. Building second on left was the home of Charles Wilson. The center building was the store of William H. Wilson. On the right was the original Parker House that Autenrieth's owned until Fridolin and Juliana Straub bought it. Photo courtesy of Christena Stevens Myers.

will have to be replaced with new ones. All that can be used is a very few 2x4. It would cost more to fix the house up and then it would not be a very good job. I think a new house to be the best in the end as you will have to have new shingles, sheathing, new 2x4 and 2x8, and sills and siding, new windows, frames and doors and frames.

So you will see that by the time the house is done it will be a new house and if you commence with a new house, everything would be level and plumb and square.

The cellar is full of water and ice and the wall is heaved quite bad. If you want me to figure on a new house about the same size, I will do so.

The ceiling in the one part is only 6 feet 4 inches high, a very low ceiling in the other part, the ceiling is 7 feet 6 inches high. The house is 48 feet long, 18 feet wide and the one part is 16 feet high and the other part is 14 feet high.

Hoping you will understand me aright. I remain respectfully yours,
Julius J. Maier

Jennie Crawford, Eldred, to Lillie Austin, Bethel
March 20, 1904
Dear Lillie,
George has been away for 10 days. He is to Shohola today. It rains. The March wind is turning me green. I will be sorry when school ends. I'll have no money

and will have to work like sin.
Now that I am trying to write, every kid asks a question. I have 27 here today so I can afford to write to you in school.
Don't criticize my spelling. I am trying to watch Charlie Rundle and Leo Morgan. They are cute kids. What kind of truant officer have you? The one we

Julius Maier as a young man. Julius Maier kept meticulous, detailed records. He at one time worked for Thomas Sidwell. Photo is courtesy of the Bosch Family.

Zane Grey Buys Property

In 1904 Zane Grey left his New York City dental practice to become a professional writer. With the help of his future wife Lina (Dolly) Roth, Zane bought 3 acres with a house and barn in Pennsylvania from the Holberts (mentioned in Chapter 5) for $1,425. The land was just south of the junction of the Delaware and Lackawaxen Rivers, and north of the Roebling Bridge—some 5 miles west of Shohola.

Zane had met Lina at the Delaware House in Lackawaxen where he and his brother liked to hike and fish.—*Information from several sources.*

have is worse than none. Well as you see I am laboring under difficulties. I will stop. Please come out.
Jennie J. Crawford

Jennie Crawford, Eldred to Lillie Austin, Bethel
April 24, 1904
Dear Lillie,
George was up in Delaware County. He said he hollered at you when he came through Bethel, but did not know whether your recognized him or not.

I was at Middletown, Otisville, and to Port Jervis. I went to see Lottie Scott and Aunt Matt. They were all well. I saw no one but Aunt Matt. Milt was downtown and Uncle John is laying flagstone up in Germantown.

We have the sitting room cleaned. Aunt Maud Crawford has been operated upon. She is in Christ's Hospital Jersey City. The tumor weighed 16 pounds. She is in a very critical condition.

Edna Beufve and Mr. Deale were over two weeks ago tonight. Bertha Wilson has been to the city and has had the measles along with her visit.

Alex Wait is home. You know he intended to learn stenography when he left.

Lottie S. has a good place. Jack Myers has moved in his new home. Crandall's folks have not moved yet.

I have three or four new photos: Harry Wormuth, Mary Beufve, Lottie Scott, and Eva and Olive Wormuth.

Aunt Etta's folks were up here to supper while I was away, but invited us all down Thursday p.m. I ate a lot I can assure you.

Cleta Horton went up to Lackawaxen and came home sick with the measles.

Maiers have their house almost up. Arbutus is out nice, but I have not been after any. I believe it is going to storm.

Now Lillie, without joking, come out. I am homesick to see you.

The new Methodist Minister is all ok. I really enjoy his sermons. Belle Boyd has the sweetest smile I ever saw. With love to all,
Jennie Crawford

Abel S. and Maria Hankins Myers
In the previous letter Jennie Crandall mentioned Cleta (Myers) Horton, the daughter of Abel and Maria Hankins Myers.

Cleta Myers married Walter Horton, son of John and Anne Stanton Horton, who lived on Highland Lake. (Walter's sister Mary Elvira Horton would marry Herman Bosch; Walter's nephew Charles Horton would marry a granddaughter of Isaac and Joanna Brown Bradley.)

There is a photo of Abel and Maria Hankins Myers' family from sometime around 1906 (though not all the people in the photo are known). The photo was probably taken behind their Orchard Terrace home on the hill near the Congregational Church in Eldred.

Abel and Maria's children:

Views of the impressive Greig Boarding House. Photo in the collection of Ed Grotecloss, courtesy of Kevin Marrinan.

Photo of Orchard Terrace, home of Abel Sprague and Maria Hankins Myers. The Congregational Church is on the left, hidden by trees. Photo courtesy of Chuck Myers.

The 1900 Washer SAVES WOMEN'S LIVES.

It Washes Lace Curtains Without Breaking a Thread, and a Carpet With Ease.

While other washers clean the clothes to some extent, they do not wash all parts. They leave the wristbands, collars and worst soiled places unfinished. But with the 1900 Washer every particle of dirt is removed. This machine forces the water through the clothes and rubs them at the same time. Machine placed on trial and sold on easy payments.

Sold by Brand & Co., Monticello, N.Y.

Ad in July 1903 Republican Watchman.

Jackson Myers and his wife Jessie; Lulu Myers Scheniman; Cleta Myers and her husband Walter Horton; Archibald Myers who would marry Minnie Sergeant; Norman Myers who would marry Bertha Eldred; and Lila Myers who would marry Henry Von Ohlen.

James and Edwin Myers were Abel's sons from his first marriage. Edwin Van Schoick and Mabel Owen Myers' children: Raymond, Clifford, and Gladys were also in the photo. Raymond Myers would marry Gladys Hill, and Gladys Myers would marry Raymond Austin, thereby confusing relatives as to which Raymond and Gladys was being talked about in years to come.

Ferncliff Lodge

Jennie Crawford mentioned Jack Myers moving into his new home. Perhaps it was his boarding house called Ferncliff Lodge.

Ferncliff Lodge is 110 miles from New York City, via Erie Railroad to Shohola Station, and a conveyance to Ferncliff which is located on ridge of mountain, surrounded by pine clad hills, between Eldred and Highland Lake—15 minutes walk to either place. House has 10 rooms, 120 feet of piazza, fine well of water, and as to the table, we try to give perfect satisfaction.

Terms: Rooms occupied singly, $10 per week; two or more in room, $7.00; transients, $1.50 per day. Ferncliff conveyances will meet any train on notification. Fare, 50 cents each person. Baggage charged for according to bulk and weight.

In this next letter Joseph told about the Pine Grove Farm fire.

Joseph Maier, Eldred, to Josephine Kassles
April 25, 1904
Dear Miss,
I received your letter last Friday night, but have been so busy I did not write you before.

I am sorry to say that we will not be able to keep any boarders this year as we will not get the new house in shape to keep any boarders. Perhaps next year, if we live and keep our health.

I also wish to say that Miss Annie got your letter and would of answered same, but the address got burned up and she could not do so. All of the buildings burned up in about two hours. We did not save $25 worth of things. It was so sudden. She was very sorry to hear of your mother's death.

Hoping this will find you and all of your folks well, which is the same with us. Our regards to you and your sister Helen. I remain Respectfully yours, Joseph Maier

Joseph Maier, Eldred to Mr. J. H. Vassmer
April 25, 1904
Mr. J.H. Vassmer,

As I heard that you had potatoes for sale, I write you these few lines to inquire the price per bushel and what kind they are. I want them to plant.

Will you please let me hear from you by return mail? If you have anymore for sale or no. I have a boarding house and will want perhaps more later on.

Mr. Carner of Barryville recommended me to you. This is spot cash. I want your lowest price on same.

Hoping to hear from you soon, I remain respectfully yours, Joseph Maier

Joseph Tries to Sell his Property
It seems that Joseph Maier was discouraged and probably exhausted by the Spring of 1904. The daunting task of rebuilding Pine Grove at age 69, along with he and Juliana (also 69) caring for their gravely ill daughter, Mary Maier Bosch, must have become too much. In May 1904, Joseph Maier wrote exploratory letters [see sidebar p. 229] to New York City realtors, to discuss the possibility of selling the house and farm.—Ken Bosch.

The property was never sold, and Joseph, Juliana, Julius, and Annie moved into the new Pine Grove Farm house when it was completed.

The Abel Sprague Myers family around 1906. Front row, second from the left: Raymond Myers, Lila Myers, Clifford Myers, and Gladys Myers. Behind Gladys is her mother, Mabel Owens holding Orville Myers. Sitting in middle of the second row: Abel S. Myers. Back row from right: Walter Horton, Edwin Myers; second from the left: Archie Myers. Photo courtesy of Joan Austin Geier.

Ferncliff Lodge, boarding house of Jackson Myers. Photo courtesy of Chuck Myers.

Daniel Rowlee Schoonover

Rowlee Schoonover had worked at Shadbolts as a blacksmith since 1890.

I stayed there for 14 years on that job. And the last 5 years I was foreman over everything. Shadbolt was forever trying new ideas and I was forever experimenting.

It was about the time the first subway was built they called it the McAdo Tunnel. It ran from the bridge to Grand Central Station and it was all built with those drawn trucks.

Shadbolt was experimenting on a dump truck that would dump when released in front. I worked on it for about a year and I told him it would not work and we used to have some pretty hot arguments about it.

Well we got the first sample truck done and took it for a try out. He had a coal company bring a team down and take it up to their coal yard on Kent Avenue and put 3 ton of coal on the truck.

The driver got up on the seat and started out of the yard. When he went off the curb, the thing unlatched. Up went the truck driver and all and dumped the load of coal on the sidewalk besides hurting the driver.

Shadbolt turned around and looked at me and said, "That is not a roaring success is it?"

Of course I said I told you so and I had. Well, I had thought out a spring with a different shape and design I knew would work. He caught right on and he said to go to work and build one.

So I went to work and turned one out, and it worked fine. The first order was for 50 trucks for the tunnel job. Then we got an order for 50 more from the Brooklyn Sanitary Co. Orders came in faster than we could turn them out.

He had taken out a patent on my spring in his name. I told him he had no right for it was my idea. He said that I was working for him and it belonged to him.

Well, I quit Shadbolts in 1904. I was fed up with the city and made up my mind I was going to the country. I saw an ad in the paper for a blacksmith to do carriage work at Tuxedo [New York]. So I answered and got a telegram to come out for an interview. So I went out and got the job. I gave Shadbolt one week notice and went to Tuxedo.

—Daniel Rowlee Schoonover.

Unknown young man. Photo courtesy of the Proctor Family.

Older man holding dog. Photo courtesy of the Proctor Family.

Jennie Crawford, Eldred, to Lillie Austin
May 1904
Dear Lillie,

Dad was so pleased because your folks sent mother those berry bushes. He could hardly wait to set them out.

The exams are to Monticello, the date I have forgotten.

We have company, two horse jockeys, Louis Beufve and Frank Greening. They are talking horse so strong you can almost smell the stable.

Mom dropped a pork barrel on her big toe and is so lame she can hardly walk.

Give my love to Mrs. Austin and remember me to Jim.
Yours lovingly,
Jennie June Crawford

Jennie Crawford, Eldred, to Lillie Austin
June 4, 1904
Dear Lillie,

I have been sick for 1 week Saturday. I went to school all the week though Friday; stayed to Cleta's and went chestnutting north of Abe Myers's folks. viz: Abel M., Will O., Mr. Stanton, George, Cleta, Lulu, Lila, and Lottie.

I was about tuckered out when we got home to the village, and went to bed as soon as I swallowed my grub.

Sunday sick abed in the afternoon. Monday sick abed all day. Tuesday I've got enough spunk to get downstairs.

I'd be all right, only a pain in my side and lungs.

Styleses would not let Anna off one day or else would have went to Port to the parade. Fred Myers's young daughter weighed 9 pounds when she was born. John Onderdonk has sold his horses.

For Sale: Pine Grove Farm

Joseph Maier's house that he rebuilt. Photo courtesy of the Bosch Family.

Eldred, New York, May 2, 1904
McDonald-Wiggins Co.,
Phillips and Wells
257 Broadway, N.Y.C.

Dear Sirs:

I have a farm which I would very much like to sell for cash. It is located 3-1/2 miles from Shohola Glen; 1-1/4 mile from the Eldred P.O.

I was formerly in the Boarder business, but my house burned down last fall and as I am getting too old for this business, would like to sell.

I am building another house, but not so large as the first one. This house and the addition has 14 rooms all told with a good cellar under.

The foundation of the big house is in very good condition to build on just as it is now. The size of this foundation is 85 × 63, the size of the new house which I am now building is 26 × 38—addition 20 × 16, 2 stories high with 5 rooms in the attic; 2 barns each 30 × 50, a few other out buildings, all farm implements that is required on a farm with one team of horses and harness and wagons; 2 cows can keep 8 or 10 heads; one well by the barn and a good spring; a well in front of the house and another well that flows and has a pipe from it to the kitchen and pumps the water up in the house; 2 everlasting springs in the pasture lot and a good size brook runs through the place. Number of acres: 111-1/2 more or less 40 acres.

Cleared the rest in woodlands; nice orchard; 2 boats; several lakes within 3 miles of my farm, a good place for the right man. Will take $8,000, $4,000 cash. $4,000 first bond and mortgage can give a good title, have not any debts on the place. My place is known far and wide as I have been keeping boarders for the last 15 or 20 years.

Please send me full particulars as to how you will take my place and what percent you will ask me.

Hoping to hear from you soon.
I remain respectfully yours,
Joseph Maier
P.S. The farm faces the southeast, has the sun all day long. *[The property never sold.]*

My blind aunt has to go to the hospital again. I don't know whether it is a cancer or her eyes or consumption. She has all three.

Mark Beufve is home. Edna went to the fair. Aunt Etta and Anna, also. Everett has a new wheel and Felix Kyte [son of William and Mary A. Whitney

Idaho and Rhode Island Battleships

U.S.S. Rhode Island Battleship #17. Postcard courtesy of Mary Briggs Austin.

U.S.S. Idaho Battleship #24. Postcard courtesy of Mary Briggs Austin.

These battleship postcards were sent to McKinley Austin in 1907.

The U.S.S. Rhode Island Battleship #17 was fitted out at the Fore River Shipbuilding Company, Quincy, Massachusetts, around 1905.

The U.S.S. Idaho Battleship No. 24, the second ship of the U.S. Navy named for Idaho, was launched in December 1905, and commissioned at Philadelphia Navy Yard on April 1, 1908.—*wikipedia.org.*

Mary Maier Bosch

Mary Maier Bosch had probably received treatments for her cancer when she stayed at the Bender House, in Middletown, New York. Mary was at the home of her parents Joseph and Juliana Maier when she wrote to Mrs. Bender in June. Even though Mary was seriously ill, she expressed concern for the patients still at the Bender Home.

Mary Bosch, Eldred, to Mrs. John Bender, Middletown, N.Y.

June 6, 1904
Dear Madam,
I herewith enclose you a Post Office money order to the amount of $2.50, which is due to you for room rent I owe you and I thank you very much for the kindness you showed toward me while I stopped at your house.
Hoping the sick are getting better at your house. Will you please keep my cot and bedding a little longer for me. I will let you know what to do with them. I thank you ever so much if you will grant me this kindness.
I remain Respect. Yours,
Mrs. Mary Bosch.

Fifteen days later, Mary Maier Bosch, 45, died.

Mary, the beloved wife of William Bosch of this place died at the home of her parents, Mr. and Mrs. Joseph Maier, in this place, June 21st, aged 45 years.
She had suffered a long time of cancer on the tongue. She was a patient sufferer and died in the full hope of a blessed immortality, expressing herself many times as not only ready, but anxious to depart and be with her Savior.
She is survived by her husband, mother and father, one sister and brother, Anna

---

Kyte] is working to Styleses. George is working to A.S. Myers.
Mrs. Wait looked good the last time I saw her.
We are washing. Mom is doing the great part of it, namely the rubbing. We haven't washed enough in almost 3 weeks so you know the job before us. Just think of the ironing I have.
June Bug,
J. Crawford

and Julius; also eight children, Minnie, Charles, Lulu, Herman, Eddie, Ralph, Menzo, and Mary [Tillie], all at home.

The funeral services were held on Wednesday last at the home of her parents, and conducted by Rev. R.A. Allen. Interment in the Eldred Cemetery.

She is not dead, but sleepeth.

Jennie Crawford, Eldred, to Lillie Austin
July 15, 1904
Dear Lillie,

Daddy is better but not well. George is going to do our haying for us. I doubt if Dad will be able to do any hard work all summer. Bertha is very low. You know I was working there when I got word about Dad. The neighbors were all good to us. George has been so good to Mother.

Burt Foster is smiling at Jennie Hallock. I wish they would get married. I never wanted to be a matchmaker before.

Lottie Scott is home for a week.

Yours till I write again after you write,
Jennie Crawford

Jennie Crawford, Eldred, to Lillie Austin, Bethel
July 29, 1904
Dear Lillie,

Dad is in pretty bad shape. He gets weaker all the time. There are two lumps as big as hickory nuts and high as ordinary thimble beside a pad some what larger than a hen's egg, but not over 3/4 of an inch raised, close under his arm and the other two are down lower on his side. I don't know but doubt if he ever gets over it. Poor Mom is about worn out.

If I only could, I would go to bed and stay all day. I have N.Y. callers ahead of time and a cold with them, so you know how good I feel. George is working here yet, poor devil.

I suppose the Lord will provide, but I don't know what I am going to do. If Dad keeps this way, we will have to hire someone, or else I must stay home and if I do where will I get my dough or rather we get our dough? I hate to ask for the Eldred School and if I do I can't get it I know. I suppose we can get along. We always have.

Bertha Wilson is better. I am so glad. I haven't been to Eldred in over a week.

Can't you leave some of your farming and come out? I too have helped farm. I drive the nag when we draw in hay and walk over the stuff and try to place it. I mean haying is all done, but the swamp. George done all of it alone. Only yesterday, Mr. Maier moved with him and we hired Fred to mow a little piece with machine.

I did a big ironing yesterday. I do the work and Mom takes care of Dad. Of course not all the time. We change off.

When can you come out? I go to Shohola 2 or 3 times a week. We expect the Dr. today. I'll tell you what he says when he comes.

Clara Sergeant and Lila Myers are both very sick. They are trying to get papers to take Abe Rundle away. Leon Parker has gone with the gypsies.

I have been up 1.5 hours and haven't had breakfast yet.

The Dr. says Dad's arm will have to gather and break. It is pretty serious. He is in terrible agony. I have been asleep and would like to stay out of doors for 6 hours if I could.

Fred's folks have quite a few boarders. I have been over to Maiers, cleaned the horse stable, washed the dishes, got a bit to eat, fed the pig and horse and put some decent rags on. Oh yes, and patched a table cloth, made my bed and swept the dining room.

I should have gone to bed if I had followed my own inclination. It is six o'clock p.m. I'll close.

Lovingly, Jennie C.

Whitehall Building

Whitehall Building around 1904. Photo: Library of Congress, Prints and Photographs Division: Detroit Publishing Co.; LC-D4-17552.

The Whitehall Building was on one of the many postcards sent to Mort and Jennie Austin's family.

The Whitehall Building, built in 1902–04, had 20 floors. It was named for Peter Stuyvesant's 17th-century house, "White Hall," which had been located nearby.

Henry J. Hardenbergh, a prominent architect, was the designer.
—wikipedia.org.

Photo in Lumberland in the early 1900s. Photo courtesy of the Proctor Family.

Over on the east side of Eldred, Lon Austin received a letter from Vouletti T. Proctor, daughter of William Ross and Elizabeth Singer Proctor.

**Vouletti T. Proctor
Yacht Margaret,
to Mr. A.A. Austin, Eldred**
July 30, 1904
Dear Lon,
 I received your nice letter and was pleased to hear from you, and to know about our chickens. I am so glad you sold so many eggs. I think you had better keep the money for us. I am glad to hear that we have one pigeon and that the turtles are all right.
 Hoping this letter will find you all well.
  Your little friend,
  Vouletti T. Proctor

Jennie Crawford to Lillie Austin
August 7, 1904
Dear Lillie,
 Lillie, I am going to teach at Eldred; wages $10. I was surprised Isaac Sergeant said I had his consent the very first one. I hope I make a success of it.
 Bertha is much better, so is Dad, but he lacks much of being well yet.
 Would you send me the address to get a "Milna's Arithmetic?" I want to get an arithmetic and key.
 Success to you in exam and school matters in general.
 B. Libela and B. Lyons both tried for the school ahead of me. What do you think of that? I feel big, probably will get wizened down before I'm through.
 George Parker and May Hammond have just been here to see Dad, also Nels Hulse and Fred Myers. Mother is feeding chickens. I have just put the horse in. I have written two letters besides this one today.
 Fred's folks have lots of boarders today. They had 10 come.
 Every one and everything seems lazy. I've forgotten all I knew.
 "Old fears that hang like a changing cloud,
  Over a sunless day
  Old wrongs that wrank and clamor loud,
  Shall pass like a dream away."
 Jennie

**Joseph Maier, Eldred,
to Mr. H.O. Rosenkrans**
August 22, 1904
Dear Sir,
 Will you please be so kind as to send me 3 barrels of Higginson's White Cement for mortar and 3 barrels of common lime, and 1 barrel of Higginson's Calcined Plaster or Plaster of Paris, as they called it.
 Please send this Tuesday if you can so I can get it Wednesday and oblige,
  Respectfully,
  Joseph Maier
 This is the price you gave me when I was down to see you last June.
3 barrels white cement.........$6.45
3 barrels com. lime...............$3.30
1 Barrel plaster Paris...........$1.60
Total.....................................$11.35

Jennie Crawford to Lillie Austin
August 29, 1904
Dear Lillie,
 George is going away soon if nothing happens. I shall miss him. He was up last night. Dad is not so well. I wish I could come to Bethel with a clear conscience. If I knew everything was all OK and stay a week.
 Wasn't it awful the mill of A.S. Myers humming at 2 a.m. and the child dying at 2 p.m. I don't know when I ever felt worse for anyone than I did for them and the German Maiers folks.
 If Dad don't get better pretty soon, I believe I shall feel about 9,000 years old. Now isn't this a cheerful letter.
 Well I'll change the subject and tell you that we got to Crandalls five minutes to or after five.
 I am going to Eldred this a.m.

Walls to protect from flooding

In September 1904, more than 20 property owners along River Road—including Highland Supervisor Fred Freeman and suspension bridge owner Stephen St. John Gardner—as well as trustees of the 127th Improved Order of Red Men's and the pastor of the Baptist Church, signed an indenture ceding their lands along the banks of the river to the state of New York for one dollar, so that the Superintendent of Public Works might construct "a dyke or dykes along the bank of the Delaware River in the village of Barryville in the Town of Highland, Sullivan County, so as to discontinue the present overflow of said lands and consequent damage to highways and property in said town."

In exchange for the work to be done, the indenture also released the state from any liability for earlier flood damage, including that caused by the 1903 and 1904 overflows.

The landowners were assured that the dyke to be constructed on their property would prevent the similar flooding of their land in the future, and for the most part it has done just that, even minimizing the damage in the great flood of 1955.
—*John Conway*, Retrospect, Sullivan County Democrat, Oct. 8, 2010.

Vouletti Theresa Proctor, 1906. Photo courtesy of the Proctor Family.

and must carry wash water.
Try to come out, can't you?
Lovingly, Jennie C.

Jennie Crawford, Eldred, to Lillie Austin
September 12, 1904
Dear Lydia Earl Austin,
There are grapes ready to pick at your earliest convenience. Tell Mom Austin that Mom Crawford wants her to come and bring you and I say you come and bring your mother. Come after the grapes. Yours lovingly, Jennie C.

Sunshine Hall
A 1904 postcard of Sunshine Hall in the Austin Collection, is an invitation for a Congregational Church Reunion, October 2, 1904.

The Hall was next to the Congregational Church, and was also used for the men's Bible study meetings.

George Foster and Jennie Hallock's Wedding Announcement

Mr. A.A. Austin and Sisters
You are cordially invited
to attend the marriage of
Jennie May Hallock
to
George Lambert Foster
at the home of Charles W. Wilson
Tuesday evening, December 6,
1904, at half after eight
High Point Cottage, Eldred, N.Y.

Jennie Hallock married George Lambert Foster on December 6, 1904. Jennie, daughter of Dan and Elvira Hallock, was apparently friends with Lon, Aida, and Maria Austin.

Raymond Austin and His Grandpa, William Henry Austin
In December 1904 Raymond Austin turned 4. A couple stories are told about Raymond and his grandfather Henry Austin who

Jennie Leavenworth Austin and sons Raymond and William sitting on the front steps of the old Austin homestead house. Photo courtesy of Mary Briggs Austin.

lived with Mort, Jennie, Raymond, McKinley, and Will.

When Raymond was very young, before he could read, he evidently had a good memory of what he heard read. His father [Mort] got the newspaper—either when he went to the village in the afternoon, or it came in the mail. Mort would often read some of the items from the newspaper to Jennie.

Raymond would listen carefully and later, with his grandfather, Henry Austin, would hold the paper up as though he was reading out loud from it.

His grandfather would always comment, "It is a caution how that boy can read!"

One day the report was about a serious railroad accident. Raymond read, with his grandfather Henry marveling—until Raymond read, "A number of people were 'conveniently' killed."

His grandfather said, "What?" and took the paper and noted some other discrepancies, as well. The deception was over.

Henry liked to eat nice thick slices of warm, homemade bread with molasses. He would spoon some molasses on to a plate and dip some bread into it, bite by bite.

The problem arose when Henry had finished the slice of bread and there was still molasses on the plate. (Henry had to cut more bread.)

Then there was likely to be not enough molasses to finish the bread. (Henry had to spoon out more molasses.) There was molasses left over when bread was finished, etc. And Henry wouldn't stop until he could make it come out even—eventually grumbling because he was getting too full.

My dad, Raymond, was fascinated by this and just kept watching to see how long it would take him to come out even. One day Raymond asked his grandpa why he just didn't stop eating if he was too full. He was told to, "Run along and tend to your own affairs."—Melva Austin Barney.

In 14 years Raymond Austin would be writing letters home from Culebra in the Panama Canal Zone. In 1904 the United States began work on the massive Panama Canal Project including controlling malaria and yellow fever. The Culebra or Gaillard Cut (1913) was a great engineering feat, with a significant cost of lives. From 1904 to 1914 over 5,500 workers died.

In late October 1904, New York City's first underground line of the subway opened.

Leavenworth Descendants
It's been some time since we talked about the descendants of Sherman Buckley and Charlotte Leavenworth.

Harriet Leavenworth Palmer died December 22, 1904, in Port Jervis. Harriet's son Harry and his wife Lydia, and Lydia's daughter

1904. Jennie and sons, Raymond and Will. Photo courtesy of Mary Briggs Austin.

Sunshine Hall and Congregational Church, October 2, 1904. Postcard courtesy of Mary Briggs Austin.

Florence, lived in Benton Harbor, Michigan. At some point Harry Palmer ran a grocery store.

There is a wonderful photo of Harriet's daughter Edith Palmer Ewart with her 5 children: Victor, Willard, Elliott, Rolland, and Millie (Pamela) Ewart. The family lived in Port Jervis when Edith's husband Albert, 47, died in 1906.

Sherman S. and Maria Leavenworth still lived on the northwest side of Eldred, with their children: Anna, a teacher, Truman, Garfield (soon to be married), Martin, Charlotte, and Christina.

Anna, the oldest, had been teaching at least since 1900. There is a photo of Anna with her students at the Eldred schoolhouse which included her sister, Christina *(see p. 240)*. The photo seems to have been taken before 1906. By 1908 Anna Leavenworth appears to be teaching near Cochecton because she sent postcards to her Austin nephews from that area.

John Leavenworth's Family
Sherman's brother John Leavenworth lived out west and mined. In March 1904 his and Amelia's daughter, Ida May Leavenworth, died. Ida was 9 years old.

Ida May Leavenworth had become deaf from scarlet fever and was sent to a special school in Colorado Springs. There she came down with measles and pneumonia. She died from complications of measles.

At the time of young Ida Leavenworth's death, Ida's mother Amelia and Eber Gregory had two young children: Charlie and Nora Gregory.

Of John Leavenworth and Amelia Bradley's four daughters, only two lived into adulthood:

Mort Austin with his son Charles Raymond. Photo courtesy of Mary Briggs Austin.

Raymond Austin's Grandpa William Henry Austin. Courtesy Melva Austin Barney.

Edith Palmer Ewart and her children, Victor, Willard, Elliott, Rolland, and Millie Ewart. Edith was a granddaughter of Sherman Buckley and Charlotte Ingram Leavenworth. Photo courtesy of Cynthia Leavenworth Bellinger.

Ida May Leavenworth, daughter of John and Amelia Leavenworth. Photo courtesy of Cynthia Leavenworth Bellinger.

Charlotte (Lottie) and Hazel.

Hazel spent her early years on a cattle ranch near Dunton, Colorado. Her playmates were her sisters and a black spaniel named Curly. Years later, Hazel liked to tell the story about shooting a bear as a young girl.

One of the family's horses had been killed by a bear. Amelia, Hazel's mother, a tough lady, set a big trap and caught the bear. Her mother hustled Hazel out of bed at 5 a.m. to go see.

"I was scared stiff," she remembers. "The bear was a big old thing caught by one back leg. He was in such terrible misery that he let out a howl and tried to climb a tree. I still feel sorry for that poor bear."

Amelia handed Hazel a rifle and told Hazel to shoot the bear. I don't know how to shoot, Hazel protested (balked).

"You're gonna," replied her mother with advice to lean against a tree and aim behind the bear's ear.

"Finally, I got a bead on the back of his ear," she said. "He dropped like Humpty Dumpty. That was a big relief."

Amelia, according to Hazel, was "kind of a showoff" who wasn't afraid of anything.

Memory card for Ida May Leavenworth, daughter of John and Amelia Leavenworth. Photo courtesy of Cynthia Leavenworth Bellinger.

—Durango Herald, *March 13, 1996.*

My mother explained to me that bears were a threat to their food supply. In winter they buried carrots etc., in piles of snow for storage. Game was hung from trees. Every winter Amelia wagon-hauled bags of flour because they were snowbound for long periods.

There was a large boulder in the middle of her fields at the Fish Creek Ranch, which she [Amelia] disliked because she had to plow around it. She asked the men to get rid of it. Because it was too large to move, they packed it with dynamite and blew it up for her.—Gerald Koenig.

Hazel's sister Charlotte (Lottie) Leavenworth married Len Andeway, a Dunton storekeeper, in December 1904. In 1905 Hazel, 9, moved in with Len and Lottie Andeway and went to school.

In New York, Alden Austin was born to Charles A. and Mary Johnson Austin in 1905. Alden was a grandson of Mortimer B. and Mary L. Millspaugh Austin.

In 1905 for $28,900, the Oswego Bridge Company replaced the 1871 Decker Bridge at Pond Eddy, which had washed away in the 1903 flood.

Jennie Crawford, Eldred, to Lillie Austin
March 27, 1905
Dear Lillie,

I have just written to Nell. She has had the diphtheria. Gotlieb Metzger is dead. Frank Kelley has partial paralysis of the face.

Bertha Hulse has a young daughter. Lottie Scott is better.

Crandall's folks have sold their place. Mom washed today. Aunt Etta sprained her foot. I got my feet wet tonight coming up.

With love,
Jennie J. Crawford

Wilhelm and Charlie Bosch
In 1905 Wilhelm Bosch, a

Real Photo Postcards

1905 rotograph of the Lackawana Railway Depot, sent to Aida Austin on February 1905. Writing was not allowed on the back until 1907. Postcard courtesy of Mary Briggs Austin.

It was 1907 before the Post Office would allow a postcard to have a message written on the same side as the address. Also, by 1907 European publishers began opening offices in the U.S. for their millions of high quality post cards. Their cards made up 75% of all postcards sold in the United States. Germany's printing methods were the best in the world.

Real Photo Postcards (RPPC) seem to have started in general use in the first few years after 1900. In 1903 Kodak introduced their No. 3A Folding Pocket Camera designed for postcard-size film. The photographs could be printed on postcard backs.

Other cameras were also used to make Real Photo postcards. Some used old-fashioned glass plates that required cropping the image to fit the postcard format.

A *rotograph* was a photograph printed by a process in which a strip or roll of sensitized paper was automatically fed over the negative so that a series of prints are made, developed, fixed, cut apart, and washed at a very rapid rate.—*usps.com; wikipedia.org.*

Real photo postcard of the covered bridge at Bridgeville, N.Y., celebrating their centennial from 1807 to 1907. Postcard printed in Germany, courtesy of Mary Briggs Austin.

The New East River Bridge

"This is our new East River Bridge, opened in 1905. Wish you could see the real bridge. Lovingly, Jessie F. Hill." Postcard courtesy of Mary Briggs Austin.

Three suspension bridges were built across the lower East River in New York City to connect lower Manhattan with Brooklyn.

The above postcard to Mort and Jennie Austin is of the Williamsburg Bridge, the second one to be built after the Brooklyn Bridge. Williamsburg was started in 1896, and opened December 19, 1903, according to one source, though Jessie Hill wrote it opened in 1905.

Manhattan Bridge, the third to be built, was opened to traffic in December 1909.

The five ferry routes at the Brooklyn Landing between Grand Street and Broadway went out of business by 1908.

Jessie Hill wrote on the front of the postcard because before 1907, no written material could be on the address side of a postcard. —wikipedia.org.

Jennie Crawford, Eldred, to Lillie Austin
June 15, 1905
Dear Lillie,

Nell Crandall's baby is a girl. They call her Verna.

Mom is better but not half well.

There is a lumber wagon passing. I wonder who.

Lottie works to Rob Crandall's.

Jennie Foster has her baby in September. Cleta's new kid is a gal called Annie Marie.

Lovingly,
Jennie

Elizabeth Tether Owen, grandmother of Gladys Myers, died in June 1905. Elizabeth had been born in England. Joseph Tether was her brother. Her husband Robert had died in 1887.

William Ort, son of Frank and Mary Crandall Ort, married Bertha LaBarr, on December 25, 1905. William's brother Charlie Ort is in the school photo on p. 240. William and Bertha Ort's daughter Eleanor, would marry Emerson Lilley, born in Bethel in 1900.

Jennie Crawford, Eldred, to Lillie Austin
December 25, 1905
Dear Lillie,

In the first place I must thank you for the cream set and the clock, I don't know which I like best.

Now Lillie, its no wonder you are dead broke if you let your money fly around on every one of

widower, married the widow Mary Nellie Van Wyck Van Eastenbridge who had 4 children. Of Wilhelm's 8 children, 5 were 15 years old or younger. Wilhelm and Mary Nellie had a daughter, Christina Bosch, born in 1906.

Charles Bosch, son of Wilhelm and Mary Maier Bosch, married Helen (Lena) Miller around 1905. He and Lena first lived in Port Jervis where Charlie worked on the railroad as a fireman. We will meet them again in 1915, when they run a small boarding house not far from Highland Lake.

Brooklyn, Manhattan, and Williamsburg Bridges over the East River, 1909. Library of Congress, Prints and Photographs Division: Irving Underhill; LC-USZ62-119637; LOT 12475 no. 14.

1905 Events

The 1905 World's Fair started on June 1 in Portland, Oregon. It honored the 100th anniversary of the Lewis and Clark Expedition.

Mid-June 1905 the Nickelodeon, a storefront theater in Pittsburgh, Pennsylvania, offered moving pictures for five cents.

Ella Phoebe Sergeant and her sister Hazel. Photo courtesy of Cynthia Leavenworth Bellinger.

your peeps (you see I call myself one of your peeps) like you do on me.

Well, I don't know when we will be married, things aren't panning out as we expected. We will not commence keeping house right away, and by the way, things look now, it's hard to tell anything we'll be doing.

If I can come out I will surely come. I don't believe we can scare up a horse in a days travel.

Let me tell you of my Xmas presents. Mrs. Maier gave me a summer shirt; George, a pound of Sparrow's chocolates and more small boxes; Mom a pair of mittens and 2 pairs slacks; Edna, a bunch of artificial leaves; Dad, a cake plate and some candy; Uncle Joel, a bag of nuts; Aunt Maude a stocking bag, a hat pin, and a collar; Lillie either a clock or a cream set, but I don't know which was for Xmas.

I had a very nice Xmas, only Lillie Austin wasn't here. Darn her. I was home all day. George came up; he went home at 8 p.m. It is 20 past now.

Tomorrow we have to wash a three weeks washing. I just dread it. George and I, also his Aunt Phebe went to the Congregational Xmas tree.

What did you have for Xmas dinner? We had chicken, jelly,

Lena Miller around 1905 who married Charles Bosch. Photo courtesy of the Bosch Family.

Charles Bosch, son of Wilhelm and Mary Maier Bosch, was a fireman for the Erie Railway. Photo courtesy of the Bosch Family.

Ella Clark Howe, aunt of Ella and Hazel Sergeant. Photo courtesy of Cynthia Leavenworth Bellinger.

Anna Leavenworth's Class sometime before 1906: Row 1: Alfred Eldred, Charles Ort, Charles Rundle, Jamie Parker, Clarence Wormuth, Ernest Horton, Emerson McBride. Row 2: Hattie Schroeder, Stella Boyd, Martha Rundle, Lila Myers, Claudia McBride, Maude Horton, Caroline Autenrieth, Mildred Myers, Mildred Rundle. Row 3: Fred Stewart, Hazel Sergeant, Bertha Eldred, Emily Parker, George Eldred, Sherman McBride. Row 4: Herman Schroeder, Mabel Furver, Mabel Boyd, Minnie Sergeant, Christina Leavenworth, Earl Owen. Anna Leavenworth, Teacher. Photo courtesy of Chuck Myers.

Anna Leavenworth, teacher. Photo courtesy of Cynthia Leavenworth Bellinger.

mashed potatoes, tomatoes, Hydeen salad, mince pie, raisin cake and cocoa nut cake, coffee. Wasn't that wonderful? Now be sure and be down when exams are.

Aunt Etta and Anna are in Port Jervis. George's mother is over to Hazens. Their kid has been very sick. They say it is doubtful if Mrs. DeSilva Sr. ever gets over her sickness. You know about her eye being out.

Come out! Well I will close.
Lovingly, Jennie Crawford

Clarissa Clark Sergeant Dies
In 1905 the wife of Frank Roberts Sergeant, Clarissa Clark, died at aged 45 from "complications of goiter and heart."

The following year Frank married his second wife, Anna Hull, a widow. Frank and Clarissa's daughter Hazel (pictured in Anna Leavenworth's class above) was sent to Massachusetts to live with her aunt Ella Clark Howe. Their other daughter Ella Phoebe Sergeant we will meet in 1906.

The next chapter about Mort and Jennie Austin's Homestead Cottage, includes the letters of Jennie Crawford Crandall and others, along with postcards, photos, and other information of the people and events in the Town of Highland from 1906 to 1910.

Chapter 8
Homestead Cottage
Mort and Jennie L. Austin, 1906–1910

Home! Where hearts are a little truer,
A little nearer than the rest—
Home! Where ties are a little stronger,
Where all is given of the best.

Home where Love burns a little brighter,
And Faith stands ever at the gate—
Home! The first and last in remembrance,
The House of Hope—where all things wait.
—Blanche Lee.

View of "Homestead Cottage," owned by Mort and Jennie Austin. Photo courtesy of Mary Briggs Austin.

So wrote my grandmother, Jennie Leavenworth Austin in her scrapbook (a reused ledger) which contained a number of poems and recipes.

Jennie was a good cook and it was fun to see the many recipes in her scrapbook—main meals, plenty of wonderful desserts, and quite an assortment of pickle recipes.

The poems that Jennie had written or cut out from the newspaper and glued into her scrapbook were about what she thought was important in life—her belief in God, the importance of a warm home, being thoughtful, kind, and treating others well.

Homestead Cottage

Mort and Jennie had purchased the Collins' place on 9 acres of land for $300 from Emma Kelso Collins, wife of Tom K. Collins, in April 1905. The former Collins' home became Mort and Jennie's boarding house, *Homestead Cottage*. The house was featured on a postcard dated 1906.

Homestead Cottage could accommodate 15 guests. It was a ten minute walk to Highland Lake. The Shohola Station, where Mort met the guests, was 6 miles away. It was a mile to the Eldred Post Office.

Running a boarding house was a considerable amount of hard work. Mort and their sons (when they were older) helped Jennie with the many chores.

Just like many other boarding house owners, Mort also farmed. In 1906 McKinley was 7, Raymond was 6, and Willie (Bill) was 3. Their grandfather Henry Austin still lived with them.

Mary Ann Austin was not well in 1906. She lived with her children, Maria, Lon, and Aida. Lon provided financially for his mother and Maria, and in later years, also for Aida. Maria, Aida, and Lon seem to have run Mountain Grove House, though Aida also taught school.

Back of the Collins' home which Mort and Jennie Austin ran as Homestead Cottage. Photo courtesy of Mary Briggs Austin.

Walter and Henrietta Styles
In 1910 Walter and Henrietta Austin Styles lived on Proctor Road, possibly in their new mansion across the road from Mountain Grove House. Rev. Alonzo and Belle Austin, Henrietta's parents, were listed as living with Walter and Henrietta, though they could have lived in the old Austin homestead. Mary Beattie, friend, and Anna Abbel, servant, also lived with the Styles.

At one time Walter and Henrietta Styles lived at Mort and Jennie's boarding house. Walter, an artist, worked in New York City during the week. There was some major discord between Henrietta and Walter. Eventually—well, we will talk about that later.

Austin Photos and Postcards
Aida Austin knew how to develop film and had her own darkroom. She was especially attached to McKinley and took many photos of him. My dad would later endure the same attention.

The Austin boys received a variety of postcards from friends (possibly boarders) and their Leavenworth aunts: Anna and Charlotte.

Estella Carlin, N.Y.C., to McKinley Austin, Eldred
Date Unknown
McKinley,
My boy, I received your postals and your picture was fine.
This is the Battery Park one block from my house. There's where I play. I will send you some more. Best wishes from Papa and

Homestead Cottage, C.M. Austin, Proprietor, Eldred, N.Y. This postcard was sent by Maria Austin to her niece Lillie Austin. "Dear Lillie, I received your postal; also your picture. Think it fine. Come and see us. With love to all. Your Aunt Maria." Postcard in Austin Collection.

Mama and myself to Aunt Maria, Aunt Aida, Raymond, Willie, and all my friends.

I will send you some more.
Yours truly, Estella Carlin

In the following letter from February 1906, Jennie Crawford was not yet married to George Crandall. She continued to write newsy letters to Lillie Austin, and often mentioned George (Crandall); Crawford Road neighbors: Mr. and Mrs. Maier, Edna Beuvfe, and Fred and Mary Bradley Myers and Lottie Scott; and nearby neighbors: Raola Kelley and children of Abel Myers.

Bertha Wilson was the wife of William H. Wilson who had the store at the corner of Eldred.

Mom A. was probably Lillie's mother. Lillie's grandmother Mary Ann Austin was not well.

Jennie Crawford, Eldred, to Lillie Austin
February 27, 1906
Dear Lillie,

I have reading fever on again. I have read, "The Blue Fairy Book," by Andrew Lang which contains such edifying topics as: "How to Shudder," and "Sleeping Beauty;" "The Gable Roofed House at Snowdon," by Mary J. Holmes; what a fool story it is. "The Belle of Bowling Green," by Amelia E. Barr, a story of the war of 1812, and a darned good story too.

Then for the third time I am reading the "Virginian," by Owen Wister. I believe that is the best story I ever read. It makes you believe you are intimately acquainted with each character. "Mandolins Lovers" is a sour story; "For Lillas," by Rosa Cauf is really good. Well I have swallowed these books in about two weeks.

George Wait was buried

Jennie Austin with a boarder at the well in 1906. Photo courtesy of Mary Briggs Austin.

yesterday. He had a complication of diseases. Asthma, dropsy and the like. They say Wait dropped dead at Mrs. Wait's feet.

Floyd and Belle and Charlie Myers were up to the funeral.

I wonder why people who lived so nicely have to be separated. Not now, but in the coming years we will understand.

Mort Austin with boarding house guests. Photo courtesy of Mary Briggs Austin.

Boarders at Homestead Cottage in July 1906. Photo courtesy of Mary Briggs Austin.

And Mrs. Joseph Maier is very sick with dropsy. She has been sick over seven weeks. She is liable to die any time.

I am going downtown tomorrow to see if I can't find some link sausage for Mrs. Maier. What a funny thing to want when one is sick.

We have the pump, but it is not working yet. George works in the mill up beyond Ike Sergeant; starts at 6 a.m. and gets home about 6:30 p.m.

Fred Myers is the happy father of a boy. Ed Myers has a new boy. I tell you it is in the air. I am blamed lucky I'm not married or I should be in fear and great trembling.

We have sent to Montgomery Ward and Company again. I sent for some thread, a book, and a pair of house slippers, and am dead broke as usual.

I'm going to the Japanese social at Bertha Wilson's Thursday. Each person who eats supper gets a Japanese souvenir. Wish you could come and go.

I have been about sick. I had the grip which came in the form of sore eyes, worse than the pink eye, a sore throat, and shaky legs goes with that. Well, I got over that and carried so much water up the cellar steps that my back is almost broke yet, and then I had sore eyes this time from reading.

I am sewing for the church. I got a new blue seersucker dress. Beg some silk or worsted pieces for me from any one whom you dare ask. I must fix my corset. It is busted again. Why do clothes wear out?

Edna Beufve is in Hornelsville. This week Mrs. Wormuth was over and Lizzie Wilson and Annie Abendroth were up.

I hope Mom Austin is better. I was up to your Aunt Maria Austin's the other day. All were well. Say did Lon always have false teeth or to speak more correctly, how long has he had them?

Great guns, but it is a cold, cold night.

Say, tomorrow is the grand wedding, the widow D. and Duane Hulse. Wouldn't that jar you? She bought him a suit of clothes and paid his board up to Jack Myers. They will live in one side of Bruckner's cottage. You know Mrs. Simpson lives on the other side.

Say about your dress, get a dark sort of purplish grey, something like my mohair and trim with a bright green piping of heavy cloth (broadcloth is the most durable) velvet is the

Boarders at Homestead Cottage. Photo courtesy of Mary Briggs Austin.

McKinley Austin. Aida Austin knew how to develop film and had her own darkroom. She was especially attached to McKinley and took many photos of him. Photos in the collection of Mary Briggs Austin.

prettiest. Or get a grey plain all over grey and trim with green to match the hat. It will look cool and yet not too cool and not show spots.

Come out when you can. Did you pass? Please answer soon.

Lovingly, J.J. Crawford

Jennie Crawford mentioned Ike Sergeant in her letter. Ike (Isaac) and Elizabeth Persbacher Sergeant were the parents of Minnie Sergeant who would marry Archie Myers. Isaac was a great-grandson of Rev. Isaac Sergeant. Archie Myers and Minnie Sergeant would be the parents of Chuck Myers. There is a lovely photo of Minnie Sergeant on p. 246.

Obituaries for George Wait and Charles Calkin

Jennie Crawford's letter also talked about George Wait's death.

Mary Ann Austin's scrapbook had the obituaries of George Wait and Charles F. Calkin. George Wait was the husband of Mary C. Mills (sister of Martha Myers, Margaret Boyd, and George Mills) and father of Alexander Wait.

George A. Wait, 57, a well known and highly respected citizen of Eldred, Sullivan County, died at his home near that village on Saturday, February 24, of heart trouble after a long illness.

He was born on Long Island in 1849, and in early life removed to Eldred, where he followed the occupation of carpenter and later built and conducted a summer boarding house.

In 1880, he was united in

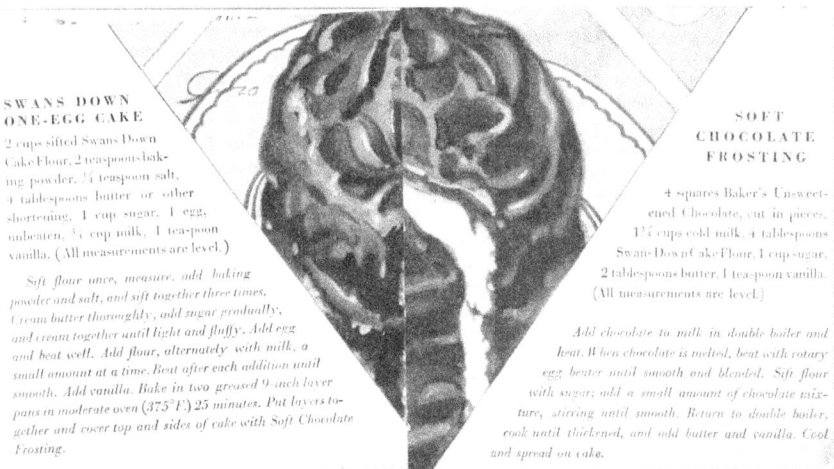

Swans Down One-Egg Cake from Jennie Austin's scrapbook. Swans Down cake flour was introduced in 1895. Recipe page courtesy of Mary Briggs Austin.

The Slonek residence and grove which overlooked the Wait Sawmill in Eldred, New York. Photo courtesy of Chuck Myers.

Minnie Sergeant, future wife of Archie Myers. Minne was also a descendant of Rev. Isaac Sergeant. Photo courtesy of Chuck Myers.

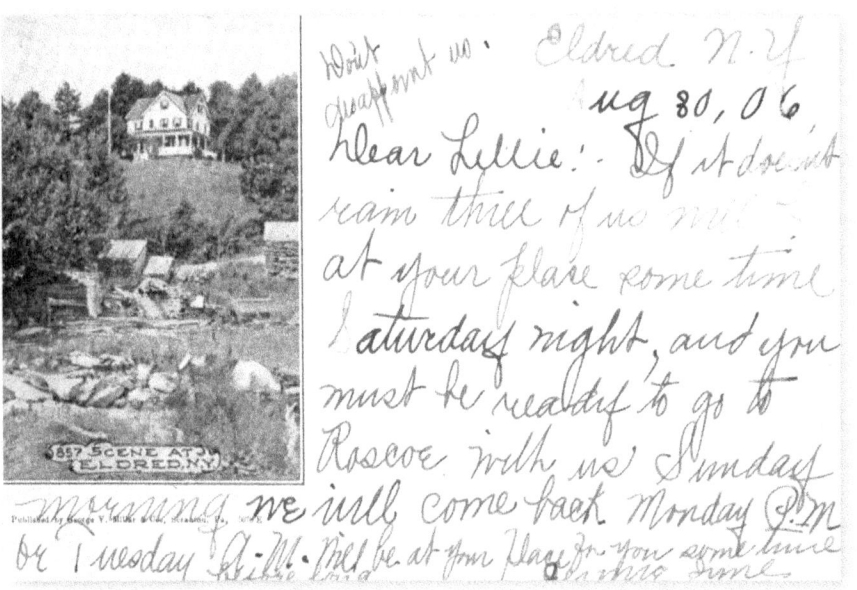

Postcard of Slonek Home sent to Lillie Austin from Jennie Crawford. Postcard courtesy of Katherine Calkin Traxler. (See p. 142.)

marriage with Miss Mary Mills of Eldred, who survives him with one son, Alexander, at home.

The funeral was held at the Eldred Congregational Church, Rev. R.W. Allen officiating, and was very largely attended.

Charles F. Calkin was the son of Oliver and Maria Gardner Calkin. Maria Calkin was the daughter of Eliza Eldred Gardner, and a niece of Mary Ann Austin.

Charles F. Calkin, 37, died at his home in Barryville, Saturday March 10, of spinal meningitis after an illness of ten days. On April 3, 1903, he was united in marriage to Miss Ida Bridge of Barryville. The sympathy of the entire community is extended to Mr. Calkin's family in this bereavement.

Jennie Crawford, Eldred, to Lillie Austin

June 23, 1906
Dear Lillie,

If it hadn't been for this darned wet weather, I could have come out, but now Dad uses the horse every dry spell at home and works him away from home when it is so rainy he can't plow. Maybe the good Lord will help me along somehow. Your black waist would look all right with a dark grey or green or navy blue, you goose. I have been ironing and my feet hurt fierce.

McDonald is helping Dad put in fodder corn. Everything we have planted we have planted in the mud. It rained last night up to about 4 a.m.

Did you see the streak in the sky at about half past 7 or 8 this a.m. It was a dark belt which seemed to divide the lighter portion of the sky from the dark cloudy part. The lighter side looked like great high waves. It was very pretty. Some claim it is the reflection of the gulf stream.

We have potatoes in bloom. The worms have about destroyed our roses. Our wire fence has come. Is there any strawberries in Bethel? I got about 3/4 of a quart the other day.

I found a dollar last Sunday and no owner. Think of it. I guess that was my lucky day. George gave me a box of Sparrow's Chocolates, too.

I am going to Mrs. Parker's to trim a hat for her. Fred's folks are tearing down their barn. Cleta [Myers Horton] has gone to Rockaway to visit. Mrs. Maier is suffering terrible now.

Hope Mom A. is well. Mother says it will soon be time to come and eat tomatoes.

Remember me to Auntie and Jimmie. Come out when you can.

Lovingly, Jennie J.

Mrs. Burnand, 26 Oak St., Paterson, N.J., to Miss Austin
July 28, 1906
Dear Miss Austin:

If you can accommodate Mabel and I for the same both as last summer, I will come up for two weeks in August. Please let me know as soon as possible.

I should like to come August 6th. Let me know who will meet us at Shohola and if the 6th will be convenient. Mabel is anxious to see McKinley and play with him again.

Hoping to hear from you soon. I remain, Yours lovingly,
Mrs. Georgia Burnand

San Francisco Earthquake 1906

In April 1906 an earthquake of at least 7.7 magnitude rocked San Francisco, California; fires burned for 3 days. At least 3,000 people died. Up to 300,000 people of a population of 410,000 were left homeless.
—wikipedia.org.

Charles Raymond, Willie, and McKinley Austin, the three grandsons Mary Ann Austin would have known before she died. Photo courtesy of Mary Briggs Austin.

Jennie Austin Recuperates
Jennie Austin had pneumonia in 1906. Since it took a long time for her to recuperate, the Austins lived temporarily in a house (which is long since gone), northeast of Eldred, on the way to Stege's Pond.

While Jennie was gaining her health back, Aida Austin ran the boarding house for them.

James Garfield Leavenworth Marries Ella Phoebe Sergeant
In August 1906 Jennie's brother Garfield Leavenworth married Ella Phoebe Sergeant.

Ella, the daughter of Frank and Clarissa Clark Sergeant, was a great-great-great-granddaughter of Reverend Isaac Sergeant who had started the Congregational Church in the area in 1799.

Garfield and Ella were married at the home near Stege's Pond where Mort and Jennie were staying.

James Garfield Leavenworth, or Garfield, as he was called,

was 6'-6" or 6'-7" tall. He was a farmer and a carpenter. He had apprenticed with Frank Sergeant, his father-in-law. Garfield played the fiddle and also made fiddles. He would be good friends with my grandfather Briggs—in 30 years.

Ella loved to work on jigsaw

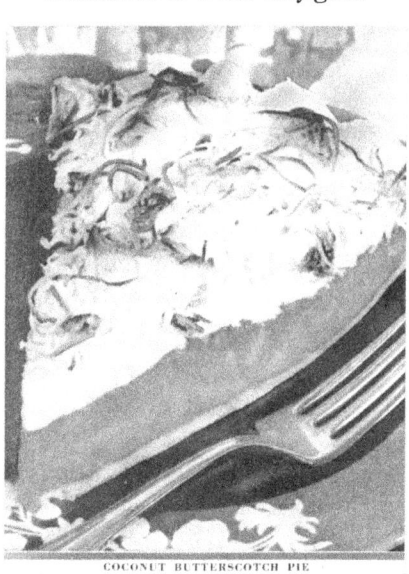

Recipe for Coconut Butterscotch Pie in Jennie Austin's recipe/poem scrapbook.

Postcard of Minnehaha Glen, Minnesota. "I was at the above place a week. Your cousin, Marie I. Neal." Postcard in the collection of Mary Briggs Austin.

puzzles and crochet. She and Garfield were Methodists. Ella's diaries add so much to this story, starting in the 1930s.

The postcard Jennie C. sent Lillie Austin on August 8, 1906, shows the Slonek House on top of the hill, and the Wait sawmill in the foreground *(also see p. 142)*.

The house would later be owned by Dr. Goodfreund and was opposite the Kyte home just past Clark Road—but before the Eldred-Yulan Road veered to the left.

Jennie Crandall, Eldred, to Lillie Austin, Bethel
August 8, 1906
Dear Lillie,
If it doesn't rain, three of us will be at your place sometime Saturday night, and you must be ready to go to Roscoe with us Sunday morning. We will come back Monday p.m. or Tuesday a.m. Will be at your place for you sometime before long.
Jennie June C.

Jennie Crandall, Eldred, to Lillie Austin, Bethel
August 15, 1906
Dear Lillie,
Thanks for the postal. Tomorrow is the M.E. Fair. The Congregational made $210 last week. Dad is to Barryville. Mother is baking rolls for the fair. I have got 30 cents for the fair. Don't you think they will get rich if they have many patrons as rich as I?
I am coming out before long, but can't tell when. Mom and I or perhaps I will come alone.
Jessie Myers (Jackson's wife) has a young son born the tenth.
Fred Myers's baby is sick again. I mean again there is a baby sick at F. Myers
Every night we have company or callers or else I am not home till late, so I am writing this morning. Effie Halstead was asking about you when she was up. I was to Crandalls the other day when your dad went by. He always looks so blamed disgusted at me that I didn't go hail him. Is your auntie to Earl's [Lillie's half brother] yet? Tell me how is Ralph [Earl's son]?
I have got to fix my corsets before I can go to town and now I must go pick what few blackberries there are. Mother has been ailing again. She has such awful times with her stomach. I just finished up the sofa pillow I had embroidered yesterday. Now I have to get the stuff to make the tick and fill it.
Belle Asendorf is home again this summer. Love to Mom A.
Lovingly,
Jennie

Nell, Vanetten, N.Y., to Lillian Austin, Bethel
August 29, 1906
Dearest Lillie,
You know my brother could not get that school for me. Another man was elected trustee and of course he had his friend, so Nell was out. If you know of any good school, will you let me know? I wrote to Sparrowbush, but they were all taken by that time. Of course, I could get one out here, but it don't seem like home to me and the wages are so small, $7 a week.
Wish you had some of our lovely apples, peaches and pears, dear. With kindest regards to your Mother and Father, and heaps of love to your own dear self, believe me as ever,
Your loving and aff. friend,
Nell

Juliana Maier Dies
Mother [Mrs. Juliana Maier] died July 25, 1906, at 8 minutes to 7 o'clock. 71 years, 6 months, 19 days.—Julius Maier.

Jennie C. had mentioned that Mrs. Maier was so very ill. Another very sad time for the Maier family. Julius Maier kept track of all Dr. Smith's visits to his mother when she was sick in 1906. The doctor was paid $3 per visit, and was at the Maier home about once a week starting in January.

G.W. Parker was paid $3 for digging the grave. Rev. Gleason was paid $3. W.H. Whitney and Mr. Porter were the undertakers; funeral expenses: $60.

On the other side of Eldred, my great-grandmother, Mary Ann Eldred Austin had been ill.

Mary Ann received a postcard from a relative (the relationship is not known) in September, the month before Mary Ann died. The postcard shows an old bridge over a stream in Minnesota, and it reminded me of Halfway Brook, the stream near the Eldred home where Mary Ann had grown up.

Marie Neal, Chicago, Ill., to Mrs. Henry Austin, Eldred
September 1, 1906

Dear Aunt Mary,
I was at the above place a week. Your cousin, Marie I. Neal

D.S., Paterson, N.J., to Mort Austin, Eldred
September 6, 1906
Dear Friend,
I am sorry your mother has not recovered, but as you say, her age is against her.
From your friend, D.S.

Mary Ann Eldred Austin Dies
Mary Ann Eldred Austin, my great-grandmother, died in October 1906. She was the last of James Eldred's children. Mary Ann was the wife of Henry Austin and mother of their ten children. Ell (James Eldred), Lon (Albert Alonzo), Maria, Aida, Mort (Charles Mortimer), and Dory (Henry Ladore) Austin were still living in 1906.

Mary Ann Austin was the grandmother of Lillie, McKinley, Raymond, and Willie Austin. Her other grandchildren, Elizabeth, Arthur (my father), and Robert Austin, were born after she died.

The following postcard was of Echo Hill. One of the initials was T.L. Perhaps Truman Leavenworth was driving the buggy. The other initials I imagine were George Crandall and Jennie C.

Echo Hill Farm House, Eldred, to Lillie Austin, Bethel
September 13, 1906
Will be out Friday morning if nothing happening to prevent.
G.L.C, J.J.C., T.L.

Fall Time
Fall was a busy time of year for the farmers who harvested and cut hay in the area. But it was also a time for friends, drinking cider, jumping in leaves, and hay wagon rides.

Postcard with Echo Hill Farm House sent to Lillie Austin. Postcard courtesy of Katherine Calkin Traxler.

Truman Leavenworth (left) with friends. Photo courtesy of Cynthia Leavenworth Bellinger.

Truman Leavenworth. Photo courtesy of Cynthia Leavenworth Bellinger.

Fall was a time for haywagon rides with friends on the Bosch farm. Menzo Bosch is driving the wagon. Photo courtesy of the Bosch Family.

Ed Bosch cutting hay at the Lake House Boarding House (in the background) during haying season. Photo courtesy of the Bosch Family.

Austin cousin, Ellsworth Clark. Photo courtesy of Katherine Calkin Traxler.

In October Aida received a postcard from James Hall, the school commissioner in Narrowsburg. *Report* possibly referred to the attendance records which were sent to the commissioner. Lillie Austin also received correspondence from Mr. Hall.

James Hall, Narrowsburg, N.Y., to Miss Aida Austin, Eldred
October 5, 1906
Dear Miss Austin,
    No report needed for the month of September. Send report for October as soon as possible.
    Yours sincerely,
    James Hall

Ida Clinton Deal was the daughter of Henry and Net Austin Clinton. Ida Deal was apparently newly married in November 1906, when she wrote her mother's first cousin Lon Austin at Mountain Grove House.

Ida Deal, Newark, N.J., to Lon Austin, Mountain Grove House
November 15, 1906
My dear Cousin,
    How you are and what you are going to do this winter? As this is the month you promised to come down and visit us, hope you have not changed your mind, for we would all love dearly to see you.
    Try and bring Maria with you.
    I hope you are all real well. Aunt Addie is with us and she joins in the invitation.
    Do write soon and tell us you will soon be with us.
    Lovingly, your cousin,
    Ida Clinton Deal

November 26, 1906
My dear cousin Lon,
    We were so pleased to hear from you, but very sorry and disappointed you could not come down and make us a visit, and to hear you had a cold. How is Maria and all the rest?
    I never will forget the pleasant time you gave me last summer and only want the opportunity of returning it whenever you can come down. I was pleased to be with you all last summer, especially to be with dear Aunt Mary and only regret it was not in my power to have eased her suffering and made her more comfortable.
    If you think of disposing of your horses in the spring, will you give us an option on Tofuey? She is such a nice horse, I would hate to see her sold to anyone who would not be good to her.
    I am going to send you a box of my wedding cake. I was

keeping it for you until you came down. It is all I have so you will have to divide with the others.
    Love and best wishes to you.
    Your affectionate cousin,
    Ida Clinton Deal

James Hall, Narrowsburg, N.Y. to Lillie Austin, Bethel

December 18, 1906
My dear Miss Austin,
    Your favor is at hand and I hasten to reply.
    I cannot possibly issue your certificate for a week or so, but that need not make any difference whatever in regard to your having all the money coming to you from the district. Go right on and make out your order and draw your money.
    I will get your certificate to you just as soon as possible.
    With the season's greetings, I remain, Very cordially yours,
    James Hall

George Crandall Marries Jennie Crawford

On December 23, 1906, George Crandall married Jennie June Crawford.

This next letter, found in the Leavenworth Collection, was written by Ellsworth Clark, son of Irvin and Laura Austin Clark. Ellsworth's brothers were Elbert and Rob Clark. The Clarks at one time lived near the Leavenworths.

Ellsworth Clark, Mill Rift, Pa., to Rob Clark, Eldred

December 31, 1906
Dear Brother Rob,
    I will write a few lines to say we are well and hope you are both the same.
    I received your letter asking if there was any show for a job fixing and I have been waiting to see O'Day, the road foreman of engines, to ask about a job for you, but have not seen him yet. His office is in Susquehanna and he is in Pennsylvania only 2 days a week. I think he is hiring some firemen as I have had some on with me in the last two weeks learning to fire. I will see him just as soon as possible, maybe today and will try and get you a job although it may be a tough job and you would be better off with less wages at something easier.
    What are you doing at present and are you married yet? Well Rob, you would be better off if you had a home of your own if you get the right kind of a wife. How is Elbert making out this winter? Is he up to Sullivan's yet?
    I would like to come up but thare is no place to stay only among strangers and there is no pleasure in doing that, but I am coming up before a great while to fish one day.
    I bought me a gasoline engine for sawing wood and making cider and expect to sight up so I can cart out rubbish out of the quarry if I want to. I have not got it running yet, but expect to this week.
    Well I must close for this time. Come down when you can and tell Elbert to come also. I will write to him this week.
    Ellsworth

M. Machin, Newark, N.J., to Aida Austin, Mountain Grove House

1907
Dear Ida,
    Shall write you a letter very soon. Hope you are resting before school opening.
    Fondly, May Machin

George and Martha Myers Become Grandparents

George W.T. and Martha Mills Myers became grandparents in 1907 when their son Charles

George Washington Taylor Myers. Photo courtesy of Cynthia Leavenworth Bellinger.

Martha Mills Myers. Photo courtesy of Cynthia Leavenworth Bellinger.

Charles Cripps Myers, son of G.W.T. and Martha Myers. Charles and his wife Lena's first son was Harold Myers. Photo courtesy of Cynthia Leavenworth Bellinger.

James Garfield Leavenworth, husband of Ella Phoebe Sergeant. Photo courtesy of Cynthia Leavenworth Bellinger.

Ella Phoebe Sergeant Leavenworth, wife of Garfield, with their daughter, Clara. Photo courtesy of Cynthia Leavenworth Bellinger.

Cripps and his wife Lena Schoonmaker Myers' son Harold Myers was born.

Sherman and Maria Leavenworth

George W.T. Myers was the brother of Maria Myers Leavenworth. Maria and Sherman became grandparents in May 1907 when Garfield and Ella Sergeant Leavenworth's daughter Clara Elizabeth Leavenworth was born in Eldred.

It was exciting to see a photo of little Clara with Phebe Owen Sergeant, her great-grandmother; Frank Roberts Sergeant, her grandfather; and her mother Ella Phoebe Sergeant Leavenworth.

Sherman and Maria Myers Leavenworth's daughter Charlotte taught in Fosterdale, New York. Their older daughter Anna continued to teach, and lived in the Cochecton area. Anna was friends with Lillie Austin.

Sherman and Maria's son Truman took summer guests for a carry-all ride around hills of Yulan and Eldred *(see p. 249)*.

A few Leavenworth family photos are part of this chapter, including one of some boarders in a play at Echo Hill Farm House.

Jennie Crandall, Eldred, to Lillie Austin
June 23, 1907

Dear Lillie,

I am sending 2 of your books, a petticoat, your green dress, and the blue waist. The machine puckered so I could scarcely get it done at all. There wasn't enough to do anything to the back. I made it fit me and that is the best I could do. Your silks I did not send. I would invest in them if you wanted to sell. I haven't got my black dress done yet.

Hope you are all well. When are you coming out? Looked for you today.

If Dad will let me have the horse, George and I are coming out; but land knows if he will let me have her or not.

The boiler at the mill is bursted, so George is working on a cupboard for his mother.

Mr. C. is getting along again. You know he has been sick.

I wish we might have a whiff of Bethel wind here. It is not warm, but hot. I am sitting here in a lump with no corset on watching George work. He raised the deuce with me and wouldn't let me iron.

Mother said to tell you she found two of your handkerchiefs which she will keep for a while at least.

Will close with love from
J.J.C.

Writer Unknown, Brooklyn, N.Y., to Aida Austin, Eldred
July 7, 1907

Dear Miss Austin,

Have your ears tingled today? We have been talking much about you today.

Mother wants to come up to your home about the 8th of August. Jessie Hill would come with her if the board could be arranged to suit our pocketbook. Could they have the rooms we occupied the first summer we

Phebe Owen Sergeant, Frank Sergeant, Clara Leavenworth, and Ella Sergeant Leavenworth, around 1908. Photo courtesy of Cynthia Leavenworth Bellinger.

From the left: Sherman S. and Charlotte Leavenworth, John Miller, Christina and Martin Leavenworth. Photo courtesy of Cynthia Leavenworth Bellinger.

Charlotte and Christina Leavenworth. Courtesy of Cynthia Leavenworth Bellinger.

Eldred is Lively

Summer Folk Making Much Out of all Kinds of Amusement

Eldred has never seen a greater patronage of all of the houses of this little resort. Social activities in the past have been rather few in number, but this season all of the sojourners have united in making much of all sorts of functions. Dances at the casinos have been well patronized and there have been other doings of a delightful nature.

Last Thursday was the event of the season at the Casino. Over 200 persons attended the function, and many elaborate costumes were noted among the summer patrons.

Straw rides form a striking part of the amusements at the resort. Among the houses that enjoyed that form of entertainment during the past week were: Echo Hill Farm House, The Arlington, Lake House, and the Pine Grove Inn. All of the rides were to Yulan…

A large buck wandered into the barnyard attached to the Orchard Terrace House last week, and upon the approach of Proprietor Myers took a flying leap over the 12-foot railing surrounding the stock pen.

A church fair was held in the Village on Saturday afternoon and evening of last week. In the evening a pleasant entertainment was rendered by a number of the sojourners, and a considerable sum was realized.
—Brooklyn Daily Eagle, *August 17, 1907.*

1907 Town of Highland Officials
Town Clerk: Wm. H. Wilson,
Commissioner: H.C. Toaspern,
Assessors: F.B. Owen, Frank Sergeant, George Mills
Inspectors: H.L. Eldred, W.B. Styles, Alvah Sergeant, George Sidwell, J.R. Myers, John Greening;
Assistant: Chris Meyer
Truant officers: A.A. Austin, Walter Tether, J.R. Myers
Board Health: W. Whitney, C. Colville
Doctor: Frank I. Smith
Justice: Isaac Sergeant
Fighting fire: Jas. Boyd
Constables: Stephen Wormuth, Robt. Crandall
Fire Warden: M.O. Sergeant
Highway implements: Wm. H. Wilson

A 1903 photo of the boarders at Echo Hill Farm House who put on a play. The lady sitting in front was Minehaha in the play. Photo courtesy of Cynthia Leavenworth Bellinger.

At the far right is possibly George W.T. Myers. Christina Leavenworth is behind the lady next to George. On the left is Charlotte, Maria, and Anna (behind Charlotte) Leavenworth. Photo courtesy of Cynthia Leavenworth Bellinger.

were at your home?

It seems so strange now when I cannot go to the country, that mother has taken such a notion to go. Such is life. People are so contrary. I should love dearly to come but can not do so this year.

I heard through Miss Crumney that you had passed through much sorrow during the past year. I sympathize very much with you all. Death comes to old and young, but when the aged leave us, we have the feeling that the work has been completed and take comfort.

At this moment, I am in my mind sitting on your piazza and breathing in the pure fresh air this lovely Sunday afternoon.

Miss Crumney retired in February, but a friend has invited her to go to Saratoga for the summer so she expects to be away in great style. Will you let me know as soon as possible what you can do for us in rooms and price. Jessie and mother join me in sending love and kind regards.

Writer unknown

George and Elizabeth Mills

In 1907 George Mills and his wife Elizabeth Gillespie ran the original Mills home where he and his siblings had grown up. George and Elizabeth's children (ages 2 to 13): Belle, James, Agnes, Alexander, George R., and Margaret (Peggy). James Mills would later own Jane Myers's boarding house. Alexander Mills would marry Minnie Meyer, whose parents would soon own the Spring House, in Barryville.

Mary Mills Wait and Alexander

Mary Mills Wait (sister to George Mills and Martha Myers), a widow, lived on Highland Lake Road with her son Alexander Wait. Mary Wait's brother-in-law William had a sawmill south of where Clark and Eldred-Yulan Roads intersected, on the west side of Eldred.

Charles W. Wilson

Charles W. Wilson (originally a brother-in-law to the Mills siblings) had a sawmill on Clark Road. A few years after his first wife Christina Mills died, Charles had married Elizabeth Hoatson Clark.

Charles and Elizabeth Wilson had a boarding house west of Board Road, just north of Eldred Corners. In 1910 Charles was Postmaster and Elizabeth was his assistant. Charles's son, Arthur Wilson and his wife also lived with Charles and Elizabeth. Elizabeth's daughter Georgia may have been at college.

The following letter from Henry Asendorf to Mort Austin, mentioned a request for lumber from Charles Wilson. Perhaps

Original Mills Boarding House on Highland Lake. George Mills Proprietor. Photo courtesy of Stuart and Geraldine Mills Russell.

Boarding House Ads and Postcards, 1906 to 1909

Fun in Sullivan County
Yulan, Sullivan County, is in the height of its summer season. Last Wednesday night was Mardi Gras at the Washington Beach Hotel on Washington Lake. About 800 people attended including several extra straw ride parties from out of town. Washington Beach Hotel has made a big success with its dances this year under the management of Lou Pfeiffer of Brooklyn.—Brooklyn Daily Eagle, *August 17, 1907.*

1908 Washington Beach Hotel. Postcard courtesy of Larry Stern.

Houses at Eldred and Yulan
Park Hotel, Echo Hill Farm House, Schewer's Mountain View House, Beechwood Cottage, Beechwood Grove House, Spring Cottage, Pine Grove Cottage, Maple Lawn House, and Mountain Rest Farm House.
—Brooklyn Daily Eagle, *August 17, 1907.*

Lake View Farm House
Accommodates 40; On Washington Lake; among the mountains; bathing, fishing and boating; good livery; large rooms; good table; beds; $7–$12. A. Kaese.—Brooklyn Daily Eagle, *July 1, 1907.*

Lake Side Cottage, Yulan
Accommodates 26; modern improvements; on Washington Lake; large airy rooms; excellent cuisine; terms on application. J. Buff.
—Brooklyn Daily Eagle, *July 12, 1907.*

Bradley House, Eldred
Elevation 1,900. 6 miles from Shohola. Good fresh vegetables. Surrounding lakes. Table fine; Proprietor good natured. H. Wells. Prop.—Brooklyn Daily Eagle, *July 12, 1907.*

West Shore Cottage, Yulan
Accommodates 40 on Washington Lake; rates $7–$10. T.W. Racine, Yulan.
—Brooklyn Daily Eagle, *July 1, 1907.*

West Shore Cottage owned by T.W. Racine. Postcard courtesy of Larry Stern.

Minisink Lodge, Yulan
Situated on Washington Lake; service first class. Yulan. McCormack & Haff.
—Brooklyn Daily Eagle, *July 5, 1908.*

Minisink Lodge on Washington Lake. Postcard courtesy of Larry Stern.

West Farm, Yulan
A quiet modern house; accommodates 40; table supplied from our own farm; large airy rooms near the lake $7–$9. Theo. West.
—Brooklyn Daily Eagle, *July 5, 1908.*

Harmony Cottage, Barryville
Fishing, boating, bathing. Charles Flieger.—Brooklyn Daily Eagle, *July 5, 1908.*

Highland Cottage, Yulan
Highest elevation on Washington Lake; strictly first class board; 10 minutes' walk to church; rate reasonable. E.J. Grannan.—Brooklyn Daily Eagle, *July 5, 1908.*

Delaware House, Barryville
Overlooking Delaware River; grounds unsurpassed, toilets, bath, fresh eggs, milk; excellent drives. $7–$8 weekly. Montgomery.—Brooklyn Daily Eagle, *July 5, 1908.*

Lake House on Highland Lake
74 guests. $6–$8 per week; piano, fishing, boating, bathing. Boat livery. Wm. Bosch.—Brooklyn Daily Eagle, *July 5, 1908.*

Oakdene, Yulan
Delightful location near Washington Lake; boating bathing fishing; large airy rooms; good table, capacity 60. Circular. W.E .Owen.—Brooklyn Daily Eagle, *July 5, 1908.*

Park Hotel, Yulan
West bank Washington Lake; accommodates 60; excellent table; boating, bathing, fishing and other amusements. A.L. Bradley.—Brooklyn Daily Eagle, *July 18, 1909.*

Parker Hotel, Eldred
Accommodates 40; boating, bathing, fishing nearby; good table, supplies, all sanitary improv. Write for terms.
—Brooklyn Daily Eagle, *July 18, 1909.*

Other Boarding Houses

1906 Postcard of Hill Side [later Side Hill] Farm owned by Mrs. John Wolff. Postcard courtesy of Larry Stern.

Henry and Belle Boyd Asendorf had started building their huge boarding house on Highland Lake.

Henry Asendorf, N.Y.C., to C.M. (Mort) Austin, Eldred
July 8, 1907
Mr. C.M. Austin,
Dear Sir,
I just wrote Chas. Wilson about sawing the balance of the lumber. I must have it on the job in a very short time as I am under contract with carpenters in Port to start very shortly. It will mean quite a little if lumber is not on job ready to start carpenters.
I have told C.W. Wilson the importance of the matter. It should all have been up there by July 1. See Wilson and write me by return mail when you expect to have all lumber on the job.
I must know as I am holding off carpenters now and they will hold me to contract for loss of time. So it is a case of cash loss to me. Write me immediately.
Yours truly, H. Asendorf

The next two letters were from friends of Mort and Jennie who were sometimes boarders.

Emma Weygandt, Luzerne, N.Y., to Mort Austin, Eldred
July 19, 1907
My Dear Mr. Austin,
I suppose you wonder why you have not heard from us. Lillie [not Lillie Austin] has been very sick with tonsillitis and Auntie was awfully afraid it would develop into something worse.
Mrs. Garbarini has just come from Bath Beach where she has been with the school children. We have gone up to Luzerne, New York.
Dr. Bok is in Milford, Conn., to stay for the summer. Mrs. Garbarini wants to know if you can put her up for 3 weeks in August.
Can you put us up? Auntie and I, maybe Lillie for 2 weeks in August? Maybe Mrs. Canefoa will come for 2 weeks. Her mother is and has been very sick, but she is getting along nicely now.
We sent 2 of our friends to you. Did they come? Miss Giannini will also come for 2 weeks in August.
How is Raymond and Willie? You have no idea how we all missed them. Remember us all to Grandpa Austin and Mrs. Austin.
Please write and let us know if you can put us up.
Best wishes to you,
Emma Deferrian Weygandt

Mayme Dassori, Bath Beach, N.Y., to Jennie Austin
August 5, 1907
Dear Mrs. Austin
Your card at hand and both Sylvester and myself wish to thank you for your kind wishes. You may expect me in Eldred the same day Mrs. Garbarini and the rest goes, which I suppose will be about next Monday, August 12, 1907.
I intend to send my trunk to Shohola about Friday or Saturday, so that I will be able

Boarding House Postcards, 1906

Highland Grove House

1906 Postcard of Daniel Hallock's Highland Lake Grove. Postcard courtesy of Larry Stern.

River View House

River View House at Minisink Ford. Postcard courtesy of Larry Stern.

Barryville-Shohola Bridge Company

An act to incorporate the Barryville and Shohola Suspension Bridge Company in Sullivan County became a law on June 11, 1907...
Menzo Quick, George Eckhart, George Mills, Alonzo A. Calkin and James K. Gardner and their successors as directors and all other persons who may hereafter be subscribers to or holders of the stock hereinafter mentioned are hereby constituted a body corporate by the name of the Barryville and Shohola Suspension Bridge Company for the purpose of purchasing, maintaining, reconstructing and managing the bridge across the Delaware River at Barryville...The corporation hereby created shall exist for fifty years...
Menzo Quick, George Eckhart, George Mills, Alonzo A. Calkin and James K. Gardner are hereby made directors of said company and shall continue in office until the first Monday of January 1908...
—Newtown Register, *September 14, 1907.*

to have it by Monday. So if Mr. Austin goes to Shohola, will you ask him to please look out for it?

If you could let me have the room that Dr. Bok had I would be very much obliged to you. Some one of the party could sleep in with me, for I intend to stay in Eldred until September. Sylvester expects to get a week off the end of August or the first part of September.

Give our love to Raymond and Sunny Jim and kindest regards to Mr. Austin, and yourself.

Mayme G. Dassori

Minnie Nelson

In May 1907 Minnie Nelson from Barryville, became a member of the Methodist Church. Minnie still attended the Methodist Church in 1935 when the Briggs family arrived, and was in several Briggs family photos.

Lon Austin and Daisy

From 1907 to 1911 Lon Austin corresponded with Daisy, a gal he met in New York City. A few excerpts from those letters have been included. Lon and Daisy seemed to be dating. Eventually, Daisy requested Lon not to write her anymore, although she changed her mind a couple times.

Ell and Emma Austin's Family

We haven't heard much from the family of Ell Austin lately. Uncle Ell and Emily had a farm in Bethel, New York. In 1907 Henry (Earl) Austin and his wife Sadie had 4 children: Ralph, Mildred, Margo, and Myrtie. Mabel, Alma, and Hazel Austin were born in the next 10 years. Earl Austin and his family lived in Callicoon at the turn of the century. Not much more is known about them.

Sophronia Parmenter lived with either her nephew Earl Austin's family, or with her sister Emily Austin's family.

Cousin Lillie Austin would soon attend Cortland Normal School. In 1907 Lillie was looking for a teaching job.

Woodside Farm House, Mrs. C. H. Calkin, Proprietress, Fosterdale, Sullivan County, New York. Lillie Austin boarded at Woodside. Postcard courtesy of Katherine Calkin Traxler.

James Hall, School Commissioner, Narrowsburg, N.Y., Lydia Austin, Bethel

August 21, 1907
My dear Miss Austin,

I wish that you had written me a few days ago for I have filled some good positions lately. Only this morning I was wondering whether or not you was located for the year.

You may be sure you will hear from me when the next good vacancy is brought to my notice.

I feel quite sure that there will be more desirable vacancies to fill later, but in the meantime, you had best keep looking around. There must be some good schools yet left in the town of Bethel.

You can refer to me as reference and I will be glad to write a personal letter of recommendation to any trustee at anytime. Should you find a position, let me know at once.

With kind regard to yourself and family, I remain,

Very cordially yours,
James L. Hall

The Calkin Family, Fosterdale

Lillie found a job teaching school in Fosterdale, less than 5 miles from Cochecton, where Anna Leavenworth was teaching. Lillie boarded at Woodside Farm House, in Fosterdale run by Mrs. Sarah Calkin, a recent widow.

Cranmer and Sarah Egan Calkin had had 4 children: Edna, Burton, Horton, and Hannah. There are letters from Edna and Hannah to Lillie included in this chapter. Burton and Hannah would play a major role in Lillie Austin's life.

Cranmer Calkin was a distant relative of Oliver Calkin who lived

"McKinley, this is I where I attend church this winter. Anna Leavenworth." Lillie Austin sent a postcard just like this one to her mother. "How do you like the calf? Lillie Austin." Postcard in the collections of both Mary Briggs Austin and Katherine Calkin Traxler.

Straub's Hotel around 1910. From the left: Ida Straub with Jack the dog. Emma Straub (Toaspern) in the white hat; Juliana and Fridolin Straub. Photo courtesy of Bill Ihlo.

in Barryville, and was married to Maria Gardner, niece of Mary Ann Eldred Austin.

Cochecton Postcard
Anna Leavenworth seems to have been living in or near Cochecton when she sent her nephew McKinley Austin a postcard of the church she attended in Cochecton. Lillie Austin sent the same postcard to her mother a few days later.

Anna Leavenworth, Cochecton, N.Y., to McKinley Austin, Eldred
October 2, 1907
McKinley,
This is where I attend church this winter.
Anna Leavenworth

Lillie Austin, Fosterdale, N.Y., to Emily Austin, Bethel
October 14, 1907
Went to church here today. Anna boards at the house which you can see part of at the left. The road over the hill goes to Tylertown.
How do you like the calf?
Lillie Austin

Tom Collins, a neighbor to the Austins, had moved to New Jersey, and wrote to Ell Austin.

Tom Collins, Sommerville, N.J., to James E. Austin, Bethel
October 21, 1907
Friend Eldred,
I thought I would write to you and let you know that we reached our new home all right and we like it very much and think it all right.
I never saw such land or ground. I plowed one day. I want to get in a piece of wheat.
All day long I did not see a stone as big as a chestnut.
This is the place to farm when a man gets to be as old as I am. I suppose it is just like the west. We have 80 acres all cleared, but very few trees.
We have plenty of neighbors within 1/2 mile of us and can see everyone of them. Good markets as can sell everything we can produce. This has been a great dairy farm. The buildings are all large and in first clap condition.
Our regards to yourself and family. Yours, T.K. Collins

J.C. Banning, Narrowsburg, N.Y., to C.M. Austin, Eldred
November 26, 1907
Dear Sir,
Thanks for your order. Received check with interest added. I did not expect or want you to add interest. A few days at anytime does not make any difference. I am pleased to have your trade on any reasonable time. I shipped your order today:

Meal 500, $7; Corn 500, $7; Oats 300, $4.50.

Thanking you for past payments. I remain yours,

J.C. Banning, Proprietor Riverside Mills, Dealer in Flour, Feed and Meal, Hard and soft coal, cedar shingles

Carrie Wait, Eldred, to Jennie Austin, Eldred
November 30, 1907
Dear Jennie [Austin],

If you only knew how pleased I was to receive your letter. It did me lots of good. I am doing nicely but only have one hand to use so you must excuse poor writing. Will be home before long. Come and see me.

Lovingly, Carrie Wait

Tom Collins, Sommerville, N.J., to J.E. (Ell) Austin, Bethel
December 3, 1907
Friend Eldred,

I received your letter on the 29th with the full amount of $8.00.

We are having our first snow tonight. It has looked like snow all day and has just reached this place. But we have had some very cold weather. I suppose that I feel it more because we are not shut in with woods like up home. The wind has full sweep, no trees to break it for miles, so I don't know what the winter will be. I will be more able to tell you next spring.

I did not get my wheat sowed. The farmers thought it was pretty late, so I took their advice. I will have it all ready for oats in the spring if we live.

You ask me if I still like it down here. Well, I don't feel the least bit homesick and you know that I said I would not say good bye to my home, nor take up the bridges as I crossed them. If we don't have good health here I

New Year Postcard for Maria Austin. Postcard courtesy of Mary Briggs Austin.

would not stay one week. So far I am content and satisfied.

Hoping that you and your family are all well, I am ever your friend. We all send our regards.

T.K. Collins

Fridolin and Juliana Straub
In 1907 Fridolin and Juliana Straub, both from Bavaria, bought the first hotel that James Y. Parker had built. The Autenrieth Family had owned the Hotel around 1900.

Fridolin and Juliana had had a beer garden in Weehawken, New Jersey, before moving to Eldred. The Straubs had five children: Julia, Fridolin Jr., Emma, Rosa, and Ida. Several of the children play a part in this story. Straub's Hotel and Bar stayed in the Straub family into the 1950s.

Anna in the following letter was a friend of Daisy.

Lon Austin, Eldred, to Anna
December 31, 1907
My dear Anna,

The long looked for, but almost despaired of letter came at last. It's not in my heart to even think one unkindly thought of the fair flower.

Tis sweet to be remembered and it seems more sweetly so when I realize that you have so much to occupy your time. Especially at this season of the year with many old friends that have long been tried and true. Joy sweeps over my being tonight to know that you find the time to give an occasional thought to your new made friend.

We had good sleighing for a few days a week or so ago. I intended to write and put you in remembrance of your promise to come up and get a sleigh ride and that very night the rain descended and spoiled the sleighing. We have good skating and if you and Daisy will come up, I'll do my best to give you a pleasant time.

The old year is dying tonight. It lies in the last throes of the midnight hour. It's laying aside its joy and blessing and opportunities, its toil and struggles of departed days, but only to give place to a bright New Year with a multitude of new blessing and opportunities and responsibilities.

May He who alone is able to give the needed grace and strength, enable us so to live and utilize the coming year that when the King shall come to gather up his jewels, we may be ready and waiting to meet him, at the brightness of his coming.

Ten minutes more and the old clock of time rings out the old and rings in the new. I must bid you good night, wishing you innumerable blessings and a Happy New Year.

Very cordially yours, Lon

Flat Iron Building

The Flatiron Building was built on a triangular-shaped lot at 23rd Street, Fifth Avenue, and Broadway. It was called the Flatiron Block, as it was shaped like a clothing iron.

Considered to be one of the first skyscrapers to be built, it was completed in 1902.

The Flatiron Building was designed by Chicago's Daniel Burnham. Its facade was limestone at the bottom and changed to glazed terra-cotta as the floors rose. It had a steel skeleton, a construction technique familiar to the Fuller Company, a contracting firm based in Chicago with considerable expertise in building such tall structures. At the vertex the triangular tower is only 6.5 feet wide; an acute angle of about 25 degrees.—*wikipedia.org.*

Flat Iron Building. Postcard from Jessie Hill in 1908. Postcard courtesy of Mary Briggs Austin.

Flat Iron Building under construction, 1902. Photo: Library of Congress, Prints and Photographs Division: Detroit Publishing Co., LC-D401-14278.

Henry Asendorf to Mort Austin
January 2, 1908
Dear Sir,

I have mailed Floyd [Boyd] checks for $100.00; 4 of $25.00 each. I expected to clean up the $179.00, but will fix up the $79.00 in a short time and in fact clean up the bill entirely.

I am sorry I could not help you out before now. I just had a 46% raise on an order I placed out west so you can see what delay cost me to date; materials for building have all gone up.

I would have sent you checks directly only I had others to send Floyd, so I sent them all together.

Yours truly,
Henry Asendorf

Floyd Boyd mentioned in the letter, was a brother-in-law to Henry Asendorf, and a first cousin to Alexander Wait.

Floyd and Alexander would have Wait & Boyd's garage in Eldred, by 1920.

Daisy to Lon Austin, Eldred
January 14, 1908
Lon,
You remarked in your letter in regards to sleigh riding up on the mountains.
Have your sisters made up their minds yet what they are going to do? If they don't go too far from the Village, they will have to have me for a boarder for I'd hate like anything to go among strangers. Daisy

Maud Crawford, Eldred, to Lillie Austin
January 5, 1908
My dear Lillie,
You were here such a short time I had no very good chance to see you. Hope you had a nice time in the city.
What a fierce day you had to ride 6 miles in the howling wind. We seem to have so much of it.
We had a very pleasant day at Verna's New Years. I spent Xmas day at Annie Maiers. A very pleasant day indeed.
I walked to Mary Myers Thursday. With love and kind wishes,
Your friend,
Maud Crawford

Tom Collins, Sommerville, N.J., to Mort Austin, Eldred
January 26, 1908
Friend Mort,
How are you getting along this winter? My wife is in the city

A 1907 postcard sent to the Willie Austin. Postcard courtesy of Mary Briggs Austin.

for today and tomorrow, so I am alone and lonesome.
I have been making fences all winter. No frost in the ground up to last Friday when we had a very heavy snow storm.
It was like the storm we had in '88. You remember it snowed all day and night and oh, the wind how it did blow—raise the hair off your head. That is what I don't like down here.
I thought of my place up there, how sheltered from these terrible winds we would be if we had those woods around the buildings. I want to have a Summer. If it is all right, we may stay a year or so.
I hope the houses are all right. I suppose you are busy getting out some lumber. Is Lon still up there?
I had a letter from Ell saying he has thought of going away from Eldred. Mort, I think he is just as well off as any place. He has his health and can make a little money.
I see so many men walking around and can't get anything to do, it is frightful. These are not tramp men, but men that will work if they can find it.
Let us hear from you. It makes us feel good to hear from home.

That is our home.
All send regards. With best wishes for your self and family.
I am ever your friend,
T.K. Collins

Lillie Austin, Port Jervis, N.Y., to Emily Austin, Bethel
February 5, 1908
Have had a splendid day in the rain. Clearing up now. Lillie

George Wells to Mr. Austin
February 10, 1908
Dear Sir:
John is very anxious for you to get the hay out of his barn, come as soon as you can conveniently.
George Wells

Jessie Hill to McKinley Austin
February 10, 1908
Dear McKinley,
Knowing how you enjoyed the papers during the summer, I thought you would like some to read during the winter. I am sending you some Sunday papers. Hope all are well. Love to all.
Jessie Hill

Lon Austin, School Trustee
Lon Austin was a school trustee around 1908, as well as a truant

First play held in Eldred's Sunshine Hall. Front row, left: John Austin, instructor. Behind John, Raola Kelley and Christina Leavenworth standing; Mildred Myers, Hazel Schroeder; Charlotte Leavenworth (check over) in plaid shawl on right. 3rd row: Bert Kyte, Ida Daily, Emily Parker Stevens, Anna Appel, Mary Kyte. Back row: Arthur Wilson, Sam Simpson, Charlie Dunlap. Photo courtesy of Cynthia Leavenworth Bellinger.

officer. It seems it was very important for teachers to fill out attendance/truant reports each day.

Lon Austin would become the only trustee on the school board, according to a story his sister Aida wrote. Aida also wrote about *the powers to be* in Eldred trying to railroad through a new $6,000 school. We will talk more about that in the next chapter.

L. Simon, Lackawaxen, Pa., to Mr. Austin, truant officer
March 6, 1908
Dear Sir:

Kindly inform Mr. Fred Hulse of Lackawaxen that his daughter Liza aged 9, and his son Irving aged 11, have been absent for four weeks, no excuse prevailing.

And oblige,
Louise A. Simon,
School No. 1, Lackawaxen

F.F. Bush, Monticello, N.Y., to Aida Austin, Eldred
March 9, 1908
Dear Madam,

I have your letter. If the will was properly executed and any of the witnesses are living, it can be proved and recorded.

Whether it is better to have it recorded, I cannot advise you and I cannot give you any advice about it without seeing the will and seeing you.

Advice by letter without knowing all about the facts is, as a general thing, good for nothing.

You did not state your grandfather's name, so that I cannot examine the records to see if the will is recorded.

Very Respectfully,
F.F. Bush, Attorney

Julius Maier's Check
In March 1908 Julius Maier, son of Joseph and Juliana Maier, worked for Thomas Sidwell—10 hours per day, 6 days a week (Monday through Saturday). He received a check on April 4th for $25.20. The check was cashed by W.H. Wilson on April 7, 1908.

Sunshine Hall where the 1908 play took place. Photo courtesy of Chuck Myers.

Emily, Forestine, N.Y., to Lillie Austin, Bethel
April 29, 1908
Dear Lillie,

I received your letter last Friday when I got home. It's the most inquisitive letter I've had for a long time.

My school will be out May 18. When will yours be out and when are you coming over?

Mother is quite well now and I hope you've gotten over your cold.

Will Schoonmaker told me last night that Phillips's (between Yulan and Barryville) was struck by lightning Monday night and burned. I don't know where he got his information and I don't know whether it was the bowling alley or one of the houses. I think perhaps Harry French might have told him as he was down that way this week. How are all your folks? Remember me to them.

Good night and answer this soon. Yours sincerely,
Emily

The First Play at Sunshine Hall
On May 19, 1908, Charlie Scheniman was chosen as head director of *The Country Store and Post Office,* the first play ever given in Eldred's Sunshine Hall. Elsie Autenrieth was the prompter for parts forgotten. The writers were Charlotte Leavenworth, Jennie and George Crandall, and anyone else who would help.

Almost every young person in Eldred had a part. Several of us got together, made up and wrote, "The Country Store and Post Office." Around 30 people were in it for 2 different nights.
—Charlotte Leavenworth.

Mary Ellery, Brooklyn, N.Y., to Lillie Austin, Bethel
June 7, 1908

Hawk's Nest: Krauss Photography in Port Jervis. Mr. Krauss is in the photo. Photo courtesy of Kevin Marrinan.

Bird's Eye view of Port Jervis, 1907. Postcard in the Defeo Collection, courtesy of Kevin Marrinan.

Eldred, September 2, 1908. Jennie Austin and Sun All. Postcard to Miss Mary Kyte. Postcard courtesy of Mary Briggs Austin.

I hope your Aunt Sophronia is better and that she and your mother will take good care of themselves and not get over tired.
Your loving fifth cousin,
Mary J. Ellery

LaBarr Family

We met the LaBarr family of Beaver Brook in *The Mill on Halfway Brook*. Jacob Daniel LaBarr, son of Calvin S. and Elizabeth Rice LaBarr, moved to New Jersey. Jacob Daniel LaBarr married Anna Mae Hankins in October 1908. Jacob Daniel worked in paper mills and had a grocery store in Hamburg, New Jersey. Jacob D. and Anna Mae LaBarr had 10 children including Jacob LaBarr, born in 1909. Jacob would be the father of Edey Werman.

My grandfather Jacob Daniel moved to New Jersey while the rest stayed in Beaver Brook.
—Edey LaBarr Werman.

Lillie Austin, Eldred, to Mrs. J.E. Austin, Bethel
July 1, 1908
Dear Mother,
I have changed plans. Will be home Monday Night. Lillie

L.M. Giannini, N.Y.C., to Homestead Cottage, Eldred
July 24, 1908
Dear Mrs. Austin,
Arrangement entirely satisfactory. Please pardon delay in answering. Kind regards to all.
Yours very truly,
L.M. Giannini

Anna Leavenworth, Beaver Brook, to Lillie Austin, Bethel
July 29, 1908
Dear Lillie,
Thanks for the card. It is a very pretty one. I imagine you are quite busy just now and as this week is about the only idle time I shall have this summer, I will write first.
Perhaps I will not be prompt to answer as Jennie [Austin, her sister] expects boarders soon and I will be there helping her.
I came up here to visit Mrs. Darling Saturday and will stay about a week. There wasn't much news of any kind when I left home. The date of our fair was settled to be the 13th of August.
The Ladies Aid held a Lawn Social at Edith McKechnie's. It was a success although the weather that night was rather cool. They cleared $20 there and $1 was collected afterward.
This has been a very slow season for boarders. We have had 17. The other houses on our road haven't any more altogether.
The mail wagon has just come. I won't be able to post this today. It is worse to have the P.O. right in the house than a mile away.
Write if you have time. Tell me all about the place and how you like it. Give my regards to Emily and don't get yourself tired out.
Lovingly, Anna Leavenworth

S.G. Dassori, Brooklyn, N.Y., to C.M. Austin, Eldred
August 5, 1908
Dear friend,
Don't forget to do what you know is right. He is nigh and you will be alright. S.G. Dassori

Port Jervis, New York, in 1908
In 1908, Port Jervis had 82 industries and establishments. Its many workers produced glassware, saws, silk, gloves and mittens and shirts. The railroad yards and shops remained a significant industry in the city until the 1960s.—www. upperdelawarescenicbyway.org.

In 1908 to get to Port Jervis from the Town of Highland, you would travel a very scenic twisting unpaved road which went beside and sometimes overlooked the Delaware River. A portion of the road known as the Hawk's Nest was not paved until 1931–1933.

Mr. Krauss started his Port Jervis photography business in 1907, and by 1910 had taken several photos of the Hawk's Nest.

Ella S., Fosterdale, N.Y., to Lydia Austin, Cortland, N.Y.
August 8, 1908
Dear Lillie,

School meeting and the Fair came off simultaneously and I think them both successes for at the first it was voted that your services be secured for the winter. Johnny was "authorized" to give a dollar more per week. I am joyful to hear it for I really think we will be together again this winter. We took in $164 at the fair, mostly net.

Don't study too hard house mate and let me hear from you as soon as you certainly know about school.

Affectionately, Ella M.S.

B. Calkin, Lake Huntington, N.Y., to Lillie Austin, Cortland, N.Y.
August 12, 1908

I got your letter and haven't time to answer it. I will be out Sunday if nothing happens. A card will have to do this time.

B.C. [Burt Calkin, Lillie's future husband.]

Sylvester Dassori, N.Y.C., to Mrs. Austin, Eldred
August 28, 1908
Dear Mrs. Austin,
Will be up Saturday.
Love to all, Sylvester Dassori

Jennie Austin and Mary A. Kyte
One of my favorite photos of my grandmother Austin is a postcard from September 2, 1908. Jennie is standing with her horse, Sun All, who was named for a famous horse at that time.

The card was addressed to Miss Mary Kyte. Mary Alice Kyte, a granddaughter of Rev. Felix Kyte, would marry Harry Wormuth. Aida Austin would write about Mary Wormuth in her 1940 diary.

Daisy to Lon Austin
September 16, 1908
Lon,
I would gladly correspond with you, but I'm afraid it will

Lake Huntington, the location from which Burt Calkin wrote Lillie Austin. Postcard in the collection of Katherine Calkin Traxler.

Photo taken from High Rock, Cochecton, New York, August 4, 1908. Postcard to Anna Leavenworth, Eldred, N.Y., from her friend, Lizzie Kruck. Postcard courtesy of Mary Briggs Austin.

1908 Model T Ford

The first production Model T left the Piquette Plant in Detroit, Michigan, on September 27, 1908. Eventually nicknamed the Tin Lizzie, it was more affordable to the average American ($850 for a 4-seat open tourer) than other cars. It was available in grey, green, blue, and red, but not black—the *only* color option in 1914.—wikipedia.org.

1908 Model T Ford. Photo: Ford Motor Company.

Emily Parmenter Austin feeding her chickens. Postal of George Ellery, courtesy of Katherine Calkin Traxler.

only keep the wound open, but I'll leave it to you. Daisy

Charlotte Leavenworth, Teacher
Charlotte Leavenworth began teaching at Fosterdale where she taught 50 students in eight grades for $540 a year, in the fall of 1908.

Lillie Austin Starts at Cortland Normal School
Lillie Austin had already taught school. But in September 1908, Lillie started teacher training classes at the Normal School in Cortland, New York. Her mother Emma Parmenter Austin wrote some endearing and newsy letters to her. In her correspondence, Emma talked about her chickens, a new road in Bethel, the need for water, the comments Ell made about missing *the girl* (meaning Lillie), and motherly advice.

George Ellery, distant cousin of Emily and Lillie Austin, sent them postals or postcards with photos of Em, Ell, Lillie, and himself, taken in the summer of 1908.

Emma Austin, Bethel, to Lillie E. Austin, Cortland, N.Y.
September 20, 1908
Dear Girlie,
Was glad to get your letter and was meaning to answer this afternoon but Sadie [son Henry Earl's wife], Sophronia, and the children came about noon which knocked that all in the head. Sophronia says she is going to stay there till November.

Well how did you get along this week? A regular servant would get about $3 and board for what you do plus working the hours you are at school. I think it is too much for you and if you can make satisfactory arrangements with Mrs. Stafford, I think you had better do so. You can't work all the time for if you do you will be apt to break down.

I got some postals from George.

We haven't had a drop of rain since you went away and we are getting a sort of water famine. We have been getting our drinking water of Mr. Heune, but last night his well failed, so today we have been without.

Chris Bunger lost a number of cattle from drinking poor water, so Dad had the further spring cleaned out for our cows. There seems to be quite a little water there, but not fit for house use. He and Willie commenced on the other spring yesterday. Going to dig it about 2 feet across and about 6 feet deep and stone it up. Quite a little water run in through the night, but very muddy. I hope they can finish it before it rains or they will have all their work for nothing.

Willie doesn't know as he can come tomorrow and Dad has to peddle Tuesday and Wednesday.

How do you like it so far? How is Geometry? If you board yourself, be sure and not go hungry because its too much trouble to cook much.

You don't know how I miss you. I never have been so lonesome.

The dog pounced on a skunk with his mouth wide open and got a dose down his throat. Dad said he was so sick he could not throw up, only gagged. Dad poured new milk down his throat, then water, but did not do any good. He got some raw meat which seemed to help him. There was but very little on his hair.

Be sure and not work too hard. Am glad your cold is better.
Your loving Mother

A. Lufburrow, Brooklyn, N.Y., to Aida Austin, Eldred
September 20, 1908
Dear Miss Aida,
Has your school opened yet? And your troubles commenced?
Love from,
A.M. Lufburrow

Emma Austin, Bethel, to Lillie E. Austin, Cortland, N.Y.

September 25, 1908
Dear Girlie,

Am glad you changed your place. You have a very nice room. How is the heat? Have you got your stove yet? Better get a wickless if you use oil.

Be sure and get up in time to have a good breakfast before going to school.

The well this morning is flowing in pretty good. Your dad said there were 22 inches.

We have had fires all around us. Babcock of Lake Huntington who had a store and Post Office got burned out. Lost $800 government money.

Made a 3 gallon jar of soy today. Dad is still butchering. Is off with cart; time he was home.

Write when you can and as often as you can.
Your loving Mother

October 1, 1908
Dear Girlie,

Washed and finished taking up my plants. Now all are in including Auntie's mums. This morning went up and finished gathering the pears. This p.m. ironed the rough dried clothes.

It rained!!! Monday, all day and night. Toward night the wind began to blow. The next morning we found there had been some little damage done. We were fortunate. Only the apple tree by the spring was turned up and one of Auntie's mums broken.

Mrs. Walker's roof went off her barn. She also lost 2 trees. Ellie Scott lost one or two trees. Charlie Dubois lost the big maple by his kitchen door. D. Stephenson lost 2 pear trees. J. Iderith's chicken house was taken out into the fields. His new barn moved 6 inches. A number of others lost trees.

Dad has the spring walled up around 4 or 5 feet; nearly level with the surface. He wants to carry it up about 2 feet above and bank around it to turn surface water.

He came over and helped me pick about a pailful of pears. When we got back, the water had run in so he dipped out about a dozen pails full. It is pretty good water.

I rec'd a letter from Mrs. Ellery Tuesday night.

If you take up gymnasium work will you have to furnish your own suit? I am glad you like your teachers. How do you like Geom. and Latin? I suppose you study evenings and don't have much time to go out, but am glad you have a good time when you do.

90, the turnpike is being surveyed to be a state road. Won't that be nice to have a macadamized road to drive over. Dad says it will make the taxes higher. They commenced at Cochecton and got about to Bethel schoolhouse this morning. There are 2 men and a woman. I thinks she is wife of one of the men.

I have bread to mix yet. Dad had beefsteak today. Said it was the tenderest he has had for quite a while. Wished the girl [Lillie] had part of it. He wonders if you get enough to eat.

Must go mix my bread. Take care of yourself and don't get sick.
Good night.
Your loving Mother

Robert Collins, brother of Tom Collins and Annie Collins, wrote McKinley Austin who lived in the old Collins' house, Homestead Cottage, owned by Mort and Jennie Austin.

Apparently Robert and Annie had visited Mort and Jennie Austin's family. Robert and McKinley had played checkers, a very Austin past time. You may remember the Austin cousins playing checkers in Aida's 1881 Diary.

Robert Collins, Madison, N.J., to McKinley Austin, Eldred
October 5, 1908
My dear McKinley,

I received your card several days ago and was glad to learn you were all well. You speak of

James Eldred Austin on 1908 postcard. Postal of George Ellery, courtesy of Katherine Calkin Traxler.

McKinley on the left standing behind his mother, Jennie Austin. Willie, Mort, and Raymond Austin. Photo courtesy of Mary Briggs Austin.

playing checkers. I have not played a game since I left Eldred, but have often wished you were down here so we might have a good one.

I only wish my sister Annie was as well as she was a year ago, we would have been with you long since.

Sister Annie is very ill and will never be any better. She is living in Newburgh and I saw her about three weeks ago. She was then very sick indeed. I have since learned that she is steadily getting weaker.

When with her, she referred to our visit at your place last September. She said, "How I did enjoy it." And how kind you folks were in doing so much to entertain us. We cannot soon forget.

This year on account of her condition, we cannot be with you, and Mrs. Collins and my daughter are so fixed they cannot go either, but sometime we hope to again.

Remember me to Aunt Maria, Ida, Uncle Lon, and your Papa and Mamma. We all hope you have had a good year this summer and may always have. Don't forget to remember me to your Grandpa and brothers.

With best wishes for yourself.
I am Sincerely yours,
R.B. Collins

Hannah Calkin, Fosterdale, N.Y., to Lillie Austin, Cortland, N.Y.
October 6, 1908
Dear Friend,
School opened yesterday and I think I shall like the teacher, but I miss you very much and it seems very lonesome at school this year.

I am sorry that I did not get out to see you before you went away, but we were so busy then that it was impossible for me to leave home.

I often think of the day I came home from Liberty. I was so sorry I did not give you some of those flowers; your mother was so fond of them. I intended to leave some for you, but I came away in such a hurry that I forgot all about them. Edna and Mother both scolded me because I did not give you some.

We are all well and hope this will fine you the same. I will be very glad to get a letter from you.

With best regards from all, I remain your Friend,
Hannah Calkin

Hannah Calkin, the sister of Burt Calkin who Lillie would marry, would become a part of Burt and Lillie's family.

Emma Austin, Bethel, to Lillie E. Austin, Cortland, N.Y.
October 8, 1908
Dear Girlie,
Was too tired to write last night. Cleaned all the hen houses yesterday afternoon. Am glad you have a chance to enjoy yourself.

How do you like the gym? Have you learned to stand on your head and wave your heels in the air yet?

Did you get your bloomers made? What kind of waist do you wear with them.

Dad often says, "I wish the girl had some of this," (whatever he thinks tastes pretty good). I guess he is afraid you won't get you enough. How are you off for money? Don't hesitate to say when you need any.

Dad does not like the idea of the state road, says it is being done mostly for the automobiles. They are to survey to Monticello. The Jeffersonville Road is to go through Fosterdale to Lake Huntington I believe. The head surveyor says this road will surely go through, but says the one from Liberty to Monticello never will, on account of mills I suppose.

I haven't heard anything about the Fosterdale school.

Take care of yourself,
Your loving Mother

In 1908, the Congregational Church Sunday School room (on the left as you look at it from the road), was added along with the front vestibule.—Chuck Myers.

Jennie Crandall, Eldred, to Lillie Austin
October 13, 1908
Dear Lillie,

Mrs. Crandall is to Port Jervis.

I hear Allen is to take the Hall to lecture in and that the Congregational Church is to get a new minister.

I've had quite a day of it. In the a.m. went up town, then Bertha and I went up to Venoge; stopped to Boyds and to Belles; had a nice time. Came home, got my dinner, canned 3 cans of citron with cranberries. Washed my breakfast dishes and had callers: Nell C. and Royal Love's wife.

Then I went to the Drawing Class and came back, peeled some potatoes, then Anna Appel came.

Young Charlotte Leavenworth. "She is a very nice girl indeed." Photo courtesy of Mary Briggs Austin.

Finally I got supper, washed dishes, mixed bread, and now am writing to you.

Read "The Ancient Law," "The Prince of Somers," and a lot of magazines; also, "Fruit of the Tree."

George's dad says, "How is Lillie?"

Mother and Dad were down Monday. I sent to Montgomery Ward and Co. for a few little things.

I feel old tonight. It is so thick in here with cigar smoke that I can hardly breathe.

Tell me about your studies and yourself. Can't you arrange to stay with me part of next summer if we are all living?

Lovingly, Jennie J. Crandall

E.M.S., Fosterdale, N.Y. to Lillie Austin, Cortland, N.Y.
October 13, 1908
My dear Lillie,

I can't go anyway for I have whooping cough not very badly, but enough so that I should stay away from people who might take it.

Charlotte Leavenworth, you may have heard, has the school and is with me. She is a very nice girl indeed. I like her personally very much and hope that she may do well with the school. If she will only be sufficiently "ugly."

Miss Bush is going to walk out and stay with us tomorrow night and get a little acquainted with Miss L., that she (Miss B.) may not feel so entirely alone when she is among an Institute of York State teachers.

All of Angie's children have the cough. Also Mary and myself who are old enough to be immune. Also Edna and all the Edlemens, Harold, and an assortment of younger Magans, and the Wormuths. And now the well part

Lillie and her 5th cousin George V. Ellery. Photo courtesy of Katherine Calkin Traxler.

of the school has been exposed, including Miss L. who has never had it.

We are very badly off for water.

Barks is getting his winter coat and looks very dark and handsome. He had his first skunk episode last week. He was not very smelly, not as skunky dogs go.

I have my outside work all done, what few apples I have gathered, are in barrels, and sent away. Also, Mr. L. bought one. Most of my garden stuff gathered and taken care of.

We are chestnutting and mushrooming. We had sausages and mushrooms (fried in the gravy) for supper last night. We had some fried plain. Tomorrow we will go again.

Lillie Austin at Cortland Normal School. Lillie is second from the left in the second row from the bottom. Photo courtesy of Katherine Calkin Traxler.

The first warm day we are going to Lake Huntington where we have permission to fish under Henry's trees.

Affectionately yours,
E.M.S.

Emma Austin, Bethel, to Lillie E. Austin, Cortland, N.Y.
October 14, 1908
Dear Girlie,

That was a pretty good hat you got, wasn't it? The other girls will be getting envious.

I don't know anything about the Fosterdale School. If it is Lottie, she will have a pretty big school for her first one. If it is Anna, the children will soon run over her.

I hope the exercises will help your hip. Do you use dumbbells and Indian clubs? Be careful when practicing on the horizontal bar and hold on tight. A fellow was visiting in Eldred one summer who broke his neck on one and had to wear a muzzle (as Lottie Bradley called it), to keep his neck straight while it was growing together again.

I haven't sold my chickens yet. The price went down to 8 or 9 cents per pound (was 14). So thought I'd keep them till the price goes up. So many are selling their poultry because the price of feed is so high. I sold a case of eggs to Corbett; brought me 31 cents.

My hens are molting so don't get many eggs. To prove to you that cleaning hen houses is not my sole occupation allow me to tell you that I took the brush hook this afternoon and cut out the old canes from one row of blackberries. Got pretty well scratched up too.

Mr. Bradley has lost 25 chickens. Thinks some one stole them. You ought to be here for someone may try to steal mine and you are a good protector.

The surveyors say this road is to be commenced in the Spring. All the telegraph poles will have to be set back and trees cut down that come within the limits of the road. Miller's stone wall and his maples will have to go I expect. The road is to be 14 ft. wide each side of center.

We will be nearer the road than ever. It will come pretty well up to the apple trees, so we can't have much comfort under the trees. But it will make all property along the road more valuable.

Mr. Miller moved his house the wrong time. If he had waited till now the state would have to pay for moving it as it pays for all damages along the road.

Am glad you are going to have a chance to see the big men and hear them speak. E.G. Lewis calls Roosevelt, Taft's wet nurse. Pity you couldn't hear Bryan too so you could judge between them.

It is about half past ten so I must stop. Take care of yourself. Hope you haven't had a cold yet.

Your loving Mother

October 21, 1908
Dear Girlie,

Dad saw Walter Scott the other day. He said it was the young Leavenworth girl that was teaching. He was mad, the parents were mad, and the children were mad because Mr. L. didn't hire you. He said he ought to have given you your price and more too.

Louie sold his father's things to settle the estate. Dad bought a tool chest with number of tools for about $2, a lot of lumber, and an old carryall wagon, without a top which he thought he could fix up for the butcher wagon (which he got for $2), and a few little things.

We have been having more fires. Day before yesterday we could scarcely see the schoolhouse the air was so thick. Last Saturday someone set Chapins Park on fire. He had a big force out fighting it. It is so terribly dry, fire travels fast. And water is so scarce. Our well has no water yet.

The further spring is nearly

dry. Dad said he could only get water enough from the other spring to fill one can and water two cows. He draws the water for the pigs and for me to wash from Jordan Brook. He is afraid he will have to draw for the cows if we don't get rain. That will be a terrible job.

I hope the ground won't freeze up before the springs get filled up. If it does we will be in a bad fix.

Your standing in Drawing is very good. I would like to know what prospect there is of your coming home at Thanksgiving.

By the way, how do you keep your stockings up if you don't wear corsets?

Geo. Wells don't like the state road any better than Dad. He says it will cost $50 a mile to keep it in repair and the taxes will have to be raised to pay it; the state won't pay for any damages done.

He says you should see some of the houses on the Jeffersonville State Road. Great big banks of dirt in front of the houses. If they cut through people's backyards, make them move their barns or houses, they won't pay for it. I don't think they can hurt us much unless they cut down our apple trees. Dad thought maybe we could get pay if they cut the maples, but I guess not. Think our nice cherry tree will have to go, too. Well we won't borrow trouble till the time comes.

Dad wants to know if you can make an estimate of what money you will want.

I am anxious to sell my chickens. Feed is so high, that I can't seem to be able to. I sent my last eggs to Corbelt (30 dozen). He paid me 32 cents. The expressage and carting were .45. That netted me about 31. They are now .35 in Monticello. I suppose they will keep on climbing. I get from 2 to 6 eggs a day.

I suppose before you write again you will have seen and heard one or both of the prospective presidents. I wonder why they selected Cortland.

Be careful and not take cold.
Your loving Mother

Jennie Crandall, Eldred, to Lillie Austin
October 25, 1908
Dear Lillie,
It is rainy here tonight.

East River Bridge postcard to McKinley Austin from Jessie in November 1908. Postcard is courtesy of Mary Briggs Austin.

Mrs. Ort was sick yesterday, but is better today. Steve Dailey's wife has had a miss slip. Norah Avery came near having one too. Every kid around one might say, has the whooping cough.

Was up to Leavenworths yesterday afternoon. Of all the days in the week, Mother and Dad came down. I met them going home.

Alex Boyd is to be married the 29th of this month I believe. Mr. Crandall has bought a new house.

Lillie going riding. Photo courtesy of Katherine Calkin Traxler.

1908 Presidential Election

W.H. Taft and J.S. Sherman were the Republican nominees. 1908 postcard sent to the Austins, courtesy of Mary Briggs Austin.

William Howard Taft, Secretary of War and close friend of President Theodore Roosevelt, was the Republican Party candidate for President of the United States in 1908.

The Democratic nominee was William Jennings Bryan.

Bryan had been defeated in 1896 and 1900 by Republican William McKinley, but Bryan was very popular with the liberal segment in the Democratic Party.

William H. Taft was elected President.

These two postcards were in the Austin Family Collection.

The full dinner pail for mine, most likely refers to the 1900 U.S. presidential slogan of William McKinley: *Four more years of the full dinner pail.*—wikipedia.org.

"Four more years of the full dinner pail" was the 1900 U.S. presidential slogan of William McKinley. This 1908 postcard was sent to Mort Austin. It is in the Austin Collection.

We gathered an awful lot of chestnuts and they are half and half now. Half worms and half chestnuts.

Lottie Leavenworth says she likes teaching first rate.

I told you Eva Wormuth's husband had his arm off didn't I?

Have had an awful cold, is better now. George is shoemaking even though it is Sunday night. It is a case of necessity.

Mother, George, and I treated our heads to a kerosene shampoo and I declare it is the first my head has stopped itching since the fourth day of July when we got so sandy going to Liberty.

Lovingly,
J.J. Crandall

**Emma Austin, Bethel,
to Lillie E. Austin, Cortland, N.Y.**
October 29, 1908
Dear Girlie,

We are having the finest rain ever. One almost wants to shout, Hurrah! Saturday it drizzled, ditto Sunday.

Monday morning it commenced to rain very gently and kept it up all day. It cleared up about 11 o'clock yesterday morning.

Last night it was bright starlight, and raining very gently. It was raining when I got up this morning and is raining still. Just a gentle rain that does lots of good.

We needed it badly enough. One spring is about dry and Dad could get but 4 pails at a time from the other. This morning the well had water enough to sink the bucket; that is about 10 or 12 inches. I guess the drought is over for this fall.

Dad is out today with his cart. Shouldn't wonder if he got damp. I took the time while he was away and cleaned the woodshed.

It is about 4 o'clock now. I put my clothes to soak last night. Expecting to wash today, so every little while, I swing the lever a few times, and if it clears in the morning, they will be ready to hang out.

I'm sorry you won't be home Thanksgiving, but it would not pay for so short a time.

Have not seen the carryall as Dad hasn't it home yet. He says it is a 2-seater, but thinks it has but one. That it is one of the first makes with a wooden axle instead of an iron one. Don't expect it will be just the thing for us to ride in, for Dad grins when he speaks of it.

I suppose when you write again, you will tell us your opinion of Taft. You won't be apt to see Bryan will you?

I wish you could tell which you liked best. Well, they will soon be over their fighting. They have both promised the same things, so perhaps it won't make much difference who wins.

I haven't sold my chickens yet. They are down to 10 cents now in Monticello. I told Dad to have the mailman find me a purchaser as they are eating too much feed. That feed given to the hens might bring me more money.

I have about 25 spring chicks to sell. If I ever do, I will send you the money. Let us know when you need the money.

I got a postal from George [Ellery] Monday saying he had been dreadfully busy. The card was a very fine picture of himself.

It is now after 9 o'clock and the stars are shining. I think I will go to bed.

Good night.
Your loving Mother

Writer Unknown, Lava, N.Y., to Lillie E. Austin, Cortland, N.Y.
November 25, 1908

1908 Christmas Postcard courtesy of Mary Briggs Austin.

This morning I took a cup of coffee for breakfast and didn't feel a bit sleepy all day. I intend to go home Wednesday this week, eat my Thanksgiving dinner at home, and come out Thursday and stay over till next week.

Freddie and Bill haven't been to school yet as they still cough (from having had the whooping cough). John was taken with appendicitis just before I came out here and was quite sick for a while, but Smith fixed him up with ice bags so that he didn't need an operation. Mother kept him out of school till he gained a little of the weight he'd lost.

I asked Miss Leavenworth if it didn't seem funny not to have any Metzgers in school. There were six of us the last time she had the school. Lottie Leavenworth had the Fosterdale school about three weeks and then got the whooping cough. I believe she is still home and Bertha Wilson is substituting for her.

I went to Institute this year with Miss Leavenworth, Lottie, and your Aunt Aida. Truman drove us out and back and out in Black Lake. The horses wanted to turn up toward Bethel. I laughed and told him it was easy to see where they'd been used to going.

Institute itself wasn't so lively this year. They didn't ask enough questions. I don't care if they do keep us hopping. I like things to be interesting.

Writer unknown

T.K. Collins, Sommerville, N.J., to J.E. Austin, Bethel
December 9, 1908
Friend Eldred,

I tell you Ell, there is nothing that would give me greater satisfaction than to sell this farm and go back to my old home. Everything looks fine here, just now grass of 4 or 3 inches high. Oats are coming through the ground nicely. Some of the farmers have their potatoes planted and are plowing for corn.

Of differences in planting here and up there I don't think is more than a week, but we have so much rain and wind never lets up. We just have had 40 hours of a heavy rain and tomorrow it will blow for a day or two. Then we will have 2 or 3 clear, then it will rain again, so it keeps it up.

I have not been well since I have been down here and for the

Barryville Glass Factory

The Barryville Glass Factory was built by William A. Gibbs & Company around 1909. It was a glass cutting shop which produced some very beautiful and famous cut glass pieces.

Glass Factory Pond was created by damming up Halfway Brook near the factory. The pond was needed for the waterwheel used to etch fine glassware for companies such as Libbey.

During a drought, the water level in Glass Factory Pond would get too low, and the wheel, of course, would not work.

Then men from the Glass Factory would sneak up at night to Highland Lake (5 or so miles northeast), and pull out the spillway or slash boards that were used to control the water flow into Halfway Brook. The water would rush out to the dammed up pond near the Barryville Factory, and there would be enough water to get the waterwheel going for a couple days. But someone would discover the boards had been pulled out and would put them back.

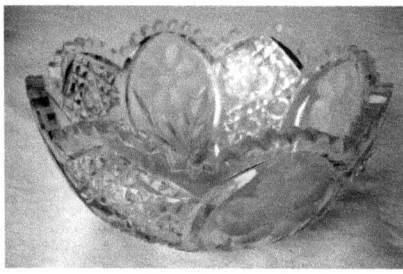

Herb and Margaret Wolff own this cut glass dish which was made at the Barryville Glass Factory. Photo courtesy of Cynthia Leavenworth Bellinger.

Halfway Brook was dammed to create Glass Factory Pond near Barryville. Slide courtesy of Charles Paulus.

past 4 or 5 weeks I have been quite sick with my old stomach troubles, but don't think that I ever had it so bad. I think it is too damp in this section. We are almost on a level with the ocean. But no doubt it is a great grape and corn belt.

You say you was down to Eldred the other day and was up to the old place. I suppose it does look lonely enough. Well, we expect to go back to it this summer or next fall. We will try and sell this for I know that my health will not permit me to live here. Hoping that you and your family are all well. All wish to be remembered to you all.
T.K. Collins

Mrs. Machin, Newark, N.J., to Miss Aida Austin, Eldred
December 25, 1908
Dear Aida,
Could not let this time of year pass without wishing you a very happy Xmas. I think of you often.
Fondly,
Mrs. Machin

Spring House
In January 1909 Chris and Meta Meyer became the new owners of the Barryville Spring House, which once belonged to George Layman. Meta Meyer bought the property from John and Annie Meyer, her in-laws, for $2,750.

Near the Parker Hotel
In 1909 Emily Parker married Howard Stevens, whom she had met when he boarded at her parents' Parker Hotel. Howard and Emily Stevens lived with her parents, James Y. and Emily Parker, at their Parker Hotel.

Several other families lived near the Parker Hotel, including Emily Stevens's brother William Parker, his wife Victoria Simpson, and their young children: James Y., William, Elsie, and Andrew Parker.

Victoria Parker's sister Nellie and her husband Robert Crandall had 2 children. Nellie Crandall was a good friend of my grandmother Jennie Austin.

George and Jennie Crawford Crandall would live near Robert and Nellie Crandall. Jennie Crandall's letters in this chapter are the last we hear of *Uncle George and Aunt Jennie* until Book 3.

Pelton Soda Factory

It is unclear when the Pelton Soda Factory (located in the former D&H Canal Office) in Barryville closed. Asher Pelton, the owner, died in 1904, but his wife Carrie lived a number of years after him. In the fall of 1909, Carrie Pelton sold the Pelton Soda Factory to her sons, Edward and Howard Pelton, for $1.

Howard Pelton was a soda water manufacturer and Edward was a soft drinks delivery man, according to the 1900 census. Howard Pelton's wife was Edith.

Back row, left: Mr. Armstrong, Charlotte Leavenworth, and Edith Pelton. First row, left: First lady was labeled Aunt Hattie Miller. Photo courtesy of Cynthia Leavenworth Bellinger.

Events in 1909

The U.S. penny was changed to the Abe Lincoln design in 1909. William Howard Taft became President. Robert Peary planted the American flag at the North Pole.

Art Rohman and His Hotel

In 1909 Art Rohman became the owner of the Shohola Glen House/Hotel near the Shohola Depot in Pennsylvania.

As I have heard the story, Art Rohman's father and friends decided that working on the railroad was not suitable for Art, so they got him the money to buy the old Shohola Glen Hotel in 1909, where he stayed (with only one vacation) until his death in 1973.—George J. Fluhr, Historian of Pike County, Pennsylvania.

After getting off the train at Shohola Depot, vacationers (as they had for many years) stopped at Rohman's Inn while waiting for a ride to the boarding houses.

Zane and Dolly Grey

The Greys lived about 5 miles west of Rohman's Inn. Zane and Dolly Grey had spent their honeymoon out West. When they returned, they lived in the old Holbert farmhouse (or cottage as they called it) that Zane had bought in 1904. Romer Grey and his wife lived next to them on the 2 acres Romer had bought and built a house.

The Holbert cottage "was not a favorable situation in which to live," Zane wrote a few winters later. "...When I awakened there was half an inch of snow on my coverlet, and a cold east wind nearly blew me out of bed. My feet are like blocks of ice all the time except when I am in bed."

Zane had also built an unheated one-room cabin (bungalow) for his office. One winter he wrote about, "huge cakes of ice floating, bumping

The Demise of Shohola Glen

Shohola Glen ended only three years after the death of its creator, John Kilgour.

Problems of passenger liability and interference with the increased volume of freight traffic on the Erie line, prompted railroad officials to terminate the Shohola Glen outings. The loss of the one dollar excursion fare, which had been the lifeblood of the Shohola resorts, resulted in the closing of the Glen in 1907.

Subsequently, in 1909, the Shohola Glen Hotel and a good portion of the Glen property passed into the hands of Art Rohman, a descendant of one of the first inhabitants of German Hill. He remained the proprietor of the hotel for the next 64 years.—Fluhr, George J., (editor), Pike County Historic Site and Scenic area survey, Vol. IV, Shohola Township, 1972, p. 10.

Eldred-Austin Cousins, 1910

The Austin cousins (children of Uncle Augustus and Aunt Maria Eldred Austin) that are known in 1910:

Alonzo Eugene and Belle Camp Austin lived in Eldred, but at some point moved to Port Jervis.

Information about their daughter Olinda Austin Ayers and her family is not known. Walter and Henrietta Austin Styles lived in Eldred. There will soon be a change in their lives.

Dr. Alonzo Eugene and Sara Hall Austin may have been in Chicago. Alonzo was a homeopathic doctor and seemed to have connections with people in high places, which he and his sister-in-law would use in 1918 to get information about their nephew.

Mortimer Bruce Austin was an attendant at the hospital. He and his wife Mary still lived in Middletown, New York. Their son and his wife, Charles Augustus and Mary Johnson Austin also lived in Middletown. They had two children, Alden and Mabel.

John Mortimer and Mary Hoatson Austin lived in Eldred. He is in the photo of a play given in Eldred. John M. Austin was a carpenter.

Henry and Net Austin Clinton lived in New Jersey. Henry was a brass finisher at a factory. Their daughter Ida Clinton Deal and her husband lived with them. Francis Deal was a brokerage clerk.

Rand (Miranda) Austin Paton, a widow, lived in Paterson, New Jersey, with her daughter Ida Paton and Ida's husband Charles Webster.

Archie R. Paton's first wife died in 1909, and he was left with 4 children under the age of 8. Archie then married Mable A. Slagle. Archie and Mabel Paton would have 4 children, including Dorothy Paton.

Edward D. Austin died in 1909.

---

into the bungalow."—From Library of Congress: LOC; HABS PA, 5371-Lack, 3.

In 1909 Mr. Grey's story about his adventures hunting mountain lions out west with Charles J. (Buffalo) Jones, a western hunter and guide, was rejected, but the next year he wrote a best selling Western.

George Mills Dies

The original Mills House on Highland Lake was some 12 miles northeast of the Greys' drafty bungalow. In February 1909 George Mills died at the age of 51. His wife Elizabeth, a very impressive woman, continued to run the Mills boarding house and raise their children: Belle, James, Agnes, Alexander, George, and Margaret.

William Henry Austin Dies

In April 1909 my great-grandfather William Henry Austin died at the age of 85. Henry had arrived around 1839, with his parents Ralph and Fanny Knapp Austin, in what was then the Town of Lumberland.

In Henry's later years he and his wife Mary Ann Eldred Austin had separated. Henry had lived with his son Mort and his family. Henry wrote very endearing letters to his children which were fortunately saved by several Austin family members.

Grandfather lived with us for as long as I can remember until he passed away, and this for us, was the first break in the family circle. McKinley (the oldest of my brothers) was 10 years and 3 months, Bill was 6 years and 1 day old, and I was 8 years and 4 months.

Grandfather had suffered with a bad cold for a few days and the doctor (Dr. F.I. Smith) had called the day before. The doctor said the cold itself was not bad enough to be dangerous under ordinary conditions, but due to age and a very weak heart, anything might be expected.

My father had gone to work on the George Beck place. About seven in the morning mother heard a noise in Grandfather's room, which was downstairs off the dining room.

She investigated and found Grandfather partly dressed lying across the bed. She surmised what had happened and ran over to our neighbor, Mr. Thomas K. Collins for help.

Mother, in her excitement, forgot to put her boots on, came back with wet feet and neglected to change shoes and stockings.

Bill and I slept in our parents room that night. Early in the morning (probably about 1 o'clock) I was awakened by my mother's coughing and half crying. She had been taken sick with pains in her chest and back, and Father, thinking he was giving her Jayne's expectorant, gave her a dose of oil of tar instead. When the doctor came he said that the oil of tar, harsh as it was, was more beneficial than the expectorant would have been.

This was the beginning of a case of pneumonia for Mother which, as I remember, kept her in bed over three weeks and made a long rest necessary for her after that. Possibly, she never did fully recover from all the effects of that siege of sickness.—Charles Raymond Austin.

William Henry Austin's funeral

Dr. Smith

The doctor who attended Mother was Dr. F.I. Smith of Shohola, Pa., a railroad station about six miles from where we lived at the time, about a mile east of Eldred, N.Y.

Dr. Smith was the first doctor I can remember and he practiced in the locality for thirty years, more or less. He was one of those dedicated men who earned for the country doctor the high reputation they so genuinely deserve. There is no doubt that he brought to that rural community, the most modern medical skill and knowledge of his time and practiced it with all conscientiousness and devotion that a human being is capable of. He was without mercenary motive, and his leniency with people who were so poor they had difficulty meeting their bills, certainly must have resulted in the doctor being victimized by some of the unprincipled element who never pay for anything if they can avoid it.

Dr. Smith, in my opinion, was unquestionably the most useful and valuable citizen that our community knew in my time there.—*Charles Raymond Austin.*

The family of Myrtie Crabtree: Ida Higginson Crabtree, Mary, Myrtie, LeRoy standing, Johnie sitting, John George Lewis Crabtree. Photo courtesy of Mary Briggs Austin.

was held at the Methodist Church on Thursday, April 9 at 1:30. Great-Grandpa William Henry Austin was buried with his wife Mary Ann Eldred.

After Henry's death, the Austin Mountain Grove House in Eldred must have been sold to Diedrich Schroeder who advertised it in the New York *New Rochelle Pioneer* paper, as a place to spend ones vacation.

Justin Bodine Dies

Justin Bodine, the original proprietor of Bodine Cottage on nearby Bodine Lake died in May of 1909.

The Briggs and Crabtree Families

The Briggs and Crabtree families lived in Nebraska in 1909. Amanda Myrtie Crabtree had a teaching certificate, and had taught first through fourth grades for 4 months. Myrtie worked for her room and board so she could attend the State Normal School in Wayne, Nebraska.

Irwin Briggs graduated from the high school in Ainsworth, around 1909. It had been too far to commute to school from the Briggs farm, so Irwin had *batched it* in town. While there in Ainsworth, Irwin saw a violin he really wanted. For graduation his father gave him that violin—the same violin that would be given to me when I was 10 years old. After high school Irwin went west and worked in the mines in Idaho.

Garfield Leavenworth

When Irwin arrived as the Methodist preacher in Highland (around 1935), he would enjoy spending time with Garfield Leavenworth who built and

This violin was given to Irwin Briggs by his father in 1909, and passed down to Louise (Austin) Smith when she was 10 years old. Photo: Gary Smith.

Kitty, William, and Ada Britt at Shohola Glen in July 1909. Photo courtesy of Richard James.

with their children, Charlie and Nora Gregory.

Mary Murray Parker Schoonover's Grandchildren

Mary Parker Schooonover's grandchildren Ada, Kitty, and William Britt visited Shohola Glen in July 1909. The girls lived in Brooklyn with their grandmother, and her children, George and Kate Parker. George Parker was a stock clerk at a wagon factory.

Being near the Big City gave the women a chance to earn some money with their piece work. Kate began making cravats—not ordinary ties—and the jobber she contacted was glad to give her materials a sum, probably not nearly what her fine work was worth. Kate's outstanding needlework was her only source of income, of "folding money," until she died.

The Britt girls…went to Public School 108 and graduated from elementary school. Both Kitty and Ada went to Andrews Methodist Church Sunday School and took night classes at P.S. 108 in secretarial skills. Both secured jobs in the Wall Street area after

Mountain Grove House ad in New Rochelle Pioneer, June 5, 26; July 17, 1909.

repaired string instruments.

In 1909 Garfield and Ella Sergeant Leavenworth's son Sherman Clinton (Goldie) Leavenworth was born in Eldred. We will talk more about the Eldred Leavenworths in the next chapter.

Hazel and Lottie Leavenworth

Out west in Dunton, Colorado, Hazel Leavenworth graduated from eighth grade. Hazel lived with her sister Lottie Leavenworth Andeway. The girls' mother Amelia Bradley Gregory and her husband Eber Gregory lived in Colorado

Christmas in Brooklyn 1911. Mary Murray Parker Schoonover and her descendants. From left in back: Kitty Britt James, Rowlee Schoonover, Thomas Wood, Alice Wood, Ada Britt Wood, Mary Murray Parker Schoonover holding Elwood James, Kate Parker, Justina Schoonover kneeling in front of Emily Schoonover Waidler, Arthur Wood. Photo courtesy of Richard James.

a stint packing perfume for Colgate's and chocolates for Loft's.

Then came dating, and if Grandma Mary approved, some courting followed. If the young man looked the least bit shifty eyed, Grandma Mary would frequently interrupt the parlor visit by winding up her big clock and loudly announcing the time.

They had girl friends. Alice O. Wood was one of them. Her brother Arthur seemed smitten with Ada, who in turn, hid when she heard his motorcycle out front. But gradually he convinced her that she'd enjoy a slow ride safely perched on the back.

Arthur did not smoke which Ada considered a big plus, nor did he drink liquor. He also had a good job and a good Cooper Union education which gave him Grandma Mary's vote.—Norma Wood James, daughter of Ada Britt Wood.

Ada later married Arthur R. Wood who had begun his career in Naval service in April 1904 as an apprentice machinist.

Kitty Britt married William Henry James. There is a photo of the Parker/Schoonover family which includes baby Elwood James, son of William and Kitty Britt James.

Caruso and the Victor Talking Machine

In 1910 Enrico Caruso, the famous singer, had been making recordings with the Victor Talking-Machine Company for 6 years.—wikipedia.org.

Aunt Aida heard Caruso sing and told me that all the things she had heard about what an objectionable person he was could hardly be credited because anyone who could sing like that could not be a really bad person. —Melva Austin Barney.

Victor and Edison Talking Machine Ad from New Rochelle Pioneer, July 1910.

Rowlee and Emily Schoonover

Daniel Rowlee Schoonover, his wife Emily Banner, their 3 children: Justina, Ethel, and William P.; and Grandmother Eliza Banner lived in Manhattan.

After leaving the Shadlot company, Rowlee worked as a blacksmith and fixed wagons at William Weygant's shop in Tuxedo Village, New York.

In 1905 Weygant and Rowlee signed up to be selling agents for some of the manufacturers at an auto show. One of the vendors (Maxwell) taught Rowlee to drive, and Rowlee drove for people that leased cars from them.

After surgery for a hernia, a Dr. Douglas was ordered by his doctor to travel only by automobile and recommended Rowlee as the driver. (Dr. Douglas, a minister, was impossible to work for.)

After a terrible test drive, Dr. D. offered Rowlee a job as chauffeur in 1906, though he did not have an auto yet. The auto arrived in 1907.
Rowlee quit the job in November 1909 after a dispute with Dr. Douglas. After a few weeks, Rowlee was rehired by William Weygant.—John Hull.

Joanna Brown Bradley Dies

It was a sad day in November 1909 for the seven Bradley children and their father Isaac M. Bradley. Joanna Brown Bradley, daughter of Mary Mercy Harding Brown Clark, died at the age of 67.

The Averys Run the Bradley House

About the time Joanna died, Isaac M. Bradley made a deal with his daughter Norah and her husband Erwin (Ernie) D. Avery, for them to run the Bradley boarding house.

The Avery family then moved

Mary Schoonover's daughter Emily Schoonover and her husband Will Waidler lived in New Rochelle, New York, in 1910.

Isaac M. Bradley and Joanna Brown Bradley. Photo courtesy of William E. Horton.

William Meyers Jr., son of William Meyers and Lottie Scott. Photo courtesy of Cynthia Leavenworth Bellinger.

1910 wedding photo of Burt and Lillie Austin Calkin. Photo courtesy of Katherine Calkin Traxler.

from White Lake where they lived, and took in summer boarders at the Bradley House.

Isaac Bradley retired and lived with the Avery family, as did his half brother John Bradley. Eventually the Bradley House became known as the Avery House.

William Meyers Jr.

There is a photo *(on page 279)* of young William Meyers Jr., Isaac M. Bradley's great-grandson. William Jr. was the son of Lottie Scott and her husband William Meyers Sr. (Jennie Crawford Crandall mentioned Lottie Scott in her letters several times.)

William Meyers Jr. would marry Anna Louise Leavenworth (who has not yet been born) daughter of Garfield and Ella Sergeant Leavenworth. This would be another Bradley-Leavenworth connection. There will be more about the other Bradley descendants in the next chapter.

In the following letter Henry Asendorf talks about a sad event regarding Bert Eldred's daughter. Perhaps the reference was to Delia Eldred, daughter of Herbert L. and Eliza Eldred, who died February 1910.

Henry Asendorf, N.Y.C., to Lon Austin, Eldred

November 30, 1909
Dear Lon,

I received your letter and was glad to hear from you. I was also pleased that the other side is a little troubled at present. Whether Aida wins out with W.W. or not, it will have a good affect on him and quiet him down.

Has anything further developed since you wrote me? I imagine they went to Monticello in regard to the assault on Bert Eldred's and Daly's daughters. I wonder how they made out?

I think if Draper were going to interfere, he would have done so long ago. It must make them sad after all the trouble of going to Albany and writing to get so little satisfaction.

Well, I hope Aida will have peace for a while anyway. I

Andrew S. Draper, Commissioner of Education. Photo in the collection of Aida Austin, courtesy of Mary Briggs Austin.

have heard nothing about the school at Venoge. I understand Mr. C. and Alex Wait were up to Narrowsburg, but did not hear any news about it.
Yours Truly,
Henry Asendorf

Andrew Sloan Draper

Andrew Sloan Draper was the first Commissioner of Education of New York and negotiated for a separate education building to be built near the New York State Capitol. The building cost about $4 million and was completed in 1911.—*wikipedia.org.*

There was a photo of Andrew Draper in Aida Austin's collection of photos and information, as well as a story Aida wrote about local school board politics that affected school District 4 in Highland.

Aida felt very strongly about education and fighting for what she thought was right.

Lillie Austin, Washington D.C., to Burt Calkin, Fosterdale, N.Y.

December 29, 1909
My dear Laddie,

Your girl is comfortably seated in her room at the Hotel Richmond. I hope you are getting on all right, and that you are careful of yourself.

I wish you were here with me, dear. I think I'd enjoy things more with you than with this crowd, although they are all right.

We missed our train in New York, and the storm had delayed traffic so that the train we did take was about 1-1/4 hour late. It was just midnight when we got to the hotel in Washington D.C.

5:10 p.m. Talk about being dog tired! We have done the Smithsonian Institution and the Natural Museum and I'm about done too.

We are going to the Library of

Left to right: A boarder from New York City, Ed Bosch, Herman Bosch, and Charlie Bosch after a hunting trip near Highland Lake in November 1912. Photo courtesy of the Bosch Family.

Charlie Bosch Sr. with a nice catch. Photo courtesy of Ken Bosch.

Congress tonight, three of us.

11:25 p.m. Have been to the Library of Congress and House of Representatives and now am dog tired. This chicken is going to bed. I wish I could see my dear laddie just a little while. I love you dear.

How I would like it if you and I could see these things together. If you hadn't been at the phone Sunday, I wouldn't have taken much pleasure in this trip.

I expect to come home Sunday on No.1 to Cochecton, but I don't think you had better try to meet me. I'd rather wait all winter than to have you take more cold.

Lovingly,
Your girl, Lillie

Burt Calkin Marries Lillie Austin
The above letter was from Lillie Austin to Burt Calkin. Burt Calkin and Lillie Austin were married in 1910. The Calkins lived in Bethel, some 14 miles northwest of the Wilhelm Bosch family.

Wilhelm and Charlie Bosch
Wilhelm Bosch and his second wife Mary Nellie Van Wyck/Van Eastenbridge, their daughter Christina; Wilhelm's children: Ed, Ralph, Tillie, and Menzo Bosch; and Mary's son, John Van Eastenbridge, lived at their Lake House boarding home, near Highland Lake in 1910.

Charlie Bosch would soon own close to 300 acres north of Highland Lake on either side of Bower Road.

Charlie Bosch's property was untouched woodland, accessible by old paths and unused dirt roads. This backwoods was used as the Bosch hunting and fishing preserve. Hunters came up yearly from the city and the Bosch men were guides.—Ken Bosch, grandson of Charlie Bosch.

Bosch Animal Stories
Hunting and fishing was a large part of life for many in the area, including the Bosch brothers. Ed Bosch wrote about the beavers and fish in nearby Mud Pond and Dry Bed Brook; and his best fishing trip ever at Stege's Pond.

When the beavers came here, they landed in Mud Pond. They built a large dam near the old road bridge and had a big house by those logs; and one at the upper end of the Pond. They cut lots of those big poplar trees down, and only took the branches and the top ends, the 6- to 8-inch size. They were cut in 4- and 5-foot lengths, and were there for a long time.

Patsy Clark [more about him in the next book] used to shoot some of them and sell the fur or skins in New York City. The Law was on them. Patsy said he found one beaver dead; a tree fell on its tail and couldn't get it off, so he died. A few years later the beavers was all over. They built a dam in the Dry Bed Brook and flooded

A delightful photo of Mary Elvira Horton with her mother, Anne Stanton Horton. Photo courtesy of Victoria Kohler.

George W.T. and Martha Mills Myers' boarding house, Lake View, on Highland Lake. George and Martha Myers were Jennie Austin's Uncle and Aunt. Photo courtesy of Christena Stevens Myers.

that big swamp.

Then they got in Steges' Lake and burrowed big holes in the banks. Some places they cut apple trees down and all kind of mischief, but some trappers made a good dollar.

Charlie [Ed's brother] and I put some pickerel and a few pails of bait fish in Dry Bed Brook and in a few years, it was good fishing there.

I was ice fishing one time up on Stege's Pond. I took my jigger and some elbow macaroni with me. It was a nice morning, not too cold. There was some other men fishing there, so I got started fishing and the fish bit so fast I couldn't take them off the hook fast enough. I caught 200 big perch and 6 big pickerel in one hour. I put them on a strong rope, and had to drag them to my car, as they were too heavy to carry. It took me all day to clean them. We put them in the freezer and we had fish for two years, the best fishing I ever had.—Ed H. Bosch.

Other Families Near Highland Lake

There were a number of other families we know who also lived in the Highland Lake Area, or near Eldred Corners, in 1910.

Anne Stanton Horton, a widow, lived nearby. Several of Anne's children lived with her, including Mary Elvira Horton who would marry Herman Bosch.

George W.T. and Martha Myers' large beautiful Lake View House was on the east side of Highland Lake, less than 2 miles (by road) from the Bosch family's Lake House. George and Martha's son Martin D. Myers was a teamster; son Charles C. Myers, his wife Lena, and their son Harold Myers lived in White Plains, New York.

The Boyd, Wait, and Mills families had boarding houses near George and Martha Myers.

Louis and Mary DeVenoge Miller lived east of Highland Lake near DeVenoge Lake. Louis, a Frenchman, also farmed. Perhaps Louis and Mary ran her father's place as a boarding house. Their neighbors were James and Margaret Boyd and their four children and Mary Wait and her son Alexander.

Thomas and Emma Collins must have moved back to Eldred. They had an adopted son, Robert (Robbie) Croft.

Gus Myers ran what was once his parent's boarding house. Edith Masvidal was the cook and Louis Basque was a helper. Perhaps Rebecca Masvidal was the housekeeper. Rebecca may have been the gal that smoked a pipe.

Herbert L. Eldred, his wife Eliza Post, their five children, and Herbert's uncle James D. Eldred, a widower, possibly lived in the home of C.C.P. and Effa Eldred, Herbert's grandparents.

Mort and Jennie Austin and their sons McKinley, Raymond, and William still ran Homestead Cottage on Collins Road.

This chapter focused mainly on Mort and Jennie Austin's family and people who lived on the east side of Eldred.

Chapter 9 starts with Jennie Austin's Leavenworth relatives who lived on the west side of Eldred, not too far from Yulan. The chapter includes Austin letters, information and photos of the families, and the known boarding houses near Washington Lake and Yulan, as well as some other ones in the Town of Highland.

Chapter 9
Echo Hill Farm House
1910–1916

Little brook, sing to me;
Sing about the bumblebee
That tumbled from a lily bell and grumbled mumblingly,
Because he wet the film
Of his wings, and had to swim,
While the water bugs raced round and laughed at him.

Little brook, sing a song
Of a leaf that sailed along
Down the golden-hearted center of your current swift and strong,
And a dragon fly that lit
On the tilting rim of it,
And rode away and wasn't scared a bit.
—*From* The Brook Song, *by James Whitcomb Riley.*

Figaro, the Leavenworth cat at the water pump. Photo courtesy of Cynthia Leavenworth Bellinger.

Blind Pond Brook still flowed behind the old Leavenworth home, Echo Hill Farm House, run by Sherman S. and Maria Myers Leavenworth.

Sherman Leavenworth had grown up in the home, as did his daughter Jennie Leavenworth Austin, my grandmother.

Jennie, her husband Mort, and their three sons lived on the east side of Eldred, near the Myers boarding house which Jennie's uncle Gus Myers ran.

Jennie's uncle George W.T. and his wife Martha lived a bit further east, and ran Lake View (mentioned at the end of the last chapter) on Highland Lake.

Soon Mort and Jennie Austin would have a new little one. And when this little one was 9 years old, she would write, *The Brook Song,* by James Whitcomb Riley in her mother's recipe and poem scrapbook.

The Leavenworths loved cats, so it was fun to find a photo of their cat, Figaro, beside the Leavenworth water pump.

Sherman and Maria had been married 35 years in 1910. Their children, Anna, Truman, Martin, Charlotte, and Christina Leavenworth lived with them at Echo Hill Farm House.

Anna and Charlotte were teachers. Charlotte would soon be her nephews' school teacher in Eldred. Christina would also teach for a few years. Christina was musical and played the organ. Christina and Charlotte, being the two youngest, were always close.

Truman was responsible to get the guests at Shohola. He also took the boarders on excursions to visit the countryside.

Echo Hill Farm House run by Sherman S. and Maria Myers Leavenworth. Photo courtesy of Christena Stevens Myers.

The Leavenworth family who lived at Echo Hill Farm House: Christina, Charlotte, Anna, Maria, Martin, and Sherman S. Leavenworth. Photos courtesy of Cynthia Leavenworth Bellinger.

Boarders in front of Echo Hill Farm House. Standing, second from left, is Charlotte, Christina is kneeling, and Maria Leavenworth is standing next to her. Martin Leavenworth is sitting, second from the right. Photo courtesy of Cynthia Leavenworth Bellinger.

Martin, you may recall, had been very ill as a child and his mind never developed past that of a 5 year old. From later stories we learn that Martin (who was well over 6 feet tall) helped by doing dishes or other such tasks. He seems to have been well cared for by his family.

Maria must have made wonderful meals. Her mother Jane Ann Myers was mentioned as a good cook in the *1881 Travelogue* of Charles E. Proctor, when he visited the area around Highland Lake.

Sherman, 67, still farmed, providing farm fresh ingredients for Maria's meals.

Guests at Echo Hill were also close to Washington Lake for swimming or boating.

There are a few photos of some boarders who stayed at Echo Hill Farm House in the Leavenworth Collection.

Garfield and Ella Leavenworth
In April 1910 Garfield and Ella Sergeant Leavenworth, their children Clara, 2, and 9-month-old Clinton (Goldie), lived on Airport Road southeast of his parents in a house that Garfield had built.

By August 1910 Garfield, Ella, Clara, and Clinton had moved to Easthampton, Massachusetts, possibly to find work. Ella's sister Hazel Sergeant lived there with their Aunt Ella Clark Howe. In August Garfield sent his sister Jennie Austin a postcard.

G. Leavenworth, Easthampton, Mass., to Jennie Austin, Eldred
August 1, 1910
Dear Jennie,
Here is a church in

August 5, 1910. "Dear Jennie, Here is a church in Easthampton for your collection." Postcard courtesy of Mary Briggs Austin.

The original Bradley Boarding House that was run by Erwin and Norah Bradley Avery and their 4 children: Laura, Beatrice, Arthur, and Gladys. Photo courtesy of William E. Horton.

William Jr. and Dorothy Meyers, great-grandchildren of Isaac Bradley. Photo courtesy of Cynthia Leavenworth Bellinger.

Easthampton for your collection.
  Your brother,
  Garfield

William and Lottie Meyers

William and Lottie Scott Meyers, their son William Jr., and daughter Dorothy lived in Garfield and Ella's home while the younger Leavenworth family was in Massachusetts. William Meyers Sr. worked at the sawmill and was a handyman. Lottie's mother Mary Frances Bradley Myers and her second husband Fred Myers Sr. and their family still ran their boarding house on Crawford Road.

Bradleys and Averys

Isaac M. Bradley (Lottie Meyers's grandfather) and his half brother John lived at the Bradley-Avery Boarding House with the Avery family: Erwin, Norah Bradley, Laura, Beatrice, Arthur, and Gladys Avery.

Isaac, John, and Erwin farmed. Erwin ran the boarding house and Avery's dairy.

The Bradley-Avery boarding house was within walking distance of fish-shaped Washington Lake where two of Isaac Bradley's children had boarding houses.

Laurel and Lake View Cottages

Abel and Viola Bradley Hazen, and their children, Mabel and Lewis, ran Laurel Cottage. Their boarding house was near the southern tip of the fish tail.

Atwell Bradley's Lake View Cottage (later Park Hotel) was north of Laurel Cottage, closer to the northern tip of the fish tail. Atwell had married Helen Heinekamp after his first wife's death. Atwell and Helen had 3 sons: Clifford (from Atwell's first marriage), George, and Clarence.

Tether Boarding Houses

Isaac Newton Bradley, his wife Jessie Tether, and their son Clifton lived in Brooklyn. Jessie was the daughter of Joseph and Anne Tether who owned two boarding houses: Washington Beach House and Washington Lake House, both on Washington Lake.

Joseph and Anne's son Walter Tether and his wife Meda Breen would later run Washington Beach House. Walter, Meda, and their son Ivan Joseph Tether (Sr.) lived in Barryville.

There is a story in the Tether family that Teddy Roosevelt visited Washington Lake House. There is also a photo of the possible former

Isaac Bradley with granddaughters, Laura and Beatrice Avery. Photo courtesy of William E. Horton.

Barryville in 1910

Some of the jobs listed in the 1910 Census included: butcher, operator, hotel owner, clerk, realtor, laborer, boarding house owner, stone mason, livery, general store, blacksmith, school teacher, soft drinks delivery man, merchant, painter, engineer, clerk, fireman, lumberman, farmer, worker at glass factory, bridge worker, artist, bookkeeper, dressmaker, fireman, cabinet maker, machinist on farm, retired, sawyer at mill, ice cream parlor worker, and housekeeper, which, as we all know, involves a number of skills.

In Barryville, John Steele was still a butcher. Irving Quick was a salesman for a general store, which most likely belonged to his father Menzo Quick. Metho and Martha Quick lived on Tow Path Road.

Robert Schoonmaker was a trainman. Simon Fredrick, from Germany, was a druggist at the pharmacy. Edward Carroll was a superintendent at a lumber mill.

Ira Austin was still a blacksmith. His wife Minerva Drake was 65. Their daughter Mabel was married to Edward Smith, a butcher. Mabel and Ed's son would be Austin Smith.

Christian and Meta Meyer, from Germany, owned the Spring House on the Delaware River. Their children (ages 8 to 20) were: Anna, John, Minnie, and Christian. Daughter Minnie would marry Alexander Mills, and they would one day run the Spring House.

Fred and Margery Schwab had been married 40 years. They had a boarding house, but Fred was also listed as a gardener.

Charles Traver, a farmer, and his wife had a 2-year-old son, John Traver. John would be a barber when he was older, and live next to the Methodist parsonage where the Briggs family lived in 1935.

Several Gardner families still lived in Barryville. James E. Gardner, his wife Rebecca, and daughter Susan lived with James's brother Stephen St. John Gardner. James E. was a merchant. Stephen and his son James K. Gardner had the general store in Shohola, Pennsylvania, at one time.

James K., his wife Ella Breen, and daughter Edna, lived near Walter and Meda Breen Tether, and their young son Ivan Joseph Tether.

Herman and Katherine Rixton had 2 daughters. Herman was a school teacher. Mary Rixton was 78.

August Clouse lived with Edward and Kate Clouse Pelton and their son Asher Pelton. August was a carpenter.

Mary E. Nelson, a widow, had a boarding house near the William Kerr family.

William Kerr and his wife lived on Canal Street with their 2 daughters, Margaret and Jesse. William's parents, John and Mary Kerr lived with them. John and Katie Greening Kerr and their 4 children lived on the Kerr homestead in nearby Lumberland.

William and Phillip Flieger lived with their parents, John and Katherine Flieger. John Flieger, 68, was a retired tailor. Charles and Katherine Flieger had 2 children. He was a laborer.

Frank Wolff was a cutter at the glass factory. His wife was Mary.

Jacob Liebla was an edger at a lumbermill. His daughter Lola was a waitress at a boarding house. Three of his sons were cutters at the glass factory.

George Carner was a Notary Public. There are letters to and from him included in this book.

Napoleon B. and Fannie White Quick lived nearby in Lumberland. Their daughter Blanche Quick would marry Herman Worzel. Blanche and Herman would be the parents of Ruth Worzel Myers, a good friend of my mother, and the wife of Chuck Myers.

Herman Worzel was the brother of Raymond Worzel. Raymond's son would marry Martha Eldred, a descendant of James Eldred through his son Abraham Mulford Eldred and his wife Elizabeth Wheeler.

John and Meta Toaspern Lass had 4 children: Jay, Charles, Helen, and Harry Lass.

Charles and Lottie Bradley Colville lived in Barryville with their daughters Ruth and Esther, and son Leslie.

Postcard of Moonlight on the Delaware, Barryville, N.Y. From the collection of Aida Austin, courtesy of Mary Briggs. Austin.

View of Tether's Washington Beach House on the northeast side of Washington Lake. Photo courtesy of Ivan J. and Jana Tether.

president with Joseph and Anne.

A number of boarding houses were or would be on Washington Lake: some new, some which we have talked about previously, others about which little is known, and some unknown.

Lake View Farm
Alfred and Sophia Kaese ran Lake View Farm boarding house on the northwest side of Washington Lake. It may have been the same as Ed Prange's Lake View Farm that was advertised in the 1880s Erie Railway booklets and the 1890s *Brooklyn Daily Eagle*.

Board at Lake View Farm. Situated in the mountains of Sullivan County, N.Y.; 6 miles from Shohola; climate pure and healthy; no malaria; elevation 1,800 feet; Washington Lake 200 feet from house; good boating, fishing and bathing; boats free to guest; large piazza; table well supplied with fresh country produce from our own farm.

Terms $6 and 7 per week; children under 10 years half price. Edward Prange, Yulan.—Brooklyn Daily Eagle, *July 10, 1892.*

Highland Cottage
Highland Cottage, a huge resort on Washington Lake, had been owned by different people. Robert Miller bought Highland Cottage for $4,000, in 1902, but died the following year.

In May 1912 Robert's widow Louisa Miller transferred the property to their daughter, Edith Miller Kalbfus.

Other Boarding Houses Near Washington Lake or Yulan
T.W. Racine owned West Shore Cottage on Washington Lake.

William and Phoebe Middaugh Owen's Oakdene was near the junction of Airport and Washington Lake Roads. William and Phoebe Owen's daughter Pearl would marry Fred Defeo.

Sophia Peterson, a widow, her daughters Anna and Malilda, and her brother-in-law Fredrick, lived at the Peterson Cottage near Yulan Corners.

Edward and Georgiana Bornstein may have lived in the LaBelle home west of the Peterson Cottage. It is thought that the LaBelle house later became Bornstein's Grand View Boarding House.

Also in Yulan was the boarding house of Fred and Mary Metzger who also owned the bowling alley with the dance floor. Fred was also the Postmaster.

John Metzger, 75, and John

Boarding House Owners, 1910

Near Highland Lake
Mort and Jennie Austin
Wilhelm and Mary Nellie Bosch
George W.T. and Martha Mills Myers
James and Margaret Mills Boyd
Elizabeth Gillespie Mills
Augustus Myers
Maria Middaugh
Stephen and Charlotte Myers
Mary Mills Wait

North, Central, and West Eldred
Greigs
Becks
Abel and Maria Myers
Fred and Juliana Straub
James Y. Parker
Sherman and Maria Leavenworth
Erwin and Norah Bradley Avery
Fred and Mary Bradley Myers
Joseph Maier

Washington Lake/Yulan
Atwell Bradley
Abel and Viola Bradley Hazen
Alfred and Sophia Kaese
Herman Barber
Adele Bodine
Charles Fleiger
Mrs. John Flieger
Wm. E. Owen
T.W. Racine
Joseph Tether
Fred and Mary Metzger
Edward and Georgiana Bornstein
Mary Wolff
Theodore West
Sophia Peterson

Barryville
Chris and Meta Meyer
Frederick and Margery Schwab
Ida Toaspern

Metzger Jr. and his wife lived nearby. One Metzger family lived in Yulan Cottage which we hear more about in Book 3.

To the east of Yulan, Adele Bodine, now a widow, ran Bodine's Cottages on Bodine Lake. Her son Henry, also widowed, helped with the boarders.

Mary Wolff, a widow, was the Proprietor of Side Hill Farm House, which seems to have become the Delaware View Inn after she died.

The Wolff and Kloss Families
The Charles Wolff family lived nearby in Tusten. Charles and his wife Jannette had six children: Carl, Frank, Agnes, Albert, Norman, and Anna. Carl would marry Frieda Kloss (sister of Lou Kloss) and they would be the parents of Herb Wolff.

Frieda Kloss lived with her parents, Ernest and Emma Kloss, who owned their farm.

Ida Toaspern
Chris Toaspern died in 1909. His widow Ida lived at the Toaspern's boarding house Maple Grove Farm, northwest of Barryville. Ida's son Walter Toaspern would marry Emma Straub, daughter of Fridolin and Juliana Straub who owned the Straub Hotel in Eldred.

Ida Toaspern's grandson Harry Lass (son of John and Meta Lass) plays a short part in our story. Ida's grandson Royden Arthur Toaspern was born to Arthur and Emma Keller Toaspern in 1911. Royden has a part in our story, as does his brother Walter (Bub). Ida Toaspern died in 1912. Maple Grove Farm was likely sold to a new owner by 1920.

John W. Johnston, Author, Dies
In March 1911 John W. Johnston died. He was the author of

Joseph Tether and guests at his Washington Lake House, which becomes the Colonial in Book 3. Photo courtesy of Ivan J. and Jana Tether.

Yulan Church Street. The Bornstein Boarding House is in the middle of the photo, this side of St. Anthony's Church. The postcard is courtesy of Kevin Marrinan.

Reminiscences, the history of the Town of Highland.

A New Sister for the Austin Boys
In March 1911 McKinley, Raymond, and Will Austin had a new sister—Elizabeth Austin. Mort and Jennie Austin, the happy parents, would have two more sons by 1915. Mort and Jennie would say they had two families as there were 8 years between Will and Elizabeth.

Joseph (l.) and Anne (r.) Tether with a guest (T. Roosevelt?) at Washington Lake House. Photo courtesy of Ivan J. and Jana Tether.

Elizabeth Austin, daughter of Mort and Jennie Austin. Photo courtesy of Mary Briggs Austin.

Robert Dale Calkin, son of Burt and Lillie Austin Calkin. Photo courtesy of his daughter, Katherine Calkin Traxler.

The Austins' New Cousin

A few months later, in August, Cousin Lillie Austin Calkin and her husband Burt Calkin had their first child, a son, Robert Dale Calkin, father of Katherine Calkin Traxler.

Robert Dale Calkin was the first great-grandchild of Henry and Mary Ann Austin. There would be 9 more—Dale's sister Dorothy Calkin, and the 8 grandchildren of Mort and Jennie Austin.

Burt and Lillie Calkin lived in Bethel, New York. Burt was a carpenter and built each of the three homes his family lived in. The first farmhouse was adjacent to where the Woodstock Music Festival took place in 1969. Burt sold that farm and built a temporary little house. Then he built a third house that the family moved into.

Hannah Calkin, Cliffside, N.J., to Burt and Lillie Calkin, Bethel
September 28, 1911

Burt and Lillie,
Was in Newark yesterday and spent last night there. Expect to go home Saturday. I am getting anxious to see my new nephew. I hear you were out home with him Sunday and I want you to be sure and go out next Sunday so I can see you. Now don't forget. I will look for you.
With love, from
Hannah

James D. Eldred and Net Clinton

James Daniel Eldred, son of C.C.P. and Effa Eldred, died September 8, 1911 in Eldred.

Cousin Net Austin Clinton, daughter of Augustus and Maria Austin, died in October 1911.

Mary Mellan

Mary Mellan's family was from Romania where her father was the mayor of a little town. He was able to get the paperwork needed to send his wife and her sisters to America so the new little one (Mary) could be born in the U.S. and have dual citizenship, making it easier to travel.

In November 1911 Mary Mellan (who lives on the east side of Eldred near her son Ed Mellan) was born in Garfield, New Jersey.

When baby Mary was 6 months old, she and her mother went back to Romania, where Mary grew up. Mary went to school with her future husband, who she would marry in the U.S. many years later. The next time we meet Mary, it will be 1927 (in Book 3), when she arrives back in the United States.

Shohola Monument

Perhaps you remember the tragic train accident of July 1864. A train with 18 cars carrying Confederate prisoners and Union Army guards was hit head on by a 50-car coal train, between Lackawaxen

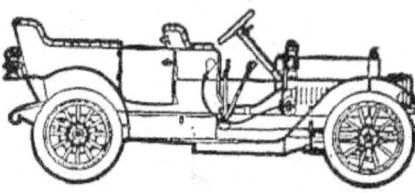

J. H. Walsh, Motor Cars
—AGENT FOR—
OLDSMOBILE AND OAKLAND Automobiles.
161 Fourth St., ELMHURST, L.I.

12 Models $1000 To $7000.   Thirty To Sixty H. P.

The above cars have a Five and Ten year reputation of which no cars built can be more highly recommended as to their reliability.
To own an Oldsmobile Autocrat, selling at $3500 is to know you have the best.
The Oakland, selling from $1000 to $1600 has set the pace for 1911.
The Oakland is made for the man who says—"SHOW ME."
Write or phone for catalogue and Demonstration.   Tel. 560 "w" Newtown

Ad from The Newtown Register, *May 30, 1911.*

Others in the 1910 Census

Mary Alice Whitney Kyte, widow of William Kyte, lived with her children Herbert and Mary Alice (who would marry Harry Wormuth).

The McBride family lived in the area. Sherman was a sawyer at a mill. He and his wife Eliza had 6 children, including their son Ezra (Buck), who would marry Laura Avery.

Robert and Katie Greig had been married 20 years and were retired. Their children Belle and Bennett; a sister, and cousin lived with them.

William Ort was a farmer. He and his wife Bertha LaBarr had been married 4 years. Their children: Eleanor and William; William's mother Mary Ort; and brothers, Charley and George, lived with them. (Eleanor Ort would marry Emerson Lilley.)

Mrs. Mary Ort (who would live to be 104) was a mid-wife and delivered several of Garfield and Ella Sergeant Leavenworth's children.

Stephen and Sarah Wormuth lived on Crawford Road. Their sons Stephen and Harry were sawyers at the mill.

John Henry and Carrie Bogert Clark had been married 23 years. John was a sawyer at a mill, and at one time worked in the acid factory in Methol, New York. Their son Ernest, 16, worked at a sawmill. Ernest would marry Eunice Hallock, 12, within the decade. Ernest and Eunice would be parents of Stella, Vernon, and Orville Clark.

Eunice's parents were Samuel and Anna M. Hallock. Eunice had 6 brothers in 1910: Oliver Lewis Hallock (ancestor of Carolyn Hallock Clark), Wilbur, Raymond (future father of Doug Hallock, who would marry Emily Knecht), Merlin, and Edgar. Eunice's brothers, Howard, Carl, and Elmer would be born in the next 7 years.

Coe Finch Young died in Kellam, Pennsylvania, in April 1910. (Coe's mother was Eliza Gardner Young, daughter of Sears and Mary Keen Gardner.) Coe Young's wife Adaline Sweezy, a teacher, died 3 years later. Their daughter Jennie Young Rauner, her husband Louis Frank Rauner Jr., and their daughter Edna lived in Manchester, Pennsylvania. Edna Rauner would marry Ellis Maudsley, who also lived in Pennsylvania.

Charles Darling and his wife Lottie Myers (daughter of Jane Ann Myers) and their daughters Ida and Agnes, lived in the Binghamton, New York area. Charles was a wholesale dealer and they had a servant, Daisy. Daughter Edith had perhaps married.

Fred Myers and his wife Mary Bradley still had their boarding house on Crawford Road. Fred and Mary had both been widowed and each had children from their first marriage, and had their own children. Fred, Mildred, Ada, and Atwell Myers were listed living with them in 1910. Daughter Della Myers had married Harry Howlett in 1909. Della and Harry would one day own the home that once belonged to C.C.P. Eldred.

Chester and Florence Hammond Middaugh's son Herbert was almost a year old. We'll hear more about Chester, a laborer, in Book 3.

Abel S. Myers, his wife Maria Hankins, and their children, Norman and Lila lived in Orchard Terrace near the Eldred Congregational Church.

Walter and Cleta Myers Horton had 2 children. Walter was a teamster and ran a store.

Edwin V. Myers, his pretty wife, Mabel Owen, and their children: Raymond, Clifford, Gladys, and Orville, lived north of Barryville, off Brook Road. There was a little wooden bridge over Halfway Brook to get to their house.

Sarah Maria Middaugh, a widow, had a boarding house. Her daughter and husband, Henrietta and George LaBarr had daughters, Hazel and Francise.

Frank and Lena Ort had a one-year-old son, John. Frank was a laborer at the mill.

Ernest Clark with his parents Carrie and John H. Clark. Photo courtesy of Emily Knecht Hallock.

and Shohola. Those who died were buried in a trench near the accident location.

In 1911 the remains of the 49 prisoners and 17 guards were relocated to the Woodlawn National Cemetery in Elmira, New York. The names of 49 Confederate prisoners of war were inscribed on the Shohola Monument on the side facing south. The names of the 17 Union guards, all privates of the 11th Veteran Reserve Corps, were engraved on the side facing north.—*civilwaralbum.com*.

There are a number of documents and letters in the Austin Collection that indicate there was some dissension in the village of Eldred relating to the education of the students.

Lon Austin, Taxpayer
Lon Austin had been a truant

Ed Bosch with his new Indian motorcycle. The Indian factory team took the first three places in the 1911 Isle of Man Tourist Trophy. Photo courtesy of the Bosch Family.

Indian Motorcycles

In the summer of 1911, the race team for the Indian Motorcycle Manufacturing Company (originally called the Hendee Manufacturing Company) took the first three places in the Isle of Man Tourist Trophy.

Over in Highland Lake, Ed Bosch drove his very own Indian Motorcycle that had been built around 1911. The Hendee Company (George Hendee and Carl Hedstrom) had produced the first American motorcycle in 1901.—*indianmotorcycle.com.*

officer and, if Aida Austin's story is correct, through a series of twists and turns at board of education meetings for the whole town, Lon became the only school trustee.

This next letter, notarized by George Carner, indicates Lon thinks something is askew with the school taxes. The education situation will be updated later in this chapter.

George Carner, Barryville, to Lon Austin, Eldred
December 29, 1911

Albert A. Austin being duly sworn deposes and says that he is a taxpayer in School District #4, Town of Highland County of Sullivan State of New York.

That on December 5, 1911, he obtained a certified copy of the school tax roll on file in the office of H.L. Eldred, School Tax Collector for said District.

That certain amounts have been added to said roll, also that the name of George Sidwell has been placed on said roll. That the said Sidwell's name is not on the assessment roll for the year 1911 and 1912. That the said H.L. Eldred committed the above named acts placing his own assessment on the property of the said Sidwell, all without authority from anyone so far as I have been able to learn.

Also, that several other names were added and corrections made that the said H.L. Eldred acknowledged verbally in the presence of myself and George Carner; that he made the above named additions and corrections. That the total amount raised by vote of the tax payers at the annual school meeting for the year 1911–1912 was $800. That the present roll by reason of said additions now calls for the sum of $10,066.00, by reason of the above your petitioner requests that you do not accept said roll without a thorough investigation.

George Carner, Notary Public

Geo. Carner, Barryville, to Lon Austin, Eldred
June 20, 1912
Dear Mr. Austin,

Yours of today arrived this evening. We will soon begin to sell milk, but Mrs. C says she will pack you a small jar of butter. We are also packing a jar for Straub. We expect to deliver tomorrow evening. If we have any over, will send some to you, also.

I had no chance to see you

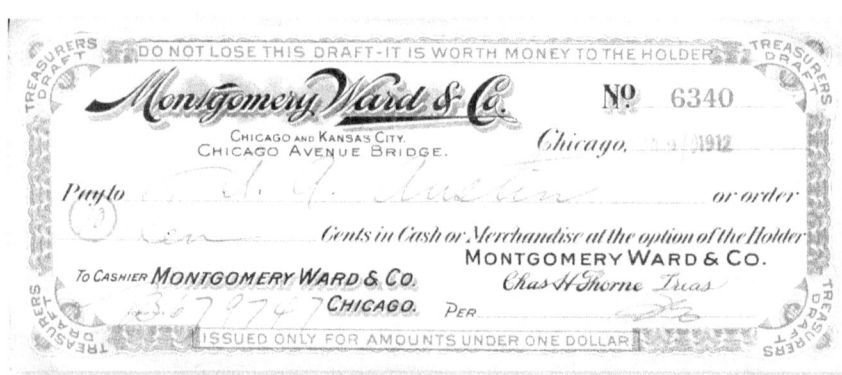

Ten cents from Montgomery Ward & Co. to Lon Austin, in 1912. In the Austin Collection.

the night of the school meeting, After the meeting, I had to make a purchase at Wilson's Store.

I haven't given up hopes of a thorough investigation of Town accounts. It is bound to come, I think. Your school district is #4; on 1908 page I find the following:

National Transit Standard Oil Pipe Line bal. 20,000. Dist #4: 8,132. The assessor apportioned the National Transit on follows:
Eldred......................6,099
Wills........................13,901
Empire and Keystone Telephone:
Eldred......................50.00
Yulan......................175
Barryville.................150

I think it would be very unwise to let anyone know where the 1908 roll is. Hope this information will be of use to you.
Yours Truly, Geo. Carner

Clifford Crandall, son of Robert and Nellie Crandall, was born on December 9, 1912. Little Clifford's siblings were Verna and Stanley. Clifford and my dad would be good friends.

Bertha Noe, Madison, N.J., to Willie Austin, Eldred
December 20, 1912
May you and your little sister and all the family have a very Merry Christmas. Bertha C. Noe

Mary Whitney, Royalton, Vt., to Jennie Austin, Eldred
December 23, 1912
Dear Jennie,
I hope you are all enjoying the Christmas season.
I intended to answer your nice letter long ago. I should love to exchange some Royalton views for Eldred views.
Remember me to all inquiring friends, Mary E. Whitney

Boarding House Ads 1910–1915

Woodbine Cottage, Yulan
Pleasantly situated; near all attractions, boating, bathing, fishing dancing; all home comforts. Address Mrs. A. John.—Brooklyn Daily Eagle, *June 12, 1910.*

West Shore Cottage, Yulan
Accommodates 40. Write T.W. Racine, Prop.—Brooklyn Daily Eagle, *June 12, 1910.*

Minisink Lodge, Yulan
On Washington Lake. Accommodates 60. Excellent table; 2 mails daily. McCormack and Haff, Proprietors. —Brooklyn Daily Eagle, *August 12, 1910.*

Mountain Grove House, Eldred
Before making arrangements for your vacation write to Diedrich Schroeder, Proprietor. Mountain Grove House, Eldred, Sullivan Co., New York.—New Rochelle Pioneer, *June 1910.*

Highland Bridge Hotel, Minisink Ford
First class Hotel and Boarding House on the Banks of the Beautiful Delaware River. Good Boating Bathing, Fishing and Hunting; $8 to $10 per week. George A. Schulz Prop.—The Newtown Register, *May 30, 1911.*

The Highland Bridge Hotel in Minisink Ford, New York, left, as viewed from Pennsylvania. Postcard courtesy of Kevin Marrinan.

Highland Lake House
120 guests; 7 miles from depot; on water. Henry Asendorf.—Brooklyn Daily Eagle, *1913.*

Mills House
40 guests Mrs. Geo. Mills.—Brooklyn Daily Eagle, *1913.*

Mountain Top Cottage in 1911. Mrs. John Flieger, Proprietor. Barryville, N.Y. Postcard courtesy of Larry Stern.

The oldest Bosch daughter, Minnie (Wilhelmina) Benedict, wrote to her aunt Annie Maier for apples for a New York City friend, Mr. Backus.

Minnie Benedict, Highland Lake, to Annie Maier, Eldred
January 17, 1913
Dear Annie,
I will take a barrel of nice apples. Please assort them for me as Mr. Backus will call in a few days to get them.
As ever yours, Minnie

Elizabeth Sergeant Dies
Elizabeth (Libbie) Persbacher Sergeant, wife of Isaac Sergeant, died January 23, 1913. Libbie and Isaac were the parents of Minnie Sergeant who would marry Archibald Myers.

Rebecca Eldred Dies
Rebecca Caroline Eldred died in February 1913. Rebecca had taught school and worked for her father C.C.P. Eldred at the Eldred Post Office. After her parents died, Rebecca went to Philadelphia and

Minnie Sergeant, future wife of Archie Myers. Photo courtesy of Chuck Myers, son of Archie and Minnie Sergeant Myers.

Archie Myers who married Minnie Sergeant. Photo courtesy of Chuck Myers.

worked in the Germantown Post Office. She then moved to Dallas, Texas, and finally went back home to Eldred and to her parents' homestead, where she died. The homestead may have gone to her nephew Herbert L. Eldred who had grown up in his Eldred grandparents' home.

Rebecca was buried in the old Eldred Cemetery with her brother, James Daniel Eldred.

Arthur Lawrence Austin is Born

Arthur Lawrence Austin, my father, arrived at the home of Jennie and Mort Austin, in March 1913. Art, named for President Chester Arthur, had blue eyes and weighed six pounds. His middle name may have been suggested by a lady boarding at their home at the time of his birth. Dad's siblings: McKinley, 14, Charles Raymond, 12, Willie, 10, and Elizabeth, 2.

Christina Leavenworth, Eldred, to Her Sister, Charlotte, Port Jervis

April 11, 1913
Dear Charlotte,

Received your letter. In regard to Mr. Sidwell's coming. He can come whenever it is convenient for him. Tell him if he has a pair of pincers or something to screw the pump together with he had better bring them, for we haven't anything for that purpose.

Have you missed your patent leather belt? I have it. Perhaps Mrs. Sidwell told you though. I forgot to put mine in my dress before I left home, so I borrowed yours. If you need a belt before I come, get one and I will pay for it.

I hope it won't rain all day, for it is my turn to lead the Epworth League [Methodist Group]. I'm afraid if it rains hard, it may be postponed till next week, then it would mean that I couldn't go to

1912 News

The Titanic sunk in 1912. It was also the year that latecomers New Mexico and Arizona became states.

The Titanic being built. Photo: Library of Congress, Prints and Photographs Division: LC-USZ62-26743; Lot 6668.

Port Jervis and stay over until Sat.

I heard Mother say sometime ago that she meant to have you look for wallpaper. Possibly we can look for it if I can manage to stay over Saturday.

Ten of us went to Barryville Tuesday night to witness the burning of the mortgage on the M.E. Church. Mrs. Van Housant (nee Proctor) lifted it. She also gave $100 for decorating the church. It was good of her, wasn't it?

Mr. Cosner was in with the rest of the order. Mother ordered some bond writing paper and envelopes. It's real nice paper too. I mentioned something about never using the house paper. Then he showed the Bond and said that he thought I would use that and so I will.

Well I'm going to write Anna so will close.

Love to all,
Christina Hayes Leavenworth

Anna Leavenworth, to Charlotte Leavenworth

April 22, 1913

1910 Town of Highland Property Values

Name	Acres	Lot	Value
Henry Asendorf	5.5 acres	Lot 24	$450
Aida Austin	2 acres	Lot 23	$10
C.M. Austin	37 acres	Lot 23	$225
A.A. Austin	9-1/2 acres	Lot 21	$475
Alonzo E. Austin	260 acres	Lots 21/22	$1,300
Ira M. Austin	2-3/4 acres	Lot 23	$400
Henry Bodine	80 acres	Lot 17	$1,000
Edward Bornstein	10 acres	Lot 16	$375
Wilhelm Bosch	50 acres	Lot 22	$600
James Boyd	5 acre	Lot 24	
Isaac M. Bradley	75; 25 acres	Lots 16, 17	$975
Atwell Bradley	5 acres	Lot 16	
August Clouse	1/2 acre	Lot 23	
Thomas Collins	76 acres	Lot 23	
George Crandall	2 acres	Lot 21	
Robert Crandall	2-3/4 acres	Lot 21	
Milton E. Crandall	200 acres	Lots 14, 15	
John Flieger	10 acres	Lot 22	$200
George Foster	50 acres	Lot 17	
Stephen S.J. Gardner	498 acres	Lots 15, 16, 21, 23	$2,775
Julia Greig Est.	2,773 acres	Lots 14, 16–21, 24, 25	$5,225
Robert Greig Est.	4,989 acres	Lots 14–21, 25	$8,500
Daniel Hallock	8 acres	Lots 22, 23, 24	$175
Mrs. E. Heyen	140 acres	Lots 17/19	$400
A.A. Hazen	56 acres	Lot 16	$1,000
William Hickok Est.	1/4 acre	Lot 24	$325
Thomas Hill Sr.	56 acres	Lot 21	$225
Chester Hulse	3 acres	Lot 23	$100
S.M. Kaese	37 acres	Lot 16	$600
John Kerr Sr.	46 1/2 acres	Lot 24	$500
LaBar Brothers	65 acres	Lots 17/18	$150
Anna Leavenworth	9 acres	Lot 18	$50
Garfield Leavenworth	28 acres	Lot 19	$150
S.S. Leavenworth	119 acres	Lots 18,19	$850
T.E. Leavenworth	28 acres	Lot 18	$100
Love and Son	HB	Lot 21	$250
Other properties	195 acres	Lot 19	$600
	5 acres	Lot 19	$25
	10 acres	Lot 18	$50
	90 acres	Lot 18	$400
	Mill	Lot 19	$200
John Metzger	75 acres	Lots 15, 16, 17	$625
Chris Meyer	1-1/2 acres	Lot 23	$1,000
Maria Middaugh	54 acres	Lots 21, 22	$350
George Mills Est.	153-1/4 acres	Lots 23, 24	$700
A.S. Myers	3 acre	Lot 21	
Gus Myers	296-3/4 acres	Lots 23, sub 10	
Jackson Myers	7 acres	Lot 21	
G.W.T. Myers	62-1/2 acres	Lot 24	
Charles F. Myers	50 acres	Lot 20	
Nelson; Gilbert Est.	160 1/2 acres	Lots 18, 23, 24	
William E. Owen	13/100 acres	Lot 16	
James Y. Parker	18 acres	Lot 20	
Pelton Brothers	1/8 acre	Lot 24	
Catherine Pelton	2 acres	Lot 16	
Peterson	25 acres	Lot 17	
Truman Racine	2-3/4 acres	Lot 16	
William Schoonover	130 acres	Lots 18/19	$500
	Mill	Lot 18	$100

The Herman Schumacher Est. had a hotel on 1/2 acre and had 3 other properties that totaled 204 acres. The Hotel was valued at $650 and the other properties totaled $800

Name	Acres	Lot	Value
Schwab	1-3/4 acres	Lot 22	

Stilling and Breckenstein had a mill on 4 acres valued at $500. They had 5 other parcels of land on Lots 16 and 17.

Name	Acres	Lot	Value
Alva Sergeant	11.5 acres	Lot 20	$200
Morgan Sergeant	66 acres	Lot 17	$275
E. Slonek	42 acres	Lot 20	$450
Edward Stage	13.5 acres	Lot 21	$50
Walter Styles	17 acres	Lot 21	$650
Fred Straub	2.5 and 2H1B	Lot 21	$1,000
Joseph Tether	195 acres	Lots 14, 16, 17	
Walter Tether	13-1/2 acres	Lots 22, 23	
Theodore West	98 acres	Lot 15	
Charles W. Wilson	188 acres	Lots 18, 20, 21	
	mill	Lot 21	
William Wilson	29-1/4 acres	Lots 18, 21	
Stephen Wormuth	40 acres	Lot 20	
John Wolfe Est.	185-1/2 acres		

A special thank you to Kevin Marrian who located and shared the 1910 tax records.

Charlotte Leavenworth, teacher. Photo courtesy of Cynthia Leavenworth Bellinger.

Christina and Charlotte Leavenworth. Photo courtesy of Cynthia Leavenworth Bellinger.

Dear Charlotte,

Your letter, the packet of notebooks, and the money all received tonight. Thanks for all.

I am suffering with a cold located chiefly in my nose and I feel like a rag.

Miss W. and I both got off a letter to an agency tonight to see whether it can get us such a position as we want.

Meanwhile I am going to write a line to Bertha. I don't think I would like it there, but I couldn't dislike it much more than this.

We had a brisk call from the truant officer this morning. The attendance in the big room was something terrible last week.

There is a new family here, the Doblingers. Mr. D. brought a little boy, Melvin, to school this morning. His card says he is backward in arithmetic and reading, but it seems to me he knows more about both than any child I ever saw of his age (he was 7) coming from the city schools.

Did you notice that Mrs. Wilson had applied for a position in Port Jervis there? She must have good grit; or else perhaps she doesn't know the circumstances.

I rec'd a fine blackboard drawing book tonight from the Davis Press, Boston. The only thing that is a drawback about it is that in much of the work one needs charcoal. If you are in any place where they sell school supplies will you enquire about it and send me some if you find it? Don't put yourself out however. I am ashamed to ask you to do anything more for me.

I am sorry Christina's hip has troubled her again, but I suspect those corsets very much. You better talk to her about wearing them.

Mother wrote me about her diet. Now there is something they call "gluten bread" for people with diabetes. Do you suppose they keep it anywhere in P.J.? Perhaps Mr. or Mrs. Sidwell would know where it could be found.

I shall be glad to get home, too. I wish I knew where I am going next winter. I always think if I were in your place I should have applied for the Johnson's principalship. I feel that Miss W. would be the better teacher for the place, but since Mr. Lewis is commissioner, of course, I know it is up to me to find my own school and I want to do it as quickly as possible.

Lovingly,
Anna

Belle Mills, The Mills House, Highland Lake, to Lon Austin
May 12, 1913
My dear Mr. Austin,

I received your letter and was glad to get such good news.

Many thanks for same.

Sincerely, Belle Mills

Charlotte Leavenworth

Charlotte Leavenworth, my great aunt, taught school for 50 years. She was 19 when she started teaching in Fosterdale. There she taught 8 grades for three years. Next, in 1911 Charlotte taught 50 students in grades 5–8 in Eldred. The following year she taught 8 grades in Tylertown.

In 1913 Charlotte taught 7 grades in Wellstown, and graduated from the Port Jervis Training Class.

In the spring of 1913, Lon Austin, the Eldred School Trustee, must have offered Charlotte a teaching job in Eldred.

Charlotte Leavenworth, Port Jervis, to Lon Austin, Eldred
May 14, 1913
Dear Mr. Austin,

Letter of Belle Mills to Lon Austin in May 1913. May 14, 1913 letter of Charlotte Leavenworth to Lon Austin. Letters in the Austin Collection.

After thinking the matter over, I have decided to take the principal room of the Eldred school this coming year, providing I pass the coming examinations which I fully intend to do.

I presume Miss Mills will have the primary department again—I hope so, but in case she shouldn't be intending to teach in that room, there is a Miss Mary Twitchell in the Teacher's Training Class at present, a daughter of Mr. John Twitchell, who will want a school next year and who in my judgment would be just the person for the position.

I expect to be home May 29th for a few days and will make the contract, if you wish, during that time. Yours truly,
Charlotte Leavenworth

**Agnes Wilson,
to Lon Austin, Eldred**
May 21, 1913
My dear Mr. Austin,
Since it will be necessary for me to accompany my daughter, next school term, and provide a home for her while she attends High School, I have not asked for this school, for the coming term, even though I would have enjoyed having it.

I want to thank you for all you have done toward making it a success this year, and trust that my successor may not meet any obstacles during her term.

My term as I understand it will close on Wednesday, June 4, 1913, and Belle's two days later. Now Mr. Austin, if you feel that you can give me a recommendation to carry away with me for future use, I will feel very grateful for it.

By the way, Raymond Myers broke the lock accidentally on the front door; one morning this

Christina and Charlotte Leavenworth picking corn on the Leavenworth Farm. Photo is courtesy of Cynthia Leavenworth Bellinger.

The Sergeant Family

Alvah Thomas Sergeant and his wife Margaret Clemens Sergeant. Photos courtesy of Cynthia Leavenworth Bellinger.

Garfield and Ella Sergeant Leavenworth lived on Airport Road before they moved to Massachusetts. Some of Ella's relatives lived near their home.

Ella's father Frank Sergeant and Anna Hull, his second wife, lived on Beaver Brook Road. Frank was a carpenter.

Frank's uncle Isaac Sergeant became a widower in 1913.

Frank's brother Alvah Thomas and his wife Margaret Clemens lived on Airport Road east of Garfield and Ella's home. Alvah was a photographer.

Charles Edgar Sergeant was also a brother to Frank. Edgar and his first wife Libby Clark were the parents of seven children including Charles Alvah Sergeant. After Libby died, Edgar married Henrietta. Two of Edgar's children lived with Edgar and Henrietta.

Charles Alvah and his wife Mary Hulse lived on Clark Road just as it went north off Airport Road; across from the Wilson Mill. They were good friends with Garfield and Ella.

Frank's sister Louella was married to Frank Kelley. Frank and Louella Kelley's daughter Raola was mentioned in Jennie Crawford's letters. We will hear more about their son Everett Kelley in Book 3.

Another sibling of Frank was Alice Sergeant Hill. Alice and her husband Thomas were the parents of John Hill. John and Esther Grinnell Hill's daughter Gladys would marry Raymond Myers, brother of Gladys who would marry Raymond Austin.

John and Esther's daughter Edna Hill would marry Oliver L. Hallock. Oliver and Edna were the grandparents of Carolyn Hallock Clark. John and Esther's son Alfred (twin of Alvin) would one day marry Elizabeth (Bessie) MacIntyre Lass.

Frank R. Sergeant and his siblings were the children of Alvah and Phebe Owen Sergeant. Alvah Sergeant (who died in 1897) was a great-grandson of Rev. Isaac Sergeant who had started the Congregational Church in Eldred.

Phebe Owen Sergeant, a widow, lived with her son Morgan (a widower in 1903) and a niece until March 1912, when Phebe died. She was the daughter of Morgan and Elizabeth Barns Owen.

Mrs. Phebe A. Sergeant, widow of Alvah Sergeant, died at her home in Eldred, Sullivan County, N.Y. on Monday morning after a long illness. She was aged 78 years, 4 months and 4 days.

For over 60 years she had lived in Eldred where she was well known and highly respected. She was a member of the Eldred Congregational Church.

The surviving relatives are three daughters, Mrs. Jane Livingston, of Yulan; Mrs. Thomas Hill, of Barryville and Mrs. S.F. Kelley, of Eldred; four sons, Charles, Frank, Morgan, and Alvah Sergeant, all of Eldred, and by 31 grandchildren and 32 great-grandchildren. The funeral will be held in the Eldred Congregational Church at 2 o'clock Wednesday afternoon.

---

week. I have asked him to see you about it, but he did not say he had, neither have I had that opportunity.

We have been talking of having the usual school picnic on the last day if agreeable to you. If not, kindly let us hear from you. Again, thanking you for many past favors,

I am Very truly yours,
Agnes J. Wilson

Edna, Cochecton, N.Y., to Lillie Calkin, Bethel
August, 25, 1913
Dear Lillie,
I can't go out this week. I didn't think about Miss Adams

when I told you I would come, but I can't leave her alone. The sick are improving.

In haste, Edna
(Burt Calkin's sister)

Belle Mills, The Mills House, Highland Lake, N.Y., to Lon Austin, Eldred
Sept. 23, 1913
My dear Mr. Austin,
I have heard that school is to open on Monday September 29th, so am writing to ask if I shall fill out and sign the contracts you left with me some time ago. If so, will you kindly let me know.

I am going to Port Jervis tomorrow for two days, but will do it as soon as I return if you say so.
Sincerely, Belle Mills

Anna L. Leavenworth is Born
Clara and Goldie (Clinton) Leavenworth, children of Garfield and Ella Sergeant Leavenworth, had a new sister in 1913. Anna Louise Leavenworth was born in October in Easthampton, Massachusetts, where Garfield and Ella still lived.

Archie Myers Marries Minnie Sergeant
Back in Eldred, Archibald (Archie) Myers married pretty Minnie Ethel Sergeant in December 1913.

Archie Myers would be in a partnership with Henry Von Ohlen who would marry Lila Myers, Archie's sister. Archie and Henry would own Von Ohlen's, a general store with a bowling alley, a dancing floor, and a player piano. The store would be opposite the Eldred Congregational Church.

In the back of the store would be a two-story addition. Archie and Minnie Sergeant Myers would live on the second floor. Henry and Lila Myers Von Ohlen would live on the first floor.

Wedding photo of Archie Myers and Minnie Sergeant. Photo is courtesy of Chuck Myers.

The Schoolhouse Problem
In the Austin Family Collection was a story written by Aida Austin about Eldred school politics that took place over several years.

Initially, the problem seemed to be that the powers-to-be tried to force the building of a new $6,000 schoolhouse on different property, based on a claim that the schoolhouse had been officially condemned. Aida had first hand information that the schoolhouse had not been condemned.

The townspeople had set up another meeting and voted in $595 to add an addition to the school. (Apparently if the amount was under $600, it did not have to go through official channels.)

Aida's story mentioned a few

Clinton, Clara, and Anna Leavenworth. Photo is courtesy of Cynthia Leavenworth Bellinger.

The Von Ohlen/Myers store. In back of the store was a two-story addition. Archie and Minnie Sergeant Myers lived on the top floor. The Von Ohlen's lived on the first floor. Photo courtesy of the Bosch Family.

more twists and turns, and behind the scenes information than the following December 1913 news account.

The village of Eldred is one of the liveliest spots in southern Sullivan. It is always somewhat of a paradox.

There is a place there called Sunshine Hall, but around its roof gathered for months the black clouds of bitterest neighborhood dissension, apparently the result of a determination to put down those in control and to pass the control to others.

Now Sunshine Hall is forgotten and for about two years, the fight has been around the schoolhouse. One faction demanded a new $6,000 schoolhouse and Superintendent Lewis has been with them. They have been in the minority however, and no special meeting would vote the money.

Last spring the district decided to build an addition to the present building and voted $600 for that purpose. The addition is nearly completed and the warrant for the collection of the tax is in the hands of the collector and most of the money gathered in.

Now comes a Mr. Austin and complains of Trustee Austin [probably Lon Austin] and with the aid of an affidavit from Superintendent Lewis to the effect

Austin Grocery Ledger, 1913–14

1 can baking powder .... .20	3 milk .... .36
5# baking powder .... .80	1 gallon molasses .... .60
3 qts. beans .... .36	2 oleo .... .56
1 broom .... .50	1 bottle peppermint .... .10
1 bottle Castoria .... .35	6# pork .... .96
1 package cinnamon .... .10	raisins .... .30
cloves .... .10	5 rice .... .40
1 can cocoa .... .30	saleratus (baking soda) .... .16
2 box cocoa .... .50	1/2 box salt .... .30
2# coffee .... .60	1 pk. salt .... .15
1 coffee pot .... .50	1 shirt .... .50
5 cornmeal .... .25	6 cakes of soap .... .25
2 cornstarch .... .16	1 pr. shoes 2.25
1 box exgrease .... .10	10 sugar .... .56
1 sack of flour 1.60	1# tea .... .50
1/4 ginger .... .10	3 tomatoes .... .30
3 kraut .... .36	3 box yeast .... .15
2# lard .... .30	Purchased from M. Quick & Company.

that the addition doesn't meet his idea of what Eldred ought to have; procures from the Vice Chancellor of the Regents an injunction order restraining the application of the tax money towards the improvements.

And while these things are going on, what sort of an idea are the children of the territory affected forming as to the solicitude of a lot of grown ups who to all appearances would sacrifice every last one of those little tots to an unholy desire to be boss.—Eldred Schoolhouse Squabble, *Monticello, N.Y. Republican Watchman,* December 12, 1913.

The end of Aida's story included an Austinesque twist. Lon Austin was sent a summons to appear at the State Education Office in Albany, with only a few days notice.

Instead, Aida Austin showed up in Albany on the appointed day, to the surprise of the Education Department. The summons meant nothing to Lon. He had farming to do, so Aida went.

The whole story, of course, was more complex. Eventually, Orchard Terrace, the boarding house of Abel Myers would be used as a school.

**Estelle Carlin
to Elizabeth Austin, Eldred**
December 12, 1913
Hello Elizabeth,
 I hope you will enjoy Christmas very much and brother too, and also Donkey. Best wishes to all, Estelle Carlin

**Estelle Carlin
to Willie Austin, Eldred**
December 23, 1913
 I hope Willie, there won't be too much snow so Sandy Claus can get to your house. Best wishes to all. Estelle Carlin

Dassoris, Somerville, N.J., to Mr. and Mrs. C.M. Austin, Eldred
December 29, 1913
Dear friends,
 Many thanks for the card. May this past year's happiest days, be the New Year's saddest.
 The best greeting to all for the New Year. Your true friends,
 C. & G. Dassori

Mary Layman Dies
In Barryville, Mary J. Layman died in April 1914. George and Mary Layman had run the Spring House in Barryville from 1885 to the early 1900s.

Willie Austin's Teacher
In Eldred, in 1914, Willie Austin had his aunt Charlotte Leavenworth for a teacher. Willie passed 5th grade according to the certificate *(see page 461)* signed by both Charlotte Leavenworth, teacher, and Frederick J. Lewis, District Superintendent. And just like in the 1950s when I went to elementary school, report cards needed a parent's signature.

In the fall of 1914, Great Aunt Charlotte taught grades 1–4 in Barryville. How did she travel the almost five miles from the Leavenworth home? She rode the U.S. mail wagon.

**Mrs. Rothman
to Mr. A.A. Austin, Eldred,**
December 23, 1914
 Best Wishes for a Merry Christmas.
 From Mrs. Rothman

Harbinger of War
At the end of June in 1914, Archduke Franz Ferdinand was

1914 Report Cards for William and Raymond Austin

William Austin's Report Card signed by his aunt Charlotte on the left; his mother's signature at the top of this column; the certificate that gives Raymond's scores on 2 tests and is signed by Frederick J. Lewis, are in the Austin Collection.

1913–14 Events

1913 and 1914 Model T Fords
There were 250,000 Ford model T cars built in 1913, the year of the first drive-in gas station. It took Ford workers 12.5 hours to build a Model T on an assembly line. In 1914 the average Model T cost $440.

1914 Model T Ford. Photo: Ford Motor Co.

Lord & Taylor
The Lord & Taylor store moved to 38th Street and Fifth Avenue in New York City in 1914.—wikipedia.org.

assassinated in Sarajevo, by a Serbian. Though assassination seemed to be common in the area, this one set off a chain reaction that eventually led to the first global war known as *The Great War* or *War to End All Wars*.

By August 23 a number of countries were involved: Austria-Hungary and Germany versus Serbia, Russia, France, Britain and Japan. (Britain's colonies and dominions offered military and financial help.)

President Woodrow Wilson declared the U.S. neutral. This would last until 1917.

Many young men from the Town of Highland would take part in this war: my uncles, McKinley (Mac) and Charles Raymond Austin; three of Wilhelm Bosch's sons; and two of Anne Horton's sons.

We'll read both Mac and Raymond Austin's WWI letters in the next 2 chapters.

Raymond Austin would write home from the Panama Canal. On August 15, 1914, the Panama Canal opened to shipping. It was 51 miles long and had taken the United States 10 years to build (work had been done by other countries starting in 1880).

Dorothy K. Calkin is Born
On Christmas Day 1914, Burt and Lillie Austin Calkin had a very special Christmas present—their daughter, Dorothy Katherine Calkin (my second cousin). Dot, as she was nicknamed, was born in Liberty, New York.

Dot's brother was Robert Dale Calkin. Dorothy is the granddaughter of James Eldred Austin, and great-granddaughter of Henry and Mary Ann Eldred Austin.

S. Dassori, Jersey City, N.J., to Mort Austin, Eldred
January 15, 1915
Dear friend Mort,
With best wishes to all from us all, for the New Year. As ever your true friend, S. Dassori

Alonzo Eugene Austin Dies
In January 1915 Cousin Alonzo Eugene Austin died at the age of 77, in his home in Port Jervis, New York. Alonzo Eugene was the husband of Isabelle Camp Austin, and son of Augustus and Maria Eldred Austin.

Alonzo E. Austin was ordained a minister, serving under the board of Home Missions of the Presbyterian Church. For 20 years he served as pastor of Camp Memorial Church in N.Y.C.

In 1879, he went to Sitka, Alaska, where he remained as a missionary of the Presbyterian church until 1898.

While in Alaska, Mr. Austin founded the Alaskan Indian Industrial School at Sitka, the territorial capital.

When he returned to New York state, he lived in Eldred and Port Jervis, and preached in various churches of this vicinity and also gave interesting lectures on Alaska.

Funeral from the residence of his son-in-law, Admiral J.G. Ayers, Port Jervis, N.Y., Monday, Jan. 18, at 2 p.m.

The surviving relatives are his wife of Port Jervis; one son: Dr. A. Eugene Austin, of New York City; two daughters: Mrs. J.G. Ayers and Mrs. W.B. Styles, of Port Jervis; one brother: Mortimer B. Austin, of New York City; three sisters: Mrs. Brown [Ida Belle]

Liquor License Holders, 1914

Barryville
Meta Meyer: Spring House Hotel

Eldred
James Y. Parker: Parker House

Fridolin Straub: Straub's German Hotel

Minisink Ford
Fred Graf: Highland Bridge Hotel

Narrowsburgh
Charles Beers: Oakland Hotel
Albert Meyer: Arlington Hotel

Yulan
Mary H. Metzger: Hotel

Pond Eddy
John McKechnie Sr.: Sky Farm
Jacob Portz: Mountain View House
William Rixton: Riverside Hotel.
—*Certificate Holders in Sullivan County, Documents of the Senate of the State of New York; 137th session, 1914; Vol. IV No. 9 Part 2.*

R.M.S Lusitania

On May 7, 1915, the *R.M.S. Lusitania*, an ocean liner owned by the Cunard Line, was torpedoed by a German U-boat, 8 miles off Kinsale, Ireland. The *Lusitania* sank in 18 minutes, and 1,198 of the 1,959 people aboard were killed; 128 were Americans.

The *Lusitania* was carrying ammunition for the Allies to use against the Germans. The U.S. threatened to sever diplomatic relations, and the Germans re-imposed restrictions on U-boat activity.—*wikipedia*.

Drawing created for the New York Herald *and the* London Sphere, *shows the "R.M.S. Lusitania" as a second torpedo hits behind a gaping hole in the hull. Photo: Library of Congress: LC-USZC4-13285.*

of New York City; Mrs. Archibald Paton [Rand], of Paterson, N.J., and Mrs. Thomas Thompson [Addie] of Newark, N.J.

Henrietta Austin

Sometime before her father's death in 1915, Henrietta Austin Styles left her husband Walter Styles, and took off with the preacher, Rev. Ralph Allen, which of course, caused no small stir.

Walter Styles, the librarian, then married Georgia Clark, a teacher who had graduated from Genesee Wesleyan Seminary. Georgia was the daughter of Elizabeth Hoatson Clark Wilson.

Elizabeth Wilson's sister Mary Hoatson was the wife of John Mortimer Austin.

Norman Myers Marries Bertha Eldred

In May 1915 Norman Myers, son of Abel and Maria Hankins Myers, married Bertha Eldred, daughter of Herbert L. and Eliza Post Eldred. Bertha was a great-

Robert Dale Calkin and his sister Dorothy Calkin, children of Burt and Lillie Austin Calkin. Photo courtesy of Katherine Calkin Traxler.

granddaughter of C.C.P. and Effa Eldred.

Norman had served with the U.S. Marines and participated in the capture of Coyotepe Hill and Barranca in the Nicaragua campaign of 1912. He then worked as an employee of the Sullivan County Highway Department.

In May 1915 in Europe, Italy joined the war. The U.S. would enter the war eventually, and both McKinley and Raymond Austin would enlist. But times were happier for the Austin family in 1915.

The Austin Children's Brother

The Austin children had a new brother, Robert Clinton Austin. Robbie was born at 11 p.m. on a hot May night in 1915.

Some of my Dad's [Raymond Austin] early impressions of his younger brothers was that he was happy to have them and thought they were pretty funny most of the time, but sometimes were pesky. They seemed to feel entitled to whatever was his and to be involved in whatever he was doing.

Uncle Bill, didn't like chicken

Burt Calkin holding his daughter Dorothy; son Robert Dale; and Burt's sister Hannah Calkin. Photo courtesy of Katherine Calkin Traxler.

Zane and Dolly Grey's Home

The home of author Zane Grey on the Delaware River near Lackawaxen, Pennsylvania. Photo: Library of Congress, Prints and Photographs Division: Historic American Buildings Survey; Jet Lowe, photographer, 1988.

Zane and Dolly Roth Grey lived near the Roebling Bridge at Lackawaxen, Pennsylvania, on the land they had bought from the Holberts. Their drafty Holbert farmhouse was next to the house and property of Zane's brother Romer.

In 1914 Romer Grey and his wife deeded their house to Zane's wife, Dolly Grey, for a dollar.

Zane Grey demolished the old Holbert farmhouse he and Dolly had lived in.

An addition and other renovations were completed on their "new" house by early spring, 1915. (There was another addition in 1916.)

Stone was hauled from Grey's bluestone quarry (he owned one-half interest) across the ice.

The building records included a letter that "master carpenter August Clouse" wrote to Zane.

August Clouse included a bill for work done by himself and his carpenters: Fred Clouse, Job Reber, and Fred Squires.

Zane, Dolly, and their 3 children stayed at the Lackawaxen house when the weather was warm—May or June until October. After the family left for California in 1918, "to assist with the production of movies based on his western novels," the Lackawaxen home continued as a summer home.—From Library of Congress: HABS No. PA-5371.

Zane Grey's first Western, *The Heritage of the Desert*, written in 1910, had become a best seller. By 1915, Zane Grey had 15 books on a variety of subjects, including baseball, westerns, fishing, and outdoor adventure.—wikipedia.org; nps.gov/upde.

and usually would not eat it except under great pressure. One day when they had chicken, Bill ate all that was on his plate, and then kept reaching back to the platter when every one else had stopped eating. Grandma [Jennie Austin] said that she was so glad that he had started liking chicken and he said, "I still don't. I just want to get rid of it."

Either Uncle Bill or Uncle Art would eat only "mashed" potatoes and the other only "smashed" potatoes. Grandma solved it by putting 2 bowls on the table and saying one was "mashed" and the other "smashed."

My Dad [Raymond] just seemed to like food, at least as far as he ever said. And that was pretty much the way he was all his life. He was really partial to Grandma's buckwheat pancakes and gingerbread. He was also partial to fish and talked about going fishing with Uncle McKinley and my mother, Gladys Myers's brothers.

Dad [Raymond] came down to play with my mother's brothers just about every day. My mother [Gladys] thought he was totally disgusting: his shirttails were always sticking out and his hair was never combed and he always went bare footed. That was just as well since one of their favorite occupations was stepping into fresh cow plops. They then could wash their feet in the brook before anyone caught them.

Except on Sundays. Then Dad would arrive in the afternoon, still dressed in his Sunday-go-to-meeting clothes, shoes, and all and hair combed, and just sat on the porch or the wall. He didn't play on Sunday. My mother thought then that he was just strange. Why did he come at all? So they all just pretty much sat and did nothing and after a while he would go home. My mother just stayed away from him.

They also went swimming and fishing in the brook in the summer. When they got to 11 or 12, they dammed up a swimming hole but they all were getting more chores to do by then—weeding gardens, leading cows out to pasture and home and helping with milking and haying, etc.
—Melva Austin Barney.

The Myers and Asendorf Families
Several Myers relatives of Jennie Austin, as well as a number of townsfolk, lived northeast of the Austins, closer to Highland Lake. Gus Myers was listed as a farmer in the 1915 Census.

Willie Austin holding Art Austin. Elizabeth looks on. Photo courtesy of Mary Briggs Austin.

Art Rohman's baseball team

Zane Grey (1872-1939) visited the tavern [Rohman's] but was also on the team. Most young men played baseball. Of course, Grey had played in college.

Art Rohman (1887-1973) also played baseball, and is in the photo. But he was also a bar owner and bartender, and probably sponsored games. Some were played on his land, probably attracting customers.

There were at least three baseball diamonds in Shohola; one was directly under the 1942 bridge and was destroyed in its building. An early diamond was in the center of town before there were many buildings. Another was near the Erie tracks. Teams included Shohola, Shohola-Barryville, and the Barryville Braves, more recent but before WWII.

Many small communities had teams that traveled to nearby communities on a Saturday or Sunday.

We are talking about a local sport that was a significant social item in communities from the late 1800s to the start of World War II when most of the men went to war. —*George J. Fluhr, Historian for Pike County, Pennsylvania.*

George W.T. and Martha Mills Myers retired from running their huge, beautiful Lake View House in 1915. Their son Charles C. Myers, a carpenter, would run Lake View. Charles's wife Lena Schoonmaker had died in 1914, and he was left with sons Harold and George, a baby. George would be adopted by Henry and Belle Boyd Asendorf.

Henry and Belle Boyd Asendorf had built a huge boarding house next to Lake View. Belle Asendorf and Charles Myers were first cousins. So Charles's son George was adopted by a relative, and was then known as George Asendorf.

In 1916 Charles C. Myers married Elizabeth Ferguson. His brother Martin David Myers married Mary Elizabeth Fee. Mary had worked at Lake View.

Isabel Asendorf's parents, James and Margaret Mills Boyd, still had a boarding house on Highland Lake. Some of their children lived with them. Floyd Boyd was a carpenter, his sister Mabel was a Postmaster.

The Austin children: Raymond and Art on the mule. Willie on the right, Elizabeth on the left. They would have one more brother, Bob. Raymond was happy to have his younger brothers "and thought they were pretty funny most of the time." Photo courtesy of Mary Briggs Austin.

Art Rohman's baseball team in 1910. Back row left: Art Rohman, Walt Toaspern. Seated on far right: Zane Grey; Art Toaspern seated next to Zane Grey. Photo courtesy of George J. Fluhr, Historian for Pike County, Pennsylvania.

Eldred News, February 23, 1915

Mr. and Mrs. J.R. [Jackson] Myers spent Wednesday in Port Jervis.

Sunday was A.S. [Abel] Myers' 80th birthday. He had two pretty birthday cakes and many expressions of good will from his many friends.

Many were remembered with cards from Mr. and Mrs. Clinton Rohman. They were married in Port Jervis last Wednesday.

Dick Schroder is making arrangements to have his barn rebuilt as he is anxious to get his stock home once more.

Mrs. Alvin Hill and daughter made quite a long visit with her mother, Mrs. Edgar Sergeant.

The sleighing is fine now. So many are logging again.

Louis Basque attended store while J.R. [Jackson] Myers was in Port Jervis and his many friends were glad to see him in his old place.

The Scouts met in Sunshine Hall Saturday night after their business meeting and exercises. Mrs. Archie Myers [Minnie Sergeant] served cocoa and cake to them.

Wilbur Foster started Saturday for Connecticut to work in the powder factory. Leo Dailey accompanied him. Mr. Foster's family remains here for a while.—Republican Watchman.

Abel Sprague Myers. "Sunday was A.S. Myers' 80th birthday." Photo courtesy of Chuck Myers, a grandson of Abel.

William Henry Horton and his wife Catherine Sutherland; John Horton, a teamster; Ernest Horton, a farmer; and Mary Elvira Horton.

William and Catherine Horton's son Charles would marry Beatrice Avery, who lived in the Bradley Boarding House near Washington Lake.

There is a great photo of Anne Horton (the white handle of a revolver sticking out of her blouse) and her daughter Mary Elvira Horton.

Mary E. Horton, an energetic, hard working young lady, with a variety of interests, would marry Herman Bosch. They would be so helpful to Aida Austin when she was older.

Wilhelm and Mary Nellie Van Eastenbridge Bosch still had the Lake House northwest of Highland Lake. Soon Wilhelm would retire and one of the sons would run the Boarding House for them.

Charlie Bosch, his wife Lena Miller, and their sons Charlie, Willie, and Eddie (who died in 1918) lived less than a mile from the Lake House. Charlie and Lena had bought a boarding house with 300 acres on Bower Road in 1915, and had summer boarders for a few seasons.

Near Mill/Stege's Pond

The Greigs and Becks still had huge houses—north of Eldred Corners, near Mill/Stege's Pond.

In the early 1900s the long, narrow Mill Pond may have been called Sidwell's Pond because Thomas and Katie Sidwell lived nearby. When Thomas Sidwell died, Katie married her third husband, Edward A. Stege.

Katie Gordon Sidwell Stege

Katie Stege was known as *The Woman who talked to the birds*.

The Asendorf Highland Lake Inn. Photo courtesy of the Stuart and Geraldine Mills Russell.

The Hallock, Horton, and Bosch Families Near Highland Lake

Daniel Hallock, a widower after his wife Elvira Horton died in 1914, had a boarding house near Highland Lake. Daniel's sister-in-law, Anne Stanton Horton, a widow, lived with her children:

Eldred News, March and August 1915

Abel A. Hazen has purchased a new automobile of the Studebaker type. Mr. Hazen is learning to operate his machine and will use it in carrying his summer guests from and to Shohola station. Mr. Hazen's boarding house is finely located on Washington Lake and is an ideal retreat for many city people.

Miss Margaret Metzger, daughter of Supervisor Metzger, is the newly appointed Postmaster of this place...

We are informed that A.A. Bradley contemplates making additions to his dwelling by way of enlarging it and adding a bath and a toilet.

Messrs. Colville and Weber acting as appraisers and Supervisor Metzger as administrator, have made a complete inventory of the personal effects of the late Mrs. Bodine. We understand that a public sale of the above goods will take place some time the coming month.

We are glad to say that Mrs. Lawrence Crandall is quite well again.

Mr. and Mrs. Joseph Tether intend leaving their farm at Washington Lake and will make their future home in Hawley, Pa. They have worked hard all their lives and have earned a needed respite from the pressing activities of life. Their son Walter Tether of Barryville will quit his present occupation at that place and settle down on the old homestead to till the soil. May peace and prosperity attend them one and all in their new relations in life.—Republican Watchman, *March 24, 1915*

Mock Wedding

Brooklynites were among the guests to take first honors at the masquerade which was held this week at Metzger's Hall. The guests of the Park Hotel at Washington Lake went in body and presented a mock wedding...

Houses in the area: Lake House, Park Hotel, Washington Lake House, Bradley House, Echo Hill Farm. —Brooklyn Daily Eagle, *Aug. 15, 1915.*

Others in 1915

Joseph Meyer, a glass cutter, and his wife Florence Van Eastenbridge had a son Raymond. Florence was the daughter of Mary Van Eastenbridge Bosch and Mary's first husband.

Alexander and Ida Wait had two children. His mother Mary Wait lived with them. Alexander, a carpenter, and his cousin Floyd Boyd would soon have a garage in Eldred called Wait & Boyds.

In 1915 Maggie Dunlap, a widow, and her sons: Charles, George, and Harold, lived in the area. Harold would one day have Dunlaps Restaurant on the southeast corner of Eldred.

Webster and Ida LaBarr farmed.

Elbert Clark, an Austin cousin, was a stone mason. Harry Wormuth, a sawyer, was married to Mary Kyte, a granddaughter of Felix Kyte.

Fred and Margery Schwab who had had a boarding house in Barryville, were listed as farming.

Charles and Lottie Bradley Colville and their 3 children lived in Barryville. Charles farmed. Their daughter Ruth would soon write letters to her friend McKinley Austin. Ruth had a sister Esther and a brother Leslie.

Stephen St. John Gardner, 79, was retired and lived in Barryville with his daughter Kate.

Stephen's son James K. Gardner, his wife Ella, and their daughter Edna, 24, also lived in Barryville. James K. was a merchant as was his uncle James E. Gardner.

Ira Austin was still a blacksmith in Barryville. His wife Minerva Drake and daughter Minnie were listed as doing housework.

Edward and Katie Stege were included in the 1915 Highland Census. William and Bertha Ort had 3 children: Eleanor, William, and Florence.

James and Cora Cox Clark had a daughter Sarah Clark. A very nice photo of Sarah at graduation was in the collection of Lillie Austin Calkin. James Clark, a sawyer, was a son of Garrett and Catherine Clark. Garrett Clark was a brother to George Case Clark whose son, John Henry Clark, was a sawyer.

Sarah Clark, daughter of James and Cora Clark. Photo courtesy Katherine Calkin Traxler.

Charlie Bosch on left with boarders. "Charlie and Lena Bosch had summer boarders for a few seasons." Photo courtesy of the Bosch Family.

William H. Horton. William's son Charles would marry Beatrice Avery. Photo courtesy of William E. Horton.

Herman Bosch would marry Mary Horton and eventually have a dairy farm. Photo courtesy of Victoria Kohler, granddaughter.

Mary Elvira Horton and her mother, Anne Stanton Horton. Notice Anne's white-handled revolver. Photo courtesy of Victoria Kohler.

Tin Pan Alley

In the late 1800s and early 1900s, there was money to be made selling sheet music. Publishers had offices in New York City, West 28th Street between 5th and 6th Avenue—called Tin Pan Alley because of the noise. —wikipedia.org.

Katie's first husband, Mr. Gordon, had made his money in the music publishing business, which included (it seems) a song titled, *Father, Dear Father.*

Mrs. Stege lived in one of the several ramshackle old houses on the estate despite the fact that she was supposed to be very wealthy and to have a fortune made in the music business.

The one thing that the natives of Eldred knew best about Mrs. Stege was that they didn't dare poach or hunt or fish on her estate. For, though the old woman usually shunned the company of humans, it was apparent to all that she loved all animals and especially the wild birds and beasts of the woods.

Deer roamed her estate without fear during the hunting season. Raccoons, opossums, wild turkeys and geese all were numbered among her pets. Thirty-five cats—blue-blooded Persians all—stalked through her house. It was reported in the village meat market that she spent $35 a month on liver to feed them alone. She bought grain for the birds and the deer. She spent her days wandering among them on the estate. Her nights were spent in the company of her feline pets.

Katie Stege sang and whistled to the birds. They ate out of her hand. No laborer on the farm was allowed to harm any one of the countless animals, nor could he so much as cut down a tree or a bush. There's no doubt that Mrs. Stege could afford to indulge her fancy for animals no matter what the cost. When her will was probated, it was discovered that her estate amounted to more than $300,000.—Sunday Mirror Magazine, *February 27, 1938, p. 2.*

Some of the townspeople, including Julius Maier and Ed Bosch worked for Katie who apparently paid very low wages. The Bosch family lived about a mile and a half east of Mrs. Stege. Ed Bosch wrote down some of his memories of working for her and others.

(The section of wall that Ed Bosch helped Hipe and Steve Dailey build was to the east of the section of the stone wall that Thomas and Bennett Greig had built in 1886.)

When I worked for Mrs. Sidwell—Mrs. Stege after she married Mr. Stege, I got a job taking care of the cows; milked them twice a day. I took the cows and oxen up Rt. 55 to the old Boyd Place to graze in the morning. In the afternoon, I got them back and milked them.

In between when I had time, I did other work like helping Hipe Dailey put that little section of wall on Stege Hill. Mrs. Stege was going to have the stone wall all around that curve, but she changed her mind so that small section is all we did.

We had a derrick made out of two lumber wagon wheels and a long tongue to get those rocks up there. Steve Dailey helped get the rocks up. It took a long time to get those rocks in place. Sometimes it took several men to bear down on the tongue of the derrick.

I also cooked for Steges— pancakes as big as a silver dollar and a lot of them. The cats was always on the table when they were eating.

So one day, I quit. I didn't get enough money.

Katie Stege in the only photo of her, taken in 1880 after her marriage to Stephen Gordon. Sunday Mirror Magazine, *February 27, 1938, p. 2, courtesy of Bosch Family.*

Wall by Stege's Pond. Falls and arches (built by Thomas Greig) are in the background. "Mrs. Stege was going to have the stone wall all around that curve, but she changed her mind so that small section is all we did." Photo courtesy of Cynthia Leavenworth Bellinger.

Frank Owens and one of the Clarks put the big stone wall up. I dug most of the trench around Sidwell's graveyard. I got 12-1/2 cents per hour, $1.25 for 10 hours of work.

I went to work in a sawmill for the Daileys for $1.50 for 9 hours. Then worked for Mr. Proctor for $1.71 for 9 hours. Proctor had 70 men working for him in the summer. In the winter about 15 worked on the park fence. I flattened one side of the post so one side was straight to nail the wire on.—Ed H. Bosch.

In Lumberland

In nearby Glen Spey, Franz August and Anna Marie Schwarz ran the boarding house, Pine Terrace Farm. August, Anna Marie, and son Walter had been in Glen Spey for 7 years in 1915. Walter would marry Ella Getz, who would be born in 1918. Ella's family moved to the

Ed and Herman Bosch when they worked for Mr. Proctor. Man on left unknown.

Crew working for Mr. Proctor. Ed Bosch has the hammer; Herman and Ralph Bosch are also in the group. Photos courtesy of the Bosch Family.

Bosch Farm and Boarding House around 1910. Photo courtesy of the Bosch Family.

area from Benton, Pennsylvania, about the same time the Schwarz family had moved.

Franz Schwarz had been a concert violinist with the New York Symphony Orchestra that performed the first opera ever in New York City at the old Metropolitan Opera House. Mr. Schwarz thought "Glen Spey had the best water in the entire world."

Franz August Schwarz, was my Grandfather. He was a graduate of Leipzig Conservatory in Germany and played at the first Metropolitan opera house in N.Y.C.

They retired here and bought Pine Terrace Farm in 1910 and ran a boarding house.

Grandmother was the adopted daughter of Victor Eckstein, owner of the notorious Luchows Restaurant. Franz served as the Lumberland Town Clerk also.
—Frank V Schwarz, Town of Lumberland Historian.

Lumberland was also the home of the MacKenzie/McKenzie estates and Brookwood, the estate of William Ross Proctor. Brookwood Manor and Farm on 5,000 acres, was 1,400 feet above the Delaware River in the Town of Lumberland. The main farm building was 350 feet long and could accommodate 150 animals.

Howard Stevens worked at the Brookwood Horse Stables. He was an expert in choosing excellent horses and was sent to Chicago to purchase horses for the Proctor Stables. There is a photo of Howard at the Brookwood Stables with a number of horses and their groomsmen *(see page 312)*.

Howard and Emily Stevens
Howard and Emily Parker Stevens lived in the Parker Hotel with her parents James Y. and Emily Parker, who owned the hotel. Howard and Emily Stevens would be the parents of Christena (Teenie), who knew my grandmother Jennie Austin and my father Art Austin.

Emily Stevens would be the Postmaster at the Eldred Post Office which would often be in a room of the Parker Hotel. In the 1930s my dad would work for her.

Emily Stevens's brother, William Parker, his wife Victoria Simpson, and their children: James Y., William, Elsie, and Andrew Parker lived nearby. Andrew would have Parker's Store when he was older.

Sherman Leavenworth Family
On the west side of Eldred, Sherman Leavenworth continued farming and running Echo Hill Farm House. Maria was not very well, probably due to her diabetes.

Anna Leavenworth was teaching school, as was Charlotte. Charlotte was at the start of her very long teaching career. For 50 years she would teach several generations of students including nephews and nieces, great nephews and nieces, as well as many descendants of the children in town.

Truman Leavenworth was

Pine Terrace Farm owned by Franz August Schwarz. Photo courtesy of Frank V Schwarz.

Maney's Mill in Glen Spey in 1917. Photo is courtesy of the Proctor Family.

The Parker House where Emily Parker Stevens grew up. The Post Office was sometimes located here. Postcard courtesy of Christena Stevens Myers.

Brookwood Barn's prize horses. Howard Stevens stands in the center holding two white horses. Photo courtesy of Christena Stevens Myers.

Howard and Emily Parker Stevens. Photo courtesy of Christena Stevens Myers.

a teamster. Martin helped out in the ways he could. Christina Leavenworth was a music teacher.

Jennie Leavenworth Austin and her family continued to run Homestead Cottage on the east side of Eldred.

Garfield Leavenworth Family
Garfield and Ella Sergeant Leavenworth and their children: Clara, Anna, and Clinton, lived in Massachusetts and would for a few more years.

Edith Palmer Ewart
Edith Palmer Ewart was the daughter of Harriet Leavenworth Palmer. Edith's first husband Albert had died, and Edith had married Frederick Ewart, Albert's brother.

In 1917 Edith, and her 5 children: Victor Ewart and his wife Kathryn Blohm; Mr. and Mrs. Willard Ewart; Elliott, Millie, and Rolland Ewart, lived in Detroit, Michigan.

Edith Palmer Ewart's brother Harry Palmer lived in Benton Harbor, Michigan, with his wife Lydia and her daughter Florence.

The Leavenworths in Colorado
Out west in Colorado, Hazel Leavenworth, daughter of John Leavenworth and Amelia Bradley (Gregory) lived near Dunton, with her sister Lottie and Lottie's husband Len Andeway.

Hazel Leavenworth had to work for her room and board for high school because they were so poor. She graduated with a class of about 50 from Durango High School in 1914.

John Leavenworth (always with a flask in his pocket)

returned to the ranch for his daughter Hazel's graduation. Hazel watched him ride off down the creek afterwards until he vanished from her sight. He never looked back. She never saw him again.

Hazel Leavenworth earned a teaching certificate and taught in a red, one-room schoolhouse in Dunton, Colorado. Each day she had to arrive early and start the fire in the wood stove.

John Ellis Leavenworth Dies
In March 1916, John Ellis Leavenworth died in California.

John Leavenworth abandoned my mother, Amelia Bradley, and eventually went to California to work in the gold mines. He died of lung disease from the dust, called, miner's silicosis. John died alone in a rented room in Bakersfield, California, and was buried there in a Potter's Field.—Hazel Leavenworth Koenig as told to Marialyce Koenig Kornkven and Gerald L. Koenig.

Irwin Briggs Meets Miss Crabtree
The Briggs Family of Irwin Briggs lived 800 miles northeast of Dunton, Colorado, in Ainsworth, Nebraska.

Blond, blue-eyed, Marium Indianola (Indy) Clark Briggs was a piano teacher. Curly brown

A lovely photo of Hazel Leavenworth. Photo courtesy of Marialyce Koenig Kornkven.

haired and brown-eyed Clinton Briggs was a music and elementary teacher and also farmed. Harry Irwin Briggs was the oldest of their 11 children.

Myrtie Crabtree was a school teacher and boarded at Clinton and Indy Briggs' Farm. (Indy would one day visit her son Irwin, his wife Myrtie, and children, in Barryville, New York.)

The Briggs girls kept telling their teacher, Miss Crabtree, "Wait 'til you see our brother!"

Myrtie's first impression of Irwin was not very positive. He had worked in the mines in Idaho and had gotten in with the wrong crowd.

His fellow workers taught him to drink by putting liquor in his eggnog. Irwin had been in a couple mine cave-ins; had a little toe amputated because it had been crushed so badly; and nearly died from drinking too much alcohol, before he returned to his home.

Irwin said he was running away from God's call to be a preacher. Myrtie consented to go with Irwin and his sister Verna to a revival meeting at the church and Irwin, "got right with the Lord."

Irwin and his sister went to Taylor University in Indiana, where he studied for the ministry.

Myrtie went to Chicago and stayed with her Grainger cousins and Aunt Sarah Crabtree Gill. She saved $7 of the $9 per week that she earned as a housekeeper.

Irwin Briggs would quit his studies to enlist in the war. Myrtie Crabtree would write to him.

Rowlee and Emily's New Arrival
Early in 1916 little Mary Murray Schoonover joined her siblings: Justina, Ethel, and William—

Garfield and Ella Sergeant Leavenworth and their children: Clara, Anna, and Clinton, lived in Massachusetts. Photos courtesy of Cynthia Leavenworth Bellinger.

The family of Clint and Indy Clark Briggs. Their children by age starting with the oldest: Irwin, Ira, Verna, Orie, Charlotte, Carl, Howard, Catharine, Lewis, Grace, and Floyd Briggs. Photo courtesy of Mary Briggs Austin.

the children of Rowlee and Emily Banner Schoonover.

Well, in 1914, I bought the Central Garage at Monroe, New York, and moved over there. It was a fine garage. I had plenty of work and went fine until the winter of 1916 and there came snow early and stayed late. I would get up in the morning and the snow was as high as the gas pumps and at that time, they did not plow out the roads and no one used their cars and the war scare was on and you could not get any parts for cars and the expenses was going on and I was about crazy.

I hung on through the next year just about breaking even with bad debts and discounting notes. The war had broken out and there was no business and you could not get anything to do business with. I will admit that I was very much discouraged. I hung on until the Lusitania was sunk [May 7, 1915] and that made me mad. At that time the Y.M.C.A. was wanting men to go overseas to go in the transport and wanted mechanics to do work. I applied and had no trouble to get with the Y.M.C.A. as a mechanic.—Daniel Rowlee Schoonover.

Rowlee's memoirs from his time working for the Y.M.C.A. in WWI are included in the next 3 chapters.

Emma, Kate, and the Britt Girls

Rowlee's sister Emily and her husband Will Waidler lived in New Rochelle, New York.

Sometime around World War I, Will and Em Schoonover Waidler bought Green Farm in the hamlet of Purling, near Cairo, New York. Perhaps the goal was to run a boarding house and have hay as a cash crop.

Emily Waidler and her half sister Kate Parker, who had cared for Kitty and Ada Britt as they grew up, continued to be a part of the girls' lives.

Kitty and Ada's brother William Britt married and had a son William Britt. But William Britt Sr. died young.

William and Kitty Britt had a son Elwood James.

Arthur Remington and Ada Britt Wood had a daughter Norma Beverly Wood. There is a photo *(see p. 316)* of Mary Murray Parker Schoonover holding little Norma Wood and Mary Murray Schoonover, the youngest daughter of Rowlee and Emily.

Kate lived with us winters ever since I could remember and had spent every summer with her half sister Emily and her husband Will Waidler where ever they lived upstate, on whatever farm.

To me, our family when I was growing up consisted of my parents, my younger brother

James Eldred Descendants in 1916

Frank (Benjamin Franklin) Eldred was a son of Abraham Mulford and Elizabeth Wheeler Eldred. Frank lived with his son Judson Eldred, or visited his other children from 1912 to 1916. In January 1916 Frank accidentally put a pitchfork through his foot.

John Eldred, son of Frank Eldred, was a successful farmer and also a cattle dealer. He cut his leg rather seriously with a scythe while haying in July 1916.

At the time, John and Minnie Sears Eldred had 8 children, including Orvis Rutledge Eldred, future father of Richard O. Eldred who would write, *The Eldred Family*.

Another son of Frank Eldred, Lewis Laforde Eldred, and his wife Cora Sisson lived in West Damascus, Pennsylvania. Lewis and Cora had 8 children including Harvey Eldred. —*Eldred, pp. 71, 96*.

Lewis Carmichael, son of Zophar and Sarah Eldred Carmichael, had died in Iowa in 1912. Leonard George Watson, son of Lina (Lewis's daughter) and Frank Watson, married Daisy Raper in 1913. Leonard and Daisy's daughter Elizabeth Jeannette Watson was born in February 1918.

Expert Mechanics Wanted

The Y.M.C.A. wants 200 expert automobile mechanics and a large number of special men for motor transport drivers for overseas service...

Must be between 31 and 50 years of age, in thorough sympathy with the U.S. war programme. Those with German or Austrian parentage cannot be taken. Men with families will be paid sufficient to take care of the family. Apply to Overseas Motor Transport, Y.M.C.A. 347 Madison Ave., NYC.—Republican Watchman, 1917.

Hay Wagon at Green Farm with Will Waidler, husband of Emily Schoonover Waidler. Photo courtesy of Richard James.

Bob; Aunt Kitty and Uncle Will James and Elwood, my cousin; my father's sister, Aunt Alice Wood; and definitely Great-Aunt Kate Parker. On the fringes in the "country" which was any place the Waidlers were then living, were Aunt Em and Uncle Will.

There was also my first cousin William Britt in Port Jervis who with his mother Bertha and later her second husband Clarence, I seldom saw, but when I did it was always so nice.—Norma Wood James, daughter of Ada Britt Wood.

Maria Austin Dies

In Eldred, in April of 1916, Maria Adelaide Austin died. Maria seemed to be the quiet Austin sister, but the few letters of hers that were saved showed the Austin dry sense of humor.

Miss Maria A. Austin, aged 61, died of grip and paralysis April 13, 1916, at her home in Eldred, where she was born and always lived. She leaves two sisters and four brothers—Miss Aida A. Austin, Alonzo A., Charles M., and Henry [Dory] Austin of Eldred, and James Eldred [Ell] Austin of Bethel.—Sullivan County Record of Jeffersonville, N.Y.

Homestead Cottage Burns Down

The Homestead Cottage on Collins Road that Mort and Jennie Austin ran, burned down in 1915 or 1916.

Mort and Jenny then purchased Mountain Grove House, which seems to be the Austin house, built around 1894. (Chapter 12 has more about Mountain Grove.)

McKinley Attends Mount Hermon

In the fall of 1916, Mort and Jennie Austin said good bye to their oldest son McKinley who attended Mount Hermon School for Boys in Massachusetts.

Mount Hermon was founded in 1881, by evangelist D.L. Moody. Sixteen was the minimum age to attend.

To help young men of very limited means to get an education such as would have done me good

William Waidler and his wife Emily Schoonover Waidler. Photos courtesy of John Hull.

Mary Murray Parker Schoonover holding Granddaughter Mary Murray Schoonover (left), and Great-Granddaughter Norma Beverly Wood. Photo courtesy of Richard James.

Mountain Grove House, 1915. Mort and Jennie Austin and their family moved here after their Homestead Cottage Boarding House burned down. Photo courtesy of Mary Briggs Austin.

Art and Mary

In the Austin Collection of photograph albums is one called *Me and Mary*. Aunt Aida took the photos. It is interesting because the little boy is my dad Art Austin, but the little girl, though named Mary and with blond hair, is not my mother. How do I know that? My mother is 12 years younger than my dad, and was not born yet. Photos courtesy of Mary Briggs Austin.

when I was their age.
—D.L. Moody (1837-1899).

The Mount Hermon campus was surrounded by 1,100 acres on the wooded banks of the Connecticut River in western Massachusetts, near the borders of Vermont and New Hampshire.

The Bible was the primary tool for instruction in the early days, and it was accompanied by a rigorous academic program similar to that of other private secondary schools of the era.

Manual labor, called "Cooperative Housekeeping," was required of all students. Girls worked ten hours per week helping with meals or cleaning dormitories. Boys performed janitorial, laundry, kitchen, and farm work.

After Moody's death in 1899, his eldest son, William, continued his father's work at the Northfield Schools [Mount Hermon and Northfield Seminary for Young Ladies].

Henry Cutler was headmaster at Mount Hermon from 1890–

12th Annual Library Reception

Monticello, N.Y., *Republican Watchman,* **May 11, 1917**

Miss Minnie Meyer led off with a piano solo and it was of such par excellence that it made the other participants hustle to keep the pace. Miss Anna Meyer and Miss Edna Gardner followed with a piano duet that was especially fine.

Adelbert M. Scriber, the editor of the *Watchman,* was an invited guest and was introduced by John C. Metzger Jr., one of the trustees of the Hall, as the first speaker of the evening. Mr. Scriber talked on thoroughness.

Mrs. Minnie E. Myers was on the program for a vocal solo and did her part beautifully. That is the word that was coined especially for Mrs. Myers' solo.

Miss Christina H. Leavenworth was another vocal soloist and acquitted herself splendidly. She possesses a sweet voice.

Another pleasing number was a vocal duet by Mrs. Minnie E. Myers and Miss Raola Kelley. Miss Kelley is the Postmistress of Eldred and she sings as well as she handles the mail. Their voices harmonized well.

...Miss Edna Gardner closed the program with a piano solo.

The town of Highland has some fine talent, and it showed itself to good advantage on Thursday night...

In the beginning, Sunshine Hall Library was a Sunday School library with about two dozen books. W.B. Styles, the treasurer and librarian of the present institution went to New York City and talked library and worked library among his friends. The patriotic people of Eldred took up the cry and in a year's time, the two dozen books had grown to 700, and year after year new books were added until now 7,000 volumes grace the shelves of Sunshine Hall and are a standing invitation to every visitor to read.

In 1901 Miss Beattie, a New York lady known for her good deeds, erected a building 28 × 120 feet, two-stories high, for the children of Eldred and called it the Community Center. In the building she put a gymnasium and appliances helpful to children's development and especially designed for their recreation...

The community center graduated finally from a gymnasium to a library. When Miss Beattie died, the revenue to run the library stopped. Then the splendid library had to be maintained by public funds or private subscriptions...

Many good hearted citizens have contributed...Among them are J.Q. Feary, who is connected with steel. He gave 390 books. E.J. Johnson, superintendent for Mr. Proctor, donated 90 books. Mr. Proctor gave $125.

Among the gifts which are prized very much is the scenery of scenic sittings for the large room, four full sets which were presented by William Ross Proctor. They were painted by his brother Charles Proctor, a professional artist.

The library is open from 8:30 to 5 o'clock, and in charge of Mr. Styles. Many people use it as a reading room, where they find in addition to the listed books, 31 of the best magazines.

It is certainly one of the finest institutions in Sullivan County and we believe the only public library maintained by subscriptions...The *Watchman* congratulates the people of Highland and the people of the county generally on having so fine a place of learning.

The officers and managers elected for 1917 are as follows:

President, Charles F. Scheniman; Vice-president, Morgan O. Sergeant; Secretary, Robert S. Greig; Financial Secretary, Samuel J. Hallock; Treasurer and Librarian, W.B. Styles; Assistant Librarian, Herbert L. Eldred.

Trustees: Dr. A. Eugene Austin, W.B. Styles, Erwin D. Avery, W.H. Wilson, C.F. Scheniman, F.R. Sergeant, John C. Metzger, Jr.

Councilors: Charles W. Wilson, John E. Hill, Archibald A. Myers, Julius J. Maier, C. Edgar Sergeant, David E. Crandall, Fred D. Heyen, Wilber Foster, James K. Gardner, Isaac Sergeant, John M. Austin, Frederick J. Lewis, George L. Crandall, Alex Wait, Stephen A. Myers, George Sidwell, John G. Love, Dr. Frank I. Smith, Edward R. Kalbfus, Howard Pelton, Charles M. Colville.

1915 Program with similar numbers played. Program courtesy of Victoria Kohler.

SUNSHINE HALL LIBRARY
Eldred, New York

OFFICERS

President	Charles W. Wilson
Vice President	Frank R. Sergeant
Secretary	Robert S. Greig
Financial Secretary	Morgan O. Sergeant
Treasurer	W. B. Styles
Librarian	
Assistant Librarian	H. L. Eldred

TRUSTEES

John M. Austin	J. R. Myers
L. A. Blackman	C. F. Scheniman
John Hill	C. E. Sergeant
Frank M. LaBarr	George Sidwell
F. J. Lewis	Alex. Wait
A. A. Myers	W. H. Wilson
F. D. Heyen	Julius J. Maier
John Love	S. J. Hallock
George L. Crandall	George Boyd
Clarence Wormuth	Wilber Foster

PROGRAM

Piano Duet	Miss Anna Meyer / Miss Edna Gardner
Solo	Miss Christina H. Leavenworth
Reading	Miss Raola Kelley
Piano Solo	Miss Mary Rixton
Duet	Mrs. Minnie E. Myers / Miss Raola Kelley
Solo	Miss Stella Boyd
Reading	Mrs. George L. Crandall
Solo	Mr. E. A. Northrop
Piano Solo	Miss Edna Gardner
Solo	Miss Virginia Northrop

REFRESHMENTS

Mt. Hermon School where McKinley attended for a year. Postcard courtesy of Mary Briggs Austin.

McKinley Austin. Photo courtesy of Mary Briggs Austin.

1932.—School archivist Peter Weis, nmhschool.org.

A letter signed by Ambert Moody is in the Appendix, p. 462.

McKinley Austin, Mount Hermon, Mass., to Aida Austin, Eldred
April 6, 1916
Dear Aunt,
I am getting along all right and I like the place very well.
All the fellows I have met so far are nice. There is one from India that I have met. He's all right too.
Give my regards to all and tell them I'll write soon.
Your nephew, McKinley

Mrs. Tuzza, Bronx, N.Y.C., to Mr. and Mrs. Austin, Eldred
December 22, 1916
Mr. and Mrs. Austin,
Greetings from Mrs. Tuzza.

Changes Ahead in 1917
The year 1917 would bring many changes. A cloud would hang over the Christmas season for the next two years; and even longer for some of our friends and relatives in the Town of Highland.

On January 31, 1917, Germany announced their U-boats would engage in unrestricted submarine warfare. German submarines sank three American merchant vessels on March 17.

Though President Woodrow Wilson had earlier declared the U.S. neutral, in April the U.S. entered the war, *The Great War, The War to End All Wars.*

Once again men in the villages of Highland township would be fighting in a war, but this time they would fight overseas.

Men from the town, descendants of early settlers, future residents, and relatives of future citizens of Highland, play a part in another horrid War.

"A cloud would hang over Christmas time for the next couple years; and even longer for some of our friends and relatives in the Town of Highland." Undated Christmas Card in the collection of Mary Briggs Austin.

Chapter 10
Dear Soldier Boy
World War I: April 1917–May 1918

My Tuesdays are meatless
My Wednesdays are wheatless
I am getting more eatless each day.
My house is heatless
My bed is sheetless
They've all been sent to the Y.M.C.A..
The bar rooms are treatless
My coffee is sweetless,
Each day I get poorer and wiser
My stockings are feetless
My trousers are seatless
Oh how I do hate the Kaiser.
   Quite a poem, is it not? Well let's hope that there will soon be an end to this awful war.—Your friend, Ruth Colville.

McKinley at his Aunt Aida's home. Photo courtesy of Mary Briggs Austin.

The United States entered World War I on April 6, 1917.

Mort and Jennie Austin's sons Mortimer McKinley (Mac) and later Charles Raymond enlisted. Their grandfather Sherman S. Leavenworth had fought in the Civil War. His brothers Hezekiah and Atwell had died near the end of the War.

Mac and Raymond would write letters home, just as their grandfather Sherman had done.

Ruth Colville, daughter of Charles and Lottie Bradley Colville, was a friend of McKinley and wrote several letters to Mac while he was in the service. Ruth quoted the poem at the beginning of this chapter in one of her letters.

By 1917 Mort and Jennie must have been resettled at Mountain Grove, which we will talk about in Chapter 12. Their family at home included: Raymond, 16, Bill, 14, Elizabeth, 6, Art, 4, and Bob, 2.

Aida and/or Lon lived in the old Austin homestead which Dr. Alonzo E. Austin owned. They apparently paid him rent.

Chas. Dassori, Jersey City Heights, N.J., to Mort Austin
June 5, 1917
Dear friend Mort,
   Hello Mort and co.! How is things? It's a long time since we have seen each other last. Isn't it a shame this dreadful war is being carried on. Everything is going up. Gussie [his wife] said it is just awful the way the prices of eatables and etc. is going up.
   Well, at any rate, I (with the Almighty's grace) expect a newcomer in the early part of August sometime. Let em come

Irwin Briggs was sent to Ft. Riley, Kansas, for training. Photo courtesy of Mary Briggs Austin.

and the more the merrier.

Say Mort, there is a young friend of ours who would like to go away the last 2 weeks in July with her young niece, and we suggested your place. She is a good soul. If you are taking boarders Mort, do you think you could take her and her niece?

I am back at it again Mort. I am thinking seriously of going to Florida this coming fall. I have already corresponded with one of the railroads for a freight checking position which I am now doing. I am very anxious to get away from this climate and its winters.

As ever, your true friend,
Chas. S. Dassori

McKinley Austin to His Family
July 7, 1917
I have arrived safely. I have been accepted and am at Ft. Slocum. Your son, McKinley

Irwin Briggs, Ft. Logan
On July 7, 1917, Irwin Briggs (dark brown eyes, dark brown hair, a ruddy complexion, 5'-10" tall) enlisted in the army at Ft. Logan, Colorado.

Irwin had not completed his first school year at Taylor University. He would later return to finish his degree to become a minister. It would be 1935 before he arrived in the Town of Highland as the Methodist pastor.

Pvt. Briggs was sent to Ft. Riley, Kansas, for training. He asked to be placed in the Medical Corps and was with the 89th Infantry. A couple pages from Irwin's instructional guide, *Drill Regulations and Service Manual for Sanitary Troops, U.S. Army*, from 1914, are in this chapter.

Both McKinley and Irwin would be stationed in France.

In this next letter, Jennie Austin must have sent Mr. and Mrs. Dassori one of her pickles in honor of their new arrival.

Charles Dassori, Jersey City Heights, N.J., to Mort Austin
July 31, 1917
Dear Friend Mort,
Say, I had a good hearty laugh over that parcel your wife sent me by Mrs. Beltrame. The picklet I put it in a barrel and it's half ripe already. The onions are devoured also.

I took the parcel along with me last Sunday (just as you sent it) over to the hospital where Gussie is and let her open it; well we had some laugh over it.

I've got another (stem winder) I mean a boy Mort, so that makes it four boys and one girl.

Mort, I was to have my vacation starting August 6, but things was arranged for me to have it now. So you see, I am now a he she or two in one: Chief cook and bottle washer and dish slinger.

Say Mort, shall we charter Pullman cars when we go west; or shall we cut down expenses and ask for cut rates on freight cars. We could put a stove in one of them and cut a hole in the roof for a pipe.

Gussie wishes to be remembered to all. Many thanks again for the parcel.

As ever your true friend,
Chas. Dassori

McKinley Austin, Chattanooga, Tenn., to Aida Austin, Eldred
August 4, 1917
Dear Aunt,
I am here and like it better

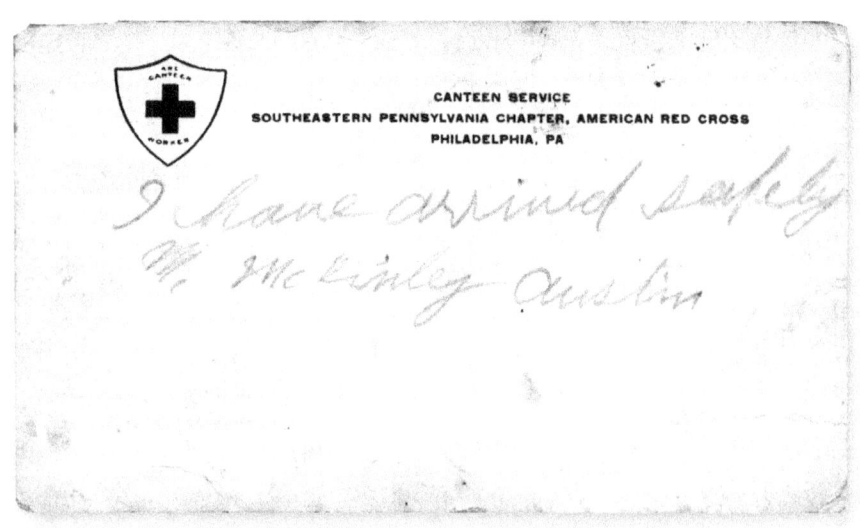

July 7, 1917, postcard from McKinley Austin. I have arrived safely. M. McKinley Austin. Postcard courtesy of Mary Briggs Austin.

Popular Pickles and Preserves
A Variety Which Will Suit All Tastes and Ages

FORTIFIED with a shelf of pickles and "company preserves" any woman will be in a mood to welcome guests expected or unexpected. Some of the following recipes may be old friends of yours but probably some will be new.

Pickled Onions

Peel the smallest onions you can obtain, place in strong brine for 2 days, then lay in fresh water for 1 day. Pack closely in jars, fill with best vinegar cold. Run knife 2 or 3 times when packing, in jars and once after onions are all in just to make sure there is no air. Carefully packed and sealed air tight these will keep for years.

Chow-Chow

One quart of cucumbers, (small), 1 quart of onions, 2 heads of cauliflower and 3 green peppers, sliced. Make a brine or cover with 1½ cups of salt. Let stand 24 hours, then scald them in the brine. Drain. To

Carrot Jam

Wash and scrape or peel large carrots, cut in inch pieces and weigh. To three pounds allow 6 cups of sugar, 6 large lemons and 2 ounces of blanched almonds cut into strips. Steam the carrots until tender, then press through a sieve. Add the grated yellow rind and strained juice of the lemons, the sugar and shredded almonds and heat slowly. Simmer for 20 minutes, stirring very often, then put up in jars.

Sweet Pickled Prunes

Pick over, wash and soak four pounds of large prunes for 24 hours. Then steam for 20 minutes. Boil together for 10 minutes, 4 cups of sugar, 2 cups of vinegar, 1 ounce each of whole cloves and stick cinnamon, and ¼ ounce of ginger. Add the prunes, simmer very gently until tender, then can and seal.

Pickled Pears and Peaches

Eight pounds of fruit, 8 cups of sugar, 1 quart of vinegar, ½ ounce of cinnamon and clove and ¼ ounce

Grandma Jennie Austin had quite a number of pickle recipes in her scrapbook. It sounds like she must have sent their friends the Dassoris at least one pickle. Scrapbook page courtesy of Mary Briggs Austin.

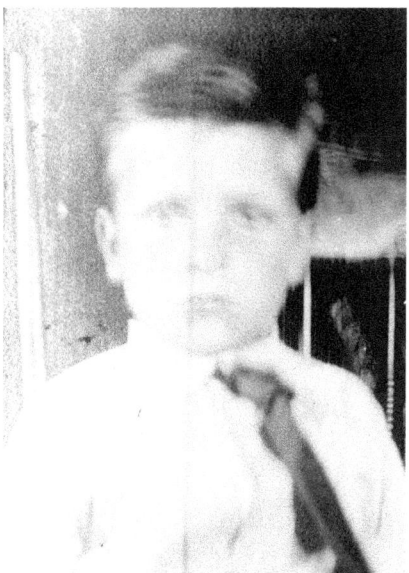

than at Fort Slocum. We get better food and the officers seem better, though we had a fine sergeant there.

It took over 34 hours to come here, counting from the time we left the barracks at Ft. Slocum, till we got here.

If I am lucky, and come back, I wouldn't miss this for five thousand dollars. The trip down to here was worth a year of a man's life. I'll never forget it. I am sure.

For the present, my address is: Mortimer Austin, 11 U.S. Inf., F Company, Military branch, Chattanooga, Tennessee.

Your nephew, McKinley

McKinley Austin, Chattanooga, Tenn., to His Family, Eldred
August 4, 1917
To all family, relations, friends,

I am very well and certainly like this place. We left Port Jervis on the morning train instead of the 12:15. Of the 15 applicants,

only 2, Al Delaney and I went. We were examined at Poughkeepsie and a bunch of us, 13 in all, were sent to Ft. Slocum. We got there late at night. Sunday we were examined again and four were sent back. Also we were vaccinated and inoculated for typhoid. My vaccination didn't take, but the inoculation did.

Monday we got our uniforms and were assigned to our squads. Tuesday afternoon, we were told to get ready to go South. And we were examined again. About 7:30, we left our barracks, turned in our blankets and marched to the parade ground. The commander inspected us. Then we were sent aboard a ship and sent down the East River.

All the way down, everybody on shore was waving. Every boat was saluting and the factory whistles were blowing. The Battery was crowded with people cheering, waving and throwing their hats in the air. I saw the

McKinley Austin's younger siblings: Elizabeth Austin and unknown lady; Art Austin, my father; and Robbie Austin. Photos courtesy of the Austin Family.

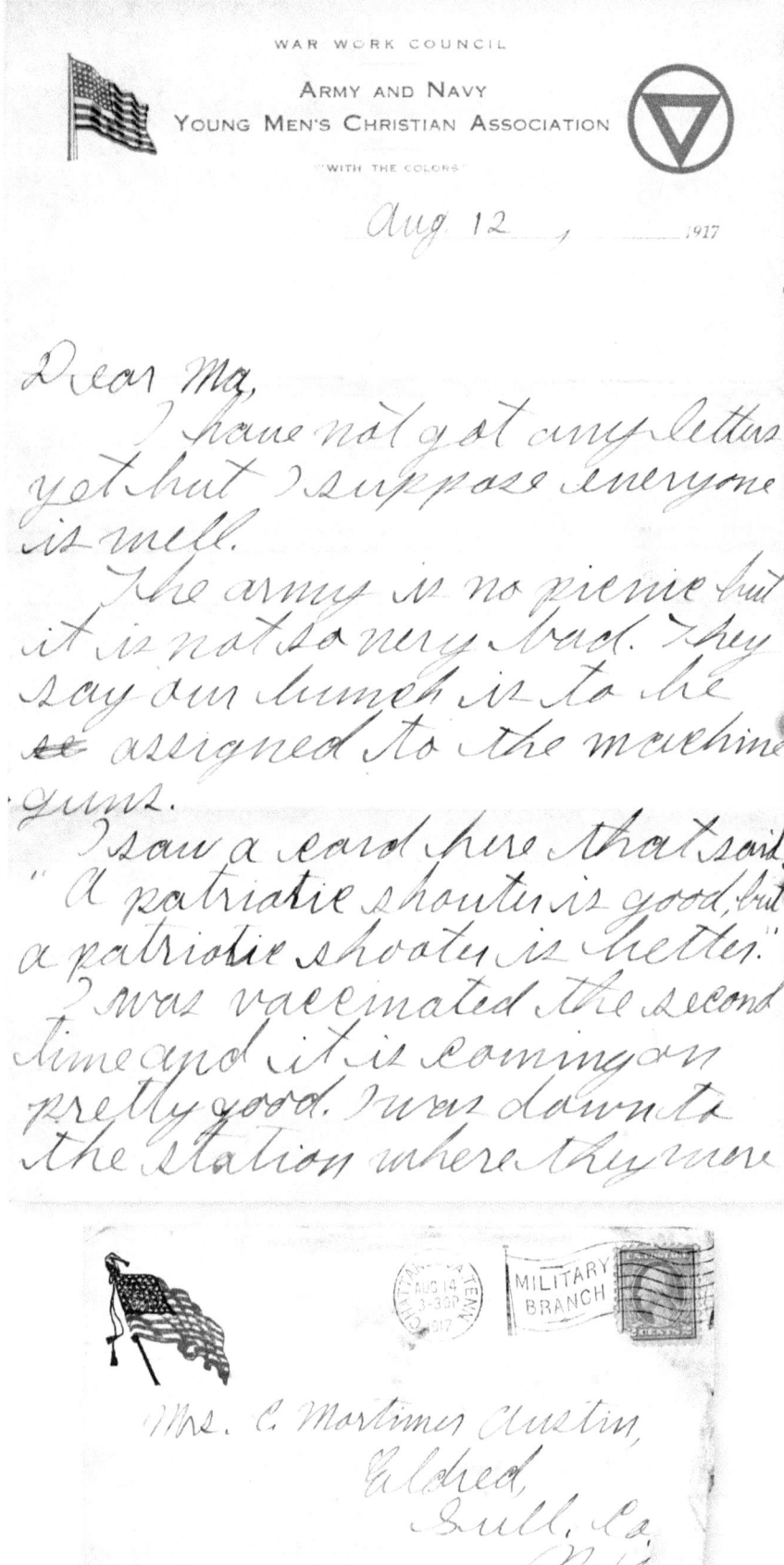

August 12, 1917 letter on Y.M.C.A. stationery from McKinley Austin to his mother. Letter in the collection of Mary Briggs Austin.

Brooklyn Navy Yard, Brooklyn Bridge, Statue of Liberty, and other noted places.

They shipped us from Jersey City through on a special train. We were well received everywhere. As we went through the towns, we would sing and cheer and wave to the crowd. My throat and arms got tired, but I never had so much fun before in my life. We certainly got some welcome.

In one East Tennessee town there was a little girl about eight years old holding a baby about the size of Robbie standing by the track and waving to us.

The country through east Tennessee is very beautiful and so are the girls. The ladies of this region are very good looking and nice acting girls. They have a ladylike way that a good many of the northern girls, especially those from the city, have not. And they dress properly for which I think counts a good deal toward making a lady. Of course, I may have only seen the best sort of them, and may later see the short skirted, loud mouthed, painted, over dressed female that we see too much of in our cities.

Give my regard to all our town and soon I will begin writing to my friends up there.

From Mac, otherwise,
Mortimer Austin

Charlotte Hall, mentioned in the next note, was the sister of Sara Hall Austin, wife of Dr. Alonzo E. Austin.

Sara Austin, Eldred, to Mort and Jennie Austin, Eldred
August 7, 1917
Dear Mortimer and Jennie,

The children of the Sunday School Class are invited to spend Sunday afternoon, August 19th from 3:30 to 5 o'clock for Sunday

Songs and stories and Bible verses.

We would be glad to have Raymond, Willie, Lawrence [Art], and Elizabeth come too.

Very Sincerely yours,
Sara Hall Austin
Charlotte C. Hall

Army Stationery

Mac and later Raymond usually wrote their letters on stationery from the Y.M.C.A. It seems there was a choice between paper with a Y.M.C.A. or Knights of Columbus letterhead.

McKinley Austin to Jenny Austin
August 12, 1917
Dear Ma,

I have not got any letters yet, but I suppose everyone is well. The army is no picnic, but it is not so very bad. They say our bunch is to be assigned to the machine guns.

I was vaccinated the second time and it is coming on pretty good. I was down to the station where they were unloading watermelons and a man dropped one of the melons on my sore arm.

Most of the officers are good, but there are two I don't like. One is a sergeant who thinks that hollering is the only way to learn a man. The other is a conceited kid corporal. Jimmy Sullivan says he would like to meet them again when the war is over.

Sullivan is an Irish sailor. He had been in the Merchant Marine and has been through the danger zone lots of times without seeing any U boats. His boat helped pick up survivors from other ships three times. He says every port in France is full of German prisoners. He says that there are no soldiers in Europe that can match the British in bayonet

Postcard of Mountain Grove House where Mort, Jennie, Raymond, Will, Elizabeth, Art, and Robbie Austin lived in Eldred. Postcard in the Austin Family Collection.

fighting. I thought the French were better, but I have heard a good many say not. Just got your letter [double underlined].

From your son,
McKinley

Bosch Family

Wilhelm Bosch's son Ed joined the Army sometime in 1917. Wilhelm's sons Ralph and Herman Bosch would also serve in WWI. Charles Bosch had served in the Army in 1900. In 1917 Charles and Lena Miller Bosch ran a boarding house north of Highland Lake. Their sons: Charlie Jr., Willie, Eddie, and Henry (Whipple) Bosch.

1917 photo of Menzo Bosch, Ed Bosch, Mary E. Horton, Herman Bosch, and John Horton. Photo courtesy of the Bosch Family.

Mary Elvira Horton married Herman Bosch in August 1917. Photo courtesy of Victoria Kohler.

Herman Bosch Marries Mary Horton

In August 1917 Herman Bosch married Mary Elvira Horton. Herman and Mary were country neighbors of Aida and Lon Austin and would be helpful to Aida when she was older.

McKinley Austin to His Brother

August 24, 1917
Dear brother,

How are you? I am getting along well now. I did have a very sore arm, but it is a good deal better now.

We have bayonet drill now and rifle practice. Our captain showed us some trenches modeled after the best and newest types and gave us a talk about transverses, parapets, etc. and their uses. Our lunch is in with the regulars now.

McKinley

Sara Austin to Mort and Jennie Austin, Eldred

September 3, 1917
Dear Mortimer and Jennie,

We would be very glad to have a visit with you before we return. Will you give us the pleasure of your company with us at dinner on Sunday, September 9th at one o'clock that we may all keep the Lord's Day together? We are all proud of Mortimer McKinley Austin and we will be glad to talk of him with you in the place where he was born.

Hoping to welcome you to the old cottage on the hill.

Very Sincerely Yours, Sara Hall Austin, Charlotte C. Hall

McKinley Austin to Mort Austin

September 5, 1917
Dear Father,

We had a holiday today as this is the day when the drafted men were called. There was a big parade in Chattanooga. My company was not in it fortunately and I had a day off. I watched the men march down Market St. They took about three quarters of an hour passing. The drafted men marched behind the soldiers. There were a number of Civil War veterans in the parade wearing their old uniforms of blue or gray.

I bet the drafted men will be sick of war soon. We got some hard drill at first, but I don't think it was anything to what the conscripts get. Some of our non commissioned officers were transferred to train the National Army as the conscripts are called, and from the way most of the regulars feel and speak of the "d---- slackers" they won't be shown as much consideration as we were.

Some of our men got awful lectures at first and the NC officers say that a man that has to be made to fight, doesn't deserve to be shown the patience a volunteer deserves. I don't mean they will be ill treated because of the rules in the discipline that forbid striking a man and all that. But they will probably get some savage calling downs and be reminded they were forced to fight for their country.

At noon a couple of the boys and I were down on Market St. I was just going to look for a restaurant when a fellow came up to us and said. "Boys, there's a lunch for you soldiers at the courthouse."

The lunch was served by the "Daughters of the Confederacy" and they sure treated us fine. They seemed to be afraid we won't get enough to eat and they kept urging us to eat some more.

One of the fellows with me tormented the other by making

out that the other wanted more to eat and the poor guy was as full as he could be. The first fellow would say, "Shorty wants some more cake."

Then a girl would come over with a plate of cake and offer it to "Shorty" who would protest that he didn't want any more. The girl would think he was bashful and insist on his taking it while we enjoyed ourselves immensely.

We made out that "Shorty" was the big eater of our company, but that he was bashful out among company. So the ladies tried to feed him all the more. When he got outside he gave us a calling down.

One of the old ladies told us that she had seen both armies in the Civil War and the men in camp in 1898, but that the lads in camp now were the best behaved soldiers she had ever seen.

Good bye and best wishes from your son,
McKinley

George Carner, Barryville, N.Y. to Mort Austin, Eldred
September 10, 1917
Dear Mort Austin,

Enclosing check $49.52 and money order $2.28 to apply on note dated May 3/17, from month amount $9,000 as follows on Principal $50.00. Interest $1.80; Balance due on note $40.00

Think you have done very well. This is war times you know. It will be all right to pay the balance next month.

Yours Truly,
Geo. Carner

Aida Austin, Eldred, to McKinley Austin
September 15, 1917
Dear McKinley,

It is nearly nine o'clock, but I will write you a few lines as I have so little time during the week.

Robbie Austin, McKinley's youngest brother. Photo courtesy of Mary Briggs Austin.

Dr. Austin's folks went back to the city yesterday and it seems rather lonesome. I will have the house this week and so be home every night.

I was rather disappointed when I came home Friday and did not find a letter at the Post Office from you, but I suppose you are kept pretty busy.

Dr. Austin has not returned from Maine yet and so we have not been able to learn anything definite with regard to this place, but I think we will get it all right.

Your father and mother with the three youngest were up for a little while this afternoon. Your father is working on the road now. Raymond worked awhile, but thought he was not getting enough and so left. I don't know what he intends to do.

Willie seems to hate to go to

Charlie and Lena Miller Bosch had a boarding house north of Highland Lake. These boys are 3 of their sons: Charlie Jr., Eddie, and Willie, in 1917. Photo courtesy of Ken Bosch.

November 3, 1917. "I am sending you some pictures I had taken in Chickamauga (Georgia)." McKinley is in front, second from the right. Photo in the Austin Collection.

school, so I will have to give him his work after school each day. I was in hopes I would not have to do any school work after school this year, but I do not like to make him go when he dreads it so.

Uncle Lon is very busy with the fall work. We had a very heavy frost three nights in succession and everything is killed. Miss Hall's flowers were just beginning to look fine. Everything was so late this year.

Maggie Dunlap was in for some butter tonight. She said Harold wrote to you sometime ago, but has not heard from you yet. Dr. Austin's wife received your letter.

Do write soon.
With love, Aunt Aida

Aida Austin, Eldred, to McKinley Austin
September 20, 1917
Dear McKinley,
I have not had a letter from you in 2 weeks. This makes the 5th that I have written to you. I will register this to you to make sure of your getting it. I had a letter from Mrs. Carlin last night. She said she had just written to you. Do let me hear from you.
With love,
Aunt Aida

The Carlins, Brooklyn, to McKinley Austin
September 1917
Dear friend McKinley,
I got your card and also a letter from Aunt Aida. It was some surprise to us as I thought you weren't old enough. It seems only a short time since you were quite small.

I hope you enjoy the life and that it agrees with you and that you get to be a healthy robust man as it is great outdoor life.

I have some friends away like you and they all like it real well and they tell me they are treated grand and that their health improved, so I hope and pray to God that the war will be over before they will have to send any more of our Americans.

Aunt Aida and Uncle Lon must have felt awful at you going away from them as they were so used to having you with them and also your parents and the family. But I hope you nor any more of the boys won't have to.

Take care of your health and be a good boy and let us hear from you when you get a chance as we all join in sending our best wishes to you in hopes God will save you and all our Americans.

*Hoping to hear from you soon,
Mr. and Mrs. and Estelle Carlin*

Isaac Sergeant Dies

In September Isaac Sergeant died at age 83. Isaac was the great-grandson of Rev. Isaac Sergeant and the grandfather of Chuck Myers, friend of my parents.

Isaac Sergeant, an old and highly respected resident of Highland, died at Eldred, September 30, 1917, after a long illness, aged 83.

Deceased was born at Yulan and was the son of Ethel B. Sergeant and Lettie Gardner Sergeant. The greater part of his life was spent in that section of the country.

Mr. Sergeant was a member of Company A of the 40th New York Infantry in the Civil War. For over 50 years he was a member and deacon of the Eldred Congregational Church and for a long time was superintendent of the Sunday school. He had held various offices in the Town of Highland.

The surviving relatives are one daughter, Mrs. Archie A. Myers, of Eldred, and one sister, Mrs. A.S. Hait, of Rutherford. The funeral will take place at 1:30 on Wednesday afternoon in the Eldred Congregational Church.

Several other people who have been a part of our story died in 1917: James Y. Parker, husband of Emily Parker and father of Emily Parker Stevens; Abel S. Myers, husband of Maria Hankins, and

War Stamps and Certificates

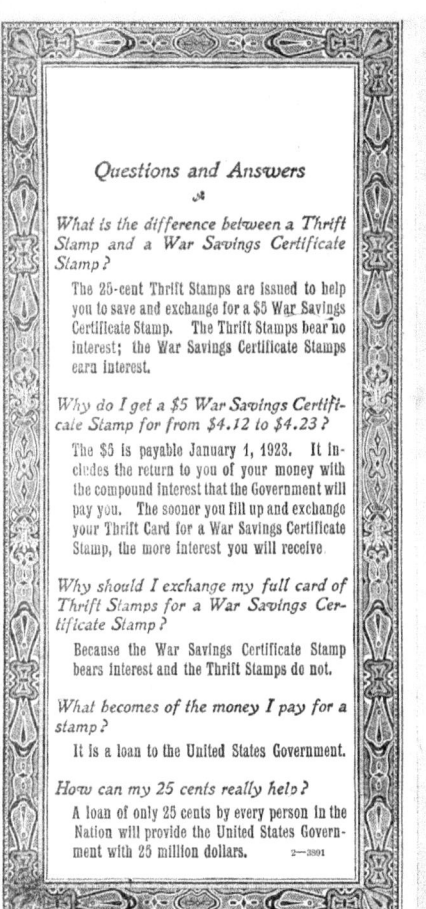

U.S. Thrift Card in the collection of Mary Briggs Austin.

War Saving Stamps and Certificates were provided for in the bond act of September 24, 1917, and put in operation December 3.

Thrift stamps cost 25 cents each, but did not accrue interest.

Sixteen thrift stamps on a thrift card could be exchanged for a war-savings stamp.

The war-savings stamps were to be affixed to certificates containing spaces for 20 stamps.

It had a face value of $100, if dated January 2, 1918. It matured January 1, 1923, when the Government said it would redeem it for $100.

If the 20 spaces were filled during December, 1917, or January, 1918, the cost was $4.12 for each stamp, or $82.40 for the full certificate.

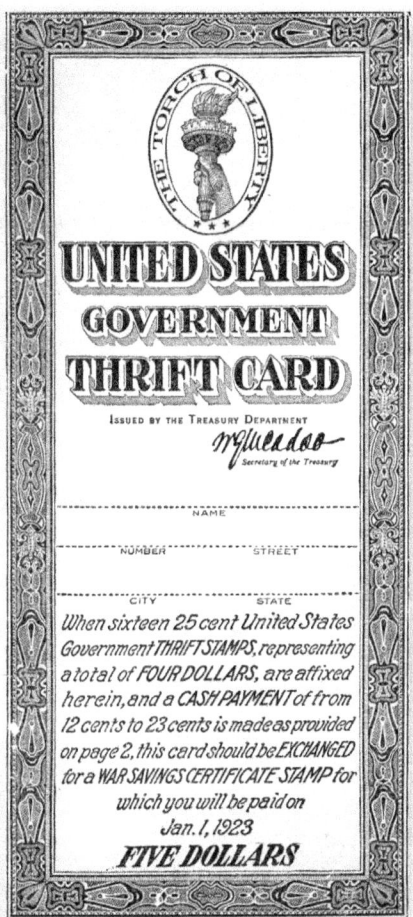

Inside of the U.S. Thrift Card in the collection of Mary Briggs Austin.

McKinley (on the left) with a friend at Chickamauga, Georgia, possibly at Crawfish Springs, mentioned in his November 3, 1917 letter. Photo in the Austin Collection.

father of 8 children including Archibald Myers and Edwin Van Schoick Myers; both George W.T. Myers and his wife Martha Mills Myers; and Addie Austin Thompson.

McKinley Austin, Chickamauga Park, Ga., to Jennie Austin
October 7, 1917
Dear Ma,
    I am sorry you were worried about me. I might say though that it is best to always believe the best; you'll hear of the worst. I have learned since I joined the army not to worry.
    I would have written sooner this time, but we had 24 hours in the trenches, a long hike, and a couple of sham battles and I have been so tired when the day's work was over, I didn't feel like writing. The strike is over and we can go to Chattanooga when it doesn't interfere with our duties.
    October 9th: Aunt Aida was here yesterday. I thought I made it clear in my letter that I was out of the hospital and what ailed me. She said the folks told her that my letter didn't say what was the matter or whether I was out of the hospital.
    I was glad to see her, but I thought it was foolish to come down here. McKinley

McKinley Austin, Chickamauga Park, Ga., to Mort Austin
November 3, 1917
Dear Father,
    I got out of the hospital alright. I wish I could get off and come home for a couple of weeks, but they are only giving short passes now.
    I am sending you some pictures I had taken in Chickamauga. One of the pictures is of me on the bridge below Chickamauga, another of two fellows from the 52nd down at Crawfish Springs, another of another fellow and me at the same place and the other of a place on the road to Chickamauga.
    Tell Aunt Aida I'll send her the pictures too, and that I'll write soon.
    But I am busy straightening my things out after being in the hospital and have not much time.
    Your son, McKinley

McKinley Austin, Chickamauga Park, Ga., to Mort Austin
December 4, 1917
Dear father,
    I am on guard at Ft. Oglethorpe just now. I'll be through and go back to our quarters the 11th. We go on guard every other day. My company goes on at 4 p.m. today. Then we come off at 4 p.m. tomorrow and rest till Thursday.
    Unless the rules are changed in our regiment, no furloughs will be given and no passes for over ten days. We have now a system for giving passes. A person who has been in the army:
4 months can get a 6-day pass
5 months can get a 7

6 months can get a 8
8 months can get a 9.

As it costs almost $45.00 with the new war tax on tickets and it takes near two days, I don't think it worthwhile getting a six day pass. I would only be home two days. Most likely we will be here in March, then I'll see if I can get a 9-day pass. I would like to see home before I go to France as I think the war will last some time.

The climate here averages much warmer than home. There are spells of cold weather, but they do not last long. The average type of weather here is the sun is very hot in the middle of the day. It gets cool about four o'clock and is very cold by morning (of course it isn't as cold as it is home then. The nights are cool all the year.

This part of Georgia is much colder than the average as we are in the mountains. The sudden changes in the weather are the worst here. The ground never is frozen very deep and soon thaws out, I am told. So far the ground has not been frozen as I have noticed. This is another disadvantage as it allows the "hookworm" to spread among the people. If a person understands how to prevent the spread of this trouble, there is no danger and cure is easy and certain.

If a person has a good warm house and uses sense, this wouldn't be a bad place to live. Work is not so well paid as it is in the North, but rents are lower and I believe land is cheaper.

Of course, it takes money to buy a farm in good condition. There are several companies here who will put money on farmlands at reasonable rates.

To give you examples, I will send you some advertisements of farms for rent or sale, running from 4 to 7,000 acres. Raymond was thinking of coming here and getting work. I'll put in some labor advertisements. Well, I've got to get ready to go on guard now.

From your son, McKinley

Mary Myers is Born

Mary Myers, daughter of Martin D. and Mary Fee Myers, was born in 1917. Martin D. Myers was the son of George W.T. and Martha Mills Myers.

Hazel Leavenworth

In 1917 Hazel Leavenworth, daughter of John Leavenworth and Amelia Bradley, traveled from Colorado to Eldred, New York, to meet her grandfather Isaac Bradley, and other family members. Hazel then went to New York City where she worked at the Irwin National Bank in the Woolworth Building. Hazel was so accurate with her accounts, that when she left to go back to Colorado, the bank personnel were reluctant to let her go.

There are some postcards Uncle Ell Austin wrote in late 1917 to his grandchildren, Robert Dale and Dot Calkin, children of Burt and Lillie Austin Calkin.

Ell Austin, Barre Place, Mass., to His Grandchildren, Bethel
November 25, 1917

Boarding Houses Ads 1917

Highland Lake House
Accommodates 35. Good table, fresh vegetables and milk. Large airy rooms; boating, bathing, fishing; telephone; mail delivered. Rates on application. H. Sulzbach, Eldred.
—Brooklyn Daily Eagle, *July 3, 1917.*

Barth House
Accommodates 40. All improvements. Telephone and mail service. Good home table. Airy rooms overlooking lake. All amusements; terms on application. P. Barth, Eldred.
—Brooklyn Daily Eagle, *July 3, 1917.*

Highland Cottage, Yulan
Splendidly situated on Washington Lake accommodates 125; fine roads; dancing, bathing, fishing tennis; garage $12 to 14; Booklet. E. V. Kalbfus.—Brooklyn Daily Eagle, *July 3, 1917.*

Montgomery Lake Cottage
Lake on premises. Boating, fishing, bathing. Own farm produce. G. Stidd, Eldred.—Brooklyn Daily Eagle, *July 3, 1917.*

Sunset View House, Highland Lake
Boating fishing bathing. Own farm produce. J. Loerch Stewart.
—Brooklyn Daily Eagle, *July 3, 1917.*

Sunset View Lodge on Highland Lake. Postcard courtesy of Larry Stern.

View from Montgomery Lake. Postcard courtesy of Larry Stern.

McKinley at his Aunt Aida's home. Photo courtesy of Mary Briggs Austin.

Master Robert D. Calkin,
My dear boy,
    I was very glad to receive your card of the 13th and was proud to learn you could write a card all alone. I think you must be learning very fast.
    The man here has some Billy goats but he will not sell them. It is quite cold here, but no snow as yet.
    Be a good boy and bring Mama lots of wood. Help Mama and Daddy all you can.
    With love, Grandpa

Miss Dorothy K. Calkin,
Dear Lassie,
    Your kind letter with Mama's received today although I can't quite read it, I was glad to know you tried to write and did it the best you could. You formed your marks very good and you will soon be able to write a long letter.
    Love from Grandpa

Lone Scout Magazine Letters
Sometime in December 1917, Raymond Austin sent his brother Mac Austin's Chattanooga, Tennessee address to the *Lone Scout Magazine*, asking *Lone Scout* readers to write to Mac.
    Lone Scouts was a rural Scout program started in 1915 by William Boyce who had started the Boy Scouts in 1910.
    Girls from rural areas across the United States saw Mac's address in the *Lone Scout* magazine (often their brother's) and wrote to him. The girls described their looks and their daily lives in the cold winter of 1918. They wrote about school, which was often 6 days a week. Basketball was played by both boys and girls. Some families had cars. Kodak cameras were popular. Besides winter sports, movies were popular and the young ladies often liked to go dancing. Many of the girls helped out the Red Cross in some way.
    Nearly all of the girls insisted on a photo of Mac. However, the gals often did not have a photo of themselves, but would promise to send him a photo when the lighting was better or the film was developed. They always seemed to have some excuse.
    The letters from these young ladies were from January and February 1918. Mac's address was:
    Mr. Mortimer Austin
    Company F, 11th U.S Infantry
    Military Branch,
    Chattanooga, Tennessee

    There were no letters after the end of February. Excerpts are included from most of the *Lone Scout* letters in this chapter.

Marnie Henry, DeBeque, Colo., to McKinley Austin
January 4, 1918
Dear Mortimer,
    I have just read a letter your brother Raymond has written to "Lone Scout" telling about you, so I decided I would write to you.
    There has been train load after train load of soldiers passed through our town here, some

Browning Automatic Rifle

1918 Browning Automatic Rifle. Photo: Public Domain, U.S. Marine Corps.

In 1917 John Browning was awarded a government contract for the M1918, a light weight automatic rifle that he designed. The M1918 was originally meant to be fired from the shoulder for soldiers in trench warfare.
    Colt's Firearms Manufacturing Company had an exclusive concession to manufacture the B.A.R. (Browning's patent was owned by Colt). But Colt was at peak capacity manufacturing the Vickers Machine for the British Army. Colt requested a delay in production of the B.A.R. so they could expand their manufacturing output.
    The request was denied because of the urgent need to replace the second rate weapons then being used. Winchester Repeating Arms Company became the prime contractor, but work did not begin until February 1918.
—wikipedia.org.

> ### Lone Scouts
>
>
>
> In one of the Boy Scout of America's lesser-known programs, nearly 400 boys around the world participate as Lone Scouts.
>
> Lone Scouting was born in 1915 when William D. Boyce, who had incorporated the B.S.A. five years earlier, decided that rural boys had little chance to join troops and founded the Lone Scouts of America so they could participate in Scouting.
>
> The L.S.A. attracted boys in droves, mainly through the magazine, *Lone Scout*. The B.S.A. absorbed the L.S.A. in 1924, which added more than 45,000 boys to its enrollment.
> —Robert Peterson, Scouting Alone, October 2001. Badge source: wikipedia.org.

Red Cross Poster from WWI showing a Red Cross nurse attending an injured man and his family. Library of Congress, Prints and Photographs Division: Chromolithograph; LC-USZC4-7707.

were going East and some West. They looked splendid in their Uniforms.

One boy, a friend of ours died at Kauf Kearney, California, and the remains were sent back here for burial. It was very sad. He was just 18 years.

How do you like the training campus? I think the war is sad, yet it is for such a just cause. We (everyone) are trying to do all we can to help out.

I am going to school and this year they are having school on Saturday, so we do not have much time for any work.

For fear I am imposing, I will not write much more, but I love all the soldiers and we are so proud of our U.S. boys.

I should be glad to hear about your army life and about yourself.

I am sorry you were sick and hope you have good health and all the happiness and brightness that *the New Year of 1918 can possibly hold in store for you.*

Best wishes to you from your unknown friend,
Marnie Henry

George Sidwell, CAC 7 Co., Fort Amador, Canal Zone, to McKinley Austin
January 5, 1918
Dear Old Mack,

Well this is the date you get a little older and tomorrow I do the same. Did four hours guard this morning. It is pay day and I go on pass this p.m., so will have time to write no more.

Drew just $13 yesterday. That is all that is left after my four liberty bonds bills, $.25 wounded soldiers fund, collected from loans $1.65, which left me just $8.40. When I went to town, I spent $5.20 for little odds and ends.

While in the city, I made up my mind to see the place. You talk of slums in New York, London, Chicago, but believe me they

"Mortimer, I have joined the Red Cross Nurse." Poster promoting the opportunities a nurse would have. Photo: Library of Congress, Prints and Photographs Division: LC-USZC4-7455.

cannot begin to compare with the city of Panama. [a long letter]
Yours,
George R. Sidwell

Jewell Hamilton, Vandervoort, Ark., to McKinley Austin
January 1918,
Kind friend,
Saw your address in "Lone Scout." Thought I would write you a few lines. Hope this will find you OK.
How do you like the Army? I have several friends who have gone to the Army. Oh it is so lonesome and makes me so sad to see them go. Miss Jewell Hamilton

Ottie Godsey, Peerless, Ind., to McKinley Austin
January 4, 1918
Dear Soldier Boy,
I saw an article that your brother had published in the "Lone Scout" magazine in which your name and address was given.
Although I am only a school girl living in a small town, I would enjoy corresponding with you. And if you will write, I will prove to you that us country girls can write as interesting letters as our city cousins.
Sincerely yours,
Ottie Godsey

Emily Crystal Falls, Mich., to McKinley Austin
January 4, 1918
Hello Mac,
Saw your brother's letter telling of you in my brother's "Lone Scout" and thought I would drop you a line.
I am still a High School girl, but am going to graduate this year. I like school real well because I think it is a place where you can have fun as well as study. How did you enjoy it before you left for the army?
Do you have skating where you are now? We have a grand rink where the athletic sports are held in the summertime.
The boys always want us to play "crack the whip" which we most of the time refuse because it isn't so very much fun to come home soaking wet every night, do you think so?
School is going to start here on Monday again. I think we will have lots of fun this week because our first basketball game of the season is going to be held Friday, and that means yell practice which I like very much.
We have a swell team and came very near winning the U.P. [Upper Peninsula] Championship last year.
How do you like the army? Please tell me about some of the things you do down there because I know that Michigan isn't the only state in the Union.
And please won't you send me a picture of yourself? It looks like I have a film in my Kodak now and have been waiting for the sun

to come up for about a week, but then it just keeps on snowing.

There is no more news in this town, whatsoever.

Do you dance? I went to a dance here in our City Hall New Year's Eve and as usual, had a good time.

Well, I guess I had better hang up the receiver as I hear some of my friends downstairs. Please excuse my writing, but I will promise to do better next time, if you give me the chance,
Sincerely,
Emily Neugebauer

Kate Lancaster, Elizabethtown, Ky., to McKinley Austin
My Dear Friend,
Your most welcome letter came the other day and I sure was delighted to hear from you.

We have been having some real bad weather in Kentucky. There is ice all over the ground at present and you sure have to watch your step or you will be walking on your hands instead of your feet. I sure would hate to drill this kind of weather and especially at Fort Oglethorpe.

My friends, Mr. and Mrs. F.G. Voight, have a drugstore in Chattanooga.

Have you been up on Signal Mountain since you have been at Chickamauga Park? You sure ought to go before you leave. I have a cousin stationed at Ft. Oglethorpe.

I will have to stop now and prepare my French for tomorrow.

Hoping to receive your picture real soon, I remain,
Sincerely,
Kate Lancaster

Cleo Morris, Porterville, Calif., to McKinley Austin
January 6, 1918
My dear friend Mortimer!

Eldred Red Cross

Red Cross Tireless Workers
The women of our local Red Cross are working most industriously for it as will be seen by the following report of the shipments this week:

Box 19, monthly allotment of 25 hot water bottle covers, value $5.

Box 20, 60 sweaters, 20 mufflers, 15 helmets, 115 pairs wristlets, and 80 pairs socks all hand knitted, value $490. The 80 pairs of socks alone show how busy the women are. The numerous auxiliaries are doing their share of this.

The Eldred Auxiliary has just raised $100 from a supper and contribution besides increasing their membership and sewing and knitting steadily. They have wisely taken a subscription for the *Red Cross Magazine* for their Sunshine Hall Free Library.—Republican Watchman, Monticello, N.Y.

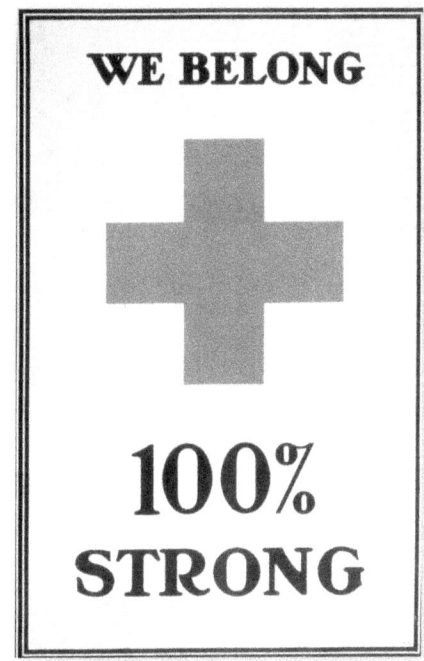

Red Cross Poster. Library of Congress, Prints and Photographs Division: LC-USZC4-7456.

As I am unknown to you, I have made up my mind to write you a few lines thinking perhaps you would enjoy a letter from a "Little California girl."

I have a kid brother; he was reading in a paper and your name was there, and he dared me to write to you.

How long have you been training and how do you like it? Suppose you boys get awfully lonesome.

A bunch of Porterville and Visalia boys were home at Christmas and New Year. We sure had some time. We had dances every eve. In Visalia, they give the "Yama-Yama" dance. My chum and I dressed in pink Yama Yama costumes.

I finished my schooling in 1916. Suppose you finished before enlisting? I sure would like to go to some of those eastern states.

And when do you think you'll leave old U.S.A.? I have an uncle in France now. That is we think he's there.

Mortimer, I have joined the Red Cross Nurse. But I am not sure that I'll pass my exams. I trained for 6 months in Los Angeles. I sure want to go. My folks are scared I will pass. But leave it to Toots, ha! ha!

I have a boyfriend in San Francisco in the Navy who leaves for New York soon. Also have a friend in New York in the Aviation squadron. I hear from them twice a week. I write to 5 different ones and have pictures of each. I surely would be pleased to have yours.

And if there is any of the California boys there, tell them you received a letter from me. And I wish them all good luck.

Do you get to go to any dances. I suppose you dance.

WWI barracks. Irwin Briggs was at Ft. Riley, Kansas. Photo courtesy of Mary Briggs Austin.

My that is all we think about here.

My father has a lemon and grapefruit grove, so I came out to help pick the grapefruit. Something I never did before.

And I sure would be delighted to have a nice long letter from you and picture too.

Mac, keep your enthusiasm up and don't get cold feet. Wishing you the very best of luck and happy year. So good by. With love.

I am a true friend,
Cleo Morris

Ila White, Duraham Okla., to McKinley Austin
January 7, 1918
Soldier Boy,

After seeing your name in the "Lone Scout" which your brother sent in, I thought I would write to you. Many of our brothers and friends are called away to protect our flag. I haven't any brother in the army, but two cousins.

We are doing our bit for our country. Some of us who are several miles from a camp, haven't any idea of what our country is doing to protect herself and it is our duty to do everything we can to win the war.

Almost every person, even children have joined the Red Cross. I think there is nothing nicer than our Red Cross organization. The older ones make the hospital garments and we younger ones hem the pillow cases and knit.

As my letter is getting long, I will describe myself and close. I am five feet four inches tall, have light hair, blue eyes and a fair complexion. Age 17 years, weigh 124 pounds.

Would like to hear from you,
Ila White

Annie Herald, Equality, Ill., to McKinley Austin
January 7, 1918
Dear Soldier Boy,

For I will call you that because Mrs. Siddell is directing me. She is President of the Red Cross Committee, and she has directed 5 girls to write to all soldier boys that she gets an address from. I was the only girl to come to the meeting this afternoon and this is what I have to do.

I like my work and she has a son in the military band. I have to write about 15 soldier boys. I get a letter nearly every day and I take them to my president to read to everyone there.

She got your address out of a "Lone Scout," a real boy paper. She also told me to say she was proud of all Lone Scouts and to say it was a fine boy organization.

I have a brother of 12 that belongs to the Lone Scouts of America. If there are any boys who want to write to me or my president, address them to me as I am secretary and get the letters.

I am 15 years of age and in the 8th grade in school. I have 2 brothers and one sister and no father. All of my brothers are younger than me and so is my sister who I love more than anything else.

Do you smoke and have you got a testament? If you have not, we will send you one. I have sent two dozen to France, and have got some more ready to send.

Good bye and answer please.
Annie Herald

Maggie Dempsey, Warrior, Ala., to McKinley Austin
January 8, 1918
Dear Unknown friend,

I will rite you a short letter as I seen your name in Lone Scouts. I like to receive letters from soldiers. I have a brother that hasn't gone yet, but guess he will half to go before the war is ended.

I have many friends at Camp Pike, so I wood like very much to hear from you as I am a girl of 19 years old, 5 feet tall, weight 125; black hair, black eyes, dark complexion.

So please send me one of your pictures, and I will send you one of mine. Hope to hear from you soon and a long letter, so I will say, Good By. From your friend,
Maggie Dempsey

Anne Rassine, Olney, Ore., to McKinley Austin

January 8, 1918
Mortimer Austin,

Perhaps you wonder how a girl almost from the other end of the continent from where you are stationed, has got your name and address.

My oldest brother gets the boys' magazine, "Lone Scout," and as I usually always read every copy of them, I chanced to read your brother's letter, where he gave your address and name.

As he didn't say that girls were not allowed to write, I am writing to you, although I presume that this isn't the only letter that you have received from girls.

My home is in a small country village called Olney, ten miles from Astoria, the largest seaport city in Oregon. We only have a stove, hotel, post office, pool room, jitney station, and dance hall. The people live quite close together, although some farms are quite large, which makes the distance to the nearest neighbors quite long.

My brother, who is younger than I am, is a real patriot. He certainly would fight for his country if he only was old enough. He is what every true hearted American boy must be.

Mortimer Austin, you surely must be very loyal to your mother country to have enlisted at the age of 18 in Uncle Sam's service.

I'm sure you did what was right. For you have a just cause to fight for and if needed to give your life and all. God's blessing will rest on every true hearted American is my belief.

I am a country girl, not 17 yet, am considered pretty by some and quite the opposite by others.

I love the country. I wouldn't exchange it for the city, not for worlds. I think I have to get used to the city life because I am going to college next winter.

We have quite a large number of Red Cross workers in Astoria, although Olney's share in the Red Cross work is comparatively small. I have joined the annual Red Cross and I'd like to be a Red Cross nurse some day, but my parents object, so I can't even think of it.

I close this letter with a sincere wish for that you (an unknown stranger) will have a happy new year (although we all have our doubts to that) and my good wishes for a joyous birthday.

I remain, Yours truly,
Anne Aline Rassine

Jewell Hamilton, Vandervoort, Ark., to McKinley Austin
January 8, 1918
Kind friend,

Saw your address in "Lone Scout," and thought I would write. Hope this will find you ok.

How do you like the army? I have several friends who have gone to the army. Oh it is so lonesome and makes me sad to see them go. There is a boy in the camp you are in that lived here. I was writing to a boy in Texas. He left for France. I haven't heard from him since.

My brother takes "Lone Scout" of which he is a member. I saw your address and thought I would write to pass the time.

Arkansas is awfully rough and dry. We haven't had a good rain since about August. There are lots of measles around here. I had them last June.

A friend,
Miss Jewell Hamilton

Lela Sperline, Wenatchee, Wash., to McKinley Austin
January 10, 1918
My Dear Friend,

For that I am sure you will be. I doubt you could ever guess

Irwin Briggs. Caption on photo reads: "The principal part of a soldier is his feet. He must march, march, march and he must have shoes large enough to be comfortable and give his feet room to spread out." Photo courtesy of Mary Briggs Austin.

January 17, 1918 envelope sent to McKinley Austin by Vera Allen from Cates, Indiana. "Do you think you will have to go to France?" Envelope in the Mary Briggs Austin Collection.

where I got your address. Your brother is a "Lone Scout," is he not?

My brother is also a "Lone Scout," and I generally read his papers. I noticed your brother's article, so I decided to write to you as I have been told several times that soldier boys get so lonesome.

I suppose you are wondering who in the world I am. My name is Lila Sperline. I have medium dark brown hair, blue eyes, and a light complexion. I am 5 feet 7 inches tall and weigh about 120 pounds. No, I am not pretty. I have freckles which spoils my beauty. Poor me. I will be 17 this month.

I would like to be an aviatrix.

I am in school today, but I can't study much as I broke my glasses and haven't gotten them fixed yet and my eyes bother me a good deal. Don't you feel sorry for me? I'm sure you do now.

Hoping that you will think me nice enough to write to.

I am an unknown friend,
Lela Sperline

Beatrice Hanson, Keatchie, La., to McKinley Austin
January 10, 1918
Dear Soldier boy,

I know you will be puzzled to receive a letter post marked Keatchie, but I was looking over the "Lone Scout," and found a letter from your brother and he gave your address and said that he would like for someone to write to you. So I thought I would write because I feel that everyone should try to cheer the boys that are in service.

I have a brother in the Army who is cooking for Co. G, 19th Infantry at Freeport, Texas. He likes it fine. He enlisted at Shreveport, Louisiana, last May and we haven't seen him since.

Well, it is getting late.

So by, by, and answer soon,
Beatrice Hanson

Bessie McCoy, Dante, Va., to McKinley Austin
January 10, 1918
Mr. Mortimer Austin,

Please pardon me for writing as I am a stranger, but I hope you will not think hard of me for I seen your address in the "Lone Scout," where your little brother was asking us all to write you cheerful letters. I hope you are satisfied and having a jolly good time.

I have two brothers that will start to Petersburg, Virginia, to the training camp the 15th of February. I am sorry to see them leave, but the time is now at hand that our dear American boys will have to go.

I wish you all God speed and a safe return back to the ones that love you all.

I will be pleased to hear from you and others also.

Yours truly, Bessie McCoy

Emily Neugebauer, Crystal Falls, Mich., to McKinley Austin
January 11, 1918
Dear Friend Mac,

Received your most welcome letter. Last night we had our first basketball game and believe me, it was a good one. We played Iron Mountain and of course won.

Have you been in Tennessee since you left home? Some of the boys from here have been to Washington, Texas, and New York, but I guess their next journey will be to France, don't you think so?

I am taking the following subjects: U.S. history, English 8, Physics, and Commercial Arithmetic.

The other day up in Physics lab, the boys took a frog from one of the jars and took it down into the assembly room with them. They put it in the girls desks and dangled it in front of their faces. You should have heard the yelling, but it was soon ended and resulted in two of the boys being sent home because the Principal caught them in the act.

Please tell me something more

about yourself, Mt. Hermon, and the army.
As Ever,
Emily Neugebauer

Ottie Godsey, Peerless, Ind., to McKinley Austin
January 13, 1918
Dear Mr. Austin,
Thank you very much for writing me such a nice letter. Now you said that you preferred the country girls to those from the city. Now you must be joking, for you know we are supposed to be stupid and half witty girls.

I like the farm life. I am a Kentuckian and Mama is there now visiting and I am doing the farm work. We live just south of the little town of Peerless on a small little farm in the southern part of Indiana.

We have a nice little school here with just a two-roomed building and teacher. My teacher is a man and all of us like him for a teacher. I am in the eighth grade.

But I am not in school this week, nor last. I am staying at home and doing the work while Mama is away.

You said you was having cold weather in Tennessee. It was 18 degrees below zero last night. The snow blew in drifts several feet deep and is still snowing. The railroads are even blocked. Just one train has passed today.

I am a brunette, have blue eyes, light complexion, weigh about 110 pounds, not very tall, and will soon be 17 years of age.

I would be pleased to receive your picture, but haven't any at present of myself suitable to send you, now.

I remain, the school girl,
Ottie Godsey

Maggie Dempsey, Warrior, Ala., to McKinley Austin
January 14, 1918
Dear Friend,
Great pleasure I take in answering your most kind and welcome letter which I received to day. Shure glad to hear from you.

I live in farming country and mining camp area, 2 miles from Warrior.

There are plenty of girls. But the boys are scattered. They have just about all been called away.

Good by. Answer soon to your friend,
Maggie Dempsey

Ruth Colville, Barryville, to McKinley Austin
January 15, 1918
Dear Friend,
Received your letter last week. We were glad to hear that you were still in America.

We haven't any horses this winter, so I hardly ever get to Eldred or in fact anywhere. They had a box social in the fall and another one around Thanksgiving, but I was in

Some Bugle calls in Irwin Briggs's "Drill Regulations and Service Manual for Sanitary Troops, U.S. Army," 1914. Book courtesy of Mary Briggs Austin.

Brooklyn, so naturally I did not get to that one.

It certainly has been a very cold winter. 30 degrees below zero some of the time, but we really haven't much to kick about in that direction as we have plenty of wood.

I have a cousin who is a major in the Aviation Corp. I have not heard since where he went.
Ruth Colville

Vera Allen, Cates, Ind., to McKinley Austin
January 17, 1918

Word War I tents. Photo courtesy of Mary Briggs Austin.

January 22, 1918 envelope from Cleo Morris, Porterville, California. "I am out on my Dad's Ranch until we can sell out." Envelope courtesy of Mary Briggs Austin.

Dear Friend,
As I saw your address in the paper. I will write you a few lines.
I am about 5 feet 2 inches in height, have brown eyes and hair am fair complected. I will graduate this winter.
There are just three in our family, my mother, brother, and myself. My father died about 8 years ago.
If you write, will you please send me a description of yourself and also a picture if you have one? I have heard that the soldiers can't write anything about their camps, so I don't suppose it would do any good to ask you to tell me anything about camp life.
Do you think you will have to go to France? Hoping to hear from you soon.
Your friend,
Vera M. Allen

Rachel Hidden, Boyd, Minn., to McKinley Austin
January 1918
Dear Mortimer,
It is the same with me as it was with you. I have been very busy this last week and did not get time to write before.
Last Sunday, 6 of us girls walked to a little town 7 miles from here. We walked both ways so it was about 14 miles. We started at 4 o'clock and came home half past 8. We were so tired when we came home that most of us went right to bed.
I certainly am glad you sent your picture. But I feel ashamed to send this letter without mine. I had some taken, but they were not good as they were not developed and it takes so long when I have them developed. But I will try my best to have one next time. I would like to hear from you the same.
Your friend,
Rachel Hidden
S.W.A.K.

Katheryn Lancaster, Elizabethtown, Ky., to McKinley Austin
January 19, 1918
Dear Soldier boy,
I suppose you will wonder where in "Sherman's Version of War" I got your name.
My brother takes the "Lone Scout" and one day when it was snowing real hard and I couldn't go outdoors because I had such a bad cold. So I was looking at the "Lone Scout" magazine and happened to read a piece about you written by your brother.
I am sending you my picture which I hope will meet with your approval. If it does, I will be expecting an answer soon.
Sincerely,
Kathryn Lancaster

Ila White, Durham, Okla., to McKinley Austin
January 20, 1918
Dear Friend,
Your letter received Friday. Was glad to hear from you.
It has been real cold here. There is snow on the ground now. We sure need some kind of moisture. We did not raise any crops at all this year or last. We live on a farm 21 miles from Canadian City, Texas.
There are just 4 in our family. I haven't any mother. She died when I was only several years old. I have one sister and one brother. My sister is going to Lawton to the State School. She will graduate next year. My brother is only 12 and he is at home with Papa and I. I have been keeping house ever since I was 12. I have went to school every winter. This is my first year in high school.
We visited Camp Douiphau Thanksgiving. We saw them drilling and working in the trenches. After dinner we went out to see the airplanes. It was certainly a sight to us because we had never been to a camp before. The boys that were there were to leave for France the 15th of this month.
When do you all have to leave? I guess this terrible war will last until the old Kaiser is killed. But when Uncle Sam gets all of

his boys over there, things will change and we will show them what our flag can do.

Well, I will close with best wishes and hoping to hear from you. Ila White

Anna Betsa, Lopez, Pa., to McKinley Austin
January 22, 1918
Dear Sir,

I thought I would drop you a few lines and see if you would correspond with me. I am a girl of 18 years.

I will not tell you how I got your address now, but if you write to me, I will tell you later on and I would like to have you send me your picture.

Your loving friend,
Anna Betsa

Rachel Hidden, Boyd, Minn., to McKinley Austin
January 22, 1918
Dear Friend Mortimer,

I thought I would answer your letter which I received this morning. You certainly are busy with your drilling if it is like you had written.

Our teacher is looking this way so mad. I suppose she will come around this way and grab it.

I am ashamed to send this because I have written so poorly against yours, but I will do better next time if I can.

We have been knitting for the Red Cross in school.

I remain as your friend,
Miss Rachel Hidden

Bonnie Osburn, Rossville, Ga., to McKinley Austin
January 22, 1918
Dear Friend,

I received your letter yesterday and was glad to hear from you. Your brother of Eldred, New York, told me about you

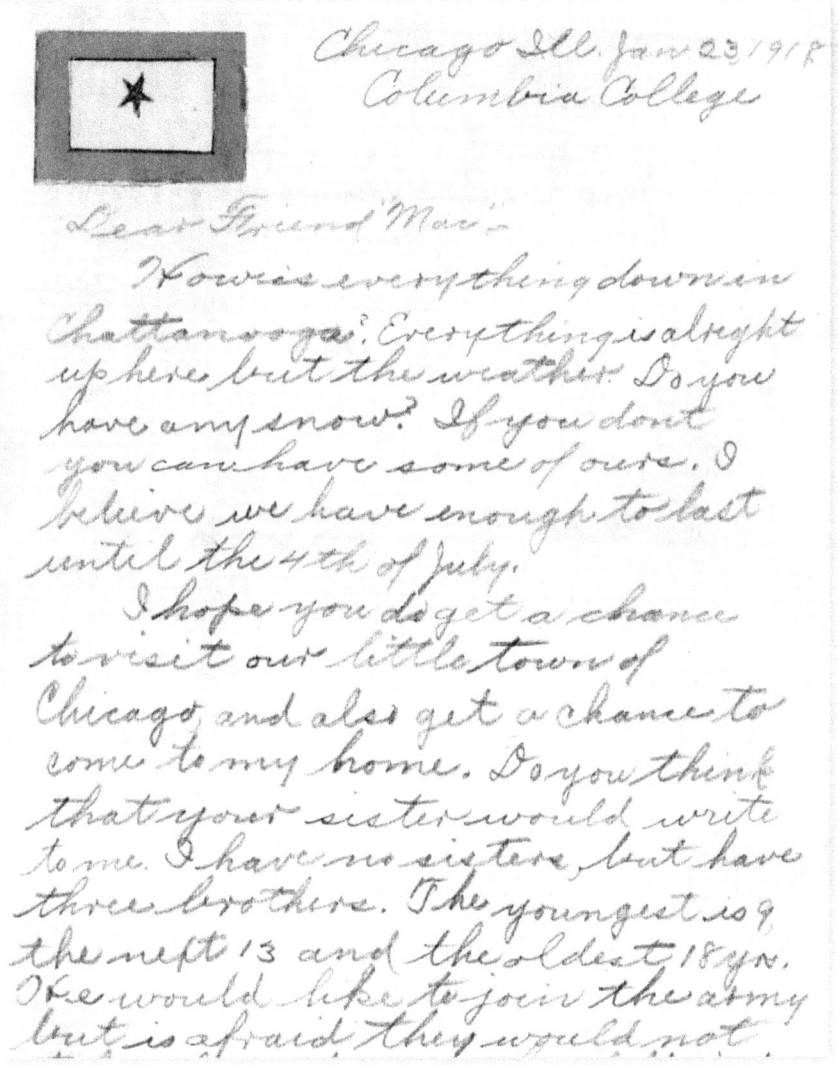

January 23, 1918, Chicago, Illinois. From Helen Hamilton. "The star in the flag is for you." Letter courtesy of Mary Briggs Austin.

and about you going to school at Mount Hermon, Massachusetts, and about you going to the hospital twice.

How are you getting along with the mumps? I have had them.

I will close, wishing to hear from you again this week.
Yours truly,
Bonnie Osburn

Cleo Morris, Porterville, Calif., to McKinley Austin
January 22, 1918
My dear friend Mac,

Your most interesting letter received some few days past. And must say, I surely was delighted to hear from you. I don't know how many different soldiers we Porterville girls write to, so far.

When you come home for good, first come out, I suppose I'll be here. If I am not, plenty more. Come and we'll feed you on grapefruit.

I am out on my Dad's Ranch until we can sell out. But goodness, I don't know how long that will be. It's lemon and grapefruit 100 acres.

Mac, I sure feel sorry for you if you don't get to go home before leaving. I hope you can.

Be sure and send a photo.
Best wishes old pal,

Page from Irwin Briggs's Drill Regulations and Service Manual for Sanitary Troops, U.S. Army, 1914. Book courtesy of Mary Briggs Austin.

Good by and good luck (answer soon),
Cleo (Toots)

Leila Sperline, E. Wenatchee, Wash., to McKinley Austin
January 23, 1918
Dear Friend Mortimer,

I wrote some time ago, but I was afraid it would not reach you, so am writing again.

I am 5 feet 7 inches tall, weigh about 120 pounds and am 17 years of age, last Saturday.

Last Friday evening I was sitting at the piano with one of my girlfriends who had come to see me when the door opened and what do you suppose? It was a bunch of young folks. When they stepped inside, the door they yelled, "Surprised!" And they sure were right for I was never so surprised in my life as I was then. We had an excellent time, at least I did, even if it was a surprise party.

I have blue eyes, medium dark brown hair, and a light complexion. I am not pretty but am not ashamed of my face by any means. I wear my hair in curls part of the time and my girl friends say I look real "cute" with curls even if I am 17.

How do you like army life? Do you boys get very lonesome? I imagine you would. I think I would like to be an aviatrix pretty well. I have a friend who is over in France, who is only nineteen, too.

I suppose you wonder where I got your address, don't you? Your brother is a Lone Scout, is he not? Well, my brother is also a Lone Scout, and I almost always read his "Lone Scout" papers. Your brother put an article in the paper and told all about you, your age and the month of your birthday and gave your address. I had been told several times to write to soldiers as they were generally lonesome, so that is why I am writing to you.

Well I had better close as it is getting late. So Good bye. Please answer right away as I am waiting for an answer.

Adios Senor, Your unknown friend, Leila B. Sperline

Celia Hayat, Springwood, Va., to McKinley Austin
January 23, 1918
Dear Mr. Austin,

Your little brother had your name printed in a paper and I saw it and thought it was my duty to write to you.

I am a young girl of 16, have light hair and blue eyes. I live on a farm near Springwood, Virginia.

Do they train you very hard down there? I hope they do not. Won't you be glad when you get back home once more? I feel so sorry for the boys that have to leave their parents and sweet hearts. My beau got kind of jealous when I told him I was going to write to you.

Answer soon. Please send me one of your pictures.
Celia Hayat

H. Hamilton, Columbia College, Chicago, Ill., to McKinley Austin
January 23, 1918
Dear Friend Mac,

How is everything down in Chattanooga? Everything is alright up here, but the weather. Do you have any snow? If you don't, you can have some of ours. I believe we have enough to last until the 4th of July.

I hope you do get a chance to visit our little town of Chicago and also get a chance to come to my home. Do you think that your sister would write to me? I have no sisters, but have three brothers. The youngest is 9, the next 13, and the oldest 18 years. He would like to join the army, but is afraid they would not take him because his left index was blown off.

I am 5 ft. 4 in. tall; have dark brown hair and eyes. I do not consider myself good looking. You will be disappointed in me, I'm afraid. I am 16 years old and my favorite stone is the blue sapphire. You were just 19 this month, weren't you?

I go to Columbia Business College and am taking up the bookkeeping course. I expect to take the Civil Service examination when I finish.

I am not very good at writing letters, but if you can read this writing and want me to write, I guess I will have to do the best I can. I will give you a picture of me on one condition, that you send me one of you first.

My nickname begins with M, too. The star in the flag is for you.

Hoping you will write soon, I am Your Friend,
Helen "Major" Hamilton

Annie Herald, Equality, Ill., to McKinley Austin
January 23, 1918
Dear Friend,
For that is what you are to me now. I was glad to hear from you as I am from others. This is nite at my home and almost my bedtime because you see, I have been out on the hill coasting with the kids and I love the sports myself, if they are outdoors sports as coasting and wading snow. I do not know how to skate and I do not want to know because I nearly got my arm broke last winter when trying to learn.

Well, I am real sorry for your brother. Hope he will get in next time he tries. There was some boys down here tried to get in, but couldn't so they came back to school and said they guess they could go to school and they are doing fine now, better than when they went to the station.

How would you like my picture? Please send me yours if you don't mind, because you see, you talk so frankly in your letter. I like it and so did Mrs. Siddels.

I am glad you like your new life. I am glad you do not smoke, as all boys do, almost all I know.

Talk about cold weather, the snow has been 24 inches deep. We have not see the ground for 4 weeks and I think more.

Well, I will say Good bye. Answer soon, from your loving friend,
  Miss Annie E. Herald
  Reindeer love the mountains
  Rabbits love the hills
  I like my soldier brother
  God knows I always will.

Ottie Godsey, Peerless, Ind., to McKinley Austin
January 24, 1918
Dear Mr. Austin,
I received your letter this morning just a few minutes before school time.

What are you doing now? Still drilling I suppose.

I have been sick and unable to attend school for some time, but was able to go this morning.

January 26, 1918 photo of Maggie Dempsey from Warrior, Alabama. Photo courtesy of Mary Briggs Austin.

You surely did have a pleasant time when you went to boarding school. We have nice times here at school. You see the Domestic Science Class has a oil stove and sewing machine. So we cook on the stove and make aprons and things on the machine.

We made candy the other evening at school and the teacher helped us of course. And then after we made the candy, the teacher dismissed school, so all we had to do then was to feed the boys with candy.

It is getting warmer, but the snow isn't melting. It must have been awful cold back at your home. It has been colder here than it has been for 6 years.

We are going to have a patriotic meeting at Bedford, a little town south of here, Wednesday, and the teacher is going to take us all. I am almost sure we will enjoy ourselves, as it is to be an all day affair.

Your Camp is situated in a historic little place, isn't it? We just had the Battle of Chickamauga as our history lesson a few days ago.

So you are in quarantine for the mumps? I have had them and I don't think they are anything pleasant.

I wish you could send me your picture. I like your nickname.

Don't forget to write to your friend, Ottie Godsey

B. Hanson, Keatchie, La., to McKinley Austin
January 24, 1918

Dearest Friend,

Will try to answer your most highly appreciated letter. I was helping mother wash when I got your letter. She was looking for a letter from my brother in the Army and sent my little brother to the mailbox to get the mail.

Well, since you have described yourself to me, I will describe myself to you. I am only 14 years of age, 5 ft. and 5 in. tall; weigh about 120 pounds; blonde hair and brown eyes. Will send you a picture of myself later on. I haven't any now.

If you have any pictures of yourself be sure and send me one for I'm crazy to see one.

We are having some bad weather here. It has been snowing and sleeting and it is melting.

Well, I am having a fine time going to school. I go to a graded school. We will start to practice playing basketball as soon as it gets dry enough, and when we all get our suits. We are going to have our pictures made and I will send you one.

Well, news is as scarce here as meat (ha. ha.), so I will have to bid you by by. Answer soon.

Lovingly yours,
Beatrice Hanson
Wrote with a pen, bottled with a tear, sealed with a kiss and sent to my dear.

McKinley Austin, Chickamauga Park, Ga., to Aida Austin
January 24, 1918
Dear Aunt,

We have had bad weather. It was warmer today and the mud is about up to my ankles. We are busy drilling now. There is nothing to tell you. We are not allowed to tell much anyway. There was a bit of verse on our bulletin board:

"Soldiers, beware, enemies ears are everywhere.

"A wise old owl lived in an oak

"The more he saw the less he spoke

"The less he spoke, the more he heard,

"Soldier, imitate that bird."

There is no need of worrying over me. We are getting good food and we have as good care as can be given us. I am feeling good and am getting fatter. You would be surprised to see me now.

Did you see the letter Raymond wrote about me to the "Lone Scout?" I met a fellow in Chickamauga who asked if I

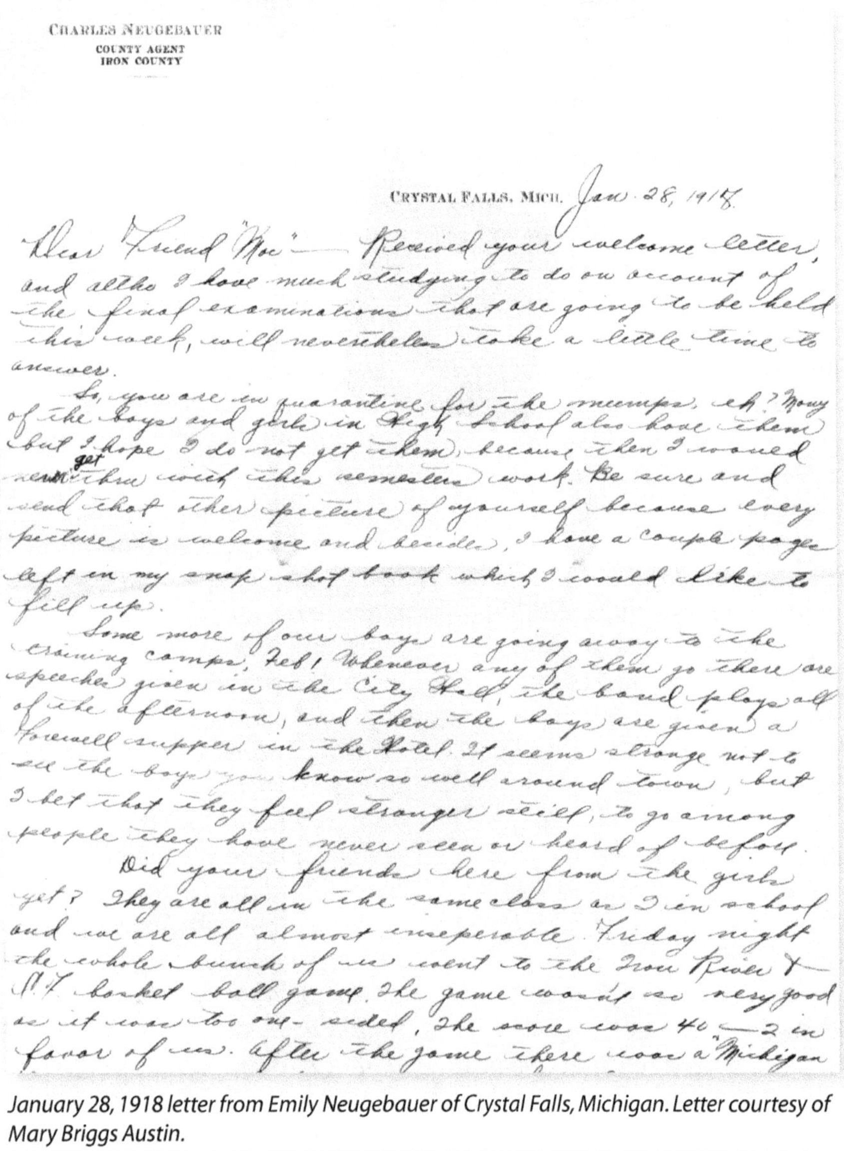

January 28, 1918 letter from Emily Neugebauer of Crystal Falls, Michigan. Letter courtesy of Mary Briggs Austin.

"knew Private Mortimer Austin, F Company, 11th infantry." I told him I did. He had seen that letter. He was a nice fellow.
Well, good by,
Your nephew, McKinley

Maple Thompson, Robinson, Ill., to McKinley Austin
January 25, 1918
Dear Mac,
You will no doubt be surprised to receive this letter. I secured your address from a friend of yours. Do you think you will ever go to France? I certainly hope not. Did you enlist or was you drafted? Mother is president or something of the Red Cross in this town and wants me to knit, but—nothing doing. I couldn't be still that long. Be sure and answer.
Yours,
(Miss) Maple G. Thompson

Bessie McCoy, Dante, Va., to McKinley Austin
January 25, 1918
Mr. Mortimer Austin,
I received your letter and was more than pleased to hear from you. I hope these few lines will find you enjoying your life.
Say! I was surprised to hear your little brother was a man. (ha ha) Please don't write him the joke.
Well I guess you would love to know what kind of looking creature I am that is so fast to write you.
I am 5 feet and 3 inches high, weigh 130 pounds; dark brown hair and bonny brown eyes, 21 years old. I will soon be an old maid. I hope you are sorry for me. (ha ha)
I am sending you one of my horrible looking photos and would love for you to send me one of yours. Excuse bad writing

McKinley Austin at his Aunt Aida's home. Photo courtesy of Mary Briggs Austin.

and all mistakes. Answer soon.
Yours truly,
Bessie McCoy

Maggie Dempsey, Warrior, Ala., to McKinley Austin
January 26, 1918
Dear Friend,
Was shure glad to read another letter from you, but was sorry to know you didn't send me one of your pictures as I am sending you one of my pictures. It was taken about a year ago.
I hope you all are having a good time out there.
My sister said she was going to rite to some of those boys out there. But said she would like for them to rite first. O say, I never did ask you if you had been married. I might be writing to a married man for all I know as you know I can't say, but you can hope not as I am quite lonesome this eve. No one here but me.
But I hope the war will end some time soon and I will get to

see you and all of my friends who is in Camp. I am your friend,
Maggie Dempsey

Laura Watson, Main St., Winton, N.C., to McKinley Austin
January 27, 1918
My dear unseen friend,
Seeing your name in the paper that you would like to hear from someone, I decided to write.
How do you like army life? Would you like to have a description of myself? Here goes: tall, slender, brown eyes, dark hair. If you have a photo of yourself, send it to me.
Somewhere in France, I have a 20-year-old brother fighting the Germans.
Do you think you will ever have to go to France? I hope not if we correspond. Haven't you a brother named Raymond? He was the chap that put your name in the paper. I guess I must close and go to super.
Please write me as soon as possible. Lovingly,
Laura May Watson

Emily Neugebauer, Crystal Falls, Mich., to McKinley Austin
January 28, 1918
Dear Friend Mac,
Received your welcome letter and although I have much studying to do on account of the final examinations that are going to be held this week, will nevertheless take a little time to answer.
So you are in the quarantine for the mumps, eh? Many of the boys and girls in High School also have them, but I hope I do not get them, because then I would never get through with this semester's work.
Be sure and send that other picture of yourself because every picture is welcome and besides,

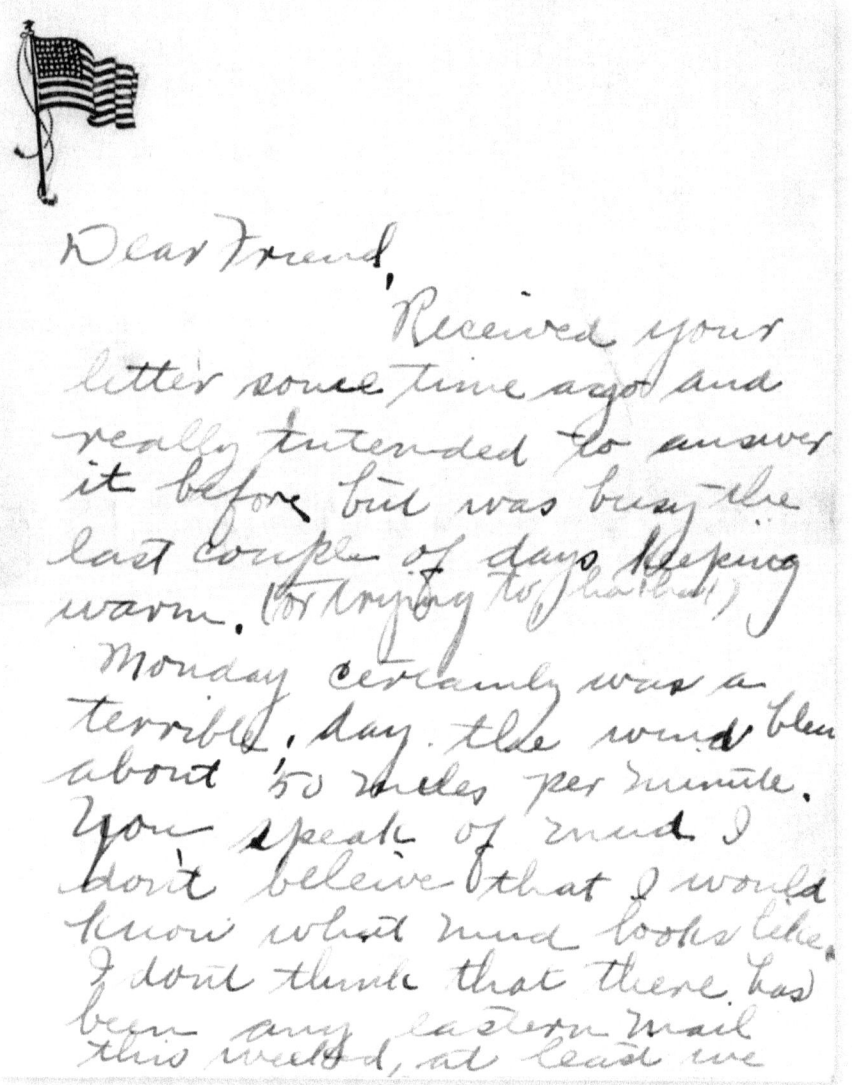

February 7, 1918 letter from Ruth Colville in the collection of Mary Briggs Austin.

I have a couple pages left in my snap shot book which I would like to fill up.

Some more of our boys are going away to the training camps, February 1. Whenever any of them go there are speeches given in the City Hall, the band plays all of the afternoon and then the boys are given a Farewell Supper in the Hotel.

It seems strange not to see the boys you know so well around town, but I bet that they feel stranger still to go among people they have never seen or heard of before. Did your friends hear from the girls yet? They are all in the same class as I in school and we are all almost inseparable.

Friday night the whole bunch of us went to the Iron River and I.R. Basketball game. The game wasn't so very good as it was too one sided. The score was 40 to 2 in favor of us.

After the game there was a Michigan Day program held in the High school assembly which was composed mostly of themes that the English class had written with a little music in between.

On the morning of the same day, we girls took our dinner to school and believe me, we had a good time.

We each had our turn of playing the piano while the other girls were eating, and then after we were through with that, we changed hats and coats and went downtown. We were nearly late for school, which would have been awful sad indeed because then we would have had to stay in the Principal's office while the whole school were practicing yells for the game. But we got there just in time, and so had our chance of yelling as loud as the rest of the bunch.

Saturday night, fifteen of us were going bob riding, but changed our minds when we went outside because it was so cold.

I wasn't going to venture outside later, but Myrtle Brooks came down and got me and then we went to the show. After the show she came over to our house, where we entertained ourselves for the rest of the evening, drumming on the piano and playing cards.

Nothing exciting has happened so far today. I might go to a dance tonight given by the Red Cross. That's if my mother will let me. Excuse the writing as I am in a terrible hurry.

As ever,
Emily Neugebauer

Jewell Hamilton, Vandervoort, Ark., to McKinley Austin
January 31, 1918
Dear Friend,

I received your letter and I was glad to get it. I am glad you like the army for those who go against their will are not contented.

My oldest brother that is single thinks he would like the army, but Mama don't want him to go. He tried to get in the Navy when he was 16, but he was too young.

Well, I will let you know how

I look. I am 5 ft. 3 inches tall; weigh 125 pounds; light hair and curly too, and got blue eyes.

I have two single brothers, and two married, and have two sisters that are married. My oldest brother that is single is a school teacher, has a second grad certificate. He goes to school at Vander Vooort. I go to Marble Hill. It is a small country school. I am in High 6th.

Haven't went to school any since November. I like school fine. I went to church yesterday. I belong to the Missionary Baptist Church. I joined a year ago last October.

Do you belong to any church? All our family belongs to that church, but my youngest brother. I have a sister in California. She has been there for 8 years.

I will close wishing you good luck and this to find you well.

Answer soon and excuse me for waiting so long to answer
Your friend,
Jewell Hamilton

Vera Allen, Cates, Ind., to McKinley Austin
February 1, 1918
Dear Friend,
I received your letter and was glad to hear from you.

You wanted to know how the weather was in Indiana. It is a little cold. It freezes one day and thaws the next. It has been 23 degrees below zero. There is some snow on the ground, but it has been on for about four weeks.

One of my old schoolmates, who went and enlisted, is at your camp.

I expect you wonder where I found your address. I found it in the magazine, "Lone Scout". One of your brothers had written a letter to the magazine telling them about you. He seemed to be very proud of you. He signed his name, C. Raymond Austin.

Will you please tell me if they have churches at your camp?

Hoping to hear from you soon,
Your friend,
Vera M. Allen

Rachel Hidden, Boyd, Minn., to McKinley Austin
February 3, 1918
Dear Friend Mortimer,
You said when you went to school you had double seats. We have just single seats and we can't whisper, but we write notes instead. Our teacher is so sly as an old fox.

Your friend,
Rachel Hidden

Ottie Godsey, Peerless, Ind., to McKinley Austin
February 4, 1918
Dear Mr. Austin,
I was very glad to get your letter this morning. But was sorry to hear that you had had the mumps. I had the mumps about three years ago, but I didn't suffer any from them, only when I tried to eat something sweet or sour.

You must be having nice weather if there isn't any snow there. It is awful cold here. There is a large snow and about an inch of sleet on top of the snow.

Answer soon,
Ottie Godsey

Annie Herald, Equality, Ill., to McKinley Austin
February 5, 1918
Dear Friend,
Will try and answer your most kind and welcome letter. You asked me to answer your letter soon.

I went to school today and made 90 on all lessons. I like to study, and geography is my favorite study.

The weather is so bad I cannot get my picture taken and the first time the sun shines, I am going to have it taken. I had them taken a few months ago, but they were no good. The weather is still good for coasting and the snow is 30 inches deep with about 3 inches sleet and that froze over and can skate anywhere you want to. We have not seen the ground here for a month before Christmas.

Your loving friend,
Miss Annie Herald
Reindeer love the mountains
Rabbits love the hills
I love my soldier boys
God knows I always will.

Maple Thompson, Robinson, Ill., to McKinley Austin
February 6, 1918
Dear Mac,
Well, you did indeed answer that horrid, horrid letter. I hope you tore it up.

I want to apologize about Bobby. It was the truth, but I shouldn't have written it to you. I am very sorry.

Today in algebra class, Mr. Hedden threatened to throw me out of the window because I never exercised my cerebrum getting three pages of algebra problems.

Daddy says I am the leader of Mischief Makers in this town. But I just can't help it.

The other day, one of the Seniors dared me to put a torpedo or something under the Professor's chair and I did. I always take a dare, though I shouldn't.

The result was that he (the professor) caught his trousers on fire and Sidney Beans, the boy who dared me to put it under there, burnt his trousers trying to save the professor. Sidney ruined his trousers and also played part of hero. So therefore,

February 11, 1918 envelope, possibly from Helen Hamilton's February 8th letter. Notice the cancellation: "Food will win the war." Envelope courtesy of Mary Briggs Austin.

though he has about a dozen suits, a different one every day almost, the high school gave him money enough for a good pair of trousers. He bought a real cheap pair, black and white checked, and kept the rest of the money. He certainly is a joke. He always wears these particular trousers to this class. He is a peck of fun.

Miss Taylor, my sewing teacher said that if they advertised for the most mischievous girl, she certainly would name me. I try to be good, but It's almost impossible.

Daddy bought my sister a new "Super Hudson" for her birthday. She is just learning to drive it. I don't think I shall learn. I don't care much for machines. Too many accidents. Daddy has a Cadillac. I think they are fun.

Well, I think I had better close and get to work on my algebra or Mr. Hedden will mop the floor up with me. Also I have my French to get, but Marie, my sister's maid is French and she helps me or at least tries to.

Please send some soldier boys addresses. My girl friends want some.

Lots of love. As ever,
Maple G. Thompson

Ruth Colville, Barryville, N.Y., to McKinley Austin
February 7, 1918
Dear friend McKinley,

Received your letter some time ago and really intended to answer it before, but was busy the last couple of days keeping warm (or trying to, ha ha).

Monday certainly was a terrible day. The wind blew about 50 miles per minute. You speak of mud. I don't believe that I would know what mud looks like.

Aunt Norah [Norah Bradley Avery] said that there were several Sundays when there wasn't anyone except the minister and Christine that ventured out to church.

Every cold day, I make a new vow that I will not stay here another winter, but I suppose that I will not have courage when it comes to the pinch, to get a job.

Belle Mills is teaching here now. Went to visit the school the other day with Anna and it surely was a circus. I never saw so many methods of "spit ball" throwing in my life, but well, I guess she is about as good as the average teacher.

Your friend, Ruth [Colville]

Anne Rassine, Astoria, Ore., to McKinley Austin
February 8, 1918
Dear Friend,

I'm staying in Astoria now till the end of this month. Astoria is a large city and besides it is a seaport city.

The municipal and public docks which makes it a large commercial city were built a few years ago. This city is on a hill and of course part of it is built on Columbia River. Columbia River is about six miles wide at the part right opposite Astoria.

Olney has very few girls and almost all have gone away to different cities. Only the little

February 8, 1918. Nurse drawn by Helen Hamilton. "How do you like the picture I am sending you?" Drawing courtesy of Mary Briggs Austin.

S.S. Tuscania

The S.S. Tuscania, mentioned in a letter from Anne Rassine, was a luxury liner named after a town in Italy. She was torpedoed February 5, 1918, by the German U-boat, UB-77 while carrying 2,013 American troops to Europe. Over 200 people were lost, mostly American troops.
—worldwar1.com

S.S. Tuscania. Photo: wikipedia.org, public domain.

school girls are left; but there are quite a few boys and also old women. The men all have come to work in Astoria at the ship yards. Astoria has three large ship yards. And each one has three large ships under construction at present.

My father is coming to work at the shipyards also, next Monday.

The shores of Washington look hazy and blue in the distance. Oregon is just as mountainous as Washington. But I love the mountains. My home is in the mountains and I love it there, although I've been dreaming of prairies sometimes. But that is because I read so many books about prairie life. Do you read much? I certainly am a real bookworm.

At home I always read during spare time. In the evenings I read almost until midnight. It seems to me like a mania already for me to be so fond of books.

Music is another thing that I like. The people with whom I stay have many musical instruments and almost every evening we have a sort of concert. I myself can't play on any musical instrument yet to amount to anything, but when I get my violin, I'm going to learn.

Well, how are you making it out there? When will you have to go to France? We have had great discussions about that ship, Tuscania that was torpedoed now lately.

I hope to goodness that such a fate will never be yours as it was for those who perished in that disaster.

Astoria is full of soldiers and sailor boys. I suppose every city is at this time.

Right close, only a few yards from this house, at the ship yards are many guards. Many of them are inclined to be quite friendly with some girls, but to me they've never said a word.

All the girls out here have soldiers for sweet hearts except me. Savvy? I'm too young for a sweetheart yet. Eh! What do you say?

I guess this is about all, so good night and I wish Sweet Dreams for you. Especially about that sweet girl you left behind.

I remain Yours, Sincerely,
Anne Rassine

Helen Hamilton, Chicago, Ill., to McKinley Austin
February 8, 1918
Dear Friend Mac,

I can't send you a good picture of myself at present, but if you wait for a couple of weeks, I will be able to.

I think you are good enough looking for anyone. Aren't you kind of scared about going over with all these ships sinking? I wish no one had to. My cousin is in training at Camp Mills, New

Cyrus Rouillon

Cyrus Rouillon. Photo courtesy of Gisele Rouillon Leavenworth.

Cyrus Rouillon in Paris, France, would be the father of Gisele Rouillon who would marry James Leavenworth.

Cyrus fought in World War I and was gassed in southern France. The commander said that each man was responsible to get himself back home.

Since Cyrus lived in Paris, he traveled at night by foot. In the day he hid out in barns or wherever so as not to be detected by the Germans. Cyrus served again in WWII because it took everyman to protect their own country.

York, and must be on his way for we never hear from him.

Our school has a service play now. A Chinese boy and our Arithmetic teacher have joined the aviation corps.

Recently our school gave a costume dance and I went as a Red Cross nurse. I took second prize. There is going to be another dance on February 22.

It takes nine days for mail to reach Chicago from Chattanooga, so that is why you don't get answers quicker than you do.

How do you like the picture [of a nurse] I am sending you? I never can draw a face very well, but I can draw most anything else.

The snow has started to melt here and the streets are awful muddy. We will have to go to school in boats pretty soon.

Thank you for the picture. Write soon. Your friend, Helen Hamilton

Flossie Fraser, Gainsboro, Saskatoon, Canada, to McKinley Austin
February 9, 1918
Dear Friend,
I am a very interested reader of "Lone Scout" and enjoy reading the letters which are in it, so here goes for a spiel to you.

First I had better give you a description of myself. I have red hair, one glass eye and can't see out of the other; one big ear and one small ear; have a large nose with a wart on the end of it; feet which might serve for scoop shovels; arms which dangle a mile out of my coat sleeves and am about the size around of a small elephant, weigh about 190 pounds. Do I suit you? If not, you must be hard to please. I have six brothers and no sisters.

Gainsboro is a small village of about 400 inhabitants. There are two stores, a bake shop, two hardware stores, a hotel, a private boarding house, a Chinese restaurant, a creamery, and three churches. There is a large brick school with four rooms in it.

There are trees along nearly every street. There is a river at the south side of town which we skate on in the winter and swim in summer. We can't skate on it now though. It is covered with snow and there is no rink. It fell in.

There are movies here every Wednesday night, but I don't go very often.

There aren't many boys. They have all enlisted.

I hope you will find time to answer and will do it.
Yours truly,
Flossie Fraser

Beatrice Hanson, Keatchie, La., to McKinley Austin
February 9, 1918
Dearest Mac,
How are you this cold morning? Fine I hope. I am enjoying the best of health now.

We are having some cold weather here now. It looks as if it might snow this morning.

I hope we will have some pretty weather because we are looking for my brother home from the army at any time. He wrote us that he thought he could get a furlough home for a few days.

We live about 30 miles south west of Shreveport, Louisiana, about 5 or 6 miles from any town. It is a hilly country and has lots of timber. We have two school houses and two churches. We have lots of parties and dances. I do not go to the dances myself. All of our family are members of the Baptist Church except the two little boys. Do you belong to any church?

I am a forward for our basketball team.

I received your picture all ok. Sure was glad to get it. Was not disappointed at all. I have not been able to get a camera to take my picture yet without breaking it. Ha Ha.

I will close for this time.
Answer soon to your devoted friend, Beatrice Hanson

Leila Sperline, E. Wenatchee, Wash., to McKinley Austin
February 9, 1918
My dear friend,
I was very glad to hear from you again.

I go to High School every day. By the time I get the work done in the morning it is time to start as I have to start about ten till eight, and when I come home I get supper and wash the dishes and then get two or three lessons. I haven't much time left, so please excuse me for not writing before.

Oh, yes, I would like being an aviatrix. If the Germans did shoot me there wouldn't be much lost. I know I would like to be one.

I'm not ashamed of my "bean" either. He is an awfully cute fellow. He has a Dodge car, too. I see him every day.

Tell some of your friends that I would be very glad to correspond with any of them.

Write soon. Your friend,
Leila Sperline

Grace Nelson, Hutchinson, Minn., to McKinley Austin
February 10, 1918
Dear Mr. Austin,
It may be a surprise to receive a letter from a girl whom you have never heard of before, unless you have received letters from other strange girls.

I saw your name and address in a "Lone Scout" paper and chose you as a soldier to write to. I imagine it is pleasant to receive letters when you are away from home.

I live in a beautiful little town of about 3,000 people,

which is situated on a branch of the Mississippi River. You may have heard of this place before, although it is not altogether probable.

I attend High School and find very little time for anything else beside my school work as we have school six days a week. I have been studying Chattanooga, Tennessee, in one of my subjects at school and I have become rather interested in that place.

It is about 34 degrees above zero today, which is certainly extra ordinary winter weather.

I hope you will find time to answer my letter. I would be very much pleased if you would.

Your new friend, Grace Nelson

Valentine Greetings from Anne Rassine of Astoria, Oregon, courtesy of Mary Briggs Austin.

Emily Neugebauer, Crystal Falls, Mich., to McKinley Austin
February 10, 1918
Dear Friend Mac,

How are you and your friends getting along? I passed my examinations alright, which I am certainly thankful for, but now I have another half year of hard work before me. Our Senior play is getting along fine, and we expect to give it sometime this month.

You know, our class pledged $145 to the Red Cross and we are giving this play to raise some of the money.

That picture of yourself was real good. When was it taken? All of the girls send you and your friends their best regards.

Well, I will now have to close and study my History because I am trying to get out of the exams.

Answer soon. Sincerely,
Emily Neugebauer

Anna Betsa, Lopez, Pa., to McKinley Austin
February 11, 1918
Dear Friend,

I received your letter which I was anxious to get.

I would like to know what nationality you are. I am a Real Russian girl hoping you shall not mind it. I have brown hair and brown eyes and about 2 inches smaller than you are.

Wouldn't you please mind telling me where your home is in Sullivan County? And is it a big city? I do not live in a city and I don't care to be in one. I work in a silk mill and I like my job.

I bet the army fellows have swell times out there. I wish I could go out there to see you. But hoping I shall see your picture soon, which you promised me. Have you any sisters or brothers and do your parents live yet? My parents live and all my sisters and brother are married except me.

Have you another girl that corresponds with you. If you have I would not like to break your friendship which would not be nice. I will close with best regards to you. Do not forget to answer this letter and send the picture along.

Your loving Friend,
Miss Anna Betsa

Ottie Godsey, Peerless, Ind., to McKinley Austin
February 12, 1918
Dear Mr. Austin,

I received your letter and picture last night and I certainly am proud of your picture.

So you are having warm weather now. Well, you aren't any better off than we are for it is warm here. The snow has melted and it is very muddy, but the way the wind is blowing, I think the mud will soon dry, if it doesn't rain.

I am in school today and the boy that sets across the aisle from me is the meanest boy I ever knew. He begins teasing us girls when the bell rings at morning and keeps it up till we are dismissed at night.

I am sorry I can't send you one of my pictures this time, but think I will have one to send next time I write.

My grandmother is spending a

A Few of the Soldiers from the Town of Highland

World War I soldiers in Eldred, Town of Highland. "You heard that Ernest Clark, John Horton, and Abel Hulse are also drafted?"
—Letter of Ruth Colville. Photo courtesy of Chuck Myers.

Drafted in the Town of Highland
Some of the men drafted in the Town of Highland listed in the, Monticello, Republican Watchman. Some of the men were exempted.

Ashauer, William.............................. Eldred
Burck, Frederick Wm...................... Eldred
Bosch, Menzo.................. Highland Lake
Bosch, Ralph .... Highland Lake
Boyd, George Alfred ..... Highland Lake
Beufve, Raymond Alfred .... Yulan
Bosch, Edward H. .... Eldred
Bosch, Herman .... Highland Lake
Cox, Joseph...................................... Eldred
Clouse, Clarence I. ....Barryville
Crandall, Lawrence G. .... Yulan
Conrad, William Walter .... Eldred
Conklin, Henry...........................Barryville
Campbell, Harry B. .... Minisink Ford
Clouse, Fredrick Joseph..........Barryville
Dunlap, Charles John .... Eldred
Dunlap, George Franklin.............. Eldred
Davis, Henry Winfred..............Barryville
Eldred, George Ely .... Eldred
Flieger, Philip..............................Barryville
Fletcher, Robert E. ....Barryville

Freeman, Charles Homer ....Barryville
Greig, Bennett Alan....................... Eldred
Greig, T. Robert.............................. Eldred
Horton, John .... Eldred
Hathaway, Roy Elihu .... Eldred
Hill, William ....Barryville
Hessberger, Ruben.......... Minisink Ford
Hegenbart, John .... Eldred
Hill, Alvin.. Eldred
Haas, Howard Frank...................... Eldred
Hulse, Abel .... Eldred
Kelly, Chris Martin............ Minisink Ford
Kalin, John Campbell .... Eldred
Livingston, Ralph Edward............. Yulan
Lassly, Sherman............................. Eldred
Loerch, Henry John....... Highland Lake
Larson, Lars .... Eldred
Myers, Abel Jackson .... Eldred
Mills, Jas. G. .... Highland Lake
McBride, Ezra Sanford .... Eldred
McBride, Emerson .... Eldred
Meyer, John William.................Barryville
McNamara, Wm. A. .... Minisink Ford
Meyer, Joseph............................Barryville
McQuirk, John J.........................Barryville
Myers, Norman Beck.................... Eldred

Mitchell, Edgar............................... Eldred
Miller, Robert Henry .... Yulan
Ort, Geo. Anthony .... Eldred
Ort, Charles.................................... Eldred
Rider, William Ross .... Yulan
Racine, Lawrence........................... Eldred
Rixton, Leon Lee ....Barryville
Rundle, Robert George................ Eldred
Staal, Paul .... Yulan
Straub, Fridolin Jr........................... Eldred
Steward, John .... Eldred
Stanton, Walter.............................. Eldred
Schumacher, Edward ....Barryville
Stevens, Howard .... Eldred
Toaspern, Walter Cole ....Barryville
Van Eastenbridge, John..........Barryville
Wormuth, Clarence....................... Eldred
Wells, Earl Irving............................ Eldred
Wells, Raymond............................. Eldred
West, Charles Daniel...................... Yulan
Wolff, Frank John ....Barryville
Wargans, Gustave Eldred............. Yulan
Wolff, Carl Joseph ....Barryville
Wells, Chester................................ Eldred
Welti, Fred ....Barryville

List courtesy of Bill Ihlo.

few months with us and she has taught me how to knit. I think I will knit some things for the Red Cross as most of the school girls are knitting for the Red Cross.

Well, I must close as I have two or thee days work of outlining to do and have about an hour to do it in. Don't you pity me?

Yours Sincerely,
Ottie Godsey

George Carner, Barryville, to Mort Austin, Eldred
February 12, 1918,
Dear Mr. Austin,

Yours at hand and I am sorry to have made you so much bother over the $1.80 interest. I have a complete record of the $90.00 note including payment of $50.00 and interest $1.80. I neglected to put down the page in index. We were looking at a record of the $1,500 Mortgage on which the note was not recorded.

Yours truly,
G. Carner

Laura Watson, Winton, N.C., to McKinley Austin
February 14, 1918
Dear Mac,

You said to call your name Mac. I also think it sounds friendly. Don't you? I received your letter of recent date with great pleasure. I am so glad I have found a nice friend and I know you are as nice as you can be.

Mac, please send me a photo of yourself. I am crazy to see what you are like. Ha! Ha!

I am not as old as you are, just 13, but if you think me too young to write to, don't write, but I know you are nicer than that, so you see I have a good opinion of you.

I am at least 5 feet tall. I am

Reporting to the Local Board

Failure to report promptly at the hour and on the day named is a grave military offense for which you may be court-martialed...

Upon reporting to your Local Board, you will not need, and you should not bring with you, anything except hand baggage. You will not be permitted to take trunks or boxes with you on the train.

You should take only the following articles: A pair of strong comfortable shoes to relieve your feet from your new regulation marching shoes; not to exceed four extra suits of underclothing; not to exceed six extra pairs of socks; four face and 2 bath towels; a comb, a brush, a toothbrush, soap, tooth powder, razor, and shaving soap.

It will add to your comfort to bring one woolen blanket, preferably of dark or neutral color. This blanket should be tightly rolled, the ends of the roll should be securely bound together and the loop of the blanket thus formed slung from your left shoulder to your right hip.

You should wear rough strong clothing and a flannel shirt, preferably an olive drab shirt of the kind issued to soldiers.—*From letter sent to Herman Bosch, courtesy of Victoria Kohler.*

foolish over playing the piano. I can play real well. I want some war time rag music.

What church do you belong to? I am a Baptist.

I am going to move in May, but will send you my new address. What was your home town before you went into the service for U.S.? What did you do before joining the Army?

Write me a long, long letter

John Horton, son of Anne Stanton Horton, lived near Highland Lake. Photo courtesy of Victoria Kohler.

Ernest Horton, son of Anne Stanton Horton, lived near Highland Lake. Photo courtesy of Victoria Kohler.

Some Town of Highland soldiers in 1918: Charlie MacIntyre on far left; Herman Bosch on far right; John Horton in the middle with two unidentified men on either side. Photo courtesy of the Bosch Family.

and send me a photo please.
Lovingly, Laura May

Vera Allen, Cates, Ind., to McKinley Austin
February 14, 1918
Dear Friend,
I received your most welcome letter last Tuesday. I was glad to get your picture and wish to thank you for it. I am sending you a picture of my self.
You said you was having nice weather down there. We have been having bad weather here for the last few days. It hailed here today.
I have been having the toothache for the last four days and the side of my face is swollen until it is about twice as large as it should be. You must excuse this writing as my tooth aches so, I can hardly write. I close, hoping to hear from you again soon.
Your unknown friend,
Vera M. Allen

Annie Herald, Equality, Ill., to McKinley Austin
February 17, 1918
Dear Friend,
Will try to answer your most kind and welcome letter I received a few days ago. I love your picture. We have had an examination. It was easy as pie and I got through with writing 2 days which ended in having cramped fingers.
I go to the show on Friday nite; went this week and Johnson bought me back. The reason I ask if you cared for me writing to other boys was because one boy got mad. My! I don't care for him anyway.
Wish I could have seen you in a parade. Bet it was a fine sight.
Will send you one of my pictures when I get the Kodak fixed. Answer soon.
From your loving friend,
Miss Annie Herald

Jewell Hamilton, Vandervoort, Ark., to McKinley Austin
February 17, 1918
Dear Friend,
I received your letter and picture and sure was glad to get it. I went to church this morning and I went yesterday. We have Church twice every month and singing every first Sunday.
I had a party here Friday night. We have candy pullings

and just parties and candy breakings. I have had two candy pullings; one candy breaking, one party. Wish you could be here to our next one which will be next week sometime.

No, I have never seen a parade. Vandervoort is a small town. They never have nothing much here. Well I am sending you a picture of myself. It isn't a good one at all.

Your true friend,
Jewell Hamilton

Helen Hamilton, Chicago, Ill., to McKinley Austin
February 18, 1918
Dear Friend Mac,

I am sending you this picture taken in the early winter.

I have heard that they were going to take some of the boys from Chattanooga to France. Mac, if you are among them, will you still keep on writing to me? I feel as if I had found a good friend in you. Tell your "Lone Scout" brother that I'm glad he put your address in the best of magazines.

How would you like to have the new song just out in Chicago. This is a sample of the chorus:

There's a long, long trail that
  winds through no man's land
  in France,
Where the shots and shells
  are bursting
All around on every hand
There'll be lots of work
  and drilling
Till our dreams can all come true
And someday we'll show
  the Kaiser
What the U.S. boys can do.

I hope you don't get any of the ground glass. Chicago papers said that a lot of sugar and salt in the Chattanooga camp was full of it.

I will close now as our school bell is ringing and I have to go to work. Don't forget to write soon, Mia Americo Soldato.
Your Friend,
Helen M. Hamilton

Maggie Dempsey, Warrior, Ala., to McKinley Austin
February 18, 1918
Dearest Mortimer,

Great pleasure I take in answering your most kind letter which I received and was sure glad to hear from you. I hope you are all right.

I sure did not have a nice time today as my old sweet heart has just left and believe me kiddo, I sure am glad of it.

Wish it had of been you instead of him, for you care better to me than he does and I hope I will see you soon.

From your friend,
Maggie Dempsey

Anna Betsa, Lopez, Pa., to McKinley Austin
February 21, 1918
Dear Friend,

I received your letter and picture which I was very glad to get. I have no picture just now of myself. I would like to have you do me a favor. You wrote to me in the last letter that there is a Russian fellow in the same company with you. So one of my girlfriends I told about this Russian fellow, so she said to write you and ask that fellow for his address and you can send it to me in the next letter.

From your friend,
Anna Betsa

Maple Thompson, Robinson, Ill., to McKinley Austin
February 21, 1918
Dear Mac,

Was it really you that wrote or your ghost. I had given up hopes

Fred (Fridolin) Straub Jr., son of Fridolin and Juliana Straub who owned Straub's Hotel. "I also heard that the company that Fred Straub is with was to have started with that ship which was sunk, but was quarantined just before it started."—Letter of Ruth Colville. Photo courtesy of Betty Ihlo Morganstern.

of your answering my letter. Your picture was lovely and I had some taken, but I will have some more taken when we once more see a sunny day.

My sister asked me why I didn't knit or do something useful. I replied, "Let me tell you I have made three socks and they are probably now on the feet of our soldiers."

"Three," she said, "why three?"

"I had no more wool and there are plenty of one legged men anyhow." She hasn't spoken to me since.

I am going to make some fudge. Do you like it? If so, answer by return mail and I will send you

"Here is a picture of our high school." Crystal Falls Michigan High School. Postcard from Emily Neugebauer, February 25, 1918, courtesy of Mary Briggs Austin.

some. Also do you like to read?

We have lots and lots of magazines and I will gladly send them if you wish.

You have my sympathy by the barrels if you had to walk that distance and carry almost 100 pounds. That was a good one about the shots. It's a wonder you didn't get caught though.

I would have liked to see you. I suppose you think I am a question box, but be sure to answer my questions.

Lots of love,
Maple Georgia Thompson

In February Ruth Colville from Barryville wrote some more local news to McKinley. Ruth was a granddaughter of Isaac Bradley.

Ruth Colville, Barryville, N.Y., to McKinley Austin
February 21, 1918
Dear Friend McKinley,

I received your letter and was of course glad to receive it. I won't write very much because I walked over to see Uncle Fred and Aunt Mary [Bradley Scott] Myers today and am very tired.

You heard that Ernest [Clark] has been drafted? John Horton and Abel Hulse are also drafted, I believe. There are quite a number to go from this town on the 23rd, but I don't know yet who they are. I guess that Ernest's folks are quite (what shall I say disturbed?) about Ernest's going.

I saw Edith Sergeant today and she said that they thought that you must have started for "Somewhere in France" because quite a little of your mail (among other things a couple of registered letters) had been returned to Eldred. Of course, all that I know is what she said about it and how she found out I don't know. I told her that you were still on this side and let it go at that, but thought you should know about it.

I also heard that the company that Fred Straub is with was to have started with that ship which was sunk, but was quarantined just before it started.

Raymond Davis is in France, I believe.

You simply can't imagine what you have missed by not being here this winter. They say that its the coldest winter ever remembered. Last week was rather warm though and the weather was very pleasant.

But I haven't been able to get to Eldred. I guess that Mr. and Mrs. Asendorf are in the south again this winter.

One day this week, one of Mr. Harry Dunlap's oldest girls was stricken blind in school. They say that it is caused by a blood clot on the optic nerve and that is too far back in the head to operate. Is it not truly a dreadful thing?

Dad is reading a "Johnny Chuck" story and if I get some of it mixed up with this letter, well just lay it to my natural craziness.

I haven't done anything very much this winter except get fat and I surely have done that. But just the same, I helped Dad with the wood last week.

Men are very scarce and some of them don't want much pay. Some of them $2.50 a day and they are just the ones who get to work about 9:30 and quit in time to get a little wood up for themselves.

Well to cut my long story short, mother and I helped. I didn't do much except rake it up, but believe me, it made my muscles sore, but they soon got over that and am feeling fine as a fiddle.

Oh I heard the other day that Walter Toaspern (you know him do you not?) is at the same place (Waco, Texas) as my cousin Clifford Colville and he is also in the aviation corps. Is that not odd?

Well I am getting really dreadfully tired and so will have to say "Good-Night."

Write once in a while and let us know what you are doing and where you are. Do you have any idea of moving soon?

Your friend, Ruth Colville

Emily Neugebauer, Crystal Falls, Mich., to McKinley Austin
February 22, 1918
Dear Friend Mac,
I received your letter yesterday.
We have not had any bob riding now for about 2 weeks because just about every 2 or 3 days, we have terrible blizzards. You can imagine how cold it is as last week a man was frozen to death. The next morning some people found him standing up.
This being National song week, we have music every morning for a whole hour. I don't mind it in the least as then we get out of Physics class.
Tomorrow as it is Washington's birthday, we are also going to have a program which will last the whole afternoon. The high school girls in the are now organizing basketball teams. Tonight we had our first practice and of course the Seniors won.
Myrtle Brooks just came down now, so I guess I will have to close in order to get to the Red Cross. Excuse the newsless letter, but I will try to do better next time.
As Ever,
Emily

Grace Nelson, Hutchinson, Minn., to McKinley Austin
February 22, 1918
Dear Mr. Austin.
I really was surprised and also much pleased to receive your letter which showed that you appreciated my letter.
I suppose it is proper that I should describe myself in this letter. I omitted it last time because I wanted to be sure of an answer before I did.
I am 16 years of age, 5 feet, 5-1/2 inches tall; I have dark brown hair and dark brown eyes.

February 26, 1918. Postcard from Burl Nation, courtesy of Mary Briggs Austin.

You said you were the oldest of 5 boys and 1 girl. It happens that I am the oldest of 5 girls and 1 boy.
I am very glad you mentioned things concerning camp life because I am very much interested in it. We have had the pleasure of having several people from different branches of service in High School. We have a 20 minute assemble period every day in which we have music, speeches, readings, etc.
I am sure I would be interested in anything concerning training, etc. that you would care to write. How long have you been in training?
If you happen to have 2 friends, or know of 2 boys who would like to write to someone else, I have 2 girl friends who would be glad to correspond with them; one being 18 and the other 15.
I just returned from a basketball game in which our team was defeated for the first time, on our own floor, this year. I feel so completely disgusted with our team that I think about the only way to forget about it is to go to bed. It is now 5 minutes after 1 o'clock. I would be very glad to receive an answer to this letter also.
Your friend,
Grace Nelson

Annie Herald, Equality, Ill., to McKinley Austin
February 24, 1918
My Dearest Friend,
I will take the pleasure of answering your most kind and welcome letter I received this morning. I was glad to hear from you. I went to the show Friday and Saturday nite both. They were fine. The Friday nite show was "The Fatal Ring." I have been going to it for about 8 or 9 weeks.
Hope you do not have to go across the Atlantic to fight. Anyway do not have to fight a real battle.
Well guess I will quit. Answer soon. Your loving friend,
Annie Herald [15]

Emily Neugebauer, Crystal Falls, Mich., to McKinley Austin
February 25, 1918
Dear friend Mac,
Here is a picture of our High School. Terrible blizzard outside, so don't know yet if I will attempt to mail this now.
Say hello to the other boys for me. Emily

Postcard to McKinley Austin
February 26, 1918
Hello, how are you? Fine I hope. I had a sweet time at school the other day. We had four examples in algebra for examination and I worked one of them. I don't know any news to write so I will close hoping to hear

from you soon.
I am your friend,
Burl Nation

Jennie Austin, Eldred, to McKinley Austin
Monday February 26, 1918
My dear McKinley:
At last I have gathered enough ambition to write. Also, I begin too realize that Dad and I are growing old when the cold weather affects us as it has this winter, we were certainly glad to hear you were having good weather. It is beginning to be pretty decent here.
Raymond seems to write quite long letters to you, so I suppose he keeps you supplied with all the news.
Clarence Wormuth is in France. Aunt Lottie and Christina [Leavenworth] had a card from him since he got there. They claim one of the McBride boys are there, too.
Did Raymond tell you that your Grandmother [Maria Myers Leavenworth] had been very sick? She was taken sick Christmas Day and is not able to go out yet. We all feel quite worried about her. Aunt Lottie [Charlotte Leavenworth] teaches at Barryville and walks home nearly every night, but that is not as bad as some of your walks. Can you cook yet and what (if you do)?
Your time must be nearly all taken up with training etc., and that letter writing Raymond got you in. He certainly likes to write letters. I would laugh if he only got a letter shower from a lot of girls himself.
Where you are, is it part of Ft. Oglethorpe? Mr. Beck's youngest son is at that Fort, the one that used to own the donkey.
About the insurance, I certainly appreciate your thoughtfulness and hope you will come safely home after this war is over and in a course of a few years take out an insurance policy in the name of Mrs. McKinley Austin. Dad is insured in the Maccabees and they gave him an insurance paper and we have it here. Do they manage with yours? I dare say it is a government affair.
Willie says you never answered his last letter. It might have miscarried somewhere, so when you answer this, write to him and I will understand that it is an answer to this. It seems to be so laborious for Willie to write a letter. I know they are not breezy like Raymonds.
This letter is for Dad too. He says sometime he will get started and write such a long letter that it will take you until the end of the war to read it. Well goodnight.
Love from all, Mother

Emily Neugebauer, Crystal Falls, Mich., to McKinley Austin
February 28, 1918
Dear Friend Mac,
Just arrived home from school and thought I would drop you a line. A few of the girls are again coming over tonight, so I suppose we will as usual enjoy ourselves. The girls send you their best regards.
As Ever, Emily

McKinley Austin in Eldred
In March, McKinley had a leave to go home before his outfit left for France, as the next letter indicates.

McKinley, Chattanooga, Tenn., to Mort Austin
March 14, 1918
Dear father,
I got here all right. The train was late into Jersey City and I missed my train. I was 14 hours late, but as I got the conductor to sign a paper telling the reason, I think it will be all O.K.
Well I will write soon. Tell Aunt Aida that I am here all right. With love to all the family.
Your son,
McKinley

C. Dassori, Jersey City Heights, N.J., to Mort Austin, Eldred
March 21, 1918
Dear Friend Mort,
Don't you think it's about time I answered your last letter? Really I've had my hands so full I didn't know where I was standing.
But some Saturday of next month April, I would like to take a trip up there and stop over until Sunday evening with you, with my little girl if you'll have room for us.
I would like to see the man together with you about renting a house for the summer months for my family. I've had Edna sick with diphtheria a few weeks. Thank God everything came around nicely and she is doing fine.
Say Mort, I am at the same old thing again, and that's of going south. I was thinking of going there while the family is up in Eldred if I can get hold of a place for them.
I have an offer from Savannah, Georgia, with the Sea Board Air line R.R. for the first of May. I am going to make the trip this season either to Savannah, Georgia, or to Jacksonville, Florida, whichever place I like best and can get employment there.
I'm going to rent a small farm and go into the poultry and hog raising on a small scale for a starter. It would be a good idea for

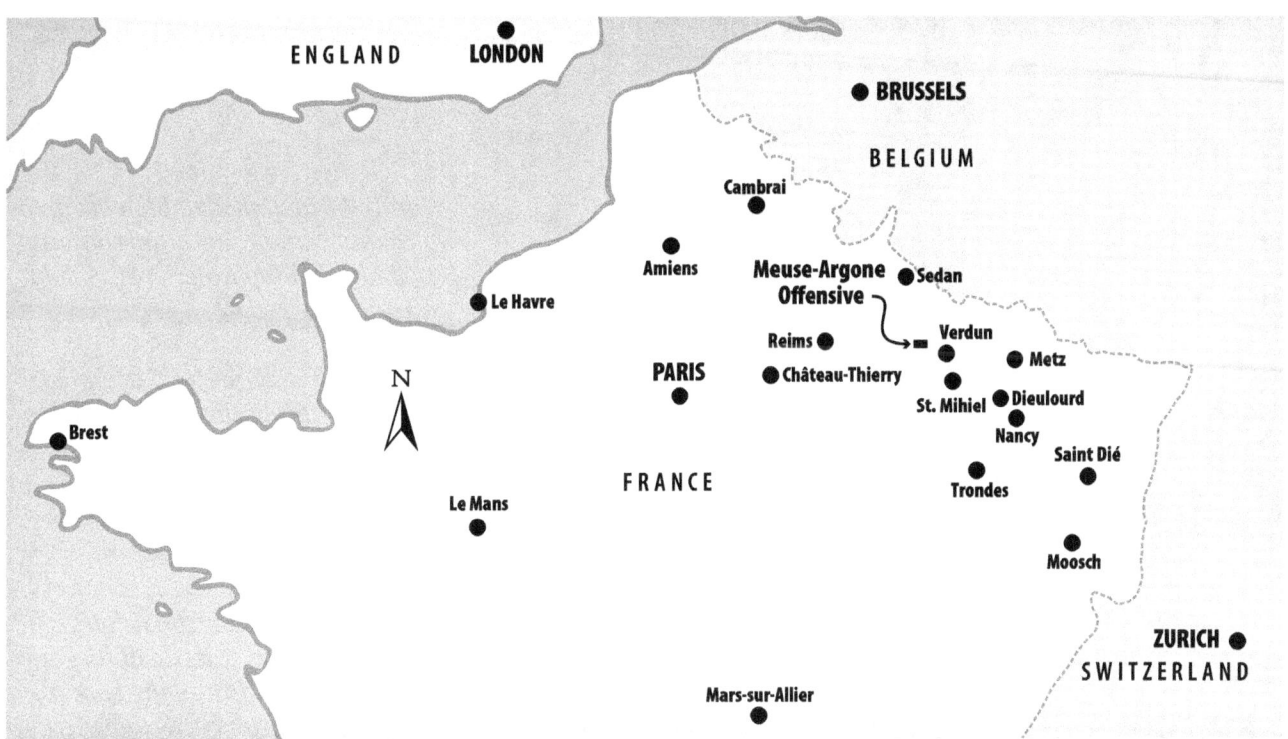

Map of France. Brest is where McKinley's outfit landed. Château-Thierry, Saint Dié, St. Mihiel, Verdun, Cambrai, Sedan, and the Meuse-Argonne Offensive are mentioned in Chapter 11. Map: Gary Smith.

two of us Mort. What say you? Will close for the present,
    Hoping to hear from you soon. Love to all from us all.
    As ever your true friend
    Chas. S. Dassori

Maria Myers Leavenworth Dies
Jennie mentioned that her mother Maria Leavenworth had been ill. Her mother, my great-grandmother, Maria Myers Leavenworth died in March 1918.

Aunt Christine told me that her mother was a "very understanding person" and taught them not to be judgmental; I have seen one photo of her with a dog, and she looks very kind and gentle. —Melva Austin Barney.

Mrs. Maria Myers Leavenworth, wife of Sherman S. Leavenworth, died at her home, Echo Hill Farm, near Eldred, Sullivan County, on Monday, March 25, 1918, of diabetes. She was 64 years of age.
She was the daughter of Martin D. Myers and Jane Ann Myers. On December 18th, 1874, she was united in marriage with Mr. Sherman S. Leavenworth.
Mrs. Leavenworth was a life long resident of Eldred and for many years conducted the Echo Hill Farm House, which had a big patronage as a summer boarding house.
She was an excellent Christian woman, devoted to her home and family and was held in high esteem in the community of which she had so long been a resident.
The surviving relatives are her husband, at home; and children: J. Garfield Leavenworth, of Easthampton, Mass.; Mrs. C. M. Austin, of Eldred; Truman, Martin, Anna, Charlotte and Christine Leavenworth, of Eldred.—Port Jervis Union Gazette, *March 26, 1918.*

George James Clark Enlists
We last talked about George James Clark, a descendant of Wilmot and Mary Van Auken Clark and grandson of George and Harriet Covert Clark, in Chapter 6.
    George J. Clark, his wife Mary Higgins, and their two daughters lived in New York City. In February 1917, Mary died giving

---

Russian Revolutions

There were a series of revolutions in Russia in 1917. In March 1917 Tsar Nicholas II abdicated. By early November 1917, the Bolshevik Party, led by Vladimir Lenin, had overthrown the Provisional Government in St. Petersburg.
    In Russia, in March 1918 the Bolshevik Party headed by Lenin, signed a peace treaty with Germany. Russia was out of the war, but they would continue to have unrest in their country.—wikipedia.org.

Mary Parker Schoonover and Great Granddaughter Norma Beverly Wood. Photo courtesy of Richard James.

S. Deyo Hull, future husband of Justina Schoonover, was a Yeoman third class on the U.S.S. Arizona in April 1918. Photo courtesy of John Hull.

birth to their son James Joseph Clark.

In March 1918 George James Clark went to Toronto, Canada, and enlisted for the Canadian Over-Seas Expeditionary Force. George, 32, was 5 foot 7-1/2 inches tall with medium complexion and brown eyes and brown hair.

Mary Costello Clark, a widow and mother of George J. Clark, cared for his two daughters. Little James J. Clark was cared for by another family member.

McKinley Austin, Chattanooga, Tenn., to Aida Austin
March 31, 1918
Dear Aunt,

I was very glad to get those pictures. They were real good. We are having fine weather here now. I did not send anymore this month because I owed some and there are some things that I want to buy to take across with me. But I expect to have a good deal to send back next month.

My corporal is attending sniper's school and I have had to lead the squad. I don't like it very much.

I am expecting to be transferred to the Machine Gun Company. I would rather stay with F Company, but I have noticed that a good many things that have happened to me lately, really unimportant themselves, have resulted in advantage to me. And while I am not superstitious, I think it best not to try to change that everything is coming for the best.

Perhaps you understand what I mean? I suppose I could get another man sent in my place, but I think whatever happens is for the best.

Your nephew, McKinley

Rowlee Schoonover, Y.M.C.A. Mechanic
Rowlee Schoonover, we learned in the last chapter, had applied to work for the Y.M.C.A. as a mechanic. He was accepted and sailed on the *Oresia S.S.* for France on April 4, 1918.

S. Deyo Hull Enlists in the Navy
Solomon Deyo Hull, Rowlee's future son-in-law, had enlisted in the U.S. Navy for 4 years, April 19, 1917. In April 1918, Deyo had been a Yeoman third class on the U.S.S. Arizona for 7 months.

When Deyo joined the Navy in WWI they made him a yeoman taking care of ship stores because of his clerking experience.—John Hull.

The U.S.S. Arizona operated out of Norfolk throughout the war, serving as a gunnery training ship and patrolling the waters of the eastern seaboard from the Virginia Capes to New York.

An oilburner, she had not been deployed to European waters owning to the scarcity of fuel oil in the British Isles—the base of other American battleships sent to aid the Grand Fleet.—ussarizona. org/history.

The U.S.S. Arizona plays a part at the end of the war.

Mary Parker Schoonover
Ada Britt's husband Arthur R. Wood worked as a civilian for the Navy. There is a photo of Arthur and Ada's young daughter Norma Beverly Wood with her

Y.M.C.A.

McKinley sent a postcard to his brother Willie with the following information about the Y.M.C.A.:

The American Y.M.C.A. Program is being carried by over 2,000 secretaries to millions of enlisted men—American soldiers and sailors in U.S. and overseas; also to French, Russian and Italian armies, and to prisoner of war camps—to help give these men a home touch and to show them that somebody cares.
—*National War Work Council of the Y.M.C.A.'s of the United States.*

great-grandmother Mary Parker Schoonover.

McKinley Sails to France

On April 24, 1918, McKinley Austin (11th Infantry) left Hoboken, New Jersey, on the *U.S.S. Leviathan*. They arrived on May 2, in Brest, France.

On May 8 they arrived at Bar-sur-Aube, southeast of Paris. They were trained there until June 1. Six days later, the 11th Infantry moved east to Alsace (German territory at the beginning of the war) in the Vosges Mountains. There the regiment was attached to a French Division.

Irwin Briggs Leaves for France

On May 10, 1918, Irwin Briggs left with the advanced party from 89th Infantry Division which was assigned to the IV Corps, American Expeditionary Forces (A.E.F.).

He most likely sailed from Camp Upton on Long Island, New York, to England and onto France, where we will next meet him at the St. Mihiel offensive in September in the Medical Corps taking the wounded from the field to the hospitals.

Myrtie Crabtree, the school teacher that Irwin met at his parents' farm in Nebraska, was with her relatives in Chicago. Myrtie would write to Irwin while he was in France.

Geo. Sidwell, Riegelsville, N.J., to Mort Austin, Eldred

May 10, 1918
Dear Sir:

In the past three months have lost two hands out of five because of the draft.

I have your letter of Dec. 18th. It occurred to me that the position as herdsman might interest you as you have boys 15

Irwin Briggs in France. Photo courtesy of his daughter, Mary Briggs Austin.

and 17 years of age. Could use the boys to advantage through the summer months and give them work in mill during winter. The position pays $50 per month, house rent, garden, potatoes, table fruit and milk.

If interested wire at my expense.

Yours truly, Geo. L. Sidwell

George J. Clark Leaves for England

George James Clark left Halifax, Canada, with the Canadian 1st Battalion on May 16, 1918. They arrived in Liverpool, England, May 27.

In May 1918 Herman Bosch received his induction notice from the local board for Sullivan County.

George Pelton, Monticello, N.Y., to Herman Bosch, Eldred

May 20, 1918
The President of the United States to Herman Bosch:
Greeting: Having submitted yourself to a local board composed of your neighbors for the purpose of determining the place and time in which you can best serve the United States in

Myrtie Crabtree, the school teacher Irwin had met, wrote to him when he was in France. Photo courtesy of her daughter, Mary Briggs Austin.

Wilhelm Bosch, owner of Lake House, had three sons who served in WWI. Photo courtesy of the Bosch Family.

the present emergency, you are hereby notified that you have now been selected for immediate Military service.

From and after the day and hour just named you will be a soldier in the military service of the United States.

Geo. Pelton

Herman Bosch, husband of Mary Horton. Photo courtesy of Victoria Kohler.

Ed Bosch, one of Wilhelm Bosch's three sons. Photo courtesy of the Bosch Family.

Ralph Bosch, son of Wilhelm Bosch, served in WWI. Photo courtesy of the Bosch Family.

Herman Bosch was inducted into the Army on May 27, 1918, as a Private in Company D, 51st Pioneer Infantry. Herman (blue eyes, brown hair, 5 feet 5 inches tall), a sheet iron worker, would be in France by June 30, 1918.

Some Highland Servicemen
Way too many sad good byes would be said to the servicemen from the Town of Highland or those who would one day live in Highland—whether they had volunteered or been inducted.

Letters would be anxiously awaited. Some of the Austin letters mentioned several of the town's soldiers.

Walter Toaspern served in the U.S. Army Hospital Corps as a chauffeur; Fridolin (Fred) Straub Jr. served overseas with the U.S. Army, 303rd Engineers, Co. E.

Some families had more than one serviceman.

Anne Stanton Horton had 2 sons, John (who fought in France) and Ernest Horton, and a son-in-law, Herman Bosch.

Herman Bosch was the son of Wilhelm Bosch, who as mentioned earlier, had 3 sons: Ed, Ralph, and Herman involved in the war effort. Ed Bosch quickly rose to the rank of sergeant.

Ed Grotecloss Jr., future husband of Belle Greig, also fought in WWI. Belle was the daughter of Robert and Kate Greig who owned the huge boarding house near Stege's Pond.

Ed Grotecloss Jr., Herman Bosch, Irwin Briggs, and McKinley Austin would all be at the battles of St. Mihiel and the Meuse-Argonne in France, though it is unknown if it was realized in later years.

March 14, 1918 envelope from McKinley Austin to his father, courtesy of Mary Briggs Austin.

McKinley Austin. Photo courtesy of Mary Briggs Austin.

Chapter 11
Another Soldier Boy
World War I: May 1918

Dear Pa, Ma, brothers, and sister,
I am still in Middletown. We expect to leave early Monday morning for Ft. Slocum, and I may not have a chance to write soon again.
The recruits got tickets or a pass at a hotel for a free night's lodging and a ticket that gets them a 50 cent meal at the French restaurant.
They surely use us great. The officers are civil and ready to talk to a certain extent. There are two other recruits here besides me.
It costs $2.50 per head a day to keep us here the way the government does; $1.50 for meals and $1.00 for lodging.
Well I hope you are all well as I am, for I am sure enjoying myself.
With love to all,
Raymond

Raymond Austin in World War I. "I hope you are all well as I am." Photo in the Austin Family Collection.

So wrote Charles Raymond Austin from Middletown, New York, on May 18, 1918, to his parents Mort and Jennie Austin, and his siblings, Willie (Bill), 15, Elizabeth, 7, Art, 5, and Bob, 3.

Charles Raymond Austin Enlists
Raymond wanted to enlist even though he was underage. Finally, after many tries, Charles Raymond Austin enlisted in the U.S. Army. It would be a few months before he was 17.

My Dad lied about his age to enlist in the army. He was several months short of his 17th birthday. The recruiting office was in the post office in Port Jervis. I don't remember how he kept making trips there (it was 20 miles from Eldred).
The recruiting officer came to know him, but couldn't take him. Finally, one day, the officer said, "Why don't you go for a walk around the block and come back 8 months older?"
So he walked around the block, came back, and the fellow acted as though he had never seen him before and took down his birth date as April 1900, rather than December.—Melva Austin Barney.

Letters from Two Soldiers
Mort and Jennie had two sons fighting in *The Great War—The War to End All Wars*. (Apparently Willie tried to get in also, but he could not.)

The Austins would be anxious to receive letters from McKinley in France, and Raymond who would be stationed in the Panama Canal Zone.

Letters to and from McKinley or Raymond Austin, photos, ads and news articles from New York Newspapers, and other

Raymond holding his little brother Robbie (Bob). Photo courtesy of Joan Austin Geier.

information and photos of relatives and townsfolk are included in this chapter which starts in May 1918 with Raymond's enlistment and ends in December 1918.

In mid-June, Raymond was recuperating at the Base Hospital according to this next letter.

Raymond Austin, Base Hospital, Camp Merritt, N.J., to Bill Austin
June 16, 1918
Dear brother William,

I didn't get any letters yet, however I am writing to tell you I am on the convalescent list. I haven't felt ill hardly at all, but I was broke out something awful and I guess I fooled the doctors.

They use us great here, ice cream every day for dinner; toast and eggs, cornflakes and cocoa for breakfast, or shredded wheat, petti-john or grape nuts.

There are about 30 beds in this ward and about two thirds as many patients.

Camp Merritt Hospital ranks up well among those in the U.S. There must be 2,000 cases altogether and I have heard rumors of 4 deaths. I hear that sometimes for 3 weeks at a stretch there are no deaths at all.

I hope that father will be all right when this reaches you. Tell him to look for me home early next month if I am still here. Ma said you expected boarders shortly. Who are they?

We will probably stay at Camp Merritt till July 15, as I hear that they haven't got an extra transport on hand. If my company goes and leaves me in the hospital, I am going to transfer to an overseas company if possible.
Raymond

Vosges Mountains, France
From mid-June to mid-July, the 11th Infantry Mortimer McKinley Austin was with, worked their way from Moosch, Alsace, in the Vosges Mountains to the Saint Dié Sector—66 kilometers (41 miles) west. McKinley was in the Machine Gun Company. His outfit took part in the Vosges Mountains, St. Mihiel, and Meuse-Argonne offensives in northeastern France.

Hindenburg Line
Germany had built a major defensive fortification system in northeastern France. Known as the Hindenburg Line, it included concrete bunkers, heavy belts of barbed wire, tunnels for moving troops, deep trenches, dug-outs, command posts, and machine gun emplacements—excellent protection for German machine gunners.—*From wikipedia.org.*

Raymond Austin, Camp Merritt, N.J., to Mort and Jennie Austin
June 17, 1918
Dear Father and Mother,

I received the letter addressed to the Base Hospital today. They let me up today and I am feeling fine. I have inspected the whole ward.

I wish you would send me a bundle of Lone Scouts and Christian Advocates as I am allowed to read now.

I will probably be here till July first, so don't worry about me taking pneumonia.

Ice cream every day for dinner. Today we had creamed chipped beef, macaroni and tomato sauce, baked potatoes, bread, butter, and coffee or milk. For breakfast we had toast, boiled eggs, cocoa, and corn flakes.

Mac's letter is with the rest of my stuff being fumigated.

Well it's supper time, so will close. Write soon.

I am with love your son,
Raymond

Raymond Austin, Camp Merritt, N.J., to Mort Austin, Eldred
June 21, 1918

Art Austin saluting. Photo courtesy of Mary Briggs Austin.

Dear Father,

I am very glad you are better now. Mother told me you didn't feel good, but she didn't mention the doctor giving you medicine. However it is just as well she didn't, or all is good that ends well.

I hope Willie will like his job on the hill and if he don't work under Kinney, I believe he will be all right.

Mrs. O'Brien, Joe Hayden, and his mother came up to see me yesterday, but they couldn't get in as the measles ward is always under quarantine. They sent me a note by a dispatcher telling me to write her at her home address at Brooklyn.

I may leave the hospital tomorrow. But I am in no hurry to. They use us too good here for me to be anxious to leave soon.

Well, write soon and give my love to all the folks. Hoping you are all well. I am your loving son,
Pvt. Chas. R. Austin

Herman Bosch Leaves for France
Herman Bosch was assigned to Co. B, 2nd Anti Aircraft, Machine Gun Battalion, on June 24, 1918. It must have been hard leaving his wife Mary E. Horton and baby Herman Bosch Jr.

Battle of Belleau Wood, France
Rowlee Schoonover was a mechanic for the Y.M.C.A. He was in France in June 1918, when the Battle of Belleau Wood took place northeast of Paris.

I remember I was sent up to Belleau Woods on a Sunday and that was the first real fight the Americans was in. They was the Marines at Belleau Woods and I was on a hill overlooking the fight. It lasted the afternoon until dark and started at daylight the next morning, and they drove the Germans out of the woods the next forenoon. It was terrible.
—Daniel Rowlee Schoonover.

Daniel Rowlee Schoonover in Europe during WWI. Photo courtesy of John Hull.

Le Collett, France, June 26, 1918
Early on the morning of June 26, the Germans attempted to raid the positions held by Companies I and L. The raid was repulsed with losses to the enemy.—Sergeant John G. Popp, 11th Infantry History.

Pvt. M.M. McKinley, 11 U.S. Inf., France, to Jennie Austin
June 27, 1918
Dear Mother,

Mary E. Horton Bosch, wife of Herman Bosch, holding their son Herman Bosch Jr. Photo courtesy of Victoria Kohler.

Gas Warfare in World War I

Both Irwin Briggs and Cyrus Roullion (and probably many of the others in this story) experienced Gas Warfare.

Until the first world war, it was considered uncivilized to use poison gas. The French fired tear-gas grenades against the Germans in August 1914, the first month of the war. Two months later, the German army fired chemical irritants or tear gas. Chlorine gas was used by the Germans in April 1915.

Phosgene gas (with a delayed affect of up to 48 hours after inhalation) was used by both German and Allied armies.

The Germans used mustard gas against the Russians in September 1917. Mustard gas was also used by the Allies. An almost odorless chemical, it caused internal and external blisters several hours after exposure; could burn lungs and cause blindness, and severe burns; and stayed in the soil for weeks after release.

Gas protection first included cotton pads dipped in a solution of bicarbonate of soda held over the face. By 1918 when the use of poison gas

Our boys in France learning to correctly use gas masks. Photo: Library of Congress: Keystone View Company, LC-USZ62-92733.

was widespread, filter respirators were available.

Deaths from gas after May 1915 were rare, but gas victims would still have a debilitating life after being gassed.—firstworldwar.com

Mustard gas caused the most gas casualties on the Western Front. Both chlorine or mustard gas could cause blindness.

Respiratory disease was another common affliction caused by the gas attack. Some died from tuberculosis.—wikipedia.org.

Just a few lines to let you know I am all right. I have been to the trenches and like them better than drilling. It was bad when it rained, but on good days, I like it.

The Germans shelled us once or twice but the more I see of artillery bombardment, the less I am afraid of it.

The trench rats scared me a couple of times when I was on guard. When they run around, they make a lot of noise and I thought once that it was a German in the next bay when it was only a rat. [They reportedly grew to the size of cats!]

Did Raymond ever join? I think it will do him good. I wish you would send me the address of the Eldred boys who are in the Army.

I will close hoping you are well. I am Your loving son,
McKinley
Machine Gun Co.

Raymond Austin, Camp Merritt, N.J., to His Family, Eldred
June 30, 1918
Dear Father, Mother, Brothers, and Sister,

There's some mistake. We didn't leave this morning and probably will not go till Wednesday, maybe not then.

When I go to Panama, it will probably be nearly a month before you hear from me as it takes nine days to go down and probably more. It will likely be two weeks before I can get assigned to a regiment so as I can give you an address.

However, I'll write you at the first opportunity. Don't worry if you don't hear from me for if anything happens to me, the government will send a telegram something like this: "Soldier 377340 has been wounded" or "Killed" or "is missing" whatever the trouble is. If I am hurt, I will be classed as wounded or if I die of disease, I'll be classed as killed.

With the insurance information, if you think it necessary, tell them my age, which was 18 years on May 6, 1918. Don't forget that the penalty for enlisting under age is 6 months at hard labor and a dishonorable discharge from the service. However I don't consider it necessary to tell them my age.

When I get to Panama, I'll send you my company and regimental address, also my number if they change it. Have I ever had any broken bones or serious illness, no?

Tuesday we hiked to the Hudson River. We went down the side of the Palisades on a narrow path four abreast for a mile. The road was almost straight up and down and it doubled back and forth 3 times to the 100 yards.

The Palisades are brown rock and run almost straight up and down at one place. I saw them. I think they are 200 feet high. The river there is about three quarters of a mile wide. We saw two transports at anchor farther down.

When we left camp for the hike, we had seventy men and three officers. We came back with forty men and two officers in the

"Tarzan of the Apes"

Our patrons have read this wonderful story in the papers and no doubt are very anxious to see the screening of this wonderful story.

Those who have not read the story will enjoy the picture as it is claimed by the producers to be the best work they have ever accomplished.

SATURDAY
JUNE 29TH, 1918
THE LYCEUM

Two Shows Only

7.30 and 9.45

Adults: 28 Cents   Children: 11 Cents

Buy War Savings Stamps

Buy-Buy From Uncle Sam or its Bye-Bye for You and Uncle Sam

Ad in the Republican Watchman, *June 1918.*

Boarding Houses Ads, 1918

Two 6-room cottages on easy terms; also Washington Beach Hotel; bathing beach and dance hall; all part furnished. For full details write W. T. Tether, owner.—Brooklyn Daily Eagle, *May 25, 1918.*

Highland Cottage
Splendidly situated on Washington Lake. Accommodates 125; fine roads, dancing, bathing fishing, tennis, garage; $12 to $14. E.V. Kalbfus. —Brooklyn Daily Eagle, *June 25, 1918.*

Highland Cottage owned by Edith Kalbfus in 1917. Postcard courtesy of Larry Stern.

Bodine Cottages on Lake Bodine
Accommodates 30; cuisine Francaise. Bathing, fishing, and boats free; $12 up. H. Bodine.—Brooklyn Daily Eagle, *June 25, 1918.*

Side Hill Farm House
Own farm produce; $12 to $14 per week. Henri Darrieusecq, Proprietor, Barryville.—Brooklyn Daily Eagle, *June 25, 1918.*

Side Hill Farm House owned by Henri Darrieusecq in 1918. Postcard courtesy of Larry Stern.

Sunset View House
Accommodates 75. Boating, bathing, fishing; own farm produce. J. Loerch Stewart, Highland Lake.—Brooklyn Daily Eagle, *June 25, 1918.*

Bradley House, Eldred
Large airy rooms; excellent table; everything fresh from our farm. Circular. E.D. Avery.—Brooklyn Daily Eagle, *June 25, 1918.*

---

ranks. The rest were straggling along in the rear.

Yesterday they sent us out into the country in an auto truck to get sod. We got two loads of sod and we got a ride through a little village. We crossed a railroad at least every mile. The gardens here are growing fine.

Most of the roads are macadam, but on our hike we went over some cobblestones that nearly broke some fellow's ankles. On the way back, we made a forced march and every once in a while, someone would drop out. The hike was 9 miles. Five of which we made at forced march.

With love to all,
Raymond

July 4, 1918
Dear Folks,

I expect to leave here tomorrow morning at 2 a.m. I don't think they are bluffing now, for we can't leave the company street, so I will mail this letter. I'll have to sneak out of here to do it.

Sunday had a 9-hour pass to Patterson, N.J. Our expenses were all paid for and we went out in private autos. The Y.M.C.A. gave us a supper which I surely enjoyed. Well, don't worry if you don't hear from me for 2 or 3 weeks. I was glad to get the package, but no letter direct from home has reached me.

Will write as soon as possible with love to all, Raymond

McKinley Austin, 11th U.S. Inf., France, to Jennie Austin
July 7, 1918
Dear Mother,

I got your letters all right. And I got one from Raymond. He was still at Camp Merritt. If he goes to Panama, he may see George Sidwell, if George is still there.

It must be hard for you to see us go, but you have been very brave. If all the mothers in America were like you, there would not have been a need for a draft. I think the reason we boys, who are no braver than the average, were so quick to go, was that we have always been taught that we have a duty to our country. Some seem to think that their country should protect

Art, Elizabeth, Bob Austin, and a friend, holding flags. Photo courtesy of Mary Briggs Austin.

"Aunt Aida sent me a couple of pictures of the children saluting. They certainly looked comical, especially Robbie." On left: a friend, Elizabeth, Bob (Robbie) and Art Austin. Photo courtesy of Mary Briggs Austin.

them, but shouldn't call on them to help.

I am getting along well. We have been lucky so far. This is a fine place for a summer home, but we have some bad neighbors.

Give my regards to all. Tell Aunt Aida I will answer her soon. But it is hard to get time. I have several letters now.

Hoping to hear from you soon, I am your loving son, McKinley

Saint-Dié-des-Vosges, France
By July 14, 1918, the 11th Infantry was at Saint Dié, France, near the Vosges Mountains, at least 400 kilometers (249 miles) east and a bit south of Paris.

Battle of Château-Thierry
On July 18, 1918, General John J. (Black Jack) Pershing led the American Expeditionary Force (A.E.F.) at the Battle of Château-Thierry, northeast of Paris.

I was in Château-Thierry the morning the Germans was drove out of there. I took the first load of supplies there and put them in what had been the City Hall with half the roof blown off.—Daniel Rowlee Schoonover.

After the Château-Thierry battle, Rowlee was sent to Italy.

St. Mihiel Offensive Planned
In July the Allied commanders agreed on a strategic offensive plan which included an attack at St. Mihiel, France, some 150 kilometers (93 miles) northwest of Saint-Dié-des-Vosges.

The assault was to start on September 12. The 11th Infantry would be part of this operation.

St. Mihiel was around 40 kilometers (29 miles) southeast of Verdun, where 306,000 German and French soldiers had died in one of the longest and most devastating battles of WWI.

McKinley Austin, 11th U.S. Inf., France, to Aida Austin
July 27, 1918
Dear Aunt Aida,

I have started to write to you several times, but something always bothered. I have been busy, so would only write one letter to the folks and expect they tell you what I write.

I have been so busy, or so lazy that I have not written lately. But I thought you might worry. I got the pictures all right. They were good.

You wanted to know about this country. There are some of the prettiest places here I have ever seen, but I prefer Sullivan County. I have seen pictures home that look just like the country here.

How is everything in Eldred? I suppose nearly everyone of the boys have either gone or expect to go soon.

I can't think of anything much to write, so I will close.

Your loving nephew, McKinley

R. Austin, Culebra, Panama Canal Zone, Ancon Hospital, Panama, to Mort and Jennie Austin, Eldred

Art Austin holding a flag. Photo courtesy of Mary Briggs Austin.

July 27, 1918
Dear Folks,

I arrived at Colon, Panama, OK, only I was just recovering from the mumps which I took on board ship. I also got seasick from being confined in the ship's hospital and I couldn't eat much.

My stomach was all upset and nothing looked good to me. But I hadn't been on land half an hour before I was as hungry as a bear.

Don't worry about me, as I am going to join my company tomorrow (Sunday), so the lieutenant who is the surgeon tells me.

Well I'll try to tell you about my trip in the order that things happened.

We got up at 2 o'clock in the morning on July 5. We ate breakfast at about 3. But it was nearly 6 before we marched out of camp Merritt. We entrained at Dumont for Hoboken which we reached at about 10:30.

We surely looked good with our rolls slung over our shoulders. We marched through Hoboken to the docks where the Red Cross gave us a cup of coffee and a sandwich.

By 12 we were all on the "Killpatrick" and at 1:10 we began to move. That night at about 7 or 8 o'clock, we saw seven small whales. We saw porpoises almost every evening. On the third night we saw the glow from the lights at Newport News, Virginia, and we saw the light from a search light nearly 30 miles away. We saw land for the first time on the fourth day when we passed Palm Beach, Florida.

The next day, I went to the ship's hospital which was a disgrace to the U.S. Navy. There were only five pairs of slippers for 16 men. They were all men and only one fellow took any interest in the sick men.

The food we got to eat during the whole voyage was the worst I ever tasted. It was almost inedible and anyone who was seriously sick would have surely died.

Through the portholes I saw several very mountainous islands. We also passed the northeastern coasts of Cuba. We ran into San Juan, Puerto Rico, on the tenth day. I could see the crowds through the portholes. Everyone wears a straw hat there.

All the soldiers who were well went ashore on a hike and got some fruit and coconuts. We didn't get any, although one of the medical men paraded around the hospital eating fruit.

On the 18th of July, we left San Juan. We came through the Caribbean Sea and it was surely rough. On the 20th the hospital got so crowded that I and some others were moved out on the deck. That night for supper, I ate my first meal since going to the hospital. The next night it rained and our bed and blankets got wet and stayed that way 'til we landed at Colon, Panama, on July 23.

They took us off the boat in the afternoon. I walked, but some had to be carried on stretchers. By the time I got on the train, I was feeling as well as ever.

There are surely a lot of railroads here. We came from Colon to Ancon, 57 miles in about one and a half hours. The railroads run on embankments raised out of the swamps in many places. On both sides there was nothing but water with the stumps of trees standing about it. Here and there an island of 2 to 5 acres raised 15 or 20 feet above the water. It is on these that the natives have their farms.

Hunt for Slackers

New York's draft cleanup, the detection and putting into uniform of young men who fooled themselves into thinking that they could save their precious skins by evading the selective service law, started on a prodigious scale. More than 42,000 were caught in New York's boroughs and the nearby cities of New Jersey.

A great specially organized police force of 20,000 men began what is officially called a canvass of the city and metropolitan district, including Hoboken, Jersey City, and Newark…

The proportion of proved slackers was probably less than 3 per cent. The others had left their draft credentials at home or were not of conscript age. The hunt will go on. The canvassers have been asked to be more careful than many of them were the first day.

One of the most important immediate results of the concerted raid was the arrest and identification of five actual deserters from the United States Army.—Republican Watchman, Monticello, July 1, 1918.

Rowlee Schoonover worked for the Y.M.C.A. in France and Italy during WWI. Photo courtesy of John Hull, his great-grandson.

At Ancon, I helped unload the men who were on stretchers from the train and put them in ambulances. Then I climbed on the back of an ambulance and rode up to the hospital.

With love to all, Raymond

**Raymond Austin, Camp Gaillard, Panama Canal Zone,
to Mort and Jennie, Eldred**
August 3, 1918
Dear Folks,

I came out of the Ancon hospital OK except for my uniform which got filthy dirty from being kicked about in the ship's hospital.

Three other men came out with me. One had no hat, leggins, or socks, and his pants were about six inches too short. His beard was about half an inch long and was red at that. He had brought a blanket to Ancon with him, so of course, he had to carry it on his arm. The other two had all their uniform, but they were all smeared with tar and grease from the ship.

We left the hospital about noon. I never felt so cheap in all my life as I did when I got out on the street in my dirty clothes and with out my leggins.

Aug. 4: I write my letters on different dates as I am continually being interrupted.

This is the wet season down here. It rains some every day and the roads are all sticky and slippery. I have heard old veterans speak of Virginia mud, but Panama mud is a reality to me now in fact, big clods of it are sticking to my shoes now.

We are quartered in tents now which remind me of Ft. Slocum. But our food is ten times better. We have to eat outside and today we ate in the rain. Nevertheless, I got enough. Something has given me an awful appetite and I will soon gain back what I lost on the "Killpatrick."

I haven't had any letters from you since the 27th of June and I am beginning to be quite worried.

Have you heard from Mac yet?

I wish you would send me a bundle of "Democrats," "Rural New Yorkers," "Farm and Homes," "Christian Advocates," and any other papers except "Lone Scout." Save them 'til I come home.

While I was in the hospital someone stole a pair of pants and a suit of underwear off me. Some of the fellows lost their blankets or mess kits, so I was comparatively lucky.

Has any one else volunteered since I left?

What kind of crops have we this year?

I'm going to write grandfather as soon as I can afford it.

With love to all,
Raymond, 33rd U.S. Inf.

**McKinley, France,
to Jennie Austin, Eldred**
August 9, 1918
Dear Mother,

I hope you will pardon me for not writing sooner. But when I had paper, I did not have time and when I had time, I could not get paper. Have you heard from Raymond lately? I have had one letter from him.

I don't suppose there are so many city boarders up this year.

Aunt Aida sent me a couple of pictures of the children saluting. They certainly looked comical, especially Robbie. Is Willie still working at Proctor's?

Tell Grandfather that I will write him sometime. When I get back home, we will have

Rowlee Schoonover in Italy, World War I

Rowlee Schoonover was hired as a mechanic for the Y.M.C.A. He first went to England, then Paris, then was eventually transferred to Italy.

I had just got the garage running OK [in France] when I was ordered to Italy. Well, I got my movement papers ready and started for Italy. I went by train from Paris to Tureno, Italy; then to Verona.

I had gotten acquainted with a man by the name of Dr. Naylor. He was a very fine man and he was sent to Italy to open the Y down there, for we had three battalions of Americans in Italy and an ambulance core.

When he got down there, he found things in a very bad way. It had been organized by another man and everything had been run any old way and no one cared how things went. So Dr. Naylor had his troubles and that was why he sent for me.

There was a lot of rich men's sons that was deferred from the army and was in the Y, but Dr. Naylor was a good deal like me. He had no use for that kind and when they would go to him with complaints, he would ship them back to France.

I remember there was a man that had charge of transportation that came from New Jersey. He had bought all the trucks, cars, and motorcycles, and they had sold him 3 second-hand Fords. I found they was in an Italian repair shop, and went to see what was the trouble. They told me they could not get parts. They were 1913 to 1914 models. I loaded the lot of them in trucks and took them to Milan where he had bought them.

The Milano Agency had the whole of Italy. I told them I wanted them replaced with new cars or I would notify the Ford Motor Company in the States that they had sold old cars for new. I knew that the Ford Company would take away their agency. I got the new cars and I had no more trouble with them. That man got sent back to the States. I had a heck of a time to get things running OK, but I went to Colonel Wallace of the Ambulance Corps at Montova and he gave me a detail of 5 Soldiers who were good men and we did our own repairs.

I had my troubles with them sky pilots. They was forever in trouble with the trucks. There was nothing but shell torn roads and not a place to get anything to eat and no place to sleep until you got to Teresta and that had been taken over by the Italian Army.

Then I must tell you about the other trip I had. They had the drive on and was pushing the Austrians back from the Piave River and we was following the army.

An old feller, Judge Evans from Des Moines, Iowa, and a very nice man wanted to go. So I took him along. We got started and the bridges had been blown out. We had to detour; half the time we were lost. We kept going all night and just at daylight we came to a good sized town.

The judge was half frozen. He had a blanket over his head and he said, "Dan, how I would like to have a cup of hot coffee."

I told him we was in the English Zone and that the English drank tea, but I would find him some if I could. I went over to the commissary and asked a Tomy if they had any coffee. He told me they had some coffee beans, but had no way to grind it.

I got some beans and put them in a rag and got a couple stones and pounded out some ground coffee, built a fire on the street and put the coffee over to boil in my mess kit and the judge got warmed up and was OK.

Well, we got back OK.

There was orders to go up to Mt. Grappa with two truck loads of beef. I took along a feller named Johnson from the Navy. He was a Dr.'s son from New York City and a very nice boy.

We got up in the mountains and had to stop for the Austrians was shelling the road from a camp down below and they had their guns trained on a corner of the road and they sure kept that spot hot. The Italians would not go in and get their wounded with their ambulances, so the Americans went in to bring out the wounded. One of our ambulances got a square hit and there was nothing left of it.

Another time I was going over the mountain to Fuma. On top of the mountain I saw two little kids a walking along, boy and girl. I do not think that they was over 6 and 8 years old. I stopped and picked them up. They did not want to get in the truck at first, but I took them up on the seat with me and I found out they had been sent to the store at town to get some cornmeal.

They was very cold. Although the snow was not so deep, it was very cold and a very high wind. I wrapped them up in a blanket and they got nice and warm and I let them off in front of their home.—Daniel Rowlee Schoonover.

Rowlee Schoonover in an airplane during WWI. Photo courtesy of John Hull.

Raymond Austin with his mother Jennie. Photo courtesy of the Austin Family.

some time swapping war stories. Raymond will talk for a week steady when he gets back.

I am getting along well. Except in a big drive there is not much danger, so you need not worry about me. Give my love to all.

Your loving son, Mac

Aida Austin, Eldred, to McKinley Austin, France
August 11, 1918
Dear Nephew,

The letter I commenced to you the forepart of last week, I did not get finished until the last of the week, but as I have planned to send you a letter every Monday, I will write you a few lines tonight so as to send it off in the morning.

I have just answered Mrs. Carlin's letter. She is at Long Beach with her cousin. Will be there until September. Fred Morgan is home for a few days. I have not seen him.

I think I told you in one of my letters, that George Sidwell is at one of the camps in one of the southern states. He is attending some kind of a school. His father was telling your dad that at Panama they wanted George to drill for an officer, but George didn't want to be an officer. It is quite comical to hear about the different fellows from this place being officers.

The Congregational Church had their fair last Thursday and Friday and took in a little over $300 the first day. I did not hear how much they took in the second day. I don't know when the Methodists have their fair.

Dr. Austin and Joe Ayers [husband of Olinda, Dr. Austin's sister] came up yesterday in Joe's car, but went back today. We have been having some fearfully hot weather, but it is cooler now again. I hope you haven't had such hot weather over there.

I will close as I want to write to Cousin Tina tonight. She has married a rich rancher and lives in Montana. She sent me a souvenir of Montana. One of the scenes is of the Custer Battlefield as it is today.

Be sure and send my letters to Barryville, N.Y., box 26.

Hoping to hear from you soon.
Your loving aunt, Aida

Raymond Austin, Camp Gaillard, Culebra, Canal Zone, to Bill Austin
August 12, 1918
Dear Brother,

It is quite warm here, but no more so than it is in New York during August.

I suppose you have heard from Mac again. I wrote him a letter day before yesterday. It will probably be 2 months before I get an answer.

Has anyone else from Eldred enlisted? Also has any news been heard from Fred Straub, George Dunlap, or any of the fellows who went over?

I suppose by the time this reaches you, Mrs. Tuzza and the others will be thinking of going home. Give all the people my best regards and tell them I am glad I joined the army although I am not a crack Soldier. We drill a couple hours every day. I am no expert at drilling, but I like it very well. We have half-an-hours exercise every morning which I don't like so well. But it's got to be done, so I do my best, which is none too good.

Hoping that all of you are well and will write soon.

I am your brother,
Raymond

Sherman S. Leavenworth, grandfather of McKinley and Raymond Austin. "I'm going to write Grandfather as soon as I can afford it." Photo courtesy of Cynthia Leavenworth Bellinger.

Raymond Austin, Camp Gaillard, Culebra, Canal Zone, to his family
August 16, 1918
Dear Folks,

I just received two letters from Willie and one from Mother. I also received letters from four Lone Scouts who read some articles I wrote for our paper. They are from Wisconsin, Kentucky, New Jersey, and South Carolina. I'll probably have more letters soon.

We had a nice little hike this morning. We were over to the canal. From where we were, there was a good view of Culebra cut from the south side. The water in the canal is very muddy. We saw a dredge at work removing the dirt that works up from the canal bottom, after one of the officers explained a good deal about machinery that operates the "little ditch."

We have signed the payroll twice and I expect to hear the old bugle say "pay day" almost any morning. The money and the stamps came together (thanks for them). The stamps are worthless here anyhow. They were stuck tight to the letter. Don't risk any of Ma's letters until I am assigned.

I have $7.60—enough to buy stamps writing paper, and bananas—and that's about all I can buy here anyhow.

How is Grandfather getting along this summer? And have you heard from Uncle Ell lately?

With love to all, Raymond

Aida Austin, Eldred, to McKinley Austin, France
August 19, 1918
Dear McKinley,

We have been having a few cold days and it seems good after the terribly hot weather we had.

Doctor Austin didn't get up Saturday, but is coming Tuesday and will stay a week. Tommie Collins is getting around again, but has to use his crutches. I think I told you about his falling from an automobile and breaking his ankle just before Robbie Croft was called to the Army.

Your dad's and Uncle Lon's

> ## Sullivan County Resorts
>
> *Sullivan County Resorts Still Alive with Guests*
>
> **Eldred Sojourners**
> The Labor Day weekend finds many Brooklynites enjoying country life at Eldred's Bradley House and Echo Hill Farm.
>
> **Yulan Guests Sleep Outdoors**
> The delightful weather of the past few weeks has kept everyone in the best of spirits. Living out of doors during the day has been supplemented by sleeping out of doors at night. The fad is prevalent throughout this section, especially among the younger people.
>
> Brooklynites are at Highland Cottage and the Washington Lake House.
>
> **Highland Lake Colony**
> The large number of bathers and of boats to be seen at Highland Lake give evidence that the last week of August has been a busy one for proprietors of the hotels.
>
> Guests from Brooklyn are at Highland Lake House and Sunset.
> —Brooklyn Daily Eagle, *September 1, 1918.*
>
>
>
> *The Joy Riders of Highland Lake, N.Y. Postcard courtesy of the Bosch Family.*

Fridolin (Fred) Straub Jr., son of Fridolin and Juliana Straub. "Has any news been heard from Fred Straub?" Photo courtesy of Betty Ihlo Morganstern.

buckwheat looks fine. Uncle Lon talks of getting a small mill so that he can grind his own grain this year. He had a fine piece of wheat and gathered it last week. He has a yearling that he is going to put into beef this fall, so with our wheat and buckwheat, meat and vegetables, and fruit that I am putting up, our living won't cost so very much and we will be able to save quite a little toward a payment on the place. I am going to put up some plums and crab apples this week.

The only thing lacking is the chickens. Lon doesn't seem to want to bother with them. But the doctor's wife and I both want chickens. We two are planning

Wedding ceremony, Art Austin as preacher. Photo courtesy of Mary Briggs Austin.

Art Austin, the preacher, using a phone book to perform the wedding ceremony. Photo courtesy of Mary Briggs Austin.

on the quiet about them, for I am sure I could make them pay, and I think you will find a fine flock of chickens on the place when you get back.

I see by the papers, the government is going to make some provision with regard to the education of the boys under 21 when the war is over. So perhaps you will be able to go through Cornell before you settle down as a farmer. I do hope you can, for it will mean so much to you later in life.

Sunday slipped by again without my writing to you. Dr. Austin was in quite a while in the morning and Ell came up in the afternoon and stayed to tea. Your folks were going to take Ell out home. They were going to get Bert Eldred to take him then, but his automobile broke down on his way back from Lackawaxen, and they couldn't go.

Ell expects to go down to Virginia to work this winter. He told Dr. Austin he would buy this place of him if he was able. But he said, "I suppose that would take a good lot of money."

The Doctor said, "Not such a great deal." This is the only hint we have had with regard to what the doctor would ask for the place. Although we have had quite a few talks with the doctor about the place, we have never asked him anything about what he wanted for it. We thought we better wait until we were ready to make a payment. He says they don't want to sell the house and yard, but will make arrangements so that you will have that, too, when they are through with it.

Your dad says Ell took your address and Raymond's and said he was going to write to you both. He liked the largest picture of yours the best.

With love from all,
Aunt Aida

St. Mihiel, France, August 30, 1918

On August 30, 1918, the first American Army under Gen. Pershing's own command, took over the entire St. Mihiel Front with four Army Corps assembling the 1st, 4th, and 5th American and the 2nd French Colonial Corps.

On that day, Marshal Fock... proposed two new jobs for the American Army. The first was to be an attack between the Meuse and the Argonne Forest, on September 15th by the 2nd French Army supported by from 4 to 6 American Divisions.

At a meeting 3 days later, General Pershing insisted that the American Army be employed as a unit, and not piecemealed out... Pershing asked for the Muese-Argonne Sector. Fifty kilometers of the front from the Argonne to Port sur-Seille well to the east of St. Mihiel was placed under Pershing's command together with all the French divisions then

Town Square of St. Mihiel, France, 1918. Photo: Schutz Group Photographers. Library of Congress, Prints and Photographs Division: Call Number LOT 6944 no. 15 (OSE); 6a35216u.

in that zone.—Gen. Liggett, from Saturday Evening Post, *June 4, 1927*.

Col. George S. Patton Jr.
General Pershing had earlier ordered the creation of a tank force to support A.E.F.'s infantry. In August 1918 Colonel George S. Patton Jr. (who was involved with training tank brigades) was placed in charge of the 1st Provisional Tank Brigade (later called 304th). Patton would command the French Renault tanks driven by Americans at the St. Mihiel Offensive.—From wikipedia.org.

11th Infantry Leaves for St. Mihiel, France, Sept. 6, 1918
On September 6, 1918, the 11th Infantry left for St. Mihiel.

On September 6 George James Clark was with the Canadian 3rd Battalion in northern France. The 3rd Canadian Infantry Battalion was part of the First Canadian Division and had been given the task of breaking through the German Hindenburg Line near an unfinished portion of Canal du Nord, in France, 290 kilometers (180 miles) northwest of St. Mihiel, where McKinley Austin, Ed Grotcloss Jr., and Irwin Briggs were located.

Raymond Austin, Co. M., Balboa, Canal Zone, to Mort Austin
September 9, 1918

Dear Father,

I received your letter while I was still at Culebra. We are quartered on the pier, so we see practically everything that goes on. There was a big Japanese vessel here bounding for Chile with about 500 Japanese, Chinese, and Korean emigrants on board. I have several pieces of Chinese, Japanese, and Australian money I will send home when I have a chance. I will also send some photographs if they will let me.

Sept. 11: The money order came yesterday. Thank you ever so much for it. I have not had a chance to cash it yet, but expect a pass around Saturday or Sunday and will do it then.

I have been permanently assigned to Company "M" so my address will be sure from now on. I wish you would send the pictures now and also Mac's letters. I have almost expected one from him myself. It would seem good to read some of his letters just now.

I am on guard today and was just relieved a few moments ago. I am watching the electric station this time. My orders on this post are, "To allow no one to pass with out a check. To arrest all suspicious persons and to examine all packages."

What did Uncle Ell say about my enlisting? Did he think I did wrong?

They are using us fine here and any one who knows enough to obey orders will not get in any serious trouble. I ran across one overbearing sergeant at Ft. Slocum and that's about all.

It is getting warmer here and believe me it takes lots of ice cream and soda to keep me comfortably cool.

So some of the people would like to see me? What does Uncle Lon and his consort say now?

When I think of the four long years that Grandfather [Leavenworth] fought through and of your cousins [Austins] and

Yours Truly on the "March France. 1918

Irwin Briggs on the March in France, 1918. Photo courtesy of Mary Briggs Austin.

Browning Automatic Rifle

By June 1918, Winchester was in full production of the Browning automatic rifle (B.A.R.), and delivered 4,000 guns. In July there were 9,000 units produced.

Both the Colt and Marlin-Rockwell Corporations began soon after Winchester was in full production. The three companies produced 706 rifles per day, and a total of 52,000 B.A.R.s were delivered by the end of the war.

The Browning automatics began to arrive in France by July 1918.

B.A.R. Used in Action

The U.S. Army's 70th Infantry Division, the first unit to receive the Browning automatic rifles, used them in action for the first time on September 13, 1918.

The Browning Automatic Rifles were used extensively during the Meuse-Argonne Offensive and would impress the allies. France would request 15,000 automatic rifles to replace what they had.
—wikipedia.org.

Mother's uncles [Hezekiah and Atwell Leavenworth] who never came home, it would be a disgrace to the whole family if I should want to quit now.

Don't worry, for if anything happens, I will tell you the truth, and conceal nothing. With love to all, Your son, Raymond
Co. M. 33rd U.S. Inf.

St. Mihiel, Sept. 12–19, 1918
Our [11th Infantry, McKinley Austin's group] barrage started at 1 a.m. on September 12. The regiment got in position for jumping off at 4:30 a.m., and the attack started at 5 a.m.

The Division Front was held by 10th Brigade. The 11th Infantry was on the right, the 6th Infantry was on the left, each regiment had one battalion in the front line. The 357 Infantry (90th Division) was on our right.

The 3rd Battalion, an assault battalion, followed and then 2nd Battalion Regiment reached all objectives on scheduled time, taking 100s of prisoners…

On September 13, a short, but fierce counter attack of the enemy was broken up by the regiment.

About midnight September 15, the regiment relieved by 61st Infantry, moved into an intermediate position and remained there until September 16.—Sergeant John G. Popp.

The French Renault tanks designed to cross 6-foot trenches in dry weather, had to navigate trenches 8 feet deep and 10 to 14 feet wide "in horrible mud."

Irwin Briggs, Medic, St. Mihiel, France
Irwin Briggs, a medic, went to the front lines to get the wounded and the dying during the St. Mihiel battle. He would also help at the next major battle, the Meuse-Argonne. There is a photo of some of the ambulances in his group. (Irwin received letters and photos from his future wife Myrtie Crabtree while he was in France.)

Raymond Austin, Balboa, Canal Zone, to Mort Austin, Eldred
September 19, 1918
Dear Mother,
The papers and magazines you sent me arrived tonight. As I am doing guard duty quite often now, I wish you would please excuse the interval between and also the briefness of my letters.
Hoping you, father, Bill and the kids are as well as I am.
Your loving son, Raymond

Raymond Austin, Balboa, Canal Zone, to Bill Austin, Eldred
September 19, 1918
Dear Brother,
I haven't seen much here to write about that would pass the censor, so don't think I am forgetting you because my letters are short.
I broke my rifle yesterday and I guess that's the climax to my "hoodoo" streak of luck. Everything has gone smoothly since that and I am picking up confidence again.
Believe me, it's hot down here. They tell me the sun here drives some men crazy, especially weak minded ones. I suppose that you all will have serious apprehensions for me after hearing this.
Howsoever, I believe I'll get back as sane as I left. Though that may not be saying much.
We had a tug of war yesterday between the front and rear ranks. It was exciting sport while it lasted, even if we were out pulled in the end.
Your brother, Raymond

McKinley Austin, 11th U.S. Inf., France, to Jennie Austin
September 19, 1918

"French Renault tanks going through Vaux." Photo: Library of Congress, W.E. Troutman, Inc., LC-USZ62-114712.

Dear Mother,

I was glad to hear from you. I have been busy lately and have not written as I should. I am well and feel as if I will be lucky.

I only wish that I could tell you more about where I have been during the past couple of weeks. You wouldn't blame me for not writing more. I certainly thought enough about you when I was laying in a shell hole with the German shells throwing dirt and stones all over me.

They are tricky fighters without much idea of honor. Their artillery and machine guns are fair, but their infantry is not much good. It may be I have not seen their good troops yet, but I think we can lick them anytime we have half a chance.

I got a letter from Raymond, a few days ago. He seems quite well satisfied. I think both of us will be more contented with home when we get back.

We are not allowed to get parcels without having permission from some officers and I don't know as I need anything much now anyway. It is surprising just how little a person really needs. I hope George Dunlap was not badly wounded. Well, I will close with love, Your son, McKinley

McKinley Austin, 11th U.S. Inf. A.E.F., to Aida Austin
September 22, 1918
(received Oct. 23)
Dear Aunt,

I am writing to let you know I am well. So far I have received all your letters. They did not come in rotation for I got your fourth, 3 days after your sixth.

I have not written as I should because we have been busy and when I get a while off, I like to rest.

I got the pictures all right. If

The Ambulance Corps that Irwin Briggs was in. Photo courtesy of Mary Briggs Austin.

you see Lena, tell her I got her letter and wrote once from over here. Her picture is not as good looking as she is, but I knew who it was.

I am glad to hear you are getting along so well on the farm. Next year I may be home to help, of course we can't be sure. If it is possible to get the land, do so.

When I come back, I will have a couple of hundred dollars or more to help with. I think that I will be lucky here. I have been so far. Well, give my love to all.
Your nephew, McKinley

Mort Austin on Jury Duty
In September Mort Austin was on jury duty in Monticello, New York. His wife Jennie Austin wrote him letters addressed to the care of Mrs. Fowler, Monticello, N.Y.

Jennie Austin, Eldred, to C.M. Austin, Monticello, N.Y.

Art, Elizabeth, and Robbie (Bob) Austin. Photo courtesy of the Austin Family.

"I thought of you when I was laying in a shell hole with the German shells throwing dirt and stones all over me." Mortimer McKinley Austin. Photo courtesy of Mary Briggs Austin.

September 25, 1918
Dear Mort,
Received your letter tonight and will write a few lines. You have been away 2 days and it seems about that many weeks.

You got another nice letter from Raymond. I will send it with this. He has been moved to Balboa. I think that is on the Pacific coast. Wasn't Balboa the one who discovered the Pacific Ocean?

I only wish we could feel as easy over Mac as we do him. I paid Raymond's Red Cross money over today. They was after it.

Elizabeth still gets along well in school. Little Anthony made me a short call after school today. He is a bright kid.

Willie is feeling alright again, so don't worry about him or us. We are feeling fine, but only wish you were here. Still it is a good rest for you and likely you will have to work hard all winter.

I will certainly be good, for I have no chance to be bad.

Take good care of yourself.
With lots of love, Jennie

Anthony Hirsch Sr.
Little Anthony may have been the young son of Anthony Hirsch Sr. who would marry Christina Leavenworth. Anthony Sr. had boarded at Echo Hill Farm where Christina's father Sherman and her siblings Charlotte, Truman, and Martin lived.

Anthony Sr., (a pastry chef in Manhattan) had immigrated to the United States in 1906 and was naturalized in 1914. His first wife (mother of little Anthony) and their young daughter had died from the Spanish flu that killed so many in New York City. Years later, Christina would comment to her daughter Charlee Hirsch, that there were so many funerals in New York City because of the influenza, that she (Christina) dreaded the sound of the parade music that went with the continuous funeral processions because of so many deaths.

Montfaucon, France
Montfaucon was in northeastern France at an elevation of 1,200 feet. To the east was the Meuse River; to the west the Argonne Forest. The German (seemingly

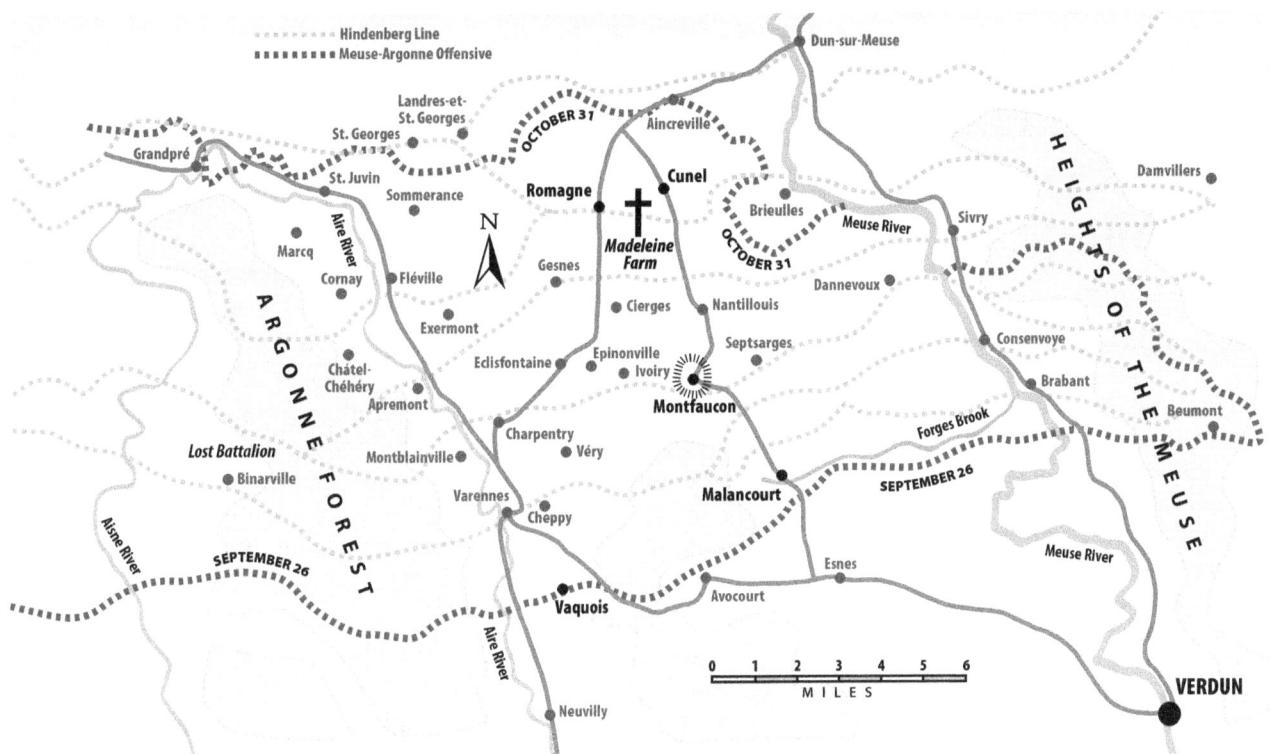

Meuse-Argonne Offensive in Northeastern France. Verdun is in the lower right hand corner. The Argonne Forest is on the left; the Meuse River is near the right of the map. North from Montfaucon in the middle of the map, is Madeleine Farm, Romagne (sous-Montfaucon), and Cunel. The Lost Battalion is shown on the middle left in the Argonne Forest. Sedan, not shown, is further north. Map: Gary Smith.

impregnable) Hindenburg Line crisscrossed the area.

The Germans had their well-protected three-story headquarters on top of Montfaucon. From that high vantage point the Kronprinz (Crown Prince) could observe the surrounding entrenchments for miles around.

The special feature of the place, however, was a powerful reflecting telescopic periscope mounted on a gun carriage and put in place on the first floor with the tube running through the tower and out the roof.—Barber, J. Frank (Chairman), History of the Seventy-ninth Division U.S. Army A.E.F., 1917–1920, *p. 123.*

Meuse River, Argonne Forest
The Argonne Forest was a wild unfriendly, thickly forested, hilly area. A small stream, the Aire River, flowed along the eastern edge of the Argonne Woods.

The Meuse River, east of Montfaucon, flowed in a very winding path from southern France, north through Sedan, France, and on into Belgium and the Netherlands.

Between the little Aire River and the Meuse River was the narrow open valley where the Meuse-Argonne Offensive would take place.

In this region were Romagne-sous-Montfaucon, Cunel, and Madeleine Farm—the villages where McKinley Austin's outfit would fight.

The Meuse Argonne sector extended from the river Meuse on the east to the western edges of the Argonne Forest on the west. It was the most important and difficult of all theaters of war on the Western Front.

The densely wooded heights

Anthony Hirsch Sr. holding son Anthony Hirsch Jr. "Little Anthony made me a short call after school today." Anthony Sr. would marry Christina Leavenworth. Photo courtesy of Cynthia Leavenworth Bellinger.

> ### Dr. Pierce's Pleasant Pellets for the Spanish Influenza
>
> Avoid crowds, coughs and cowards, but fear neither germs nor Germans! Keep the system in good order, take plenty of exercise in the fresh air and practice cleanliness. Remember a clean mouth, a clean skin, and clean bowels are a protecting armour against disease.
>
> To keep the liver and bowels regular and to carry away the poisons within, it is best to take a vegetable pill every other day, made up of May apples, aloes, jalap, and sugar-coated, to be had at most drug stores, known as *Dr. Pierce's Pleasant Pellets*. If there is a sudden onset of what appears like a hard cold, one should go to bed, wrap warm, take a hot mustard foot-bath and drink copiously of hot lemonade.—Dr. L.W. Bowers.

of the Argonne Forest was only a small portion of the whole sector, but perhaps the strongest and most formidable held by the Germans.

It was considered so impregnable (and the Germans a high vantage point), that the attack by the Americans/French included the necessity of outflanking the Forest on both sides rather than by wresting it from the enemy by frontal attacks.—Moss, Col. Jas. A., and Howland, Col. Harry S., America In Battle, *1920, pp. 213–215.*

The Meuse-Argonne Offensive

Marshal Ferdinand Foch, head of the French Army and appointed Supreme Commander of the Allied Armies, and British commander Field Marshal Haig, planned the Meuse-Argonne Offensive (M.A.O.) to start on September 26, 1918.

The objective of the Meuse-Argonne Offensive was to break through the German defenses, supply lines, and communication center; and capture the railroad hub near the northeastern city of Sedan, France, some 64 kilometers (40 miles) from the German observatory at Montfaucon. Nearly all the supplies for the German army in France went to Sedan.

If successful, the offensive would cut off communication between the left and the right wings of the German Army. The goal included driving the Germans from the rugged terrain between the Argonne Forest and the Meuse River where they had been entrenched for four years. This meant breaking through the Hindenburg Line.

The Kreimhilde Stellung [part of the Hindenburg Line] was a rough trench line with barbed wire guarded by covering positions in front which was especially strong in the Romagne Forests… the series of woods which were the wilderness of this campaign.

This trench system continued eastward along the heights to the southern outskirts of Romagne and Cunel. From these different hills, crowned with woods, the enemy had almost perfect observation as far south as Montfaucon.—Gansser, Emil B., History of the 126th Infantry in the War with Germany, *1920, pp. 163–167, 171.*

The whole region was masked and tortuous, one of dense woods and thickets, steep and rocky ridges, valleys and ravines.

In front was a devastated area. The whole constituted the strongest position on the western front and the Allies had put it down as impregnable for all practical purposes.—Gen. Liggett, Saturday Evening Post, *May 7, 1927, pp. 28, 29.*

Meuse-Argonne Offensive Plan

The Meuse-Argonne Offensive plan called for the American, Belgian, British, and French Armies to attack in a line from Flanders to the Meuse. The M.A.O., at a horrendous cost of lives, was credited for leading directly to the Armistice on November 11.

Aida Austin's Research of the Meuse-Argonne Offensive

Aida Austin researched this battle and hand wrote 10 pages of the information from, *America in Battle*, *Colliers* magazine, and the *Saturday Evening Post*. Aida also sailed to France in 1923. Some of her photos and postcards of Montfaucon, Madeleine Farm, Romagne-sous-Montfaucon, and Cunel are in this chapter. The devastation of the land and towns could still be seen five years after the war ended.

"How well prepared and equipped was the Army?" asked Aida.

The short answer: "The major portion of U.S. troops were mostly untried and inexperienced."

This next quote Aida copied from the *Saturday Evening Post* which featured information from General Hunter Liggett. Gen. Liggett directed the final phases of the Meuse-Argonne offensive and the pursuit of the German forces until after the Armistice.

Some of the divisions were without artillery. Nearly all American divisions were short in some sort of equipment. Artillery brigades received their guns one day and were off to the front the next. They were short of transportation and animals.

Horses were on their way, but would be too late. Browning machine guns, heavy artillery, and tanks and tractors were coming from home…The different corps headquarters had had only 4 days on the ground to familiarize themselves with the situation. The divisional commands had even less.

The artillery brigades of some divisions had been attached to the divisions for the first time in the last 24 hours. Artillery units which had horses used their horses to bring up the guns of units which had none.

Our men were exhausted by their hard marching and arduous labors, and our officers by the pressure of their responsibilities and their apprehension in trying to have all details ready.

Marshal Foch postponed the attack from the 25th to the 26th, the understanding being that the French 4th Army was not yet ready…These 24 hours were valuable to our engineers, who occupied in the Saint Mihiel operation, could not arrive until the day before the attack…

We had not enough engineers to look after 2 great battles at once. Our engineers having arrived 36 hours before the attack were very short of material.

Aside from the 28th and 77th, the 33rd had had some little experience. The officers of the others knew little in practice of the technique of how to keep their men in formation through the barbed wire and across the sea of craters and in face bursts of machine guns and sudden concentration of gas and other shell fire, and of the methods of overcoming machine gun nests.
—Palmer, Frederick, Colliers, March 22, 1919, pp. 6, 7.

Influenza Pandemic of 1918

The 1918 influenza pandemic, often called the Spanish Flu, killed between 20 and 40 million people—more people than were killed in WWI. An estimated 675,000 Americans died from the flu. Half of those from the U.S. who died in Europe, died from the influenza virus—43,000 servicemen.

The 1918 Spanish flu was caused by an unusually severe and deadly Influenza A virus strain of subtype H1N1. The pandemic lasted from 1918 to 1919, spreading even to the Arctic and remote Pacific islands. Current estimates are that 50 million to 100 million people worldwide died.

One source said the disease was first observed at Fort Riley, Kansas, in March 1918. The disease came to be called the Spanish Flu because so many died (8 million) in Spain in May.

The virus returned to the US in Boston in September 1918. In October 1918, the virus killed almost 200,000. One-fourth of the U.S. and one-fifth of the world was infected with the influenza.

One of the complications was hemorrhaging from the ears, nose, stomach, and intestines. Many of the deaths were from a secondary infection, bacterial pneumonia.

The public health departments distributed gauze masks to be worn in public. Funerals were limited to 15 minutes. *wikipedia.org.*

The miserable roads began to have their effect on the second day. As the infantry advanced, it lost the proper support of the artillery which was unable to follow. The engineers toiled furiously, but the task was an appalling one.—Gen. Liggett, Saturday Evening Post, *June 4, 1927.*

Meuse-Argonne: First Phase September 26 to October 3, 1918
It was foggy around 5:30 a.m. Thursday, September 26, when about 600,000 American troops (most of them inexperienced) and their 2,700 artillery guns opened fire on 60,000 well entrenched Germans. The Meuse-Argonne Offensive, the largest American campaign of WWI, had begun.

The main U.S. effort took place north and northwest of the town of Verdun, between September 26 and November 11, 1918. It was about 32 kilometers (20 miles) from Verdun to Montfaucon. The American battlefront stretched some 25 kilometers (15 miles) from the Argonne Forest to the Meuse River.

Montzeville, just behind the American lines in the Meuse Argonne sector, 1919. Photo: Library of Congress Prints and Photographs Division: Schutz Group Photographers, Lot 6944, no. 40; 6a35481.

Montfaucon showing German observatories and fortifications captured by the American Forces, September 27, 1918. Photo: Library of Congress, Prints and Photographs Division: Schutz Group Photographers, Lot 6944 no. 26; 6a35296.

Observatory for the Kronprinz (Crown Prince). Image in Verdun book, courtesy of Victoria Kohler.

Church in Montfacucon. Image in Verdun book, courtesy of Victoria Kohler.

Col. Patton Wounded

On September 26 Col. Patton Jr. was wounded in the left leg while leading six men and a tank in an attack on German machine guns. Patton's orderly Private First Class Joe Angelo saved Patton and was awarded the Distinguished Service Cross. Col. Patton, of course, plays a major role in the next war, but as a General.—*wikipedia.org*.

Montfaucon, Sept. 27, 1918

It was rainy most of September 27. Mud and heavy, wet uniforms slowed things down. Engineers fixed shell holes and laid communication wire on the ground. The wire didn't work when wet, and was constantly being cut by heavy traffic. Ambulances received priority, ammunition second, artillery, then food. Montfaucon was captured by noon.

North of Montfaucon, the Germans were ready with hundreds of German machine guns and snipers, and another division for support. Little if any progress was made by the American troops by evening.

On September 27 George James Clark was about 220 kilometers (137 miles) northwest of Montfaucon. He was with the Canadian forces which smashed through the Hindenburg Line at a dry section of the Canal du Nord near Cambrai (as planned).

Trench warfare in the old sense was now over. The opposing armies had all accepted this new system of thin outpost lines in the fox holes, while the machine gunners moved their guns skillfully about in forming criss-cross zones of fire.—Gansser, p. 197.

The Americans did not capture Montfaucon on September 26.

The ruins of Montfaucon from a German observation position. It was captured by the American Army, September 27, 1918. Photo: Library of Congress, Prints and Photographs Division: Schutz Group Photographers, Lot 6944 no. 27; 6a35304.

Raymond Austin, Balboa, Canal Zone, to Mort Austin, Eldred
September 27, 1918
Dear Father,

I received your letter yesterday. I was delighted with the pictures. The children have not changed so much after all. Although Bob seems bigger to me. Did you send Mac any pictures?

So you will be glad when the last battle is fought. I think we all will be. I don't like to discourage you, but I feel we will see quite a while of it yet. Our loss to date has been about 25,000 men, so you see we haven't fought a single big battle yet and I feel sure there are some big fights in store for us yet. We'll win though, cost what it may.

Tell Bill not to enlist until he is at least 17 years old, unless we should get hard up for men, and I don't believe we will. There are enough between 18 and 40 to do up this job good and proper.

There is nothing much worth writing that would pass the censor. I am glad you are sending the papers every week. I sure do enjoy reading them. By the way, if you can get any books on military drill, tactics, etc., send them to me. I think you could get them in any city like Port Jervis at a bookstore.

Hoping you and the rest are all well and happy as I am. If you have any to spare, please send more pictures.
With love to all,
Raymond

Meuse-Argonne, France, September 28, 1918
A runner was sent back with a message: "For God's sake send us litters, blankets and food."

The word came back that nothing could be done on account of lack of transportation.

At this time there were 800 men at the dressing station. German airplanes were dropping bombs on the station. It was raining all the time. The men had summer underwear and no overcoats and many of them laid for hours on the ground without litters.—Hoffman, Cap. Harry H., Scrap Book No. VI, p. 1, Feb. 17, 1919.

McKinley Austin, 11th U.S. Inf. to Lena Hill, Town of Highland
September 28, 1918
Dear Lena,

Did you get the other letter I wrote? It was so long ago I forgot when. I got a letter from you that you wrote just after I left the states. I got your picture from my aunt. It was good, but you are much better looking than the picture.

Well, how is everything in Eldred now? I hope to be back there by this time next year or sooner.

It is now about 14 months since I enlisted in the army and I will be glad when the war is over. We are doing our best to get it over soon, too. The Allies are winning everywhere now, and

Before and after. House transformed into an observatory for the Kronprinz's (Crown Prince) and taken by the American Army on the 26 of September 1918. Postcard of Aida Austin in the collection of Mary Briggs Austin.

Mountain Grove House
C. M. AUSTIN, Proprietor.

Situated 5 Miles From Shohola Station.   Can Accommodate 40 Guests.
Overlooking the Village.   Two Daily Mails.
Telephone Connection.

Eldred, Sullivan Co., N. Y., _____ 191_

Wednesday noon
My dear Mortimer:—
Just received your letter and was glad to hear you were well, we all feel fine but this damp weather I keep the children in the house, Verna told me she heard there were a lot of cases of diphtheria in Barryville but I doubt it our phone don't work right so I can not find out, but I am careful here. I got a letter from Ray I will send it to you, tonight I am going to

October 2, 1918. Letter from Jennie Austin to her husband who was on Jury duty in Monticello, New York.

America is doing her share.

I heard from my brother Raymond. He is in Panama now. He seems to like the army pretty well. I guess I will close now. Write soon. Hoping you are well.

I am your friend, McKinley

**Dieulourd and Trondes, France
September 29, 1918**
On September 29, while stationed at Dieulourd, 3 enemy shells caused a great number of casualties in 1st Battalion. On October 1, Battalion Regiment Headquarters established at Trondes [102 kilometers (63 miles) to Montfaucon].
—Sgt. John J. Popp.

The first phase of the great American offensive had spent itself without reaching its first objective and with the enemy's strongest defensive positions still unconquered.—Gansser, p. 170.

Raymond Austin, Balboa, Canal Zone, to Mort Austin, Eldred
October 1, 1918
Dear Father,
Your letter from Monticello received today. I was very glad to hear from you. I saw your name on the jury list, so was not surprised. Did they try many interesting cases this session?

1918. Concrete bombproof dugouts of the German Army operating in the Argonne Forest; behind front lines positions, east of Le Four de Paris. Photo: Library of Congress, Prints and Photographs Division: Schutz Group Photographers; Lot 6944 no. 35; 6a35445.

The Lost Battalion

The Lost Battalion affair occurred during the attack in the Argonne Forest in October 1918. Companies A, B, C, E, G, H, 308th Infantry; Company K, 307th Infantry; and Companies C, D 306th Machine Gun Battalion were isolated by the Germans.

These organizations, or detachments therefrom, comprised the approximate force of 550 men under command of Major Charles W. Whittlesey, which was cut off from the remainder of the 77th Division and surrounded by a superior number of the enemy near Charlevaux, in the Forest d'Argonne, from the morning of October 3, 1918, to the night of October 7, 1918.

Without food for more than 100 hours, harassed continuously by machine gun, rifle, trench mortar and grenade fire, Major Whittlesey's command, with undaunted spirit and magnificent courage, successfully met and repulsed daily violent attacks by the enemy.

They held the position which had been reached by supreme efforts, under orders received for an advance, until communication was re-established with friendly troops.

On the fourth day a written proposition to surrender received from the Germans was treated with the contempt which it deserved.

When relief finally came, approximately 194 officers and men were able to walk out of the position. Officers and men killed numbered 107.

The officers and men of these organizations during these 5 days of isolation continually gave unquestionable proof of extraordinary heroism and demonstrated the high standard and ideals of the U.S. Army.
—Robert Alexander, Major General, U.S. Army, Commanding, April 15, 1919; worldwar1.com.

View of the Delaware River near the Hawk's Nest in New York. Lost Battalion is inscribed on a brick in the wall. Photo: Gary Smith.

"Lost Battalion" (possibly referring to the lost soldiers) is inscribed on top of the wall running alongside the Delaware River on the Hawk's Nest Road north of Sparrowbush.

I have been on the rifle range or gallery twice. The first record I made was 13 scores out of 75 possible points. There was only one fellow who was as low as I was. The second time at 75 yards, I shot 30 points, a trifle above the average. The rifle we use for target practice weighs 8 pounds and shoots .22 shot cartridges.

I didn't get the papers yet, but probably will before long. Mother said she was going to send me a package. I would advise her not to send things to eat for any perishable things will sure "perish" before they get here. However, I could use towels, handkerchiefs, soap, 3-in-1 oil, shoe polish, etc. It would leave me nearly all of my $7.00 each

Robbie Croft, October 7, 1918. "The one in the field where the cattle are, was taken across the road from the house. He was not quite near enough to the camera to tell who it is, but the one near the silo looks just like him." Aida Austin photo courtesy of Mary Briggs Austin.

"We have soldiers, too." Robbie Croft, October 7, 1918. Photo in letter of Aida Austin courtesy of Mary Briggs Austin.

month. I would also like my razor.

Have you heard from Mac lately? I suppose he has had a hand in the fighting by this time. I wish I could be with him now.

I think Bulgaria's surrender is the very first sign that the balance is beginning to swing in our favor. Turkey again cut off from German aid, will soon quit. Germany and Austria-Hungary may fight on indefinitely and we will probably meet with bloody Czechs before Metz, Strasburg, and the other Rhine fortresses fall. I hope next year will end it. Am enclosing some pictures and Chinese, Japanese, and Austrian money.

Your son, Raymond

Jennie Austin, Eldred, to C.M. Austin, Monticello, N.Y.
Wed. Noon, Oct. 2, 1918
My dear Mortimer,

Just received your letter and was glad to hear you were well. We all feel fine, but this damp weather I keep the children in the house. Verna told me she heard there were a lot of cases of diphtheria in Barryville, but I doubt it. Our phone don't work right, so I can not find out, but I am careful here.

I got a letter from Ray. I will send it to you. Tonight I am going to get Mac's letters and the pictures together and send to him.

If Willie don't feel well any morning, I won't let him go to work. Mr. Scheineman is home sick today and besides, he got a sliver in his eye putting on the roof of his building.

I will be glad when you get through "courting" for it is certainly lonesome without anyone to scold.

Well, Elizabeth is ready to go back to school so I must close.

With love from all, Jennie
X Arthur's kiss, X Elizabeth's kiss, X Robbie's kiss, X mine, X Willie's

Raymond Austin, Balboa, Canal Zone, to Jennie Austin, Eldred
October 3, 1918
Dear Mother,

I am in the best of health and spirits and am enjoying life as well as it is possible to in Panama.

I got a letter last night from Uncle Ell which I will answer directly as soon as we come off lock guard. Will also write Grandfather a letter then.

I hear that there's a song going in the states that runs, "Take down your service flag, your boy's in Panama." Is that true?

Have you heard from Mac lately? I have been thinking a lot about him recently. To say I am worried would be unsoldier like and to say uneasy or anxious is altogether too mild an adjective for this case.

Take it from me, I'll be glad to see snow again. I want no more of this "continual summer districts."

Give me apples and peaches any time hereafter, against bananas and oranges, and I'll match the pine tree against the palm any day. New York may not be the best state in the union, but the United States is the best place in the world.

I have given up all hopes of seeing France as a soldier. I'll not feel very proud when I get home.

Your loving son,
Raymond

Meuse-Argonne, Second Phase October 4 to October 28, 1918
The second and the hardest phase of Meuse-Argonne Offensive in France started on October 4 and lasted through the month.

Autumn was now upon us in earnest. The nights were penetrating cold and the ground where the men had to lie moist from the chill rains which turned *paths and roads into sloughs. Mist interfered with aerial and artillery observation.*—Colliers, March 29, p. 5.

Robbie Croft mentioned by Aida Austin in the next letter was the adopted son of Tom and Emma Kelso Collins.

Aida Austin, Eldred, to McKinley Austin, France
October 7, 1918
Dear McKinley,
I see by the papers that the soldiers are going to be allowed to have Christmas presents, and that the Christmas labels are being distributed to the soldiers. It will seem so good to be allowed to send you a little something again.

It wouldn't surprise me at all if the war ended before Christmas, but it isn't likely that things will be settled enough so that many of the soldiers will get back much before spring.

I got Robbie Croft's picture a few days ago and am sending you some. The one in the field where the cattle are, was taken across the road from the house. He was not quite near enough to the camera to tell who it is, but the one near the silo looks just like him. I haven't heard yet whether he has gone across, but he expected to go soon, when he was home.

Quite a number will be in the next draft from Eldred. I don't know just who. I suppose Raymond Myers will be one of them. But there isn't much possibility of any of them getting to France. Jim Parker, being on the railroad, will escape being called.

We are having some beautiful weather, but I suppose the winter will soon set in now.

I had a letter from Mrs. Carlin

Romagne-sous-Montfaucon: The Great Street. Postcard of Aida Austin from 1923, from the collection of Mary Briggs Austin.

last week. They were all well, but dreading the winter. I can stand the winter better than I can the hot weather.

Lon had a letter from Dr. Austin a few days ago. Miss Hall had been quite sick, but was getting better.

We are all well and hoping that you are. If there is anything special you want, let me know so that I can send it when I send your Christmas.
With love,
Aunt Aida

Herman Bosch in France
Herman Bosch fought in the Meuse-Argonne Offensive from October 10 to November 11, 1918. He is known to have shot down at least one German plane.

Cunel, France, October 11, 1918
On October 11 the attack was renewed early in the morning… Progress was bitterly contested by heavy machine-gun fire and by flanking artillery support, as on previous days.

During the night of October 11-12, the relief of the 80th Division and certain elements of the 4th Division, by the 5th Division, was successfully carried out. The corps front was now held by the 5th Division on the left and the 4th Division on the right.—Ireland, Maj. Gen. M.W. The Medical Department of the U.S. Army in the World War, Vol. 8, 1925, p. 692.

The French landscape was devastated. Villages were in ruins, forests were gone; roads were filled with craters and muddy. The American troops had to trudge through mud and face icy winds and rain. By October 11 the Argonne Forest had been cleared but a foothold had not been gained in the area to the east toward the Meuse River.

Jennie Austin, Eldred, to McKinley Austin, France
October 12, 1918
My dear Mac,
Just a few lines while I have time. I see in the papers in order to send a package to the soldiers that the soldier one sends the package to must first get a label and send it to the one he expects to receive a package from.

I hope you have sent yours before this as they claim no

packages will be accepted without the labels in it. If you don't get a Christmas package, it will be because we have received no label.

The Spanish Influenza is sweeping the country here, even our school is closed for awhile. No cases being nearer than Shohola, as we know of. We often wonder how you are and if you have escaped it. You must be careful and it is a worry to know at times.

You must be in places where you can not be careful. We have a joke on Dad coming home from Monticello. He met a soldier who had been wounded in France and for a month had been in the hospital of Otisville. He was on his way home and Dad fell in with him at Port Jervis and became so interested that he was carried on beyond Shohola. The conductor was kind enough to slow the train down and let him off at Lackawaxen.

I am afraid my pencil is so dim by the time this reaches you, you will not be able to read it. But Elizabeth is learning to write with pen and ink. It is impossible to find a decent pen in the house.

Willie is still working at Procters. Dad expects to work for John Love some as he gathers his garden.

Well I must close as Dad is going to the [post] office. It has been over a month since we heard from you, so we are looking for a letter every day.
Love from all,
Mother
[The letter was returned.]

Montfaucon, France, October 12 and 13, 1918

McKinley's outfit arrived in the vicinity of Montfaucon on October 12.

They suffered casualties as a result of heavy shelling from enemy guns the next day. The 11th Infantry took up a position around Ferme de la Madeleine that evening, the night of October 13.

Battle of Romagne-sous-Montfaucon, France, October 14–17, 1918

At the Battle of Romagne-sous-Montfaucon (October 14–17), the Americans launched a series of costly frontal assaults that finally broke through the main German defences of the Hindenburg Line.

The enemy waiting until the forward movement is commenced, throws down a terrific barrage upon our front so that the division going 'over the top' at daylight (October 14th) with the 9th Brigade (60th and 61st Infantry) on the right, and the 10th brigade, 6th and 11th Infantry on the left, is immediately plunged into a perfect storm of shell fire which inflicts heavy casualties in its ranks at the very outset of the advance.
—Moss and Howland, p. 287.

McKinley is Hit

It was our [11th Infantry's] first day in the Argonne drive and we went over at 8 the morning of the 14th of October. We hadn't gone far when we were held up by the German machine guns.

They [Germans] were firing on us from three different directions and there wasn't enough of the boys left to advance farther so we were forced to stop and dig in.

The Corporal of his squad being a casualty, [I] made [McKinley] Austin as I knew him, Squad leader and when we reached the hill which was Madelaine Farm, the German's made it so hot for us we could not advance further. So I directed him to put his gun into action on the west of the hill.

Then I went on seeing the other gun put into action which was even more perilous and came back.

Seeing him on the side of the hill I asked him if he had the gun in action.

He said, no. He came back for a shovel.

I paid no more attention to him then and went on to report to Capt. Dashiell who was killed later.
—Sgt. John Popp letter.

At Madelaine Farm after this company had gained its first objective, [Mac] was put in command of the 6th squad (acting as corporal).

In order to consolidate the position and to prevent a successful German counter-attack, [Mac] took his machine gun and his squad of men forward to a shell hole.

It was a dangerous mission for artillery and machine gun fire was heavy. Finding the hole not deep enough to provide cover for the gun and all the men, he returned to the trench and obtained a shovel. Most any other man in his position would have sent one of the men of the squad back for the shovel, but [Mac] chose to run the danger himself.—Letter from Allen Maxwell; Captain 11th Infantry Commanding Company.

The first thing we did was to get our machine guns placed in case of a counter-attack. It was while engaged in this that McKinley was shot.

A shell hole a little advanced was selected so as to allow no dead space. [McKinley] made a dash for the hole and saw he was about to fall into it. The Germans opened up with a machine gun and one of the bullets hit him…and he fell.
—Harold Fraley letter.

On the return trip to the shell hole he was struck in the breast by a machine gun bullet and although badly wounded, he continued forward and gave the shovel to his squad, who then dug in and held their position.
—*Cap. Allen Maxwell letter.*

Looking around, I seen your son [Mac] fall forward into the hole he was placing the gun in. Running over to him, I asked him where he was hit. He said stomach. So I pulled him back off the crest of the hill, bandaged him and placed him in a hole and covered him up with blankets where he died a few hours later.
He was the best gunner we had in the Company and his loss meant much to those who had to depend on him to keep the German's head down.—*Sgt. John G. Popp letter.*

We saw him fall. As the way in which he fell was queer we called to him and asked if he was hit. He told us he was, and we immediately made a rush for the hole.
Well we got him out all right and brought him back down the hill a piece and applied first aid. The only words he uttered was "It's hell boys."
He never made a groan and just drew his legs up a little, I suppose to ease the pain.
We wrapped him up in a blanket and he died within an hour. There was nothing removed from his body as long as I was there which was about two days, when I was hit in the leg and went to the hospital.—*Harold Fraley letter.*

During a lull in the fighting, Mac was brought back to the trenches for Medical Aid. All efforts were in vain and about an hour later, he passed away. He realized that his wound was fatal and took the knowledge like a man and like a soldier, never once complaining and only regretting that he would be unable to fight on.—*Cap. Allen B. Maxwell letter.*

Mortimer McKinley Austin was killed October 14th in the Argonne Forest Drive. He was killed near a small town called Cunel. I was with him when he died. But was wounded later in the day...Chaplain McVeigh was in charge of the burying party.
—*Lt. G.L. Edwards, 11th Infantry.*

The fighting was fierce and I guess it was more luck than anything else that I got out alive. We went in with about a 170 men and came out with something like 25 or 30 of the original number.
—*Harold Fraley letter.*

It would be November 17th before Mort and Jennie Austin heard about their son McKinley's death, at Madeleine Farm, France. The Austins would first be told that McKinley died on October 21, 1918. The date would later be changed to October 14, 1918.

The 11th Infantry went "over" the morning of October 14, and

The area of Madeleine Farm, France, where McKinley was killed. Photo taken by Aida Austin, June 1923, from the collection of Mary Briggs Austin.

remained in action continuously until October 22, when the regiment moved into support position.—*Sgt. John Popp.*

Raymond Austin, Culebra, Canal Zone, to Bill Austin, Eldred
October 17, 1918
Dear Brother Bill,
I am back at Culebra again. Our company has done its shift at Lock Gave, and is back to its headquarters again.
I have had a couple letters from Father and Mother and I will answer them soon.
There is not much to write about here. This climate takes a person's [energy] and it is really hard work even to write a letter.
If I was you, I would go to school this winter. You have passed your regents in the subjects you

Fields north of Madeleine Farm. Photo taken by Aida Austin, June 1923, from the collection of Mary Briggs Austin.

Romagne-sous-Montfaucon: The Ruins of the Church. Postcard of Aida Austin, courtesy of Mary Briggs Austin.

tried. In January, you may get some more of them and by June you could go over the top.

"Hang good jobs and big pay" [underlined twice] when you are so young and so near high school. Remember I was much older than you before I got any of my regents. I got tired of living on Father's money alone. That's why I got my first job at Proctor's.

You have worked all summer and I know you have earned a winter's schooling. Father and Mother are both anxious. I am sure that you will. Don't be afraid that you will run short of money for I will help you and I think Mac will too.

I have learned since I came to this army, that it's the educated men who are the officers and the rest are like me, more or less.

I am your brother,
Raymond

George James Clark in England

In October George James Clark was having troubles with his feet. On the 24th he was sent to England for treatment of trench foot.

Trench foot was a serious problem for many soldiers fighting in the First World War. Men stood for hours in waterlogged trenches without being able to remove wet socks or boots. Gradually their feet would become numb and their skin would turn red or blue. An infection would set in. If left untreated, trench foot could turn gangrenous and result in an amputation.

Raymond Austin, Culebra, Canal Zone, to Mort Austin
November 3, 1918
Dear Father,

I received your welcome letter several days ago, but we have had a hike and a field meet since, so have not had much time to write.

We hiked 7 or 8 miles, only two fell out of our company. It was quite hot and I had a headache for a couple of hours after we got back.

In the field meet yesterday, M Company made a good start. But Company L had the ranking officer, so what he said went. They disqualified us twice. Once they disqualified both of our runners for one man's error.

We took first prize in the walking contest; also in the squad competition. Altogether we won about 25 points. We have a pretty good ball team and I hope we will keep on building up.

Have you heard from Mac lately? I have written him several letters from Panama and as yet I have heard nothing from him. It looks to me like the war is going through its last stages.

I am feeling fine except the heat and I don't get along very good. There are few cases of influenza here. But no such thing gets me.

All I wish is that I was in the states. But I don't worry about that for I expect to come back soon, so don't be worrying about me. With love to you all,
Son Raymond

Romagne-sous-Montfaucon. The remains of a Fortlet at the place called, "The Ground of Boeuil." Enormous pieces of armored cement weighing 10,000 kilograms have been projected 50 metres in consequence of the explosion. Postcard of Aida Austin from 1923, in the collection of Mary Briggs Austin.

Armistice, November 11, 1918
The regiment again went into action November 3rd in the Meuse drive and remained in action to the end of the fighting November 11 at 11 a.m.

Our line held until November 12 when the regiment was relieved by the 6th Infantry and the 60th Infantry when the Army of Occupation (3rd Army) was formed on November 17, this regiment was made a part thereof.—Sgt. John Popp.

Mort and Jennie Austin Notified of McKinley's Death
November 17, 1918
Mr. and Mrs. C.M. Austin, of Eldred, Sullivan County, on November 17th received a telegram from the War Department at Washington informing them that their son, McKinley Austin, had been killed *in action somewhere in France on October 21st.*—Port Jervis Union.

Meuse-Argonne Cemetery
Mortimer McKinley Austin was buried in isolated Grave #828, in the Meuse-Argonne American Cemetery east of the village of Romagne-sous-Montfaucon, France.

The Austins later learned that the chaplain at McKinley's burial was J.P. Van Horn, 11th U.S. Infantry, and that McKinley was

"The little bridge provisionally repaired." Romagne-sous-Montfaucon. Postcard of Aida Austin from 1923, in the collection of Mary Briggs Austin.

Romagne-sous-Montfaucon. "The Little Street. In the end, the Ruins of the Church." Postcard of Aida Austin from 1923, in the collection of Mary Briggs Austin.

Eldred Boy Killed in France

Mr. and Mrs. C.M. Austin, of Eldred, Sullivan County, on November 17th received a telegram from the War Department at Washington informing them that their son, McKinley Austin, had been killed in action somewhere in France on October 21st.

"Private Austin enlisted in the U.S. Army early in the war while home from his studies at Mount Hermon Seminary, Northfield, Mass. He was a bright and popular young man. Two of his grandfather's brothers gave their lives for their country on Southern battlefields during the Civil War; his grandfather, S.S. Leavenworth, having served during the great conflict, is now living in Eldred as one of its most highly respected citizens."—The Port Jervis Union, November 25, 1918.

buried with one identification tag and the other one was put on the cross over the grave.

Raymond Austin, Camp Gaillard, Canal Zone, to Family in Eldred
November 17, 1918
It would be worse than useless to try to express my thanks (on paper) for the box you sent me. The razor is a good one. Luckily for me it's a safety for now that there is no chance of a German bullet getting me, I'd hate to die by a razor.

Well, Mac will soon be home now. Probably next spring or next summer. Some fine day you will see the top of a military hat coming over the steps and it will be me you see next.

I am getting somewhat used to the climate and the last hike didn't tire me much. We made the last mile mostly up hill at quick time. Possibly a dozen fell out.

They are using us fine, as always well fed and quartered.

Did I ever tell you that our present quarters are in full view of Culebra—also part of the Perdio Miguel (Peter McGill) Locks.

I wrote a letter to Grandfather sometime ago. Did he get it?

With love to all,
Raymond

A.E. and Sally Austin, Charlotte Hall, N.Y.C., to the Austins
November 19, 1918
Dear Mortimer and Jennie, Raymond, Willie, Elizabeth, Lawrence and Robert,

To you all we send our sympathy with you in the sorrow this sad news brings. I have telephoned to several parties and have written (in Eugene's name) to the Sec'y of War, Baker, Washington, and to the

American Red Cross here for any information in regard to McKinley. It is possible that the information is in error. We can only trust to God.

We are all sharing this sorrow and this suspense with you.

McKinley was noble and loyal to the highest things of life. He was brave and gentle. He was a young man of high principles.

Mr. Walter Styles's letter came at once to us with your message. Everyone must sympathize with you all for McKinley was universally respected.

Affectionately and with sympathy,
Eugene and Sally [Sara] Austin, and Charlotte Hall

Raymond Austin, Culebra, Canal Zone, to Jennie Austin
November 23, 1918
Dear Mother,

I received your letter a few days ago. Many thanks for the money order. I was surprised and terribly sorry to hear of our neighbors awful misfortune. I sincerely hope that they are all well again. I am thankful that none of you have been sick. Don't worry about me for influenza is very rare here abouts.

I was very glad to read Mac's letter. I have written him several.

We had a hike the other day, but it didn't tire me much. Several dropped out though. We also had about half a miles double time. I started about third from the east and finished with only six men and an officer ahead of me. Only about ten ran all the way around. I have a notion to try for the football team for lack of better excitement.

The climate doesn't bother me much now although I could stand old Sullivan County much better. I wonder who will be the gladdest

Meuse-Argonne Cemetery

Romagne-sous-Montfaucon, American Cemetery, principal entrance, the Hotel-House and offices. Postcard of Aida Austin in the collection of Mary Briggs Austin.

Crosses in the Romagne-sous-Montfaucon Cemetery where McKinley Austin was buried initially. Postcard of Aida Austin in the collection of Mary Briggs Austin.

The Meuse-Argonne Cemetery covers 130 acres and holds the largest number of American dead—14,246—in Europe. Most of those buried in the cemetery died during WWI's Meuse-Argonne Offensive.

A short distance from the Meuse-Argonne Cemetery, just where the Romagne-Cunel Road turned down into the village of Romagne, was a war monument with the following:

This point: the left west Romagne boundary of 5th division in the attack of October 14, 1918, Meuse-Argonne offensive.

The National Cemetery is located on terrain wrested from the enemy on that day by the 10th Infantry Brigade, 5th Division.

The last verse of *Flanders Fields*, by John McCrae, was written on back of McKinley's gravemarker photo:

*To you from failing hands we throw
The torch; be yours to hold it high!
If ye break faith with us who die
We shall not sleep, though poppies grow
In Flanders fields.*

McKinley Austin's grave marker at the Meuse-Argonne Cemetery in France. Photo courtesy of Mary Briggs Austin.

The Distinguished Service Cross, the highest American award to heroes, is being presented by General Pershing to a lieutenant colonel attached in the Second Division Headquarters. The citation was for conspicuous gallantry and intrepidity under fire. Photo from The Port Jervis Union, *November 25, 1918, courtesy of Mary Briggs Austin.*

Certificate stating that Mortimer McKinley Austin died with honor in the service of his country. Certificate courtesy of Mary Briggs Austin.

Mac or myself when we get back. I hope he gets home first and I think he will.

You can hardly imagine how lazy and listless a person grows down here. I used to like to write letters, but now I can hardly keep my mind on one thing for a minute. This is H—L on earth so far as the climate and looks of the place goes.

But they feed us fine. We have exceptionally good officers and as we won't be here much longer, I can amuse myself some way or another for a few months. We may come back in January. But far more likely, it will be May or June.

Very shortly we will go on the rifle range and probably in January, we will go through the war maneuvers at Cuerra. So that time will go fast.

Could you send me an arithmetic? I'm going to some school when I come back so I may as well improve my time here. I think I shall go to work at a factory and then go to school nights. I could save money that way to go on up.

Did you get those books I wrote for? Also can you find my Esperanto books? If so, I wish you would please send them to me.

Tell Elizabeth I was glad to hear from her and will send her some postcards. Am returning Mac's letter. Please send me more if you have them.

With love to all,
Raymond

Marion Sidwell, Port Jervis, N.Y., to Jennie Austin, Eldred
November 24, 1918
My dear Mrs. Austin,

There has been nothing connected with the war, or any other sad experience for years that brought such a shock to us as when we learned last Monday of the tidings that reached you the day before. It seemed as if I could not have it so, that your big splendid boy had given all.

I wish I could say something comforting. You see, next to my very own, McKinley came closest to my heart for George often said and repeatedly has written when he was in Panama, that "Mack" was his only friend. Of course there are boys he cares for, but your boy was the only one he ever had in the intimate inner circle of his heart.

The Indian tribe they had formed as boys they took along with the years—the language, the signs, their calendar and names. Only last Sunday, I found "Ahmek's" Christmas message to "Humn" in one of laddie's pockets. There were their vows one of which was the clean white life they were to lead. Things I come across accidentally, and as intimate and holy. I mention it to you only to show the clean white thought and life of your boy.

These past few years have tried us as by fire, and we mothers have tried to watch our boys with a faith and courage equal to their own. It has not been easy, this giving up, but we have been so proud of our soldier boys, proud that they volunteered.

Believe me, you and yours have our deepest sympathy—more than this we are sharing your grief for it is ours too.

May you feel that the Eternal God is your refuge and the comforting touch of the Everlasting Arms in these days of your grief.
Yours most sincerely,
Marion Sidwell

Arthur Howlett, Albany, N.Y., to Lon Austin, Eldred

Thanksgiving Day, 1918
My Dear Friend Lon,
My thoughts were turned to you by this newspaper clipping of the casualty list and I began wondering if it was your brother Mort or his boy. But whichever it was, it proves you were loyal and the boy was not afraid to pay the price for liberty.

What a wonderful Thanksgiving Day for America, but sad for the families of the boys that will not come back.

But what a wonderful victory and so much sooner than we had hoped for. We had prayed for victory and while we were yet praying, the powers of darkness were falling.

Well brother, 20 years go I worked with you on Proctor Hill, so time lies on a pace and a great task is ahead of the American people to reconstruct.

Well Lon, write me how you are and give my sympathy to the family of the Hero. They had something real to give while I had only money, but glad to be alive to help in the great struggle.

I am with the Albany Hardware and Iron Co.
Very truly yours,
Arthur E. Howlett

Rev. Taylor, Avon Methodist Church, N.Y., to Mort Austin
November 26, 1918
Dear brother Austin,
I read in yesterday's paper of the death of Mortimer McKinley Austin of Eldred, N.Y., and can have no doubt that it is my dear friend, your son McKinley. Is it possible that this is so?

It was a great shock to me when I read the name. I haven't seen the names of any others from out there if there have been others wounded or killed.

Has this great privilege come

Jennie Austin, Gold Star Mother

The Service Flag of Jennie Austin, courtesy of Mary Briggs Austin.

It was a custom of families of servicemen to hang a Service Flag in the window of their homes. The Service Flag had a star for each family member in the military. Living servicemen were represented by a blue star, and those who had lost their lives were represented by a gold star.

This is the Austin flag with a gold star because of McKinley's death, and a blue star for their son Raymond who also served during World War I.

to McKinley alone out there, to make the supreme sacrifice for liberty and the rights of humanity?

I know what a terrible blow this has been for you all, but also feel sure that you realize the great honor and glory that has come to him in giving his life and to you in giving a son in the greatest conflict for the truth and honor that the world has ever known.

God bless you in this hour of need and your wife and children. What a blessing to know that Jesus gave His life and understands our hearts and needs and sympathizes with us.

It is surely a great comfort to you to know that McKinley was a Christian. His ideals were high and I feel sure that in enlisting (for he must have enlisted being too young for the draft), he did it with a noble purpose to serve God and his fellow man and make his life count for the most. This he has done.

He lived more in those months of service probably than many of the rest of us if we reach fourscore years.

My prayer is that God may comfort your hearts and grant the fulfillment of the ideal world order and freedom for which dear McKinley laid down his life.

Yours in sympathy and love,
Charles W. Taylor, Pastor

War Department, Washington D.C, to A. Eugene Austin, M.D., N.Y.C.
November 29, 1918
Sir:

I regret to advise that this office has received no further information concerning the death of Private Mortimer McK. Austin, Machine Gun Company, 11th Infantry, than that he was killed in action October 21st, 1918.

For further information and details concerning his death you should write to his Commanding Officer:

Commanding Officer
Machine Gun Co., 11th Infantry
American Expeditionary Force

Respectfully, M.F. Lerovin
Adjutant General

Charlotte Hall, to the Austins
November 30, 1918
Dear Mortimer and Jennie and all dear to McKinley,

With this a letter goes to France to the Commanding Officer of Madeline Gen. Company 11th Infantry asking for further information and details concerning McKinley.

I wrote him how McKinley was the oldest of his family, universally beloved and respected, the first man to enlist from Eldred. As soon as the answer comes, it shall go to you as this does, at once.

We trust One whose love and wisdom and comfort is infinite. He is with McKinley and McKinley is with Him where the dear boy is, and we shall surely meet again.

Lovingly from us all,
Charlotte C. Hall

American Red Cross Letter to A. Eugene Austin, N.Y.C.
December 3, 1918

With deep sympathy for your loss that we inform you from the official report that Private Mortimer McKinley Austin was killed in action.

For further particulars concerning his death, we have asked our Paris office to get all possible details from his comrades or anyone who can give any information.

We regret very much we can not expect this report for at least six weeks because of the overcrowded mails, but shall communicate again with you just as soon as we hear.

Message from Herbert Hoover

Addressed to the Housewives of New York State and Every Worker in the Ranks of Food Conservation.

Your work during the last year has had more to do than you may realize in the achievement of the American people, which will be one of the remembered glories of this titanic struggle. That achievement was not only the provisioning of the armies and the allies until victory; it was the demonstration that there was no power in autocracy equal to the voluntary effort of free people.

The essential feature of this plan was that individual conscience should rule under the guidance of local leadership. It was then, your work which made the devotion of 20,000,000 households fruitful.

As we come to the end of that undertaking we are summoned to a still larger task—to provision the allies and the liberated nations of Europe, which face not hunger alone, but the collapse of all that holds their civilization together unless a steady stream of food supplies can be kept flowing to them to repair their gravest deficiencies and in far greater volume than by utmost stress was sent last year.

The President of the United States has asked me to take charge for this Government of this relief work; to perfect and enlarge the arrangements for foodstuffs to the populations of Belgium and France now being released and to organize and determine the need of provision to the liberated peoples of southern Europe to prevent such debacle as has taken place in Russia.

I am asking the Federal Food Administration to join forces with the new organization of relief, holding their staffs intact as far as possible, and I hope that each of you will respond to the call which will be made upon you by your Federal Food Administrator, that the same splendid support which was given to the prosecution of the war may be devoted to establishing the peace and security of the world.

—Article in *Port Jervis Union*, November 25, 1918.

Raymond Austin, Culebra, Canal Zone, to Bill Austin, Eldred
December 6, 1918
Dear Brother Bill,

I believe I owe you a letter so will write you a few lines tonight. I celebrated my birthday by doing a day's kitchen police. Not a happy celebration either, believe me.

We are trying out on the rifle range now. I believe I can do good enough in the preliminaries to be allowed to shoot for record. I hope to make sharp shooter if all goes well. I feel pretty sure I can make marksman without any trouble.

Since I got that letter, I have had hard work to do anything. Say why don't you get the "Official bulletin" Oct. 21st up and look over the casualties. You can get them at any Post Office. Miss Kelly would be glad to let you look over them.

I have found more Austins on the lists, but not Mac. I also found two George Dunlaps, one from Oswego, N.Y. Many of the "killed in action" often turn up to be wounded or to have been isolated during the battle and returned later.

How does the dispatch read? Does it say "was killed" or "was reported killed in action? These are very improbable hopes. But some how I can't believe it. I am praying I am right.

Mac probably wrote you a letter before he went into the battle if it comes, I wish you would send it to me.

Raymond

Raymond Austin, Culebra, Canal Zone, to Mort Austin, Eldred
December 8, 1918
Dear Father,

You doubtless have received my other letter which I wrote immediately upon the receipt of

Anthony Hirsch, husband of Christina Hayes Leavenworth. Photo courtesy of Cynthia Leavenworth Bellinger.

your letter of November 17.

Although I scarce dare think Mac is still alive, I think there is a possible chance of the report being a mistake. I have gone over the casualties down to October 16. A fellow by the name of J.M. Austin of N.Y. state was killed or died around October 20 the list was made out about Nov. 15th. There are also many other Austins listed, mostly all killed. There is a little hope of confusion of the names.

I wish you would send me a copy of the words used by the telegram. Also, compare the serial number given by the telegram and the one on Mac's insurance policy.

These are surely sad days for me and I can tell how you all must feel.

Do not think I am all alone with this sorrow confined to myself. We are all brothers to a great extent and we feel and sympathize for each other.

You have all been very brave. Pray for fresh strength and trust that the message is false.

Christina Hayes Leavenworth married Anthony Hirsch on December 1918. Photo courtesy of Cynthia Leavenworth Bellinger.

Trusting you are all well.
Love to all, your son,
Raymond

Christina Hayes Leavenworth Marries Tony Hirsch

Mr. Sherman S. Leavenworth announces the marriage of his daughter Christina Hayes
to

Investigation of Failure at Argonne

An article that Aida Austin copied.

Gov. Henry Allen of Kansas addressed the House Rules Committee this morning in advocacy of a formal searching investigation of the alleged failure of the American Command at the battle of the Argonne to provide the infantry with adequate artillery and aircraft support. According to Governor Allen, this failure was supplemented by the failure of the Medical Corps that resulted in a 50 per cent increase in mortality among the severely wounded.

A letter from a Lieutenant Colonel stated: Our artillery failed us and did not support us after the first few hours. We fought the German machine guns and hand grenades with our service rifles only.

Official report signed by Cap. Truman and sent back by runner from the advancing infantry to post commander:

During the entire day our troops were continually pelted with our own artillery. Our own artillery was more destructive to our men than the enemy. Our airplanes have been of little use to us in combating enemy planes. I have sent 5 different messages to the artillery this morning to lengthen our range. Short fire is doing more to undermine our morale than anything else.

There is not a telephone in the organization: no signal flares left and we have no way to communicate except by runner. Our regiment has no more than 1,000 men left.

The regiment went in with the full strength of 3,000, commented Governor Allen at this point.
—*Scrap book No. VI, February 17, 1919, p. 1, Report by Captain Harry H. Hoffman.*

Mr. Anthony V. Hirsch on Sunday, December 8, 1918, Eldred, New York

Anna and Jennie's sister Christina Leavenworth married Anthony Hirsch in December 1918.

Anthony Sr., Christina, and Anthony Jr. were living in Manhattan in 1920. Anthony Sr. owned his own bakeshop. In Book 3 Anthony and Christina's daughter Charlee (my dad's first cousin) will be born. The Hirsch family would eventually leave New York City because Anthony's Bakery would lose business when they re-routed or repaired the street that went by his store.

Raymond Austin, Culebra, Canal Zone, to the Austins, Eldred
December 8, 1918
Dear Folks,

Just a few lines to let you know I have found McKinleys name on the casualty list of November 25.

As soon as you receive any word, hope you will send it to me as it worries me day and night. I am doing my best to stand up to it like a soldier and I hope you all will remember that this is a soldier's family and will act accordingly.

They are examining our equipment and I hear the war maneuvers are coming off sooner than expected. After them our time here will in all probability be short.

The weather is very hot now, the dry season is here and drilling is pretty warm work.
Raymond

Anna Leavenworth, to Jennie Austin, Eldred
December 12, 1918
Dear Jennie,

I've intended to write to you from day to day. I can't write much at night and it gets dark so soon after school is out that I don't get much writing done at the schoolhouse.

There has been a great deal of sickness and death here. Three deaths in family of Miller's just below the schoolhouse—the father, infant son, and the best child they had in their family, a big boy about 14. My school was very small for about 2 weeks, but now I have about 22.

I wonder very much how things are going at home. Christina said she would send me an announcement soon as they were married. I expected it Tuesday night, but when it didn't come last night, I began to feel worried. They say, "No news is good news", but it is hard to believe it so far away. I am willing to come back if any of them are sick and they know it.

My knees ache every day, but I get up free from it in the mornings. At first, I thought I was getting influenza, but guess it is something that will last longer. I guess I'm getting rheumatism,

I hope you have kept as well as the rest of your family and I would like to know how Raymond is getting along. Will stop as it is really quite dark in room now and I must leave. Glad it is coming moonlight.
Lovingly,
Anna

Ira McBride Austin Dies

Two people who have been a part of this story died in December 1918: Ira McBride Austin and Stephen St. John Gardner. Mary Murray Parker Schoonover also died sometime in 1918.

December 2, 1918, Ira McBride

Austin, one of the oldest and most highly respected citizens of the town of Highland Sullivan County, died this morning at his home in Barryville after a short illness.

Deceased was born in Barryville and was the son of Mr. and Mrs. Benjamin C. Austin. He was a veteran of the Civil War, and for many years conducted a blacksmith and wagon making shop in Barryville. He had served as Justice of the Peace and Town Clerk of the town of Highland.

On May 10th, 1866, he was united in marriage with Miss Minerva Drake of Barryville. Mr. and Mrs. Austin celebrated their 50th or golden wedding anniversary at their home in Barryville on May 10th, 1916.

Besides his wife, at home, he is survived by three sons, Frank D., of Clifton, NJ., Ralph W. of Elkhorn, West Virginia, and Lou E. of Port Chester, N.Y.; three daughters, Mrs. Mabel Smith and Miss Minnie Austin of Barryville; and Miss Nellie Austin of Olean, New York, and one sister, Mrs. Harriet A. Liebla of Barryville.

Stephen St. John Gardner Dies
Stephen St. John Gardner died December 16, 1918. He was 83. Stephen was the son of James K. and Eliza Eldred Gardner, and a grandson of James Eldred. Stephen was a first cousin to my grandfather Mort Austin and his siblings, Aida, Ell, Lon, and Dory. A 1900 biography on Stephen:

He is always courteous, kindly and affable, and those who know him personally have for him a warm regard. A man of great natural ability, his success in business has been uniform and rapid, and he has ever supported those interests which are calculated to uplift and benefit humanity. He and his estimable wife both hold membership in the Congregational Church.—Beers & Co. (pub.), Commemorative Biographical Record of Northeastern Pennsylvania, *Chicago, 1900.*

Descendants of Mary Murray Parker Schoonover: Unknown boy, Justina Schoonover, Elwood James, and Norma Wood. Photo courtesy of Richard James.

Marry Murray Parker Schoonover
Mary Murray Parker Schoonover died in 1918, in Purling, New York. She was buried nearby in a cemetery in Cairo, New York.

Mary, the second wife of Perry Schoonover, had a number of descendants in 1918: four children: George Parker, Kate Parker, Emily Schoonover Waidler, and Daniel Rowlee Schoonover; seven grandchildren, and two great-grandchildren: Elwood James and Norma Wood.

Eldred Austin, Barre, Mass., to Mort Austin, Eldred
December 18, 1918
Dear brother Mort,

Your letter dated December 17 at hand. I was very sorry to hear that McKinley was killed and feel his untimely death with you all. There is a great comfort in knowing he died in action in a good cause. It is with pride I think of your boys, not only of those that got in the army, but of Will for the grit and the willingness he showed when I was at your house to get in the fight.

I am sorry to hear Jennie and the children were sick and hope they are well now.

I received a letter from Lillie last week. She said they are all well.

John Parmenter's youngest daughter died in Chicago a short time ago from influenza.

Is Tom and Emma Collins in Eldred this winter or did they go to the city?

I don't know of anything here that would interest you so will close with love to all.

Eldred [James Eldred Austin]

WWI Medals and Awards

Bronze medal awarded to Cyrus Rouillon for being gassed in WWI. Medal courtesy of Gisele Rouillon Leavenworth.

Awards of Irwin Briggs in WWI: WWI service in France medallion; Evacuation Company No. 1, Evacuation Hospital No. 37, WWI Honorable Discharge pin.

The Allied Dead

When down the world low summer winds come creeping,
Where fame still guards the portal of her braves,
Dreams go back to seek some lost mate sleeping
Beneath the sod that knows four million graves
Roll back the few brief summers intervening
And most of them were laughing boys at play
Light hearted dreamers down the world careening
Through fields of sport across a golden day.

Where are they now, from all their early glory,
Where the last star through somber silence gleams
Four million crosses tell their simple story
As the long night drifts in above their dreams.
Season by season they have slept on dreaming
Maybe of old hikes through the battered loam
Who knows? Maybe of far lights gleaming
Over old friends back at a place called Home

Dust unto dust amid the shell torn places,
What is the message that a ghost might send
We took the road that led from last embraces
To the lone cross that marked the journey's end.
—Poem in the collection of Aida Austin.

Wm. Lozier, Hoboken, N.J., to Friend Austin
December 19, 1918
Dear Friend Austin,
   The news about poor McKinley has just reached me and it goes without saying that I was grieved at his sad fate.
   I shall not attempt anything by way of consolation for, alas, in such cases, there is no consolation, but time.
   I had just begun to settle myself in the belief that as no news was good news, we could all meet together again under more changed and happier circumstances, than last season, shake hands and congratulate all around. That God may help you to bear up under it and that you will accept this expression of my sincere sympathy in your trouble.
   As you no doubt have received many such tokens of condolence, I will not burden you with the necessity of replying until we next meet.
   I am most sincerely your friend,
   Wm. A. Lozier

Raymond Austin, Quarry Heights, Canal Zone, to Jennie Austin
December 23, 1918
Dear Mother,
   I came down here to Quarry Heights Friday. I started a letter to you but was called on guard before I could finish it. I received yours and Bill's letters and the package. Many thanks for it. Everything came in handy.
   Don't worry about me being sick for if I am sent to the hospital, I'll drop you a line before I go so you will know.
   I heard that our battalion will sail for Camp Meritt on January 22, 1919. I hope so, but hardly believe it. They say that a few have already gone.

I suppose by now you have had some news from the Red Cross investigation. Perhaps they may have some of McKinley's personal belongings, letters, watch, etc. I have found out that the 11th Infantry is in the 5th division (not corps) and is in the army of occupation.

I believe the last letter of Macs I saw was dated September 19. He must have written a letter between then and October 21st.

I guess the U.S. has lost terrible for the number engaged 700,000 men (U.S.) were engaged and 262,000 fell. I really believe our next war is only a few years off and I think President Wilson sees it. I hope he can carry out his war program for 1926. Lord Raldon says that "Wilson's ideas are almost damnable," and I guess Japan seconds the motion.

We are doing guard duty now. I was on guard on Pier 18 night before last.

My letters must have been held up as I write once or twice every week.

*Send my mail to Culebra.
Raymond*

F.F. Cutler,
Mount Hermon School, Mass.,
C.M. Austin, Eldred
December 26, 1918
Dear Mr. Austin:

I am sorry to hear that your boy has been taken from you. He, with others of our Mount Hermon boys, has made the supreme sacrifice, and of these we are proud, but we miss them from our list.

I appreciate your kindness in giving me the information, and wish to express to you our sympathy with you in the great loss which has come to you.

*Yours sincerely, F.F. Cutler
Office of the Principal*

Martin D. and Mary Myers
Martin David Myers, and his wife of two years, Mary Fee Myers, had a daughter Ethel Myers in December 1918. Ethel lived to be almost three years old. Martin D. was the son of George W.T. and Martha Mills Myers.

Raymond Austin,
Quarry Heights, Canal Zone,
to His Family, Eldred
December 31, 1918

I am very glad you are all well and hope you will continue. So you were lucky to have all pulled safely through the influenza.

What kind of a wedding did Aunt Christina have? I hope she is well now. I hear the influenza has started up again.

I got a $2 money order at Culebra some time ago, but I think I told you about it. Many thanks for it. Also, the lot of things you sent me.

It sure puts heart in a fellow to know that the folks are still thinking of him.

I expect I'll be home sometime in May or June.

*Don't worry about me for I feel fine.
Raymond*

Men Still in the Service After the Armistice
Though an Armistice had been called on November 11, 1918, it would be some months before all of the servicemen were back in the United States.

Irwin Briggs and Mars, France
Irwin Briggs, Private 1st Class in Evacuation Hospital #37, worked (starting in January) at the large Hospital Complex in Mars-sur-Allier (Mars), France. The Hospital at Mars had 700 buildings and covered 33 acres, and was located at the railhead. The hospital units

Irwin Briggs remained in France after the Armistice. He worked at the Mars Hospital Complex in Mars-sur-Allier, France. Photo courtesy of Mary Briggs Austin.

were conveniently grouped on either side of the train tracks that led into the center. There was a road, water, sewerage, and lighting facilities.

Mars averaged 8,098 patients and could expand to 20,000 patients. It had a nearby 4,000 bed convalescent camp.

Deyo Hull and U.S.S. Arizona
Deyo Hull, Yeoman first class, was aboard the U.S.S. Arizona, part of the honor escort convoying President Woodrow Wilson to Brest, France, on December 13, 1918. The Arizona then headed to New York where she arrived on the afternoon of Christmas Day.

Chapter 12
The next chapter begins with growing up at Mort and Jennie Austin's Mountain Grove House. It includes some 1919 letters, boarding houses by 1920, as well as the soldier boys coming home and a wrap up of World War I.

WWI Soldiers in the Town of Highland

Memorial Plaque to the WWI Soldiers in the Town of Highland, New York. ★ signifies those wounded. Those who died in battle were listed in the middle as Highland Martyrs. Photo courtesy of the Bosch Family.

Died in battle (Martyrs)
McKinley Austin
Frank E. Clouse
Henry J. Loerch
C. Dewey Liebla
Edwin T. Wolfe

Triumphant from the Marne to the Argonne, 1917, 1918
These are our boys who helped drive home Washington's liberty wedge over there and here in each war zone with the precious lives in pledge. Our citizens presented this table because Americans won the world's applause and for all who fell that right may emerge freed from the sting of autocracies scourge.

Raymond Austin
Claude Angell
William Ashaur
Raymond Beufve
Herman, Edward, Ralph Bosch
George J. & Ernest W. Beck ★
Ferman Beck
Joseph Cox
Edwin L. Crail
William W. Conrad
Clarence I. Clouse
George F. Dunlap ★
Raymond Davis
George E. Eldred
Joseph Glaab
John Horton
Ernest Horton
Abel Hulse
Raymond J. Keller
Martin E. Kendrigen
Jay H. Lass
George Liebla
Ralph & Emmet Livingston
Emerson & Ezra McBride
John C. Metzger ★
Fred Metzger
Wesley & Fred Morgan
Edgar Mitchell
John McQuirk
Harvey Myers
Earl C. Owen ★
Fridolin Straub
Edward Schumacher
Walter C. Toaspern
Matthew Vollmer
Raoul Will
Everett Wells
Carl J. Wolfe
Clarence Wormuth

The following men were also listed as being in WWI, in the 1930 Census. Some may have moved to the town after WWI. Others, like Charlie MacIntyre, must have been left off accidentally. John Morgan, Frederick Hensel, George F. Cantwell, Harry Baker, Lewis Edwards, Charles Frey Jr., John Meyer, Tracy Myers, Charles R. MacIntyre, Harry Siegel, Ernest Timmerhof, Frederick Bye, Arthur Hartung, Herman Cox.

Chapter 12
Mountain Grove House
The Austin Family, 1919–1920

On the whole, though, my early years were happy ones. I liked the noon hours, the recesses, and the nights after school when we played a wide assortment of games.

I always looked forward, however, to the time when school would be out, for I never was too fond of studying, and besides, my parents ran a small summer boarding house to which a few families brought their children year after year.

The summer season was the most pleasant time of all, for then the school bell did not interrupt the baseball games or the hours spent swimming with my city friends.—Art Austin, September 22, 1948.

Art Austin at his home, Mountain Grove House, around 1920. "When they played Robin Hood, I was Friar Tuck." Photo courtesy of Mary Briggs Austin.

Mountain Grove House was the small boarding house where my dad Art Austin grew up. Mort and Jennie Austin, Art's parents, ran Mountain Grove, the boarding house the family had moved to after their Homestead Cottage had burned down around 1915.

Though a small boarding house by comparison to others in the town, the Austin's house could accommodate 30 guests in its large, airy rooms. One of Jennie's letters indicated they had a phone.

Mountain Grove had been in Mort's Austin family from 1884 to 1908. The original 1884 house did not have a railing around the front porch.

Mountain Grove was set on a spacious lawn with spruce trees at an elevation of 1,800 feet, and had a nice view of the surrounding country. There was good fishing, boating, and swimming a mile away at Highland Lake. Casinos were nearby.

The cost to stay at Mountain Grove House was $15 per week and up; or $3 per day. Grandpa Mort would pick guests up at Shohola, 5 miles away. The cost was $1 for the scenic ride back, and 50 cents for trunks.

Mort and Jennie Austin
Jennie's homemade meals were made from fresh vegetables, eggs, and milk. Included in this chapter are a few of Jennie's recipes (mostly desserts), and quite a list of the names of pickle recipes.

Grandma [Jennie Austin] was a great cook and made wonderful meals, delicious food, roasts, and chicken.—Joan Austin Geier.

Grandma was always busy. She did all the cooking and baking for the boarding house, and of course, for her family—including the bread.

Those people were certainly well fed on fresh food. One of the things that impressed me as a

Art, Jennie, Elizabeth, Gladys Myers, and Mort at the breakfast table in their Mountain Grove House. "For breakfast, he liked buckwheat pancakes, the batter for which was always in a big pitcher." Photo courtesy of Mary Briggs Austin.

Mort Austin with his horse. "Grandpa had a horse who did general farm work." Photo courtesy of Mary Briggs Austin.

small child was how she served green beans or peas or carrots in cream and butter.

One person from New York said the veggies were good, but, "They don't taste nice and fresh like you can buy in the city."

Grandma made gingerbread men on occasion and bread rolls or biscuits in interesting shapes.

Grandpa was another hard worker. It seems that he had always gone out before I was up and returned only briefly during the day. For breakfast, he liked buckwheat pancakes, the batter for which was always in a big pitcher.

Grandpa had a horse who did general farm work. In the summer, Grandpa brought vegetables (which he would help pre-wash in tubs at the outside pump) from the garden to the house on him in some kind of baskets on each side.

He sometimes helped clear up the dining room after the boarders' supper as well as in the kitchen.—Melva Austin Barney, granddaughter.

The Austin Family, 1919–1920

In 1919 Mort and Jennie's son Raymond Austin (Melva and Joan's father) was still in the Army in the Panama Canal Zone. Bill Austin, 16, worked at Proctors; Elizabeth (the only daughter) was 8; Art Austin (my dad) was 6; and the youngest, Bob or Robbie, was 4.

My dad Art Austin told what it was like to live in Eldred from about 1919 to 1925.

I grew up in a three-story boarding house with a basement and an attic with lots of old stuff. We had our own bedrooms unless there were boarders.

In winter sometimes we slept together to keep warm. We ice skated on Bosch's Pond a mile or two up the road and did a lot of sleigh riding until they sanded the roads.

The ice house kept things cold. We cut ice and packed sawdust around it and it would last all summer. We had an ice box.

We had kerosene lights at first. At the end we had gasoline. It had a generator, but one had to be careful. They gave a brilliant light. When electricity came, we had our own generator. Then the lines came through.

In the summer I carried water up and helped with the dishes. We had hand fans and would get under trees to keep cool. We closed windows during the day. We went swimming in the swimming hole, Highland Lake, or sometimes in the town brook. There was a place to swim on each side of Highland Lake. I swam with my brother Bob.

On the fourth of July we had sparklers and shot off fire crackers. One year we shot them up with a bow and arrow.

The town would have an ice cream social during the summer. Churches would have a fair. You could eat and they would sell handcrafts.

We had a 5 and 10 cent store when things were five and ten cents. Candy gum was 1 cent, a candy cigar cost 5 cents.

We never went out over night. We took picnics. One day we hooked up the horse and took a trip to the falls. We went because they were going to put in a dam and it was going to be destroyed.

At one time an uncle [Dory Austin] stayed with us a year or so.

I got a spanking because I threw a stick at a cat. I didn't mean to hit him. He was on the wood pile.

August 1920. Bob Austin in front of his mother, Jennie Austin; Elizabeth Austin is on the right; Art Austin is on the left. Mountain Grove is in the background. Photo courtesy of Joan Austin Geier.

We used to catch lightning bugs. I didn't do much fishing or camping. Raymond was an outdoors person. He belonged to the Lone Scouts.

When they played Robin Hood, I was Friar Tuck. They also played Fox and Chicken, Snap the Whip, Hunter and Deer, Cowboys and Indians, and Kick the Rock.

It wasn't good bicycle country. We made a slingshot out of a tube of rubber. We had a wagon.

I played baseball and basketball. We had baseball, bats, and gloves. I had a broken arm from playing ball and catch.

We didn't have a tooth fairy, but we had birthday cake and candles for birthdays.

Mountain Grove House, Family, and Boarders

Mountain Grove House. Photo courtesy of Mary Briggs Austin.

Art and Bob Austin. Photo courtesy of the Austin Family.

Bob Austin lower right with children of boarders. Mountain Grove in the distance. Photos courtesy of Mary Briggs Austin.

Boarders at Mountain Grove House. Photos courtesy of Mary Briggs Austin.

Herman Bosch and others cutting and harvesting ice blocks on Bosch Pond. "We ice skated on Bosch's Pond a mile or two up the road."
—*Art Austin. Photo courtesy Victoria Kohler and Ken Bosch.*

My dog King was a St. Bernard. A woman who lived in the city gave him to me. Before that, I had a black dog named Rover. One dog would dig a hole for Raymond to get out.

There was usually a horse, a cow, and chickens. We always gave the horses buckets of water. Once father noticed the horses raising their heads. He looked and found the frogs Raymond had put in the buckets of water.

Guns were around the house. I had a 22. My older brothers went hunting some.

We didn't have a radio when we were little. The first one had all kinds of batteries, wet and dry. We had an antenna, but still had lots of static. We went to town to pick up the Sunday papers.

I walked to the two-room schoolhouse in town. Sometimes I came home for lunch. Math was my favorite, and I disliked English. I always got poor grades in handwriting and art. I did very well in math and history.

I didn't play hooky from school. Not more than once anyway. I liked school as much as you were supposed to.

Bob Austin, Bill Austin, and Elizabeth Austin. Photos courtesy of Mary Briggs Austin.

Gladys Myers and Elizabeth Austin. Photo courtesy of Melva Austin Barney.

On Valentine's Day we sent cards. Halloween was mostly tricks. We didn't go up and ask. We would soap windows, ring church bells, take a carriage apart and put it together in some ridiculous place. We didn't dress up; others did.

At Christmas time, we cut our own tree. We had a few candles because the old ones were dangerous. We hung stockings around the tree, but not every year, only me and Bob, the others were much older. I got a sleigh once. We always got oranges and nuts. At church they had a Santa Claus who passed out candy after Christmas Program.

Trains were the main source of transportation. There were street cars in Port Jervis. Our first car was an old model T when I was about a year old. We took railroad trips to Port Jervis or to the City.—Art Austin.

Gladys Myers

Gladys Myers helped Mort and Jennie at Mountain Grove. Her father Edwin Van Schoick Myers was a very good friend of Mort. Edwin and his wife Mabel Owen had 4 children: Raymond, Clifford (cutter at the glass factory), Gladys, and Orville. One day Gladys would become Mrs. Raymond Austin.

My mother had worked for her [Jennie Austin] when she was a girl. She always liked Grandma and Grandpa Austin, but thought their sons were strange creatures. —Melva Austin Barney, daughter.

In January 1919 Mort and Jennie had still not heard specifics regarding the death of their son McKinley in October 1918 in France. The details would come in several letters, the last of which would arrive in November 1919.

Raymond Austin continued to write home from the Canal Zone where he had been sent after he had enlisted for World War I.

In this last chapter of *Echo Hill and Mountain Grove* (from 1919 to 1920), information and photos of the Austin family, relatives, neighbors, and the known boarding houses in the Town of Highland are interspersed with the letters of Raymond, Uncle Ell, and others.

Raymond Austin, Canal Zone, to Bill Austin
January 3, 1919
Dear brother Bill,

Many thanks for the box of candy that arrived today. Another fellow in our tent also got a box of sweetcakes, etc., and the tent had quite a feast. We put guards at the tent door to keep out the rest of the company.

I guess we leave here on January 15 for Culebra and a few days later I believe we will "March on Shearear" for war maneuvers.

We may be there for a month. There are 60 men going to a place called David, 250 miles up the coast. I hope that I am on the list. Lately, I have almost hoped for a revolution somewhere. Since Mac was killed, time hangs heavy on my hands.

It's hard to tell just when we will come home. Probably about mid-May at the longest.

Have you any further particulars of Mac? The 11th Infantry is in the 1st Army Corps and fought under General Hunter Liggett. I saw where a fellow in the 11th company E, I believe, was wounded in the Argonne fighting.

If the letters he [Mac] wrote to Rosie and Lena are dated after September, I would almost believe he had made a mistake in the month or if they were dated between September 1st and 11th, it could be mistaken for November.

Did he say anything about being in a hospital? Many men were there when their regiments left for the fighting and being unaccounted for in the confusion were erroneously reported killed

---

Clam Chowder

100 clams
3 qts. carrots
2 qts. onions
1-1/4 peck potatoes
2 heads of cabbage
2 bunches celery
1 bunch parsley
2 qts. tomatoes
3-1/2 lb. salt pork
1/4 cayenne pepper
1/4 black pepper
Salt to taste

Dice the pork and fry until brown.
Add the onions, brown.
Put pork and all in liquid 2 hours.
Add potatoes and clams.

Jennie Austin's recipe from her scrapbook.

Elizabeth Austin, Jennie Austin, and Jennie's friend. Photo courtesy of Mary Briggs Austin.

Charles Raymond Austin and his sister Elizabeth Austin. Photo courtesy of the Austin Family.

or missing in action. Also, did he speak of any particular event.

I suppose the states are going wild over the homecoming soldiers.

I suppose Elizabeth is still going to school. I will write her a few lines soon.

Tell Arthur and Bob that every man should be a soldier when there is a war. There is no better time to begin than now. Make them proud of poor Mac and as anxious to be willing to serve our country as he was.

I'll say it's pretty hot here, but at present, we don't drill any and only walk post 5 hours out of 72. I consider this to be a snap.

The winter is well along up there now and pretty cold too, I expect. I want you all to be careful and not get sick for I believe to loose another one of you would just about do me up.

I am returning the telegram with this letter. Praying you all are well as I am and will write soon. With much love to all.
Your Brother,
Raymond

Aida Austin Writes Rev. McVeigh
On January 11, 1919, Aida Austin wrote to Rev. Wm. J. McVeigh, Chaplain, 11th U.S. Infantry, A.E.F., France, and asked for more information on names of some of the members of McKinley's company.

Raymond Austin, Canal Zone, to Bill Austin
January 14, 1919
Dear Brother,
Your letter of December 29 just received. Needless to say, I was very glad to hear from you. I suppose by now you have had more details about Mac from the Red Cross. Don't fail to send me any details you may get immediately.

I am glad you are having a mild winter and I hope it keeps up. Although, I am afraid you will have a late spring and they won't send us home during bad weather. When the 29th Infantry went back, many soldiers died from diseases caused from the change of climate. We have only been here a few months. However, most of them had from 4–10 year's service here. I'll take my chances any day.

I never got Fred Morgan's letter. What company and regiment does he belong to? What

Uncle Wiggily and other Animal Stories

Jennie used to read Uncle Wiggily stories from the Herald Tribune *Newspaper to her boys. Art spoke about it.—Mary Briggs Austin.*

Uncle Wiggily, one of the many animal characters in the book of the same name, was an elderly rabbit, lame from rheumatism. Some of the animals are friendly, some mischievous but harmless, others are out to nibble on Uncle Wiggly's ears.

Uncle Wiggily's author, Howard Roger Garis, also wrote Tom Swift books and some of the Bobbsey Twins books under pseudonyms.

I have very fond memories of my dad reading to us (complete with expression and/or dialect) a number of animal books with mischievous animals including, Garis's amusing *Uncle Wiggily*; rascally Br'er Rabbit in *Uncle Remus,* by Joel C. Harris; and Kipling's delightful *Just-So* tales.

Book cover in the Public Domain.

Bob and Art Austin. "Jennie used to read Uncle Wiggily stories to her boys." Photo courtesy of Joan Austin Geier.

---

camp is he at?

According to reports, 20 men from M company who have dependants are booked for a discharge. Also we hear that men are coming from the states in February to relieve the 33rd. They will be in quarantine for 30 days so we may possibly leave here in April. Then we would be held in detention for a month in the states.

Some how I feel that I will be discharged and come home next July. If things keep up in South America, we may have to go down there and cool things off.

Raymond

Dr. Alonzo Eugene Austin in New York City and his sister-in-law Charlotte Hall were quite active in writing letters to the 11th Infantry personnel to find out the circumstances of McKinley Austin's death.

Allen B. Maxwell, Captain of the 11th Infantry Machine Gun Company, wrote Dr. Austin in January 1919. On finding out that Dr. Austin was not McKinley Austin's father, Capt. Maxwell resent the same letter to Mort Austin in March. The letter can be read in its entirety in the Appendix, p. 466.

Captain Maxwell, MG Co. 11th Inf., to Dr. A.E. Austin
January 19, 1919
Dear Sir:

As commanding officer of the MG CO. 11th Inf., I answer your letter of inquiry regarding the death of your son Mortimer McKinley Austin.

I was in a different division at the time of the death of your son, but by questioning men in the Company who were present during that engagement, I am enabled to give you the following information—most of which was given by Sergeant Popp who was in command of the section...

All the men of the Company state that your son was one of the most likable men in the company. None were braver and the reason he was killed was because he was too brave really. I shall not attempt to assuage your grief with mere words of sympathy.

Perhaps the knowledge that he died as the bravest of the brave, facing toward the enemy, leading his men forward to a point in advance even of our own lines, may somewhat lessen your suffering. I sincerely hope so.

Believe me to be very truly yours,
Allen B. Maxwell

Eldred Austin, Barre, Mass., to Mort and Jennie Austin, Eldred
January 19, 1919
Dear Brother Mort,

Your letter received some time ago. I have been sick the last 2 weeks, so have not written many letters.

I received a letter from Raymond and answered that letter for I thought he was so far away from home and alone and waited for yours until I was well. I am feeling quite well now and went to work last Thursday. There is quite a lot of sickness around here. I received a letter from Lillie a few days ago. She has been sick with the flu, but was around when she wrote.

Last Friday it was 12 below zero, the coldest so far this winter. It is warm now and no sleighing. The ice is 8 inches to 12 inches thick now and it looks as if we are not going to have much snow or cold weather this winter. Still it is quite a while until spring and we may have all the winter we want.

Is Tom Collins in Eldred this winter or did they go to the city for the winter?

I hope you are all well now.

Dear Jennie,

I come to you in this your hour of sorrow with sympathy from the depths of my heart while you mourn the loss of your boy,

I feel we can all thank God that he gave his life in a noble cause. While your heart bleeds for your boy, we can feel grateful that God has given you other children to comfort you while many a mother has given her all in this cruel war.

Love to all,
Eldred

Raymond Austin, Quarry Heights, Canal Zone, to Mort Austin

January 25, 1919
Dear Father,

Your more than welcome letter of January 7 received a day or two ago. Would have answered sooner, but was on guard the 23rd and 24th, and as there was inspection at 9 a.m. this morning, until now there has been no convenient opportunity.

I am glad you are having Mac brought home. We cannot better use his insurance than in that way. It will be hard to come home without him. But it will be easier to have his grave where we can care for it.

I got a letter from Uncle Ell a few days ago. I am glad to see how he has changed his opinion of joining the Army.

The weather up here, while altogether too hot, is not so bad as at Culebra. There is no reveille or retreat to stand, and we are only supposed to do 5 hours guard in the days. Although just now some men are in the hospital and I have to go on again at 4 o'clock. However on guard once in a while is easy enough.

There are some more rumors around about us going to the states in March. The Puerto Rican soldiers attached to the military police go back to their regiment on the 27th and I hear they sail for Puerto Rico on February 7.

Raymond

Charlotte C. Hall, N.Y.C. to the Mort Austin Family

February 11, 1919
Dear Mortimer and Jennie, Raymond, William, Elizabeth, Lawrence, and Robert,

It is a great sorrow to enclose this letter [from Allen Maxwell, January 19, 1919] which tells that our McKinley has paid the supreme sacrifice on the altar of our world's freedom in France.

In all your mourning, we mourn with you. His death is a great loss to you all. It was like him to ask that the insurance, should he give his life, be used

Jennie Austin's Pickle Recipes

Pickles
Pickled Onions
Chow-Chow
Pepper Relish
Green Tomato Pickle
Pickled Corn
Preserved Tomatoes
Carrot Jam
Sweet Pickled Prunes
Pickled Pears And Peaches
Apple Relish
Uncooked Mustard Pickles

Pickled Beets
Mustard Pickles
Thousand Island Pickles
Sour Cucumber Pickles
Uncooked Jackson Pickles
Uncooked Pickles
Sliced Ripe Cucumber Pickle
Easy Pickles
Mango Relish
Uncooked Mixed Pickles
Sweet Chopped Pickle
Pickles From Oregon

Mustard Pickles
Salt Pickles
Dill Pickles
Green Tomato Pickles
Tomato Relish
Pepper Hash
Pepper Relish
Sweet Cucumber Pickle
Bread And Butter Pickles
Short Order Pickles
—*Jennie Austin's recipe from her scrapbook.*

The sawmill across from the original Jane Ann Myers Boarding House. "I believe the old mill whose foundation is still somewhat visible was probably there at the time of the Myers or maybe even before, as there was a lot of lumbering in the area."—Geraldine Mills Russell. Photo courtesy of Stuart and Geraldine Mills Russell.

for the education of his sister and brothers.

We love McKinley. His going home is also a great loss to us. We had high hopes that sometime his home would be where his great-grandfather Austin lived.

As the letter of inquiry was written on paper like this, Capt. Maxwell evidently thought McKinley was Eugene's son. I am writing him that he has not that honor, but that McKinley's parents will receive the letter and will want to reply.

[Dr.] Eugene and Sally [Austin] write in messages of sincere sympathy with you all. These pages are from them as truly as from me. Our united prayers are for you all. In loving memory of McKinley, and full of sympathy with your sorrow.

Also, please give our congratulations to his Grandfather Leavenworth, that he had so soldierly, so truly patriotic grandson.

Please give him and his family our sympathy in their loss.
Charlotte C. Hall

Lt. Edwards answered some of the questions Aida had asked in her January letter to Chaplain McVeigh. Lt. Edwards's entire letter can be read in the Appendix.

Lt. G.L. Edwards, Y.M.C.A., Luxemburg, to Aida Austin
February 14, 1919
Dear Miss Austin,
Chaplain McVeigh gave me your letter concerning Mortimer Austin MG Co. 11th Inf....I was with him when he died, but was wounded later in the day and cannot say where he was buried.

I don't know anything about his personal belongings for I was taken to a hospital on the same day that he was killed, but am trying to learn something about it. When I do, I'll be sure to let you know at once. Chaplain McVeigh has gone to the States and he was in charge of the burying party.

My dear lady it grieves me to have to write this information. But I am the only officer with the company that was with them there. However you will be glad to know that he died like a true

Estonian Army Forced to Retire

Esthonian Army Forced to Retire (by Associated Press) London, Feb. 19.—Esthonian troops have been forced to fall back before the Bolshevik forces in the region of Pskov, according to an official statement issued by the Esthonian headquarters.

Lenine and Trotzky are Reported Near Break
Stockholm, Feb. 19.—Serious differences of opinion have arisen between the Moscow Soviet headed by Premier Lenine and the Petrograd Soviet headed by Leon Trotzky, over the allied proposal for a conference on the Princes Islands, according to a dispatch from Helsingfors [Helsinki].

Lenine, it is said, wishes to accept the invitation for a conference on account of the economic situation of Russia, which is declared to be hopeless. Trotzky at Petrograd is declared to be of the opinion that the occupation of the Ukraine offers the possibility of food and fuel supplies for the Soviet Government. Trotzky who is Minister of War, is sending all available troops into the Ukraine.

Bolshevik forces operating in the Ukraine, according to advices from Kiev, have suffered several severe defeats at the hands of the Ukrainians.—The Tri-States Union, February 20, 1919. [Lenine was the given spelling.]

American doing his duty. He was well liked by both officers and men of the company, and we are proud to have had such a man.

If there is anything I can do for you in anyway, please let me know. I'd be only too glad to do it.

*Yours very respectfully,
G.L. Edwards
1st Lt. 11th inf. NYC*

Families who Lived to the East of the Austins

Several of the families who have been a part of our story lived to the east of the Austin family, not far from Highland Lake.

Thomas and Emma Kelso Collins seem to have moved back to Eldred from New Jersey.

Rebecca (Aunt Becky?) Masvidal (63, Spanish, and single) worked for Gus Myers. Unfortunately, the photo of "Aunt Becky" who smoked a pipe has been lost. The sawmill near Gus Myers's house may have been there in the early 1800s.

Daniel Hallock, 80, was widowed. His sister Martha Hallock may have lived with him.

Mary Mills Wait had been a widow for 13 years. She ran a boarding house and lived with her son Alexander Wait, his wife Ida, and their 2 daughters. Alexander was listed as a carpenter.

James and Margaret Mills Boyd (perhaps retired from running a boarding house) still had children at home: Mabel was a Postmaster; George was a carpenter; and Stella was an assistant Postmaster.

Floyd and Helen Kalbfus Boyd had a daughter Elizabeth. Floyd was a carpenter. Wait & Boyd's Garage owned by Floyd Boyd and his cousin Alexander Wait was listed in a 1919 ad.

Elizabeth Mills, a widow for 10 years in 1919, continued to run the original Mills boarding house

After the Armistice

After the Armistice, the Italians had a great many Austrian prisoners. They made the prisoners carry water in their German helmets from the irrigating ditches and pour it on roads to settle the thick dust.

The Austrians had taken over one million prisoners in the first big drive. When the Armistice came, they turned them all loose to go home. The Italians would not help them. They claimed it was their fault that they lost the first drive.

To get even, they made them walk. At night, they herded them in a field and gave them soup. At daybreak, they turned them loose and let them walk. No one was allowed to carry any of them.

I used to feel so sorry for them. Some were barefooted; some had rags wrapped around their feet. They would run by the side of the trench and cry for Panny (bread).

I would take a bunch in the truck and tie down the curtains. When we would come to a barrier, the Italians would make them get out and make us go on. I would wait until they came along and then pick them up again.

Some of them was very nice people and some lived 100s of miles down in the southern part of Italy.

One time I was going up in Mt. Grappa and there was 10,000 prisoners coming out—the worst looking lot of human beings that I had ever seen. They had been bottled up in the mountains without any supplies for months. All they had to eat was dry, hard, yellow corn on the cob. They was dirty and unshaven; you could smell them long before they came in sight. They was marching four abreast and taking up the whole width of the road. A Scotch soldier was in front and one in the rear. They did not cause any trouble.

It was on that trip that I saw Victor Emmanuel, the King. A motorcycle patrol came along and crowded us off the road and everything had to stop. A touring car with the top down stopped just a little above where I was. I hollered to the driver of the truck in front of me, "What the Hell are they making all the fuss about?"

He put his fingers on his lips to motion me to keep still. Just then a man popped up in the back seat and looked at me and said, "You're from New York, aren't you?" and laughed. He was a very small man and he had a cap on that came down to his ears.

My interpreter, Tom, had an Italian mother and an English father. His mother kept their home up near the Austrian border. He had not seen her since the war had come.

This was after the Armistice, and we had plenty left in the warehouse. So Parks and I made up a large box of supplies and took Tom along to his mother's place and what a reunion that was. I know she cried, Tom cried, Parks cried, and of course, old Dan cried. She said she had been under the Austrian rule from the beginning of the war. But she was like all of them. She had buried some wine up in the woods. She went and dug it up and we had a very nice visit.—*Daniel Rowlee Schoonover.*

Rowlee Schoonover on the right. Photo courtesy of John Hull.

Mary Horton Bosch holds Herman Bosch Jr. Photo courtesy of Victoria Kohler.

on Highland Lake. Six children were still at home: Belle was a teacher; James was a chauffeur for the boarding house; Agnes was a servant at the boarding house (probably helping her mother); Alexander was a carpenter; George and Margaret.

Charles Myers, his second wife Elizabeth, their daughter Eleanor (born in April 1920), and his son Harold Myers lived at Lake View House on Highland Lake.

George Myers Asendorf lived with his parents Henry and Isabelle Boyd Asendorf in their huge boarding house on Highland Lake during the summer months.

Charles Myers's brother Martin David Myers and his wife Mary Fee had two young daughters: Mary Myers and Ethel Myers. Son Martin D. Myers Jr. was born in 1920. Martin Sr. was a chauffeur.

Wilhelm Bosch's Lake House was leased (1915) and run by Otto Schreib (whose daughter Paula would marry Ralph Bosch). Wilhelm and Mary Nellie Van Eastenbridge Bosch were retired, but lived there with their children Ralph and Christina. In the next book, Lake House becomes Green Meadows.

Mary Elvira Horton Bosch cared for Herman Bosch Jr. while she waited for Herman Sr. over in France. Herman Bosch would be honorably discharged in March. He would have a sawmill and dairy farm. The Bosch Pond Art Austin talked about at the beginning of this chapter, would be built on Herman and Mary Bosch's property near Proctor Road south of Collins Road. We will read more about Herman and Mary in Book 3, when Aida Austin mentions them in her early 1940s diary.

Raymond Austin, Canal Zone, to His Parents and Sister, Eldred
February 16, 1919
Dear Folks,

I was very glad to receive your three letters of January 23, 25, and 28. It was nearly 3 weeks since I had heard from you and I had begun to feel uneasy.

I came back to Culebra, February 6 to be examined for discharge on the grounds of my allotment. I have turned in my equipment and have been kept very busy.

There are a number of others who are waiting discharges and as we don't drill, we do most of the work.

I would have written to you long ago, but I have had very little time. Just when I will get home is guess work, but unless the breaking off of the Armistice holds, our discharge is up. I expect to see you around March 10th to 20th, maybe sooner. A few men have already gone back.

I am satisfied now that Mac is among the killed. According to one account I have seen, the 11th lost 399 men killed, 141 wounded and 226 missing and another account gives it as 339 men killed.

One of Mac's friends in F Co., was Aloucious Delaney of Port Jervis. Maybe if you can locate his folks, he may know something

Several names in the list of the Socony Gasoline Dealers are familiar: Wait & Boyd of Highland Lake; Quick & Co., Barryville; J.R. Myers, Eldred; T.W. Racine and Son, Eldred; R. Wells, Eldred; Henry Asendorf, Highland Lake; Clarence Van Gorder, Glen Spey.—*Republican Watchman, 1919.*

Wilhelm Bosch at his Lake House Store around 1920. The signs read: Boats To Let: $2 per week. Cigars, Candies, Ice Cream, Soda Water, Souvenir Post Cards. Photo courtesy of the Bosch Family.

about the details of Mac's death.

At Quarry Heights, I saw the names of 2 or 3 men who were wounded in the 11th infantry in September, so would know nothing of the casualties of October. Two officers from the 11th were cited for bravery. One was killed.

Clarence Wormuth is among the 10,000 missing. I am very much afraid that our losses will not stop there. This may yet turn out to be our bloodiest war.

I am glad you are having such an easy winter. You must all take care of yourselves as I want to see you all well when I come home.

Tell Fred Morgan I got his letter and I would have answered it, but did not know whether to send it, being as he was getting out so soon.

I have no intention of reenlisting. Keep your eyes open and if you see any good job. I'll jump at it the next day after I land home. By all means stay in by the fire during the bad weather. I think I can fix anything that is liable to go wrong.

The cake and the nuts were surely great. We (about 14) divided the cake and all said it was fine. I was very glad to get it. Many, many thanks for them.

Love to all, Raymond

Dear little sister,

I was very glad to see that you are learning to write so nice. You must go to school every day and by and by you will learn enough to be a school teacher.

I am coming home soon and I will be glad to see you and Arthur and Robbie again.

Don't send any papers from the government or Red Cross to me as I will not be here when they come and they might get lost.

With much love, your brother, Raymond

F.F. Cutler, Mount Hermon School, Mass., to C.M. Austin
February 17, 1919

My dear Mr. Austin:

I am very sorry to hear of the death of your son. He made an excellent record here at Mount Hermon. He was on the honor list of students both terms he was here and had an absolutely perfect record in attendance upon all his classes and appointments.

About 1,300 of our boys have been in military service; 42 of them have made the supreme sacrifice. We have sorely missed the boys here at Mount Hermon, but have been glad that they have been able to help in the settlement of these great questions.

I sympathize with you in these days when you must feel so keenly the loss of your boy.

Yours sincerely, F.F. Cutler
Office of the Principal

The *Port Jervis Tri-States Union* of February 20, 1919 ran an account of the death of McKinley from the new information the Austins had received.

Eldred, February 17, 1919
Tri-States Union, Port Jervis

It is a raw, cold day, so different from the spring weather of last week.

Mr. and Mrs. Ernest Clark came in town to spend Sunday with her parents last Saturday. They found plenty of mud on their way here in their car.

There was some excitement Tuesday evening over the law suit at Justice Eldred's. Even the ladies turned out. Barryville was well represented as both parties resided in that place.

Mr. John Love lost one of his horses to paralysis. His mate is all right again and is being worked today.

Mr. A.T. Sergeant is slowly recovering from his severe illness. Mr. Alvin Hill is getting better slowly. He does not like the "flu." Mrs. Webb LaBarr has been confined to the house for a few days. Mr. N.B. Myers was hit by a limb on the knee in the woods the other day and has not been able to work since.

Mrs. M. Hoatson [Marietta West Eldred] was ill a few days last week with Neuralgia. She is staying with Mrs. C.W. [Elizabeth Hoatson] Wilson.

The singing class will meet Wednesday evening in Sunshine Hall. All are invited. The Union Sunday School is steadily growing. We hope all in the village will join. Rev. Mr. Fletcher held services in the Congregational Church Sunday evening. He sang a beautiful solo, which was enjoyed by all.

There will be a lecture in Sunshine Hall on Friday evening by Rev. Mr. Watters, of Port Jervis. He comes well recommended, and we hope all will go and hear him.

The play, *Cranberry Corners*, is being practiced three evenings a week at Sunshine Hall. Some say it is as good as *Red Acre Farm*.

A number from here attended the dance in Red Men's Hall, at Barryville, on Saturday night.

Mr. Frank LaBarr was called to see his mother last Friday, as she was very ill. She is about the same. The many friends of Mr. Ed Sergeant are glad he is feeling so much better. He has been ill for over two weeks.

The social last Thursday evening at Sunshine Hall was a success in spite of the rain. Jack [Myers] has opened his billiard room.

"Mr. and Mrs. Ernest Clark came in town to spend Sunday with her parents." Ernest and Eunice Hallock Clark were married September 18, 1918, at her parents' home in Hillside. Eunice's parents were Samuel and Anna May Buchanan Hallock. Ernest's parents were John Henry Clark and Carrie Etta Bogert. Photo courtesy of Emily Knecht Hallock.

The February 20 headline read: *Attempt Made to Assassinate Premier Clemenceau*. The *Tri-States Union* cost $1.50 per year in 1919.

Raymond Austin, Culebra, Canal Zone, to his parents, Eldred
February 23, 1919
Dear Folks,
Just received mother's letter with the copy of Captain Maxwell's account of Mac's death at the battle of Madeline Farm. I hardly know what to say. My pride in him overcomes much of my grief.

The object of God in taking one so dear to us is very hard on our frail minds to perceive. We are all "tried by fire," also we are promised that no "grief too heavy to bear" shall be imposed upon us. With implicit confidence we can look into eternity unwavering calmness. With love to all,
Raymond

From Mountain Grove House to Eldred Corners
Mountain Grove on Proctor Road was less than a half mile from the center of Eldred. In Book 3, we read how Aida Austin (who lived a bit further away) walked to the *Village*, as she called it, every day; sometimes twice—in 1940 when she was 79.

Whether walking or riding to Eldred, the Austins would cross Halfway Brook. On the right was the old C.C.P. Eldred house where Herbert and Eliza Post Eldred probably lived (though they will soon move); next the Van Ohlen store (at some point the residence of the Van Ohlens and Archie and Minnie Sergeant Myers); and then the Straub Hotel of Fridolin and Juliana Straub and their children. On the corner was William H. Wilson's store. William and Bertha Boyd Wilson had a young son Forest.

North of the Wilson Store were the huge homes of the Greigs and Becks. Kate Greig was a widow. Her daughter, Isabelle Greig Kelso, was also a widow. Belle would marry Edward Grotecloss Jr., from Brooklyn. Ed and Belle Greig Grotecloss would have a son Edward Grotecloss III, and build

The original Abel Myers home, on the left, which became the Eldred schoolhouse. Photo courtesy of Chuck Myers.

a large boarding house near the Greigs.

Ed Grotecloss Jr. fought at St. Mihiel and Meuse-Argonne. He received a Silver Star for heroism and a special citation from Gen. John J. Pershing.

Back near Eldred Corners opposite Straub Hotel was the schoolhouse. Next to the schoolhouse was the Congregational Church.

Behind the church and schoolhouse was Orchard Terrace, originally owned by Abel S. Myers. In the next book it will be used as a school.

From Eldred Corners South
Left (south) onto Brook Road at Eldred Corners went towards Barryville. On the left (east) was a store probably owned by Jackson Myers; and next to it was the Parker House where Emily Parker, a widow, lived.

273,079 is total of U.S. Casualties

Washington, Feb. 18.—Revised figures bring the total American casualties in the European war to 273,079, an increase of 10,356 over the incomplete figures announced November 30, by General March.

Of this large aggregate, 69,055 are dead from all causes. Those killed in action or who died from wounds number 46,476, an increase of 6,112 over the early figures.

The complete summary follows:

Killed in action	32,776
Died of wounds	13,700
Died of disease	19,719
Died, other causes	2,860
Wounded	190,886
Missing	7,733
Prisoners	5,400
Total	273,079

While increases are shown in the number killed in action, died of wounds, and other causes, a decline is shown in the number of missing, which originally was 14,290. This is due to the fact that the status of many of the missing has now been determined. Some of them were found in hospitals, others in detachments not their own, and still others are now known to be dead whose fate a few days after the Armistice it was not possible to learn.

Germany's Losses
Late estimates of German losses made on the basis of German press reports, show that Germany's dead may number 2,000,000. Her total casualties so far as reported up to October 24, were 6,066,762. The dead numbered 1,611,104, but this total was not complete for that period and there were two weeks and a half of fighting after this which was extremely costly for the German armies.—Tri-States Union, *1919.*

Brook Road in Eldred Corners looking south towards Barryville. On the left is possibly Jackson Myers's store. The next building is the Parker Hotel where Emily Parker, and Howard and Emily Stevens lived. Photo courtesy of Kevin Marrinan.

Howard and Emily Stevens

Emily's daughter Emily Stevens and her husband Howard Stevens lived at the Parker House. Emily Stevens was the Postmaster. Howard was a teamster and worked at a diary farm.

The first Post Office was in the C.C.P. Eldred house, which was across from the Library. It was also in the building which is now the Bethany Church at some point.

In that era, the Postmasters changed as the politics changed in Washington, D.C. [depending on who was President]. My mother, Emily Stevens, was Postmaster and still was when I was born in 1920. Then when things went Republican, Mr. Sparks was appointed.

When Roosevelt was elected my Mom was re-appointed (following an exam) and then the policy was changed. Mom had the Post Office in the Parker House and Mr. Sparks moved it to the corner where the liquor store is now.—Christena (Teenie) Stevens Myers.

In 1920 Howard and Emily Parker Stevens' delightful daughter Christena Stevens was born. Christena would one day also be the Postmaster. She would marry Martin D. Myers Jr., son of Martin D. and Mary Fee Myers, a descendant of Jane Ann Myers.

Emily Parker Stevens's brother William Parker was a carpenter. William and Victoria Parker had 4 children: James Y. (a herdsman on a dairy farm), William, Elsie, and Andrew (who would have Parker's Store).

Eldred Corners to the Leavenworths

If Jennie Austin visited her father Sherman S. Leavenworth, or her

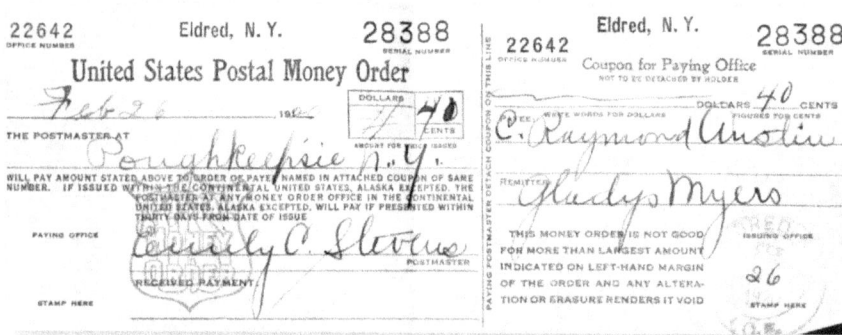

Money order sent to Raymond Austin by Gladys Myers; signed by Emily Stevens. Courtesy of the Austin Family.

siblings: Anna, Charlotte, Truman, and Martin, on the west side of town, she would continue past the Wilson Store (owned by William H. Wilson) at Eldred Corners and onto Eldred-Yulan Road.

Opposite William Wilson's store on Eldred's northwest corner was a building that seems to have been owned by Charles Wilson. His son Arthur Wilson would later own the A&P store there.

Charles and Elizabeth Hoatson Clark Wilson's home was north of the building at the corner and set back off Board Road. Their family included: Arthur Wilson, his wife Abby, and their son Robert; Joseph and Julia Wilson Cox; and Marietta West Eldred Hoatson, 76. Arthur Wilson worked at a grain company and Joseph Cox was a carpenter.

As Jennie Austin continued northwest on Edred-Yulan Road, she would come to a Y in the road. The land between the two roads was called Becker's Woods. The property would one day have a house on it, and one day the Austins would own that house.

Eldred-Yulan Road curved left and went past Maier's Pine Grove Farm and the Fred Myers Boarding House. (Fred and Mary Bradley Myers's daughter Ada lived with them.)

Jennie would continue on Airport Road on the right to visit her family.

Sherman S. Leavenworth seems to still be running Echo Hill Farm House as a boarding house in 1919. There are photos of him with boarders. Truman lumbered wood. Anna and Charlotte were still teachers.

Others on Airport Road

The Kelley, Meyers, and Middaugh families also lived on Airport Road.

Frank and Louella Sergeant

Becker's Woods (between the two roads) would one day have a Boarding House, and one day the Austins would own it. Eldred-Yulan Road is to the left. Airport Road, to the right, went past the Leavenworth and Bradley-Avery Boarding Houses. Photo courtesy of Chuck Myers.

Kelley's son Everett was over 7 feet tall. There will be a fun story about him in Book 3. Everett was an automobile machinist.

William Meyers Sr. was a lumberman. He and his wife Lottie Scott Meyers lived in Garfield Leavenworth's home as Garfield's family was still in Massachusetts. The Meyers had 2 children: William and Dorothy. William Meyers Jr. would marry a daughter of Garfield and Ella Sergeant Leavenworth.

Chester Middaugh was a teamster on a dairy farm. He and his wife Florence had a son Herbert. Chester and Florence play a part in Book 3.

In March 1919 Raymond Austin wrote home. He was still in the Canal Zone, and trying to track down an account of his brother's death.

Raymond Austin, Culebra, Canal Zone, to Mort and Jennie, Eldred
March 11, 1919
Dear Folks,
I would have written long ago, but I found I had no more stamps so I had to wait to payday,

Julius Maier with a calf beside the Maier barn on the Maier property of their Pine Grove Farm on Crawford Road. Photo courtesy of the Bosch Family.

Anna Leavenworth was a teacher. Photo courtesy of Cynthia Leavenworth Bellinger.

Charlotte Leavenworth on the left with boarders; Sherman Leavenworth is on the right. Photo courtesy of Cynthia Leavenworth Bellinger.

Charlotte Leavenworth and her dad, Sherman S. Leavenworth. Photo courtesy of Cynthia Leavenworth Bellinger.

Christena Stevens [Myers], shown here with my grandmother Jennie Leavenworth Austin, sent me this photo.

which is today. I am very sorry, but I could not help it. I hope you haven't worried about me for I have been well and on duty all the time. I got your letters also, the papers. I was awful glad to get them.

Say, can you get another paper with the account of Mac's death? A chum of mine who had a brother blown to pieces at the battle of St. Mihiel would like to have the account of Mac that was published in the Democrat.

It's just a year ago today Mac left us the last time and it is just about the same time that he left the house. I little thought then that it was the last time we would ever see him. It seems harder than ever to bear. But every time I remember that each name under the "killed in action," means another sorrowing family.

I feel convinced that all this suffering is the work of the Almighty and that He has his own deep motives for them and some day, each wound will be appeased and will be made plain to us.

They issued us back our equipment again and we went on a 13-mile hike and were out 2 days.

Evidently there has been a hitch in the demobilization down here for men are going out in small bunches and so far I have not been lucky. Mine is class B which is next in line to class A.

My discharge is approved of, but they lack transport service as the transports are carrying Puerto Rican troops homeward. The U.S. soldiers go back 1st class on passenger ships.

The rainy season is near at hand and I hope to leave here

before it arrives. I have seen enough of it last summer and fall.

Well, I must go on fatigue now, hoping you are all well and will write soon.

I am with love to all,
Raymond

Herman Bosch Returns Home, March 18, 1919

We hope we are going to enjoy better weather the next few days than we have been having. It was so foggy that it was very disagreeable.

Private H. Bosch of Highland Lake, N.Y., who returned home from overseas last Friday evening, was in town yesterday calling on his many friends. He gave some very interesting accounts of his life while on the battlefield. We are glad that here is a man who speaks so highly of his general, so many forget this. Private Bosch brought home a number of curios; also his gas mask. If one wants to enjoy a few hours in his company, they will learn much that has been hearsay.—Newspaper clipping.

Cap. Allen B. Maxwell to Mort Austin

March 18, 1919
Mr. C.M. Austin,

The effects of your son, the late Mortimer M. Austin, have not yet been received and that in numerous instances it was impossible to retrieve any effects.

[Also included was the letter first sent to Dr. Austin in January.]

Believe me to be very truly yours, Allen B. Maxwell

George James Clark

The last time we talked about George James Clark he was being treated for trench foot in England. George J. rejoined the Canadian 12th Reserve by January 1919. He returned to Canada on the H.M.S. Celtic in March, and was discharged on March 20, 1919.

Back in Eldred not far from where George James Clark's ancestors lived in the early 1800s, was Washington Lake. There were a number of boarding houses near or on Washington Lake.

Boarding Houses Near or On Washington Lake

Erwin and Norah Bradley Avery ran the original Isaac Bradley boarding house. Their children: Laura, Beatrice, Arthur, and Gladys.

Norah's father Isaac Bradley and his half brother John Bradley, also lived with the family, as did George Litman, a servant.

Alfred and Sophia Kaese owned Lake View Farm House. Their children: Lola, Albert, and Charles.

Abel and Viola Bradley Hazen ran Laurel Cottage. Their son Lewis, and their daughter Mabel and her husband William Ashauer, lived with them. Abel was listed as a carpenter; William worked on the farm.

Atwell and Helen Bradley ran Park Hotel. Sons Clifford, George, and Clarence Bradley helped keep it a lively household.

Washington Beach postcard courtesy of Kevin Marrinan.

Hindenburg Party Protests

London, Feb. 19.—Advice received from Berlin by way of Basel are to the effect that the Pan German Military Party, headed by Field Marshal von Hindenburg, bitterly resents the new clauses in the Armistice, especially those limiting the German army to the size of a simple police force (according to a Paris report, 250,000 to maintain order), the supervision of control of ammunition factories, and the demand that Germany pay the expenses of the allied armies of occupation on the Rhine.

These conditions, it is complained, will throw out of work thousands of German officers, from General down, while the army of 600,000 volunteers reported by the German press to have been organized must be disbanded...
—Tri-States Union, *Feb. 20, 1919.*

A rowboat ride on Washington Lake. The building on the left, Minisink Lodge. West Shore Cottage on the far right, was originally owned by the Racines. Both Minisink Lodge and West Shore Cottage would become part of Cantwell's West Shore Lodge. Photo courtesy of Kevin Marrinan.

Joseph Tether had retired from running Washington Lake House. His wife Anne had died in September 1916.

Walter and Meda Breen Tether

Abel and Viola Bradley Hazen's Boarding House. Photo courtesy of Larry Stern.

Washington Lake House. Walter Tether third from the left. Photo courtesy of Ivan J. and Jana Tether.

ran Washington Lake House. They had a son Ivan Joseph Tether. Thomas O'Grady, 76, a servant, lived with them.

Henri Darriensecq was listed as Manager of Washington Beach House in 1919 and 1920. Later Walter Tether would run the Beach House.

Mrs. Edith Miller Kalbfus ran Highland Cottage.

Minsink Lodge was run by M.A. McCormick. Minisink Lodge and West Shore Cottage (owned at one time by T.W. Racine) becomes part of Cantwell's West Shore Lodge in Book 3.

An old friend of the Austin family, Robert Collins, wrote a sympathy letter to the Mort and Jennie, in March 1919.

Robert Collins, Madison, N.J. to Mort Austin, Eldred
March 25, 1919
My dear Mort,

I received a Tri-States *paper confirming the report I saw in the N.Y.* Tribune *last year that McKinley was killed in action.*

The report is very well written and shows the interest the officers took in looking after their men. Their desire to afford all the information attainable under the circumstances most difficult and distress to their relations.

McKinley was your first born and the first of your little group to pass from your companionship, not by ordinary disease, but in the shock of battle, a struggle for home and country and God against the most uncalled for cruel diabolical of wars the world has ever known.

I remember McKinley with pleasure. He was a bright and cheerful youth. We spent a good many pleasant hours at the checkerboard together. He could outplay me easily. His ready wit, keen and alert mind enabled him to see how he could move his checkers for my defeat. I was often overwhelmed as in certain moves he took man after man.

Had he lived, I have no doubt that he would have risen to a high position in his company. It was his ambition to do his best and so it was on that fatal day, with no fear for himself in the midst of the greatest danger, he jumped to the need of making the defense of his company more secure—he was determined to win.

My prayer is that the good Lord may bless and keep you all in his ways. Heaven is only a little way from the earth, and when the time comes for our removal, it will be but a step from this life to the better one on high.

With the wish that Raymond may soon be home and with best wishes for the dear old village of Eldred and its people,

I am Yours truly, R.B. Collins

Raymond Austin, Culebra, Canal Zone, to Mort and Jennie Austin
March 25, 1919
Dear Folks,

I left the hospital today. I was only in six days for a slight touch of malaria, but am OK now.

I got Bill's letter. Many thanks for the money. It will come in very handy.

Ten men left this company for home yesterday. We may leave April 3rd. I find that the allotment men have turned in their equipment again anyhow. I hope they are done fooling now and will get us off the zone shortly. I've had 8 months of Panama and my stomach's full of it.

One of the letters I wrote to Mac September 12th at Balboa, came back to me marked:

"Returned to writer. Killed in action Oct. 23, 1918."

That's just five months and two days ago. Do you hear anymore about getting him home or about getting any of his personal effects? It will surely seem lonesome without him when I get home.

I hope I get out of here before anything comes of our trouble with Japan. I am more than ready to fight, but the idea of scraping in these jungles don't suit me.

So Mrs. Tuzza and Nettie are with you now? I am glad mother has company for I know how she must have felt all alone during the day. I have been busy continually, yet it bothers me all the time.

I am with love to all,
Raymond

Soft Ginger Cookies

5 to 6 cups sifted flour
2 tsp. baking soda
2 tsp. ginger
1/2 tsp. salt
1 cup shortening (lard or butter)
1-1/2 cups sugar
1 egg, slightly beaten
1 cup molasses
1 cup sour milk

1. Mix and sift flour, baking soda, ginger and salt together until light and fluffy.
2. Add egg and beat well. Add molasses.
3. Add flour, alternately with milk, a small amount at a time, beating until blended after each addition.
4. Turn into greased, shallow pans, and pat out 1/2 inch thick.
5. Bake in hot oven 400 degrees for 15 to 20 minutes
6. Cut in squares. Makes about 4 dozen cookies.

Jennie Austin's recipe from her scrapbook.

West Farm

West Farm, pleasantly situated among the mountains of Sullivan County, accommodating 35 guests, offers an ideal spot for a pleasant vacation.

Its cozy nooks, lawn swings, pretty walks, croquet, piano, radio, etc., afford the opportunity to while away many happy hours.

Near amusement hall and casino. Convenient to Catholic and Protestant churches.

Beautiful views of the country may be had. Boating, bathing, fishing. Baseball diamond. An ideal trout stream runs through our property.

Just a short distance from the house are two fragrant pine groves with swings and seats. We are sure you will find it a good place for rest and recreation.

Good, wholesome, home cooking. Pleasant airy rooms. Electric lights. Good roads leading to and from, make West Farm easy of access by auto.

Rates: On application.—*West Farm booklet information.*

Theodore West and his son Charles West sitting on the porch of their West Farm. Photo courtesy of Virginia West Palmer.

The West Farm

It has been some time since we talked about Theodore and Phebe West. Their West Farm, west of Washington Lake's tail and north of Yulan, may have been run by their son Charles West by 1920.

Yulan Souvenir Folder. Yulan Post Office. Courtesy of Helen Hensel Oset.

Charles and Selma Werner West had two young children, Theodore and Selma. They had moved from Brooklyn back to Eldred in 1916.

Near Yulan
There were some boarding houses south of Washington Lake near Yulan.

Henry Bodine, 62, and his wife Blanche ran the Bodine Cottages on Bodine Lake. They had 2 young children, Paul and Blanche.

Edward and Georgianna Bornstein had a boarding house on Beaver Brook Road which would be called Grand View Farm.

The Peterson family included, Sophia Peterson, daughter Anna, a dressmaker, and brother-in-law Frederick, 83.

Elizabeth Austin, Eldred, to Raymond Austin, Culebra, Canal Zone
Spring 1919
Dear Raymond,
I want you to send me two wrings, that will be all I will ever ask for.
What is the name of the Easter Rabbit?
Are you coming home Easter?
xxxxxxxx
Your sister, Elizabeth

Raymond Austin, Culebra, Canal Zone, to Mort and Jennie Austin
March 28, 1919
Dear Folks,
I received your more than welcome letters yesterday at mail call and am taking the first opportunity to answer.

I think at last the time is near when we sail for the good old U.S. The men with allotments have turned in all their equipment and are supposed to sail for New Orleans between April 3rd and 7th. Our destination is Camp Shelby, Mississippi, where we will be at least a month in quarantine. In all probability I'll see you between May and July. Probably about the middle May.

Of course, all kinds of delays, etc., are likely to occur. So I set July as a late date. Anyhow, I'll have two service chevrons which is more than a good many will have.

If things keep up, I'll probably be back in uniform before I have been a civilian life long. Somehow I feel that we are near another big war.

It comes out now that we were not supposed to come here, but were to go "over there," to be trained and used to fill up the losses made in the fighting regiments. New Orleans is the embarkation point for Panama and it was through a mistaken order that any Merritt men came here.

I got a letter from Uncle Ell and he said Cousin Lillie never received any answer to the letter she wrote me. I wrote to her last December. I am writing to her now, but if you see any of them, explain to them how some of our mail has been mixed up.

Of course none of us would ever want to use the insurance. I believe he [McKinley] wanted it used for the children's education

Bornstein's Grand View Farm. Postcard courtesy of Kevin Marrinan.

so it would be no more than proper to use the balance that way when they are old enough. It will take well over $1,000 probably to bring him home.

One of my friends is going home on a furlough of 30 days and I told him to stop off and see you all on the way back. His name is Clinton E. Fields, I think I mentioned him to you before. He will be able to tell you a good many things about what has happened since I was in Camp Merritt with him and I'll be glad to see someone who has seen you all, should I be here when he gets back, which probably I won't be.

Well, I will close now hoping you are all well as I am and will write soon.

I am with much love to all,
Raymond

Rowlee Schoonover

Rowlee Schoonover was home by May 1919. He received the Italian War Cross for his work of Director of Motor Transportation for the Y.M.C.A. Rowlee wrote the following in his memoirs for his daughter Justina Schoonover.

I had stayed long after the Armistice and wanted to get back to the States. I had got rid of all the cars and stock we had on hand and was waiting for orders to go home. I was all ready to leave from Genoa for I had letters that your mother [his wife, Emily] was sick and for me to come home at once and I was worried.

Instead of sailing from Genoa direct to N.Y., I got a telegram to report to Headquarters at Paris. So I went to Paris and reported at HQ and was told to report at the Red Cross HQ.

They told me that I would be sent with a convoy of trucks loaded with food for the starving people in Constantinople and that I should have charge of everything there; that I had been recommended very highly for the job. They did not ask me if I could or would like to go, but I must go.

That did not set well with me. I told them that I was on my way to N.Y. and there was where I intended to go. I went back to the Y HQ and got my orders to sail from Brest.

There was no passage from Brest for 12 days, so they sent me over to a little Brittany town called Tressee—a little fishing town on the Brittany Coast.

I spent 12 days there and

Bodine Cottages

A modern summer resort with all improvements for the convenience and amusement of patrons.

Bodine's Cottages were the pioneers in the summer boarding house business in the vicinity of Sullivan County, New York. What is now Bodine Cottages, one of the best known of the smaller resorts in the eastern resort territory, was established in 1880 as a small farm boarding house with a capacity of 12 guests.

The rooms have been refurnished frequently and everything about the resort has been kept modern and in good condition. There are 30 large, airy rooms; a double piazza extends all around the main building. Running water and baths in some rooms.

Bodine Lake, which is the property of the owner of the resort, is kept well stocked with pickerel, bass, perch, etc., and there are two other lakes within 15 minutes' walk. There is also good gunning in season.

Bodine's Cottages also make a direct appeal to the winter sports enthusiast. Coasting, fishing through the ice, and skating are among the diversions of these cold weather guests.

Amusements, Casinos nearby, tennis, basketball, fishing, swimming, boating, radio, saddle horses and golf nearby.

Bodine's Cottages have been known for the excellent meals that are served. The cuisine is French-American. Eggs and vegetables are supplied from nearby farms.

Catholic Church about 6 minutes' walk from the house.

Auto conveyance from station .75, trunk $1.00. Pulmonary patients not entertained. Make reservations early. Write today.

Post Office 15 minutes' walk from house. Two daily mails.

Rates reduced in accordance with the times. Children $5.00 and up. Transient $3.00 to $3.50 per day.

All rooms have electric lights, but not all have running water.

Rooms in Cottage Annex: $16.00, 2 or more in room; single $18.00 each.

In Main Building 2 or more in room, $18 each; single $19 each, with private bath, $22; 2 or more in room, $20 each.

Bungalows: 2 in room, $18 each; single, $20 each.

106 miles from N.Y. on Erie R.R. Shohola Station.

—*Bodine Brochure, date unknown.*

Bodine Cottages. Postcard courtesy of Larry Stern.

Deyo Hull in Guantanamo shortly before he left the Navy with an Honorable Discharge as Chief Yeoman, U.S.S. Arizona, in August 1919. Photo courtesy of John Hull.

enjoyed it very much. It was during Easter Week and to see them people come in for Easter Sunday services. They had two wheel carts and big Normandy horses and the carts was very nice with landscape pictures painted on the bodies and Papa and Mama on the seat. Mama with her lace cap and big flowing skirts; Papa with his tight pants and round crown hat with wide rim with two streamers down his back and the kiddies sitting in the back in the straw.

We had a very nice trip home. I got through the clearing process that night and I hired a taxi to take me home to E. N.Y., 77 Logan St., and I sure was glad to see you all and it was a very happy homecoming for all hands. Your mother was no time in getting OK.—Daniel Rowlee Schoonover.

Deyo Hull

Justina Schoonover's future husband Deyo Hull was Chief Yeoman aboard the U.S.S. Arizona, which arrived in New York City from Constantinople, Turkey, on June 30, 1919. From February until June, the battleship had been in several countries including, Guantanamo Bay, Cuba.

Deyo Hull was honorably discharged from the U.S.S. Arizona on August 21, 1919.

I am not exactly sure how Justina and Deyo met. They both lived in Monroe at the time. Deyo would have been recently back from the war (WWI) and taken a job with a bank in NYC (handsome guy in uniform). Justina was a student at Cooper Union. Both were train commuters to the City. My dad told me where he thinks Rowlee's car shop was, which would have Justina walking past Deyo's home on her way to the station. —John Hull.

Charles Dassori, Jersey City Heights, N.J., to Mort Austin
June 1, 1919
Dear Friend Mort,

Some train. I had to stand up half the way home. We got home safe.

When I got home my Brother Joe and Mrs. Beltram was there. They wanted to know how Eldred was. I told them it is fine, that there isn't anything better than country life. Now Mort, if there is anything that I can do for you, don't be a bit backwards in telling me what it is. I am always ready for you and yours.

D.R. Schoonover Awarded Italian War Cross

Daniel R. Schoonover of Brooklyn who recently arrived from Italy where he had been serving with the Y.M.C.A. as Director of Motor Transportation, is one of the few secretaries in Italy who has been decorated. He has the Italian War Cross and the service bar with a star representing front line work on the Plave. Schoonover went to France last summer arriving just in time for the Château-Thierry offensive. He has the distinction of having carried the first load of supplies into the Château-Thierry Courthouse. Although the road was heavily shelled, he managed to arrive safely with his truck.

For his efficiency in organization and handling motor transportation he was sent to Italy in the fall. During the terrific fighting on the Piave, when all the bridges across the river had been destroyed by Austrian shell fire and the hastily constructed pontoon bridges were found inadequate for the heavy American trucks, Schoonover volunteered his lighter trucks and for two days supplied all the troops in his sector.—Brooklyn Daily Eagle, *May 4, 1919.*

Walking on path near the Delaware River in Barryville. Photo possibly taken by Aida Austin, courtesy of Mary Briggs Austin.

Am getting sleepy will close for the present trusting you are all enjoying good health. Love to all from my fleet.

Your true friend, Chas. Dassori

Raymond Austin was home at least by July as we find out in this next letter written by Ell Austin to his brother Mort.

Ell Austin was apparently working in Rushville, New York. By 1919 Ell and his wife Emma Parmenter Austin were divorced. It's hard to understand what happened to a marriage which seemed (from Emma's letters in the 1880s) so full of love and concern at the start.

Ell Austin, Rushville, N.Y. to Mort Austin, Eldred
July 20, 1919
Dear Brother Mort,

I was glad to hear that Raymond got home. I wrote to Raymond two weeks ago, but am not sure that he received my letter, for Lillie doesn't seem to receive all of my letters. Lillie writes me she was at Liberty July 4, and Raymond carried the colors. You and Jennie must have been very glad to have Raymond home again. I suppose Will and the other children were happy to see Raymond.

The Rochester paper said that Eckstein's boarding house at White Lake has burned.

Jennie and you must be very busy now with boarders. Think the farmers here are about 2/3 done haying and have about 1/8 of their wheat cut.

Write whenever you get time. Love to all, Ell

There is a photo with Ell displaying a very tall stalk of corn. The little girl in the photo may be his granddaughter Dot Calkin.

Menzo and Ed Bosch. Photo courtesy of the Bosch Family.

Dot and her brother Robert Dale Calkin lived with their parents in Bethel, where their mother Lillie Austin Calkin taught school. Ell Austin sometimes lived with Burt and Lillie Calkin; and sometimes Emma Parmenter Austin and her sister lived with the Calkin family.

Ed Bosch, August 13, 1919
I got out of the Army August 13, 1919. Came home and Web LaBarr and I cut logs for John Love until the snow got so deep, 30 inches in the woods.

So I went to New York, got a job building pool tables and bowling alleys for Wagner and Adler Co. at 30 Union Square, New York. I made out OK because I always did the best I could do…I worked on alleys for 30 years or so.—Ed Bosch.

Sgt. John Popp wrote Mort Austin in August. Sgt. Popp included several names of men who witnessed McKinley's death. Raymond Austin wrote to one of the men—Harold Fraley—and received a letter later in the year. Sgt. Popp's entire letter can be read in the Appendix, p. 466. *The History of the 11th Infantry*

Ell Austin, famous for his corn. Possibly his granddaughter Dot Calkin is holding up the top from the balcony. Photo in the Austin Collection.

mentioned in Sgt. Popp's letter is on p. 465.

Sgt. Popp, Chicago, Ill., to Mort Austin, Eldred
August 30, 1919
Mr. C.M. Austin, Eldred
Dear Sir,

Received your letter sometime ago and must apologize for not answering sooner. I have enclosed a complete history of the 11th Inf. during the war…

He was well liked and very popular among the men and

Spring House owned by Chris and Meta Meyer. Photo courtesy of Kathy Datys.

The Ira Austin House in Barryville. Photo courtesy of Christina Watts.

The old Hotel of John Schumacher had been added on to and was called Clouse's Casino. Photo courtesy of Kevin Marrinan.

among those few who lived a clean life while over there.

Yours very truly, John G. Popp

Barryville, New York

Some of the townspeople we have met still lived in Barryville.

Arthur Toaspern Sr. (son of Chris and Ida Heyen Toaspern) was Superintendent of Highways. Arthur and his wife Emma Keller had 2 sons: Royden Arthur and Walter (whose names could easily be confused with their father, Arthur, and their uncle Walter). Art Sr.'s brother, Walter, marries Emma Straub in Book 3.

John and Meta Toaspern Lass had 4 children that lived with them: Jay, Charles, Helen, and Harry Lass.

Aida Austin taught at the Barryville schoolhouse at some point. One of her students was Jessie Kerr, the daughter of William Kerr.

The William Kerr family lived on the Canal Tow Path, near the old Pelton Soda Bottle Factory. William Kerr and his wife Mary had 5 daughters: Margaret, Jessie, Mary, Ruth, Helen; and the youngest, a son, John (Jack).

In 1919/1920 many people worked at the Barryville Glass Factory by Glass Factory Pond. Howard Pelton was a foreman for glass factory. His wife was Edith.

Chris and Meta Meyer were the hotel keepers of the Spring House on River Road. Their children were: Anna, John, Minnie, and Chris.

James K. and Ella Breen Gardner, their daughter Edna, and his sister Katie McElroy Gardner, also lived on River Road. Edna taught music lessons. James K. Gardner was a merchant. Ella was a sister of Meda Breen Tether, the wife of Walter Tether. Walter and Meda had a home in Barryville and

Boarding Houses in 1919 or 1920

Here is a list of some of the Boarding Houses mentioned in various sources.

Eldred
Straub's Hotel, Fridolin Straub
Mountain Grove House, Mort Austin
Parker Hotel, Emily Parker
Echo Hill Farm House, Leavenworth
Bradley House, Erwin Avery
Pine Grove Farm, Joseph Maier
Myers House, Fred Myers

Near or On Highland Lake
Highland Lake House, Asendorfs
Sunset View House, Catharine Loerch
Mills House, Elizabeth Mills
Lake House, Wilhelm Bosch
Lake View, Charles C. Myers
Myers House, Gus Myers
Stephen A. Myers
Anton and Mary Rennenberg
Chris and Freida Koester
Peter and Mary Barth
Lake Side Cottage, Mary Wait

Lake Side Cottage, home of Mary Wait. Postcard courtesy of Larry Stern.

Washington Lake
Highland Cottage, E.V. Kalbfus
Minisink Lodge, M.A. McCormick

Washington Beach, Henri Darrieusecq
Park Hotel, Atwell Bradley
West Shore Cottage

Near Yulan
Bodine Cottages, Bodines
Grand View Farm, Bornsteins
Yulan Cottage, Metzgers
John and Edith Birr

Minisink Ford
Mountain House, Mrs. W.M. Gregory

Barryville
Spring House, Chris Meyer
Torwood Farm, Kerr Family
Handsome Eddy Farm, A. Schwab

Boarding House Ads 1919–1920
Highland Cottage
Splendidly situated on Washington Lake. Accommodates 124. Fine roads. Dancing, bathing, fishing, tennis. Garage. $14 to $15. E.V. Kalbfus. —Brooklyn Daily Eagle, *July 1, 1919.*

Bodine Cottages, Bodine Lake
All modern improvements. Cuisine Francaise. Acc. 50. Auto garage; ideal location; $12 and up.—Brooklyn Daily Eagle, *July 1, 1919.*

Washington Beach Hotel, Yulan
Wonderful Bathing Beach; fishing, dancing, pool; terms $14 to $16 per week. Henri Darrieusecq manager. —Brooklyn Daily Eagle, *July 1, 1919.*

Torrwood Farm, Barryville
For a quiet resting place on top of Sullivan County Mountains, come to Torrwood Farm. John H. Kerr, Prop. Barryville, Long distance telephone. Terms $10 to $12 per week. Automobile services.—Brooklyn Daily Eagle, *July 1, 1919.*

Torwood, the old homestead of the Kerr Family. Postcard courtesy of Larry Stern.

Mountain House, Minisink Ford
Boating, bathing fishing; board $14 and $15. Mrs. W.M. Gregory, Lackawaxen.—Brooklyn Daily Eagle, *July 3, 1919.*

Washington Beach Hotel
Electric light, bathing, fishing, dancing free, first class cooking. $18 up. Henri Darrieusecq.—Brooklyn Daily Eagle, *July 25, 1920.*

Minisink Lodge, Yulan
Homelike hotel; 1800 feet on Washington Lake; bathing, fishing. M.A. McCormick.—Brooklyn Daily Eagle, *July 25, 1920.*

---

ran Washington Lake House, as mentioned earlier in this chapter.

Fred and Margery Schwab were in their 70s and probably retired from their boarding house business.

Charles and Lottie Bradley Colville's children were: Esther, Leslie, and Ruth. Charles lumbered wood. Ruth, who wrote to McKinley during the war, would marry Herbert Deveraus.

Minerva Austin, widow of Ira Austin, had several family members living with her: daughter Minnie A.; daughter Mabel, her husband Edward Smith, and their son Austin Smith, 9 months. Ed Smith worked at the glass factory.

The old Hotel of John Schumacher had been added on to and was called Clouse's Casino—a place for eating and drinking. In the 1920s there would be another Clouse Casino (Bar and Grill). It would become Reber's.

It would be 1935 before the Briggs family arrived in Barryville.

Irwin Briggs and Myrtie Crabtree
Irwin Briggs returned to the United States in July and was discharged at Camp Dodge, Iowa,

Amanda Myrtie Crabtree wrote to Harry Irwn Briggs when he was in France in WWI. Irwin married Myrtie on September 2, 1919. Photos courtesy of Mary Briggs Austin.

on July 14, 1919. He was given a bonus of $127.49.

Irwin Briggs married Amanda Myrtie Crabtree in September 1919 in Ainsworth, Nebraska.

Irwin said, "Why don't you come home (there were 10 miles between his parents and mine) and we will be married?"

So I came home.

September 2, 1919, he and my folks met me at the train. I went to my home for a wedding supper my mother had prepared. I was so excited I couldn't eat.

After supper I got into my wedding dress, every stitch I made by hand. Brother Johnie took us in a car with my sister Mary and his brother Carl to Ainsworth Methodist Church Parsonage, and we were married.

Irwin called his mother on the telephone: "Is this Mrs. C.L. Briggs? Mrs. H.I. Briggs wants to talk to you."

They said she had to find a chair to sit down on. Irwin's younger sister, Verna, was getting married the next day and they were so busy with those preparations, they didn't pay any attention to him as he got his and his brother's suits cleaned, and pressed them himself.

Irwin told me that two of his younger brothers had already gotten married and he wanted to get married before Verna.

Gingerbread

1/2 cup Crisco
1/2 cup sugar
1 cup molasses
2 eggs
1 tsp. cinnamon
1 tsp. cloves
1 tsp. ginger
1 tsp. salt
1 tsp. soda
3 cups sifted flour
3/4 cup hot water

1. Mix.
2. Pour into Criscoed shallow 8x12 baking tin.
3. Bake in at 350 for 30 minutes.

—Jennie Austin's recipe from her scrapbook.

Verna was so upset that he'd been able to pull this off that she said we couldn't see her before the wedding. The next day we went out to see them all, and his sister Verna was married in the evening, September third. We stayed at my folks' home until time to go to college, Taylor University, in Upland, Indiana. We went by train.

At Taylor University, we rented a four-room house (small I suppose), on the campus for $60 a year. Furnishing the house, I had my dresser and mirror my brother had made. We got a new mattress from Montgomery Wards with money I had put in the bank. I had $350 saved from that job and besides, I was always lending money and I got that paid back; at least $100 I'd loaned out.

My mother gave me the quilts my grandmother Crabtree had made and never been used. Irwin had a pair of blankets.—Amanda Myrtie Crabtree Briggs.

The following year Irwin and Myrtie Crabtree Briggs went to seminary in Taylor, Indiana. They lived on the $150 a month government compensation for the loss of hearing Irwin had during the war; and any work that he could find.

Back in Eldred in November, the Austins received more information on Mac's death. Harold Fraley had responded to Charles Raymond Austin's letter. Mr. Fraley's complete letter can be read in the Appendix, pp. 462, 466.

Harold Fraley, Camp Gordon, Atlanta, Ga., to Raymond Austin
November 9, 1919
Charles Austin, Eldred, New York
Dear Sir:
My mother sent me your letter from my home in New Jersey.

Some Eldred-Austin Cousins, 1920

Margaret Paton, daughter of Archie Paton and his first wife, Mary Brown. Photo courtesy of Darren Foster.

Late November 1919, Cousin Rand (Miranda) Austin Paton died in Patterson, New Jersey.

In Paterson, on Friday November 21, 1919, Miranda Austin Paton wife of the late Archibald H. Paton died. Relatives and friends are invited to attend the funeral on Tuesday, November 25, 1919, from the home of her daughter [Ida], Mrs. Charles R. Webster. 313-15th Avenue at 2:30 o'clock p.m. Interment at Cedar Lawn.

Dorothy May Paton, Rand Austin Paton's granddaughter, was a year and a half old. Dorothy, was the daughter of Archie R. Paton (little Archie or Buddy, in *Aida Austin's 1881 Diary*) and Mable Slagle, his second wife. Dorothy's siblings were Mabel, Archibald C., and Marjorie Paton.

Dorothy Paton never knew

Cute little Dorothy Paton, daughter of Archie Paton and his second wife Mabel Slagle. Photo courtesy of her grandson, Darren Foster.

the children from her father's first marriage to Mary Brown: Margaret, Effie, Archie Jr., and Donald Paton.

Cousin Mortimer Bruce Austin and his wife Mary Millspaugh lived in Middletown, New York, in 1920. Their son Charles Augustus Austin was a tinsmith. Charles A. and Mary Johnson Austin had two children, Alden and Mabel.

I am very glad to give you the details of your brothers death, as I was on the spot and saw him get hit...
I am glad to tell you that your brother died like a man and facing death bravely. We were good friends and I was sorry to see him go...

I am happy to be of service to you and if there is anything else I can do, don't hesitate to ask it.
Sincerely yours,
Harold Fraley, 5th MP Co.

Ambert Moody to Mort Austin
In November and December, Mort Austin received letters from

Norma Wood, Elwood James, and their uncle Will Waidler. Photo courtesy of Richard James.

Black Chocolate Cake

2 cups brown sugar
3 eggs, save one white for icing
1/2 cup lard
1/2 cup sour milk

1. Melt 2 squares chocolate in 1/2 cup boiling water and cool.
2. Add to other ingredients:
    2 cups of flour
    1 ts. baking powder
    1 ts. soda
    1 ts. vanilla
    Pinch of salt
3. Mix baking powder with flour.
4. Dissolve soda in sour milk.

Jennie Austin's recipe from her scrapbook.

Ambert Moody of the Northfield Schools (Mt. Hermon), where McKinley had attended.

The November 12 letter mentioned a resolution passed by the trustees of Northfield Schools regarding the 63 Mount Hermon men who gave their lives for their country. The December letter *(see p. 462)* from Mr. Moody said that the newspaper account about McKinley's death, which Mort had sent the Northfield Schools, would be kept on file.

Raymond Austin went to school in Poughkeepsie in 1920. His future brother-in-law, Orville Myers, wrote him.

Orville Myers, Eldred, to Raymond Austin, Poughkeepsie, N.Y.
February 26, 1920
Dear Raymond,
We got snow on Monday and we got snow for Tuesday and for a change we got snow Wednesday, and so as to break from the old routine, we got snow on Thursday and for another change we got snow the rest of the week.
Orville Myers

In March, Mort and Jennie Austin received an invitation from the American Legion.

Boarding House Season, 1920

At Yulan there has been no let up in the season since it began in earnest, about the middle of July. Although many guests went back the end of July, August vacationists are more than filling the places vacated.

At Highland Lake, the fish are biting better than they did in previous years and many anglers are summering at the resorts to partake of their favorite sport.

Other houses mentioned: Bodine Cottage; Yulan Cottage; Highland Cottage; Bradley House, Eldred; Sunset View; Mills House, and Park View.—Brooklyn Daily Eagle, *August 8, 1920.*

American Legion, Monticello, N.Y., to Mort and Jennie Austin
March 14, 1920
Celebration and Reunion and presentation of the French Memorial Certificates held at Monticello, N.Y., on May 14, 1920, at 11 o'clock.
In the afternoon, the inscription on the monument will be unveiled...preceded by a parade of ex service men, G.A.R., D.A.R., firemen, Monument Association, Red Cross, cadets, several bands, and other organizations.
French Government Official War Certificates will be presented to the nearest of kin.

The Parker/Schoonover Family
Chapter 1 of *Echo Hill and Mountain Grove* started with Rowlee Schoonover telling about his father Perry Schoonover taking him on a raft trip down the Delaware River.

You probably recall that after Perry's first wife Ann Mary

Austin died, Perry married Mary Murray Parker, a widow with 3 children. Perry and Mary also had 2 children, Rowlee and Emily.

Will and Emily Waidler lived in Cairo, New York. Their Green Farm was probably sold in 1920. George Parker lived with the Waidlers.

In the summers Kate Parker lived with her niece Ada Britt Wood, her husband Arthur Wood, and their daughter Norma Beverly Wood. Kate's other niece, Kitty Britt James and her husband William James had a son, Elwood James.

After the war Rowlee had taken a job in Santo Domingo maintaining cars under contract.

When Rowlee returned to the States (after a series of negotiations), he worked again as a chauffeur for Rev. Douglas.

In June 1920 Justina Schoonover, daughter of Daniel Rowlee and Emily Banner Schoonover, married Solomon Deyo Hull, son of George and Alice Deyo Hull. (Alice was a widow at the time of the wedding.)

Justina's parents: Rowlee and Emily Schoonover; siblings: William, Ethel, and Mary Murray Schoonover; Aunt Kate Parker; and cousins: William, Kitty Britt, and Elwood James, and Arthur R. and Ada Britt Wood attended the wedding.

Deyo and Justina Hull spent their honeymoon on the farm in Cairo owned by Justina's uncle Will and aunt Emily Waidler.

We will meet some of Perry and Mary's descendants again in Book 3, including Rowlee who eventually returns to Eldred.

Several of our Town of Highland friends died in 1920: William Owen died at the age of 63 (he had been a mail carrier for Yulan/Eldred); Fridolin Straub died at age 57; Austin friend Tom K. Collins died at the age of 76; and Helen Bradley, 44, second wife of Atwell Bradley, died.

Amelia Bradley Gregory

Atwell Bradley's sister Amelia Bradley Gregory lived in Colorado with her husband Eber Gregory and their children Charlie and Nora Gregory.

We will meet Amelia again in Book 3, when she visits her hometown. My uncle Bob Austin remembered her visit.

Hazel Leavenworth Marries Eugene Koenig

In Chapter 10, Amelia's daughter Hazel Alice Leavenworth worked at Irwin National Bank in New York City. When Hazel was offered a teaching job in Dunton, Colorado, she resigned herself to becoming an old maid, and left New York City.

1920

The United States population topped 100 million in 1920.

The first radio broadcast was in Pittsburgh, Pennsylvania.

Jennie Austin enjoyed listening to the radio as we shall learn from one of her letters in Book Three.

In 1920 the jobs in the area were: farmer, electrician, laborer, store keeper, worker at steel corporation, teamster, mason stone worker, blacksmith, carpenter, shoemaker, mailman, wood chopper, garage owner, watchman, dairy farms, saw mill, wood lumberer, telegraph or telephone operator, superintendent of highways, railroad worker, Supervisor of Highland, cutter at glass factory, waitress, chauffeur, bookkeeper, truck driver, musical instructor, instrument maker, officer on sailing vessel, and of course housekeeper.

Hazel Leavenworth married Eugene Koenig in June 1920. Photo courtesy of Marialyce Koenig Kornkven.

Amelia Bradley Gregory in the middle of the photo with the dark wrap. Eugene Koenig is to the right of Amelia. Photo courtesy of Marialyce Koenig Kornkven.

But Hazel had a nice surprise awaiting her—Eugene Koenig. Eugene, from Milwaukee, Wisconsin, was a foreman at the Rosebud Silver Mine, in Dunton.

My dad, Eugene Koenig was born in Ironwood, Michigan, March 24, 1890. He was an electrician.

Eugene became acquainted with mines as a scout for the mines his dad was promoting.

He learned assaying at a school in Los Angeles. Then he worked 2 years at Reward Mine to learn the business. At Yucca, Arizona, he did mill and assay work for 2 years, and was paid good wages.

Eugene quit working in Yucca when WWI broke out, but was not drafted because the County's quota was up. He did do work as a foreman in a TNT factory during WWI.

His father became interested in the Rosebud Mine in Dunton, Colorado, and sent him there. —Gerald Koenig.

In June 1920, Eugene Koenig and Hazel Leavenworth were married. The newlyweds moved to Milwaukee, Wisconsin, the next year.

My mother [Hazel Koenig] did not learn to read until she was over 10 years old. She proved an excellent student; I saw her exam grades for the Colorado teacher's exam and they were tops, yet she never mentioned that to us in all the years we were in school. She was a fast talker, a fast thinker, and loved to read and learn.

My father used to tutor her in science subjects they were interested in. He had even less eduction, but could learn anything.

Eugene went to Milwaukee to work for Newport Chemical Co. in Carrolville.—Gerald Koenig.

Descendants of Harriet Palmer
Edith Ewart (daughter of Harriet Leavenworth Palmer) lived in Detroit. Edith's children: Victor and Kathryn Ewart had 2 children; Willard's wife had died in 1919; Millie had graduated as a student nurse at Children's Free Hospital in Detroit, in 1919; Elliot and Rolland were still single.

Harriet's son Harry Palmer ran a grocery store. He and his wife Lydia lived in Chicago.

Calkin Family in Bethel
In 1920 Ell Austin's daughter Lillie and her husband Burt Calkin lived in Bethel, New York (population 1,849), with Robert Dale, 9, and Dot, 6 (in December). Cousin Lillie taught school in Bethel.

Charles Dassori, Los Angeles, Calif., to Mort Austin, Eldred
July 7, 1920
Dear friend,
The climate here is fine. We enjoyed the trip very much. A letter will follow shortly. We are all well, trusting you are all the same.

Love to all from all. Friend,
Chas. Dassori

Charles Dassori, Scranton, Pa., to Mort Austin
August 30, 1920
Dear friend Mort,
Well here I am again Mort, in Scranton, Pa. Say Mort, do you think there is any prospects of my securing a position in Yulan?

I do not like it here in Scranton, Pennsylvania, and Gussie said she is willing to go to Yulan if there is any way of my making a living for the family.

The reason of suggesting that place is, she would like to be near the church. I am also stuck on Eldred. I think between you and I, we ought to be able to dope out some kind of business to go into and make good. Have you anything in mind Mort we could venture in?

California is a pretty state of what I have seen, but I couldn't get rooms there. The climate there is just grand. Mort, I also have the name and address of the Land Commissioner who has charge of the sale of land (farms)

Eldred Family, 1920

Herbert Lincoln Eldred was a descendant of C.C.P. and Effa Eldred. Herbert and his wife Eliza Post lived in Eldred, New York. They had three children at home. Their daughter Bertha Eldred was married to Norman Myers, and they had two young sons. Herbert and Eliza's son, George Ely Eldred married Bertha Hill, daughter of Thomas and Alice Sergeant Hill.

John Franklin and Lewis Laforde Eldred were sons of Frank and Almira Barnes Eldred. Frank Eldred's parents were Mulford and Elizabeth Wheeler Eldred.

John Franklin and Minnie Sears Eldred's son, Orvis Rutledge Eldred would be the father of Richard Orvis Eldred who wrote, *The Eldred Family.*

Lewis Laforde and Cora Sisson Eldred lived in Carbondale, Pennsylvania. In February 1920, Cora died during the Spanish influenza epidemic. Lewis's 9 children were also sick with the Spanish flu. Son Harvey Eldred would be the father of Martha Eldred Worzel.—*Eldred, p. 103.*

Velvet Cake

1 cup grated chocolate or cocoa
1/2 cup hot water over to melt it
1-1/3 cups brown sugar
1/2 cup butter
1/2 cup sweet milk
3 eggs—separate yolks and whites
2 cups flour
3 ts. baking powder
1 ts. soda dissolved in a little hot water

Cream sugar and butter.
Add chocolate, egg yolks, milk, soda.
Add flour with baking powder
Add whites of eggs beaten stiff.
Bake 25 minutes in moderate oven.
Mrs. W.M.S.
—*Recipe from Jennie Austin's scrapbook.*

Others in the 1920 Census

Morgan Sergeant, a carpenter, his wife Alice and his sister-in-law Ellen Spiers, lived on Airport Road.

Frank Sergeant, a millwright in a sawmill, his second wife Anna Hull and her sister Jennie Hull lived on Highland Lake Road; as did Edgar, Henrietta, and Edith Sergeant.

Walter Styles, 58, Librarian, his wife Georgia Clark, 30, and his parents Charles and Sarah Styles lived on Proctor Road.

Frank LaBarr was a dairy farmer. He and his wife Mabel had 4 children.

Annie Rothman, 55, lived near Mort and Jennie Austin.

Edwin LaBarr worked at a sawmill. His wife's name was Bessie. His mother Caroline was a widow.

Charles Ort lived with his parents, Frank and Mary Ort. Frank was a shoemaker.

William Ort, a teamster, and his wife Bertha LaBarr had 4 children: Eleanor, William, Florence, and John.

Carl, Albert, Norman, and Anna Wolff were children of Charles and Janette Wolff. Carl would marry Frieda Kloss, sister of Lou Kloss whose *Memoirs* we have read.

Harry Wormuth and Mary Kyte were married. Harry was a sawyer at a lumbermill, probably his own.

A descendant of Felix and Eliza Kyte, Frank Crouch Kyte, had married Hazel A. Robinson in 1918.

Verna, Stanley, and Clifford were the children of Robert and Nellie Crandall. Two of Maggie Dunlap's sons lived with her. George was a herdsman at a dairy barn. Harold was a laborer cutting logs and would have the Dunlap Restaurant in Eldred. Charles Dunlap, Maggie's other son, was married to Selma.

Jackson Myers was a merchant with a general store. He and his wife Jessie had 4 children. Louis Basque had worked for Gus Myers in 1910. In 1920, Louis Basque lived with Jackson and Jessie Myers and worked as a salesman in a general store.

Emma Clouse was a widow. Her son Roy was a carpenter at a dairy farm. Her son Ralph was a salesman at a general store.

John Weber from Bavaria was a sawyer at a lumber mill, as was Edward Fish. George Beck, 74, was an artist/sculptor.

Samuel Hallock was a lumberer. He and his wife Anna Buchanan had 9 sons, ages 3 to 21. Their only daughter Eunice Hallock was married to Ernest Clark. Stella Adelaide Clark, daughter of Ernest and Eunice Hallock Clark, was born January 21, 1920, in Tylertown, New York. Ernest, Eunice, and Stella lived at the home of his parents, John Henry and Carrie Etta Bogert Clark.

Lottie Myers (daughter of Jane Ann Myers) and her husband Charles Darling lived in Binghamton, New York. Their daughter Ida and her husband Walter Whitmarsh lived with them.

Stephen A. and Charlotte E. Myers were the parents of Kathryn, Stanley, and Marie.

George Foster was a lumber teamster. He and Jennie Hallock Foster had 13 children, including Herbert Foster, future father of Douglas Foster who would marry Dorothy Knecht.

Wilson and Ida Davis Knecht had moved from Pittston, Pennsylvania, to Shohola, in 1919. Wilson and Ida would be the grandparents of Emily Knecht Hallock and Dorothy Knecht Foster.

James and Cora Clark had Grandson Alvin living with them. James was an edger in a sawmill. John and Kate Love lived west of Eldred. He was a lumberman.

Charles and Jennie Traver and their young sons, John and Charles lived in Barryville.

Emerson, Ezra (Buck), Walter, and Mabel were children of Sherman and Eliza McBride.

August Clouse, a carpenter, lived with his son Frederick, also a carpenter, and his wife Emma and their sons, Joseph and Raymond.

Susan Gardner, daughter of James E. and Rebecca Rider Gardner, was a sales person at a grocery store.

Maria Gardner Calkin, a widow, lived with her daughter Lillie.

John H. and Katherine Greening Kerr were the proud parents of Charlie Kerr born in December 1920.

Dora Schumacher, a widow, lived with her son Harry, granddaughter Lillian Schumacher, and servant Katie Glaab.

Edward and Catharine Schumacher had two sons, Charles and Arthur.

Milton Crandall, a widower, lived with his son Lawrence, his wife Matilda, their son Leonard, and Milton's daughters Bertha and Amy.

John and Esther Hill and their family lived on Board Road. John Hill was a machinist on a dairy farm. Their daughter Agnes was a seamstress in an underwear factory; son Edgar worked at a hat factory. John and Esther Hill's other children: Gladys, Lena, Edna, and twins, Alvin and Alfred.

On Yulan Mail Road: Frank and Katherine Owen and 5 children; Thomas and Myrtle Hill and daughter; Thomas and Alice Hill and son; George and Alice Carner and nephew; Katherine Fleiger and grandson John; and Herman and Isabel Barber.

On River Road: Ella Watson and her brother George; Fred Freeman, Town of Highland Supervisor; and Frank and Mary Wolff. Frank was a cutter at the glass factory

William Wait was 72; his wife Carrie was 58. Her mother Phebe Parker lived with them.

Napoleon B. and Fannie White Quick were the parents of Ralph, Blanche, and Horton Quick; and the grandparents of Ruth Worzel Myers, a good friend of my mother.

The Parker Hotel, northwest of the original James Eldred house. Photo courtesy of Christena Stevens Myers.

Art Austin petting a calf. Photo courtesy of Mary Briggs Austin.

owned by the Atchison, Topeka, and Santa Fe Company at very reasonable prices and terms—from Kansas to Arizona.

How is things going with you Mort? How is the family? We are all enjoying good health, thank God, and trust you are all doing the same.

I remain, Your true friend,
Chas. S. Dassori

Town of Highland, 1920

As this book closes in 1920, Boarding Houses have become a major form of financial support for those in the Town of Highland's hamlets. The Houses would continue into the 1960s. Some new ones would be built. Some would change names or owners, some would burn down and would not be rebuilt.

Gone were the larger lumber companies and the D&H Canal first mentioned in *The Mill on Halfway Brook*. Family sawmills continue, and a larger one, Narrowsburg Lumber Company, would start in 1927.

Farewell to Eldred

Book 3, *Farewell to Eldred*, is the final book in the series, *Memoirs from Eldred, New York, 1800–1950*. It gives the account of my relatives, the Leavenworths and Austins, their families and friends, and the boarding houses in the Town of Highland from 1920 until 1950, when my parents move to Michigan.

Garfield and Ella Sergeant Leavenworth and their children, Clara, Clinton, and Anna Leavenworth (in Easthampton, Massachusetts) move back to Eldred. Their son James Roberts—the future father of Cynthia, David, and Nancy—is born. Gisele Rouillon, the future Mrs. James Leavenworth, is born in Paris.

Echo Hill Farm House continues for some years. We will meet Charlee Hirsch, the daughter of Anthony and Christina Leavenworth Hirsch.

We will keep updated with the descendants of John and Amelia Bradley Leavenworth, and Harriet Palmer Leavenworth.

Mort and Jennie Austin continue to run Mountain Grove House another 15 years. Both happy and very sad times are ahead for Mort and Jennie and their family: Raymond, William, Elizabeth, Art, and Bob.

Raymond Austin will marry Gladys Myers, daughter of Edwin and Mabel Owen Myers. They will have 4 wonderful daughters—Melva, Joan, Margie, and Dawn Lee—grandchildren for Mort and Jennie Austin and Edwin and Mabel Owen Myers.

Lon, Ell, and Aida Austin continue to be a part of the story as does Lillie Austin Calkin and her family.

The Briggs family, including my mom Mary Briggs (3 weeks old) head east from Nebraska. But it is another 10 years before they finally arrive in Barryville, where Irwin pastors the Pond Eddy, Barryville, and Eldred Methodist Churches.

There is another horrendous war. Art, Bill, and Bob Austin; their cousin Jim Leavenworth; distant cousin Martin D. Myers; friend Chuck Myers, and many others from the area fight in another World War.

Farewell to Eldred is the story of the daily lives of friends and relatives, both new and old, as told by photos, scrapbooks, postcards, letters, diaries, documents, yearbooks, and stories that have very fortunately been preserved by family and the many friends and relatives of those who once lived in the Town of Highland.

The Brook Song

View of Leavenworth home from Blind Pond Brook. Photo courtesy of Cynthia Leavenworth Bellinger.

The Introduction to this book, *Echo Hill and Mountain Grove*, started with the poem, *The Brook Song*, by James Whitcomb Riley. You may remember, Elizabeth Austin wrote the poem in her mother Jennie Austin's scrapbook of recipes and poems.

Brooks played an important part in the Town of Highland and in the lives of my ancestors.

In *The Mill on Halfway Brook*, the James Eldred family settled at the end of 1815, in an old cabin with a sawmill, near the middle of Halfway Brook. That location would later be the southeast corner of the village of Eldred.

James Eldred was Charles Mortimer Austin's grandfather. Mort Austin (born in 1865) grew up in the Austin homestead that was to the east of Halfway Brook.

Blind Pond Brook went behind the Leavenworth home where Jennie Leavenworth Austin was born in 1880.

*Little brook! Little brook!
You have such a happy look
Such a very merry manner, as you
    swerve and curve and crook.
And your ripples, one and one,
Reach each other's hands and run
Like laughing little children in
    the sun!*

*Little brook sing to me;
Sing about the bumblebee
That tumbled from a lily bell and
    grumbled mumblingly,
Because he wet the film
Of his wings, and had to swim,
While the water bugs raced round
    and laughed at him.*

*Little brook, sing a song
Of a leaf that sailed along
Down the golden-hearted center of
    your current swift and strong,
And a dragon fly that lit
On the tilting rim of it,
And rode away and wasn't scared
    a bit.*

*And sing, how oft in glee
Came a truant boy like me,
Who loved to lean and listen to your
    lilting melody,
Till the gurgle and refrain
Of your music in his brain
Wrought a happiness as keen to him
    as pain.*

*Little brook, laugh and leap!
Do not let the dreamer weep:
Sing him all the songs of summer till he
    sink in softest sleep;
And then sing soft and low
Through his dreams of long ago
Sing back to him the rest he used to
    know!*

The Brook Song by James Whitcomb Riley. Written by Elizabeth Austin for third grade in her mother Jennie Austin's scrapbook.

Bibliography

Books and Booklets

Abbott, John N.,
Mountain Lake and Cataract: Summer Homes and Rambles Along the Erie Railway, New York, Lake Erie and Western Railroad Company, Hopcraft & Co. N.Y., 1882 and 1883
Summer Excursion Routes, New York, Lake Erie & Western Railroad, Sunshine Publishing Company, Philadelphia, 1881
Summer Homes and Rambles on the Picturesque Erie, New York; Lake Erie & Western R.R., 1886
Summer Homes and Rambles on the Picturesque Erie, New York, Lake Erie & Western R.R., 1885, Google Digital Book

Barber, J. Frank (Chairman),
History of the Seventy-ninth Division U.S. Army A.E.F., 1917–1920, Steinman & Steinman, Lancaster, PA, 1922

Beers & Co., J.H. (pub.), *Commemorative Biographical Record of Northeastern Pennsylvania*, Chicago, 1900

Eldred, Richard O.,
The Eldred Family: Elisha Eldred of Minisink, New York, and His Descendants, Baltimore: Gateway Press, Inc., 1988

Erie Railway Tourist, Erie Railway Company, 1874

Farmer, L.P.,
Picturesque Erie Summer Homes, Passenger Department, N.Y., L.E. & W.R.R., 1888 and 1890
Picturesque Erie Summer Homes, Passenger Department, N.Y., L.E. & W.R.R., 1889, Google Digital Book

Fluhr, George J.,
Pike County, 1975
Quarries, Kilgour, and Pike County, PA, 1984
Rohman's Inn, Shohola Glen Hotel, a History, 1999
Shohola: History of a Township, 1992

Fluhr, George J., and McKay, John S., *An illustrated Historic Survey of Shohola Township, 1979*

Gansser, Emil B., *History of the 126th Infantry in the War with Germany*, Grand Rapids, Michigan, 1920

Ireland, Maj. Gen. M.W.,
The Medical Department of the U.S. Army in the World War, Vol. 8, 1925

Johnston, John Willard,
Reminiscences, Town of Highland Cultural Resources Commission, 1987

Moss, Col. Jas. A., and Howland, Col. Harry S.,
America In Battle: With Guide to the American Battlefield in France and Belgium, Geo. Banta Publishing Co., Menasha, Wisconsin, 1920

Osterberg, Matthew M.,
Matamoras to Shohola, Arcadia Publishing, 2002
The Delaware and Hudson Canal and the Gravity Railroad, Arcadia Publishing, 2003

Smith, Louise E.,
Aida Austin's 1881 Diary, Halfway Brook, 2010
Grandma and Me, Austin-Smith Books, 2007
The Mill on Halfway Brook, Halfway Brook, 2010

Whan, Clara Jean Briggs, *Briggs Heritage*, 1985

Other Information Sources

A Century of Church Life: Centennial of the First Congregational Church of Eldred Celebrated, "The Tri-States Union," Vol. XLIX. No. 33. Port Jervis, N.Y., August 17, 1899

Historic Walking/Driving Tour of Barryville, New York, Highland Renaissance/Highland Pride, 2007

Barber, Gertrude A.,
Records of the First Congregational Church in the Town of Lumberland, Sullivan County, New York
Records of the Barryville Congregational Church, 1836 to 1927
Record of the Methodist Episcopal Church, Barryville, N.Y., 1931

Congregational Church Centennial (1899) booklet

Methodist Centennial and 150-Year booklets

Werman, Edey, *Sullivan County Cemeteries*: usgwarchives.org/ny/sullivan/cemeteries/cemeterytoc.htm

Website Sources of Interest

Books (old) on CD: betweenthelakes.com
Conway, John, *Retrospect:* sullivanretrospect.com
Encyclopedia online: wikipedia.org
Halfway Brook *Publishing*: halfwaybrook.com
Minisink Valley Historical Society: minisink.org
Office of Medical History: history.amedd.army.mil
Old New York Newspapers: fultonhistory.com/Futon.html
Proctor Family: sandpond.org
Shohola Area History: shohola.org
Sullivan County Historical Society: sullivancountyhistory.org
Town of Bethel: townofbethel.com
Town of Highland: townofhighlandny.com
Town of Lumberland: townoflumberland.org
Upper Delaware Scenic Byway: upperdelawarescenicbyway.org
World War I History: worldwar1.com

Appendix

Charles Mortimer Austin Ancestors 438

Jennie Louisa Leavenworth Ancestors.. 439

Some Austin Descendants 440

Some Leavenworth Descendants.. 441

Some Bradley Descendants 442

Some Rev. Isaac Sergeant Descendants 443

Some James and Polly Mulford Eldred Descendants.. 444

Some Abel Sprague Myers Descendants 445

News Articles about Stephen St. John Gardner and his Family 445

Leavenworth Family Memorabilia.. 446

Poems in Mary Ann Austin's Scrapbook.. 449

Wm. Henry and Mary Ann Austin Family Letters, etc. 451

Mort Austin's Autograph Book 453

Mort Austin Letters and Documents 456

Aida Austin's Autograph Book... 458

William and McKinley Austin's Report Cards 461

McKinley Austin, World War I 462

History of the 11th Infantry 465

Letters to Mort and Jennie Austin on McKinley's Death 466

Mountain Grove House 468

Headstones in the Old Eldred Cemetery... 469

Charles Mortimer Austin Ancestors

4 Ralph AUSTIN
b. 16 May 1784
bp. Connecticut
m. 25 Dec 1806
mp. Greenwich, Connecticut
d. 4 Jun 1863
dp. Westchester Co., New York

William Henry AUSTIN
b. 13 Mar 1824
bp. Westchester Co., New York
m. 9 Jan 1849
mp. Halfway Brook, Sullivan Co., New York
d. 6 Apr 1909
dp. Eldred, Sullivan Co., New York

5 Fanny KNAPP
b. 29 Apr 1788
bp. Stamford, Connecticut
d. 6 Jun 1861
dp. Halfway Brook, Sullivan Co., New York

Charles Mortimer AUSTIN
b. 27 Mar 1865
bp. Halfway Brook, Sullivan Co., New York
m. 14 Oct 1897
mp. Barryville, New York
d. 4 Jun 1937
dp. Eldred, Sullivan Co., New York

6 James ELDRED
b. 7 Oct 1777
bp. Minisink, Orange Co., New York
m. 12 Feb 1826
mp. Halfway Brook, Sullivan Co., New York
d. 12 Apr 1857
dp. Halfway Brook, Sullivan Co., New York

Mary Ann ELDRED
b. 3 Dec 1827
bp. Halfway Brook, Sullivan Co., New York
d. 5 Oct 1906
dp. Eldred, Sullivan Co., New York

7 Hannah HICKOK
b. 18 Jul 1789
bp. Southbury, Litchfield Co., Connecticut
d. 2 Apr 1869
dp. Halfway Brook, Sullivan Co., New York

8 Joshua AUSTIN
b. 1748
bp.
m.
mp.
d. Jul 1828
dp.

9 Mary
b. 1758
bp.
d. 1809
dp.

10 Samuel KNAPP
b. 29 Dec 1768
bp. Stamford, Connecticut
m. 29 Nov 1787
mp. Stamford, Connecticut
d.
dp.

11 Naomi PALMER
b. abt 1766
bp.
d. 1827
dp. Stamford, Connecticut

12 Elisha ELDRED
b. 15 Feb 1753
bp. New England
m. abt 1775
mp.
d. 18 Oct 1804
dp. Minisink, Orange Co., New York

13 Mary HULSE
b. 20 Jan 1755
bp.
d. 18 Sep 1837
dp. Halfway Brook, Sullivan Co., New York

14 Asa HICKOK
b. 4 Jun 1754
bp. Woodbury, Litchfield Co., Connecticut
m. 29 Dec 1777
mp. Woodbury, Litchfield Co., Connecticut
d. 23 Mar 1836
dp. Bradford Co., Pennsylvania

15 Hester (Esther) HINMAN
b. 23 Oct 1759
bp. South Britain, New Haven Co., Connecticut
d. 23 Apr 1844
dp. Bradford Co., Pennsylvania

16 Joshua AUSTIN
b. Feb 1718/19
d. 10 Oct 1801

17 Tryphena HATHAWAY
b. 17 Jun 1729
d. 2 May 1802

18 b. d.

19 b. d.

20 Samuel KNAPP Sr
b. 9 May 1744
d. 22 Dec 1810

21 Susannah SCOFIELD
b.
d.

22 b. d.

23 b. d.

24 ELDRED
b.
d.

25 b. d.

26 James HULSE
b. abt 1728
d. abt 1791

27 Mary ARNOT
b. 1731
d. 1784

28 Justice HICKOK
b.
d.

29 b. d.

30 Ebenezer HINMAN
b.
d.

31 b. d.

Jennie Louisa Leavenworth Ancestors

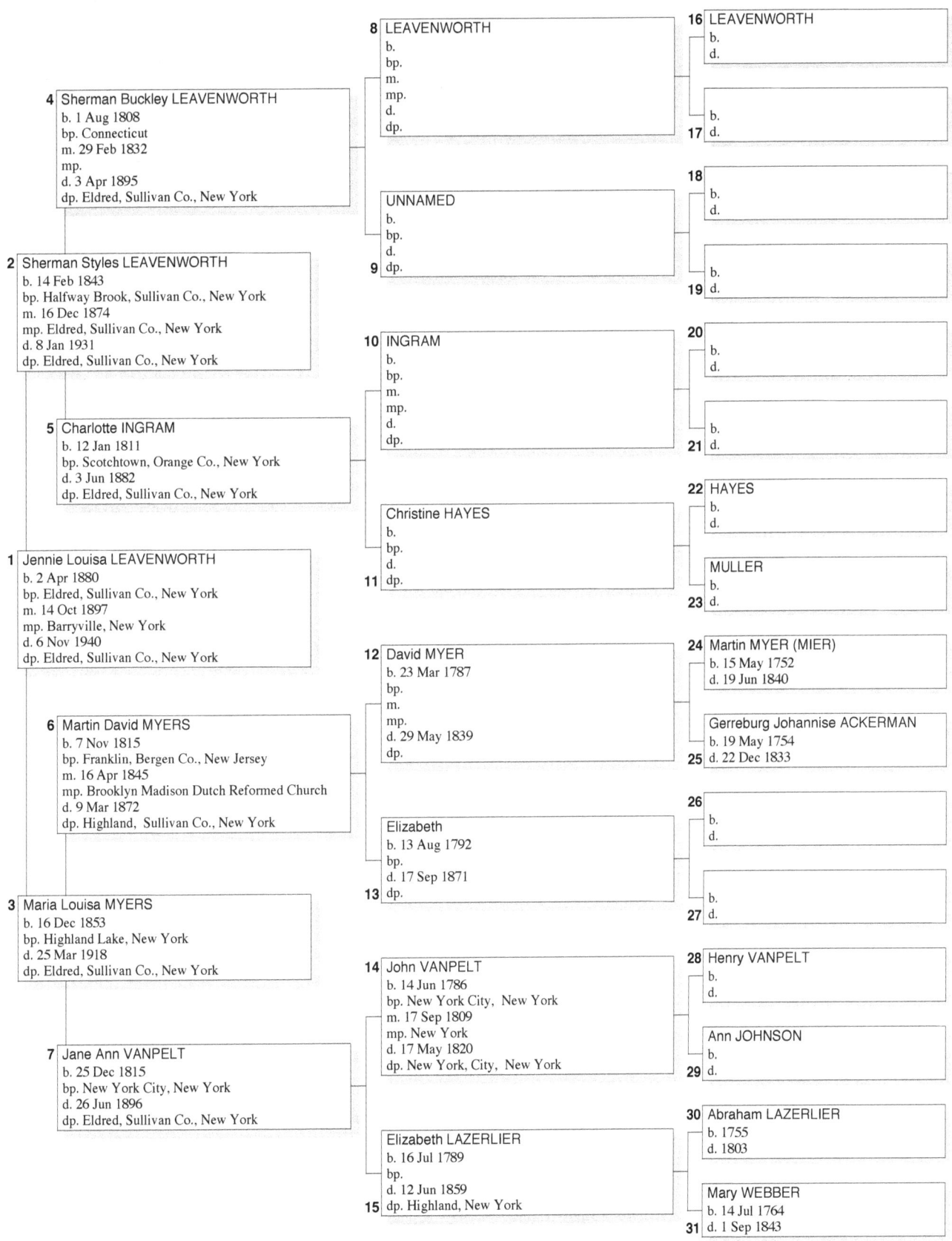

Some Austin Descendants

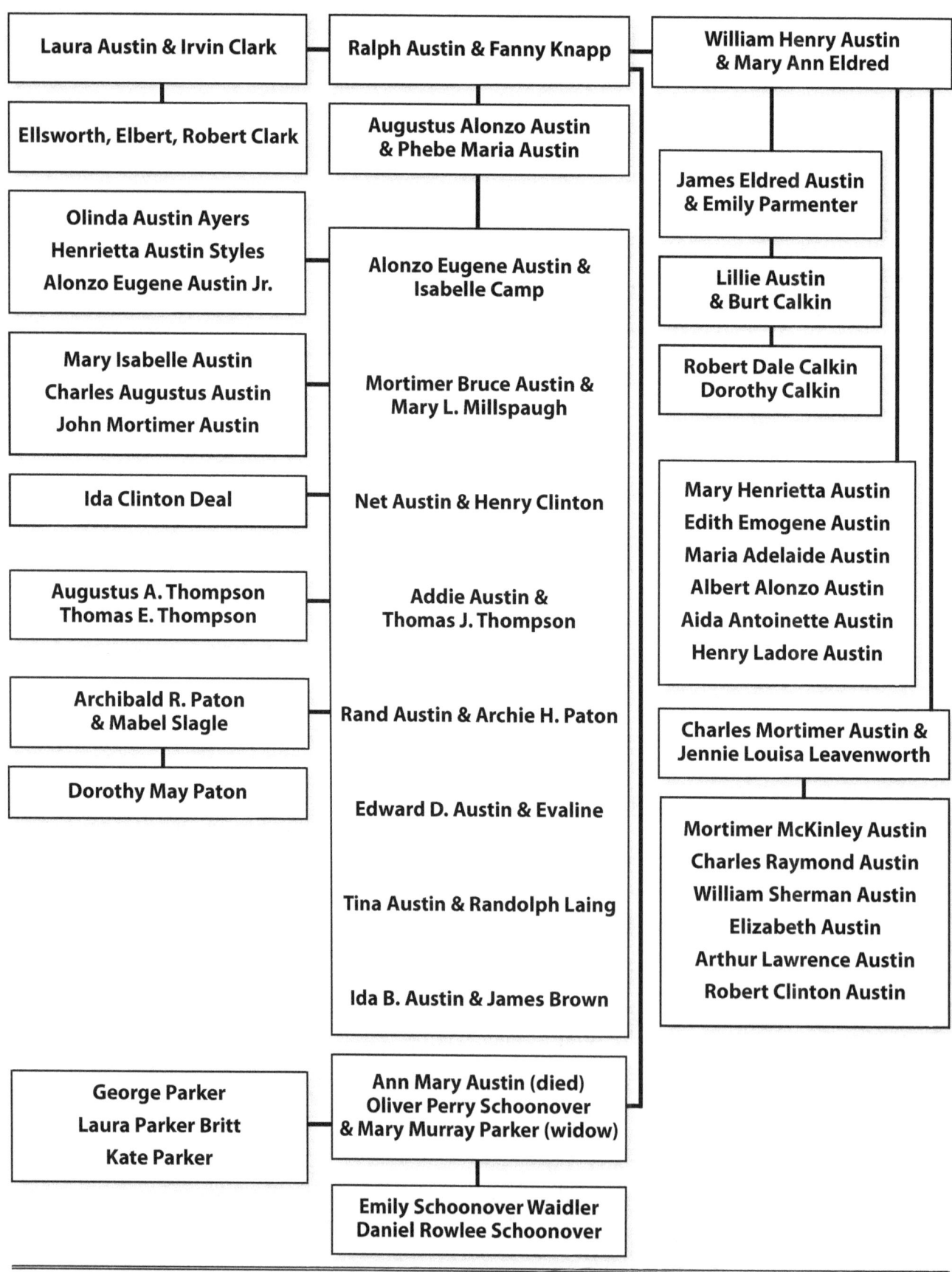

Some Leavenworth Descendants

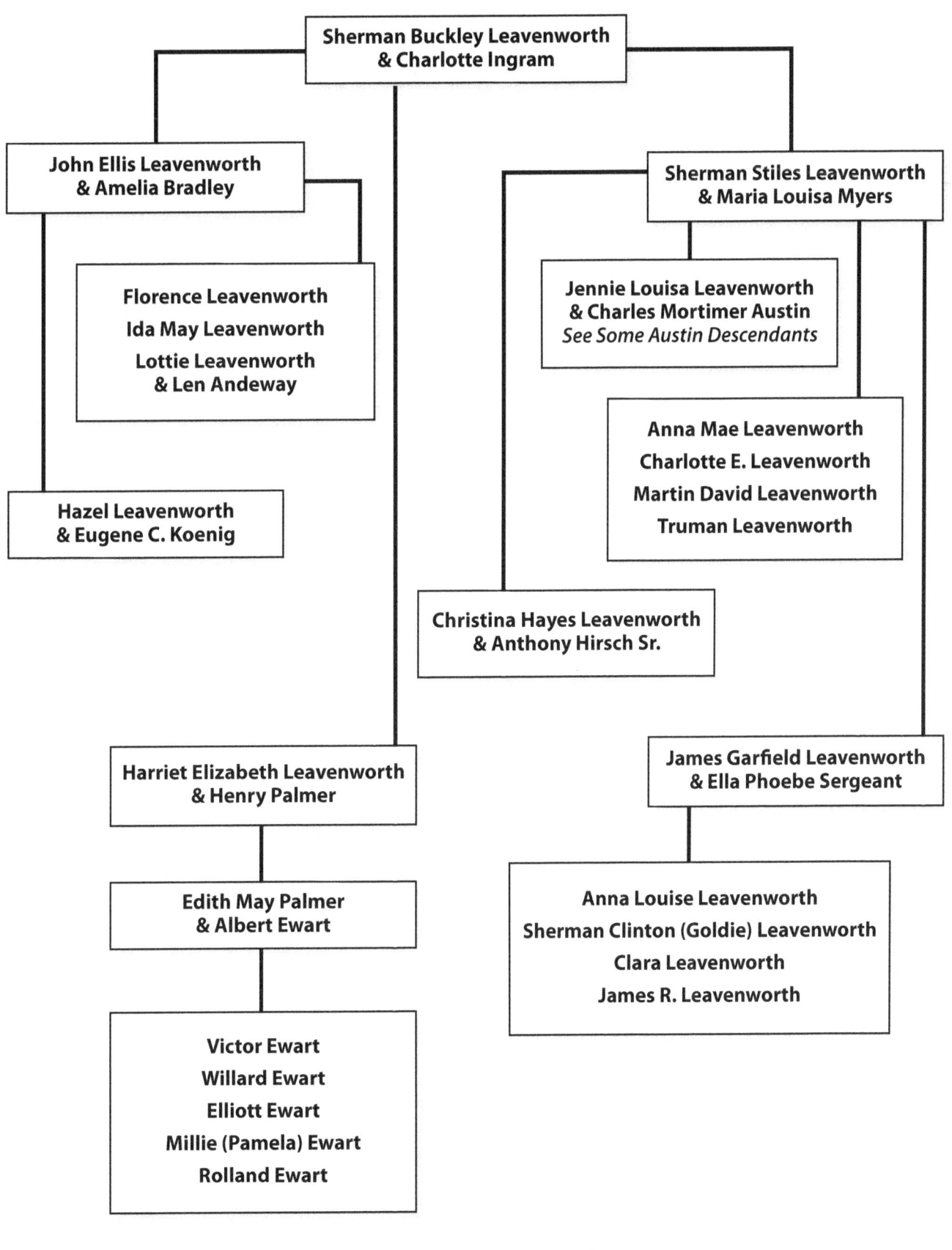

Some Bradley Descendants

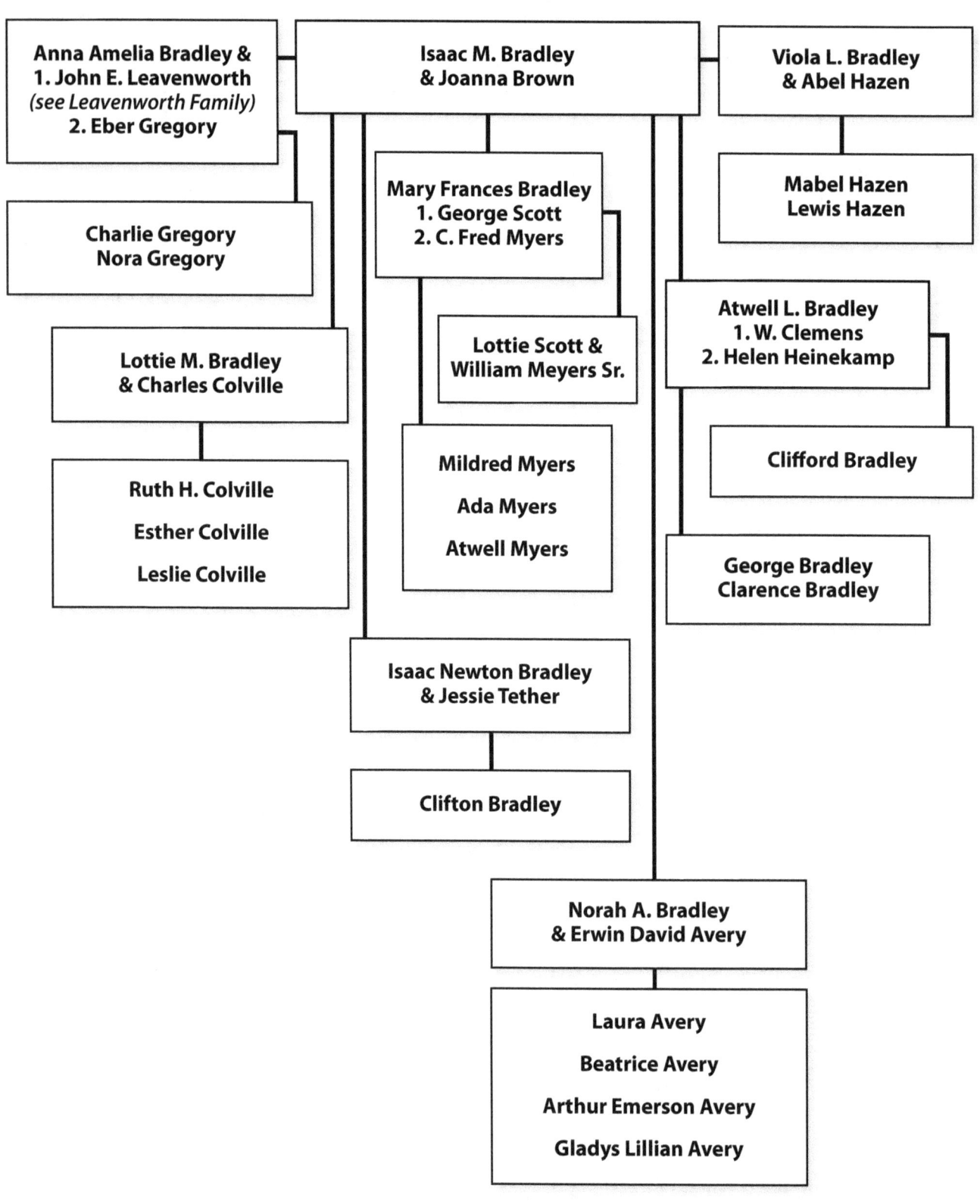

Some Rev. Isaac Sergeant Descendants

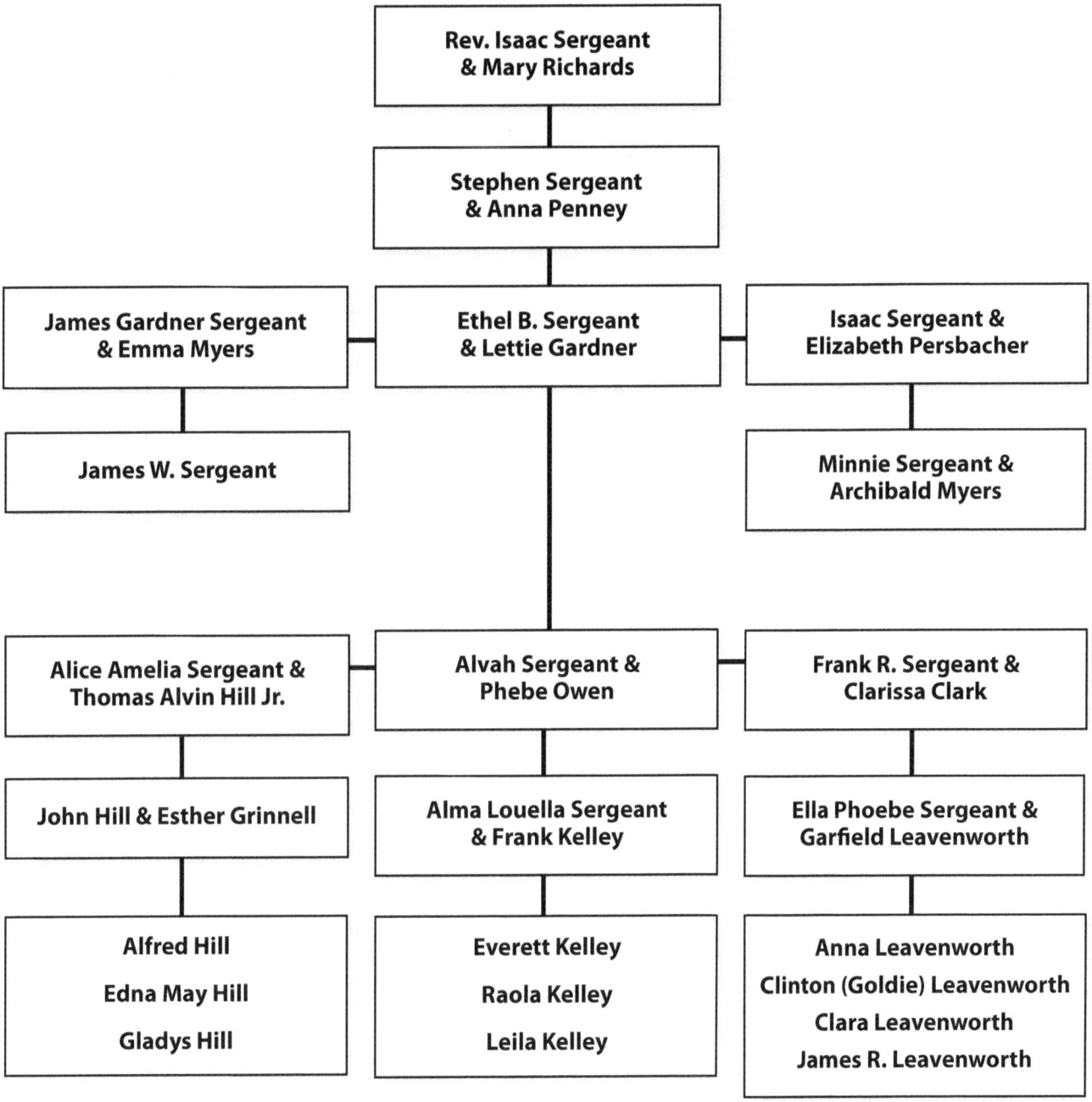

Some James Eldred and Polly V. Mulford Descendants

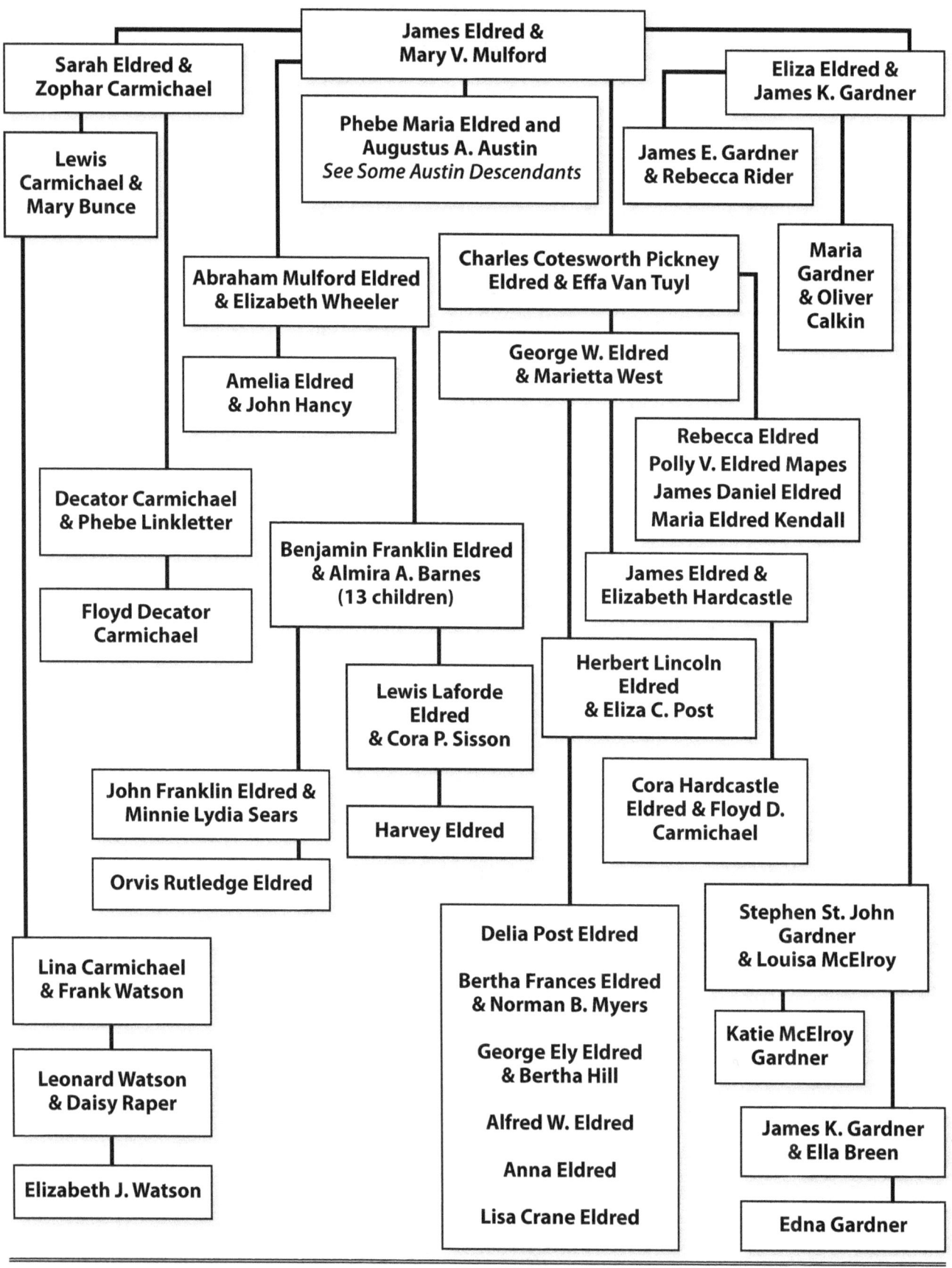

Some Abel Sprague Myers Descendants

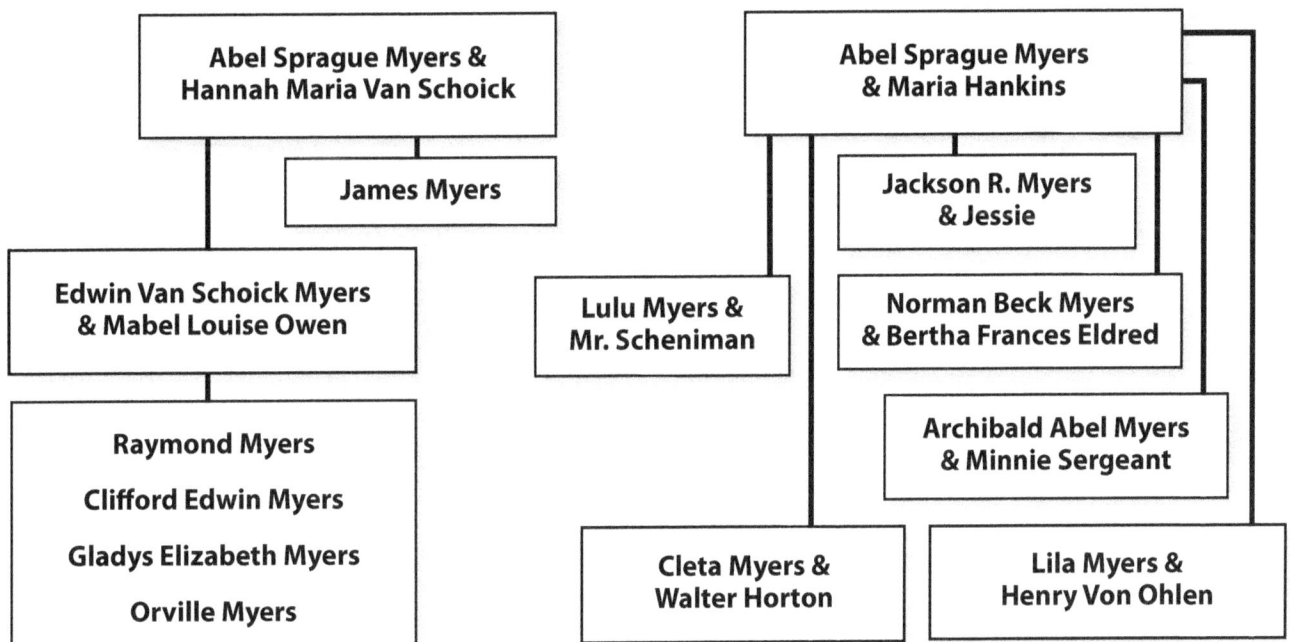

News Articles about Stephen St. John Gardner and Family

Scarlet Fever at Barryville
The district school at Barryville has been closed on account of the Scarlet Fever. There has been four deaths in that place from it, three of them were members of the school. The first was Mina Cortright, 16 years of age, who had just won a prize of $10 for the best attendance scholarship and deportment. The teacher and scholars attended the funeral on the 2nd and the next night Lizzie, daughter of Jacob Beck, aged 7 years died, and she was not buried when Herbert, youngest son of Hon. S. St. John Gardner, died.—Republican Watchman, *December 17, 1880.*

Mary L. Gardner Dies
Mary L., youngest daughter of Stephen St. John Gardener, died on Monday of last week in her 13th year, and was buried the following Wednesday in the Eldred Cemetery. The parents and relatives of the deceased have our sincere sympathy…

Mr. Christian has completed the dam across the Halfway Brook. He expects to build a saw and gristmill during the coming year.
—Republican Watchman, *December 26, 1884.*

Stephen St. John Gardner Running for County Member of Assembly
For the Assembly no more fit or deserving man could have been found than Stephen St. John Gardner…

Mr. Gardner is a businessman of the village in which he resides and has many warm friends in the western towns. In 1861 he was elected to the Assembly and served in that body in the year 1862. He was the youngest member of the body, yet his record of services was of the highest character and one of which his constituents were justly proud. He is a man of fine intellectual attainments and is looked upon in all the country in which he has been engaged in business as the poor man and laborers' friend. No better nomination could have been made.
—Republican Watchman, *October 1893.*

Margaret Terns Gardner Dies
Margaret, wife of Hon. Stephen St. John Gardner died at her home at Barryville…of apoplexy. She had been on the piazza ten minutes before taken ill…

The deceased was the second wife of Mr. Gardner by whom she is survived and the following step children: James and Katie at home and Myers of California…—Port Jervis Gazette, *1902.*

April 1914 News
Stephen St. John Gardner of Barryville has regained his health and will attend to business.

The glass factory at Barryville is running on full time giving employment to many people in that vicinity.—Republican Watchman, *April 16, 1914*

Leavenworth Family Memorabilia

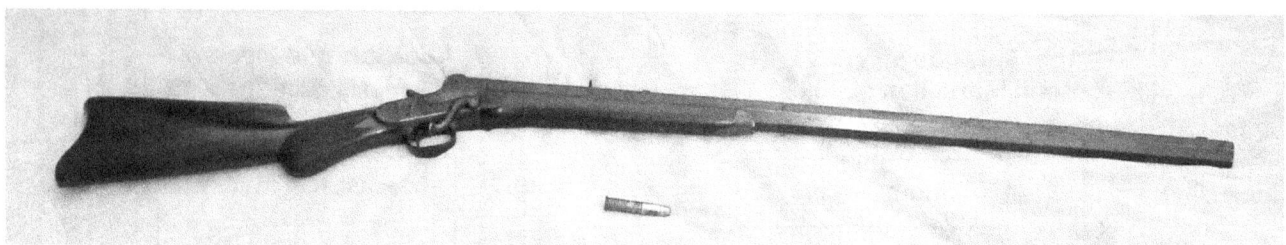

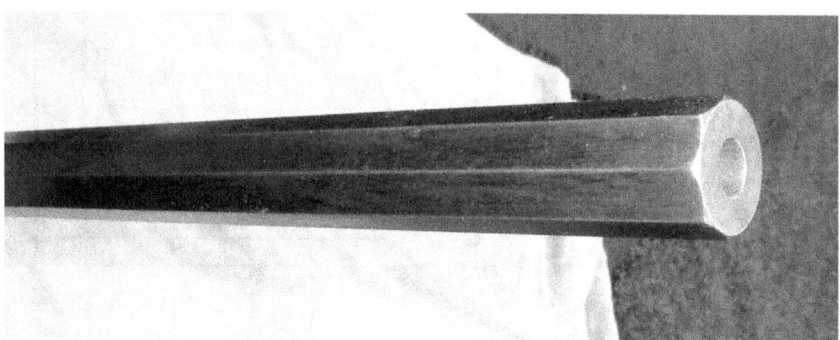

Sherman S. Leavenworth's 1898 Remington Hepburn rifle. Photos courtesy of Norm Bohs.

Death certificate of Sherman B. Leavenworth. Courtesy of Cynthia Leavenworth Bellinger.

OBITUARY.

SHERMAN B. LEAVENWORTH.

Mr. Sherman Buckley Leavenworth, one of the most highly respected citizens of Eldred, Sullivan county, died at his home, in that place, at 3 30 o'clock this morning. Several years ago he sustained a stroke of paralysis, which was followed, at various intervals, by lighter strokes, which ultimately ended in his death.

Mr. Leavenworth was born in Connecticut and was 86 years of age, 60 years of which he resided in Eldred. Upon coming to Eldred he purchased a tract of land, in the clearing of which he immediately engaged. From this land and the improvements made on it by clearing it, he developed one of the most productive farms in that whole district, which consists of about 150 acres.

About 45 years ago he was converted to the Methodist Episcopal church and twenty years ago, joined the Congregational church, at Eldred, of which he was a member at the time of his death.

Three of Mr. Leavneworth's son's served in the war of the Rebellion; Hezekiah, who contracted a disease while in the service, and returned home and died shortly afterwards at Eldred; Atwell, who died during the third year of the the war and was buried in South Carolina, and Samuel, now residing at Eldred

He is survived by two sons, Samuel S. Buckley, at home, with whom he resided and John, of Denver, also by one daughter, Mrs Harriet E. Palmer, wife of Mr. H. W. Palmer, of Port Jervis.

The funeral will take place from his late residence at 3 o'clock on Friday afternoon. Interment at Eldred.

Obituary is courtesy of Carolyn Hallock Clark.

Leavenworth Family Memorabilia (cont'd.)

FAMILY RECORD.

BIRTHS.	BIRTHS.
Anna May, Oct. 5, 1875 Death Oct. 29, 1958	MORTIMER AUSTIN AND Jennie Louisa LEAVENWORTH their Children
Truman Ellis June 1, 1878 Death	McKinley
Jennie Louisa April 2, 1880	Charles Raymond
James Garfield June 22, 1882 Death July 24, 1957	
Martin David June 29 1884	
Charlotte Elizabeth July 25 1889	Jas. Garfield Leavenworth and Ella Sergeant their children
Christina Hayes March 18, 1894	Clara
	Clinton
	Anna
	Jas. GA

Leavenworth Bible page courtesy of Ric Schroedel.

Elizabeth Owen, servant of the Leavenworths in 1880. Photo courtesy of Cynthia Leavenworth Bellinger.

Leavenworth Civil War Story
During the Civil War, a stack of material and equipment, including ties and black powder for the Railroad was stored across from Minisink Ford, in Lackawaxen, Pennsylvania.

Two Leavenworth relatives, the story goes, would get the guard drunk and steal the black powder used to get stumps out. They put it in containers and stored it in different places, including Beaver Swamp.

Either lightning or a brush fire touched off a fire. As it burned, the randomly placed black powder containers started on fire, and went off. It frightened the people in town, as they thought they heard Confederate cannons and that the Rebels had arrived.
—*Norman Bohs.*

Leavenworth Family Memorabilia (cont'd.)

"Port Jervis Union"

OBITUARY. Mar. 26 1918

Mrs. Maria Myers Leavenworth.

Mrs. Maria Myers Leavenworth, wife of Sherman S. Leavenworth, died at her home, Echo Hill Farm, near Eldred, Sullivan county, on Monday, March 25th, of diabetes. She was 64 years of age.

Deceased was born December 16th, 1853, and was the daughter of Martin D. Myers and Jane Ann Myers. On December 18th, 1874, she was united in marriage with Mr. Sherman S. Leavenworth. Mrs. Leavenworth was a life long resident of Eldred and for many years conducted the Echo Hill Farm House, which had a big patronage as a summer boarding house.

She was an excellent Christian woman, devoted to her home and family and was held in high esteem in the community of which she had so long been a resident.

The surviving relatives are her husband, at home; and the following-named children: J. Garfield Leavenworth, of Easthampton, Mass.; Mrs. C. M. Austin, of Eldred; Truman, Martin, Anna, Charlotte and Christine Leavenworth, of Eldred.

Obituary for Maria Myers Leavenworth, courtesy of Carolyn Hallock Clark.

Mrs Maria M Leavenworth

Mrs Maria Meyers Leavenworth, wife of Sherman S. Leavenworth, died at her home at Eldred, Monday aged 63 years. The deceased was born in New York city, the daugter of Martin D and Jane Ann Myers. She had resided at Eldred for a number of years. On Dec. 16, 1874, she was united in marriage with Sherman S. Leavenworth who with the following children survive. J. Garfield of East Hampton, Mass; Mrs C. M. Austin of Eldred, and Truman, Martin, Anna and Christine at home. 1 April 1918

Obituary for Maria Myers Leavenworth, courtesy of Emily Knecht Hallock.

Mr. Sherman S. Leavenworth
announces the marriage of his daughter
Christina Hayes
to
Mr. Anthony V. Hirsch
on Sunday, December the eighth
one thousand nine hundred and eighteen
Eldred, New York

Wedding announcement for the marriage of Anthony Hirsch and Christina Hayes Leavenworth. Announcement courtesy of Cynthia Leavenworth Bellinger.

Poems in Mary Ann Austin's Scrapbook

Two Glasses By Ella Wheeler Wilcox
There sat two glasses filled to the brim,
On a rich man's table, rim to rim.
One was ruddy and red as blood,
And one was clear as the crystal flood.
Said the glass of wine to his paler brother:
"Let us tell tales of the past to each other;
I can tell of banquet, and revel, and mirth,
Where I was king, for I ruled in might;
For the proudest and grandest souls on earth
Fell under my touch, as though struck with blight.
From the heads of kings I have torn the crown;
From the heights of fame I have hurled men down.
I have blasted many an honoured name;
I have taken virtue and given shame;
I have tempted the youth with a sip, a taste,
That has made his future a barren waste.
Far greater than any king am I,
Or than any army beneath the sky.
I have made the arm of the driver fail,
And sent the train from the iron rail.
I have made good ships go down at sea,
And the shrieks of the lost were sweet to me.
Fame, strength, wealth, genius before me fall,
And my might and power are over all!

Ho, ho! pale brother," said the wine,
"Can you boast of deeds as great as mine?"
Said the water-glass: "I cannot boast
Of a king dethroned, or a murdered host,
But I can tell of hearts that were sad
By my crystal drops made bright and glad;
Of thirsts I have quenched, and brows I have laved;
Of hands I have cooled, and souls I have saved.
I have leaped through the valley, dashed down
    the mountain,
Slept in the sunshine, and dripped from the fountain.
I have burst my cloud-fetters and dropped from the sky,
And everywhere gladdened the prospect and eye;
I have eased the hot forehead of fever and pain;
I have made the parched meadows grow fertile with grain.
I can tell of the powerful wheel of the mill,
That ground out the flour and turned at my will.
I can tell of manhood debased by you,
That I have uplifted and crowned anew;
I cheer, I help, I strengthen and aid;
I gladden the heart of man and maid;
I set the wine-chained captive free,
And all are better for knowing me."
These are the tales they told each other,
The glass of wine and its paler brother,
As they sat together, filled to the brim,
On a rich man's table, rim to rim.

There's Only One
There's only One on whose dear arm
We safely lay our thoughts to rest;
There's only One who knows the depth
Of sorrow in each stricken breast.

There's only One who knows the truth
Amidst this world's deceit and lies;
There's only One who knows each case
With just, unselfish, candid eyes.

There's only One who marks the wish,
Nor cruelly severely blames;
There's only One too full of love
To put aside the weakest claims.

There's only One whose pity falls
Like dew upon the wounded heart;
There's only One who never stirs,
Though enemy and friend depart.

There's only One, when none are by,
To wipe away the fallen tear,
There's only One to heal the wound
And stay the weak one's timid fear.

There's only One who's never harsh,
But tenderness itself to all;
There's only One who knows each heart.
And listens to its faintest calls.

There's only One who understands
And enters into all we feel;
There's only One who views each spring,
And each perplexing wheel in wheel.

There's only One who can support
And who sufficient grace can give
To bear up under every grief
And spotless in this world to live.

There's only One who will abide
When loved ones in the grave are cold;
There's only One who'll go with me
When this long, painful journey's told.

There's only One I'm sure will watch
O'er every dear one whom I love;
There's only One can sanctify
And bring them safe to Heaven above.

Poems in Mary Ann Austin's Scrapbook (cont'd.)

O Blessed Jesus! Friend of friends!
Come bide us 'neath Thy sheltering arm;
Come down amidst this wicked world,
And keep us from its guilt and harm.

Thou are the One the only One
For whom no love too warm can flow;
Thou are the One, the only One
In whom there's perfect rest below.
—Hymn.

Undertake for Me
Is xviii., 14
By H.W.M.
Full of wanderings, Lord, am I,
Watch me, guide me with Thine eye.
Let thy light, thy cheering light,
Lead my straying steps aright.
Full of wanderings, bear my plea;
Saviour, undertake for me.

Full of longings, Lord, am I,
Thou canst all my need supply.
Feed my hungry, fainting soul,
Purge from guilt and make me whole,
Full of longings, hear my plea;
Saviour, undertake for me.

Full of weakness, Lord am I,
On Thy strength I must rely;
Now to me Thy love impart,
Grant me, Lord, a trusting heart.
Full of weakness, hear my plea;
Saviour, undertake for me.

Full of coldness, Lord, am I,
Help me, save me, is my cry.
At Thy feet I humbly bow,
Comfort, healing, grant me now,
Full of coldness, hear my plea;
Saviour, undertake for me.

Full of vileness, Lord am I,
Wash me, cleanse me, or I die.
Let Thy blood for sinners shed,
Be my ransom from the dead.
Full of vileness, hear my plea;
Saviour, undertake for me.

What Matters
What matters how the time goes by,
    If ever with its flight
Our feet keep pace with steady tread
    In duty's path of right?
If every passing year could say
    A year of duties done,
Of wisdom gained, of added strength,
    Of vict'ries fairly won.

What matters though time swiftly flies,
    When youthful days are gone,
If in the way our Master leads
    Our feet are hast'ing on.
If we have wept with those who weep
    Rejoiced when they are glad,
Give cooling drink and kindly word
    To thirsty one and sad.

If we have scattered wide the seed
    Of wisdom, truth and love,
The fruits of which shall make our world
    Like unto that above,
If we have freely cast our bread
    Upon the waters wide,
Nor stopped to watch its onward course
    Upon the swelling tide;

If in the war 'twixt bad and good
    We've boldly taken stand,
Defended right, opposed the wrong,
    Obeying God's command,
Then let the days glide swiftly on,
    And brown hair turn to gray,
And feeble pulse and falt'ring step,
    And human strength decay.

God over all is just and good;
    He slumbers not nor sleeps.
And over childhood's youth and age
    His loving watch e'er keeps.
—Odell, Illinois.
by Augusta Leonard, for the *Witness*.

Wm. Henry and Mary Austin Family Letters, etc.

Drawing by Gussie Thompson at the end of his December 10, 1882 letter; a second letter of Gussie. Both letters courtesy of Melva Austin Barney.

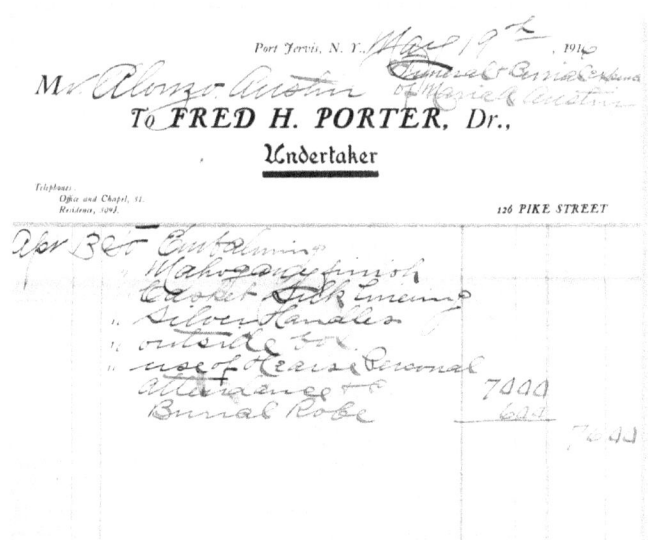

Bill for Maria Austin's funeral that was paid by Lon Austin. Courtesy of Mary Briggs Austin.

Eldred Manse, Feb. 24.

Henry Austin

Dear Brother,
In view of approaching "Town Meeting" I have been requested by our Deacons here to preach two "Temperance Sermons."

The first will God willing be given this Sunday morning, the 20th the following Sunday evening. My presentation of the subject is different from the common view and knowing you to be interested in the training of the youth of our land I believed you would like to hear these sermons. They are carefully prepared.

The week after the "Donation" we expect to have a good visit with your family.
Your Brother and true friend,

Edward W. Fisher

Letter (1880 to 1883) to Henry Austin, courtesy of Mary Briggs Austin.

William Henry and Mary Ann Austin Family and Relatives

Signatures for a church group (p. 130) from Henry Austin's Carting book, courtesy of Mary Briggs Austin.

December 31, 1881 page from Aida Austin's 1881 Diary. Diary courtesy of Mary Briggs Austin.

Wedding announcement for Dr. Alonzo Eugene Austin and Sara Hall.

Mort Austin's Autograph Book

Autographs

Mary F. Bradley
Eldred Sull Co N Y

To my Friend

Fear God and keep his Commandments
for this is the whole duty of man
Mrs O P Schoonover

Eldred
February 3d 1884

Mortimer
Remember now thy Creator in the days of thy youth,
Eldred, February 3th 1884
O P Schoonover

Mary F. Bradley, Mrs. O.P. Schoonover, O.P. Schoonover.

My Dear Son
Remember your Creator in the days of your youth
Seek out ways of wisdom and truth
Earthly pleasures my Son bring no but pain
Then my Child seek heavenly joys to gain
May God watch over you
to Heaven and keep you from evil,
through Life
Mary A Austin
Eldred

To My Son
Whatever you have to do, my boy,
Be sure you do it right;
If life is but a battle, boy,
Be faithful in the fight.

With high resolve and holy,
With purpose firm and true,
Let us go forth with meekness,
God's will and work to do.
W. H. Austin
Eldred Sullivan Co
New York Feb 2nd 1884

Friend Mortimore
Be not overcome of evil
but overcome evil with good
Chas C P Eldred
Eldred N Y
Feb 6 1884

Always your friend
James W. Sergeant
Feb 6th 1884

Mary A. Austin (mother), W.H. Austin (father), Chas. C.P. Eldred (uncle) and James W. Sergeant (friend).

Mort Austin's Autograph Book (cont'd.)

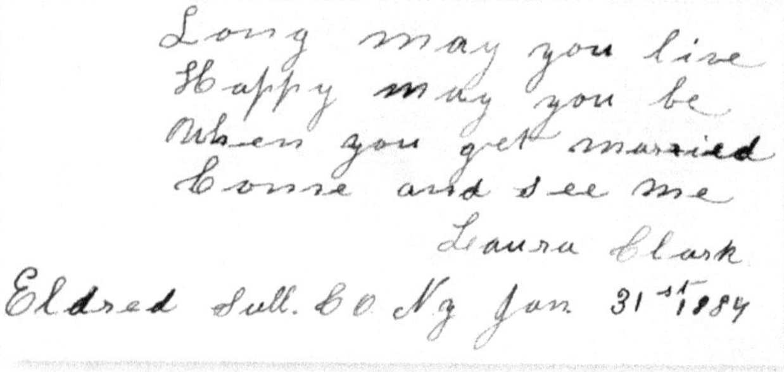

Long may you live
Happy may you be
When you get married
Come and see me
　　　　Laura Clark
Eldred Sull. Co Ny Jan 31st 1884

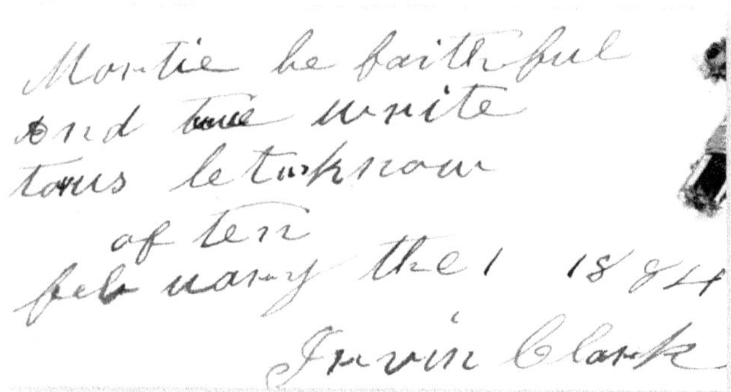

Mortie be faithful
and true write
to us let us know
often
february the 1 1884
　　　　Irvin Clark

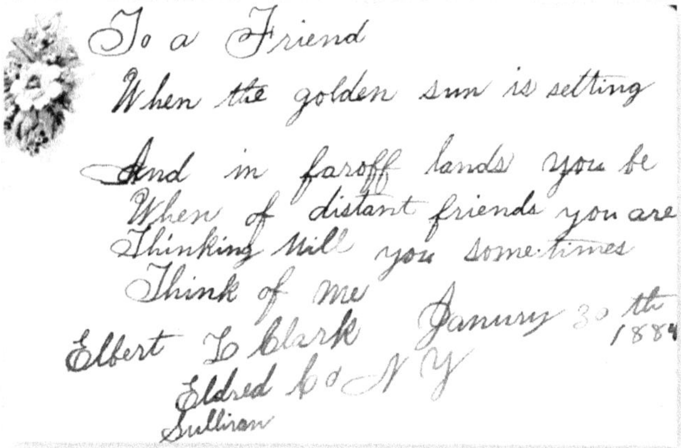

To a Friend
When the golden sun is setting
And in faroff lands you be
When of distant friends you are
Thinking will you sometimes
　Think of Me
Elbert L Clark　January 30th 1884
　Eldred Co N Y
　Sullivan

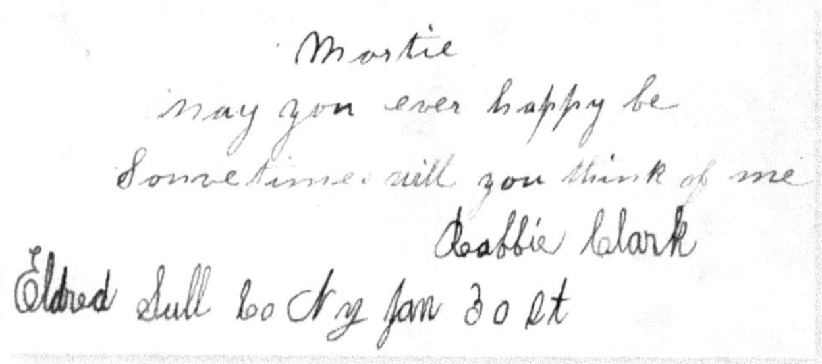

Mortie
may you ever happy be
Sometimes will you think of me
　　　　Robbie Clark
Eldred Sull Co Ny Jan 30 st

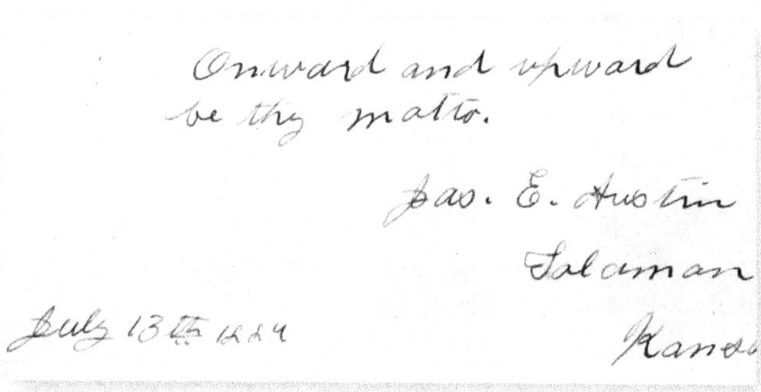

Onward and upward
be thy motto.
　　　　Jas. E. Austin
　　　　Salaman
July 13th 1884　　Kansas

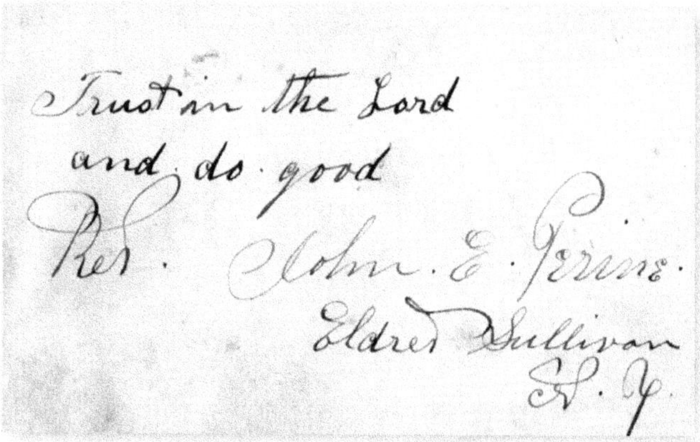

Trust in the Lord
and do good
Rev. John E. Perine.
　Eldred Sullivan
　　N. Y.

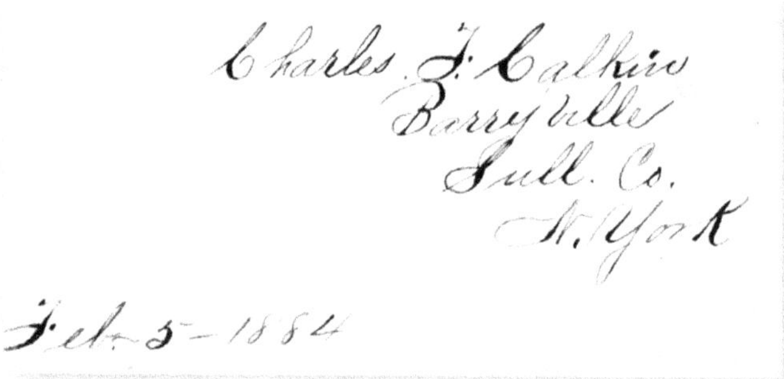

Charles F. Calkin
　Barryville
　Sull. Co.
　　N. York
Feb. 5 – 1884

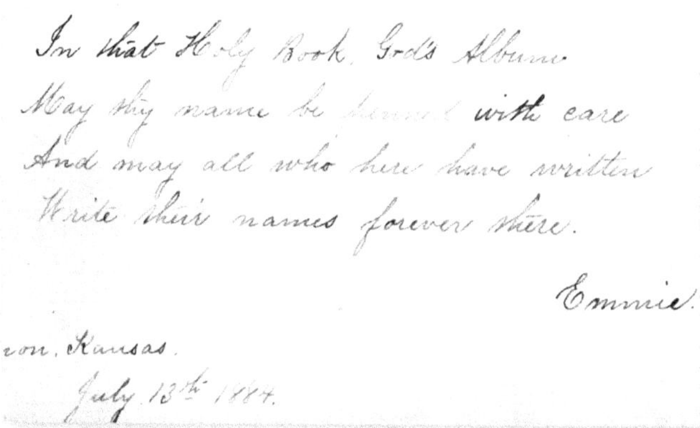

In that Holy Book, God's Album
May thy name be honored with care
And may all who here have written
Write their names forever there.
　　　　Emmie
son, Kansas.
July 13th 1884.

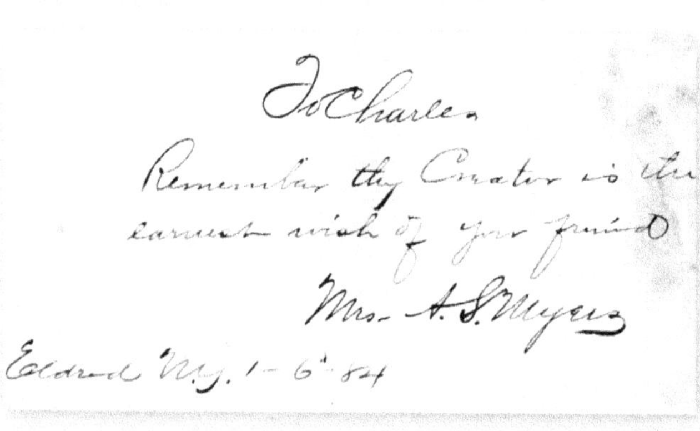

To Charles
Remember thy Creator is the
earnest wish of your friend
　　　　Mrs. A. S. Myers
Eldred N.y. 1 – 6 – 84

Top left: Laura Clark (aunt), Irvin Clark (uncle), Elbert and Robbie Clark (cousins), Jas. E. Austin (brother), John E. Perine, Charles F. Calkin (cousin), Emmie (sister-in-law) and Mrs. A.S. Myers (wife of Abel Sprague Myers.

Mort Austin's Autograph Book (cont'd.)

Edwin V. Myers
Eldred
N.Y.
February 6th 1884

To Charlie

From a friend

Lottie Bradley
Jan 6 1884   Eldred Sull Co NY

Cousin Mortie,
Bring a willing sacrifice—
Thy soul to Jesus' feet;
Stand in him, in him alone,
All glorious and complete.
Rebecca C. Eldred
Feb. 6th 1884

Bertha S. S. Collins,
Stapleton,
Staten Island,
New York.

Nelly E. Kendall

Edwin V. Myers, Lottie Bradley, Aida, sister.   Rebecca C. Eldred (cousin), Bertha S.S. Collins, Nelly Kendall (cousin).

Mort Austin Letters

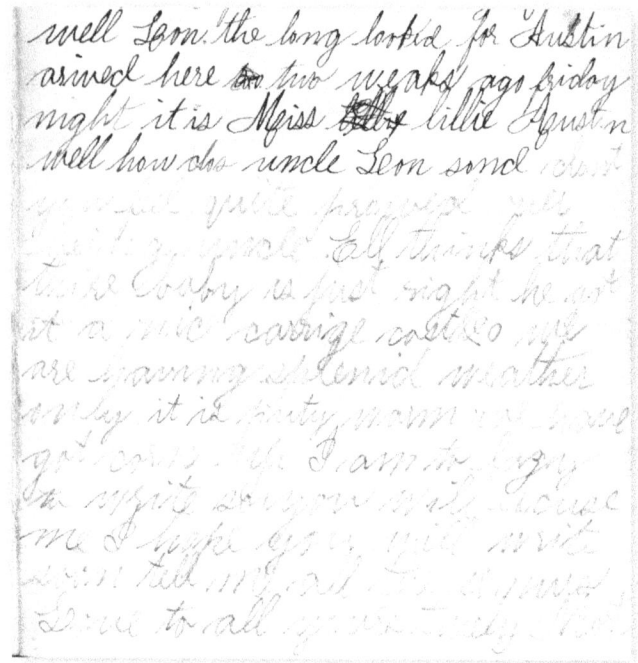

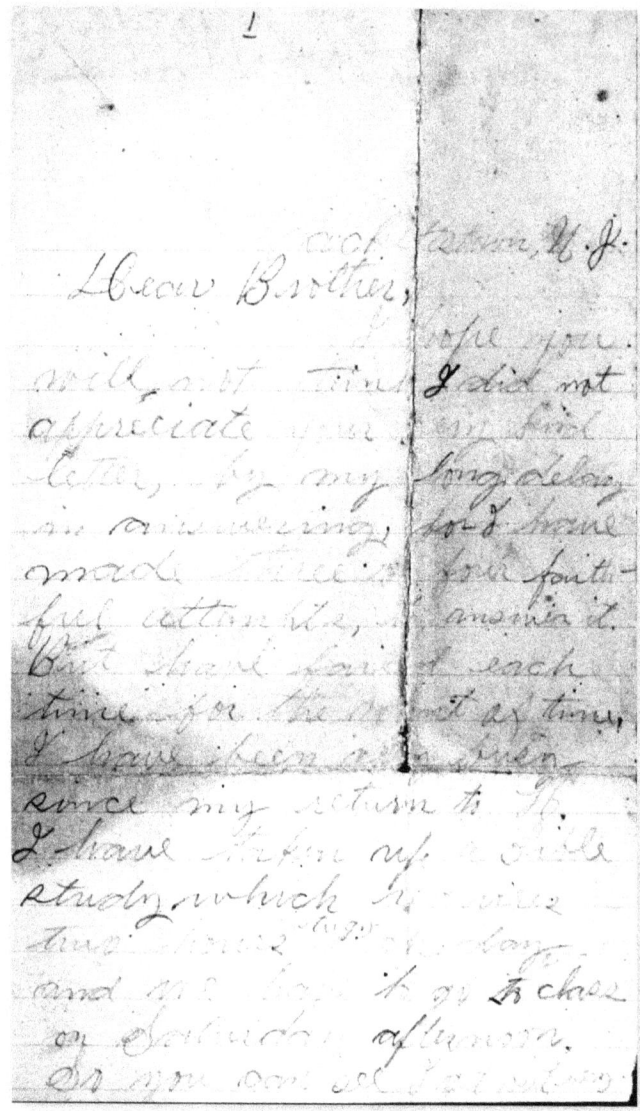

Envelope and page from 1884 letter to Lon Austin about the birth of Lillie Austin. Letter courtesy of the Austin Family. See p. 96.

Letter to Lon Austin from Hackettstown, New Jersey, where Mort went to Seminary. Letter courtesy of Mary Briggs Austin.

One of Mort Austin's calling cards courtesy of the Austin Family.

Another of Mort Austin's calling cards courtesy of the Austin Family.

Mort Austin Documents

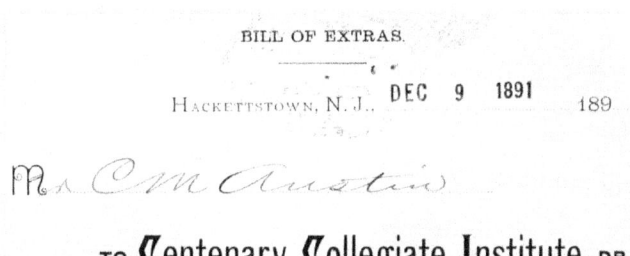

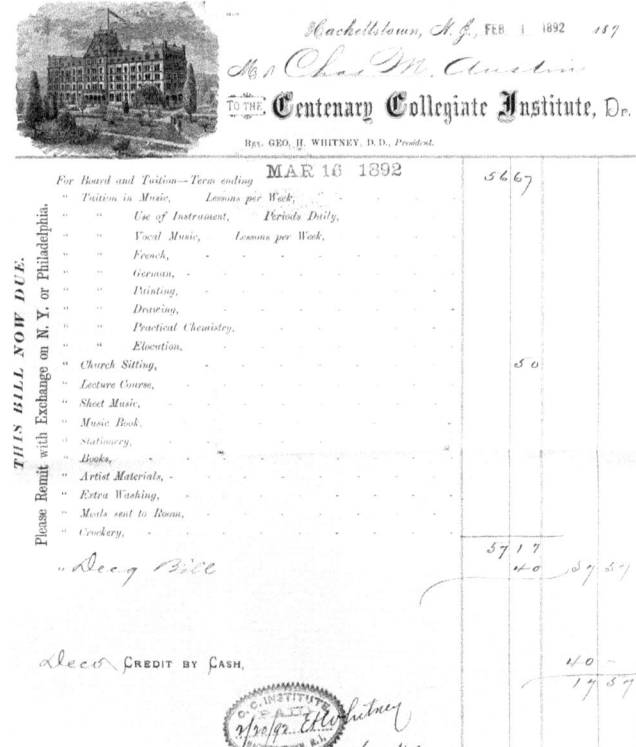

Bills from Centenary Collegiate Institute of Hackettstown, New Jersey, where Mort Austin went to college. Courtesy of Mary Briggs Austin.

Freight costs and envelope for the Austin Homestead Cottage. Courtesy of Mary Briggs Austin.

Aida Austin's Autograph Book

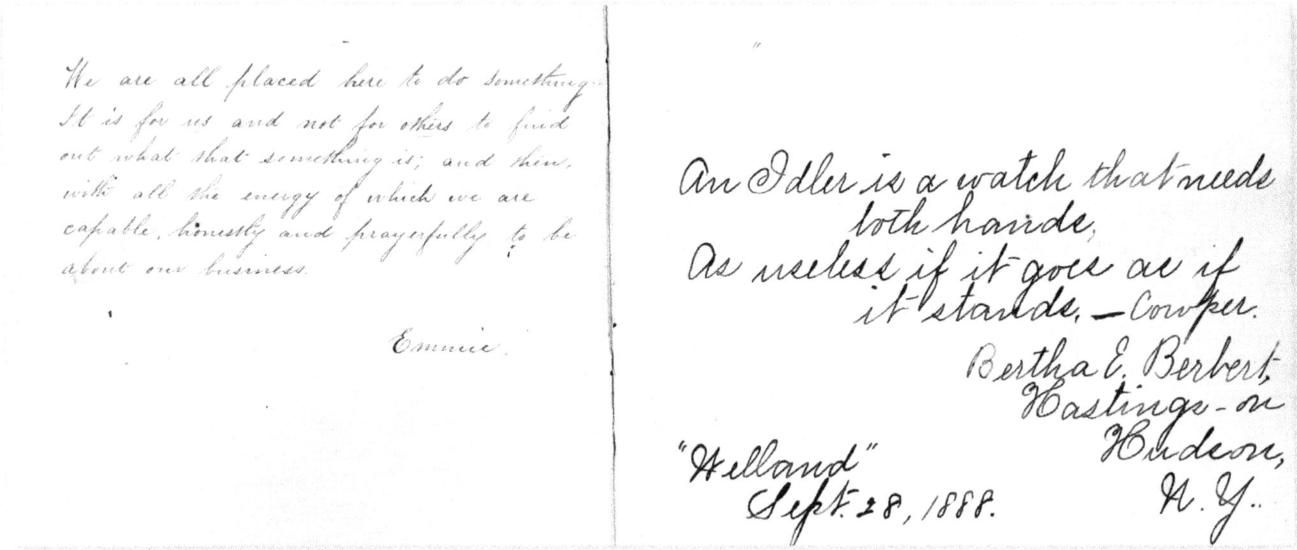

We are all placed here to do something.
It is for us and not for others to find
out what that something is; and then,
with all the energy of which we are
capable, honestly and prayerfully, to be
about our business.

Emmie

An Idler is a watch that needs
both hands,
As useless if it goes as if
it stands. — Cowper.

Bertha E. Berbert,
Hastings-on-
Hudson,
N.Y.

"Helland"
Sept. 28, 1888.

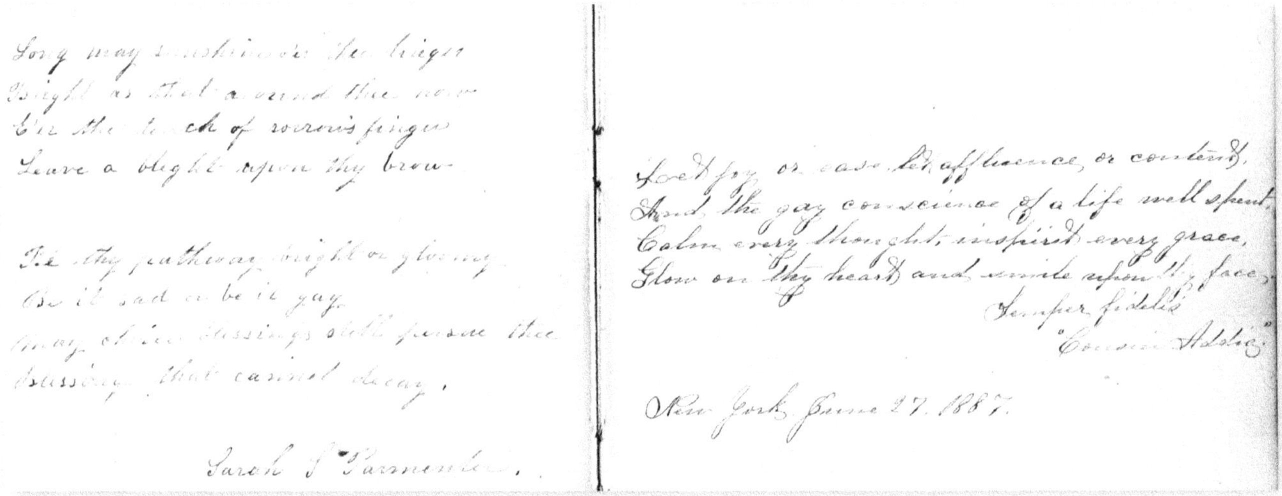

Long may sunshine's ray beam
Bright as that around thee now
Err the touch of sorrow's finger
Leave a blight upon thy brow.

Tis thy pathway bright or gloomy
Be it sad or be it gay
May choice blessings still pursue thee
Blessings that cannot decay.

Sarah S. Parmenter

Tired of joy or ease, of affluence, or content,
And the gay conscience of a life well spent,
Calm every thought, inspirit every grace,
Glow on thy heart and smile upon thy face.

Semper fidelis
"Cousin Addie"

New York, June 27, 1887.

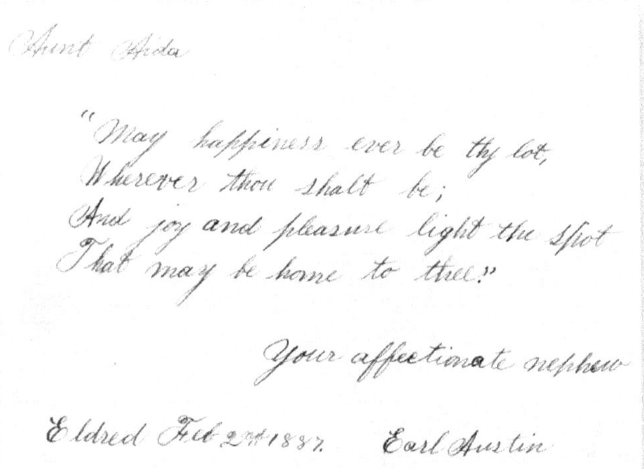

Aunt Aida

"May happiness ever be thy lot,
Wherever thou shalt be;
And joy and pleasure light the spot
That may be home to thee."

Your affectionate nephew

Eldred Feb 2nd 1887. Earl Austin

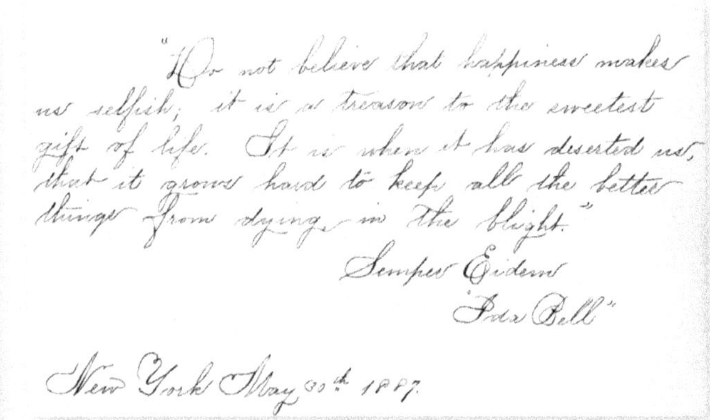

"Do not believe that happiness makes
us selfish; it is a treason to the sweetest
gift of life. It is when it has deserted us,
that it grows hard to keep all the better
things from dying in the blight."

Semper Eidem
"Ida Bell"

New York May 20th 1887.

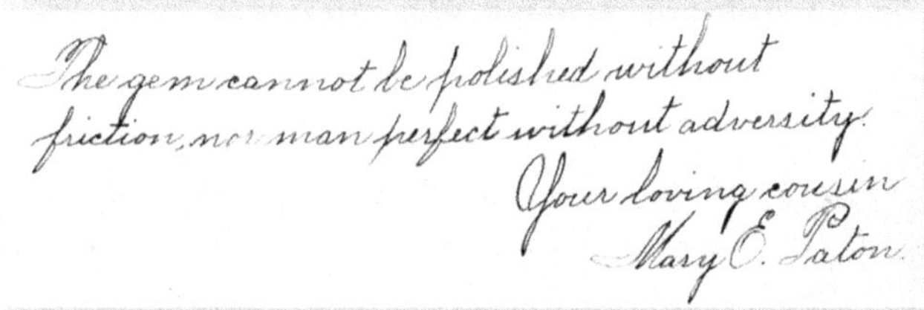

The gem cannot be polished without
friction, nor man perfect without adversity.

Your loving cousin
Mary E. Paton.

Top left: Emmie (Parmenter, Aida's sister-in-law), Sarah S. Parmenter (Emmie's sister), Earl Austin (Emmie's son). Top right: Bertha E. Berbert, Cousin Addie, Cousin Ida Belle, Cousin Mary E. Paton.

Aida Austin's Autograph Book (cont'd.)

In compliance with your request, with pleasure do I sign myself.

Very sincerely
Your friend
Geo. W. Braisted

Oct. 6— 1887.

To Aida:

These few lines to you are tendered
By a friend, sincere and true;
Hoping but to be remembered,
When I'm far away from you.

Yours truly
William F. Braisted

New York Oct. 11, 1887.

May your life have just enough
    shadow
To temper the glare of the sun

Your friend
Laura Braisted
New York

Oct. 16th 1887.

"We meet and part—the world is wide;
We journey onward side by side
A little while, and then again
Our paths diverge; a little pain
A silent yearning of the heart
For what has grown of life a part;
A shadow passing o'er the sun,
Then gone, and light again has come:
We meet and part, and then forget;
And life holds blessings for us yet."

Mary Ellermeyer,
Kittanning,
Penna.

"Welland" Jan. 3, 1889.

When the name that I write here is
    dim on the page
And the leaves of your album are
    yellow with age,
Still think of me kindly and do not forget
That, wherever I am, I remember you yet.

Sincerely your friend,
Gertrude Bellew,
New Milford,
Pa.

Oswego Normal School,
Jan. 17, 1886.

Top left: George W. Braisted, William F. Braisted, Laura Braisted. Top right: Mary Ellermeyer, Gertrude Bellew.

Aida Austin's Autograph Book and a Letter

> Seven little words
> I'm going to write
> Remember me Aida
> With all your might
>   Your loving friend
>   Lulu Bloom
>   Phillipsport,
>   N.Y.
> Eldred, July 12th, 1872.

> As a Normalite,
>   Strive to keep the golden rule and learn your lessons well at school.
>
> "Dear friend and fellow traveller to the tomb."
>
> "No man can do anything well, who does not esteem his work of importance."
>
> Don't forget the days in "27" or the evening polka in stocking feet.
>   Your loving friend
>   Alida D. Hall.
>   Bloomfield,
>   Essex Co.,
>   N.J.

Autographs of Lulu Bloom and Alida D. Hall.

> Aida A. Austin.
>   December 21st 1886.
>
> "Go forth thou little volume
> I leave thee to thy fate,
> To love and friendship truly
> Thy leaves I dedicate."

Page from Aida's Autograph Book; Letter Aida wrote to her brother on June 6, 1885.

> Oswego, N.Y.
>   June 6, 1885.
> Dear Brother,
>   Will you please meet me at Lackawaxen next Wednesday, June 10, at 6.44 P.M.? I can not go to Shohola as there is no train on the "Erie" which connects with the "Delaware" train, and stops there. So I will have to get off at Lackawaxen.
>   Hoping to see you all soon, with love I remain
>   your loving sister,
>   Aida.

William and McKinley Austin's Report Cards

New York State Education Department

County of Sullivan

This is to certify that William Austin a pupil in district no. 4, town of Highland, has satisfactorily passed the examination for the 2nd term of the Fifth grade, based on the State elementary course of study for the public schools, and is qualified to pursue the course prescribed for the following term.

Charlotte Leavenworth, Teacher
Frederick J. Lewis, District Superintendent

[Dated] June 30, 1914

1914 report card for William Austin, signed by his aunt Charlotte Leavenworth and Frederick J. Lewis, Superintendent. Card in the Austin Collection.

We take pleasure in announcing that M. McKinley Austin has won the following distinction in his record at Mount Hermon School

Honors, Spring Term, 1916

Henry F. Cutler, Principal

Mount Hermon School
Mount Hermon
Massachusetts

1916 Certificate for McKinley Austin from Mount Hermon School in Massachusetts. Card in the Austin Collection.

Mount Hermon School Report Blank

Mount Hermon, Mass., JUL 27 1916

Report of M. M. Austin

for the SPRING term ending JUL 1 1916

Abbreviations Used

FORMS
- I. First Form.
- II. Second Form.
- III. Third Form.
- IV. Fourth Form.
- V. Fifth Form.
- VI. Sixth Form.

TERMS
- A, First Term.
- B, Second Term.
- C, Third Term.
- D, Fourth Term.
- E, Fifth Term.

SCHOLARSHIP GRADES
- E, Excellent.
- G, Good.
- M, Medium.
- L, Low.
- F, Failed.

(Passing Mark, "L")

CONDUCT AND WORK GRADES
- A, Satisfactory.
- B, Unsatisfactory.
- C, Retained on Probation.
- D, Dismissed.

Length of term, 15 weeks

Name: M. M. Austin

Tardiness Exc. ___ Unexc. ___
Absences Exc. ___ Unexc. ___
Conduct: A / A
Work: B / A
Gymnasium (2): ___

	A	B		A	B
Bible			Music		
Bible (2)	III	E	Penmanship (5)		
English (3)	II	G	Spelling (5)		
English (4)					

The number following a subject indicates number of recitations per week.

DAILY SUBJECTS	A	B	C	D	E
Languages					
English Grammar		G			
Latin					
Greek					
French					
German					
Mathematics					
Arithmetic					
Algebra					
Geometry—Plane		E			
Geometry—Solid					
Trigonometry					

DAILY SUBJECTS (Cont.)	A	B	C	D
Science				
General				
Physiology				
Hygiene				
Zoology				
Botany				
Physics				
Chemistry				
Agriculture				
Agriculture		E		
Horticulture				
Animal Husbandry				
Dairying				
History				
United States				
Advanced U. S. (3)				
Advanced Civics (3)		G		
Greek (3)				
Roman (3)				
English (3)				

Signed H. F. Cutler, Principal

1916 report card for McKinley Austin from Mount Hermon School. Card is in the Austin Collection.

McKinley Austin, World War I

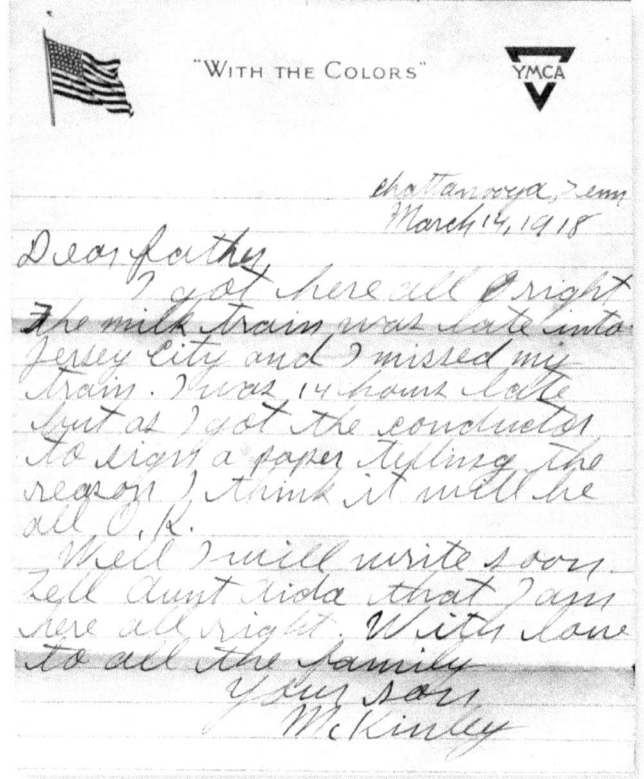

Top Left: Letter McKinley wrote to his father Mort Austin. Right: Letter to Mort Austin from Ambert Moody in December 1919. Bottom left: Letter of Jennie Austin to her son McKinley Austin. Courtesy of Mary Briggs Austin. Letter of Harold Fraley to Raymond Austin, courtesy of Raymond's daughters: Melva, Joan, Margie, and Dawn Lee.

McKinley Austin, World War I (cont'd.)

AMERICAN EXPEDITIONARY FORCES,
HEADQUARTERS SERVICES OF SUPPLY,
TRANSPORTATION CORPS,
OFFICE OF GENL. SUPT. TRANSPORTATION,
RAILWAY DEPARTMENT.

11, April 1919.

My dear General:--

As per your request I am attaching hereto record obtained from our Grave Registration Service Bureau with respect to Private Mortimer M. Austin. I am sending it in duplicate and hope it will furnish the family all the information desired; if, however, it does not, and there is anything further in connection therewith that I am able to do, you have but to command and I will secure pleasure in endeavoring to execute your desires.

With kindest regards to you and the Madame, and assuring you of most pleasant memories of some delightful evenings at your home, I am,

Sincerely yours,

General Taufflieb,
44 Rue DeVillejust.
Paris (France).

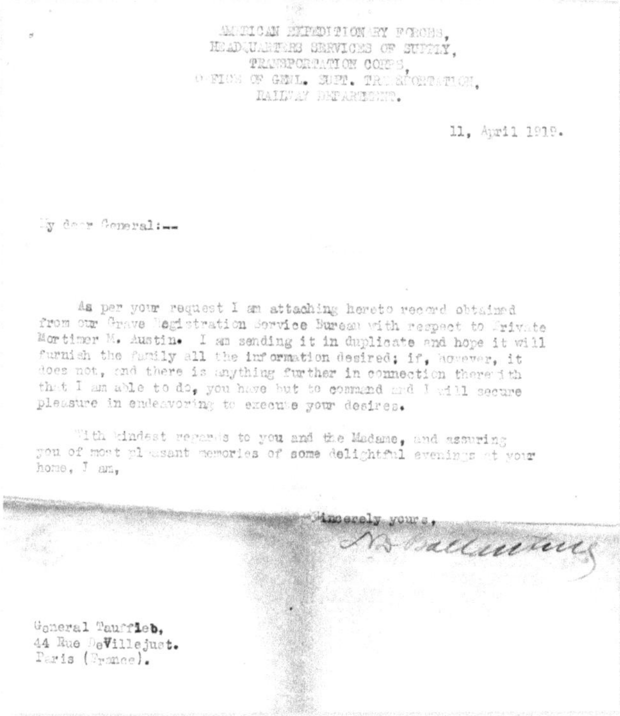

Paris, France
April 11, 1919

American Expeditionary Forces, Headquarters Services of Supply, Transportation Corps, Office of Genl. Supt. Transportation, Railway Department.

My dear General:

As per your request I am attaching hereto record obtained from our Grave Registration Service Bureau with respect to Private Mortimer M. Austin. I am sending it in duplicate and hope it will furnish the family all the information desired; if, however, it does not, and there is anything further in connection therewith that I am able to do, you have but to command and I will secure pleasure in endeavoring to execute your desires.

With Kindest regards to you and the Madame, and assuring you of most pleasant memories of some delightful evenings at your home, I am,

Sincerely yours,
N.D. Ballauture

General Taufflieb
44 Rue DeVillejust
Paris (France)

MORTIMER M. AUSTIN, Private (#735644).

Killed in Action Oct. 21, 1918.

Buried in isolated Grave
#628, in Commune of -
Romagne-sous-Montifaucon,
Department of MEUSE.

- - - - -

Direction - Map 35 North-East; Position
of coordination - EAST 3066.63, NORTH 285.43,
Scale 1 to 500.

- - - - -

NEAREST KIN -
Charles M. Austin (Father),
Eldred, New York, USA.

- - - - -

Chaplain at Burial - J. P. Van Horn, 11th U.S. Infantry.

- - - - -

Burial and location confirmed; one identification tag buried with body and the other on cross over grave.

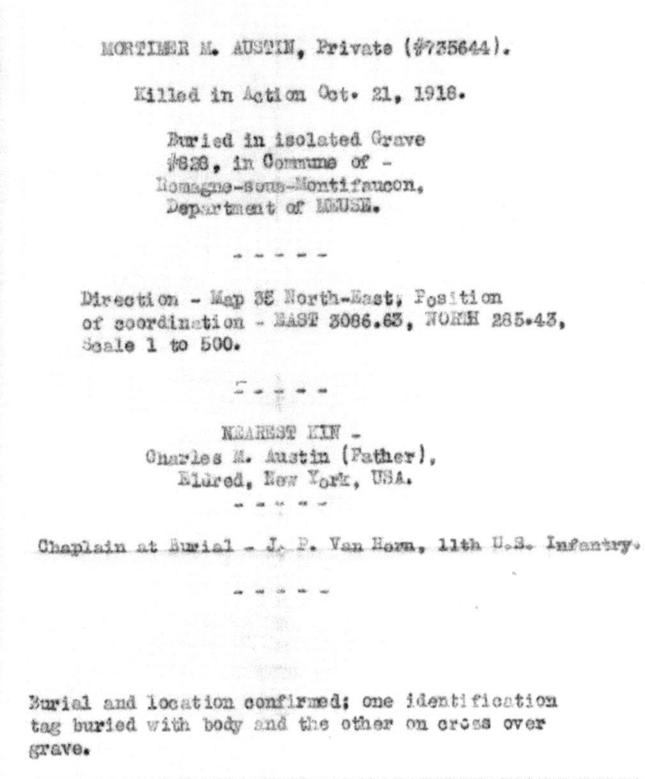

Information where McKinley was buried in Mary Briggs Austin Collection.

WAR DEPARTMENT,
THE ADJUTANT GENERAL'S OFFICE,
WASHINGTON.

THE INCLOSED CERTIFICATE IS ISSUED BY DIRECTION OF THE PRESIDENT, WHO WISHES TO EXPRESS HIS DEEP AND SINCERE SYMPATHY.

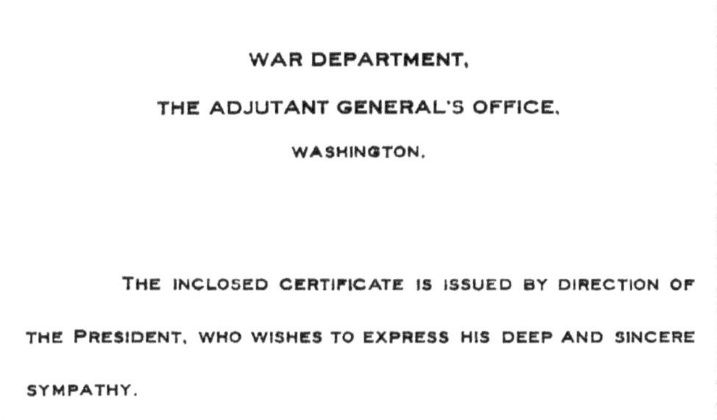

Sympathy certificate from Washington D.C. on McKinley Austin's death sent to his parents, Mort and Jennie Austin. Certificate courtesy of Mary Briggs Austin.

Letter to General Taufflieb is courtesy of Mary Briggs Austin.

Obituaries for McKinley Austin, WWI

AUSTIN DIED FACE TO THE FOE

Eldred Volunteer Was Fatally Wounded in Going from Shell Hole to Trench for Shovel

Mr and Mrs C. M. Austin have received particulars of their son's death on the battlefield of France. Mortimer Austin, who was reported killed in action Oct. 21, was one of the first boys of Eldred to volunteer at the beginning of the war. So far as is known he is he only soldier from the town of Highland to die for his country.

The following information is gleaned from a letter written by Capt. Allan B. Maxwell of the Machine Gun company of the 11th Infantry.

As commanding officer of M. G. Co., 11th Inf., I answer your letter of inquiry regarding the death of your son, Mortimer McKinley Austin. I was in a different division at the time of his death but by questioning men in the company who were present during that engagement, I am enabled to give you the following information, most of which was given by Sergeant Popp, who was in command.

At Madelaine Farm, after this company had gained its first objective, your son was put in command of the sixth squad, he acting as corporal. In order to consolidate their position and to prevent a successful German counter attack, your son took his machine gun and his squad of men forward to a shell hole. It was a dangerous mission, for arillery and machine gun fire was heavy. Finding the hole not deep enough to provide cover for the gun and all the men, he returned to the trench and obtained a shovel. Almost any man in his position would have sent one of the men of the squad back for the shovel, but your son chose to run the danger himself. On the return trip to the shell hole he was struck in the breast by a machine gun bullet and although badly wounded, he continued forward and gave the shovel to his squad, who then dug in and held their position.

During a lull in the fighting he was brought back to the trench for medical aid. All efforts were in vain, however, and about an hour later he passed away. He realized that his wound was fatal and took the knowledge like a man and a soldier, never once complaining and only regretting that he would be unable to fight on. All of the men of his company state that your son was one of the most likable men in the company, that none were braver, and the reason he was killed was because he was too brave.

He died as the bravest of the brave, face to the enemy, leading his men forward to a point in advance even of our own line.

Corp. Austin leaves besides his parents, three brothers and one sister at home, one brother who is serving in the 33rd Infantry, and a host of friends in Eldred and neighboring villages mourn his early even though brave death.

Date of McKinley's Death
Though later information said McKinley was killed on the 14th of October, a letter to Mort and Jennie said October 21, 1918.

Pvt. Mortimer McKinley Austin
MG Gun Co., 11th Inf.
Eldred, N.Y.

Killed in action October 21; Isolated in the community of Romagne-sous-Montfaucon. Map coordinates: Verdun 35 NE; North 285 and East 08.8.

Identified by Tag on cross and 3 tags on body. Removed June 10, 1919 to grave 69 Section 43 Plot 2, Romagne-sous-Montfaucon.

CORPORAL AUSTIN KILLED WHILE AIDING HIS MEN

Eldred's First Soldier Met Death While Beyond Advanced Line.

Eldred, N. Y., Feb. 17. — Through the efforts of Dr. Eugene A. Austin, of New York City, the following account of the death of Corporal Mortimer McKinley Austin has been received by his family at this place. He was born at Eldred January 5th, 1899, and was the first one to offer his services to his country in this locality. He enlisted in June, 1917. Later his brother, Charles Raymond Austin, enlisted, and is now serving in Panama.

McKinley was respected and loved by all who knew him and the entire community sympathize with the family in their loss.

The letter follows:

Machine Gun Co., 11th U. S. Inf., A. P. O. 745, A. E. F.
Mr. C. M. Austin, Eldred, N. Y.,
Dear Sir:—As commanding officer of the M. G. Co., 11th Inf., I answer your letter of inquiry regarding the death of your son, Mortimer McKinley Austin.

I was in a different division at the time of the death of your son, but by questioning men in the company who were present during that engagement, I am enabled to give you the following information, most of which was given by Sergeant Popp, who was in command of the section.

At Madelaine Farm after this company had gained its first objective, your son was put in command of the Sixth Squad (acting as corporal). In order to consolidate the position, and to prevent a successful German counter attack, your son took his machine gun and his squad of men forward to a shell hole. It was a dangerous mission for artillery and machine gun fire was heavy. Finding the hole not deep enough to provide cover for the gun, and all the men, he returned to the trench and obtained a shovel. Most any other man in his position would have sent one of the men of the squad back for the shovel, but your son chose to run the danger himself. On the return trip to the shell hole he was struck in the breast by a machine gun bullet, and although thus badly wounded, he continued forward and gave the shovel to his squad, who then dug in and held their position. During a lull in the fighting he was brought back to the trenches for medical aid. All efforts were in vain, however, and about an hour later he passed away.

He realized that his wound was fatal and took the knowledge like a man and like a soldier, never once complaining and only regretting that he would be unable to fight on.

All the men of this company state that your son was one of the most likable men in the company, none were braver, and the reason he was killed was because he was too brave really. I shall not attempt to assuage your grief with mere words of sympathy. Perhaps the knowledge that he died, as the bravest of the brave, facing toward the enemy, leading his men forward to a point in advance even of our own lines, may somewhat lessen your suffering. I sincerely hope so. Believe me to be, Very truly yours,—
ALLEN B. MAXWELL, Captain 11th Infantry, Commanding Company.

History of the 11th Infantry

A brief History of the 11th Infantry during the War sent to Mort and Jennie Austin in a letter by Sgt. John G. Popp.

This regiment left Camp Forest, Georgia, April 16th, 1918, embarked from Hoboken, New Jersey, on the U.S.S. Leviathan, April 24th, 1918 and arrived in Brest, France, May 2nd, 1918.

They left Brest on May 6, 1918, and detrained at Bar-sur-Aube, May 8, 1918. They were in training in that area until June 1.

On May 18, a standard of colors were presented to the regiment in behalf of the descendants of the French officers who fought with us during the Revolution. The regiment moved from here to Brienne-le-Chateau and entrained on June 2, arriving at Le Thillot on June 4. Regimental Headquarters were established at St. Maurice.

On June 7, this regiment moved to Moosch, Alsace. This area was German territory at the beginning of the war. While here the regiment was attached to the 77th Div. (French).

From here the regiment moved on June 13 for the trenches of the Arnould Sector, arriving at Le Collet June 14. The first casualties were suffered that evening.

While moving up to the trenches, Captain M.W. Clark was severely wounded and Private Jos. Kanerski, Co. I was killed by enemy shell fire.

Early on the morning of June 26, the enemy attempted to raid the positions held by Companies I and L. The raid was repulsed with losses to the enemy.

July 1, at 2 a.m., the enemy again attempted a raid on outposts held by Co. G and H. Both were driven off with loss of one officer killed and several men wounded.

July 3, regiment took over sub-sectors Bichstein and Gaschney of the Arnould Sector. Regimental PC at Camp Nicolas. Regiment remained in this sector until July 14.

July 15 embussed to St. Die Sector. Regimental Headquarters at Denipaire. The first prisoner captured by the Fifth Division was taken on July 23rd by a patrol composed of men of Co. I, 11th infantry, 2nd Lieut. H.S. Sper, commanding.

July 28, second prisoner was taken by patrol commanded by Lieut. J.S. Guise of Co. L.

When Frappelle was taken by 6th Infantry on Aug. 17, Co. A, 11th Infantry cooperating with that Regiment.

August 22, the Regiment left the trenches. This ended our position warfare. August 25, arrived at Archette. Embussed from here, August 30 to Neuvillers Area.

Left for St. Mihiel Area September 6.

St. Mihiel: Our barrage started at 1 a.m. September 12. Regiment got in position for jumping off at 4:30 a.m. September 12. The attack started at 5 a.m. Division Front held by 10th Brigade, 11th Infantry on right, 6th Infantry on left, each regiment having one battalion in front line. The 357 Infantry (90th Division) was on our right.

3rd Bn. was assault battalion; followed and then 2nd Bn. Regiment reached all objectives on scheduled time, taking hundreds of prisoners.

Bois des Sauix, Bois des Grandes Portions, Bois de la Rappes, Bois St. Claude, Vieville-en-Haye and Bois Gerard were all taken by this regiment September 12.

On September 13, a short, but fierce counter attack of the enemy was broken up by the regiment.

About midnight September 15, the regiment relieved by 61st Infantry, moving into intermediate position and remained there until September 16.

On September 29, while stationed at Dieulourd, three enemy shells caused a great number of casualties in 1st Bn.

On October 1, Bn. Reg. Hdq. established at Trondes.

On October 4, embussed from Foug to a camp near Lampere. October 5, regiment moved to Foret de Neese. October 11, moved to Bois de Cuiay and on October 12, to the vicinity of Montfaucon.

October 13, casualties were suffered here as the result of heavy shelling from enemy guns. Took up position around Ferme de la Madeleine the night of October 13.

(Here is where your son was killed on October 14, 1918.)

Went "over" morning of October 14, and remained in action continuously until October 22, when regiment moved into support position.

On October 21, Bois des Rappes was taken by the regiment. The taking of this position is the subject of letters of commendations by Army and Corps Commanders.

The regiment again went into action November 3rd in the Meuse drive and remained in action to the end of the fighting November 11 at 11 a.m.

During the fighting from November 5 to the 11, this regiment took from the enemy: Liny-Devant-dun Hill 260, on November 5; Bois du Fayel, Nervaux, Bois de Bussy, Fontaines, les Fonzy Bois, Bois Chassogne, Bois de Failles, Croix Morand, and Bois du Corrol on November 6; Hill 308, Brndeville, and Hill 373 on November 7; Bois de Remoiville, Bois de Monoel, Jametz and Lemoiville, on November 9; Louppy on November 10.

Our line held until November 12 when the regiment was relieved by the 6th Infantry and the 60th Infantry when the Army of Occupation (3rd Army) was formed on November 17, this regiment was made a part thereof.

December 16, the regiment was transferred to the 2nd Army. This regiment was again transferred to the 3rd Army April 1, 1919.

Casualties of Regiment:
Killed in Action 437; Missing 177; Total 2538
Prisoner captured: Officers and men: 700, 1 nurse
Depth advanced: 27 kilometers

Letters to Mort and Jennie Austin on McKinley's Death

Letter from Allen B. Maxwell
MG CO. APO 745, 11th Inf,
January 19, 1919
Dr. A. Eugene Austin, N.Y., N.Y.
Dear Sir:

As commanding officer of the MG CO 11th Inf., I answer your letter of inquiry regarding the death of your son Mortimer McKinley Austin. I was in a different division at the time of the death of your son, but by questioning men in the Company who were present during that engagement, I am enabled to give you the following information—most of which was given by Sergeant Popp who was in command of the section.

At Madelaine Farm after this company had gained its first objective, your son was put in command of the 6th squad (acting as corporal). In order to consolidate the position and to prevent a successful German counter-attack, your son took his machine gun and his squad of men forward to a shell hole. It was a dangerous mission for artillery and machine gun fire was heavy... Finding the hole not deep enough to provide cover for the gun and all the men, he returned to the trench and obtained a shovel.

Most any other man in his position would have sent one of the men of the squad back for the shovel, but your son chose to run the danger himself. On the return trip to the shell hole he was struck in the breast by a machine gun bullet and although thus badly wounded, he continued forward and gave the shovel to his squad, who then dug in and held their position.

During a lull in the fighting, he was brought back to the trenches for Medical Aid and all efforts were in vain however and about an hour later, he passed away. He realized that his wound was fatal and took the knowledge like a man and like a soldier, never once complaining and only regretting that he would be unable to fight on.

All the men of the Company state that your son was one of the most likable men in the company. None were braver and the reason he was killed was because he was too brave really. I shall not attempt to assuage your grief with mere words of sympathy. Perhaps the knowledge that he died as the bravest of the brave, facing toward the enemy, leading his men forward to a point in advance even of our own lines, may somewhat lessen your suffering. I sincerely hope so.

Believe me to be very truly yours, Allen B. Maxwell

Letter from G.L. Edwards, Y.M.C.A., Luxemburg
February 14, 1919
Dear Miss Austin,

Chaplain McVeigh gave me your letter concerning Mortimer Austin MG Co. 11th Inf.

I regret to have to tell you that he was killed October 14th in the Argonne Forest Drive. He was killed near a small town called Cunel. I was with him when he died. But was wounded later in the day and cannot say where he was buried. I don't know anything about his personal belongings for I was taken to a hospital on the same day that he was killed. But am trying to learn something about it. When I do, I'll be sure to let you know at once.

Chaplain McVeigh has gone to the States and he was in charge of the burying party.

My dear lady it grieves me to have to write this information. But I am the only officer with the company that was with them there.

However you will be glad to know that he died like a true American doing his duty. He was well liked by both officers and men of the company, and we are proud to have had such a man. If there is anything I can do for you in anyway, Please let me know. I'd be only too glad to do it.

Yours very respectfully,
G.L. Edwards
1st Lt. 11th inf. N.Y.C.

Letter from John Popp, Chicago, Ill.
August 30, 1919
Mr. C.M. Austin, Eldred, N.Y.
Dear Sir,

Received your letter sometime ago and must apologize for not answering sooner.

I have enclosed a complete history of the 11th Inf. during the war.

Not being able to see you personally, when I came through Camp Meills, I will try to explain in writing how he was killed.

The Corporal of his squad being a casualty, made Austin as I knew him Squad leader and when we reached the hill which was Madelaine Farm, the German's made it so hot for us we could not advance further, so I directed him to put his gun into action

Letters to Mort and Jennie Austin on McKinley's Death (cont'd.)

on the west of the hill. Then I went on seeing the other gun put into action which was even more perilous and came back. Seeing him on the side of the hill I asked him if he had the gun in action. He said no, he came back for a shovel.

I paid no more attention to him then and went on to report to Capt. Dashiell who was killed later.

Looking around, I seen your son fall forward into the hole he was placing the gun in. Running over to him, I asked him where he was hit. He said stomach.

So I pulled him back off the crest of the hill, bandaged him and placed him in a hole and covered him up with blankets where he died a few hours later.

He was well liked and very popular among the men and among those few who lived a clean life while over there.

He was the best gunner we had in the Company and his loss meant much to those who had to depend on him to keep the German's head down

I will enclose names of men in my section who came back and you can find their addresses by writing to the Society of the Fifth Division, United States Army Veterans of the World War, WA DC Yours very truly, John G. Popp 108 S. La Salle St., Chicago, Ill.,

Siemanski; Hutchison (witness to his death); Harold Fraley; Wendling, Naperville, Ill., who was wounded getting Austin's 1st aid pouch; Covey Hilton; Chapman; John G. Popp.

Letter from Harold Fraley, Camp Gordon, Atlanta, Ga.
November 9, 1919
Charles Austin, Eldred, N.Y.
Dear Sir:

My mother sent me your letter from my home in New Jersey and I am very glad to give you the details of your brothers death, as I was on the spot and saw him get hit.

It was our first day in the Argonne drive and we went over at 8, the morning of the 14th of October. We hadn't gone far when we were held up by the German machine guns. They were firing on us from three different directions and there wasn't enough of the boys left to advance farther so we were forced to stop and dig in. The first thing we did was to get our machine guns placed in case of a counter-attack. It was while engaged in this that your brother was shot. A shell hole a little advanced was selected so as to allow no dead space. Your brother made a dash for the hole and saw he was about to fall into it, the Germans opened up with a machine gun and one of the bullets hit him in the abdomen and he fell.

We saw him fall as the way in which he fell was queer we called to him and asked if he was hit. He told us he was and we immediately made a rush for the hole. Well we got him out all right and brought him back down the hill a piece and applied first aid. The only words he uttered was "It's hell boys." He never made a groan and just drew his legs up a little. I suppose to ease the pain.

We wrapped him up in a blanket and he died within an hour. There was nothing removed from his body as long as I was there which was about two days when I was hit in the leg and went to the hospital.

We were not allowed to bury anybody as there was special men for that work. I have heard of them taking money and things off of a man that had gone west and never turning them in but, don't know how true it is. Everything of that nature was supposed to be sent to the nearest relatives.

I am glad to tell you that your brother died like a man and facing death bravely. We were good friends and I was sorry to see him go. The fighting was fierce and I guess it was more luck than anything else that I got out alive. We went in with about a hundred and seventy men and came out with something like twenty-five or thirty of the original number.

I am happy to be of service to you and if there is anything else, I can do, don't hesitate to ask it.
Sincerely yours, Harold Fraley
5th MP Co.

Mountain Grove House

HIGHLAND LAKE

BOATING AND BATHING AT SAND BEACH, HIGHLAND LAKE

SCENE IN SULLIVAN COUNTY

MOUNTAIN GROVE HOUSE is reached by the Erie Railroad from Chambers St. or West 23rd St. Ferries to Shohola, Pa., then five miles by auto over a beautiful country road to the House, which is 1,800 feet above sea-level.

All guests are promptly met when notified. Transportation $1.00 from Shohola to House. Trunks 50c. Rates, $15 per week up. Transients, $3 per day.

C. M. AUSTIN, Prop.,
Eldred, Sullivan County, N. Y.

Mountain Grove House letterhead; Mountain Grove House booklet; and Mort Austin's calling card. Collection courtesy of the Austin Family.

Headstones in the Old Eldred Cemetery

AUSTIN

Austin Marker in the Eldred Cemetery. Photo: Gary Smith.

Father, William Henry Austin. Photo courtesy of Cynthia Leavenworth Bellinger.

Gravestone for William Henry and Mary Ann Eldred Austin. Photo courtesy of Gary Smith.

BOSCH

Mary Maier Bosch. Photo courtesy of Ken Bosch.

BRADLEY

Wilhelmena Clemens, wife of Atwell Bradley. Photo courtesy of Cynthia Leavenworth Bellinger.

BUNCE

Gravestone of George Bunce. Photo courtesy of Cynthia Leavenworth Bellinger.

Alonzo Eugene Austin, brother of William Henry Austin. Alonzo was: Pioneer missionary to the Alaskan Indians. Photo courtesy of Cynthia Leavenworth Bellinger.

Maria Austin, Henry's daughter who died in 1916. Photo courtesy of Cynthia Leavenworth Bellinger.

Headstones in the Old Eldred Cemetery (cont'd.)

CLARK

Mahlon Irvin and Laura Austin Clark. Photo courtesy of Gary Smith.

Mercy Harding Brown Clark, wife of George Case Clark. Photo courtesy of Cynthia Leavenworth Bellinger.

George and Harriet Covert Clark. Photo courtesy of Cynthia Leavenworth Bellinger.

George Case Clark, husband of Mercy Harding. Photo courtesy of Cynthia Leavenworth Bellinger.

COLLINS

Thomas K. Collins. Photo courtesy of Cynthia Leavenworth Bellinger.

DEVENOGE

Dr. Leon and Catharine DeVenoge monument. Photo courtesy of Cynthia Leavenworth Bellinger.

Headstones in the Old Eldred Cemetery (cont'd.)
ELDRED

Polly V. Eldred first wife of James Eldred. Photo courtesy of Cynthia Leavenworth Bellinger.

James Eldred. Photo courtesy of Cynthia Leavenworth Bellinger.

Hannah Hickok Eldred, second wife of James Eldred. Photo courtesy of Cynthia Leavenworth Bellinger.

James Eldred and his sister Rebecca C. Eldred, children of C.C.P. Eldred and his wife Effa Van Tuyl. Photo courtesy of Gary Smith.

Charles C.P. Eldred and Effa Van Tuyl Eldred. Photo courtesy of Cynthia Leavenworth Bellinger.

C.C.P. Eldred. Photo courtesy of Cynthia Leavenworth Bellinger.

Headstones in the Old Eldred Cemetery (cont'd.)
GARDNER

Monument to James K. and Eliza Eldred Gardner from original brochure, courtesy of Victoria Kohler.

Robert, Herbert, and Mary L. Gardner, children of Stephen St. John Gardner. Photo courtesy of Cynthia Leavenworth Bellinger.

Stephen St. John Gardner and his second wife, Maggie Terns. Photo courtesy of Cynthia Leavenworth Bellinger.

Gardner Monument Brochure
That thy days may be long in the land is amply verified by the erection of a beautiful Iconic monument to the memory of esteemed parents, the Honorable James K. Gardner and Eliza Eldred Gardner, in the Eldred Cemetery, Eldred, New York, it being over half a century since the former place of interment was first marked by a marble memorial, now disintegrating, proving the bonds of love are more enduring than stone, thus do we honor ourselves by honoring Father and Mother...

The monument is a twelve foot monolith seven and one half tons approximate weight and is built of Beton steel construction, an artificial stone, pronounced by connoisseurs a perfect imitation of sandstone both in color and texture and on account of its extreme hardness which time imparts, our leading architects and engineers are substituting for marble, stone, granite, etc. in some of their best structures and is considered superior to that used in the walls and dome of the Pantheon in Rome and the aqueducts...

The foundation is four and one half feet underground...On the east front upon the plinth stands the American Eagle a watchful guardian maintaining the dignity and majesty of the Law as did James K. Gardner when his fellow citizens esteemed him worthy and so elected him to the offices of judge and assemblyman. The Fasces (bundle of rods with axe) being the symbol of the civic official.

On the inscription panels are the olive branches (emblems of peace) representing the four surviving members of the family and are placed there in loving remembrance of their revered Parents, the two sons on one panel, the two daughters on the other, whose combined ages aggregate two hundred and ninety-four years...

The family plot, 32 by 9 feet, imparts the elegance of simple harmony to the ensemble in which 5 of the 7 sons and 2 daughters of the eleven children are interred beside the Parents.

Designed and executed by George Beck, sculptor, Eldred, N.Y.

View of the Gardner area. Photo courtesy of Cynthia Leavenworth Bellinger.

APPENDIX • 473

Headstones in the Old Eldred Cemetery (cont'd.)

HICKOK

KYTE

Old Hickok section. Photo courtesy of Cynthia Leavenworth Bellinger.

Rev. Felix and Eliza Greiger Kyte and their daughter, Elizabeth T. Kyte. Photo courtesy of Cynthia Leavenworth Bellinger.

MILLS

MYERS

Alexander and Margaret Gillies Mills. Photo courtesy of Cynthia Leavenworth Bellinger.

George W.T. Myers and his wife Martha Mills. Photo courtesy of Gary Smith.

Jane Ann Van Pelt Webb Myers. Photo courtesy of Cynthia Leavenworth Bellinger.

Old Eldred Cemetery entrance. Photos of Mary Briggs Austin.

Orville, first child of Edwin and Mabel Myers. Photo courtesy of Cynthia Leavenworth Bellinger.

Headstones in the Old Eldred Cemetery (cont'd.)
TETHER, SERGEANT, STIDD, SCHOONOVER

Elizabeth Tether, wife of Robert Owen. Photo courtesy of Cynthia Leavenworth Bellinger.

Ethel and Lettie Gardner Sergeant. Photo courtesy of Cynthia Leavenworth Bellinger.

William Stidd and his wife Mary Hickok. Photo courtesy of Cynthia Leavenworth Bellinger.

Isaac Sergeant and his wife Elizabeth Persbacher and 2 children who died young. Photo courtesy of Cynthia Leavenworth Bellinger.

O.P. (Oliver Perry) Schoonover, father of Daniel Rowlee Schoonover and Emily Schoonover Waidler. Photo courtesy of Cynthia Leavenworth Bellinger.

Index

Note: When a last name had varied spellings, one version was used to be consistent.

A

Abendroth, Annie, 211, 244
Adams, Martha, 5
Alaska
    Hoonah, 27
    Sitka, 26, 27, 29, 199, 302
Alaskan Indian Industrial School, 302
Albany Normal School, 107
Alexander's Hotel, 11
Allen
    Henrietta Austin Styles, 27, 29, 97, 100, 170, 186, 191, 209, 242, 276, 302–3, 440
    Henry (Gov.), 396
    Ralph, Rev., 231, 246, 269, 303
    Vera, 337, 345, 352
American Red Cross,129, 330–335, 339, 343–4, 348–9, 351, 355, 367, 376, 391, 394, 399, 407, 413, 423
Anderson, Linda Guenther, vii
Andeway
    Len, 237, 312, 441
    Lottie Leavenworth, 83, 158, 236, 237, 278, 312, 441
Angell, Claude, 400
Appel, Anna, 262, 269
Arlington (Eldred), 220, 253
Arlt, Joe, vii
Arthur, Chester (Pres.), 41, 50, 294
Asendorf
    George (Myers), 305, 412
    Henry, 75, 157, 254, 256, 260–1, 280, 293, 295, 305, 354, 412, 427
    Isabelle Boyd, 74, 75, 88, 157, 225, 248, 256, 305, 354, 412
Ashauer
    Mabel Hazen, 150, 286, 419, 442
    William, 350, 419
Atkins, Martha, 138, 198
Austin
    Addie, *see Thompson*
    Aida, 5, 19, 23–8, 30, 39, 40, 45, 46, 52, 55, 57–8, 60–2, 64, 67, 72, 89, 90, 93–5, 97–101, 105, 107–113, 116–7, 125, 129, 130, 143, 165, 171–177, 183, 191, 194, 202–3, 233, 241–2, 247, 249–252, 262, 265–6, 274, 280, 292, 295, 299, 301, 306, 315, 318–20, 324–6, 328, 342, 358, 366, 370, 372, 375, 378, 384–5, 387, 388–90, 397–8, 407, 410, 412, 414, 426, 435, 440, 452, 458, 459, 460
    Albert Alonzo (Lon), 5, 19, 23–4, 28, 31–5, 37–39, 42, 44–48, 53, 55, 57–8, 60, 63, 89–91, 94–6, 100, 102–4, 106–117, 120, 129–30, 165, 169–175, 184–186, 188–191, 193–4, 199, 200, 202–3, 213–4, 216, 232–3, 241, 244, 249–50, 253, 257, 259, 261–2, 265, 280, 291–2, 295–7, 299–301, 315, 319, 324, 326, 371, 393, 397, 435, 440, 444, 456
    Alden, 237, 276, 429
    Alma, 257
    Alonzo Eugene Sr., 26–7, 29, 97, 100, 170–1, 190–1, 197, 199, 202, 209, 242, 276, 295, 302, 440, 469
    Alonzo Eugene Jr., 27, 29, 170–1, 185, 190–1, 199, 202, 209, 276, 302, 317, 322, 325–6, 370, 372, 385, 390–1, 394, 408, 410, 440, 452
    Ann Mary, *see Schoonover*
    Antoinette (Net), *see Clinton*
    Arthur Lawrence, 121, 249, 294, 305, 316, 319, 321, 361–2, 366, 367, 372, 375, 384, 390, 401–4, 406, 408, 412, 434–5, 440
    Augustus Alonzo, 25–7, 29, 36, 58, 60–1, 88, 168, 209, 276, 440
    Benjamin C., 19, 397
    Bertha, 19
    Carol J., v
    Charles Arthur, v
    Charles Augustus, 29, 34, 209, 237, 276, 429
    Charles Mortimer, iv, xii–xiv, 23–5, 32–3, 35, 41–7, 55, 58, 63–4, 89, 90, 92, 94, 96, 100, 102, 107, 109, 111, 113–6, 118, 126, 130, 133, 145, 165, 168–75, 178–9, 183–4, 186–90, 192, 194–6, 201–2, 209, 212–3, 218, 234–5, 240, 241–3, 249, 254, 256, 258, 260–1, 263, 267, 268, 276, 282–3, 288–90, 294–5, 302, 315, 319–20, 322, 324–5, 328, 351, 356, 359, 361, 368, 371, 373–4, 375–6, 381–2, 384, 387–90, 393–5, 397, 399, 401–2, 406, 408–9, 413, 417, 419–422, 424–5, 427, 429–30, 432–3, 435, 440–1, 453–7, 466–8
    Charles Raymond, 179, 204, 218, 226, 233–4, 235, 241, 247, 256, 268, 276–7, 282, 289, 294, 298, 301–3, 305, 319, 330, 361–8, 370–1, 373–4, 381–2, 384, 387, 388, 390–3, 395–6, 398–400, 402–3, 405–7, 409, 412–4, 416–7, 421–2, 425, 429–30, 435, 440
    Dawn Lee, *see Segarra*
    Edith Emogene, 26, 30, 90, 95, 440
    Edward, 25–6, 29, 209, 276
    Elizabeth, 249, 289–90, 294, 301, 305, 319, 321, 361, 366, 375, 384, 390, 402–3, 405–7, 422, 435, 440
    Emily (Emma) Parmenter, 90–2, 96, 100, 105, 110, 114–5, 120–1, 123–8, 165, 184, 195, 200, 202, 208, 244, 257, 263, 266, 268, 270, 272, 425, 427, 440, 454, 458
    Evaline, 209, 440

Frank, 19, 140, 397
Gladys Myers, 72, 179, 226–7, 291, 298, 304, 402, 406, 416, 435, 445
Harriet, *see Liebla*
Hazel, 257
Henrietta, *see Allen*
Henry Earl Slocum, 100, 105, 110, 122, 124–6, 128, 165, 184, 195, 202, 257, 458
Henry Ladore (Dory), 23–25, 44–5, 47, 88, 109, 115, 122–3, 130, 169, 199, 202, 249, 315, 397, 403, 440
Ida Belle, *see Brown*
Ira McBride, 19, 110, 137–41, 155, 212, 287, 295, 307, 396–7, 426
Isabelle (Belle) Camp, 27, 29, 97, 100, 170, 202, 209, 276, 302, 440
James, 186
James Eldred (Ell), 5, 24, 33–4, 38–9, 63, 64, 88–92, 94–6, 100, 104, 110–12, 114, 116, 120–1, 124, 126–8, 130, 165, 170–1, 184, 195, 200, 203, 206, 249, 257–9, 267, 273, 302, 329, 372, 397, 425, 432, 435, 440, 454
Jennie Louisa Leavenworth, iv, xii–xiv, 20, 64, 69, 73, 83, 85, 88, 141, 145, 165, 179, 186–90, 192, 195, 201, 206, 209, 218, 234, 240–1, 243, 245, 247, 256, 259, 264, 265, 267–8, 274, 276, 282–3, 285, 288–90, 293–4, 301, 311–2, 315, 319–24, 328, 356–7, 361–3, 365, 368, 370, 374–6, 382, 384–5, 387, 389–94, 398–9, 401–3, 406, 407, 408–9, 416–8, 421, 422, 430–1, 433, 435, 440–1, 462, 466–7
Joan, *see Geier*
John Mortimer, 29, 34, 97, 209–10, 218, 262, 276, 303, 317, 440
Julia, 58, 186, 193
Justina (Tina), *see Laing*
Laura, *see Clark*

Lou, 19, 140, 397
Lydia (Lillie), *see Calkin*
Mabel (d/o Henry Earl), 257
Mabel (d/o Charles A.) 276, 429
Mabel, *see Smith*
Margie, *see Maglione*
Margo, 257
Maria, 24–6, 35, 37–40, 43, 44–5, 47, 52, 55–8, 60–2, 89, 115, 129, 186, 194, 202, 233, 241–2, 244, 249, 315, 440, 451, 469
Mary Ann Eldred, 17, 23–5, 30, 34, 37, 39, 43, 45–7, 57, 60, 63, 73, 88–9, 92–3, 96, 101, 111, 115–6, 165–7, 171, 175, 186, 192–3, 202–5, 207–9, 241, 243, 245, 247–9, 258, 276–7, 290, 440, 449–53, 469
Mary Briggs, iv, xii, 14, 152, 316, 435
Mary Isabelle, *see Hurtin*
Mary Henrietta, 24, 44, 48
Mary Hoatson, 97, 210, 218, 276, 303
Mary Johnson, 209, 237, 276, 429
Mary Letitia Millspaugh, 29, 34, 58, 209, 218, 237, 276, 429, 440
Mary M., v
Melva, *see Barney*
Mildred, 257
Minerva Drake, 19, 137–8, 287, 307, 397, 427
Minnie, 19, 140, 307, 397, 427
Miranda (Rand), *see Paton*
Mortimer Bruce, 26, 29, 34–6, 38, 94, 97, 209, 218, 237, 276, 302, 429, 440
Mortimer McKinley, 139, 195, 201, 202, 204, 218, 234, 241–2, 245, 247, 249, 258, 261, 267, 276, 282, 289, 294, 302–3, 307, 315, 318, 319–26, 328–49, 351–56, 358–60, 362–3, 365–6, 368, 370–1, 373–7, 381, 385–94, 400, 410, 419, 429, 440, 461–4, 466–7
Myrtle, 257
Nellie, 19, 140, 397
Olinda (Linnie), *see Ayers*

Phebe Maria Eldred, 17, 25–7, 29, 34–6, 38, 55–6, 58, 61, 166, 168, 205, 207, 209, 276, 440, 444
Ralph and Fanny Knapp, 168, 276, 440
Ralph, (s/o H. Earl), 202, 257
Ralph Waldo, 140, 397
Robert Clinton, 69, 169, 249, 303, 319, 321, 325, 361, 362, 366, 375, 384, 390, 402–5, 408, 431, 435, 440
Sadie LeRoy, 184, 195, 202, 257
Sara (Sally) Hall, 190, 209, 276, 322–4, 390–1, 410, 452
William Henry, 21, 24–5, 33, 43–5, 47, 55, 57–8, 88–9, 92–6, 98, 101, 104, 112–3, 115–6, 126, 130, 165, 168–70, 175, 179, 195, 198–9, 202, 207, 218, 233–5, 241, 249, 256, 276–7, 290, 440, 451–3, 469
William Sherman, 218, 234, 241, 247, 249, 256, 268, 276, 282, 289, 293–4, 301, 305, 361, 362, 370, 374, 384, 387, 390, 395, 405, 406–7, 435, 440, 461
Autenrieth
Caroline, *see Penney*
Elsie, 263
Autenrieth Hotel, 141–2, 212, 224, 259
Avery
Arthur, 286, 306, 308, 419, 442
Beatrice, *see Horton*
Erwin D., 149, 279, 286, 288, 317, 365, 419, 427, 442
Gladys, 286, 419, 442
Laura, *see McBride*
Norah Bradley, 69, 88, 149, 187, 271, 279, 286, 288, 346, 419, 442
Ayers
Charles H., 191, 209
David, 21
Joseph Garrish Jr., 191, 209
Joseph Garrish Sr., 97, 191, 209, 302, 370
Olinda (Linnie) Austin, 97–8, 191, 209, 276, 302

INDEX • 477

B

Baker
   Harry, 400
   Rev., 181
Banner
   Eliza, 191, 279
   Emily, *see Schoonover*
Barber, Belle and Herman, 19, 135
Barns/Barnes
   Almira, *see Eldred*
   Elizabeth, *see Owen*
   Ida, 23
Barney, Melva Austin, iv, xii, 30, 179, 187, 189, 234, 279, 304, 357, 402, 406, 435
Barnum Circus, 2
Barnum, P.T., 50
Barryville Glass Factory, 274, 287, 426–7, 433, 445
Barryville-Shohola Bridge, 9, 10, 73, 132–4, 223, 256
Barth, Peter and Mary, 329, 427
Barton, Clara, 129
Basque, Louis, 157, 282, 306, 433
Beattie, Mary, 242, 317
Beaver Brook, 20, 66
Beaver Brook Bridge, 66
Beaver Brook Mill Pond, 65–6, 135
Beaver Brook Road, 136, 298, 422
Beaver Swamp, 66, 447
Beck
   Elizabeth (Mrs.), 49, 150–2
   Ernest W., 400
   Family, 20, 150, 172, 288, 306, 414
   Ferman, 400
   Florence, 199
   George Jr., 178, 186, 400
   George, 150–1, 205, 276, 356, 433, 472
   Jacob and Lizzie, 445
   Lulu, 130
Becker's Woods, 143, 145, 417
Beers, Charles, 302
Bellew, Gertrude, 105, 108, 459
Bellinger
   Cynthia Leavenworth, iv–vii, xii, 434
   Richard, v
Benedict, Minnie Bosch, 154, 202, 204, 231, 293

Bennett
   Arlene Wolff, vii
   James G. Sr. and Jr., 177
Berbert, Bertha E., 105, 459
Betsa, Anna, 339, 349, 353
Beufve
   Edna, 225, 244
   Louis and Mark, 229
   Mary, 225
   Raymond, 218, 350, 400
Birr, John and Edith, 427
Black, James, 198
Blaine, James, 41
Blind Pond, 66–7, 141, 143
Blind Pond Brook, xiii, xiv, 66–8
Blizzard of 1888, 118–120
Blohm, Kathryn, *see Ewart*
Bodine
   Adele, 72, 136, 288–9, 307
   Blanche, 422, 427
   Blanche (daughter), 422
   Henry, 136, 289, 295, 365, 422, 427
   Justin, 21, 66, 71–2, 135–6, 277, 289
   Paul, 422
Bodine Cottages (Little Pond Cottage), 71–2, 131, 135–6, 277, 289, 365, 22–3, 427
Bodine Lake (Little Pond), xiv, 65–6, 72, 135–6, 277, 289, 365, 422–3, 427, 430
Bogert
   John and Amanda Hogencamp, 86
   Carrie Etta, *see Clark*
   D.W., 73, 75
Bohs,
   Linda Leavenworth, v
   Norman, v, 68, 447
Bok, C. Soule, 169, 183, 196
Bolton
   Jessie, 199
   Mr., 109
Bornstein
   Edward, 288, 295, 422, 427
   Georgiana, 288, 422, 427
Bosch
   Alice, *see Reisen*
   Charles (Charlie) Sr., 154, 203, 231, 238–9, 281–2, 306, 308, 323

   Charles (Charlie) Jr., 306, 323, 325
   Christina, 238, 281, 412
   Edward, 76, 153–4, 203–4, 231, 250, 281–2, 292, 309–10, 323, 350, 360, 400, 425
   Eddie (s/o Charlie Sr.), 306
   Fred Bosch, vi
   Heinrich Wilhelm (Boesch), 76–8, 137, 152–4, 202, 204, 237, 255, 281, 288, 295, 302, 306, 323, 359–60, 412–3, 427
   Helen (Lena) Miller, 238, 239, 306, 323
   Henry (Whipple), 323
   Herman, 101, 154, 202–4, 231, 281–2, 306, 308, 310, 323–4, 350–2, 359, 360, 363, 385, 400, 405, 412, 419
   Herman Jr., 363, 412
   Ken, vi, 78, 152, 154, 227, 281
   Lulu, 154, 202, 204, 231
   Margo Bosch, *see Meyer*
   Mary Elvira Horton, 75, 101, 154, 203, 281–2, 306, 308, 323–4, 363, 412
   Mary Maier, 76, 101, 137, 152, 153, 202, 204, 227, 230, 469
   Mary Nellie Van Wyck/Van Eastenbridge, 238, 281, 288, 306, 307, 412
   Menzo, 154, 203–4, 231, 250, 281, 323, 350, 425
   Paula Schrieb, 412
   Ralph, 154, 203–4, 231, 281, 310, 323, 350, 360, 400, 412
   Robert (s/o Herman), vi
   Tillie, 154, 203, 231, 281
   Wilhelmina (Minnie), *see Benedict*
   William (Bill), vi
   Willie, 306, 323, 325
Bower, John, 5
Boyd
   Alex, 271
   Bertha, *see Wilson*
   Elizabeth, 411
   Floyd, 75, 260–1, 305, 307, 411
   George, 350, 411
   Helen Kalbfus, 411
   Isabelle, *see Asendorf*

James, 21, 74, 111, 130, 154, 157, 171, 183, 193, 212, 253, 282, 288, 295, 305, 411
Mabel, 240, 305, 411
Margaret Mills, 74, 157, 193, 282, 288, 305, 411
Stella, 240, 411
Bradley
Anna Amelia, *see Gregory*
Atwell, 69, 149, 212–3, 255, 286, 288, 295, 307, 419, 427, 442
Charlotte Perry, 70–1
Clarence, 286, 419, 442
Clifford, 149, 213, 286, 419, 442
Clifton, 286, 442
George, 286, 419, 442
Helen Heinekamp, 286, 419, 431, 442
Isaac (Isaac M.'s father), 69, 70
Isaac M., 21, 29, 69–71, 148, 154, 174–5, 178, 279, 280, 286, 295, 329, 419, 442
Isaac N., 69, 71, 150, 286, 442
Jessie Tether, 71, 150, 286, 442
Joanna Brown, 23, 29, 69, 70, 71, 83, 86, 148, 279, 442
John Perry, 70–1, 92, 148, 280, 286, 419
Lottie, *see Colville*
Mary Frances, *see Myers*
Mary Larkin, 69
Norah, *see Avery*
Viola, *see Hazen*
Wilhelmena Clemens, 149, 212–3, 442, 469
Bradley House, 71, 135, 148, 155, 208, 255, 280, 306, 307, 365, 371, 419, 427, 430
Brady, John, 27
Braisted
George, 26, 28–9, 459
Laura, 25–6, 28–31, 35, 62, 105, 459
Otis, 26
Sr., Mr. and Mrs., 26
William, 26, 29, 105 459
William Jr., 26, 28, 29
Bramble Brae, 173–4
Breen
Charles, 212
Ella, *see Gardner*
Meda, *see Tether*

Bridge, Ida, *see Calkin*
Briggs
Amanda Myrtie Crabtree, 117, 160, 212, 277, 313–4, 359, 427–9, 435
Carl, 428
Clint/Indy's Children, 314
Clinton, 117, 160, 277, 313–4
Irwin, 117, 139, 160, 212, 247, 277, 313–4, 320, 334–5, 359, 360, 364, 373–5, 398–9, 427–9, 435
James T., 160
Marium (Indy) Clark, 117, 160, 313–4
Mary, *see Austin*
Verna, 428
Britt
Ada, *see Wood*
John, 99, 100–1
Kitty, *see James*
Laura Parker, 1, 5, 19, 23, 29, 38, 43–4, 99, 100, 180–1, 440
William Sr., 88, 100, 180–1, 278, 314
William Jr., 314–5
Britton, Nathaniel and Elizabeth, 195
Bronx Zoo, 195
Brook Road, xiv, 2, 102, 110, 135, 141, 179, 291, 415–6
Brooklyn Bridge, 7, 50–2, 238, 322
Brookwood Manor and Farm, 213, 217, 310–312
Brown
Eliza (Lizzy), 31, 61
Ida Belle Austin, 25, 29, 36, 38, 41, 44–7, 55, 61, 97, 98, 111, 191, 214–5, 302, 440
James Sr., and James Jr., 61
Joanna, *see Bradley*
Mary, *see Paton*
Mercy Harding, *see Clark*
Silas, 86
Browning, John, 330
Browning Rifle, 330, 374, 379
Brunette, Maurla, 44
Bryan, William Jennings, 270, 272–3
Buchanan
Anna May, *see Hallock*
Tillie, 203

Buck's New York Hotel, 79
Bunce
George, 21, 67, 469
Mary, *see Carmichael*
William, 67
Bunger, Chris, 266
Burnand, Georgia, 247
Bush, F.F., 171–2, 174–5, 193, 262
Busse, Madelyn Meyers, vi
Bye, Frederick, 400

C
California
Cuffey's Cove, 51, 53, 58
San Francisco, 247
Calkin
Alonzo, 17, 256
Burton, 257, 265, 268, 280–1, 290, 302, 303, 425, 432, 440
Charles, 17, 92, 139, 245–6, 454
Cranmer, 257
Dorothy (Dot) K., *see Hale*
Edna, 257, 298
Ella, 23
Ezra, 79
Hannah, 257, 268, 290, 303
Horton, 257
Ida Bridge, 246
James, 17
Katherine, *see Traxler*
Lillie Austin, 96, 110, 122–6, 165, 195, 200-2, 205–6, 208, 209–13, 215–6, 218–9, 224–5, 229, 231–3, 237–9, 242–3, 246, 248, 250–2, 257–8, 261, 263, 265–6, 268–73, 280–1, 290, 302, 329, 425, 432, 435, 440
Maria Gardner, 17, 29, 39, 55, 139, 246, 258, 433, 444
Oliver, 17, 93, 137–9, 246, 257, 444
Robert Dale, 290, 302–3, 330, 425, 432, 440
Sarah Egan, 257
Camp, Isabelle, *see Austin*
Campbell
Harry, 350
Katie, *see Persbacher*
Cantwell, George, 400
Cantwells, 149, 150, 420

Carlin, Estella, 242–3, 301, 326, 370, 385
Carmichael
    Cora Hardcastle Eldred, 17, 167, 210, 444
    Decator, 17, 210, 444
    Eliza, see Puff
    Floyd Decator, 17, 444
    Ichabod, 197
    Lewis, v, 17, 210, 314, 444
    Lina, see Watson
    Mary Bunce, 444
    Phebe Linkletter, 17, 210, 444
    Sarah Eldred, 17, 210, 444
    Stephen, 17, 173, 174
    Zophar, 17, 210, 444
Carner,
    Alice, 433
    George, 287, 292–3, 325, 351, 433
Carr, Mr., 9
Carr's Rock, 9
Carroll, Edward, 287
Carson, W.H., 23
Carter, Rev. W.J., 212
Centenary Collegiate Institute, 168–70, 173, 457
Central Park, 25–6, 29, 56
Chinatown, 183
Christian, Mr., 445
Clark
    Carolyn Hallock, vi, 161, 291, 298
    Carrie Etta Bogert, 86, 161, 291, 414, 433
    Catherine, 307
    Clarissa (Clara), see Sergeant
    Cora Cox, 307, 433
    Dan, 49
    Ernest J., 86, 161, 291, 350, 354, 414, 433
    Elbert, 29, 41, 44, 55, 63, 67, 92, 166, 182, 194, 251, 307, 440, 454
    Elizabeth Hoatson, see Wilson
    Ella, see Howe
    Ellsworth, 29, 41–2, 51, 67, 250–1, 440
    Eunice Hallock, 86, 161, 291, 414, 433
    Florence, 133
    Frank, 166, 183
    Garrett, 307
    George, 21, 67, 83, 470
    George Case, 86, 148, 307, 470
    George James, 67, 76, 198, 357, 358, 359, 373, 380, 388, 419
    George Malcome, 67, 84
    Georgia, see Styles
    Harriet Covert, 67, 84, 357, 470
    Hazel, 183
    Irving, 183
    James, 307, 433
    James C., vii
    James Joseph, 358
    John Henry, 86, 149, 161, 291, 307, 414, 433
    Laura Austin, 25, 29, 41–2, 46–7, 67, 92, 166, 168, 183, 187, 207–8, 251, 440, 454, 470
    Elizabeth (Libby), see Sergeant
    Lillie, 183
    Mahlon Irvin, 21, 29, 41, 67, 92, 115, 116, 166, 182, 183, 187, 208, 440, 454, 470
    Marium Indianola, see Briggs
    Martin Dominick, 67, 76, 198
    Mary Costello, 67, 76, 198, 358
    Mary Higgins, 357
    Mercy Harding Brown, 70, 86, 148, 279, 470
    Orville, 291
    Patsy, 281
    Phebe Hazen, see Myers
    Robert, 29, 41, 67, 92, 183, 194, 251, 440, 454
    Sarah, 307
    Stella, see Leavenworth
    Thomas W., 86
    Vernon, vi, 291
    Wilmot and Mary Van Auken, 67, 83, 357
Clark Road, xiv, 62, 67, 142-3, 187, 248, 254, 298
Clemens
    Margaret, see Sergeant
    Mrs. Anthony, 213
    Wilhelmena, see Bradley
Click, Marnette Watson, v
Clinton
    Antoinette (Net) Austin, 26, 29–31, 35–6, 38, 52, 55–7, 60–1, 97–8, 102, 194, 209, 250, 276, 290, 440
    Henry, 29, 30–1, 52, 55–6, 58, 60, 209, 250, 276, 440
    Ida Belle, see Deal
Cloud, Sue Horton, vii
Clouse
    Anna, 139
    August, 19, 139, 287, 295, 304, 433
    Clarence, 139, 350, 400
    Emma, 433
    Emma Wagner, 93, 198, 433
    Frank, 400
    Fred, 139, 304, 350, 433
    Jacob, 19, 93, 198
    Kate, see Pelton
    Lewis and Lizzie, 19
    Joseph and Raymond, 433
    Roy, 432
    Solomon, Susanna, William, 19
Clouse's (Reber's), 93, 138, 427
Clouse's Casino, 138, 426–7
Cobb
    Anna, 198
    E. Mabelle and J. Florence, 130
Cold Springs Farm, 146, 141, 159
Collins
    Annie, 35, 38–9, 41–2, 44, 166, 202, 267–8
    Bertha (Bertie), see Noe
    Emma Kelso, 40, 129–30, 202, 241, 282, 385, 397, 411
    Isabelle, 40–2, 62
    James, 21, 38, 41
    Robert, 41, 166, 170, 172, 189, 195, 202, 267, 420
    Robert Croft, 384–5, 371
    Thomas (Tom), 35, 37, 41, 118, 123, 129–30, 166, 201, 241, 258–9, 261, 273, 276, 282, 295, 371, 385, 397, 409, 411, 431, 470
Collins Road, xiv, 22, 24, 45, 157, 188, 191, 201–2, 282, 315, 412
Colony
    Charles Kyte and John, 67
Colorado
    Dunton, 159–60, 236, 278, 312–3, 431–2
    Colorado Springs, 235
    Denver, 216
    Fish Creek, 83, 158–60
    Ft. Logan, 320

Rico, 160
Telluride, 160
Columbia College, 170, 340
Colville
    Charles, 71, 139, 208, 253, 287, 307, 317, 427, 442
    Clifford, 384
    Esther and Leslie, 287, 307, 427, 442
    Lottie Bradley, 69, 71, 92, 139, 270, 287, 307, 427, 442, 455
    Ruth, *see Deveraus*
Coney Island, 51, 53, 106, 182
Congregational Church
    Barryville, 132, 138–9
    Eldred, 4, 23–4, 35, 55, 62, 67, 84, 90, 129, 142, 147, 166–8, 170, 176, 195–9, 206, 211–12, 226, 233–4, 239, 246–8, 269, 298, 327, 370, 397, 414–5
Connors
    Hazel Sergeant, v, 163, 239, 240, 285
    Marion, *see Hansen*
Conrad, William W., 350
Conway, John, 219, 233
Cortland Normal School, 257, 264, 266, 270–2
Cortright
    Ada, 143
    Bill, 120
    Mina, 445
Cortright's River View House, 73, 75
Cory, Oliver, 139
Costello,
    Alfred, 76, 198
    Elizabeth, 76
    Mary, *see Clark*
Coverts, 196
Cox
    Cora, *see Clark*
    Ella Wheeler, 449
    Herman, 400
    Joseph, 350, 400, 417
    Julia Wilson, 143, 417
    W.C., 23
Crabtree
    Amanda Myrtie, *see Briggs*
    Ida Higginson, 117, 160, 277
    John, 117, 160, 277
    Johnie and Mary, 277, 428

Crail, Edwin L., 400
Crandall
    Amy and Bertha, 433
    Betsy, 20
    Clifford, 293, 433
    David, 20, 141, 205, 317
    Ezekiel, 20
    George, 141, 205, 209, 243, 249, 251, 263, 274, 295, 317
    Henry, 20
    Jennie Crawford, 138, 141, 200, 205–7, 209–13, 215, 218–9, 224–5, 229–33, 237–8, 240, 243–9, 251–2, 263, 269, 271–2, 274
    John, 20
    Lawrence, 350, 433
    Leonard, 433
    Martha, 136, 307
    Mary, *see Ort*
    Matilda, 422
    Milton, 20, 136, 159, 295, 433
    Nellie Simpson, 20, 141, 205, 238, 274, 293, 433
    Robert, 20, 141, 205, 238, 253, 274, 293, 295, 433
    Stanley and Verna, 293, 433
Crawford
    Alfred and Andrew, 138
    Henrietta Halstead, *see Sergeant*
    Jennie, *see Crandall*
    Joel, 138
    Maud, 138, 261
    Melvina, 138, 233
    Seele, 198
Crest Hill Cottage, 159, 205, 220,
Croton Aqueduct, 12
Cuddeback
    Ann Eliza Gardner, 17, 29
    Lewis, 17, 29
    Mary, 17
Custer, Anna, 198

D

D&H Canal, 1, 5–8, 11–2, 14–5, 18–9, 130–1, 138–9, 140, 162, 275, 434
Dabron, Mrs. M., 79
Dailey
    Hipe, 308–9
    Leo, 306

    Steve, 270, 308–9
Daily
    Ida, 262
    Mr., 122, 125–6
Daily's Theater, 36
Daley, Hiram, 179
Dana, Hattie S., 192
Darling
    Agnes, 74, 156, 291
    Charles, 74, 156, 291, 433
    Edith, 74, 156, 291
    Ida, *see Whitmarsh*
    Lottie Myers, 74, 156, 157, 291, 433
    Dassori, 256, 264–5, 301–2, 319–20, 356, 424, 432, 434
Darrieusecq, Henri, 365, 420, 427
Datys, Kathy, vii
Davenport
    George, 198
    Gussie and Edith, 212
Davis, Raymond, 455, 400
Deal
    Francis, 276
    Ida Clinton, 30–1, 94, 97–8, 209, 250, 276, 440
Decker, Mr., 139
Defeo
    Fred Sr., 72, 288
    Pam Fischetti, vi
    Pearl Owen, 72, 150, 288
DeKnetel, Marie, 139
Delaware House, 8, 77–9, 224
Delaware House (Barryville), 255
Dempsey, Maggie, 334, 337, 343, 353
DeSilva
    Sadie, 195
    Vic, 49
DeVenoge
    Caroline, 41, 157, 470
    Dr. Leon, 21, 32, 35, 41, 74–6, 87, 94, 107, 152, 157
    Mary, *see Miller*
Deveraus
    Herbert, 427
    Ruth Colville, 319, 337, 344, 346, 384, 427, 442
Doolittle
    Chester and George, 134, 218
    Mary, *see Layman*

Drake
  Family, vi, 14
  Minerva, *see Austin*
  Phebe, 212
Draper, Andrew S., 280
Dubos, Armandine, *see Lair*
Dunlap
  Catharine, 45
  Charles, 198, 262, 307, 350, 433
  Elizabeth J. Eldred, 167, 210
  Emily, 45
  George, 45
  George, 167, 198, 307, 350, 370, 375, 395, 400, 433
  Harold, 307, 433
  Harry, 354
  Lewis, 45
  Lewis Oliver, 45
  Maggie, 198, 307, 326, 433
  Selma, 433
  Walter, 198, 218
Dunlop, Emily, *see Eldred*

E
Eaton
  Mary, 139, 218
  Moses B., 154
Echo Hill Farm House, xiii, 68, 133, 144–5, 147, 249, 252–3, 255, 283–5, 307, 311, 357, 371, 376, 417, 427, 435
Eckhart
  George, 139, 256
  Julia, 139
Eckstein, Victor, 310
Edwards,
  G.L. (Lt.), 387, 410, 466
  Lewis, 400
Eldred
  Abraham Mulford, 17, 167, 210, 444
  Alfred, 240, 444
  Almira Barnes, 17, 167, 432, 444
  Amelia, *see Hancy*
  Anna, 444
  Benjamin Franklin, 17, 167, 210, 314, 432, 444
  Bertha, *see Myers*
  Bertha Hill, 163, 210, 432, 444
  Charles C.P., 4, 17, 20–1, 24, 29, 41, 43, 67, 92, 116, 163, 166-8, 176, 416, 444, 471
  Clara, *see Theadore*
  Cora Hardcastle, *see Carmichael*
  Cora Sisson, 167, 210, 432, 444
  Delia, 280, 444
  Effa Caroline Van Tuyl, 17, 18, 20, 29, 41, 43, 116, 163, 167, 170, 175, 444, 471
  Eliza C. Post, 167, 195, 210, 280, 282, 303, 414, 432, 444
  Elizabeth Hardcastle, 130, 167, 210, 444
  Elizabeth Justina, *see Dunlap*
  Elizabeth Wheeler, *see Travis*
  Emily Dunlop, 167, 210
  Frances Payne, 198
  George, 97, 168, 444
  George Ely, 210, 240, 350, 400, 432–4
  George W., 17, 167, 444
  Hannah Hickok, 17, 93, 205, 471
  Harvey, 432, 444
  Herbert Lincoln, 17, 43, 167, 176, 210, 280, 282, 292, 294, 317, 372, 414, 432, 444
  James, 9, 17, 141, 163, 205, 435, 444, 471
  James (s/o George W.), 17, 43, 167, 176, 210, 444
  James Daniel, 17, 19, 29, 130, 176, 198, 282, 290, 294, 444, 471
  John Franklin, 17, 167, 210, 314, 432, 444
  Judson, 167, 210, 314
  Lewis Laforde, 17, 167, 210, 314, 432, 444
  Lisa, 444
  Margaret Rutlege, 167, 210
  Maria Adeline, *see Kendall*
  Marietta West, *see Hoatson*
  Martha, *see Worzel*
  Minnie Sears, 167, 210, 314, 432, 444
  Orvis R., 167, 210, 314, 432, 444
  Polly Mulford, 17, 444, 471
  Polly Vandorsdol, *see Mapes*
  Rebecca (Becca), 17, 29, 41, 43, 92, 93, 100, 118, 130, 176, 199, 293, 444, 455, 471
  Richard O., v, 167, 210, 314, 432
  Sarah Jane, *see Wait*
Ellery
  George V., 208–9, 266, 269, 273
  Mary J., 216, 263, 267
Ellis Island, 173
England
  Liverpool, 359
  Lydd, 23
  Manchester, 20, 40
Erie Railroad, 5, 8–13, 22, 46–8, 54, 64–5, 68, 70–83, 132, 138, 155, 159, 162, 174, 217, 219, 226, 239, 275, 305, 423
Ewart
  Albert, 84–5, 147–8, 235, 441
  Edith Palmer, 69, 84–5, 147–8, 234–6, 312, 432, 435, 441
  Elliot, 147–8, 235–6, 312, 432, 441
  Kathryn Blohm, 312, 432
  Pamela (Millie), 147–8, 235–6, 312, 432, 441
  Rolland, 148, 235–6, 312, 432, 441
  Victor, 147–8, 235–6, 312, 432, 441
  Willard, 147–8, 235–6, 312, 432, 441

F
Fearey, J.W., 317
Fee, Mary Elizabeth, *see Myers*
Ferguson, Elizabeth, *see Myers*
Ferncliff Lodge, 226, 228
Fish, Edward, 433
Fisher
  Lucy, 23, 90, 93, 97, 117
  Rev. E.W., 23, 40, 42, 49, 90, 93, 118, 451
Fletcher, Rev., 414
Fleiger/Flieger
  Charles, 255, 287–8
  John, 287, 295
  Katherine (wife of John) 287–8, 293, 433
  Katherine (w/o Charles), 287
  Phillip, 287, 350
  Robert, 350
  Ron, vii
  William, 287
Fluhr, George J., vii, 9, 80, 83, 162, 275, 305

Foch, Ferdinand (Marshall), 378
Forgerson, Gardner, 72
Foster
   Darren, v
   Dorothy Knecht, vi, 433
   Douglas, 433
   George (Burt), 198, 231, 233, 295, 433
   Herbert, 433
   Jennie Hallock, 101, 154, 198, 231, 233, 238, 433
   Sarah, 198
   Wilbur, 306, 317
Fox, John, 139
Frace
   C., 93
   Charles, Mrs., 73, 75
Fraley, Harold, 86–7, 425, 429, 462, 467
France
   Belleau Wood, 363
   Brest, 357, 359
   Cambrai, 357, 380
   Canal du Nord, 373, 380
   Charsonville, 85
   Château Thierry, 357, 366
   Cunel, 378, 385
   Dieulourd and Trondes, 357, 382
   Franco-Prussian War, 85
   Le Collett, 363
   Madeleine Farm, 377–8, 386–7
   Mars-sur-Allier, 357, 399
   Meuse-Argonne, 357, 377–9, 381, 385, 389, 391
   Montfaucon, 376–80, 386
   Moosch, 357, 362
   Paris, 160, 347, 357, 463
   Romagne-sous-Montfaucon, 377–9, 386, 388–90
   Saint Dié, 357, 366
   Sedan, 357, 377–8
   St. Mihiel, 357, 367, 372–4
   Verdun, 357, 377, 379
   Vosges Mountains, 359, 362
   Wissous, 160, 287
Fredrick, Simon, 287
Freeman
   Charles, 400
   Fred, 233, 433
   Hester, 89
Frey, Charles Jr., 400
Furver, Mabel, 240

G
Gaete, Tania Leigh, iv
Gallagher
   J.P., and S., 72, 75
   Wm. 57
Gardner
   Ann Eliza, *see Cuddeback*
   Anna, 17
   Charles F., 17, 36,
   Edna, 108, 139, 211, 287, 307, 317, 426, 444
   Eliza Ann, *see Young*
   Eliza Eldred, 17, 29, 36, 39, 43, 139, 166, 197–8, 204, 205, 206, 207, 472
   Ella Breen, 108, 139, 287, 307, 426, 444
   Herbert, 445, 472
   James E., 17, 29, 39, 139, 287, 433, 444
   James K., 17, 205–6, 444, 472
   James K. (younger), 17, 39, 108, 139, 212, 214, 287, 307, 317, 426, 444
   Katie, 17, 39, 139, 307, 426, 444–5
   Lettie, *see Sergeant*
   Louisa McElroy, 444
   Margaret Terns, 17, 39, 139, 199, 214, 445, 472
   Maria, *see Calkin*
   Mary A. Greiger, 163
   Mary L., 17, 34, 39, 445, 472
   Myers, 17, 39, 43, 109, 139, 445
   Rebecca Rider, 17, 139, 287, 433, 444
   Sears and Mary Keen, 14, 163, 291
   Sears Robert, 163
   Stephen St. John, 9, 17, 23, 29, 34, 39, 80, 127, 133–4, 137, 139, 194, 197, 199, 207, 214, 233, 256, 287, 295, 307, 396, 397, 444–5, 472
   Susan, 17, 36, 138, 139, 287, 433
Garfield
   Lucretia, 41, 55
   President, 41, 54–5
Geier
   Joan Austin, iv, 52, 53, 401, 435
   Liz, iv

Geiselman, C.A., 216
General Electric, 174
Genesee Wesleyan Seminary, 303
German Hill, 9, 275
Getz, Ella, *see Schwarz*
Gibbs, William A. & Co., 274
Gill, Sarah Crabtree, 313
Gillespie
   Agnes, *see Wilson*
   Elizabeth, *see Mills*
   Helena (Nell), 97, 102–4, 106–10, 114, 199, 200
   James (Mrs.), 199
   Margaret, 199
Glabb
   Joseph, 400
   Katie, 433
Glass Factory Pond, 274, 426
Goble Quarry, 11
Goodfreund, Dr., 248
Gordon
   Katie Sims, *see Stege*
   Mr. 308
Goss, Edna, 148
Godsey, Ottie, 332, 337, 341, 345, 349
Gould, Jay, 127
Grand View Farm, 288, 422, 427
Green Acres/ Meadows, 152, 412
Green Farm, 314–5, 431
Greening
   Frank, 229
   John, 253
   Katie, *see Kerr*
Gregory
   Amelia Bradley Leavenworth, 69, 83, 148, 158–60, 235–7, 278, 312–3, 431, 435, 441–2
   Charles Eber, 160, 235, 278, 431, 442
   Charlie, 159, 235, 278, 431, 442
   Nora, 235, 278, 431, 442
   W.M. (Mrs.), 427
Greig
   Bennet, 151, 222, 291, 309, 350
   Isabella (Bella), *see Grotecloss*
   Jane, 151, 222
   Julia, 151, 295
   Kate, 150, 151, 222, 291, 414
   Mrs. T., 159, 205
   Robert, 150, 51, 222, 291, 295, 317

T. Robert, 350
Thomas, 151, 309
Greiger, Mary, *see Gardner*
Grey
    Lina (Dolly) Roth, 224, 275, 304
    Romer, 162, 212, 275, 304
    Zane, 162, 212, 224, 275, 276, 304–5
Grotecloss
    Ed Jr., 260, 414–5
    Ed III, vi, 151, 222, 414
    Isabelle (Bella) Greig, 151, 222, 291, 360, 414
Grove, A.E., 159, 205
Guenther
    Linda, *see Anderson*
    Marion Lass, vii
Guiteau, Charles, 41

H

Haas
    Berniece Wells, vi, 137
    Darlene Sutherland, vi, 29
    Richard (Dickie) Haas, vii
Haig, Field Marshall, 378
Hale, Dorothy Calkin, v, 201, 302–3, 330, 425, 432, 440
Halfway Brook, xiii, xiv, 16–8, 20, 110, 141, 152, 166, 168, 204, 248, 274, 291, 414, 435, 445
Hall
    Charlotte Chambers, 209, 322, 390, 394, 408
    Edward (Dr. and Mrs.), 190, 199
    James Hall, 250–1, 257
    Sara Frances, *see Austin*
Hallenbeck
    Chris, 161
    Emma Schwab Hallock, 14, 161
Hallock
    Adelia, 14
    Amelia E., 23,
    Anna May Buchanan, 14, 161, 291, 414, 433
    Annie, *see Pine*
    Carl, 291
    Carolyn, *see Clark*
    Charles, 48
    Daniel, 91, 101, 103, 124–5, 154, 161, 179, 233, 256, 295, 306, 411
    Daniel V., 161

Doug, 161, 291
Edgar, 291
Edna Hill, 298, 443
Elmer, 291
Elvira Horton, 101–2, 154, 233, 306, 308
Emily Knecht, vi, 161, 291, 433
Emma Schwab, *see Hallenbeck*
Eunice, *see Clark*
Howard, 291
Jennie (Murns), *see Foster*
Martha, 154, 411
Mary Brodt, 101, 161
Mary Rider, 14, 161
Merlin, 291
Oliver Lewis, 161, 291, 298
Oliver Blizzard, 14, 91, 161
Raymond S., 161, 291
Samuel Jesse, 14, 161, 291, 317, 414, 433
Stephen, 103, 154, 155
Thomas W. and Julia Van Tuyl, 91, 101
Wilbur, 291
William, 91, 101, 161
Halstead
    Effie, 248
Hamilton
    H.P., 23
    Helen, 340, 347, 353
    Jewell, 332, 335, 344, 352
Hammond,
    May, 232
    Florence, *see Middaugh*
Hancy
    Amelia Eldred, 17, 167, 210, 444
    John, 17, 210, 444
Handsome Eddy Farm, 427
Hankins, Mary and W.H., 79
Hansen, Marion Connors, v
Hanson, Beatice, 336, 342, 348
Hardcastle, Elizabeth, *see Eldred*
Hardenbergh, Henry J., 188, 231
Hartung, Arthur, 400
Hawk's Nest Road, 12–3, 79, 132–3, 263, 265, 383
Hayden, Joe, 363
Hazen
    Abel, 83, 148–9, 155, 286, 288, 295, 307, 419–20, 442
    Lewis, 286, 419, 442
    Mabel, *see Ashauer*

    Viola Bradley, 69, 83, 148, 149, 286, 288, 419–20, 442
Hensel, Frederick, 400
Herald, Annie, 334, 341, 345, 352
Heyen
    D.H., 73, 75,
    E. (Mrs.), 295
    Fred, 317
Hickok, 473
    Charles, 73, 75
    David, 21
    George, 35
    John, 19
    Justus and Mary Wells, 73, 207
    Olin, 23, 25
    William, 11, 155, 295
Hidden, Rachel, 338–9, 345
Higgins, Mary, *see Clark*
Highland Bridge Hotel, 293, 302
Highland Cottage, 155, 159, 205, 208, 255, 288, 329, 365, 371, 420, 427, 430
Highland Lake (Hagan Pond), xiv, 16, 22, 40, 45, 64, 70, 72–7, 101, 103, 137, 140, 142, 152, 153–8, 187, 193, 202, 212, 225–6, 238, 241, 254, 255, 256, 276, 281–3, 285, 288, 304–6, 323, 329, 351, 401, 403, 411–12, 427, 430
Highland Lake Grove, 154, 256
Highland Lake House, 214, 293, 329, 371, 427
Highland Lake (Hagan Pond) Road, xiv, 20, 24, 44–5, 73, 152, 170, 188, 433
Highpoint Cottage, 233
Hill
    Agnes, 433
    Alfred, 152, 298, 433, 443
    Alice Sergeant, 163, 298, 432, 433, 443
    Alvin, 298, 350, 414, 433
    Anna Crawford, 306
    Bertha M., *see Eldred*
    Elizabeth (Bessie) MacIntyre, 152, 298
    Edgar, 433
    Edna, *see Hallock*
    Elizabeth, 152
    Esther Grinnell, 163, 298, 433, 443

Gladys, *see Myers*
Jessie, 238, 252, 260–1
John, 163, 220, 298, 317, 433, 443
Lena, 381, 433
Thomas, 163, 295, 298, 432, 433, 443
Thomas and Myrtle, 433,
William, 350
Hillside, 14, 161, 414
Hindenburg Line, 362, 373, 377–8, 380, 386
Hindenburg Party, 419
Hirsch
    Anthony Sr., 145, 376–7, 395, 396, 435, 441, 448
    Anthony Jr., 376–7, 396
    Charlee, *see Schroedel*
    Christina Leavenworth, 144–6, 162, 235, 240, 253–4, 262, 283–5, 294, 296–7, 312, 317, 356–7, 376, 395–6, 435, 441, 448
Hoatson
    Elizabeth, *see Wilson*
    Marietta West Eldred, 17, 97, 167–8, 210, 414, 417, 444
    Mary, *see Austin*
    Samuel D., 97, 167, 210
Hogencamp, Amanda, *see Bogert*
Holbert
    F.J., 77
    Frederick and Mary, 162
    M.A. (Mrs.), 77
    William, 78
Homestead Cottage, 188, 201, 240, 241–2, 244, 264, 267, 312, 315–6, 401, 457
Horton
    Anne Elizabeth Stanton, 75, 102, 154, 225, 281, 282, 302, 306, 308, 360
    Beatrice Avery, 75, 154, 286, 306, 308, 419, 442
    Carrie, 154
    Catherine Sutherland, 29, 154, 306
    Charles, 75, 225, 306
    Cleta Myers, 94, 142, 225–7, 229, 247, 291, 445
    Ernest, 154, 240, 306, 351, 400
    Edith, 154

    Elvira, *see Hallock*
    John, 75, 101, 102, 154, 225
    John Jr., 154, 306, 323, 350, 351, 352, 354, 400
    Mabel, 154
    Mary Elvira, *see Bosch*
    Maud, 154, 240
    Sue, *see Cloud*
    Walter, 154, 225, 226, 227, 291, 445
    William Erwin, vii, 29, 149
    William Henry, 306, 308
Howe
    Ella Clark, 67, 239, 240, 285
Howlett
    Arthur E., 393
    Della Myers, 137, 291
    Harry, 291
    J., 189
Hull
    Alice Deyo, 431
    Anna, *see Sergeant*
    George, 431
    Jennie, 433
    John, v, 279, 358, 424
    Justina Schoonover, 192, 278–9, 313, 358, 397, 423–4, 431
    Marjorie, *see Huwa*
    Solomon Deyo, 358, 399, 424, 431
Hulse
    Abel, 350, 354, 400
    Bertha, 237
    Chester, 19, 139, 295
    Duane, 244
    Elizabeth, 19, 139
    Frederick, 19, 198, 262
    Helen Myers, vi
    Henry, 19
    James, 198
    John, 198
    Katherine, 198
    Mary, 19, 198
    Mary, *see Sergeant*
    Mary Eaton, 218
    Nels, 232
    Samuel, 19, 139
Hurtin
    Mary I. Austin, 29, 34, 209
    William, 209
Huwa, Marjorie Hull, v

I
Ihlo
    Bill, vii
    Barbara, *see Sardone*
    Betty, *see Morganstern*
Ingram
    A.J., 130
    Christina Hayes, 145
Iowa, Mondamin, 160, 212

J
Jackson, Sheldon, 27
James
    Barbara Kate, *see Stowell*
    Elwood, 278, 314, 315, 397, 430–1
    Kitty Britt, 100, 180–1, 278, 314, 431
    Norma B. Wood, 314–5, 358, 397, 430
    Richard, v, 181, 211
    William Henry, 278, 314, 431
Jervis, John B., 12
Johnson
    E.J., 316
    Mary, *see Austin*
Johnston
    John W. (author), 6, 9, 10, 19, 48, 73, 81, 94, 134, 137, 140, 162–3, 289
    John W., 73
    Napoleon B., 73, 139, 140
    Robert and Phebe, 163
Jones, Charles J. (Buffalo), 276

K
Kaese
    Alfred, 73, 150, 255, 288, 419
    Lola, Albert, Charles, 419
    Sophia, 150, 288, 419
Kalbfus
    Edith Miller, 288, 329, 365, 420, 427
    Edward, 212, 317
    Ray, 218
Kansas
    Abilene, 58
    Dayton, 90
    Fort Riley, 203, 320, 334, 379
    Lawrence, 28, 31
    McPherson, 60, 63
    Salina, 97, 104

INDEX • 485

Smoky Hill River, 90, 91, 170
Solomon City, 24, 33–5, 38, 48, 53, 63, 90, 95–6, 100, 104, 116, 120–1, 125, 184
Keller
    Helen, 216
    Raymond J., 400
Kelley
    Alma Louella Sergeant, 163, 298, 417, 443
    Everett, 163, 417, 433
    Leila, 163, 433
    Raola, 163, 205, 207, 243, 262, 298, 317, 433
    Samuel Frank, 163, 237, 298, 417, 433
Kelso
    Alice, 130
    Amanda, 5, 37
    Edward, 37, 38
    Ella J., 23
    Emma, *see Collins*
    Isabelle Greig, *see Grotecloss*
    Minnie, 23, 37, 129, 130
    Rob, 35, 37, 44, 109
    Robert Sr., 37, 38, 40, 154
Kendall
    Charles, 17, 116, 130
    Charles Sr., 17, 116
    Maria Adeline Eldred, 17, 116, 444
    Nellie, 17, 116, 176, 455
Kendrigen, Martin E., 400
Kerr
    Charles, 140, 433
    Family, 14
    Helen, 426
    Jessie, 140, 287, 426
    John and James, 140
    John (Jack), 426
    John H. and Katie Greening, 140, 287, 427, 433
    John and Mary, 139–40, 287, 295
    Margaret, 140, 287, 426
    Mary (teacher), 72
    Mary (d/o William), 426
    Ruth, 426
    William and Mary, 139–40, 163, 287, 426
Kilgour Bluestone Co., 9, 80

Kilgour, John F., 9, 10, 78–80, 82–3, 275
Kloss
    Emma and Ernest, 136, 289
    Frieda, *see Wolff*
    Karl, 136
    Lou, 4–7, 12–3, 15, 16, 81, 85, 87, 118, 133, 136, 162, 433
    Will, 136
Knapp, DeWitt, 79
Knecht
    Emily, *see Hallock*
    Dorothy, *see Foster*
    Wilson and Ida Davis, 433
Koenig
    Eugene, 431–2, 441
    Gerald, vi, 69, 159, 237, 313, 432
    Hazel Leavenworth, 69, 158–9, 236, 278, 312–3, 329, 431–2, 441
    Marialyce, *see Kornkven*
Koester
    Chris and Freida, 427
Kohler, Victoria (Vicki), vi
Kornkven
    Marialyce Koenig, vi, 313
Krauss, Mr., 263, 265
Kuhn, Kelly Leavenworth, v
Kyte
    Bronwyn, vii
    Charles Colony, 67, 143
    Charles Eldred, 67
    Clarence and Elizabeth, 199
    Elizabeth B., 143
    Elizabeth Greiger, 67, 143, 163, 473
    Felix J,. 67, 143, 229
    Felix, J.S., 197, 199
    Frank Crouch, 142, 143, 433
    Hazel Robinson, 433
    Herbert, 67, 130, 199, 262
    John Felix and Lena Leota, 67
    Mary Alice Whitney, 67, 72, 143, 291
    Mary, *see Wormuth*
    Rev. Felix, 23, 196, 197, 473
    Rev. Joseph, 197, 198, 199
    Sarah Crouch, 67
    Thomas, 199
    William, 44, 62, 72, 130, 143, 186

L
LaBarr
    Anna Mae Hankins, 198, 264
    Bertha, *see Ort*
    Bessie and Edwin, 433
    Brothers, 295
    Calvin S., 20, 198
    Caroline, 433
    Edey, *see Werman*
    Elizabeth Rice, 20, 198
    Francise, 291
    Frank, 414, 433
    George, 198, 291
    Gordon R., 20
    Hazel, 291
    Henrietta Middaugh, 198, 291
    Ida, 307, 414
    Jacob Daniel, 20, 198, 264
    Jacob, 264
    Mabel, 433
    Webster (Web), 307, 425
Lackawaxen River, xiv, 8, 9, 77–9, 162, 164, 224
Laing, Justina (Tina) Austin, 29, 36–7, 97, 98, 209, 440
Lair
    Albert and Armandine Dubos, 160
    Jeanne, *see Rouillon*
Lake House, 152–3, 202, 250, 253, 255, 281, 306–7, 329, 359, 412–3, 427
Lake Side Cottage, 208, 427
Lake Side Cottage (Yulan), 255
Lake View House, 155–7, 282–3, 305, 412, 427
Lake View Farm House (Prange), 73, 75, 135, 150, 220
Lake View Farm (Kaese), 255, 288, 419
Lake View Cottage, 286
Lambert, Rev. M.S., 23, 69
Lancaster, Kate, 333, 338
Lass
    Charles, 287, 289, 426
    Harry and Helen, 287, 426
    Jay, 287, 426
    John, 287, 289, 426
    Meta Toaspern, 19, 134, 219, 287, 289, 426
Laurel Cottage, 82, 148, 155, 220, 286, 419

Laurel Valley House, 53, 75
Layman
  George, 48, 72–3, 75, 78, 80, 133–4, 212, 218
  Mary, 134, 218
  Mary Doolittle, 134, 301
LeSatz, Louisa Gray, vii
Leavenworth
  Anna Amelia Bradley, *see Gregory*
  Anna Louise, *see Meyers*
  Anna Mae, 69, 83, 130, 142, 145, 162, 177, 235, 240, 242, 252, 254, 257–8, 264–5, 273, 283, 295–6, 311, 357, 396, 417–8, 441
  Atwell, 68, 147, 374
  Charlotte (Lottie), *see Andeway*
  Charlotte Elizabeth, 85, 144–6, 162, 235, 242, 252–4, 262–3, 266, 269–70, 272–3, 275, 283–5, 296–7, 301, 311, 356–7, 376, 417–8, 441, 461
  Charlotte Ingram, 68–9, 234, 236, 441
  Christina H., *see Hirsch*
  Clara Elizabeth, 252, 290, 299, 312–3, 434, 441, 443
  Cynthia, *see Bellinger*
  David, v, 434
  Ella Phoebe Sergeant, 85, 163, 198, 239–40, 247–8, 252, 278, 280, 285, 291, 298–9, 312, 417, 434, 441, 443
  Florence, 158, 441
  Gisele Rouillon, v, 85, 160, 347, 434
  Harriet, *see Palmer*
  Hazel, *see Koenig*
  Hezekiah, 68, 147, 374
  Ida May, 158, 235, 236, 441
  James Garfield, iv, 69, 83, 85–6, 88, 144–6, 160–3, 198, 235, 247–8, 252, 277–8, 280, 285, 291, 295, 298–9, 312, 357, 417, 434, 441, 443
  James Roberts, 85, 347, 434–5, 441, 443
  Jennie Louisa, *see Austin*
  John Ellis, 5, 69, 83, 148, 158–60, 235, 312–3, 435, 441–2
  Kelly, *see Kuhn*
  Linda, *see Bohs*
  Maria Myers, 69, 73, 81, 83, 144–6, 157, 162, 187, 235, 252, 254, 283-5, 288, 311, 356–7, 441, 448
  Martin David, 83, 145, 162, 235, 253, 283–5, 357, 376, 417, 441
  Nancy, *see Leo*
  Sherman Buckley, 21, 68, 69, 147, 204, 234, 236, 441, 446
  Sherman Clinton (Goldie), 68, 86, 278, 299, 312–3, 434, 441, 443
  Sherman Stiles, 67–9, 81, 83, 144–7, 162, 179, 218, 235, 252–3, 283–4, 288, 295, 311, 319, 357, 370, 373, 376, 390, 395, 410, 416, 418, 427, 441, 446
  Stella Clark, 86. 433
  Truman, 69, 83, 133, 144, 145–6, 162, 235, 249, 252, 283, 295, 311, 357, 376, 417, 441
Leo, Nancy Leavenworth, v, 434
Lewis, Frederick J., 296, 300–1, 317, 401
Lewis and Clark Centennial, 239
Liebla
  Harriet Austin, 397
  George and Dewey, 400
  Jacob and Lola, 287
Liggett, Hunter (Gen.), 373, 378–9, 406
Lilley
  Almond and Mary, 198
  Earl and Sharon Stewart, vii
  Eleanor Ort, 198, 238, 291, 433
  Emerson, 238, 291
Lily, Henry, 35
Lincoln, Robert T., 41
Linimous, William A., 114
Litman, George, 419
Little Pond, *see Bodine Lake*
Little Pond Cottage, *see Bodine*
Litts, Rev. H., 23, 84, 108
Livingston
  David, 177
  Emmett, 400
  Jane Sergeant, 67, 163, 298
  Ralph, 350, 400
Loch Ada (Haggai's Pond), xiv, 22–3, 65, 188, 215
Lochada, 22–3, 164, 188, 213–14
Loerch
  Catharine, 427
  Henry J., 350, 400
Lone Scouts, 330–1
Longfellow, Henry Wadsworth, 59
Lord & Taylor, 38, 40, 158, 302
Lord, Samuel, 40
Lost Battalion, 377, 383
Love
  John, 386, 414, 425, 433
  Kate, 433
Lovee, George, 31, 34–5, 46, 89, 91, 199
Lozier, William A., 398
Lusitania, 303

M

MacIntyre
  Adeline, 152
  Elizabeth (Bessie), *see Hill*
  Charles R., 152, 400
  James, 152
MacKenzie/McKenzie
  Alexander, 22
  Edward, 22, 184
  George Ross, 22, 87, 173
  Hugh and James, 22
  Lizzie, 117
  Rebecca, 22
  Rebecca (dau.) 22
Madison Square Garden, 2
Madison, Mr., 5
Maglione, Margie Austin, iv, 435
Maier
  Anna, 76, 137, 227, 261, 293
  Joseph, 76–7, 136–7, 159, 208, 218–9, 220–3, 226–7, 229, 230–2, 243, 288, 427
  Juliana, 76, 136–7, 219, 223, 227, 230, 239, 243, 244, 247–8
  Julius, 76, 137, 220, 224, 227, 248, 262, 309, 317, 417
  Mary, *see Bosch*
Maney
  Charlotte, 182
  George W., 23, 192, 221
Maney's Mill, 22, 311
Mapes
  Charles, 176

INDEX • 487

George Egbert, 17
Polly Vanorsdol Eldred, 17, 93, 116, 118, 176, 186, 444
Maple Grove Farm, 139, 219, 289
Marrinan, Kevin, vi
Masher, Sarah, 5
Massachusett, Easthampton, 285, 299, 357, 434
Masvidal
 Edith, 157, 282
 Rebecca, 282, 411
Maudsley
 Edna Rauner, 291
 Ellis, 291
 Louis, 291
Maxwell, Allen (Cap.), 387, 408–9, 414, 419, 466
McBride
 Claudia, 198, 240
 Eliza, 198, 291, 433
 Emerson, 198, 240, 350, 400, 433
 Ezra (Buck), 198, 291, 350, 400, 433
 Laura Avery, 286, 291, 419, 442
 Mabel, 433
 Sherman Sr., 198, 291, 433
 Sherman Jr., 198, 240
 Thomas, 198
 Walter, 433
McCormack/Cormick, 255, 293, 420, 427
McCoy, Bessie, 336, 343
McKechnie, Edith, 264
 John, 302
McKinley, William (Pres.), 195, 211, 272
McPhillamy, Susan VanTuyl Rider, 161
McQuirk, John, 350, 400
Mellan
 Ed, vii, 290
 Mary, 290
Merritt, Mr., 88
Methodist
 Barryville, 23, 139, 160, 210, 257, 277, 287, 435
 Eldred, 4, 23, 24, 142, 143, 147, 160, 197, 200, 206, 210, 225, 248, 277, 370, 435
 Pond Eddy, 23, 160, 210, 435

Metzger
 Barbara, 19
 Charles, 178, 183
 Christian and Follett, 19
 Fred, 135, 288, 400
 Gotlieb, 19, 237
 John, 135, 154, 288, 295
 John Jr., 289, 317, 400
 Margaret, 307
 Mary, 135, 288, 302
 Matilda, 135
 Matilda and Harriet, 135
 Regina and Robert, 19
 T.G., 192
Meyer
 Albert, 302
 Anna Leavenworth, 287, 317, 426
 Christian, 253, 274, 287–8, 295, 426, 427
 Christian Jr., 287, 426
 Florence Van Eastenbridge, 307
 John and Annie, 274
 Joseph, 307, 350
 John, 287, 350, 400, 426
 Margo Bosch, vi
 Meta, 274, 287–8, 302, 426
 Minnie, *see Mills*
Meyers
 Anna Leavenworth, 280, 290, 299, 312-3, 434, 441, 443
 Dorothy, 286, 417
 Lottie Waller Scott, 83, 137, 205, 225, 231, 237, 243, 280, 286, 417, 442
 Madelyn, *see Busse*
 William Sr., 83, 280, 286, 417
 William Jr., 83, 279, 280, 286, 417
Michigan
 Benton Harbor, 148, 235, 312
 Crystal Falls, 332, 342, 354–5
 Detroit, 265, 312
 Ironwood, 431
Middaugh
 Charlotte, *see Myers*
 Chester, 150, 198, 291, 417
 Dennis, 150
 Emma, 35
 Florence Hammond, 198, 291, 417
 Henrietta, *see LaBarr*

 Herbert, 291, 417
 Maria, 198, 288, 291, 295
 Phoebe, *see Owen*
 Sarah, 150
Miller
 Aunt Hattie, 275
 Edith, *see Kalbfus*
 Helen (Lena), *see Bosch*
 Louis, 157, 282
 Louisa, 288
 Mary DeVenoge, 44-45, 157, 282
 Robert, 208, 288
 Robert H., 350
Mills
 Agnes, 157, 254, 276
 Alexander, 21, 74, 156, 473
 Alexander, 157, 254, 276, 287
 Christina, *see Wilson*
 Elizabeth Gillespie, 156–7, 254, 276, 288, 293, 411, 427
 George, 74, 156, 157, 253, 254, 256, 276, 295
 George Ross, 254, 276
 Geraldine, *see Russell*
 Isabelle (Belle), 157, 254, 276, 296, 297, 299, 346
 James G., 157, 254, 276, 350
 Kenneth, 157
 Margaret, 254, 276
 Margaret Gillies, 74, 288, 473
 Margaret, *see Boyd*
 Martha, *see Myers*
 Mary C., *see Wait*
 Minnie Meyer, 254, 287, 317, 426, 287
 Sophia Stellwagen, 157
Mills House, 74, 76, 157, 254, 276, 293, 427, 430
Millspaugh
 Mary Letitia, *see Austin*,
 Mrs., 194
Minisink Lodge, 255, 293, 424, 427
Mistenas, Anna, 19
Mitchell, Edgar, 350, 400
Moffatt, James, 174
Montgomery Lake Cottage, 329
Montgomery Lake, xiv, 65, 72, 329
Montgomery Ward & Co., 220, 244, 269, 292, 429
Montoza Cemetery, 137

Moody
  Ambert, 318, 429, 430, 462
  D.L., 315, 316
  William, 316, 462
Moore, Elijah, 208
Mitchell, Edgar, 350, 400
Morgan
  Fred, 400, 407, 413
  John and Wesley, 400
Morganstern, Betty Ihlo, vii
Morris, Cleo, 333, 338–9
Moss, Cora F., 176-7
Mount Hermon School, 315–6, 318, 339, 390, 399, 413, 430, 461
Mount Pleasant, 135, 159
Mountain Farm House, 135
Mountain Grove House, xiii, 152, 165, 169, 176, 178, 181, 186-7, 202, 214, 241–2, 250-1, 277, 293, 279, 315–6, 319, 323, 401–4, 406, 414, 425, 427, 468
Mountain (Lake) House (DeVenoge), 152, 157, 159, 181
Mountain House (Gregory), 427
Mountain Top Cottage, 293
Muche, W.D., 96
Munger, F. C., 79
Murray, George W., 99, 180
Myers
  Abel Sprague, 18, 21, 24, 41, 43–4, 57, 86, 93–5, 125, 127–8, 140–2, 154, 163, 179, 205, 208, 212, 225, 229–30, 232, 253, 288, 291, 295, 306, 327, 350, 415, 445
  Ada, see Wells
  Archibald Abel, 84, 142, 163, 226–7, 245, 293–4, 299, 317, 328, 443, 445
  Atwell, 291, 442
  Augustus (Gus), 73–4, 127, 128, 145, 153, 157–8, 187, 282–3, 288, 295, 304, 411, 427
  Bertha Eldred, 210, 226, 240, 303, 432, 444, 445
  Bill (old), 49
  Charles Cripps, 88, 156–7, 187, 243, 251, 282, 305, 412, 427
  Charles Fred Sr., 83, 137–8, 149, 218, 229, 232, 244, 248, 286, 288, 291, 295, 417, 427, 442
  Charles Fred Jr., 137, 291
  Charles Henry (Chuck), vi, 84, 152, 245, 269, 287, 327, 435
  Charlotte (Lottie), see Darling
  Christena (Teenie) Stevens, vi, 20, 141, 205, 311, 416, 418
  Cleta, see Horton
  Clifford Edwin, 226, 227, 291, 406, 445
  Della, see Howlett
  Edwin VanSchoick, 24, 45, 72, 92, 94, 179, 226–7, 244, 291, 328, 406, 435, 445, 455
  Eleanor Mildred, see Rizzuto
  Elizabeth Ferguson, 305, 412
  Ethel, 399, 412
  George, see Asendorf
  George W.T., 21, 38, 40, 73–4, 156–7, 187, 251, 254, 282, 288, 295, 305, 328, 473
  Gladys Hill, 163, 226, 298, 433, 443
  Gladys, see Austin
  Harold, 252, 282, 305, 412
  Harvey, 137, 400
  Helen, see Hulse
  Jackson, 24, 94, 142, 225, 226, 228, 244, 253, 295, 306, 412, 414, 415, 416, 433, 445
  James, 226, 445
  Jane Ann VanPelt Webb, 40, 45, 64, 73–4, 157, 473
  Jessie, 226, 248, 433, 445
  Kathryn and Stanley, 198, 433
  Lena Schoonmaker, 252, 282, 305
  Lila, see Von Ohlen
  Lulu, see Scheniman
  Mabel Louise Owen, 72, 179, 226, 227, 291, 406, 435, 445
  Maria, see Leavenworth
  Maria Hankins, 24, 92, 94, 141, 142, 163, 179, 211, 225, 288, 291, 327, 445, 454
  Maria VanSchoick, 445
  Marie, 198, 433
  Martha Mills, 38, 73–4, 156–7, 187, 251, 282, 288, 305, 328, 473
  Martin David Sr., 156–7, 187, 282, 305, 399, 412
  Martin David Jr., 412, 416, 435, 445
  Mary, 329
  Mary Elizabeth Fee, 305, 399, 412
  Mary Frances Bradley Scott, 69, 83, 92, 137, 149, 205, 243, 286, 288, 291, 354, 417, 442, 453
  Mildred, 240, 262, 291, 442
  Minnie Sergeant, 84, 163, 197, 226, 240, 245–6, 293–4, 299, 300, 306, 317, 327, 414, 443, 445
  Moses Dewitt, 86
  Norman, 142, 210, 226, 291, 303, 350, 414, 432, 444–5
  Orville, 291, 406, 430, 445
  Phoebe Hazen Clark, 86
  Raymond, 179, 226, 227, 291, 297–8, 385, 406, 445
  Ruth Worzel, vi, 14, 152, 287, 433
  Samuel S. and Elizabeth, 76
  Sarah, 24
  Stephen A. and Charlotte E. Middaugh, 198, 288, 317, 427, 433
  Tracy, 400
Myers, Mills and Co. (Jane Ann or Gus), 64, 71, 73, 155, 427
Myers House (Fred), 137, 218, 286, 291, 417, 427

N
National Hotel, 79
Nebraska, 117, 160, 212, 277, 359, 435
  Aimsworth, 160, 277, 313, 428
  Lincoln, 117
  Wayne, 277
Nelson
  Charles, 139
  Gilbert, 139, 295
  Grace, 348, 355
  Mary, 139, 287
  Minnie, 139, 257
  Bob and Beatrice Behrens, vi
Neugebauer, Emily, 336, 343, 349, 355–6
New Jersey
  Brookside, 31, 34–5, 46, 89, 91, 199
  Garfield, 290

Hackettstown, 166, 168–74, 178, 183, 195, 456, 457
Hoboken, 359
Paterson, 68, 276, 429
New York
  Barryville (The River), xiii, xiv, 1, 5, 7, 8, 10-2, 15-9, 23, 25, 29, 39, 44–5, 48, 55, 65, 69, 72–3, 75, 77, 80, 85, 93, 102, 108–11, 113, 122–3, 131–40, 150, 154–5, 157, 159, 163, 178–9, 184, 186, 192, 194, 198–9, 205, 208, 212, 214–5, 217–20, 227, 233, 246, 248, 254–8, 274–5, 286–9, 292–4, 301–2, 305, 307, 325, 337, 346, 350–1, 354, 356, 365, 370, 384, 397, 412, 414–6, 424, 426-7, 433, 435
  Beaver Brook, 63, 198, 264
  Bethel, xiv, 20, 115, 141, 143, 151, 165, 195, 200, 202, 206, 209–13, 215, 224–5, 231–2, 238, 247–9, 251–2, 257–9, 261, 263–4, 266–8, 272–3, 281, 290, 298, 315, 329, 425, 432
  Big Eddy, 79
  Binghamton, 74, 157, 221, 291, 433
  Brooklyn, 2, 29, 31, 34, 50, 52-3, 87, 99, 102–4, 106–18, 120, 139, 152, 180, 182, 196, 199–200, 211, 215, 238, 252, 255, 263–4, 266, 278, 286, 307, 322, 326, 337, 363, 371, 414, 422, 424
  Cairo, 314, 397, 431
  Callicoon, 38, 46, 68, 70, 79, 257
  Cochecton Center, xiv, 216
  Cortland, 265–6, 268–73
  Eldred (the Village), xiii, xiv, 2, 4–5, 16, 20, 23-27, 35, 37, 38, 65, 179, 200, 206, 416
  Fosterdale, 209, 252, 257–8, 265–6, 268–70, 273, 280, 296
  Fremont, 213
  Glen Spey, xiv, 20, 22, 45, 118, 152, 166, 173, 184, 197, 199, 216, 309–11, 412
  Goshen, 68, 143, 199
  Handsome Eddy, xiv, 8, 14, 161, 199, 427
  Highland Lake (Venoge), xiii, xiv, 103, 140, 142, 152, 154–5, 292–3, 296, 299, 329, 350, 365, 371, 419
  Hillside, 14, 161, 414
  Middletown, 17, 38–9, 68, 119, 209–10, 225, 230, 276, 361, 429
  Minisink Ford, xiii, xiv, 7–8, 66, 77, 87, 162, 256, 293, 302, 350, 427, 447
  Monticello, 35, 58, 103, 107, 128, 171–2, 174–5, 209, 211, 229, 262, 268, 271, 273, 280, 359, 375, 382, 384, 386, 430
  Narrowsburg, 68, 70, 79, 250, 257–8, 280, 302
  New Rochelle, 98, 183, 277–9, 293, 314
  Otisville, 70, 83, 225, 386
  Phillipsport, 165, 172, 173, 176–7
  Pond Eddy, xiv, 7–9, 12–15, 23, 41, 68, 79, 162–3, 219, 221, 237, 302, 435
  Port Jervis, 1, 3, 8, 12–3, 22, 26, 60, 68–9, 79, 80, 87, 93, 127, 132, 148, 153, 174, 181, 185–6, 190, 193, 199, 225, 234–5, 238, 240, 261, 263, 264–5, 269, 276, 294, 296, 299, 302, 306, 315, 321, 361, 381, 386, 392, 406, 412–4
  Purling, 314, 397
  Rondout, 1, 5, 6
  Rushville, 425
  Sparrowbush, 11–2, 68, 79, 248, 383
  Tylertown, xiv, 258, 296, 433
  Wellstown, 296
  White Lake, 46, 106–7, 131, 149, 280, 425
  White Sulphur Springs, 86
  Youngsville, 86
  Yulan, xiii, xiv, 5, 16, 20, 65–6, 70, 72, 77, 85, 88, 131, 134–6, 143, 145, 148–50, 154–5, 159, 192, 205, 208–9, 218–20, 252–3, 255, 263, 282, 288–9, 293, 302, 327, 329, 350, 371, 421, 422, 427, 430–3
New York Hotel, 79
Noe
  Bertha Collins, 92, 166, 170, 172, 184–8, 190–1, 195–6, 202, 455
  Louis Albert, 195–6
Northfield Seminary, 316

O

O'Grady, Thomas, 420
Oakdene, 72, 150, 205, 220, 255, 288
Ohio
  Cleveland, 17, 54, 210
  Sand Hollow, 93, 97, 117
Onderdonck
  John, 229
  W.H.C., 155
Orchard Terrace, 141–2, 205–6, 208, 220, 225–6, 253, 291, 301, 415
Ort
  Catherine, 20
  Charles, 198, 238, 291, 433
  Eleanor, *see Lilley*
  Florence, 433
  Frank Sr., 20, 198, 433
  Frank Jr., 198, 291
  George, 198, 291
  Jacob, 20
  John, 433
  John (s/o Frank and Lena), 291
  Katie, 20
  Lena, 291
  Mary, 20
  Mary Crandall, 20, 198, 291, 433
  William, 198, 238, 291, 433
  William Jr., 291, 433
Osburn, Bonnie, 339
Oset, Helen Hensel, vii
Osier
  Augustus (Gus), 19, 35, 113, 123
  Phoebe J. Lee, 19
  Theresa, 23
Oswego Normal School, 97–100, 105, 107–8, 112–3, 125
Owen
  Basil, 150
  Earl, 240, 400
  Elizabeth (Libby), 68, 447
  Elizabeth Barns, 298

Elizabeth Tether, 72, 150, 179, 238, 474
Etta, 150
Florence, 150
Frank, 72, 208, 253, 309, 433
Katherine, 433
Mabel Louise, *see Myers*
Morgan, 298
Pearl, *see Defeo*
Phebe, *see Sergeant*
Phoebe Middaugh, 72, 150, 288
Robert, 72, 150, 179
William, 72, 150, 205, 255, 288, 295, 431
Owens, Priscilla Kilpatrick, 23
Ozenbaugh, James A., 139, 154

P

Palmer
Edith, *see Ewart*
Harriet Leavenworth, 69, 84, 147, 148, 234, 312, 432, 435, 441
Harry, 69, 148, 234–5, 312, 432
Henry, 69, 147–8, 441
James, 69, 148
Lydia, 148, 234, 312, 432
Virginia West, vi
Panama Canal, 234, 302, 331, 361, 366, 368, 370–4, 381–2, 384, 387–8, 390–1, 395–6, 398–9, 402, 406–7, 409, 412, 414, 417, 421, 422
Panic of 1893, 176
Park Hotel, 255, 286, 307, 419, 427
Parker
Adelaide, 20, 77, 141
Andrew, 20, 274, 311, 416
Benjamin, 19
Edith, 218
Elijah S., 10
Elsie E., 274, 311, 416
Emily (Emma), *see Stevens*
Emily C. Payne, 20, 76, 77, 78, 140–2, 274, 311, 327, 415, 427
George, 1, 5, 19, 29, 99, 182, 192, 278, 397, 431, 440,
G.W., 248
James Y. Jr., 20
James Young, 20, 76, 78, 140, 141, 142, 274, 288, 295, 302, 311, 327
James Y. (s/o William), 142, 240, 274, 311, 385
Kate, 1, 2, 5, 19, 23, 29, 38, 43, 99, 120, 180–2, 192, 278, 314–5, 397, 431, 440
Laura, *see Britt*
Leon, 231
Mary Murray, *see Schoonover*
Phebe, 433
Victoria Simpson, 142, 274, 311, 416
William, 20, 77, 140, 142, 274, 311, 416
William Jr., 274, 311, 416
Parker Hotel (first), 20, 35, 76, 78, 124, 140, 141, 200, 212, 224, 259
Parker Hotel (second), 142, 178–9, 184, 255, 274, 311, 415, 416, 427, 434
Parkers Glen Fountain, 10
Parmenter
Emily A. (Emma), *see Austin*
Henry and Effie, 90, 120, 125, 128
Henry Sr., 24, 60, 89–1, 128
Jere, 126–7
John Earl and Annie, 90, 397
Sarah Sophronia, 90–1, 110, 114, 120, 165, 195, 257, 458
Paton
Archibald C., 429
Archibald H., 28–9, 32, 169, 429, 440
Archibald R. (Buddy), 28–9, 169, 209, 276, 429, 440
Archibald Jr. (s/o Archie R.), 429
Donald, 429
Dorothy May, 276, 429, 440,
Effie, 429
Ida, *see Webster*
Mabel L., 429
Mabel Slagel, 276, 429, 440
Margaret, 429
Marjorie, 429
Mary, 29, 105, 458
Mary Brown, 209, 429
Miranda (Rand) Austin, 26, 28–9, 32, 35, 52, 56, 58, 61, 97, 111, 169, 209, 276, 303, 429, 440
Nettie, 28–9
Patterson, John R., 79
Patton, George S., 373, 380
Paulus, Charles, vii
Payne
Emily C., *see Parker*
Frances, *see Eldred*
Peary, Robert, 275
Pelton
Asher, 163, 275
Asher Jr., 287
Carrie, 163, 275, 295
Edith, 275, 426
Edward, 163, 275, 287
George, 359
Howard, 163, 275, 317, 426
Kate Clouse, 139, 287
Pelton Soda Bottle Factory, 139, 140, 162, 163, 275, 426
Penney
Caroline Autenrieth, 142, 240
James Cash, 142
Pennsylvania
Carbondale, 6, 432
Dingman's Ferry, 1
Easton, 3
Hawley, viii, 68, 80, 307
Honesdale, 1, 5–6, 68, 167
Lackawana, 3, 237
Lackawaxen, xiv, 7–8, 46, 50, 57, 60, 64, 70, 79, 100, 162, 207, 212, 224, 262, 290, 304, 372, 386, 427, 447
Mast Hope, 79
Mill Rift, 9, 13, 251
Parkers Glen, viii, xiv, 8–15, 68, 79, 80
Philadelphia, 3, 15, 17, 116, 129, 163, 186, 199, 221, 230, 293
Pittsburgh, 129, 213, 239, 431
Shohola, xiii, xiv, 2, 8–13, 15, 17, 22, 25, 64–5, 68, 70–3, 75, 76, 78, 80–1, 83, 100, 123, 132–3, 137–9, 145, 152–3, 155, 159, 194, 205, 208–9, 214, 216–8, 221, 223, 224, 226, 231, 241, 247, 255–7, 275, 277, 283, 287–8, 305, 307, 386, 401, 423, 433
Shohola Glen, 9, 47–9, 75, 79–83, 132, 139, 155, 159, 180, 205, 229, 275, 278
Trenton, 15

West Damascus, 17, 167, 210, 314
Perine, Rev. John E., 23, 93, 97, 98, 100, 111, 199, 454
Persbacher
    Elizabeth (Libbie), *see Sergeant*
    Jacob and Catherine Kreiter, 84
    Katie Campbell, 84
    Valentine J., 83
Perschbacher, Jacob, 9, 47, 49, 84
Pershing, John J. (Gen.), 366, 372–3, 392, 415
Pestalozzi, Johann, 99
Peterson
    Andrew, 135
    Anna, 135, 288, 422
    Matilda, 135, 288
    Sophia, 135, 288, 422
    Erick, 135
    Frederick, 135, 422
    Matilda (d/o Frederick), 135
Piermont Hotel, 157, 193
Pine Grove Cottage, 208, 220, 255
Pine Grove Farm, 76, 136, 137, 159, 208, 219, 220, 226, 229, 417, 427
Pine Terrace Farm, 309–11
Pine, Archibald and Annie Hallock, 161
Pond Eddy Bridge, xiv, 12, 14, 219, 237
Popp, John, 363, 374, 382, 386, 387, 389, 408, 425–6, 465–7
Port Jervis Training Class, 296
Portz, Jacob, 302
Post, Eliza, *see Eldred*
Potato Hill, 14
Prange
    Anna, 135
    Edward, 73, 75, 150, 288
Proctor, 35, 179, 186, 201, 309, 310, 368, 388, 402
    Ada Olive, 22
    Charles Edward, 22, 23, 74, 131, 157, 285, 317
    Charles E. (Mrs.), 216
    Elizabeth Singer, 213, 214
    Vouletti T. Singer, 22
    Vouletti Theresa, 213, 214, 232, 233
    William Fash, 22, 23, 87, 165, 188, 189, 213

William Ross, 22, 213, 214, 217, 310, 317
William Ross Jr., 213
Proctor Road, xiv, 4, 20, 22, 24, 136, 141–2, 152, 165–6, 170, 191, 202, 242, 412, 414, 433
Puff, Egbert and Eliza Carmichael, 7, 210

Q
Quick
    Ami (Mrs.), 212
    Blanche, *see Worzel*
    Frances (Fannie) White, 14, 152, 287, 433
    Hiram, 72
    Horton, 433
    Hugh (Mrs.), 23
    Ida, 23
    Irving, 137, 138, 287
    James, 139, 163, 192
    Joseph, 152
    Lucinda, 152
    Menzo, 139, 154, 175, 220, 256, 287
    Metho and Martha, 287
    Napoleon B., 14, 152, 287, 433
    Ralph, 433
    Tom, 155

R
Racine
    Charles, 73, 75, 150
    Lawrence, 350
    T.W., 150, 155, 288, 293, 412, 420
    Truman, 295
Rainer, E.M., 53
Rassine, Anne, 334, 346
Rauner
    Edna, *see Maudsley*
    Jennie D. Young, 14, 291
    Louis Frank, 291
Reber, Job, 304
Reber's Restaurant, 138, 427
Red Men's Hall, 178–9, 414
Redding, Anna, 135
Reisen, Alice Bosch, vi
Rennenberg
    Anton and Mary, 427
Reprogel, Florence, 148, 312
Rhodes, Rev. F.L., 212

Rice, Elizabeth, *see LaBarr*
Rider
    Mary, *see Hallock*
    Susan Van Tuyl, *see McPhillamy*
    William R. 350
Ridley, Edward Sr., 37
Ridley's, 36–8, 52, 53, 55–6, 60–1, 94, 110
Riley, James Whitcomb, xiii, 283, 435
River View House (Cortright), 73, 75
River View House, 256
Rixton
    Anna, Caroline, Charles, 19
    Henry, 19, 139
    Herman, 19, 93, 287
    John, 19
    Joseph, 19, 150
    Katherine, 287
    Leon, 350
    Lucy Tether, 150
    Martin, 19
    Mary, 19, 139, 287
    Mary (d/o Mary), 19
    William, 19, 79, 302
Rizzuto, Eleanor Myers, vi, 412
Roebling
    Aqueduct/bridge, xiv, 7–8, 50, 77–8, 162, 164, 224, 304
    Emily, 50
    John A., 7, 50
    Washington, 50–1
Rohman,
    Art, 275, 305
    Clinton (Mr. and Mrs.), 306
Rohman Hotel/Inn, 275
Roosevelt, Theodore (Pres.), 191, 211, 222, 270, 272, 286, 289, 416
Rose, Mary, 79
Rothman, Annie, 301, 433
Rouillon
    Blanche Olga Malinge, 84, 160
    Cyrus Albert, 160, 347, 398
    Gisele, *see Leavenworth*
    Jean Charles, 84, 85, 160
    Jeanne Lair, 160
Round Pond, xiv, 22, 74, 157
Rowley, Daniel H. and Mary, 19

Rundle
- Abram W., 17, 198, 231
- Charles, 224, 240
- Martha and Mildred, 240
- Robert, 350

Rusby
- Carrie, 139, 187
- Rev. Samuel, 139, 187, 197, 199, 212

Russell,
- Geraldine Mills, vi, 157, 410
- Stuart, vi

Rutlege, Margaret, *see Eldred*

S

Sand Pond, 22, 23
Sardone, Barbara Ihlo, vii
Scheniman
- Charlie, 263, 317
- Lulu Myers, 94, 142, 226, 229, 445

Schoonmaker
- Robert, 287
- Will, 263

Schoonover
- Ann Mary Austin, 1, 431, 440
- Daniel Rowlee, 1–5, 7, 12, 16, 19, 29, 38, 81, 99, 119, 120, 154, 179, 180–1, 192, 228, 278–9, 314, 358, 363, 366, 368–9, 397, 411, 423, 424, 431, 440
- Emily Banner, 180–1, 192, 279, 314, 431, 440
- Emily, *see Waidler*
- Ethel, 279, 313, 431
- Justina, *see Hull*
- Mary Murray, 313–4, 316, 431
- Mary Murray Parker, 1, 5, 16, 19, 29, 38–9, 92, 99, 179, 180, 182, 211, 278, 314, 316, 358, 396–7, 431, 440, 453
- Oliver Perry, 1, 2, 5, 16, 19, 29, 38, 81, 29, 99, 179, 180, 182, 211, 212, 440, 453, 474
- Peter, 16
- William, 279, 295, 313–5, 431

Schrieb
- Otto, 412
- Paula, *see Bosch*

Schroedel
- Charlee Hirsch, v, 376, 396, 435
- Matt, v
- Ric, v

Schro(e)der
- Dick, 306
- Diedrich, 277, 293
- Hattie, 244
- Hazel, 262
- Herman, 240

Schulz, George A., 293
Schumacher, 19
- Arthur and Charles, 433
- Catharine, 433
- Dora, Harry, and Lillian, 433
- Edward, 350, 400, 433
- Herman, 295
- John, 138–9, 426–7

Schumacher Pond, xiv, 19, 65–6
Schwab, 14, 161
- A., 427
- Emma, *see Hallenbeck*
- Frederick and Margery, 19, 137, 287–8, 295, 307, 427

Schwarz
- Anna Marie, 309, 310
- Ella Getz, 309
- Franz August, 309, 310
- Frank V, vii, 174, 310
- Walter, 309

Scott
- George, 83, 442
- Lottie Waller, *see Meyers*
- Mary Frances Bradley, *see Myers*

Scriber, Adelbert M., 317
Sears, Minnie, *see Eldred*
Segarra
- Dawn Lee Austin, iv, 435
- Joseph, v

Sergeant
- Alice, *see Hill*
- Alice Spiers, 433
- Alma Louella, *see Kelley*
- Alvah, 21, 67, 163, 443
- Alvah Thomas, 67, 220, 253, 295, 298, 414
- Anna Hull, 240, 298, 433
- Anna Penney, 83, 443
- Caroline, 67
- Charles Alvah, 298
- Charles Edgar, 298, 306, 317, 414, 433
- Clarence, 146
- Clarissa Clark, 41, 67, 83–5 163, 231, 240, 247, 443
- Edith, 354, 433
- Elizabeth (Libby) Clark, 298
- Elizabeth (Libbie) Persbacher, 23, 83–4, 163, 245, 293, 443, 474
- Ella Phoebe, *see Leavenworth*
- Emma Myers, 443
- Ethel, 21, 67, 83, 443, 474
- Frank Roberts, 67, 83–5, 163, 220, 247, 252, 253, 298, 317, 433, 443
- Hazel Ruth, *see Connors*
- Henrietta Halstead Crawford, 198, 298, 306, 414, 433
- Isaac, 67, 83–4, 109, 163, 197, 199, 232, 244–5, 253, 293, 298, 317, 327, 443, 474
- Isaac Rev., 23, 196, 197, 199, 443
- James Gardner, 443
- James W., 67, 92, 130, 443, 453
- Jane, *see Livingston*
- Lettie Gardner, 14, 67, 83, 163, 327, 443, 474
- Lettie Hait, 163
- Margaret Clemens, 298
- Mary Hulse, 298
- Mary Richards, 443
- Minnie Ethel, *see Myers*
- Morgan, 67, 163, 220, 253, 295, 298, 317, 433
- Phebe Owen, 67, 84, 163, 165, 252, 298, 443
- Stephen, 83, 443

Seven Oaks, 150–1
Sheldon Jackson School, 27
Shohola (Glen)
- Hotel/House, 9, 48, 72, 78, 80, 139, 214, 275
- Monument, 290
- Switchback Gravity Railroad, 6, 81–2

Shotwell, Mrs. (Sara), 4, 5
Side Hill Farm House (Hill Side), 255, 289, 365
Sidwell
- George, 253, 292, 317, 331, 359, 365, 370
- Katie Sims, *see Stege*
- Marion, 392

Thomas, 222, 262, 306
Siegel, Harry, 400
Simpson
   Nellie, see Crandall
   Sam, 262
   Victoria, see Parker
Sims, Katie, see Stege
Singer Company, 22, 87, 173
Singer
   Isaac Merritt, 22
   Vouletti Theresa, see Proctor
   William Henry, 213
Sisson, Cora, see Eldred
Skinner, Alfred, 37
Slagle, Mabel, see Paton
Slocum, Henry Earl, see Austin
Slonek
   E., 295
   Home, 142–3, 200, 206, 246, 248
Smith
   Austin, 19, 140, 287, 427
   Dr. Frank I., 248, 253, 273, 276–7, 317
   E.A., Rev., 23
   Ed, 19, 140, 287, 427
   Enos, 19
   Mabel Austin, 19, 140, 287, 397, 427
   Oliver, 184
Smith Hotel, 2
South Dakota, Bonesteel, 160
Spanish American War, 191
Speidel, Merritt C., 199
Sperline, Lela, 335, 340, 348
Spiers, Ellen, 433
Sprague
   Bill R. and H., 35
Spring House, 72–3, 75, 133–4, 157, 218, 254, 274, 287, 301–2, 426–7
Squires, Fred, 304
Stage
   Charley, 117
   Jacob, 197, 199, 214
   Martha Carmichael, 199
Stanley, Henry, 177
Stanton
   Anne Elizabeth, see Horton
   Walter, 350
Steel(e)
   John, 139, 287

George, 139
Stege
   Edward, 295, 306–7
   Katie Sims Gordon Sidwell, 201, 306, 308–9
Stege's Pond (Mill Pond), xiv, 20, 150–1, 201, 222, 247, 281–2, 306, 360
Stellwagen, Sophia, see Mills
Stern, Larry, vii
Stevens
   Christena (Teenie), see Myers
   Emily (Emma) Parker, 140–2, 240, 252, 274, 311–2, 327, 416
   Howard, 274, 311–2, 350, 416
Stewart
   Fred, 240
   J. Loerch, 329, 365
Stidd
   G., 329
   Lou, 111
   Mary Hickok, 93, 207, 474
   William, 93, 474
Stowell, Barbara Kate James, v
Straub
   Emma, see Toaspern
   Fridolin, 224, 258–9, 288–9, 295, 302, 414, 427, 431
   Fridolin (Fred) Jr., 259, 350, 353–4, 360, 370–1, 400
   Ida, 258
   Julia, 259
   Juliana Hergenhan, 224, 258–9, 288–9, 414
   Rosa, 259
Straub's Hotel and Bar, 78, 224, 258–9, 289, 302, 414–5, 427
Sturns, Joe, 5
Styles
   Charles H. and Sarah, 433
   Georgia Clark, 67, 84, 97, 143, 212, 254, 303, 433
   Henrietta Austin, see Allen
   Walter, 27, 84, 97, 100, 170–1, 185–6, 191, 194, 209, 242, 253, 276, 295, 303, 317, 391, 433
Sullivan Co. Highway Dept. 303
Sulzbach, H., 329
Sunset View House, 329, 365, 427
Sunshine Hall, 233–4, 262–3, 300, 306, 317, 333, 414

Sutherland
   Alfred, Anne Agnes, Arthur, 29
   Catherine, see Horton
   Darlene, see Haas
   Family, 14
   Irving, Martha, Norman W., 29
   Phoebe Warner, 29
   Stephen and Washington, 29
   William G., 28, 31, 48, 53, 58, 60, 63
Sweezy, Adaline, see Young

T
Taft, William Howard, 270, 272–3, 275
Taylor
   George Washington, 40
   J.R., 23
   Rev. Charles W., 394
Taylor University, 313, 320, 429
Testa, Judy Gumaer, vii
Terns
   John, 139
   Margaret, see Gardner
Terwilleger, Geo., 79
Tether
   Anne Barber, 71, 72, 149–50, 289, 307, 420
   Edward and Elizabeth Peet, 72
   Elizabeth, see Owen
   Ivan J. and Jana, vii
   Ivan Joseph Sr., 286, 287, 420
   Jessie, see Bradley
   Joseph W., 21, 71, 72, 75, 149, 150, 288, 289, 295, 307, 420
   Lucy, see Rixton
   Marianne, see Whitney
   Meda Breen, 139, 150, 286, 287, 420, 426
   Walter, 139, 150, 253, 286, 287, 295, 307, 365, 420, 426
Theadore, Clara Eldred, 167
Thiese, Bernard, 138
Thomas, Chauncey, 9, 17, 48, 78, 80, 134
Thomas Tavern, 78
Thompson
   Addie Austin, 25–6, 29, 35, 38, 44–5, 47, 52–3, 55–8, 61–3, 101, 105, 111, 186, 192–3, 195, 207, 209, 303, 328, 440

Augustus (Gussie), 26, 64, 101, 440, 451
Aunt Polly, 111
Harry, 26, 29
Maple, 343, 345, 353
Thomas J., 26, 69, 440
Thomas E., 26, 28–9, 62, 440
Tilton Seminary, 170
Timmerhof, Ernest, 400
Tin Pan Alley, 308
Tinglit people, 27
Titanic, 294
Toaspern
　Anna, 19
　Arthur, 134, 219, 289, 305, 426
　Edith, 19
　Emma Keller, 289, 426
　Emma Straub, 258–9, 289, 426
　Henry Christian (Chris), 19, 134, 219, 253, 288
　Ida Heyen, 19, 134, 219, 288–9
　Meta, *see Lass*
　Royden Arthur, 289, 426
　Walter (Bub), 289, 426
　Walter, 134, 219, 289, 305, 350, 354, 360, 400, 426
Torwood Farm, 140, 427
Town of
　Bethel, xiv, 20, 141, 257
　Cochecton, xiii, 215, 258, 265
　Highland, vii, xiii, xiv, 4, 8, 19, 20, 65, 67, 69, 74, 80, 84–5, 88, 130, 132–3, 154, 198, 201, 233, 253, 292, 295, 302, 317–8, 350, 352, 397, 400, 433, 434
　Lumberland, xiii, xiv, 4, 14, 20, 22, 29, 65, 69, 74, 87, 140, 151–2, 157, 161, 166, 168, 173, 198, 204, 207, 213, 217, 232
　Tusten, xiv, 5, 13, 20, 65–6, 136, 151, 211, 269
Traver
　Charles and Jennie, 287, 433
　Charles Jr., 433
　John, 287, 433
Travis, Elizabeth Wheeler Eldred, 17, 167, 210, 444
Traxler, Katherine Calkin, v
Treaty of Paris, 191
Tri-States Rock, 12–3
Tucker, Dan, 16, 18

Twichell/Twitchell
　Edith, 198
　H.E., 79
　Horace, 137
　John, 107, 198–9, 297
　Mary, 297
Twin Lake Farm (House), 72, 75, 152, 155

U, V

U.S.S. Arizona, 358, 399, 424
U.S.S. Maine, 191
Van Auken
　Chauncey, 198
　Sarah, 198
Van Eastenbridge
　Florence, 307
　John, 281
　Mary Nellie Van Wyck, *see Bosch*
Van Pelt, Elizabeth, 40
Vanderbilt, 11
Vans, Phil, 120
Von Ohlen
　Henry, 226, 299, 300, 414, 445
　Lila Myers, 142, 226, 229, 231, 240, 291, 299, 414, 445

W

Wagner, Emma, *see Clouse*
Waidler
　Emily Schoonover, 5, 19, 29, 38, 99, 179, 180, 278–9, 314–5, 397, 431
　Will, 180, 279, 314–5, 430–1
Wait
　Alexander, 75, 211, 225, 245, 254, 261, 280, 282, 307, 317, 411–2
　Carrie, 198, 259, 433
　George, 75, 198, 243, 245
　Ida, 307, 411
　John, 152
　Mary C. Mills, 74–5, 198, 243, 245–6, 254, 288, 292, 295, 307, 411, 427
　Sarah Jane Eldred, 17
　William, 142, 198, 201, 214, 433
Walker Lake Falls, 10
Wall Street, 197, 278
Wallace, Nancy, 176–7

Washington Beach Hotel/House, 149–50, 255, 286, 288, 365, 419–20, 427
Washington Lake House, 71, 75, 149–50, 220, 286, 289, 307, 371, 420, 427
Watson
　Daisy Raper, 314, 444
　Elizabeth J., 314, 444
　Ella and George, 433
　Frank and Lina Carmichael, 17, 210, 314, 444
　Laura, 343, 351
　Leonard George, 210, 314, 444
Watters, Rev., 414
Watts, Christina, vii
Webb
　Charles Cripps, 45
　Henry, 45–6
　John, 19
　Sarah Shotwell, 23, 45
Webber, Dorie, 150
Weber
　John, 198, 433
　Dorothy Brodmerkel, vi
　Kate, 198
Webster
　Charles, 276
　Ida Paton, 29, 111, 169, 276, 429
Weidner, David, vii
Welland Hall, 100, 112–3
Wells
　Ada Myers, 137, 291, 417, 442
　Berniece, *see Haas*
　Chester, 350
　Daniel, 21
　Earl, 350
　Everett, 400
　Raymond, 350, 412
Werman, Edey LaBarr, vi, 264
West
　Charles, 198, 421–2
　Dora, 26, 35, 39, 55, 107
　Marietta, *see Hoatson*
　Phebe, 135, 198, 421
　Samuel and Mary, 17, 97
　Selma, 422
　Theodore and Selma, 422
　Theodore, 135, 159, 198, 208, 421
　Virginia, *see Palmer*

West Farm, 135, 159, 198, 208, 220, 255, 421
West Shore Bridge, 6
West Shore Cottage, 73, 149, 150, 255, 288, 293, 420, 427
West Shore Lodge, 150, 420
Westerfield
    Edythe King, v
    Pamela, v
Wheeler, Elizabeth, see Travis
White, Frances (Fannie), see Quick
Wilkinson, Barbara Waite, vii
Whitmarsh
    Ida Darling, 74, 156, 291, 433
    Walter, 433
Whitney
    George H., 67, 72, 143, 291
    Louisa, 198
    Marianne Tether, 72
    Mary Alice, see Kyte
    Rev. Joel F., 195–8
    William H., 19, 23, 126, 199, 248, 253
Whittlesey, Charles, W. (Maj.) 383
Wicks, Ted, vi
Wilcox
    Ella Wheeler, 449
    W.C., 23
Will, Raoul, 400
Willett Street Church, 55–6, 58, 94
Williams College, 41
Williams, Ben, 18
Willis, Alice, vii
Wilson
    Abby, 417
    Agnes Gillespie, 297, 298
    Anna, 62, 118
    Arthur, 143, 254, 262, 417,
    Bertha Boyd, 74–5, 88, 193, 211, 225, 231, 243, 244, 273, 296, 414
    Charles, 62, 67, 84, 142, 143, 154, 201, 233, 254, 256, 295, 317, 417
    Christina Mills, 67, 74, 143
    Edward, 62, 67, 130, 143, 197, 199
    Elizabeth Hoatson Clark, 67, 84, 97, 143, 210, 244, 254, 303, 414, 417
    Forrest, 414
    Garret, 9, 81
    Julia, see Cox
    Mary, 41, 118
    Robert, 417
    William H., 45, 62, 67, 75, 142, 193, 211, 243, 253, 262, 295, 317, 414, 417
    Woodrow, President, 302, 318, 399
Wilson Store, 67, 141, 178, 224, 293
Winslow, Elizabeth, 5
Wisconsin, Milwaukee, 431–2
Wolf/Wolfe/Wolff
    Agnes, 136, 289
    Albert, 136, 289, 433
    Anna, 289, 433
    Carl, 136, 289, 350, 400, 433
    Catherine, 198
    Charles, 136, 289, 433
    Edwin T., 400
    Frank, 136, 289, 350
    Frank and Mary, 287, 433
    Fredericke, 136
    Frieda Kloss, 136, 289, 433
    Herb and Margaret, v, 274, 289
    Janette, 136, 289, 433
    John and Mary, 198, 255, 288–9, 295
    Margaret, 135, 198
    Norman, 136, 289, 433
    William, 135, 159, 198
Wood
    Ada Britt, 100, 180–1, 211, 278, 314, 358, 431
    Alice, 278, 315
    Arthur Remington, 278, 358, 314, 431
    Lorna, 136
    Norma Beverly, see James
    Thomas, 278
Woodbine Cottage, 293
Woodland Cottage, 208
Woodlawn National Cemetery, 291
Woodside Farm House, 257
Wormuth
    Clarence, 240, 350, 356, 400, 413
    Eva, 272
    Harry, 143, 225, 291, 307, 433
    Mary A. Kyte, 67, 72, 143, 186, 195, 262, 264–5, 291, 307, 433
    Olive, 211, 225
    Sarah E., 195, 291
    Stephen, 137, 253, 291, 295
Worzel
    Blanche Quick, 152, 287, 433
    Herman, 152, 287
    Martha Eldred, 210, 287, 432
    Raymond, 287
    Ruth, see Myers
Wright Brothers, 221

Y

Y.M.C.A., 314, 322–3, 358, 363, 365, 368–9, 410, 423–4
Young
    Adaline Sweezy, 14, 291
    Coe Finch, 14, 291
    Eliza Ann Gardner, 14, 163, 221, 291
    Jennie Dusenbery, see Rauner
Yulan Cottage, 289, 427, 430

Erie Switchback Railroad in Pennsylvania's Moosic Mountains. 1881 Erie Summer Excursion *Booklet.*

About the Author

Louise Elizabeth (Austin) Smith grew up on treeless Peach Street in Southgate, Michigan (south of Detroit). She tried writing fiction at an early age, but it never seemed to work out. Writing research papers in High School and College, however, was something at which she excelled (as long as she could use the living room floor for organizational purposes. Thanks Mom). Music and especially violin became a serious part of her life after she inherited her grandfather's violin (mentioned in Echo Hill and Mountain Grove).

Louise received a bachelor's degree in music education (Western Michigan University) and later a master's degree (Eastern Michigan University) in elementary education.

After teaching music and fifth grade classroom for ten years, Louise met and married the love of her life, Gary Smith, then a car designer for General Motors. She transferred her educational and musical skills to homeschooling their four children, now all grown and on their own.

When the youngest was in his last year of high school, Louise ran across some favorite stories her grandmother Myrtie Crabtree Briggs had told and a few photos from an aunt. Using her research skills (with the help of the internet) and the family collections that were soon shared, Louise began to compile the story of her grandparents and their ancestors.

Louise continues to enjoy researching and writing (and still needs a large area for organizational purposes. Thanks Gary). The story of the new friends and "long lost" relatives she has met and the colossal amount of photos and family information they shared, could be its own book.

Echo Hill and Mountain Grove is the fourth book published with the help of Gary who designed the covers, interiors, adjusted all of the photos, and added his professional touch. Louise and Gary reside in Cave Creek, Arizona.

Louise Elizabeth Smith with husband Gary. Photo: Chris Tingom.

Family Info Online

HalfwayBrook.com
Halfway Brook community blog, on-going projects, resources

Weezy.info
Stories and information about the Crabtree-Higginson, Austin-Leavenworth, Smith-Corbridge, and Fallin-Williams families

Eldred Corners from Book 3, Farewell to Eldred. *The second building on the left is the Parker Hotel. On the right is Arthur Wilson's store, and behind it is Wait & Boyd's garage. Postcard courtesy of Mary Briggs Austin.*

Other Books by Louise E. Smith

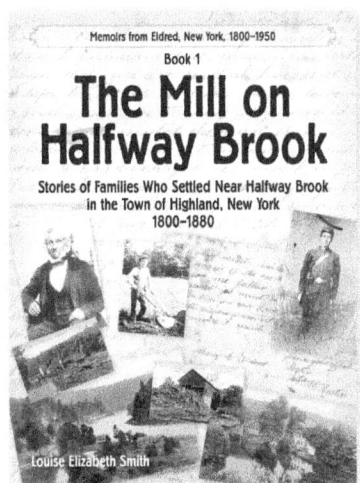

The Mill on Halfway Brook
The Mill on Halfway Brook tells of the Eldred, Austin, Myers, and Leavenworth families, their neighbors, friends, and kinsfolk that settled in what was once the Town of Lumberland, in the villages of Halfway Brook (Eldred), The River (Barryville), Ten Mile River (Tusten), and South Lebanon (Glen Spey).

The narrative weaves vignettes of townsfolk, preachers, churches, regional and national events with historical information, land documents, censuses, an 1875 biography, Congregational and Methodist Church records, over 300 photos and postcards, old and new maps, and at least 200 family letters (1845–1880).

The Mill on Halfway Brook is fully indexed with names of over 900 people, places, and events. It is the first in the series, *Memoirs from Eldred, New York, 1800–1950*.
ISBN 978-0-9826374-0-1, 8.3 × 11, 284 pages, Softcover

Aida Austin's 1881 Diary
Aida Austin started a diary at the beginning of 1881, the year she turned 20 in November. Whether in New York City with her Austin cousins or at her home in Eldred, New York, Aida wrote about her daily life: plumbers fixing pipes, dentist and doctor visits, going to Central Park, skating, sailing, shopping, getting the mail, holidays, daily visits with relatives, President Garfield's assassination, drinking tea, and raking hay.

Included at the end of the Diary are photos of Aida's parents, brothers, and some of her Eldred-Austin relatives mentioned in her diary.
ISBN 978-0-9826374-1-8, 6.7 × 9.6, 108 pages, Softcover

Grandma and Me
Amanda Myrtie Crabtree Briggs was born in 1891 in a sodhouse on her father's Nebraska homestead farm. Over the years she told her children and grandchildren the stories of her growing up as well as those of her parents and her Crabtree and Higginson grandparents—real pioneers of the west. This book is a collection of those stories and includes almost 600 photos and documents.

246 pages
8-1/2 × 11, Softcover

Available at HalfwayBrook.com

www.ingramcontent.com/pod-product-compliance
Lightning Source LLC
Chambersburg PA
CBHW081754300426
44116CB00014B/2114